THIRD EDITION

Learning PHP, MySQL, JavaScript, CSS & HTML5

Robin Nixon

Beijing · Cambridge · Farnham · Köln · Sebastopol · Tokyo

Learning PHP, MySQL, JavaScript, CSS & HTML5, Third Edition

by Robin Nixon

Printed in the United States of America.

Published by O'Reilly Media, Inc., 1005 Gravenstein Highway North, Sebastopol, CA 95472.

O'Reilly books may be purchased for educational, business, or sales promotional use. Online editions are also available for most titles (*http://my.safaribooksonline.com*). For more information, contact our corporate/institutional sales department: 800-998-9938 or *corporate@oreilly.com*.

Editor: Andy Oram
Production Editor: Kristen Brown
Copyeditor: Rachel Monaghan
Proofreader: Jasmine Kwityn

Indexer: Lucie Haskins
Cover Designer: Karen Montgomery
Interior Designer: David Futato
Illustrator: Rebecca Demarest

June 2014:   Third Edition

Revision History for the Third Edition:

2014-05-19:   First release

See *http://oreilly.com/catalog/errata.csp?isbn=9781491949467* for release details.

ISBN: 978-1-491-94946-7

[LSI]

For Julie

Table of Contents

Preface

The combination of PHP and MySQL is the most convenient approach to dynamic, database-driven web design, holding its own in the face of challenges from integrated frameworks—such as Ruby on Rails—that are harder to learn. Due to its open source roots (unlike the competing Microsoft .NET Framework), it is free to implement and is therefore an extremely popular option for web development.

Any would-be developer on a Unix/Linux or even a Windows/Apache platform will need to master these technologies. And, combined with the partner technologies of JavaScript, CSS, and HTML5, you will be able to create websites of the caliber of industry standards like Facebook, Twitter, and Gmail.

Audience

This book is for people who wish to learn how to create effective and dynamic websites. This may include webmasters or graphic designers who are already creating static websites but wish to take their skills to the next level, as well as high school and college students, recent graduates, and self-taught individuals.

In fact, anyone ready to learn the fundamentals behind the Web 2.0 technology known as Ajax will obtain a thorough grounding in all of these core technologies: PHP, MySQL, JavaScript, CSS, and HTML5.

Assumptions This Book Makes

This book assumes that you have a basic understanding of HTML and can at least put together a simple, static website, but does not assume that you have any prior knowledge of PHP, MySQL, JavaScript, CSS, or HTML5—although if you do, your progress through the book will be even quicker.

Organization of This Book

The chapters in this book are written in a specific order, first introducing all of the core technologies it covers and then walking you through their installation on a web development server so that you will be ready to work through the examples.

In the first section, you will gain a grounding in the PHP programming language, covering the basics of syntax, arrays, functions, and object-oriented programming.

Then, with PHP under your belt, you will move on to an introduction to the MySQL database system, where you will learn everything from how MySQL databases are structured to how to generate complex queries.

After that, you will learn how you can combine PHP and MySQL to start creating your own dynamic web pages by integrating forms and other HTML features. Following that, you will get down to the nitty-gritty practical aspects of PHP and MySQL development by learning a variety of useful functions and how to manage cookies and sessions, as well as how to maintain a high level of security.

In the next few chapters, you will gain a thorough grounding in JavaScript, from simple functions and event handling to accessing the Document Object Model and in-browser validation and error handling.

With an understanding of all three of these core technologies, you will then learn how to make behind-the-scenes Ajax calls and turn your websites into highly dynamic environments.

Next, you'll spend two chapters learning all about using CSS to style and lay out your web pages, before moving on to the final section on the new features built into HTML5, including geolocation, audio, video, and the canvas. After this, you'll put together everything you've learned in a complete set of programs that together constitute a fully functional social networking website.

Along the way, you'll also find plenty of pointers and advice on good programming practices and tips that could help you find and solve hard-to-detect programming errors. There are also plenty of links to websites containing further details on the topics covered.

Supporting Books

Once you have learned to develop using PHP, MySQL, JavaScript, CSS, and HTML5, you will be ready to take your skills to the next level using the following O'Reilly reference books. To learn more about any of these titles, simply search the O'Reilly website (*http://oreilly.com*) or any good online book seller's website:

- *Dynamic HTML: The Definitive Reference* (*http://oreil.ly/dynamic_html*) by Danny Goodman
- *PHP in a Nutshell* (*http://oreil.ly/PHP_nutshell*) by Paul Hudson
- *MySQL in a Nutshell* (*http://oreil.ly/MySQL_nutshell*) by Russell J.T. Dyer
- *JavaScript: The Definitive Guide* (*http://oreil.ly/javascript-tdg-6e*) by David Flanagan
- *CSS: The Definitive Guide* (*http://oreil.ly/css-tdg-3e*) by Eric A. Meyer
- *HTML5: The Missing Manual* (*http://oreil.ly/html5-tmm-2e*) by Matthew Mac-Donald

Conventions Used in This Book

The following typographical conventions are used in this book:

Plain text
> Indicates menu titles, options, and buttons.

Italic
> Indicates new terms, URLs, email addresses, filenames, file extensions, pathnames, directories, and Unix utilities.

`Constant width`
> Indicates command-line options, variables and other code elements, HTML tags, macros, and the contents of files.

`Constant width bold`
> Shows program output or highlighted sections of code that are being discussed in the text.

`Constant width italic`
> Shows text that should be replaced with user-supplied values.

 This element signifies a tip, suggestion, or general note.

 This element indicates a warning or caution.

Using Code Examples

Supplemental material (code examples, exercises, etc.) is available at *http://lpmj.net*.

This book is here to help you get your job done. In general, if example code is offered with this book, you may use it in your programs and documentation. You do not need to contact us for permission unless you're reproducing a significant portion of the code. For example, writing a program that uses several chunks of code from this book does not require permission. Selling or distributing a CD-ROM of examples from O'Reilly books does require permission. Answering a question by citing this book and quoting example code does not require permission. Incorporating a significant amount of example code from this book into your product's documentation does require permission.

We appreciate, but do not require, attribution. An attribution usually includes the title, author, publisher, and ISBN. For example: *"Learning PHP, MySQL, JavaScript, CSS & HTML5, Third Edition*, by Robin Nixon. Copyright 2014 Robin Nixon, 978-1-4919-4946-7."

If you feel your use of code examples falls outside fair use or the permission given here, feel free to contact us at *permissions@oreilly.com*.

We'd Like to Hear from You

Every example in this book has been tested on various platforms, but occasionally you may encounter problems—for example, if you have a nonstandard installation or a different version of PHP. The information in this book has also been verified at each step of the production process. However, mistakes and oversights can occur and we will gratefully receive details of any you find, as well as any suggestions you would like to make for future editions. You can contact the author and editors at:

O'Reilly Media, Inc.
1005 Gravenstein Highway North
Sebastopol, CA 95472
(800) 998-9938 (in the United States or Canada)
(707) 829-0515 (international or local)
(707) 829-0104 (fax)

We have a web page for this book, where we list errata, examples, and any additional information. You can access this page at *http://bit.ly/lpmjch_3e*.

There is also a companion website to this book at *http://lpmj.net*, where you can download all the examples from this book in a single zip file.

To comment or ask technical questions about this book, send email to *bookques tions@oreilly.com*.

For more information about our books, courses, conferences, and news, see our website at *http://www.oreilly.com.*

Find us on Facebook: *http://facebook.com/oreilly*

Follow us on Twitter: *http://twitter.com/oreillymedia*

Watch us on YouTube: *http://www.youtube.com/oreillymedia*

Safari® Books Online

 Safari Books Online (*www.safaribooksonline.com*) is an on-demand digital library that delivers expert content in both book and video form from the world's leading authors in technology and business.

Technology professionals, software developers, web designers, and business and creative professionals use Safari Books Online as their primary resource for research, problem solving, learning, and certification training.

Safari Books Online offers a range of product mixes and pricing programs for organizations, government agencies, and individuals. Subscribers have access to thousands of books, training videos, and prepublication manuscripts in one fully searchable database from publishers like O'Reilly Media, Prentice Hall Professional, Addison-Wesley Professional, Microsoft Press, Sams, Que, Peachpit Press, Focal Press, Cisco Press, John Wiley & Sons, Syngress, Morgan Kaufmann, IBM Redbooks, Packt, Adobe Press, FT Press, Apress, Manning, New Riders, McGraw-Hill, Jones & Bartlett, Course Technology, and dozens more. For more information about Safari Books Online, please visit us online.

Acknowledgments

I would like to once again thank my editor, Andy Oram, and everyone who worked so hard on this book, including Albert Wiersch for his comprehensive technical review, Kristen Brown for overseeing production, Rachel Monaghan for her copyediting, Jasmine Kwityn for proofreading, Robert Romano for his original illustrations, Rebecca Demarest for her new illustrations, David Futato for interior design, Lucie Haskins for creating the index, Karen Montgomery for the original sugar glider front cover design, Randy Comer for the latest book cover, and everyone else too numerous to name who submitted errata and offered suggestions for this new edition.

CHAPTER 1

Introduction to Dynamic Web Content

The World Wide Web is a constantly evolving network that has already traveled far beyond its conception in the early 1990s, when it was created to solve a specific problem. State-of-the-art experiments at CERN (the European Laboratory for Particle Physics—now best known as the operator of the Large Hadron Collider) were producing incredible amounts of data—so much that the data was proving unwieldy to distribute to the participating scientists who were spread out across the world.

At this time, the Internet was already in place, with several hundred thousand computers connected to it, so Tim Berners-Lee (a CERN fellow) devised a method of navigating between them using a hyperlinking framework, which came to be known as Hypertext Transfer Protocol, or HTTP. He also created a markup language called HTML, or Hypertext Markup Language. To bring these together, he wrote the first web browser and web server, tools that we now take for granted.

But back then, the concept was revolutionary. The most connectivity so far experienced by at-home modem users was dialing up and connecting to a bulletin board that was hosted by a single computer, where you could communicate and swap data only with other users of that service. Consequently, you needed to be a member of many bulletin board systems in order to effectively communicate electronically with your colleagues and friends.

But Berners-Lee changed all that in one fell swoop, and by the mid-1990s, there were three major graphical web browsers competing for the attention of five million users. It soon became obvious, though, that something was missing. Yes, pages of text and graphics with hyperlinks to take you to other pages was a brilliant concept, but the results didn't reflect the instantaneous potential of computers and the Internet to meet the particular needs of each user with dynamically changing content. Using the Web was a very dry and plain experience, even if we did now have scrolling text and animated GIFs!

Shopping carts, search engines, and social networks have clearly altered how we use the Web. In this chapter, we'll take a brief look at the various components that make up the Web, and the software that helps make it a rich and dynamic experience.

 It is necessary to start using some acronyms more or less right away. I have tried to clearly explain them before proceeding. But don't worry too much about what they stand for or what these names mean, because the details will all become clear as you read on.

HTTP and HTML: Berners-Lee's Basics

HTTP is a communication standard governing the requests and responses that take place between the browser running on the end user's computer and the web server. The server's job is to accept a request from the client and attempt to reply to it in a meaningful way, usually by serving up a requested web page—that's why the term *server* is used. The natural counterpart to a server is a *client*, so that term is applied both to the web browser and the computer on which it's running.

Between the client and the server there can be several other devices, such as routers, proxies, gateways, and so on. They serve different roles in ensuring that the requests and responses are correctly transferred between the client and server. Typically, they use the Internet to send this information.

A web server can usually handle multiple simultaneous connections and—when not communicating with a client—spends its time listening for an incoming connection. When one arrives, the server sends back a response to confirm its receipt.

The Request/Response Procedure

At its most basic level, the request/response process consists of a web browser asking the web server to send it a web page and the server sending back the page. The browser then takes care of displaying the page (see Figure 1-1).

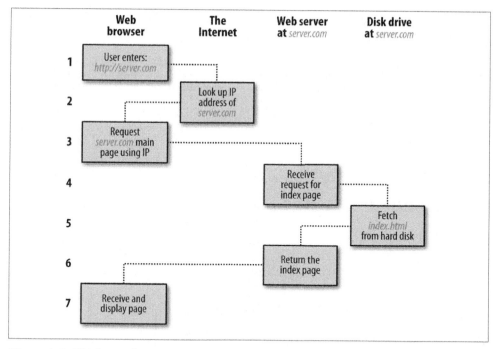

Figure 1-1. The basic client/server request/response sequence

Each step in the request and response sequence is as follows:

1. You enter *http://server.com* into your browser's address bar.
2. Your browser looks up the IP address for *server.com*.
3. Your browser issues a request for the home page at *server.com*.
4. The request crosses the Internet and arrives at the *server.com* web server.
5. The web server, having received the request, looks for the web page on its hard disk.
6. The web page is retrieved by the server and returned to the browser.
7. Your browser displays the web page.

For an average web page, this process takes place once for each object within the page: a graphic, an embedded video or Flash file, and even a CSS template.

In step 2, notice that the browser looked up the IP address of *server.com*. Every machine attached to the Internet has an IP address—your computer included. But we generally access web servers by name, such as *google.com*. As you probably know, the browser consults an additional Internet service called the Domain Name Service (DNS) to find its associated IP address and then uses it to communicate with the computer.

For dynamic web pages, the procedure is a little more involved, because it may bring both PHP and MySQL into the mix (see Figure 1-2).

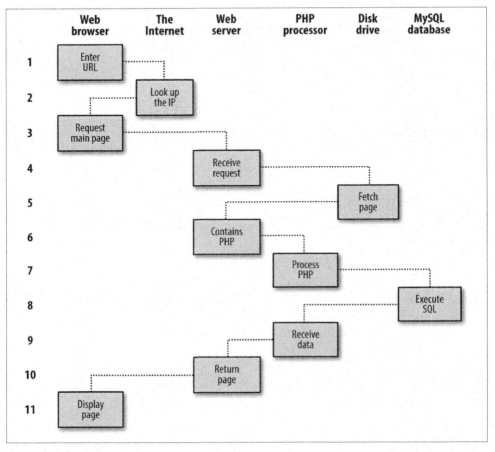

Figure 1-2. A dynamic client/server request/response sequence

Here are the steps for a dynamic client/server request/response sequence:

1. You enter *http://server.com* into your browser's address bar.
2. Your browser looks up the IP address for *server.com*.
3. Your browser issues a request to that address for the web server's home page.
4. The request crosses the Internet and arrives at the *server.com* web server.
5. The web server, having received the request, fetches the home page from its hard disk.

6. With the home page now in memory, the web server notices that it is a file incorporating PHP scripting and passes the page to the PHP interpreter.

7. The PHP interpreter executes the PHP code.

8. Some of the PHP contains MySQL statements, which the PHP interpreter now passes to the MySQL database engine.

9. The MySQL database returns the results of the statements back to the PHP interpreter.

10. The PHP interpreter returns the results of the executed PHP code, along with the results from the MySQL database, to the web server.

11. The web server returns the page to the requesting client, which displays it.

Although it's helpful to be aware of this process so that you know how the three elements work together, in practice you don't really need to concern yourself with these details, because they all happen automatically.

HTML pages returned to the browser in each example may well contain JavaScript, which will be interpreted locally by the client, and which could initiate another request—the same way embedded objects such as images would.

The Benefits of PHP, MySQL, JavaScript, CSS, and HTML5

At the start of this chapter, I introduced the world of Web 1.0, but it wasn't long before the rush was on to create Web 1.1, with the development of such browser enhancements as Java, JavaScript, JScript (Microsoft's slight variant of JavaScript), and ActiveX. On the server side, progress was being made on the Common Gateway Interface (CGI) using scripting languages such as Perl (an alternative to the PHP language) and *server-side scripting*—inserting the contents of one file (or the output of a system call) into another one dynamically.

Once the dust had settled, three main technologies stood head and shoulders above the others. Although Perl was still a popular scripting language with a strong following, PHP's simplicity and built-in links to the MySQL database program had earned it more than double the number of users. And JavaScript, which had become an essential part of the equation for dynamically manipulating CSS (Cascading Style Sheets) and HTML, now took on the even more muscular task of handling the client side of the Ajax process. Under Ajax, web pages perform data handling and send requests to web servers in the background—without the web user being aware that this is going on.

No doubt the symbiotic nature of PHP and MySQL helped propel them both forward, but what attracted developers to them in the first place? The simple answer has to be the ease with which you can use them to quickly create dynamic elements on websites. MySQL is a fast and powerful, yet easy-to-use, database system that offers just about anything a website would need in order to find and serve up data to browsers. When PHP allies with MySQL to store and retrieve this data, you have the fundamental parts required for the development of social networking sites and the beginnings of Web 2.0.

And when you bring JavaScript and CSS into the mix too, you have a recipe for building highly dynamic and interactive websites.

Using PHP

With PHP, it's a simple matter to embed dynamic activity in web pages. When you give pages the *.php* extension, they have instant access to the scripting language. From a developer's point of view, all you have to do is write code such as the following:

```php
<?php
  echo " Today is " . date("l") . ". ";
?>

Here's the latest news.
```

The opening `<?php` tells the web server to allow the PHP program to interpret all the following code up to the `?>` tag. Outside of this construct, everything is sent to the client as direct HTML. So the text `Here's the latest news.` is simply output to the browser; within the PHP tags, the built-in `date` function displays the current day of the week according to the server's system time.

The final output of the two parts looks like this:

Today is Wednesday. Here's the latest news.

PHP is a flexible language, and some people prefer to place the PHP construct directly next to PHP code, like this:

```php
Today is <?php echo date("l"); ?>. Here's the latest news.
```

There are also other ways of formatting and outputting information, which I'll explain in the chapters on PHP. The point is that with PHP, web developers have a scripting language that, although not as fast as compiling your code in C or a similar language, is incredibly speedy and also integrates seamlessly with HTML markup.

 If you intend to enter the PHP examples in this book to work along with me, you must remember to add `<?php` in front and `?>` after them to ensure that the PHP interpreter processes them. To facilitate this, you may wish to prepare a file called *example.php* with those tags in place.

Using PHP, you have unlimited control over your web server. Whether you need to modify HTML on the fly, process a credit card, add user details to a database, or fetch information from a third-party website, you can do it all from within the same PHP files in which the HTML itself resides.

Using MySQL

Of course, there's not much point to being able to change HTML output dynamically unless you also have a means to track the changes that users make as they use your website. In the early days of the Web, many sites used "flat" text files to store data such as usernames and passwords. But this approach could cause problems if the file wasn't correctly locked against corruption from multiple simultaneous accesses. Also, a flat file can get only so big before it becomes unwieldy to manage—not to mention the difficulty of trying to merge files and perform complex searches in any kind of reasonable time.

That's where relational databases with structured querying become essential. And MySQL, being free to use and installed on vast numbers of Internet web servers, rises superbly to the occasion. It is a robust and exceptionally fast database management system that uses English-like commands.

The highest level of MySQL structure is a database, within which you can have one or more tables that contain your data. For example, let's suppose you are working on a table called users, within which you have created columns for surname, firstname, and email, and you now wish to add another user. One command that you might use to do this is:

```
INSERT INTO users VALUES('Smith', 'John', 'jsmith@mysite.com');
```

Of course, as mentioned earlier, you will have issued other commands to create the database and table and to set up all the correct fields, but the INSERT command here shows how simple it can be to add new data to a database. The INSERT command is an example of SQL (Structured Query Language), a language designed in the early 1970s and reminiscent of one of the oldest programming languages, COBOL. It is well suited, however, to database queries, which is why it is still in use after all this time.

It's equally easy to look up data. Let's assume that you have an email address for a user and need to look up that person's name. To do this, you could issue a MySQL query such as:

```
SELECT surname,firstname FROM users WHERE email='jsmith@mysite.com';
```

MySQL will then return Smith, John and any other pairs of names that may be associated with that email address in the database.

As you'd expect, there's quite a bit more that you can do with MySQL than just simple INSERT and SELECT commands. For example, you can join multiple tables according to various criteria, ask for results in a variety of orders, make partial matches when you know only part of the string that you are searching for, return only the *n*th result, and a lot more.

Using PHP, you can make all these calls directly to MySQL without having to run the MySQL program yourself or use its command-line interface. This means you can save the results in arrays for processing and perform multiple lookups, each dependent on the results returned from earlier ones, to drill right down to the item of data you need.

For even more power, as you'll see later, there are additional functions built right into MySQL that you can call up for common operations and extra speed.

Using JavaScript

The oldest of the three core technologies in this book, JavaScript, was created to enable scripting access to all the elements of an HTML document. In other words, it provides a means for dynamic user interaction such as checking email address validity in input forms, displaying prompts such as "Did you really mean that?", and so on (note, however, that it cannot be relied upon for security, which should always be performed on the web server).

Combined with CSS (see the following section), JavaScript is the power behind dynamic web pages that change in front of your eyes rather than when a new page is returned by the server.

However, JavaScript can also be tricky to use, due to some major differences in the ways different browser designers have chosen to implement it. This mainly came about when some manufacturers tried to put additional functionality into their browsers at the expense of compatibility with their rivals.

Thankfully, the developers have mostly now come to their senses and have realized the need for full compatibility with one another, so they don't have to write multi-exception code. But there remain millions of legacy browsers that will be in use for a good many years to come. Luckily, there are solutions for the incompatibility problems, and later in this book we'll look at libraries and techniques that enable you to safely ignore these differences.

For now, let's take a quick look at how you can use basic JavaScript, accepted by all browsers:

```
<script type="text/javascript">
  document.write("Today is " + Date() );
</script>
```

This code snippet tells the web browser to interpret everything within the `script` tags as JavaScript, which the browser then does by writing the text `Today is` to the current document, along with the date, by using the JavaScript function `Date`. The result will look something like this:

```
Today is Sun Jan 01 2017 01:23:45
```

Unless you need to specify an exact version of JavaScript, you can normally omit the `type="text/javascript"` and just use `<script>` to start the interpretation of the JavaScript.

As previously mentioned, JavaScript was originally developed to offer dynamic control over the various elements within an HTML document, and that is still its main use. But more and more, JavaScript is being used for Ajax. This is a term for the process of accessing the web server in the background. (It originally meant "Asynchronous Java-Script and XML," but that phrase is already a bit outdated.)

Ajax is the main process behind what is now known as Web 2.0 (a term popularized by Tim O'Reilly, the founder and CEO of this book's publishing company), in which web pages have started to resemble standalone programs, because they don't have to be reloaded in their entirety. Instead, a quick Ajax call can pull in and update a single element on a web page, such as changing your photograph on a social networking site or replacing a button that you click with the answer to a question. This subject is fully covered in Chapter 18.

Using CSS

With the emergence of the CSS3 standard in recent years, CSS now offers a level of dynamic interactivity previously supported only by JavaScript. For example, not only can you style any HTML element to change its dimensions, colors, borders, spacing, and so on, but now you can also add animated transitions and transformations to your web pages, using only a few lines of CSS.

Using CSS can be as simple as inserting a few rules between `<style>` and `</style>` tags in the head of a web page, like this:

```
<style>
  p {
    text-align:justify;
    font-family:Helvetica;
  }
</style>
```

These rules will change the default text alignment of the `<p>` tag so that paragraphs contained in it will be fully justified and will use the Helvetica font.

As you'll learn in Chapter 19, there are many different ways you can lay out CSS rules, and you can also include them directly within tags or save a set of rules to an external file to be loaded in separately. This flexibility not only lets you style your HTML precisely, but it can also, for example, provide built-in hover functionality to animate objects as the mouse passes over them. You will also learn how to access all of an element's CSS properties from JavaScript as well as HTML.

And Then There's HTML5

As useful as all these additions to the web standards became, they were not enough for ever more ambitious developers. For example, there was still no simple way to manipulate graphics in a web browser without resorting to plug-ins such as Flash. And the same went for inserting audio and video into web pages. Plus, several annoying inconsistencies had crept into HTML during its evolution.

So, to clear all this up and take the Internet beyond Web 2.0 and into its next iteration, a new standard for HTML was created to address all these shortcomings. It was called HTML5 and it began development as long ago as 2004, when the first draft was drawn up by the Mozilla Foundation and Opera Software (developers of two popular web browsers). But it wasn't until the start of 2013 that the final draft was submitted to the World Wide Web Consortium (W3C), the international governing body for web standards.

With nine years for it to develop, you might think that would be the end of the specification, but that's not how things work on the Internet. Although websites come and go at great speed, the underlying software is developed slowly and carefully, and so the stable recommendation for HTML5 is not expected until after this edition of the book has been published—in late 2014. And then guess what? Work will move on to versions 5.1 and higher, beginning in 2015. It's a never-ending cycle of development.

However, while HTML5.1 is planned to bring some handy improvements (mainly to the canvas), basic HTML5 is the new standard web developers now need to work to, and it will remain in place for many years to come. So learning everything you can about it now will stand you in very good stead.

There's actually a great deal of new stuff in HTML (and quite a few things that have been changed or removed), but in summary, here's what you get:

Markup
Including new elements such as <nav> and <footer>, and deprecated elements like <font> and <center>.

New APIs
For example, the <canvas> element for writing and drawing on a graphics canvas, <audio> and <video> elements, offline web apps, microdata, and local storage.

Applications
Including two new rendering technologies: MathML (Math Markup Language) for displaying mathematical formulae) and SVG (Scalable Vector Graphics) for creating graphical elements outside of the new <canvas> element. However, MathML and SVG are somewhat specialist, and are so feature-packed they would need a book of their own, so I don't cover them here.

All these things (and more) are covered in detail starting in Chapter 22.

One of the little things I like about the HTML5 specification is that XHTML syntax is no longer required for self-closing elements. In the past you could display a line break using the <br> element. Then, to ensure future compatibility with XHTML (the planned replacement for HTML that never happened), this was changed to <br />, in which a closing / character was added (because all elements were expected to include a closing tag featuring this character). But now things have gone full circle, and you can use either version of these element types. So, for the sake of brevity and fewer keystrokes, in this book I have reverted to the former style of <br>, <hr>, and so on.

The Apache Web Server

In addition to PHP, MySQL, JavaScript, CSS, and HTML5, there's actually a sixth hero in the dynamic Web: the web server. In the case of this book, that means the Apache web server. We've discussed a little of what a web server does during the HTTP server/ client exchange, but it actually does much more behind the scenes.

For example, Apache doesn't serve up just HTML files—it handles a wide range of files from images and Flash files to MP3 audio files, RSS (Really Simple Syndication) feeds, and so on. To do this, each element a web client encounters in an HTML page is also requested from the server, which then serves it up.

But these objects don't have to be static files such as GIF images. They can all be generated by programs such as PHP scripts. That's right: PHP can even create images and other files for you, either on the fly or in advance to serve up later.

To do this, you normally have modules either precompiled into Apache or PHP or called up at runtime. One such module is the GD (Graphics Draw) library, which PHP uses to create and handle graphics.

Apache also supports a huge range of modules of its own. In addition to the PHP module, the most important for your purposes as a web programmer are the modules that handle security. Other examples are the Rewrite module, which enables the web server to handle a varying range of URL types and rewrite them to its own internal requirements, and the Proxy module, which you can use to serve up often-requested pages from a cache to ease the load on the server.

Later in the book, you'll see how to actually use some of these modules to enhance the features provided by the three core technologies.

About Open Source

Whether the open source quality of these technologies is the reason they are so popular has often been debated, but PHP, MySQL, and Apache *are* the three most commonly used tools in their categories.

What can be said definitively, though, is that their being open source means that they have been developed in the community by teams of programmers writing the features they themselves want and need, with the original code available for all to see and change. Bugs can be found and security breaches can be prevented before they happen.

There's another benefit: all these programs are free to use. There's no worrying about having to purchase additional licenses if you have to scale up your website and add more servers. And you don't need to check the budget before deciding whether to upgrade to the latest versions of these products.

Bringing It All Together

The real beauty of PHP, MySQL, JavaScript, CSS, and HTML5 is the wonderful way in which they all work together to produce dynamic web content: PHP handles all the main work on the web server, MySQL manages all the data, and the combination of CSS and JavaScript looks after web page presentation. JavaScript can also talk with your PHP code on the web server whenever it needs to update something (either on the server or on the web page). And with the powerful new features in HTML5, such as the canvas, audio and video, and geolocation, you can make your web pages highly dynamic, interactive, and multimedia packed.

Without using program code, let's summarize the contents of this chapter by looking at the process of combining some of these technologies into an everyday Ajax feature that many websites use: checking whether a desired username already exists on the site when a user is signing up for a new account. A good example of this can be seen with Gmail (see Figure 1-3).

Figure 1-3. Gmail uses Ajax to check the availability of usernames

The steps involved in this Ajax process would be similar to the following:

1. The server outputs the HTML to create the web form, which asks for the necessary details, such as username, first name, last name, and email address.

2. At the same time, the server attaches some JavaScript to the HTML to monitor the username input box and check for two things: (a) whether some text has been typed into it, and (b) whether the input has been deselected because the user has clicked on another input box.

3. Once the text has been entered and the field deselected, in the background the JavaScript code passes the username that was entered back to a PHP script on the web server and awaits a response.

4. The web server looks up the username and replies back to the JavaScript regarding whether that name has already been taken.

5. The JavaScript then places an indication next to the username input box to show whether the name is one available to the user—perhaps a green checkmark or a red cross graphic, along with some text.

6. If the username is not available and the user still submits the form, the JavaScript interrupts the submission and reemphasizes (perhaps with a larger graphic and/or an alert box) that the user needs to choose another username.

7. Optionally, an improved version of this process could even look at the username requested by the user and suggest an alternative that is currently available.

All of this takes place quietly in the background and makes for a comfortable and seamless user experience. Without Ajax, the entire form would have to be submitted to the server, which would then send back HTML, highlighting any mistakes. It would be a workable solution, but nowhere near as tidy or pleasurable as on-the-fly form field processing.

Ajax can be used for a lot more than simple input verification and processing, though; we'll explore many additional things that you can do with it in the Ajax chapters later in this book.

In this chapter, you have read a good introduction to the core technologies of PHP, MySQL, JavaScript, CSS, and HTML5 (as well as Apache), and have learned how they work together. In Chapter 2, we'll look at how you can install your own web development server on which to practice everything that you will be learning.

Questions

1. What four components (at the minimum) are needed to create a fully dynamic web page?
2. What does HTML stand for?
3. Why does the name MySQL contain the letters *SQL*?
4. PHP and JavaScript are both programming languages that generate dynamic results for web pages. What is their main difference, and why would you use both of them?
5. What does CSS stand for?
6. List three major new elements introduced in HTML5.
7. If you encounter a bug (which is rare) in one of the open source tools, how do you think you could get it fixed?

See "Chapter 1 Answers" on page 639 in Appendix A for the answers to these questions.

CHAPTER 2

Setting Up a Development Server

If you wish to develop Internet applications but don't have your own development server, you will have to upload every modification you make to a server somewhere else on the Web before you can test it.

Even on a fast broadband connection, this can still represent a significant slowdown in development time. On a local computer, however, testing can be as easy as saving an update (usually just a matter of clicking once on an icon) and then hitting the Refresh button in your browser.

Another advantage of a development server is that you don't have to worry about embarrassing errors or security problems while you're writing and testing, whereas you need to be aware of what people may see or do with your application when it's on a public website. It's best to iron everything out while you're still on a home or small office system, presumably protected by firewalls and other safeguards.

Once you have your own development server, you'll wonder how you ever managed without one, and it's easy to set one up. Just follow the steps in the following sections, using the appropriate instructions for a PC, a Mac, or a Linux system.

In this chapter, we cover just the server side of the web experience, as described in Chapter 1. But to test the results of your work—particularly when we start using Java-Script, CSS, and HTML5 later in this book—you should also have an instance of every major web browser running on some system convenient to you. Whenever possible, the list of browsers should include at least Internet Explorer, Mozilla Firefox, Opera, Safari, and Google Chrome.

If you plan to ensure your sites look good on mobile devices too, then you should also try to arrange access to a wide range of Apple iOS and Google Android phones and tablets.

What Is a WAMP, MAMP, or LAMP?

WAMP, MAMP, and LAMP are abbreviations for "Windows, Apache, MySQL, and PHP," "Mac, Apache, MySQL, and PHP," and "Linux, Apache, MySQL, and PHP." These abbreviations describe a fully functioning setup used for developing dynamic Internet web pages.

WAMPs, MAMPs, and LAMPs come in the form of a package that binds the bundled programs together so that you don't have to install and set them up separately. This means you can simply download and install a single program, and follow a few easy prompts, to get your web development server up and running in the quickest time with a minimum hassle.

During installation, several default settings are created for you. The security configurations of such an installation will not be as tight as on a production web server, because it is optimized for local use. For these reasons, you should never install such a setup as a production server.

But for developing and testing websites and applications, one of these installations should be entirely sufficient.

 If you choose not to go the WAMP/MAMP/LAMP route for building your own development system, you should know that downloading and integrating the various parts yourself can be very time-consuming and may require a lot of research in order to configure everything fully. But if you already have all the components installed and integrated with one another, they should work with the examples in this book.

Installing a WAMP on Windows

There are several available WAMP servers, each offering slightly different configurations, but the best is probably Zend Server Free Edition, because it's free and is from the developers of PHP itself. You can download it at *http://tinyurl.com/zendfree*, as shown in Figure 2-1.

Throughout this book, whenever there's a long URL to type, I use the TinyURL web address shortening service to save you time and reduce typos. For example, the URLs *http://tinyurl.com/zendfree* and *http://tinyurl.com/zenddocs* are much shorter than the URLs that they lead to:

- *http://www.zend.com/en/products/server/free-edition*
- *http://files.zend.com/help/Zend-Server-6/zend-server.htm*

Figure 2-1. You can download the Free Edition from the Zend website

I recommend that you always download the latest stable release (in this instance, it's 6.3.0/PHP 5.5 for Windows). It will probably be listed first in the Download section of the web page, which should display the correct installer for your computer out of Linux, Windows OS X, and IBM i.

During the lifetime of this edition, some of the screens and options shown in the following walkthrough may change. If so, just use your common sense to proceed in as similar a manner as possible to the sequence of actions described.

Once you've downloaded the installer, run it to bring up the window shown in Figure 2-2.

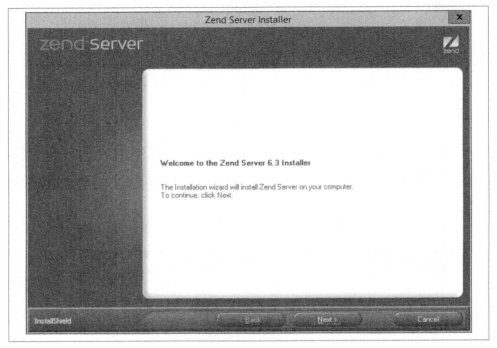

Figure 2-2. The main installation window of the installer

Click Next and accept the license agreement that follows to move on to the Setup Type screen (see Figure 2-3), then select the Custom option so that the MySQL server can also be installed.

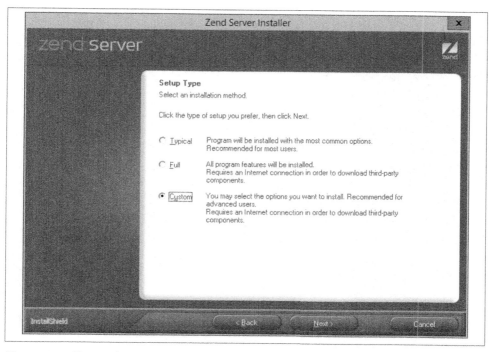

Figure 2-3. Choose the Custom install option

When the Custom Setup window appears, scroll down the list of options to the bottom and ensure that MySQL Server is checked, as shown in Figure 2-4, then click Next.

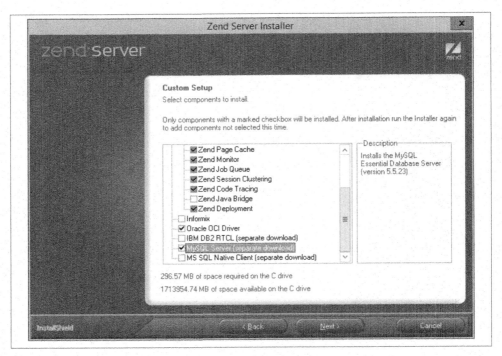

Figure 2-4. Check MySQL Server before continuing

On the following screen (see Figure 2-5), even if you already have an IIS web server installed, I recommend that you choose to install the Apache web server, because the examples in this book are for Apache. Then click Next.

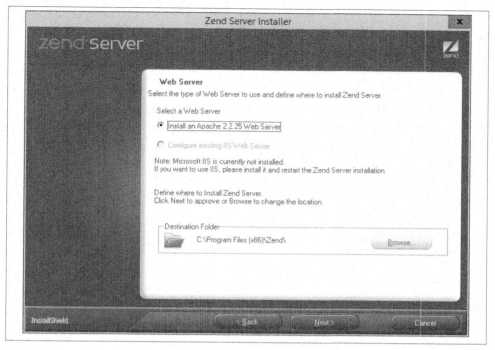

Figure 2-5. Install the Apache web server

Now accept the default values of 80 for the Web Server Port, and 10081 for the Zend Server Interface Port (see Figure 2-6) and click Next.

If either of the ports offered states that it is occupied (generally this will be because you have another web server running) and doesn't allow you to use the defaults, then try a value of 8080 (or 8000) for the Web Server Port, and 10082 for the Zend Server Interface Port. You'll need to remember these values for later when you're accessing either web pages or the Zend server. For example, instead of visiting *localhost/index.htm* in your web browser, you would use *localhost:8080/index.htm*.

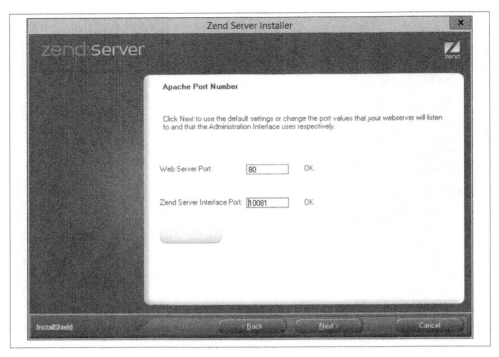

Figure 2-6. Accept the default values offered for the ports

Once the ports have been assigned, you will reach the screen in Figure 2-7, where you should click Install to start the installation.

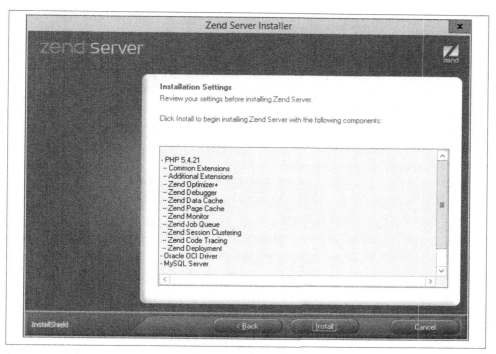

Figure 2-7. Now you are ready to click Install to proceed

During installation some extra files may be downloaded, so it may take a few minutes for the programs to get set up. During installation you might also see a pop-up dialog box from Windows Firewall. If so, accept the request to give it access. When the files have been installed, you will be notified and prompted to start using the software by clicking Finish. When you do so, your default browser will be opened with the page shown in Figure 2-8, where, to continue, you must check the box to agree with the terms.

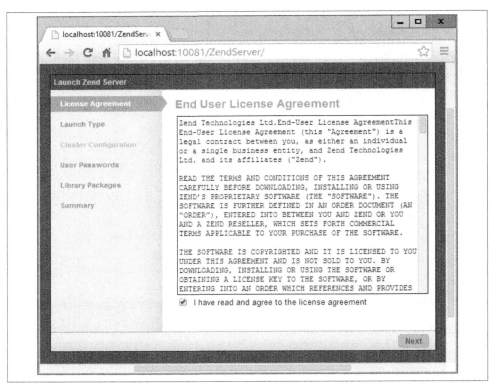

Figure 2-8. You must agree to the terms in order to use the server

Next, you are asked how you will be using the server. I recommend that you select the Development option for the purposes of working through the exercises in this book (see Figure 2-9).

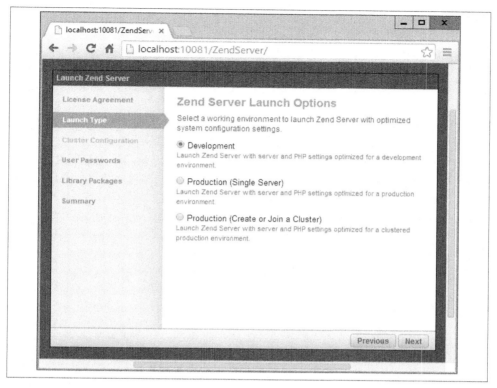

Figure 2-9. Select the Development option

Now you are ready to set a password for the user *admin* (see Figure 2-10). You do not need to enter a password for the user *developer*. Make sure you choose a password you will remember and click Next. After the library packages show as deployed, click Next again to proceed to the screen shown in Figure 2-11, where you can now click Launch to finish installation. Note that the Cluster Configuration option may not appear on the OS X version of the installer.

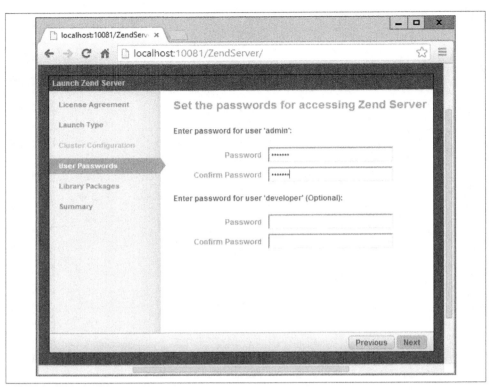

Figure 2-10. Choose your password and enter it twice

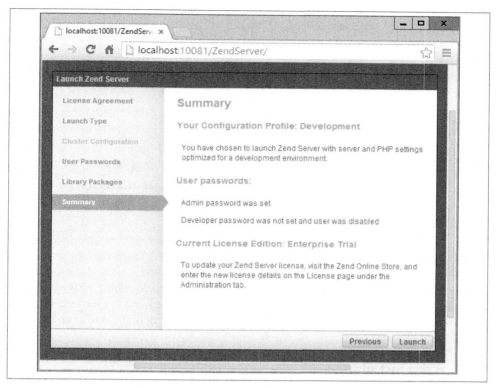

Figure 2-11. Click Submit to complete setup

After a short wait, your browser will show the Dashboard screen in Figure 2-12, which is where you can administer the server.

Figure 2-12. The Zend Server administration screen

You can return to this screen at any time by entering *http://localhost:10081* into your browser. Or, if you entered a value other than 10081 for the Zend Server Interface Port (or 10088 on a Mac), then you can get to this screen by using that value after the colon instead.

Testing the Installation

The first thing to do at this point is verify that everything is working correctly. To do this, you are going to try to display the default web page, which will have been saved in the server's document root folder (see Figure 2-13). Enter either of the following two URLs into the address bar of your browser:

```
localhost
127.0.0.1
```

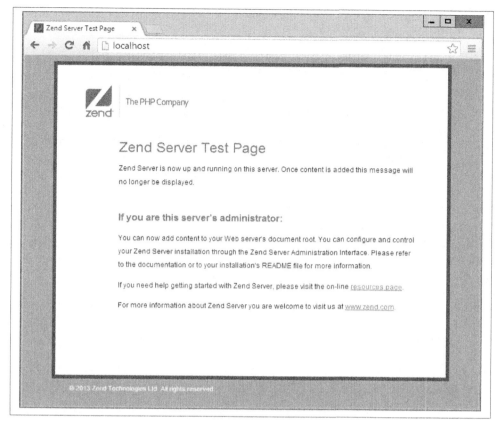

Figure 2-13. How the home page should look by default

The word *localhost* is used in URLs to specify the local computer, which will also respond to the IP address of 127.0.0.1, so you can use either method of calling up the document root of your web server.

 If you chose a server port other than 80 during installation (e.g., 8080), then you must place a colon followed by that value after either of the preceding URLs (e.g., *localhost:8080*). You will have to do the same for all example files in this book. For example, instead of the URL *localhost/example.php*, you should enter *localhost:8080/example.php* (or whatever value you chose).

The document root is the directory that contains the main web documents for a domain. This is the one that is entered when a basic URL without a path is typed into a browser, such as *http://yahoo.com* or, for your local server, *http://localhost*.

By default, Zend Server uses one of the following locations for this directory (the former for 32-bit computers, and the latter for 64-bit):

```
C:/Program Files/Zend/Apache2/htdocs
C:/Program Files (x86)/Zend/Apache2/htdocs
```

 If you are not sure whether your computer is 32-bit or 64-bit, try to navigate to the first directory and, if it exists, you have a 32-bit machine. If not, open up the second directory because you have a 64-bit computer. When they include spaces, older versions of Windows may require you to place path and filenames in quotation marks, like this:

```
cd "C:/Program Files/Zend/Apache2/htdocs"
```

To ensure that you have everything correctly configured, you should now create the obligatory "Hello World" file. So create a small HTML file along the following lines using Windows Notepad or any other program or text editor, but not a rich word processor such as Microsoft Word (unless you save as plain text):

```
<html>
  <head>
    <title>A quick test</title>
  </head>
  <body>
    Hello World!
  </body>
</html>
```

Once you have typed this, save the file into the document root directory previously discussed, using the filename *test.htm*. If you are using Notepad, make sure that the "Save as type" box is changed from "Text Documents (*.txt)" to "All Files (*.*)". Or, if you prefer, you can save the file using the *.html* file extension; either is acceptable.

You can now call this page up in your browser by entering one of the following URLs (according to the extension you used) in its address bar (see Figure 2-14):

```
http://localhost/test.htm
http://localhost/test.html
```

You should now have had a trouble-free installation, resulting in a fully working WAMP. But if you encountered any difficulties, check out the comprehensive documentation at *http://tinyurl.com/zenddocs*, which should sort out your problem.

Figure 2-14. Your first web page

Alternative WAMPs

When software is updated, it sometimes works differently than you'd expected, and bugs can even be introduced. So if you encounter difficulties that you cannot resolve, you may prefer to choose one of the various other solutions available on the Web instead.

You will still be able to make use of all the examples in this book, but you'll have to follow the instructions supplied with each WAMP, which may not be as easy to follow as the preceding guide.

Here's a selection of the best in my opinion:

- EasyPHP (*http://www.easyphp.org/*)
- XAMPP (*http://apachefriends.org/en/xampp.html*)
- WAMPServer (*http://wampserver.com/en/*)
- Glossword WAMP (*http://glossword.biz/glosswordwamp/*)

Installing a MAMP on Mac OS X

Zend Server Free Edition is also available on OS X, and you can download it from *http://tinyurl.com/zendfree*, as shown in Figure 2-15.

I recommend that you always download the latest stable release (in this instance, it's 6.3.0/PHP 5.5 for OS X). It will usually be listed first in the Download section of the web page, which should display the correct installer for your computer out of Linux, Windows, OS X, and IBM i. You may be asked to log in before you download, but you can also click a link to get the file without logging in or registering, although you'll miss out on product update emails and other news.

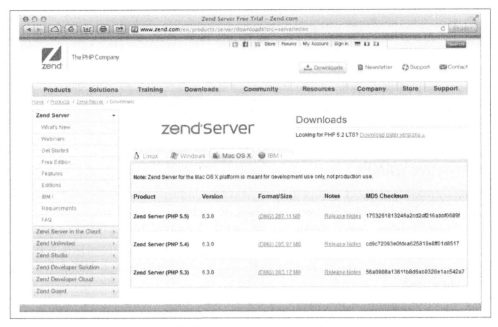

Figure 2-15. You can download the server from the Zend website

Once the installer is downloaded, double-click the *.dmg* file and wait for the download to verify, and then you should see the window shown in Figure 2-16.

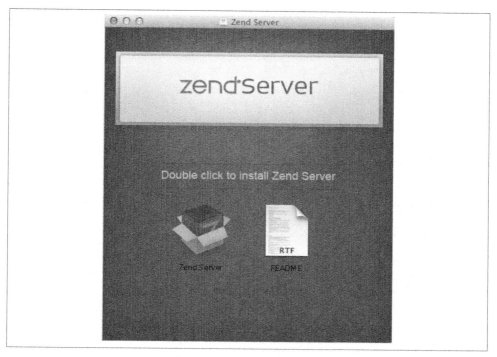

Figure 2-16. Double-click Zend Server to install it

Here you can double-click the *README* file for instructions, or double-click Zend Server to open up the installation window shown in Figure 2-17.

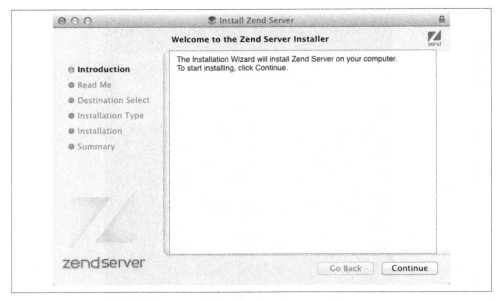

Figure 2-17. The Zend Server installer

Now click Continue, read the instructions that are displayed, and then click Continue again to reach the screen shown in Figure 2-18, where you can decide where to put the installed software (the default being Macintosh HD). Click Install when you are ready, and enter your password if prompted for it.

During installation, you may be asked whether you wish to install additional software. If so, I recommend accepting everything offered to you by clicking the Install button. Upon completion of the installation, you can click Close to close the installer.

Once the software is installed, locate the ZendServer program in your *Applications* folder and double-click it to proceed with completing the setup. This will bring up a page in your default web browser similar to that shown in Figure 2-8. Now follow the prompts you are given (shown in Figure 2-8 through Figure 2-11), in which you must accept the license agreement and choose a password before being taken to the main dashboard, as shown earlier in Figure 2-12.

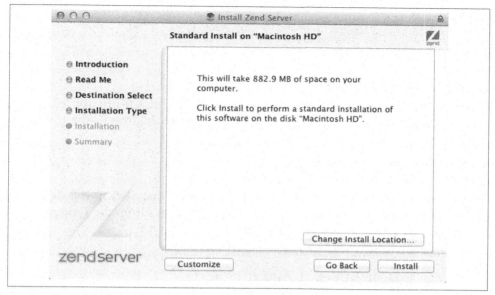

Figure 2-18. Choosing the destination for installation

Configuring MySQL

Unfortunately, the installer doesn't set up the commands needed to be able to start, stop, and restart the MySQL server, so you're going to have to do this manually by opening the Terminal and entering the following command:

```
sudo nano /usr/local/zend/bin/zendctl.sh
```

After entering your password you will now be in the Nano text editor, so move the cursor down a few lines using the down cursor key, and where you see the line that reads MySQL_EN="false", change the word false to true.

Now scroll down some more until you find these two lines:

```
case $1 in
        "start")
```

Below that, you'll see an indented line that reads:

```
        $0 start-apache %
```

Just after this line, insert a new one that reads as follows:

```
        $0 start-MySQL %
```

This will allow MySQL to start, but now you need to scroll down a little more until you get to the section that starts with:

```
        "stop")
```

Then below it, you'll see an indented line that reads:

```
$0 stop-apache %
```

Just after this line, insert a new one that reads as follows:

```
$0 stop-MySQL %
```

This will allow MySQL to be stopped. Now you can press Ctrl-X to exit from edit mode, press the Y key when prompted to save the changes, and then press Return to save the edited file.

Ensuring MySQL Starts on Booting

Unfortunately, there's another edit you have to make so that MySQL will start when your Mac does, and that's to issue the following commands from the Terminal (supplying your password in the relevant place if prompted for it):

```
cd /Library/StartupItems/ZendServer_init/
sudo rm zendctl.sh
sudo ln -s /usr/local/zend/bin/zendctl.sh ./
```

Your Mac is now configured, but MySQL has not yet been started, so now you must issue the following command (along with password if prompted) after which you should be all set to go:

```
sudo /Library/StartupItems/ZendServer_init/zendctl.sh restart
```

Testing the Installation

You can now test the installation by entering either of the following URLs into your web browser to call up the screen shown in Figure 2-13:

```
localhost:10088
127.0.0.1:10088
```

The word *localhost* specifies the local computer (which will also respond to the IP address of 127.0.0.1). And the reason for having to enter *:10088* is because many Mac computers will already have a web server running, so this avoids any clash.

You must therefore remember to place *:10088* after every *localhost* for all examples in this book. So, for example, if the filename *test.php* is being accessed, you would call it up from the browser using the URL *localhost:10088/test.php*.

If you are sure that there isn't another web server running on your Mac, you can edit the configuration file at the following URL (ensuring you have permission to do so), changing the command (at around line 40) that reads `Listen 10088` to `Listen 80`:

```
/usr/local/zend/apache2/conf/httpd.conf
```

You will then need to restart the server by opening the Terminal utility and issuing the following command (along with your password if prompted), and you will then no longer need to add the *:10088* to local URLs:

```
sudo /usr/local/zend/bin/zendctl.sh restart
```

The page that gets displayed in the browser when you go to *http://localhost* or *http://localhost:10088* is the file *index.html* in the server's document root (the directory that contains the main web documents for a domain). This is the directory that is entered when a basic URL without a path is typed into a browser, such as *http://yahoo.com*, or in the case of your local web server, *http://localhost*, and so on.

By default, Zend Server on OS X uses the following as its document root folder:

```
/usr/local/zend/apache2/htdocs
```

To ensure that you have everything correctly configured, you should now load a test file. So create a small HTML file along the following lines using Windows TextEdit or any other program or text editor (such as the popular TextWrangler), but not a rich word processor like Microsoft Word (unless you save as plain text):

```html
<html>
  <head>
    <title>A quick test</title>
  </head>
  <body>
    Hello World!
  </body>
</html>
```

Once you have typed this, save the file into the document root directory using the filename *test.htm*. Or, if you prefer, use the *.html* file extension. You can now call this page up in your browser by entering one of the following URLs (according to the extension you saved with) in its address bar (see Figure 2-14):

```
http://localhost:10088/test.htm
http://localhost:10088/test.html
```

You should now have had a trouble-free installation, resulting in a fully working MAMP. But if you encountered any difficulties, check out the comprehensive documentation at *http://tinyurl.com/zenddocs*, which should sort out your problem.

Installing a LAMP on Linux

This book is aimed mostly at PC and Mac users, but its contents will work equally well on a Linux computer. However, there are dozens of popular flavors of Linux, and each of them may require installing a LAMP in a slightly different way, so I can't cover them all in this book.

Nonetheless, many Linux versions come preinstalled with a web server and MySQL, and the chances are that you may already be all set to go. To find out, try entering the following into a browser and see whether you get a default document root web page:

```
http://localhost
```

If this works, you probably have the Apache server installed and may well also have MySQL up and running too; check with your system administrator to be sure, though.

If you don't yet have a web server installed, however, there's a version of Zend Server Free Edition available that you can download at *http://tinyurl.com/zendfree*.

All the instructions and help you need are detailed on the Download page. Follow them closely or use the provided scripts, and you should be able to work through all the examples in this book.

Working Remotely

If you have access to a web server already configured with PHP and MySQL, you can always use that for your web development. But unless you have a high-speed connection, it is not always your best option. Developing locally allows you to test modifications with little or no upload delay.

Accessing MySQL remotely may not be easy either. You may have to Telnet or SSH into your server to manually create databases and set permissions from the command line. Your web hosting company will advise you on how best to do this and provide you with any password it has set for your MySQL access (as well as, of course, for getting into the server in the first place).

Logging In

I recommend that, at minimum, Windows users should install a program such as PuTTY (*http://putty.org*) for Telnet and SSH access (remember that SSH is much more secure than Telnet).

On a Mac, you already have SSH available. Just select the *Applications* folder, followed by *Utilities*, and then launch Terminal. In the terminal window, log into a server using SSH as follows:

```
ssh mylogin@server.com
```

where `server.com` is the name of the server you wish to log into and `mylogin` is the username you will log in under. You will then be prompted for the correct password for that username and, if you enter it correctly, you will be logged in.

Using FTP

To transfer files to and from your web server, you will need an FTP program. If you go searching the Web for a good one, you'll find so many that it could take you quite a while to come across one with all the right features for you.

Nowadays I always recommend FireFTP, because of these advantages:

- It is an add-on for the Firefox web browser, and will therefore work on any platform on which Firefox runs.
- Calling it up can be as simple as selecting a bookmark.
- It is one of the fastest and easiest-to-use FTP programs that I have encountered.

 You may say, "But I use only Microsoft Internet Explorer, and FireFTP is not available for it," but I would counter that if you are going to develop web pages, you need a copy of each of the main browsers installed on your PC anyway, as suggested at the start of this chapter.

To install FireFTP, visit *http://fireftp.mozdev.org* using Firefox and click on the Download FireFTP link. It's about half a megabyte in size and installs very quickly. Once it's installed, restart Firefox; you can then access FireFTP from the Tools menu (see Figure 2-19).

Another excellent FTP program is the open source FileZilla (*http://filezilla-project.org*), available for Windows, Linux, and Mac OS X 10.5 or newer.

Of course, if you already have an FTP program, all the better—stick with what you know.

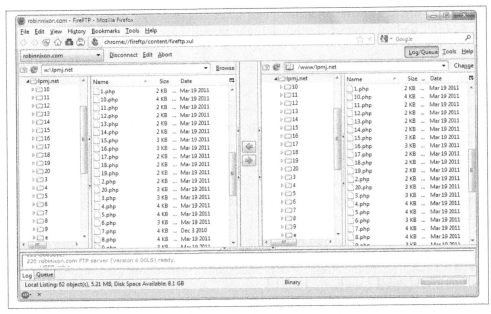

Figure 2-19. FireFTP offers full FTP access from within Firefox

Using a Program Editor

Although a plain-text editor works for editing HTML, PHP, and JavaScript, there have been some tremendous improvements in dedicated program editors, which now incorporate very handy features such as colored syntax highlighting. Today's program editors are smart and can show you where you have syntax errors before you even run a program. Once you've used a modern editor, you'll wonder how you ever managed without one.

There are a number of good programs available, but I have settled on Editra, because it's free and available on Mac, Windows, and Linux/Unix. You can download a copy by visiting *http://editra.org* and selecting the Download link toward the top left of the page, where you can also find the documentation for it.

As you can see from Figure 2-20, Editra highlights the syntax appropriately using colors to help clarify what's going on. What's more, you can place the cursor next to brackets or braces and Editra will highlight the matching pair so that you can check whether you have too many or too few. In fact, Editra offers a wealth of additional features, which you will discover and enjoy as you use it.

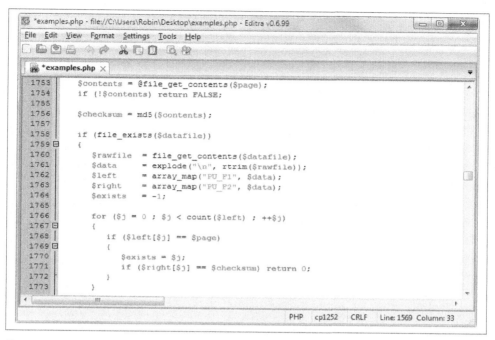

```
1753      $contents = @file_get_contents($page);
1754      if (!$contents) return FALSE;
1755
1756      $checksum = md5($contents);
1757
1758      if (file_exists($datafile))
1759      {
1760          $rawfile = file_get_contents($datafile);
1761          $data    = explode("\n", rtrim($rawfile));
1762          $left    = array_map("PU_F1", $data);
1763          $right   = array_map("PU_F2", $data);
1764          $exists  = -1;
1765
1766          for ($j = 0 ; $j < count($left) ; ++$j)
1767          {
1768              if ($left[$j] == $page)
1769              {
1770                  $exists = $j;
1771                  if ($right[$j] == $checksum) return 0;
1772              }
1773          }
```

Figure 2-20. Program editors are superior to plain-text editors

Again, if you have a different preferred program editor, use that; it's always a good idea to use programs you're already familiar with.

Using an IDE

As good as dedicated program editors can be for your programming productivity, their utility pales into insignificance when compared to *integrated development environments* (IDEs), which offer many additional features such as in-editor debugging and program testing, as well as function descriptions and much more.

Figure 2-21 shows the popular phpDesigner IDE with a PHP program loaded into the main frame, and the righthand Code Explorer listing the various classes, functions, and variables that it uses.

When developing with an IDE, you can set breakpoints and then run all (or portions) of your code, which will then stop at the breakpoints and provide you with information about the program's current state.

As an aid to learning programming, the examples in this book can be entered into an IDE and run there and then, without the need to call up your web browser.

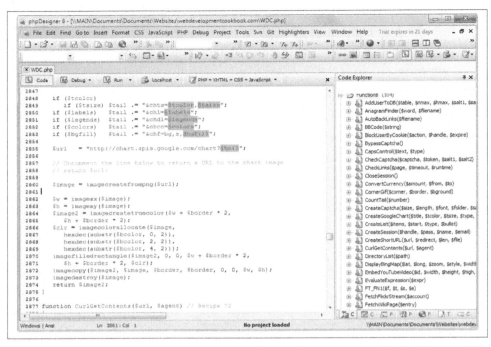

Figure 2-21. When you're using an IDE such as phpDesigner, PHP development becomes much quicker and easier

There are several IDEs available for different platforms, most of which are commercial, but there are some free ones too. Table 2-1 lists some of the most popular PHP IDEs, along with their download URLs.

Choosing an IDE can be a very personal thing, so if you intend to use one, I advise you to download a couple or more to try them out first; they all either have trial versions or are free to use, so it won't cost you anything.

Table 2-1. A selection of PHP IDEs

IDE	Download URL	Cost	Win	Mac	Lin
Eclipse PDT	*http://eclipse.org/pdt/downloads/*	Free	☑	☑	☑
Komodo IDE	*http://activestate.com/Products/komodo_ide*	$245	☑	☑	☑
NetBeans	*http://www.netbeans.org*	Free	☑	☑	☑
phpDesigner	*http://mpsoftware.dk*	$39	☑	☐	☐
PHPEclipse	*http://phpeclipse.de*	Free	☑	☑	☑
PhpED	*http://nusphere.com*	$119	☑	☐	☑
PHPedit	*http://www.phpedit.com*	$119	☑	☐	☐
Zend Studio	*http://zend.com/en/downloads*	$189	☑	☑	☑

You should take the time to install a program editor or IDE you are comfortable with and you'll then be ready to try out the examples in the coming chapters.

Armed with these tools, you are now ready to move on to Chapter 3, where we'll start exploring PHP in further depth and find out how to get HTML and PHP to work together, as well as how the PHP language itself is structured. But before moving on, I suggest you test your new knowledge with the following questions.

Questions

1. What is the difference between a WAMP, a MAMP, and a LAMP?
2. What do the IP address 127.0.0.1 and the URL *http://localhost* have in common?
3. What is the purpose of an FTP program?
4. Name the main disadvantage of working on a remote web server.
5. Why is it better to use a program editor instead of a plain-text editor?

See "Chapter 2 Answers" on page 640 in Appendix A for the answers to these questions.

CHAPTER 3

Introduction to PHP

In Chapter 1, I explained that PHP is the language that you use to make the server generate dynamic output—output that is potentially different each time a browser requests a page. In this chapter, you'll start learning this simple but powerful language; it will be the topic of the following chapters up through Chapter 7.

I encourage you to develop your PHP code in one of the IDEs listed in Chapter 2. It will help you catch typos and speed up learning tremendously in comparison to less feature-rich editors.

Many of these development environments let you run the PHP code and see the output discussed in this chapter. I'll also show you how to embed the PHP in an HTML file so that you can see what the output looks like in a web page (the way your users will ultimately see it). But that step, as thrilling as it may be at first, isn't really important at this stage.

In production, your web pages will be a combination of PHP, HTML, and JavaScript, and some MySQL statements laid out using CSS, and possibly utilizing various HTML5 elements. Furthermore, each page can lead to other pages to provide users with ways to click through links and fill out forms. We can avoid all that complexity while learning each language, though. Focus for now on just writing PHP code and making sure that you get the output you expect—or at least that you understand the output you actually get!

Incorporating PHP Within HTML

By default, PHP documents end with the extension *.php*. When a web server encounters this extension in a requested file, it automatically passes it to the PHP processor. Of course, web servers are highly configurable, and some web developers choose to force files ending with *.htm* or *.html* to also get parsed by the PHP processor, usually because they want to hide the fact that they are using PHP.

Your PHP program is responsible for passing back a clean file suitable for display in a web browser. At its very simplest, a PHP document will output only HTML. To prove this, you can take any normal HTML document such as an *index.html* file and save it as *index.php*, and it will display identically to the original.

To trigger the PHP commands, you need to learn a new tag. The first part is:

```
<?php
```

The first thing you may notice is that the tag has not been closed. This is because entire sections of PHP can be placed inside this tag, and they finish only when the closing part is encountered, which looks like this:

```
?>
```

A small PHP "Hello World" program might look like Example 3-1.

Example 3-1. Invoking PHP

```
<?php
  echo "Hello world";
?>
```

The way you use this tag is quite flexible. Some programmers open the tag at the start of a document and close it right at the end, outputting any HTML directly from PHP commands.

Others, however, choose to insert only the smallest possible fragments of PHP within these tags wherever dynamic scripting is required, leaving the rest of the document in standard HTML.

The latter type of programmer generally argues that their style of coding results in faster code, while the former says that the speed increase is so minimal that it doesn't justify the additional complexity of dropping in and out of PHP many times in a single document.

As you learn more, you will surely discover your preferred style of PHP development, but for the sake of making the examples in this book easier to follow, I have adopted the approach of keeping the number of transfers between PHP and HTML to a minimum—generally only once or twice in a document.

By the way, there is a slight variation to the PHP syntax. If you browse the Internet for PHP examples, you may also encounter code where the opening and closing syntax looks like this:

```
<?
  echo "Hello world";
?>
```

Although it's not as obvious that the PHP parser is being called, this is a valid, alternative syntax that also usually works, but should be discouraged, as it is incompatible with

XML and its use is now deprecated (meaning that it is no longer recommended and could be removed in future versions).

 If you have only PHP code in a file, you may omit the closing ?>. This can be a good practice, as it will ensure that you have no excess whitespace leaking from your PHP files (especially important when you're writing object-oriented code).

This Book's Examples

To save you the time it would take to type them all in, all the examples from this book have been archived onto the companion website (*http://lpmj.net*), which you can download to your computer by clicking the *Download Examples* link in the heading section (see Figure 3-1).

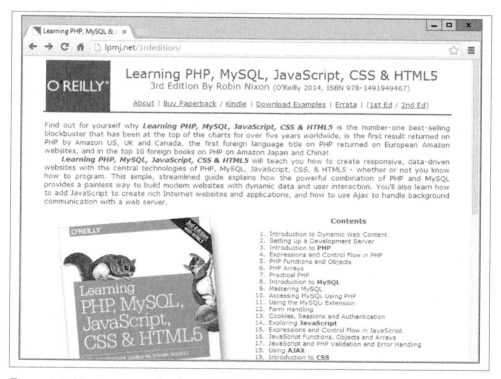

Figure 3-1. Viewing examples from this book at http://lpmj.net

In addition to having all the examples saved by chapter and example number (such as *example3-1.php*), the archive also contains an extra folder called *named_examples*, in which you'll find all the examples I suggest you save using a specific filename (such as the upcoming Example 3-4, which should be saved as *test1.php*).

The Structure of PHP

We're going to cover quite a lot of ground in this section. It's not too difficult, but I recommend that you work your way through it carefully, as it sets the foundation for everything else in this book. As always, there are some useful questions at the end of the chapter that you can use to test how much you've learned.

Using Comments

There are two ways in which you can add comments to your PHP code. The first turns a single line into a comment by preceding it with a pair of forward slashes, like this:

```
// This is a comment
```

This version of the comment feature is a great way to temporarily remove a line of code from a program that is giving you errors. For example, you could use such a comment to hide a debugging line of code until you need it, like this:

```
// echo "X equals $x";
```

You can also use this type of comment directly after a line of code to describe its action, like this:

```
$x += 10; // Increment $x by 10
```

When you need multiple-line comments, there's a second type of comment, which looks like Example 3-2.

Example 3-2. A multiline comment

```
<?php
/* This is a section
   of multiline comments
   which will not be
   interpreted */
?>
```

You can use the /* and */ pairs of characters to open and close comments almost anywhere you like inside your code. Most, if not all, programmers use this construct to temporarily comment out entire sections of code that do not work or that, for one reason or another, they do not wish to be interpreted.

A common error is to use /* and */ to comment out a large section of code that already contains a commented-out section that uses those characters. You can't nest comments this way; the PHP interpreter won't know where a comment ends and will display an error message. However, if you use a program editor or IDE with syntax highlighting, this type of error is easier to spot.

Basic Syntax

PHP is quite a simple language with roots in C and Perl, yet it looks more like Java. It is also very flexible, but there are a few rules that you need to learn about its syntax and structure.

Semicolons

You may have noticed in the previous examples that the PHP commands ended with a semicolon, like this:

```
$x += 10;
```

Probably the most common cause of errors you will encounter with PHP is forgetting this semicolon. This causes PHP to treat multiple statements like one statement, which it is unable to understand, prompting it to produce a `Parse error` message.

The $ symbol

The $ symbol has come to be used in many different ways by different programming languages. For example, if you have ever written in the BASIC language, you will have used the $ to terminate variable names to denote them as strings.

In PHP, however, you must place a $ in front of *all* variables. This is required to make the PHP parser faster, as it instantly knows whenever it comes across a variable. Whether your variables are numbers, strings, or arrays, they should all look something like those in Example 3-3.

Example 3-3. Three different types of variable assignment

```php
<?php
  $mycounter = 1;
  $mystring  = "Hello";
  $myarray   = array("One", "Two", "Three");
?>
```

And really that's pretty much all the syntax that you have to remember. Unlike languages that are very strict about how you indent and lay out your code (e.g., Python), PHP leaves you completely free to use (or not use) all the indenting and spacing you like. In fact, sensible use of *whitespace* is generally encouraged (along with comprehensive commenting) to help you understand your code when you come back to it. It also helps other programmers when they have to maintain your code.

Variables

There's a simple metaphor that will help you understand what PHP variables are all about. Just think of them as little (or big) matchboxes! That's right—matchboxes that you've painted over and written names on.

String variables

Imagine you have a matchbox on which you have written the word *username*. You then write *Fred Smith* on a piece of paper and place it into the box (see Figure 3-2). Well, that's the same process as assigning a string value to a variable, like this:

```
$username = "Fred Smith";
```

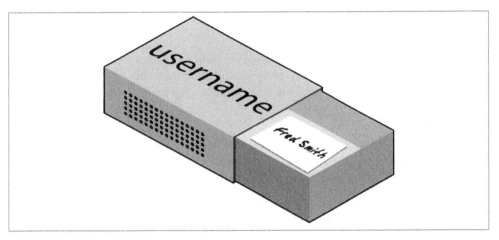

Figure 3-2. You can think of variables as matchboxes containing items

The quotation marks indicate that "Fred Smith" is a *string* of characters. You must enclose each string in either quotation marks or apostrophes (single quotes), although there is a subtle difference between the two types of quote, which is explained later. When you want to see what's in the box, you open it, take the piece of paper out, and read it. In PHP, doing so looks like this:

```
echo $username;
```

Or you can assign it to another variable (photocopy the paper and place the copy in another matchbox), like this:

```
$current_user = $username;
```

If you are keen to start trying out PHP for yourself, you could try entering the examples in this chapter into an IDE (as recommended at the end of Chapter 2) to see instant results, or you could enter the code in Example 3-4 into a program editor and save it to your server's document root directory (also discussed in Chapter 2) as *test1.php*.

Example 3-4. Your first PHP program

```php
<?php // test1.php
  $username = "Fred Smith";
  echo $username;
  echo "<br>";
  $current_user = $username;
  echo $current_user;
?>
```

Now you can call it up by entering the following into your browser's address bar:

```
http://localhost/test1.php
```

 If during installation of your web server (as detailed in Chapter 2) you changed the port assigned to the server to anything other than 80, then you must place that port number within the URL in this and all other examples in this book. So, for example, if you changed the port to 8080, the preceding URL becomes:

```
http://localhost:8080/test1.php
```

I won't mention this again, so just remember to use the port number if required when trying out any examples or writing your own code.

The result of running this code should be two occurrences of the name "Fred Smith," the first of which is the result of the echo $username command, and the second of the echo $current_user command.

Numeric variables

Variables don't contain just strings—they can contain numbers, too. If we return to the matchbox analogy, to store the number 17 in the variable $count, the equivalent would be placing, say, 17 beads in a matchbox on which you have written the word *count*:

```
$count = 17;
```

You could also use a floating-point number (containing a decimal point); the syntax is the same:

```
$count = 17.5;
```

To read the contents of the matchbox, you would simply open it and count the beads. In PHP, you would assign the value of $count to another variable or perhaps just echo it to the web browser.

Arrays

So what are arrays? Well, you can think of them as several matchboxes glued together. For example, let's say we want to store the player names for a five-person soccer team in an array called $team. To do this, we could glue five matchboxes side by side and write down the names of all the players on separate pieces of paper, placing one in each matchbox.

Across the whole top of the matchbox assembly we would write the word *team* (see Figure 3-3). The equivalent of this in PHP would be:

```
$team = array('Bill', 'Mary', 'Mike', 'Chris', 'Anne');
```

Figure 3-3. An array is like several matchboxes glued together

This syntax is more complicated than the ones I've explained so far. The array-building code consists of the following construct:

```
array();
```

with five strings inside. Each string is enclosed in apostrophes.

If we then wanted to know who player 4 is, we could use this command:

```
echo $team[3]; // Displays the name Chris
```

The reason the previous statement has the number 3, not 4, is because the first element of a PHP array is actually the zeroth element, so the player numbers will therefore be 0 through 4.

Two-dimensional arrays

There's a lot more you can do with arrays. For example, instead of being single-dimensional lines of matchboxes, they can be two-dimensional matrixes or can even have three or more dimensions.

As an example of a two-dimensional array, let's say we want to keep track of a game of tic-tac-toe, which requires a data structure of nine cells arranged in a 3×3 square. To represent this with matchboxes, imagine nine of them glued to each other in a matrix of three rows by three columns (see Figure 3-4).

Figure 3-4. A multidimensional array simulated with matchboxes

You can now place a piece of paper with either an "x" or an "o" in the correct matchbox for each move played. To do this in PHP code, you have to set up an array containing three more arrays, as in Example 3-5, in which the array is set up with a game already in progress.

Example 3-5. Defining a two-dimensional array

```php
<?php
  $oxo = array(array('x', ' ', 'o'),
               array('o', 'o', 'x'),
               array('x', 'o', ' '));
?>
```

Once again, we've moved up a step in complexity, but it's easy to understand if you have a grasp of the basic array syntax. There are three `array()` constructs nested inside the outer `array()` construct.

To then return the third element in the second row of this array, you would use the following PHP command, which will display an x:

```
echo $oxo[1][2];
```

 Remember that array indexes (pointers at elements within an array) start from zero, not one, so the [1] in the previous command refers to the second of the three arrays, and the [2] references the third position within that array. It will return the contents of the matchbox three along and two down.

As mentioned, we can support arrays with even more dimensions by simply creating more arrays within arrays. However, we will not be covering arrays of more than two dimensions in this book.

And don't worry if you're still having difficulty coming to grips with using arrays, as the subject is explained in detail in Chapter 6.

Variable naming rules

When creating PHP variables, you must follow these four rules:

- Variable names must start with a letter of the alphabet or the _ (underscore) character.
- Variable names can contain only the characters a–z, A–Z, 0–9, and _ (underscore).
- Variable names may not contain spaces. If a variable must comprise more than one word, it should be separated with the _ (underscore) character (e.g., `$user_name`).
- Variable names are case-sensitive. The variable `$High_Score` is not the same as the variable `$high_score`.

 To allow extended ASCII characters that include accents, PHP also supports the bytes from 127 through 255 in variable names. But unless your code will be maintained only by programmers who are familiar with those characters, it's probably best to avoid them, because programmers using English keyboards will have difficulty accessing them.

Operators

Operators are the mathematical, string, comparison, and logical commands such as plus, minus, multiply, and divide. PHP looks a lot like plain arithmetic; for instance, the following statement outputs 8:

```
echo 6 + 2;
```

Before moving on to learn what PHP can do for you, take a moment to learn about the various operators it provides.

Arithmetic operators

Arithmetic operators do what you would expect. They are used to perform mathematics. You can use them for the main four operations (plus, minus, multiply, and divide) as well as to find a modulus (the remainder after a division) and to increment or decrement a value (see Table 3-1).

Table 3-1. Arithmetic operators

Operator	Description	Example
+	Addition	$j + 1
–	Subtraction	$j – 6
*	Multiplication	$j * 11
/	Division	$j / 4
%	Modulus (division remainder)	$j % 9
++	Increment	++$j
--	Decrement	--$j

Assignment operators

These operators are used to assign values to variables. They start with the very simple = and move on to +=, -=, and so on (see Table 3-2). The operator += adds the value on the right side to the variable on the left, instead of totally replacing the value on the left. Thus, if $count starts with the value 5, the statement:

```
$count += 1;
```

sets $count to 6, just like the more familiar assignment statement:

```
$count = $count + 1;
```

Strings have their own operator, the period (.), detailed in the section "String concatenation" on page 58.

Table 3-2. Assignment operators

Operator	Example	Equivalent to
=	$j = 15	$j = 15
+=	$j += 5	$j = $j + 5
-=	$j -= 3	$j = $j - 3
*=	$j *= 8	$j = $j * 8
/=	$j /= 16	$j = $j / 16
.=	$j .= $k	$j = $j . $k
%=	$j %= 4	$j = $j % 4

Comparison operators

Comparison operators are generally used inside a construct such as an `if` statement in which you need to compare two items. For example, you may wish to know whether a variable you have been incrementing has reached a specific value, or whether another variable is less than a set value, and so on (see Table 3-3).

Note the difference between = and ==. The first is an assignment operator, and the second is a comparison operator. Even more advanced programmers can sometimes transpose the two when coding hurriedly, so be careful.

Table 3-3. Comparison operators

Operator	Description	Example
==	Is **equal** to	$j == 4
!=	Is **not equal** to	$j != 21
>	Is **greater than**	$j > 3
<	Is **less than**	$j < 100
>=	Is **greater than or equal** to	$j >= 15
<=	Is **less than or equal** to	$j <= 8

Logical operators

If you haven't used them before, logical operators may at first seem a little daunting. But just think of them the way you would use logic in English. For example, you might say to yourself, "If the time is later than 12 p.m. and earlier than 2 p.m., then have lunch." In PHP, the code for this might look something like the following (using military time):

```
if ($hour > 12 && $hour < 14) dolunch();
```

Here we have moved the set of instructions for actually going to lunch into a function that we will have to create later called `dolunch`. The *then* of the statement is left out, because it is implied and therefore unnecessary.

As the previous example shows, you generally use a logical operator to combine the results of two of the comparison operators shown in the previous section. A logical operator can also be input to another logical operator ("If the time is later than 12 p.m. and earlier than 2 p.m., or if the smell of a roast is permeating the hallway and there are plates on the table"). As a rule, if something has a TRUE or FALSE value, it can be input to a logical operator. A logical operator takes two true-or-false inputs and produces a true-or-false result.

Table 3-4 shows the logical operators.

Table 3-4. Logical operators

Operator	Description	Example
&&	**And**	`$j == 3 && $k == 2`
and	Low-precedence **and**	`$j == 3 and $k == 2`
||	**Or**	`$j < 5 || $j > 10`
or	Low-precedence **or**	`$j < 5 or $j > 10`
!	**Not**	`! ($j == $k)`
xor	**Exclusive or**	`$j xor $k`

Note that && is usually interchangeable with and; the same is true for || and or. But and and or have a lower precedence, so in some cases, you may need extra parentheses to force the required precedence. On the other hand, there are times when *only* and or or is acceptable, as in the following statement, which uses an or operator (to be explained in Chapter 10):

```
mysql_select_db($database) or die("Unable to select database");
```

The most unusual of these operators is xor, which stands for *exclusive or* and returns a TRUE value if either value is TRUE, but a FALSE value if both inputs are TRUE or both inputs are FALSE. To understand this, imagine that you want to concoct your own cleaner for household items. Ammonia makes a good cleaner, and so does bleach, so you want your cleaner to have one of these. But the cleaner must not have both, because the combination is hazardous. In PHP, you could represent this as:

```
$ingredient = $ammonia xor $bleach;
```

In the example snippet, if either $ammonia or $bleach is TRUE, $ingredient will also be set to TRUE. But if both are TRUE or both are FALSE, $ingredient will be set to FALSE.

Variable Assignment

The syntax to assign a value to a variable is always *variable = value*. Or, to reassign the value to another variable, it is *other variable = variable*.

There are also a couple of other assignment operators that you will find useful. For example, we've already seen:

```
$x += 10;
```

which tells the PHP parser to add the value on the right (in this instance, the value 10) to the variable $x. Likewise, we could subtract as follows:

```
$y -= 10;
```

Variable incrementing and decrementing

Adding or subtracting 1 is such a common operation that PHP provides special operators for it. You can use one of the following in place of the += and -= operators:

```
++$x;
--$y;
```

In conjunction with a test (an `if` statement), you could use the following code:

```
if (++$x == 10) echo $x;
```

This tells PHP to *first* increment the value of $x and then test whether it has the value 10; if it does, output its value. But you can also require PHP to increment (or, in the following example, decrement) a variable *after* it has tested the value, like this:

```
if ($y-- == 0) echo $y;
```

which gives a subtly different result. Suppose $y starts out as 0 before the statement is executed. The comparison will return a TRUE result, but $y will be set to -1 after the comparison is made. So what will the echo statement display: 0 or -1? Try to guess, and then try out the statement in a PHP processor to confirm. Because this combination of statements is confusing, it should be taken as just an educational example and not as a guide to good programming style.

In short, whether a variable is incremented or decremented before or after testing depends on whether the increment or decrement operator is placed before or after the variable.

By the way, the correct answer to the previous question is that the echo statement will display the result -1, because $y was decremented right after it was accessed in the if statement, and before the echo statement.

String concatenation

String concatenation uses the period (.) to append one string of characters to another. The simplest way to do this is as follows:

```
echo "You have " . $msgs . " messages.";
```

Assuming that the variable $msgs is set to the value 5, the output from this line of code will be:

You have 5 messages.

Just as you can add a value to a numeric variable with the += operator, you can append one string to another using .= like this:

```
$bulletin .= $newsflash;
```

In this case, if $bulletin contains a news bulletin and $newsflash has a news flash, the command appends the news flash to the news bulletin so that $bulletin now comprises both strings of text.

String types

PHP supports two types of strings that are denoted by the type of quotation mark that you use. If you wish to assign a literal string, preserving the exact contents, you should use the single quotation mark (apostrophe) like this:

```
$info = 'Preface variables with a $ like this: $variable';
```

In this case, every character within the single-quoted string is assigned to $info. If you had used double quotes, PHP would have attempted to evaluate $variable as a variable.

On the other hand, when you want to include the value of a variable inside a string, you do so by using double-quoted strings:

```
echo "This week $count people have viewed your profile";
```

As you will realize, this syntax also offers a simpler form of concatenation in which you don't need to use a period, or close and reopen quotes, to append one string to another. This is called *variable substitution*, and you will notice some applications using it extensively and others not using it at all.

Escaping characters

Sometimes a string needs to contain characters with special meanings that might be interpreted incorrectly. For example, the following line of code will not work, because the second quotation mark encountered in the word *spelling's* will tell the PHP parser that the string end has been reached. Consequently, the rest of the line will be rejected as an error:

```
$text = 'My spelling's atroshus'; // Erroneous syntax
```

To correct this, you can add a backslash directly before the offending quotation mark to tell PHP to treat the character literally and not to interpret it:

```
$text = 'My spelling\'s still atroshus';
```

And you can perform this trick in almost all situations in which PHP would otherwise return an error by trying to interpret a character. For example, the following double-quoted string will be correctly assigned:

```
$text = "She wrote upon it, \"Return to sender\".";
```

Additionally, you can use escape characters to insert various special characters into strings such as tabs, newlines, and carriage returns. These are represented, as you might guess, by \t, \n, and \r. Here is an example using tabs to lay out a heading; it is included here merely to illustrate escapes, because in web pages there are always better ways to do layout:

```
$heading = "Date\tName\tPayment";
```

These special backslash-preceded characters work only in double-quoted strings. In single-quoted strings, the preceding string would be displayed with the ugly \t sequences instead of tabs. Within single-quoted strings, only the escaped apostrophe (\') and escaped backslash itself (\\) are recognized as escaped characters.

Multiple-Line Commands

There are times when you need to output quite a lot of text from PHP, and using several echo (or print) statements would be time-consuming and messy. To overcome this, PHP offers two conveniences. The first is just to put multiple lines between quotes, as in Example 3-6. Variables can also be assigned, as in Example 3-7.

Example 3-6. A multiline string echo statement

```
<?php
  $author = "Steve Ballmer";

  echo "Developers, Developers, developers, developers, developers,
  developers, developers, developers, developers!

  - $author.";
?>
```

Example 3-7. A multiline string assignment

```
<?php
  $author = "Bill Gates";

  $text = "Measuring programming progress by lines of code is like
  measuring aircraft building progress by weight.

  - $author.";
?>
```

PHP also offers a multiline sequence using the <<< operator—commonly referred to as a *here-document* or *heredoc*—as a way of specifying a string literal, preserving the line breaks and other whitespace (including indentation) in the text. Its use can be seen in Example 3-8.

Example 3-8. Alternative multiline echo statement

```php
<?php
  $author = "Brian W. Kernighan";

  echo <<<_END
Debugging is twice as hard as writing the code in the first place.
Therefore, if you write the code as cleverly as possible, you are,
by definition, not smart enough to debug it.

  - $author.
_END;
?>
```

This code tells PHP to output everything between the two _END tags as if it were a double-quoted string (except that quotes in a heredoc do not need to be escaped). This means it's possible, for example, for a developer to write entire sections of HTML directly into PHP code and then just replace specific dynamic parts with PHP variables.

It is important to remember that the closing _END; tag *must* appear right at the start of a new line and it must be the *only* thing on that line—not even a comment is allowed to be added after it (nor even a single space). Once you have closed a multiline block, you are free to use the same tag name again.

 Remember: using the <<<_END ... _END; heredoc construct, you don't have to add \n linefeed characters to send a linefeed—just press Return and start a new line. Also, unlike either a double-quote- or single-quote-delimited string, you are free to use all the single and double quotes you like within a heredoc, without escaping them by preceding them with a slash (\).

Example 3-9 shows how to use the same syntax to assign multiples lines to a variable.

Example 3-9. A multiline string variable assignment

```php
<?php
  $author = "Scott Adams";

  $out = <<<_END
Normal people believe that if it ain't broke, don't fix it.
Engineers believe that if it ain't broke, it doesn't have enough
features yet.

  - $author.
_END;
?>
```

The variable $out will then be populated with the contents between the two tags. If you were appending, rather than assigning, you could also have used .= in place of = to append the string to $out.

Be careful not to place a semicolon directly after the first occurrence of _END, because that would terminate the multiline block before it had even started and cause a Parse error message. The only place for the semicolon is after the terminating _END tag, although it is safe to use semicolons within the block as normal text characters.

By the way, the _END tag is simply one I chose for these examples because it is unlikely to be used anywhere else in PHP code and is therefore unique. But you can use any tag you like, such as _SECTION1 or _OUTPUT and so on. Also, to help differentiate tags such as this from variables or functions, the general practice is to preface them with an underscore, but you don't have to use one if you choose not to.

Laying out text over multiple lines is usually just a convenience to make your PHP code easier to read, because once it is displayed in a web page, HTML formatting rules take over and whitespace is suppressed (but $author is still replaced with the variable's value).

So, for example, if you load these multiline output examples into a browser they will *not* display over several lines, because all browsers treat newlines just like spaces. However, if you use the browser's view source feature, you will find that the newlines are correctly placed, and the output does appear over several lines.

Variable Typing

PHP is a very loosely typed language. This means that variables do not have to be declared before they are used, and that PHP always converts variables to the *type* required by their context when they are accessed.

For example, you can create a multiple-digit number and extract the *n*th digit from it simply by assuming it to be a string. In the following snippet of code, the numbers 12345 and 67890 are multiplied together, returning a result of 838102050, which is then placed in the variable $number, as shown in Example 3-10.

Example 3-10. Automatic conversion from a number to a string

```
<?php
  $number = 12345 * 67890;
  echo substr($number, 3, 1);
?>
```

At the point of the assignment, $number is a numeric variable. But on the second line, a call is placed to the PHP function substr, which asks for one character to be returned from $number, starting at the fourth position (remembering that PHP offsets start from zero). To do this, PHP turns $number into a nine-character string, so that substr can access it and return the character, which in this case is 1.

The same goes for turning a string into a number, and so on. In Example 3-11, the variable $pi is set to a string value, which is then automatically turned into a floating-point number in the third line by the equation for calculating a circle's area, which outputs the value 78.5398175.

Example 3-11. Automatically converting a string to a number

```
<?php
  $pi     = "3.1415927";
  $radius = 5;
  echo $pi * ($radius * $radius);
?>
```

In practice, what this all means is that you don't have to worry too much about your variable types. Just assign them values that make sense to you and PHP will convert them if necessary. Then, when you want to retrieve values, just ask for them (e.g., with an echo statement).

Constants

Constants are similar to variables, holding information to be accessed later, except that they are what they sound like—constant. In other words, once you have defined one, its value is set for the remainder of the program and cannot be altered.

One example of a use for a constant might be to hold the location of your server *root* (the folder with the main files of your website). You would define such a constant like this:

```
define("ROOT_LOCATION", "/usr/local/www/");
```

Then, to read the contents of the variable, you just refer to it like a regular variable (but it isn't preceded by a dollar sign):

```
$directory = ROOT_LOCATION;
```

Now, whenever you need to run your PHP code on a different server with a different folder configuration, you have only a single line of code to change.

> The main two things you have to remember about constants are that they must *not* be prefaced with a $ (as with regular variables), and that you can define them only using the define function.

It is generally considered a good practice to use only uppercase for constant variable names, especially if other people will also read your code.

Predefined Constants

PHP comes ready-made with dozens of predefined constants that you generally will be unlikely to use as a beginner to PHP. However, there are a few—known as the *magic constants*—that you will find useful. The names of the magic constants always have two underscores at the beginning and two at the end, so that you won't accidentally try to name one of your own constants with a name that is already taken. They are detailed in Table 3-5. The concepts referred to in the table will be introduced in future chapters.

Table 3-5. PHP's magic constants

Magic constant	Description
__LINE__	The current line number of the file.
__FILE__	The full path and filename of the file. If used inside an include, the name of the included file is returned. In PHP 4.0.2, __FILE__ always contains an absolute path with symbolic links resolved, whereas in older versions it might contain a relative path under some circumstances.
__DIR__	The directory of the file. If used inside an include, the directory of the included file is returned. This is equivalent to *dirname*(__FILE__). This directory name does not have a trailing slash unless it is the root directory. (Added in PHP 5.3.0.)
__FUNCTION__	The function name. (Added in PHP 4.3.0.) As of PHP 5, returns the function name as it was declared (case-sensitive). In PHP 4, its value is always lowercase.
__CLASS__	The class name. (Added in PHP 4.3.0.) As of PHP 5, returns the class name as it was declared (case-sensitive). In PHP 4, its value is always lowercase.
__METHOD__	The class method name. (Added in PHP 5.0.0.) The method name is returned as it was declared (case-sensitive).
__NAMESPACE__	The name of the current namespace (case-sensitive). This constant is defined at compile time. (Added in PHP 5.3.0.)

One handy use of these variables is for debugging purposes, when you need to insert a line of code to see whether the program flow reaches it:

```
echo "This is line " . __LINE__ . " of file " . __FILE__;
```

This causes the current program line in the current file (including the path) being executed to be output to the web browser.

The Difference Between the echo and print Commands

So far, you have seen the echo command used in a number of different ways to output text from the server to your browser. In some cases, a string literal has been output. In others, strings have first been concatenated or variables have been evaluated. I've also shown output spread over multiple lines.

But there is also an alternative to echo that you can use: print. The two commands are quite similar, but print is a function-like construct that takes a single parameter and has a return value (which is always 1), whereas echo is purely a PHP language construct. Because both commands are constructs, neither requires the use of parentheses.

By and large, the echo command will be a tad faster than print in general text output, because it doesn't set a return value. On the other hand, because it isn't implemented like a function, echo cannot be used as part of a more complex expression, whereas print can. Here's an example to output whether the value of a variable is TRUE or FALSE using print, something you could not perform in the same manner with echo, because it would display a Parse error message:

```
$b ? print "TRUE" : print "FALSE";
```

The question mark is simply a way of interrogating whether variable $b is TRUE or FALSE. Whichever command is on the left of the following colon is executed if $b is TRUE, whereas the command to the right is executed if $b is FALSE.

Generally, though, the examples in this book use echo, and I recommend that you do so as well until you reach such a point in your PHP development that you discover the need for using print.

Functions

Functions are used to separate out sections of code that perform a particular task. For example, maybe you often need to look up a date and return it in a certain format. That would be a good example to turn into a function. The code doing it might be only three lines long, but if you have to paste it into your program a dozen times, you're making your program unnecessarily large and complex, unless you use a function. And if you decide to change the data format later, putting it in a function means having to change it in only one place.

Placing it into a function not only shortens your source code and makes it more readable, it also adds extra functionality (pun intended), because functions can be passed parameters to make them perform differently. They can also return values to the calling code.

To create a function, declare it in the manner shown in Example 3-12.

Example 3-12. A simple function declaration

```
<?php
  function longdate($timestamp)
  {
    return date("l F jS Y", $timestamp);
  }
?>
```

This function takes a Unix timestamp (an integer number representing a date and time based on the number of seconds since 00:00 a.m. on January 1, 1970) as its input and then calls the PHP `date` function with the correct format string to return a date in the format *Tuesday May 2nd 2017*. Any number of parameters can be passed between the initial parentheses; we have chosen to accept just one. The curly braces enclose all the code that is executed when you later call the function.

To output today's date using this function, place the following call in your code:

```
echo longdate(time());
```

This call uses the built-in PHP `time` function to fetch the current Unix timestamp and passes it to the new `longdate` function, which then returns the appropriate string to the echo command for display. If you need to print out the date 17 days ago, you now just have to issue the following call:

```
echo longdate(time() - 17 * 24 * 60 * 60);
```

which passes to `longdate` the current Unix timestamp less the number of seconds since 17 days ago (17 days × 24 hours × 60 minutes × 60 seconds).

Functions can also accept multiple parameters and return multiple results, using techniques that I'll develop over the following chapters.

Variable Scope

If you have a very long program, it's quite possible that you could start to run out of good variable names, but with PHP you can decide the *scope* of a variable. In other words, you can, for example, tell it that you want the variable `$temp` to be used only inside a particular function and to forget it was ever used when the function returns. In fact, this is the default scope for PHP variables.

Alternatively, you could inform PHP that a variable is global in scope and thus can be accessed by every other part of your program.

Local variables

Local variables are variables that are created within, and can only be accessed by, a function. They are generally temporary variables that are used to store partially processed results prior to the function's return.

One set of local variables is the list of arguments to a function. In the previous section, we defined a function that accepted a parameter named `$timestamp`. This is meaningful only in the body of the function; you can't get or set its value outside the function.

For another example of a local variable, take another look at the `longdate` function, which is modified slightly in Example 3-13.

Example 3-13. An expanded version of the longdate function

```php
<?php
  function longdate($timestamp)
  {
    $temp = date("l F jS Y", $timestamp);
    return "The date is $temp";
  }
?>
```

Here we have assigned the value returned by the date function to the temporary variable $temp, which is then inserted into the string returned by the function. As soon as the function returns, the value of $temp is cleared, as if it had never been used at all.

Now, to see the effects of variable scope, let's look at some similar code in Example 3-14. Here $temp has been created *before* we call the longdate function.

Example 3-14. This attempt to access $temp in function longdate will fail

```php
<?php
  $temp = "The date is ";
  echo longdate(time());

  function longdate($timestamp)
  {
    return $temp . date("l F jS Y", $timestamp);
  }
?>
```

However, because $temp was neither created within the longdate function nor passed to it as a parameter, longdate cannot access it. Therefore, this code snippet outputs only the date, not the preceding text. In fact, it will first display the error message Notice: Undefined variable: temp.

The reason for this is that, by default, variables created within a function are local to that function, and variables created outside of any functions can be accessed only by non-function code.

Some ways to repair Example 3-14 appear in Examples 3-15 and 3-16.

Example 3-15. Rewriting to refer to $temp within its local scope fixes the problem

```php
<?php
  $temp = "The date is ";
  echo $temp . longdate(time());

  function longdate($timestamp)
  {
    return date("l F jS Y", $timestamp);
  }
?>
```

Example 3-15 moves the reference to $temp out of the function. The reference appears in the same scope where the variable was defined.

The solution in Example 3-16 passes $temp to the longdate function as an extra argument. longdate reads it into a temporary variable that it creates called $text and outputs the desired result.

Example 3-16. An alternative solution: passing $temp as an argument

```php
<?php
  $temp = "The date is ";
  echo longdate($temp, time());

  function longdate($text, $timestamp)
  {
    return $text . date("l F jS Y", $timestamp);
  }
?>
```

 Forgetting the scope of a variable is a common programming error, so remembering how variable scope works will help you debug some quite obscure problems. Suffice it to say that unless you have declared a variable otherwise, its scope is limited to being local: either to the current function, or to the code outside of any functions, depending on whether it was first created or accessed inside or outside a function.

Global variables

There are cases when you need a variable to have *global* scope, because you want all your code to be able to access it. Also, some data may be large and complex, and you don't want to keep passing it as arguments to functions.

To declare a variable as having global scope, use the keyword global. Let's assume that you have a way of logging your users into your website and want all your code to know whether it is interacting with a logged-in user or a guest. One way to do this is to create a global variable such as $is_logged_in:

```php
global $is_logged_in;
```

Now your login function simply has to set that variable to 1 upon a successful login attempt, or 0 upon its failure. Because the scope of the variable is global, every line of code in your program can access it.

You should use global variables with caution, though. I recommend that you create them only when you absolutely cannot find another way of achieving the result you desire. In general, programs that are broken into small parts and segregated data are less buggy and easier to maintain. If you have a thousand-line program (and some day you will) in which you discover that a global variable has the wrong value at some point, how long will it take you to find the code that set it incorrectly?

Also, if you have too many global variables, you run the risk of using one of those names again locally, or at least thinking you have used it locally, when in fact it has already been declared as global. All manner of strange bugs can arise from such situations.

 Sometimes I adopt the convention of making all global variable names uppercase (just as it's recommended that constants should be uppercase) so that I can see at a glance the scope of a variable.

Static variables

In the section "Local variables" on page 66, I mentioned that the value of the variable is wiped out when the function ends. If a function runs many times, it starts with a fresh copy of the variable and the previous setting has no effect.

Here's an interesting case. What if you have a local variable inside a function that you don't want any other parts of your code to have access to, but you would also like to keep its value for the next time the function is called? Why? Perhaps because you want a counter to track how many times a function is called. The solution is to declare a static variable, as shown in Example 3-17.

Example 3-17. A function using a static variable

```php
<?php
  function test()
  {
    static $count = 0;
    echo $count;
    $count++;
  }
?>
```

Here the very first line of function test creates a static variable called $count and initializes it to a value of 0. The next line outputs the variable's value; the final one increments it.

The next time the function is called, because $count has already been declared, the first line of the function is skipped. Then the previously incremented value of $count is displayed before the variable is again incremented.

If you plan to use static variables, you should note that you cannot assign the result of an expression in their definitions. They can be initialized only with predetermined values (see Example 3-18).

Example 3-18. Allowed and disallowed static variable declarations

```php
<?php
  static $int = 0;          // Allowed
  static $int = 1+2;        // Disallowed (will produce a Parse error)
  static $int = sqrt(144);  // Disallowed
?>
```

Superglobal variables

Starting with PHP 4.1.0, several predefined variables are available. These are known as *superglobal variables*, which means that they are provided by the PHP environment but are global within the program, accessible absolutely everywhere.

These superglobals contain lots of useful information about the currently running program and its environment (see Table 3-6). They are structured as associative arrays, a topic discussed in Chapter 6.

Table 3-6. PHP's superglobal variables

Superglobal name	Contents
$GLOBALS	All variables that are currently defined in the global scope of the script. The variable names are the keys of the array.
$_SERVER	Information such as headers, paths, and script locations. The entries in this array are created by the web server, and there is no guarantee that every web server will provide any or all of these.
$_GET	Variables passed to the current script via the HTTP GET method.
$_POST	Variables passed to the current script via the HTTP POST method.
$_FILES	Items uploaded to the current script via the HTTP POST method.
$_COOKIE	Variables passed to the current script via HTTP cookies.
$_SESSION	Session variables available to the current script.
$_REQUEST	Contents of information passed from the browser; by default, $_GET, $_POST, and $_COOKIE.
$_ENV	Variables passed to the current script via the environment method.

All of the superglobals (except for $GLOBALS) are named with a single initial underscore and only capital letters; therefore, you should avoid naming your own variables in this manner to avoid potential confusion.

To illustrate how you use them, let's look at a bit of information that many sites employ. Among the many nuggets of information supplied by superglobal variables is the URL of the page that referred the user to the current web page. This referring page information can be accessed like this:

```php
$came_from = $_SERVER['HTTP_REFERER'];
```

It's that simple. Oh, and if the user came straight to your web page, such as by typing its URL directly into a browser, $came_from will be set to an empty string.

Superglobals and security

A word of caution is in order before you start using superglobal variables, because they are often used by hackers trying to find exploits to break into your website. What they do is load up $_POST, $_GET, or other superglobals with malicious code, such as Unix or MySQL commands that can damage or display sensitive data if you naïvely access them.

Therefore, you should always sanitize superglobals before using them. One way to do this is via the PHP htmlentities function. It converts all characters into HTML entities. For example, less-than and greater-than characters (< and >) are transformed into the strings < and > so that they are rendered harmless, as are all quotes and backslashes, and so on.

Therefore, a much better way to access $_SERVER (and other superglobals) is:

```
$came_from = htmlentities($_SERVER['HTTP_REFERER']);
```

> Using the htmlentities function for sanitization is an important practice in any circumstance where user or other third-party data is being processed for output, not just with superglobals.

This chapter has provided you with a solid background in using PHP. In Chapter 4, we'll start using what you've learned to build expressions and control program flow—in other words, do some actual programming.

But before moving on, I recommend that you test yourself with some (if not all) of the following questions to ensure that you have fully digested the contents of this chapter.

Questions

1. What tag is used to cause PHP to start interpreting program code? And what is the short form of the tag?
2. What are the two types of comment tags?
3. Which character must be placed at the end of every PHP statement?
4. Which symbol is used to preface all PHP variables?
5. What can a variable store?
6. What is the difference between $variable = 1 and $variable == 1?
7. Why do you suppose an underscore is allowed in variable names (e.g., $current_user) whereas hyphens are not (e.g., $current-user)?
8. Are variable names case-sensitive?

9. Can you use spaces in variable names?

10. How do you convert one variable type to another (say, a string to a number)?

11. What is the difference between ++$j and $j++?

12. Are the operators && and and interchangeable?

13. How can you create a multiline echo or assignment?

14. Can you redefine a constant?

15. How do you escape a quotation mark?

16. What is the difference between the echo and print commands?

17. What is the purpose of functions?

18. How can you make a variable accessible to all parts of a PHP program?

19. If you generate data within a function, what are a couple of ways to convey the data to the rest of the program?

20. What is the result of combining a string with a number?

See "Chapter 3 Answers" on page 640 in Appendix A for the answers to these questions.

CHAPTER 4

Expressions and Control Flow in PHP

The previous chapter introduced several topics in passing that this chapter covers more fully, such as making choices (branching) and creating complex expressions. In the previous chapter, I wanted to focus on the most basic syntax and operations in PHP, but I couldn't avoid touching on more advanced topics. Now I can fill in the background that you need to use these powerful PHP features properly.

In this chapter, you will get a thorough grounding in how PHP programming works in practice and in how to control the flow of the program.

Expressions

Let's start with the most fundamental part of any programming language: *expressions*.

An expression is a combination of values, variables, operators, and functions that results in a value. It's familiar to anyone who has taken high-school algebra:

$$y = 3(abs(2x) + 4)$$

which in PHP would be:

```
$y = 3 * (abs(2 * $x) + 4);
```

The value returned (y, or y in this case) can be a number, a string, or a *Boolean value* (named after George Boole, a nineteenth-century English mathematician and philosopher). By now, you should be familiar with the first two value types, but I'll explain the third.

TRUE or FALSE?

A basic Boolean value can be either TRUE or FALSE. For example, the expression "20 > 9" (20 is greater than 9) is TRUE, and the expression "5 == 6" (5 is equal to 6) is FALSE.

(You can combine Boolean operations using operators such as AND, OR, and XOR, which are covered later in this chapter.)

Note that I am using uppercase letters for the names TRUE and FALSE. This is because they are predefined constants in PHP. You can also use the lowercase versions, if you prefer, as they are also predefined. In fact, the lowercase versions are more stable, because PHP does not allow you to redefine them; the uppercase ones may be redefined— something you should bear in mind if you import third-party code.

Example 4-1 shows some simple expressions: the two I just mentioned, plus a couple more. For each line, it prints out a letter between a and d, followed by a colon and the result of the expressions. The <br> tag is there to create a line break and thus separate the output into four lines in HTML.

Now that we are fully into the age of HTML5, and XHTML is no longer being planned to supersede HTML, you do not need to use the self-closing <br /> form of the <br> tag, or any void elements (ones without closing tags), because the / is now optional. Therefore, I have chosen to use the simpler style in this book. If you ever made HTML non-void tags self-closing (such as <div />), they will not work in HTML5 because the / will be ignored, and you will need to replace them with, for example, <div> ... </div>. However, you must still use the <br /> form of HTML syntax when using XHTML.

Example 4-1. Four simple Boolean expressions

```php
<?php
  echo "a: [" . (20 > 9) . "]<br>";
  echo "b: [" . (5 == 6) . "]<br>";
  echo "c: [" . (1 == 0) . "]<br>";
  echo "d: [" . (1 == 1) . "]<br>";
?>
```

The output from this code is as follows:

```
a: [1]
b: []
c: []
d: [1]
```

Notice that both expressions a: and d: evaluate to TRUE, which has a value of 1. But b: and c:, which evaluate to FALSE, do not show any value, because in PHP the constant FALSE is defined as NULL, or nothing. To verify this for yourself, you could enter the code in Example 4-2.

Example 4-2. Outputting the values of TRUE and FALSE

```php
<?php // test2.php
  echo "a: [" . TRUE  . "]<br>";
  echo "b: [" . FALSE . "]<br>";
?>
```

which outputs the following:

```
a: [1]
b: []
```

By the way, in some languages FALSE may be defined as 0 or even –1, so it's worth checking on its definition in each language.

Literals and Variables

The simplest form of an expression is a *literal*, which simply means something that evaluates to itself, such as the number 73 or the string "Hello". An expression could also simply be a variable, which evaluates to the value that has been assigned to it. They are both types of expressions, because they return a value.

Example 4-3 shows three literals and two variables, all of which return values, albeit of different types.

Example 4-3. Literals and variables

```php
<?php
  $myname = "Brian";
  $myage  = 37;

  echo "a: " . 73       . "<br>"; // Numeric literal
  echo "b: " . "Hello" . "<br>"; // String literal
  echo "c: " . FALSE    . "<br>"; // Constant literal
  echo "d: " . $myname . "<br>"; // String variable
  echo "e: " . $myage   . "<br>"; // Numeric variable
?>
```

And, as you'd expect, you see a return value from all of these with the exception of c:, which evaluates to FALSE, returning nothing in the following output:

```
a: 73
b: Hello
c:
d: Brian
e: 37
```

In conjunction with operators, it's possible to create more complex expressions that evaluate to useful results.

When you combine assignment or control-flow constructs with expressions, the result is a *statement*. Example 4-4 shows one of each. The first assigns the result of the expression 366 - $day_number to the variable $days_to_new_year, and the second outputs a friendly message only if the expression $days_to_new_year < 30 evaluates to TRUE.

Example 4-4. An expression and a statement

```php
<?php
  $days_to_new_year = 366 - $day_number; // Expression

  if ($days_to_new_year < 30)
  {
    echo "Not long now till new year";  // Statement
  }
?>
```

Operators

PHP offers a lot of powerful operators that range from arithmetic, string, and logical operators to assignment, comparison, and more (see Table 4-1).

Table 4-1. PHP operator types

Operator	Description	Example
Arithmetic	Basic mathematics	$a + $b
Array	Array union	$a + $b
Assignment	Assign values	$a = $b + 23
Bitwise	Manipulate bits within bytes	12 ^ 9
Comparison	Compare two values	$a < $b
Execution	Executes contents of back ticks	\`ls -al\`
Increment/decrement	Add or subtract 1	$a++
Logical	Boolean	$a and $b
String	Concatenation	$a . $b

Each operator takes a different number of operands:

- *Unary* operators, such as incrementing ($a++) or negation (-$a), which take a single operand.
- *Binary* operators, which represent the bulk of PHP operators, including addition, subtraction, multiplication, and division.
- One *ternary* operator, which takes the form ? x : y. It's a terse, single-line if statement that chooses between two expressions, depending on the result of a third one.

Operator Precedence

If all operators had the same precedence, they would be processed in the order in which they are encountered. In fact, many operators do have the same precedence, so let's look at a few in Example 4-5.

Example 4-5. Three equivalent expressions

```
1 + 2 + 3 - 4 + 5
2 - 4 + 5 + 3 + 1
5 + 2 - 4 + 1 + 3
```

Here you will see that although the numbers (and their preceding operators) have been moved, the result of each expression is the value 7, because the plus and minus operators have the same precedence. We can try the same thing with multiplication and division (see Example 4-6).

Example 4-6. Three expressions that are also equivalent

```
1 * 2 * 3 / 4 * 5
2 / 4 * 5 * 3 * 1
5 * 2 / 4 * 1 * 3
```

Here the resulting value is always 7.5. But things change when we mix operators with *different* precedencies in an expression, as in Example 4-7.

Example 4-7. Three expressions using operators of mixed precedence

```
1 + 2 * 3 - 4 * 5
2 - 4 * 5 * 3 + 1
5 + 2 - 4 + 1 * 3
```

If there were no operator precedence, these three expressions would evaluate to 25, –29, and 12, respectively. But because multiplication and division take precedence over addition and subtraction, there are implied parentheses around these parts of the expressions, which would look like Example 4-8 if they were visible.

Example 4-8. Three expressions showing implied parentheses

```
1 + (2 * 3) - (4 * 5)
2 - (4 * 5 * 3) + 1
5 + 2 - 4 + (1 * 3)
```

Clearly, PHP must evaluate the subexpressions within parentheses first to derive the semi-completed expressions in Example 4-9.

Example 4-9. After evaluating the subexpressions in parentheses

```
1 + (6) - (20)
2 - (60) + 1
5 + 2 - 4 + (3)
```

The final results of these expressions are −13, −57, and 6, respectively (quite different from the results of 25, −29, and 12 that we would have seen had there been no operator precedence).

Of course, you can override the default operator precedence by inserting your own parentheses and forcing the original results that we would have seen had there been no operator precedence (see Example 4-10).

Example 4-10. Forcing left-to-right evaluation

```
((1 + 2) * 3 - 4) * 5
(2 - 4) * 5 * 3 + 1
(5 + 2 - 4 + 1) * 3
```

With parentheses correctly inserted, we now see the values 25, −29, and 12, respectively.

Table 4-2 lists PHP's operators in order of precedence from high to low.

Table 4-2. The precedence of PHP operators (high to low)

Operator(s)	Type
( )	Parentheses
++ −−	Increment/decrement
!	Logical
* / %	Arithmetic
+ − .	Arithmetic and string
<< >>	Bitwise
< <= > >= <>	Comparison
== != === !==	Comparison
&	Bitwise (and references)
^	Bitwise
|	Bitwise
&&	Logical
||	Logical
? :	Ternary
= += −= *= /= .= %= &= != ^= <<= >>=	Assignment
and	Logical
xor	Logical
or	Logical

Associativity

We've been looking at processing expressions from left to right, except where operator precedence is in effect. But some operators require processing from right to left, and this direction of processing is called the operator's *associativity*. For some operators there is no associativity.

Associativity becomes important in cases in which you do not explicitly force precedence, so you need to be aware of the default actions of operators, as detailed in Table 4-3, which lists operators and their associativity.

Table 4-3. Operator associativity

Operator	Description	Associativity
CLONE NEW	Create a new object	None
< <= >= == != === !== <>	Comparison	None
!	Logical NOT	Right
~	Bitwise NOT	Right
++ --	Increment and decrement	Right
(int)	Cast to an integer	Right
(double) (float) (real)	Cast to a floating-point number	Right
(string)	Cast to a string	Right
(array)	Cast to an array	Right
(object)	Cast to an object	Right
@	Inhibit error reporting	Right
= += -= *= /=	Assignment	Right
.= %= &= |= ^= <<= >>=	Assignment	Right
+	Addition and unary plus	Left
-	Subtraction and negation	Left
*	Multiplication	Left
/	Division	Left
%	Modulus	Left
.	String concatenation	Left
<< >> & ^ |	Bitwise	Left
?:	Ternary	Left
|| && and or xor	Logical	Left
,	Separator	Left

For example, let's take a look at the assignment operator in Example 4-11, where three variables are all set to the value 0.

Example 4-11. A multiple-assignment statement

```php
<?php
  $level = $score = $time = 0;
?>
```

This multiple assignment is possible only if the rightmost part of the expression is evaluated first and then processing continues in a right-to-left direction.

 As a beginner to PHP, you should avoid the potential pitfalls of operator associativity by always nesting your subexpressions within parentheses to force the order of evaluation. This will also help other programmers who may have to maintain your code to understand what is happening.

Relational Operators

Relational operators test two operands and return a Boolean result of either TRUE or FALSE. There are three types of relational operators: *equality*, *comparison*, and *logical*.

Equality

As we've already encountered a few times in this chapter, the equality operator is == (two equals signs). It is important not to confuse it with the = (single equals sign) assignment operator. In Example 4-12, the first statement assigns a value and the second tests it for equality.

Example 4-12. Assigning a value and testing for equality

```
<?php
  $month = "March";

  if ($month == "March") echo "It's springtime";
?>
```

As you see, by returning either TRUE or FALSE, the equality operator enables you to test for conditions using, for example, an if statement. But that's not the whole story, because PHP is a loosely typed language. If the two operands of an equality expression are of different types, PHP will convert them to whatever type makes best sense to it.

For example, any strings composed entirely of numbers will be converted to numbers whenever compared with a number. In Example 4-13, $a and $b are two different strings, and we would therefore expect neither of the if statements to output a result.

Example 4-13. The equality and identity operators

```
<?php
  $a = "1000";
  $b = "+1000";

  if ($a == $b)  echo "1";
  if ($a === $b) echo "2";
?>
```

However, if you run the example, you will see that it outputs the number 1, which means that the first `if` statement evaluated to TRUE. This is because both strings were first converted to numbers, and 1000 is the same numerical value as +1000.

In contrast, the second `if` statement uses the *identity* operator—three equals signs in a row—which prevents PHP from automatically converting types. $a and $b are therefore compared as strings and are now found to be different, so nothing is output.

As with forcing operator precedence, whenever you have any doubt about how PHP will convert operand types, you can use the identity operator to turn this behavior off.

In the same way that you can use the equality operator to test for operands being equal, you can test for them *not* being equal using !=, the inequality operator. Take a look at Example 4-14, which is a rewrite of Example 4-13 in which the equality and identity operators have been replaced with their inverses.

Example 4-14. The inequality and not identical operators

```php
<?php
  $a = "1000";
  $b = "+1000";

  if ($a != $b)  echo "1";
  if ($a !== $b) echo "2";
?>
```

And, as you might expect, the first `if` statement does not output the number 1, because the code is asking whether $a and $b are *not* equal to each other numerically.

Instead, it outputs the number 2, because the second `if` statement is asking whether $a and $b are *not* identical to each other in their present operand types, and the answer is TRUE; they are not the same.

Comparison operators

Using comparison operators, you can test for more than just equality and inequality. PHP also gives you > (is greater than), < (is less than), >= (is greater than or equal to), and <= (is less than or equal to) to play with. Example 4-15 shows these operators in use.

Example 4-15. The four comparison operators

```php
<?php
  $a = 2; $b = 3;

  if ($a > $b)  echo "$a is greater than $b<br>";
  if ($a < $b)  echo "$a is less than $b<br>";
  if ($a >= $b) echo "$a is greater than or equal to $b<br>";
  if ($a <= $b) echo "$a is less than or equal to $b<br>";
?>
```

In this example, where $a is 2 and $b is 3, the following is output:

```
2 is less than 3
2 is less than or equal to 3
```

Try this example yourself, altering the values of $a and $b, to see the results. Try setting them to the same value and see what happens.

Logical operators

Logical operators produce true-or-false results, and therefore are also known as Boolean operators. There are four of them (see Table 4-4).

Table 4-4. The logical operators

Logical operator	Description
AND	TRUE if both operands are TRUE
OR	TRUE if either operand is TRUE
XOR	TRUE if one of the two operands is TRUE
NOT	TRUE if the operand is FALSE, or FALSE if the operand is TRUE

You can see these operators used in Example 4-16. Note that the ! symbol is required by PHP in place of the word NOT. Furthermore, the operators can be lower- or uppercase.

Example 4-16. The logical operators in use

```php
<?php
  $a = 1; $b = 0;

  echo ($a AND $b) . "<br>";
  echo ($a or $b)  . "<br>";
  echo ($a XOR $b) . "<br>";
  echo !$a          . "<br>";
?>
```

This example outputs NULL, 1, 1, NULL, meaning that only the second and third echo statements evaluate as TRUE. (Remember that NULL—or nothing—represents a value of FALSE.) This is because the AND statement requires both operands to be TRUE if it is going to return a value of TRUE, while the fourth statement performs a NOT on the value of $a, turning it from TRUE (a value of 1) to FALSE. If you wish to experiment with this, try out the code, giving $a and $b varying values of 1 and 0.

> When coding, remember to bear in mind that AND and OR have lower precedence than the other versions of the operators, && and ||. In complex expressions, it may be safer to use && and || for this reason.

The OR operator can cause unintentional problems in `if` statements, because the second operand will not be evaluated if the first is evaluated as TRUE. In Example 4-17, the function `getnext` will never be called if `$finished` has a value of 1.

Example 4-17. A statement using the OR operator

```php
<?php
  if ($finished == 1 OR getnext() == 1) exit;
?>
```

If you need `getnext` to be called at each `if` statement, you could rewrite the code as has been done in Example 4-18.

Example 4-18. The "if ... OR" statement modified to ensure calling of getnext

```php
<?php
  $gn = getnext();

  if ($finished == 1 OR $gn == 1) exit;
?>
```

In this case, the code in function `getnext` will be executed and the value returned will be stored in `$gn` before the `if` statement.

Another solution is to simply switch the two clauses to make sure that `getnext` is executed, as it will then appear first in the expression.

Table 4-5 shows all the possible variations of using the logical operators. You should also note that `!TRUE` equals FALSE and `!FALSE` equals TRUE.

Table 4-5. All possible PHP logical expressions

Inputs		Operators and results		
a	b	AND	OR	XOR
TRUE	TRUE	TRUE	TRUE	FALSE
TRUE	FALSE	FALSE	TRUE	TRUE
FALSE	TRUE	FALSE	TRUE	TRUE
FALSE	FALSE	FALSE	FALSE	FALSE

Conditionals

Conditionals alter program flow. They enable you to ask questions about certain things and respond to the answers you get in different ways. Conditionals are central to dynamic web pages—the goal of using PHP in the first place—because they make it easy to create different output each time a page is viewed.

There are three types of non-looping conditionals: the if statement, the switch statement, and the ? operator. By *non-looping*, I mean that the actions initiated by the statement take place and program flow then moves on, whereas looping conditionals (which we'll get to shortly) execute code over and over until a condition has been met.

The if Statement

One way of thinking about program flow is to imagine it as a single-lane highway that you are driving along. It's pretty much a straight line, but now and then you encounter various signs telling you where to go.

In the case of an if statement, you could imagine coming across a detour sign that you have to follow if a certain condition is TRUE. If so, you drive off and follow the detour until you return to where it started and then continue on your way in your original direction. Or, if the condition isn't TRUE, you ignore the detour and carry on driving (see Figure 4-1).

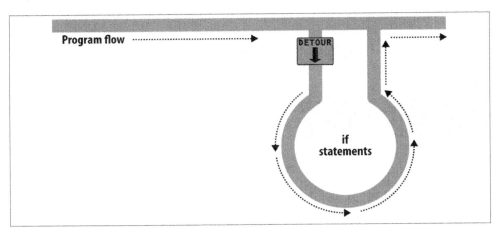

Figure 4-1. Program flow is like a single-lane highway

The contents of the if condition can be any valid PHP expression, including equality, comparison, tests for 0 and NULL, and even the values returned by functions (either built-in functions or ones that you write).

The actions to take when an if condition is TRUE are generally placed inside curly braces, { }. However, you can ignore the braces if you have only a single statement to execute. But if you always use curly braces, you'll avoid having to hunt down difficult-to-trace bugs, such as when you add an extra line to a condition and it doesn't get evaluated due to lack of braces. (Note that for space and clarity, many of the examples in this book ignore this suggestion and omit the braces for single statements.)

In Example 4-19, imagine that it is the end of the month and all your bills have been paid, so you are performing some bank account maintenance.

Example 4-19. An if statement with curly braces

```php
<?php
  if ($bank_balance < 100)
  {
    $money        = 1000;
    $bank_balance += $money;
  }
?>
```

In this example, you are checking your balance to see whether it is less than $100 (or whatever your currency is). If so, you pay yourself $1,000 and then add it to the balance. (If only making money were that simple!)

If the bank balance is $100 or greater, the conditional statements are ignored and program flow skips to the next line (not shown).

In this book, opening curly braces generally start on a new line. Some people like to place the first curly brace to the right of the conditional expression; others start a new line with it. Either of these is fine, because PHP allows you to set out your whitespace characters (spaces, newlines, and tabs) any way you choose. However, you will find your code easier to read and debug if you indent each level of conditionals with a tab.

The else Statement

Sometimes when a conditional is not TRUE, you may not want to continue on to the main program code immediately but might wish to do something else instead. This is where the else statement comes in. With it, you can set up a second detour on your highway, as in Figure 4-2.

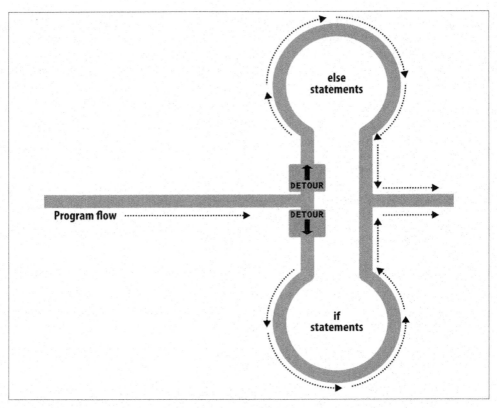

Figure 4-2. The highway now has an if detour and an else detour

With an `if ... else` statement, the first conditional statement is executed if the condition is TRUE. But if it's FALSE, the second one is executed. One of the two choices *must* be executed. Under no circumstance can both (or neither) be executed. Example 4-20 shows the use of the `if ... else` structure.

Example 4-20. An if ... else statement with curly braces

```php
<?php
  if ($bank_balance < 100)
  {
    $money        = 1000;
    $bank_balance += $money;
  }
  else
  {
    $savings      += 50;
    $bank_balance -= 50;
  }
?>
```

In this example, now that you've ascertained that you have $100 or more in the bank, the else statement is executed, by which you place some of this money into your savings account.

As with if statements, if your else has only one conditional statement, you can opt to leave out the curly braces. (Curly braces are always recommended, though. First, they make the code easier to understand. Second, they let you easily add more statements to the branch later.)

The elseif Statement

There are also times when you want a number of different possibilities to occur, based upon a sequence of conditions. You can achieve this using the elseif statement. As you might imagine, it is like an else statement, except that you place a further conditional expression prior to the conditional code. In Example 4-21, you can see a complete if ... elseif ... else construct.

Example 4-21. An if ... elseif ... else statement with curly braces

```php
<?php
  if ($bank_balance < 100)
  {
    $money        = 1000;
    $bank_balance += $money;
  }
  elseif ($bank_balance > 200)
  {
    $savings      += 100;
    $bank_balance -= 100;
  }
  else
  {
    $savings      += 50;
    $bank_balance -= 50;
  }
?>
```

In the example, an elseif statement has been inserted between the if and else statements. It checks whether your bank balance exceeds $200 and, if so, decides that you can afford to save $100 of it this month.

Although I'm starting to stretch the metaphor a bit too far, you can imagine this as a multi-way set of detours (see Figure 4-3).

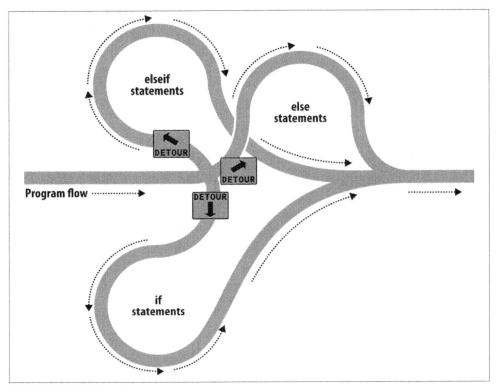

Figure 4-3. The highway with if, elseif, and else detours

An else statement closes either an if ... else or an if ... else if ... else statement. You can leave out a final else if it is not required, but you cannot have one before an elseif; neither can you have an elseif before an if statement.

You may have as many elseif statements as you like. But as the number of elseif statements increases, you would probably be better advised to consider a switch statement if it fits your needs. We'll look at that next.

The switch Statement

The switch statement is useful in cases in which one variable or the result of an expression can have multiple values, which should each trigger a different function.

For example, consider a PHP-driven menu system that passes a single string to the main menu code according to what the user requests. Let's say the options are Home, About,

News, Login, and Links, and we set the variable $page to one of these, according to the user's input.

If we write the code for this using if ... elseif ... else, it might look like Example 4-22.

Example 4-22. A multiple-line if... elseif... statement

```php
<?php
  if      ($page == "Home")  echo "You selected Home";
  elseif ($page == "About") echo "You selected About";
  elseif ($page == "News")  echo "You selected News";
  elseif ($page == "Login") echo "You selected Login";
  elseif ($page == "Links") echo "You selected Links";
?>
```

If we use a switch statement, the code might look like Example 4-23.

Example 4-23. A switch statement

```php
<?php
  switch ($page)
  {
    case "Home":
        echo "You selected Home";
        break;
    case "About":
        echo "You selected About";
        break;
    case "News":
        echo "You selected News";
        break;
    case "Login":
        echo "You selected Login";
        break;
    case "Links":
        echo "You selected Links";
        break;
  }
?>
```

As you can see, $page is mentioned only once at the start of the switch statement. Thereafter, the case command checks for matches. When one occurs, the matching conditional statement is executed. Of course, in a real program you would have code here to display or jump to a page, rather than simply telling the user what was selected.

> With switch statements, you do not use curly braces inside case commands. Instead, they commence with a colon and end with the break statement. The entire list of cases in the switch statement is enclosed in a set of curly braces, though.

Breaking out

If you wish to break out of the `switch` statement because a condition has been fulfilled, use the `break` command. This command tells PHP to break out of the `switch` and jump to the following statement.

If you were to leave out the `break` commands in Example 4-23 and the `case` of Home evaluated to be TRUE, all five cases would then be executed. Or if `$page` had the value News, then all the `case` commands from then on would execute. This is deliberate and allows for some advanced programming, but generally you should always remember to issue a `break` command every time a set of `case` conditionals has finished executing. In fact, leaving out the `break` statement is a common error.

Default action

A typical requirement in `switch` statements is to fall back on a default action if none of the `case` conditions are met. For example, in the case of the menu code in Example 4-23, you could add the code in Example 4-24 immediately before the final curly brace.

Example 4-24. A default statement to add to Example 4-23

```
default:
    echo "Unrecognized selection";
    break;
```

Although a `break` command is not required here because the default is the final substatement, and program flow will automatically continue to the closing curly brace, should you decide to place the `default` statement higher up it would definitely need a `break` command to prevent program flow from dropping into the following statements. Generally, the safest practice is to always include the `break` command.

Alternative syntax

If you prefer, you may replace the first curly brace in a `switch` statement with a single colon, and the final curly brace with an `endswitch` command, as in Example 4-25. However, this approach is not commonly used and is mentioned here only in case you encounter it in third-party code.

Example 4-25. Alternate switch statement syntax

```php
<?php
  switch ($page):
    case "Home":
        echo "You selected Home";
        break;

    // etc...
```

```
    case "Links":
        echo "You selected Links";
        break;
  endswitch;
?>
```

The ? Operator

One way of avoiding the verbosity of if and else statements is to use the more compact ternary operator, ?, which is unusual in that it takes three operands rather than the typical two.

We briefly came across this in Chapter 3 in the discussion about the difference between the print and echo statements as an example of an operator type that works well with print but not echo.

The ? operator is passed an expression that it must evaluate, along with two statements to execute: one for when the expression evaluates to TRUE, the other for when it is FALSE. Example 4-26 shows code we might use for writing a warning about the fuel level of a car to its digital dashboard.

Example 4-26. Using the ? operator

```
<?php
  echo $fuel <= 1 ? "Fill tank now" : "There's enough fuel";
?>
```

In this statement, if there is one gallon or less of fuel (i.e., if $fuel is set to 1 or less), the string Fill tank now is returned to the preceding echo statement. Otherwise, the string There's enough fuel is returned. You can also assign the value returned in a ? statement to a variable (see Example 4-27).

Example 4-27. Assigning a ? conditional result to a variable

```
<?php
  $enough = $fuel <= 1 ? FALSE : TRUE;
?>
```

Here $enough will be assigned the value TRUE only when there is more than a gallon of fuel; otherwise, it is assigned the value FALSE.

If you find the ? operator confusing, you are free to stick to if statements, but you should be familiar with it, because you'll see it in other people's code. It can be hard to read, because it often mixes multiple occurrences of the same variable. For instance, code such as the following is quite popular:

```
$saved = $saved >= $new ? $saved : $new;
```

If you take it apart carefully, you can figure out what this code does:

```
$saved =                          // Set the value of $saved to...
        $saved >= $new            // Check $saved against $new
    ?                             // Yes, comparison is true ...
        $saved                    // ... so assign the current value of $saved
    :                             // No, comparison is false ...
        $new;                     // ... so assign the value of $new
```

It's a concise way to keep track of the largest value that you've seen as a program progresses. You save the largest value in $saved and compare it to $new each time you get a new value. Programmers familiar with the ? operator find it more convenient than if statements for such short comparisons. When not used for writing compact code, it is typically used to make some decision inline, such as when you are testing whether a variable is set before passing it to a function.

Looping

One of the great things about computers is that they can repeat calculating tasks quickly and tirelessly. Often you may want a program to repeat the same sequence of code again and again until something happens, such as a user inputting a value or reaching a natural end. PHP's various loop structures provide the perfect way to do this.

To picture how this works, take a look at Figure 4-4. It is much the same as the highway metaphor used to illustrate if statements, except that the detour also has a loop section that—once a vehicle has entered—can be exited only under the right program conditions.

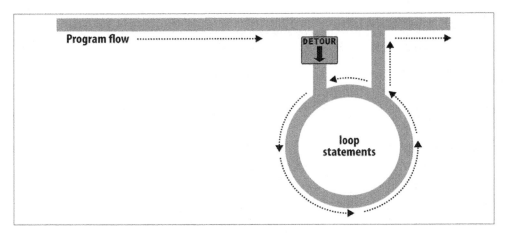

Figure 4-4. Imagining a loop as part of a program highway layout

while Loops

Let's turn the digital car dashboard in Example 4-26 into a loop that continuously checks the fuel level as you drive, using a `while` loop (Example 4-28).

Example 4-28. A while loop

```php
<?php
  $fuel = 10;

  while ($fuel > 1)
  {
    // Keep driving ...
    echo "There's enough fuel";
  }
?>
```

Actually, you might prefer to keep a green light lit rather than output text, but the point is that whatever positive indication you wish to make about the level of fuel is placed inside the `while` loop. By the way, if you try this example for yourself, note that it will keep printing the string until you click the Stop button in your browser.

 As with `if` statements, you will notice that curly braces are required to hold the statements inside the `while` statements, unless there's only one.

For another example of a `while` loop that displays the 12 times table, see Example 4-29.

Example 4-29. A while loop to print the 12 times table

```php
<?php
  $count = 1;

  while ($count <= 12)
  {
    echo "$count times 12 is " . $count * 12 . "<br>";
    ++$count;
  }
?>
```

Here the variable `$count` is initialized to a value of 1, then a `while` loop is started with the comparative expression `$count <= 12`. This loop will continue executing until the variable is greater than 12. The output from this code is as follows:

```
1 times 12 is 12
2 times 12 is 24
3 times 12 is 36
and so on...
```

Inside the loop, a string is printed along with the value of $count multiplied by 12. For neatness, this is also followed with a <br> tag to force a new line. Then $count is incremented, ready for the final curly brace that tells PHP to return to the start of the loop.

At this point, $count is again tested to see whether it is greater than 12. It isn't, but it now has the value 2, and after another 11 times around the loop, it will have the value 13. When that happens, the code within the while loop is skipped and execution passes on to the code following the loop, which, in this case, is the end of the program.

If the ++$count statement (which could equally have been $count++) had not been there, this loop would be like the first one in this section. It would never end and only the result of 1 * 12 would be printed over and over.

But there is a much neater way this loop can be written, which I think you will like. Take a look at Example 4-30.

Example 4-30. A shortened version of Example 4-29

```php
<?php
  $count = 0;

  while (++$count <= 12)
    echo "$count times 12 is " . $count * 12 . "<br>";
?>
```

In this example, it was possible to remove the ++$count statement from inside the while loop and place it directly into the conditional expression of the loop. What now happens is that PHP encounters the variable $count at the start of each iteration of the loop and, noticing that it is prefaced with the increment operator, first increments the variable and only then compares it to the value 12. You can therefore see that $count now has to be initialized to 0, not 1, because it is incremented as soon as the loop is entered. If you keep the initialization at 1, only results between 2 and 12 will be output.

do ... while Loops

A slight variation to the while loop is the do ... while loop, used when you want a block of code to be executed at least once and made conditional only after that. Example 4-31 shows a modified version of the code for the 12 times table that uses such a loop.

Example 4-31. A do ... while loop for printing the times table for 12

```php
<?php
  $count = 1;
  do
    echo "$count times 12 is " . $count * 12 . "<br>";
  while (++$count <= 12);
?>
```

Notice how we are back to initializing $count to 1 (rather than 0) because the code is being executed immediately, without an opportunity to increment the variable. Other than that, though, the code looks pretty similar.

Of course, if you have more than a single statement inside a do ... while loop, remember to use curly braces, as in Example 4-32.

Example 4-32. Expanding Example 4-31 to use curly braces

```php
<?php
  $count = 1;

  do {
    echo "$count times 12 is " . $count * 12;
    echo "<br>";
  } while (++$count <= 12);
?>
```

for Loops

The final kind of loop statement, the for loop, is also the most powerful, as it combines the abilities to set up variables as you enter the loop, test for conditions while iterating loops, and modify variables after each iteration.

Example 4-33 shows how you could write the multiplication table program with a for loop.

Example 4-33. Outputting the times table for 12 from a for loop

```php
<?php
  for ($count = 1 ; $count <= 12 ; ++$count)
    echo "$count times 12 is " . $count * 12 . "<br>";
?>
```

See how the entire code has been reduced to a single for statement containing a single conditional statement? Here's what is going on. Each for statement takes three parameters:

- An initialization expression
- A condition expression
- A modification expression

These are separated by semicolons like this: for (*expr1* ; *expr2* ; *expr3*). At the start of the first iteration of the loop, the initialization expression is executed. In the case of the times table code, $count is initialized to the value 1. Then, each time around the loop, the condition expression (in this case, $count <= 12) is tested, and the loop is entered only if the condition is TRUE. Finally, at the end of each iteration, the modification expression is executed. In the case of the times table code, the variable $count is incremented.

All this structure neatly removes any requirement to place the controls for a loop within its body, freeing it up just for the statements you want the loop to perform.

Remember to use curly braces with a for loop if it will contain more than one statement, as in Example 4-34.

Example 4-34. The for loop from Example 4-33 with added curly braces

```php
<?php
  for ($count = 1 ; $count <= 12 ; ++$count)
  {
    echo "$count times 12 is " . $count * 12;
    echo "<br>";
  }
?>
```

Let's compare when to use for and while loops. The for loop is explicitly designed around a single value that changes on a regular basis. Usually you have a value that increments, as when you are passed a list of user choices and want to process each choice in turn. But you can transform the variable any way you like. A more complex form of the for statement even lets you perform multiple operations in each of the three parameters:

```php
for ($i = 1, $j = 1 ; $i + $j < 10 ; $i++ , $j++)
{
  // ...
}
```

That's complicated and not recommended for first-time users. The key is to distinguish commas from semicolons. The three parameters must be separated by semicolons. Within each parameter, multiple statements can be separated by commas. Thus, in the previous example, the first and third parameters each contain two statements:

```php
$i = 1, $j = 1   // Initialize $i and $j
$i + $j < 10     // Terminating condition
$i++ , $j++      // Modify $i and $j at the end of each iteration
```

The main thing to take from this example is that you must separate the three parameter sections with semicolons, not commas (which should be used only to separate statements within a parameter section).

So, when is a while statement more appropriate than a for statement? When your condition doesn't depend on a simple, regular change to a variable. For instance, if you want to check for some special input or error and end the loop when it occurs, use a while statement.

Breaking Out of a Loop

Just as you saw how to break out of a switch statement, you can also break out of a for loop using the same break command. This step can be necessary when, for example, one of your statements returns an error and the loop cannot continue executing safely.

One case in which this might occur is when writing a file returns an error, possibly because the disk is full (see Example 4-35).

Example 4-35. Writing a file using a for loop with error trapping

```php
<?php
  $fp = fopen("text.txt", 'wb');

  for ($j = 0 ; $j < 100 ; ++$j)
  {
    $written = fwrite($fp, "data");

    if ($written == FALSE) break;
  }

  fclose($fp);
?>
```

This is the most complicated piece of code that you have seen so far, but you're ready for it. We'll look into the file handling commands in a later chapter, but for now all you need to know is that the first line opens the file *text.txt* for writing in binary mode, and then returns a pointer to the file in the variable $fp, which is used later to refer to the open file.

The loop then iterates 100 times (from 0 to 99) writing the string data to the file. After each write, the variable $written is assigned a value by the fwrite function representing the number of characters correctly written. But if there is an error, the fwrite function assigns the value FALSE.

The behavior of fwrite makes it easy for the code to check the variable $written to see whether it is set to FALSE and, if so, to break out of the loop to the following statement closing the file.

If you are looking to improve the code, the line:

```php
    if ($written == FALSE) break;
```

can be simplified using the NOT operator, like this:

```php
    if (!$written) break;
```

In fact, the pair of inner loop statements can be shortened to the following single statement:

```php
    if (!fwrite($fp, "data")) break;
```

The break command is even more powerful than you might think because if you have code nested more than one layer deep that you need to break out of, you can follow the break command with a number to indicate how many levels to break out of, like this:

```
break 2;
```

The continue Statement

The continue statement is a little like a break statement, except that it instructs PHP to stop processing the current loop and to move right to its next iteration. So, instead of breaking out of the whole loop, PHP exits only the current iteration.

This approach can be useful in cases where you know there is no point continuing execution within the current loop and you want to save processor cycles or prevent an error from occurring by moving right along to the next iteration of the loop. In Example 4-36, a continue statement is used to prevent a division-by-zero error from being issued when the variable $j has a value of 0.

Example 4-36. Trapping division-by-zero errors using continue

```php
<?php
  $j = 10;

  while ($j > -10)
  {
    $j--;

    if ($j == 0) continue;

    echo (10 / $j) . "<br>";
  }
?>
```

For all values of $j between 10 and -10, with the exception of 0, the result of calculating 10 divided by $j is displayed. But for the particular case of $j being 0, the continue statement is issued and execution skips immediately to the next iteration of the loop.

Implicit and Explicit Casting

PHP is a loosely typed language that allows you to declare a variable and its type simply by using it. It also automatically converts values from one type to another whenever required. This is called *implicit casting*.

However, there may be times when PHP's implicit casting is not what you want. In Example 4-37, note that the inputs to the division are integers. By default, PHP converts the output to floating point so it can give the most precise value—4.66 recurring.

Example 4-37. This expression returns a floating-point number

```php
<?php
  $a = 56;
  $b = 12;
  $c = $a / $b;

  echo $c;
?>
```

But what if we had wanted $c to be an integer instead? There are various ways in which we could achieve this, one of which is to force the result of $a/$b to be cast to an integer value using the integer cast type (int), like this:

```php
  $c = (int) ($a / $b);
```

This is called *explicit* casting. Note that in order to ensure that the value of the entire expression is cast to an integer, we place the expression within parentheses. Otherwise, only the variable $a would have been cast to an integer—a pointless exercise, as the division by $b would still have returned a floating-point number.

You can explicitly cast to the types shown in Table 4-6, but you can usually avoid having to use a cast by calling one of PHP's built-in functions. For example, to obtain an integer value, you could use the intval function. As with some other sections in this book, this one is mainly here to help you understand third-party code that you may encounter.

Table 4-6. PHP's cast types

Cast type	Description
(int) (integer)	Cast to an integer by dropping the decimal portion.
(bool) (boolean)	Cast to a Boolean.
(float) (double) (real)	Cast to a floating-point number.
(string)	Cast to a string.
(array)	Cast to an array.
(object)	Cast to an object.

PHP Dynamic Linking

Because PHP is a programming language, and the output from it can be completely different for each user, it's possible for an entire website to run from a single PHP web page. Each time the user clicks on something, the details can be sent back to the same web page, which decides what to do next according to the various cookies and/or other session details it may have stored.

Although it is possible to build an entire website this way, it's not recommended, because your source code will grow and grow and start to become unwieldy, as it has to account for every possible action a user could take.

Instead, it's much more sensible to split your website development into different parts. For example, one distinct process is signing up for a website, along with all the checking this entails to validate an email address, determine whether a username is already taken, and so on.

A second module might well be one for logging users in before handing them off to the main part of your website. Then you might have a messaging module with the facility for users to leave comments, a module containing links and useful information, another to allow uploading of images, and more.

As long as you have created a way to track your user through your website by means of cookies or session variables (both of which we'll look at more closely in later chapters), you can split up your website into sensible sections of PHP code, each one self-contained, and therefore treat yourself to a much easier future developing each new feature and maintaining old ones.

Dynamic Linking in Action

One of the more popular PHP-driven applications on the Web today is the blogging platform WordPress (see Figure 4-5). As a blogger or a blog reader, you might not realize it, but every major section has been given its own main PHP file, and a whole raft of generic, shared functions have been placed in separate files that are included by the main PHP pages as necessary.

The whole platform is held together with behind-the-scenes session tracking, so that you hardly know when you are transitioning from one subsection to another. So, as a web developer, if you want to tweak WordPress, it's easy to find the particular file you need, modify it, and test and debug it without messing around with unconnected parts of the program.

Next time you use WordPress, keep an eye on your browser's address bar, particularly if you are managing a blog, and you'll notice some of the different PHP files that it uses.

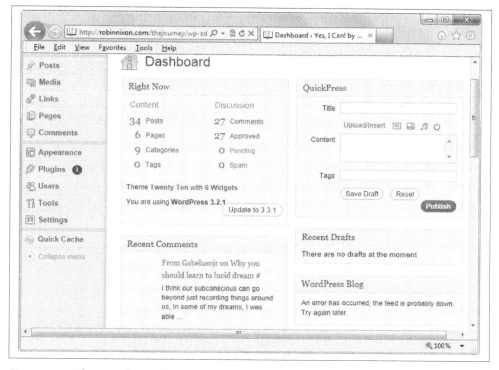

Figure 4-5. The WordPress blogging platform is written in PHP

This chapter has covered quite a lot of ground, and by now you should be able to put together your own small PHP programs. But before you do, and before proceeding with the following chapter on functions and objects, you may wish to test your new knowledge on the following questions.

Questions

1. What actual underlying values are represented by TRUE and FALSE?
2. What are the simplest two forms of expressions?
3. What is the difference between unary, binary, and ternary operators?
4. What is the best way to force your own operator precedence?
5. What is meant by *operator associativity*?
6. When would you use the === (identity) operator?
7. Name the three conditional statement types.

8. What command can you use to skip the current iteration of a loop and move on to the next one?

9. Why is a for loop more powerful than a while loop?

10. How do if and while statements interpret conditional expressions of different data types?

See "Chapter 4 Answers" on page 641 in Appendix A for the answers to these questions.

CHAPTER 5

PHP Functions and Objects

The basic requirements of any programming language include somewhere to store data, a means of directing program flow, and a few bits and pieces such as expression evaluation, file management, and text output. PHP has all these, plus tools like `else` and `elseif` to make life easier. But even with all these in our toolkit, programming can be clumsy and tedious, especially if you have to rewrite portions of very similar code each time you need them.

That's where functions and objects come in. As you might guess, a *function* is a set of statements that performs a particular function and—optionally—returns a value. You can pull out a section of code that you have used more than once, place it into a function, and call the function by name when you want the code.

Functions have many advantages over contiguous, inline code. For example, they:

- Involve less typing
- Reduce syntax and other programming errors
- Decrease the loading time of program files
- Decrease execution time, because each function is compiled only once, no matter how often you call it
- Accept arguments and can therefore be used for general as well as specific cases

Objects take this concept a step further. An *object* incorporates one or more functions, and the data they use, into a single structure called a *class*.

In this chapter, you'll learn all about using functions, from defining and calling them to passing arguments back and forth. With that knowledge under your belt, you'll start creating functions and using them in your own objects (where they will be referred to as *methods*).

PHP Functions

PHP comes with hundreds of ready-made, built-in functions, making it a very rich language. To use a function, call it by name. For example, you can see the `print` function in action here:

```
print("print is a pseudo-function");
```

The parentheses tell PHP that you're referring to a function. Otherwise, it thinks you're referring to a constant. You may see a warning such as this:

```
Notice: Use of undefined constant fname - assumed 'fname'
```

followed by the text string `fname`, under the assumption that you must have wanted to put a literal string in your code. (Things are even more confusing if there is actually a constant named `fname`, in which case PHP uses its value.)

Strictly speaking, `print` is a pseudo-function, commonly called a *construct*. The difference is that you can omit the parentheses, as follows:

```
print "print doesn't require parentheses";
```

You do have to put parentheses after any other functions you call, even if they're empty (i.e., if you're not passing any argument to the function).

Functions can take any number of arguments, including zero. For example, `phpinfo`, as shown here, displays lots of information about the current installation of PHP and requires no argument (the result of calling this function can be seen in Figure 5-1):

```
phpinfo();
```

The `phpinfo` function is extremely useful for obtaining information about your current PHP installation, but that information could also be very useful to potential hackers. Therefore, never leave a call to this function in any web-ready code.

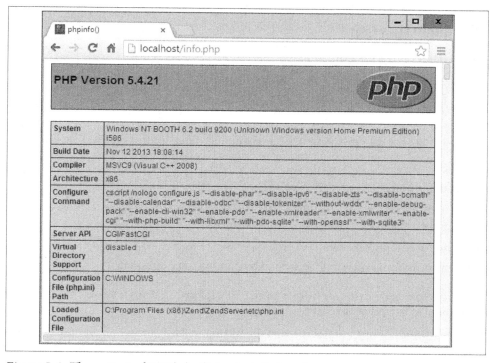

Figure 5-1. The output of PHP's built-in phpinfo function

Some of the built-in functions that use one or more arguments appear in Example 5-1.

Example 5-1. Three string functions

```php
<?php
  echo strrev(" .dlrow olleH"); // Reverse string
  echo str_repeat("Hip ", 2);   // Repeat string
  echo strtoupper("hooray!");   // String to uppercase
?>
```

This example uses three string functions to output the following text:

Hello world. Hip Hip HOORAY!

As you can see, the `strrev` function reversed the order of characters in the string, `str_repeat` repeated the string `"Hip "` twice (as required by a second argument), and `strtoupper` converted `"hooray!"` to uppercase.

Defining a Function

The general syntax for a function is:

```
function function_name([parameter [, ...]])
{
    // Statements
}
```

I'll explain all the square brackets, in case you find them confusing. The first line of the syntax indicates that:

- A definition starts with the word `function`.
- A name follows, which must start with a letter or underscore, followed by any number of letters, numbers, or underscores.
- The parentheses are required.
- One or more parameters, separated by commas, are optional.

Function names are case-insensitive, so all of the following strings can refer to the `print` function: `PRINT`, `Print`, and `PrInT`.

The opening curly brace starts the statements that will execute when you call the function; a matching curly brace must close it. These statements may include one or more `return` statements, which force the function to cease execution and return to the calling code. If a value is attached to the `return` statement, the calling code can retrieve it, as we'll see next.

Returning a Value

Let's take a look at a simple function to convert a person's full name to lowercase and then capitalize the first letter of each name.

We've already seen an example of PHP's built-in `strtoupper` function in Example 5-1. For our current function, we'll use its counterpart, `strtolower`:

```
$lowered = strtolower("aNY # of Letters and Punctuation you WANT");echo $lowered;
```

The output of this experiment is:

any # of letters and punctuation you want

We don't want names all lowercase, though; we want the first letter of each name capitalized. (We're not going to deal with subtle cases such as Mary-Ann or Jo-En-Lai for this example.) Luckily, PHP also provides a `ucfirst` function that sets the first character of a string to uppercase:

```
$ucfixed = ucfirst("any # of letters and punctuation you want");echo $ucfixed;
```

The output is:

`Any # of letters and punctuation you want`

Now we can do our first bit of program design: to get a word with its initial letter capitalized, we call `strtolower` on a string first, and then `ucfirst`. The way to do this is to nest a call to `strtolower` within `ucfirst`. Let's see why, because it's important to understand the order in which code is evaluated.

If you make a simple call to the `print` function:

```
print(5-8);
```

The expression `5-8` is evaluated first, and the output is `-3`. (As you saw in the previous chapter, PHP converts the result to a string in order to display it.) If the expression contains a function, that function is evaluated first as well:

```
print(abs(5-8));
```

PHP is doing several things in executing that short statement:

1. Evaluate `5-8` to produce `-3`.

2. Use the `abs` function to turn `-3` into `3`.

3. Convert the result to a string and output it using the `print` function.

It all works, because PHP evaluates each element from the inside out. The same procedure is in operation when we call the following:

```
ucfirst(strtolower("aNY # of Letters and Punctuation you WANT"))
```

PHP passes our string to `strtolower` and then to `ucfirst`, producing (as we've already seen when we played with the functions separately):

`Any # of letters and punctuation you want`

Now let's define a function (shown in Example 5-2) that takes three names and makes each one lowercase with an initial capital letter.

Example 5-2. Cleaning up a full name

```php
<?php
  echo fix_names("WILLIAM", "henry", "gatES");

  function fix_names($n1, $n2, $n3)
  {
    $n1 = ucfirst(strtolower($n1));
    $n2 = ucfirst(strtolower($n2));
    $n3 = ucfirst(strtolower($n3));

    return $n1 . " " . $n2 . " " . $n3;
  }
?>
```

You may well find yourself writing this type of code, because users often leave their Caps Lock key on, accidentally insert capital letters in the wrong places, and even forget capitals altogether. The output from this example is:

```
William Henry Gates
```

Returning an Array

We just saw a function returning a single value. There are also ways of getting multiple values from a function.

The first method is to return them within an array. As you saw in Chapter 3, an array is like a bunch of variables stuck together in a row. Example 5-3 shows how you can use an array to return function values.

Example 5-3. Returning multiple values in an array

```php
<?php
  $names = fix_names("WILLIAM", "henry", "gatES");
  echo $names[0] . " " . $names[1] . " " . $names[2];

  function fix_names($n1, $n2, $n3)
  {
    $n1 = ucfirst(strtolower($n1));
    $n2 = ucfirst(strtolower($n2));
    $n3 = ucfirst(strtolower($n3));

    return array($n1, $n2, $n3);
  }
?>
```

This method has the benefit of keeping all three names separate, rather than concatenating them into a single string, so you can refer to any user simply by first or last name, without having to extract either name from the returned string.

Passing by Reference

In PHP, prefacing a variable with the & symbol tells the parser to pass a reference to the variable's value, not the value itself. This concept can be hard to get your head around, so let's go back to the matchbox metaphor from Chapter 3.

Imagine that, instead of taking a piece of paper out of a matchbox, reading it, copying it to another piece of paper, putting the original back, and passing the copy to a function (phew!), you simply attach a piece of thread to the original piece of paper and pass one end of it to the function (see Figure 5-2).

Figure 5-2. Imagining a reference as a thread attached to a variable

Now the function can follow the thread to find the data to be accessed. This avoids all the overhead of creating a copy of the variable just for the function's use. What's more, the function can now modify the variable's value.

This means you can rewrite Example 5-3 to pass references to all the parameters, and then the function can modify these directly (see Example 5-4).

Example 5-4. Returning values from a function by reference

```php
<?php
  $a1 = "WILLIAM";
  $a2 = "henry";
  $a3 = "gatES";

  echo $a1 . " " . $a2 . " " . $a3 . "<br>";
  fix_names($a1, $a2, $a3);
  echo $a1 . " " . $a2 . " " . $a3;

  function fix_names(&$n1, &$n2, &$n3)
  {
    $n1 = ucfirst(strtolower($n1));
    $n2 = ucfirst(strtolower($n2));
    $n3 = ucfirst(strtolower($n3));
  }
?>
```

Rather than passing strings directly to the function, you first assign them to variables and print them out to see their "before" values. Then you call the function as before, but put an & symbol in front of each parameter, which tells PHP to pass the variables' references only.

Now the variables $n1, $n2, and $n3 are attached to "threads" that lead to the values of $a1, $a2, and $a3. In other words, there is one group of values, but two sets of variable names are allowed to access them.

Therefore, the function fix_names only has to assign new values to $n1, $n2, and $n3 to update the values of $a1, $a2, and $a3. The output from this code is:

```
WILLIAM henry gatES
William Henry Gates
```

As you see, both of the echo statements use only the values of $a1, $a2, and $a3.

 Be careful when passing values by reference. If you need to keep the original values, make copies of your variables and then pass the copies by reference.

Returning Global Variables

You can also give a function access to an externally created variable by declaring it a global variable from within the function. The global keyword followed by the variable name gives every part of your code full access to it (see Example 5-5).

Example 5-5. Returning values in global variables

```php
<?php
  $a1 = "WILLIAM";
  $a2 = "henry";
  $a3 = "gatES";

  echo $a1 . " " . $a2 . " " . $a3 . "<br>";
  fix_names();
  echo $a1 . " " . $a2 . " " . $a3;

  function fix_names()
  {
    global $a1; $a1 = ucfirst(strtolower($a1));
    global $a2; $a2 = ucfirst(strtolower($a2));
    global $a3; $a3 = ucfirst(strtolower($a3));
  }
?>
```

Now you don't have to pass parameters to the function, and it doesn't have to accept them. Once declared, these variables remain global and available to the rest of your program, including its functions.

In order to retain as much local scope as possible, you should try returning arrays or using variables by association. Otherwise, you will begin to lose some of the benefits of functions.

Recap of Variable Scope

A quick reminder of what you know from Chapter 3:

- *Local variables* are accessible just from the part of code where you define them. If they're outside of a function, they can be accessed by all code outside of functions, classes, and so on. If a variable is inside a function, only that function can access the variable, and its value is lost when the function returns.
- *Global variables* are accessible from all parts of your code.
- *Static variables* are accessible only within the function that declared them but retain their value over multiple calls.

Including and Requiring Files

As you progress in your use of PHP programming, you are likely to start building a library of functions that you think you will need again. You'll also probably start using libraries created by other programmers.

There's no need to copy and paste these functions into your code. You can save them in separate files and use commands to pull them in. There are two types of commands to perform this action: `include` and `require`.

The include Statement

Using `include`, you can tell PHP to fetch a particular file and load all its contents. It's as if you pasted the included file into the current file at the insertion point. Example 5-6 shows how you would include a file called *library.php*.

Example 5-6. Including a PHP file

```
<?php
  include "library.php";

  // Your code goes here
?>
```

Using include_once

Each time you issue the include directive, it includes the requested file again, even if you've already inserted it. For instance, suppose that *library.php* contains a lot of useful functions, so you include it in your file, but also include another library that includes *library.php*. Through nesting, you've inadvertently included *library.php* twice. This will produce error messages, because you're trying to define the same constant or function multiple times. So you should use include_once instead (see Example 5-7).

Example 5-7. Including a PHP file only once

```php
<?php
  include_once "library.php";

  // Your code goes here
?>
```

Then, whenever another include or include_once is encountered, if it has already been executed, it will be completely ignored. To determine whether the file has already been executed, the absolute file path is matched after all relative paths are resolved and the file is found in your include path.

 In general, it's probably best to stick with include_once and ignore the basic include statement. That way, you will never have the problem of files being included multiple times.

Using require and require_once

A potential problem with include and include_once is that PHP will only *attempt* to include the requested file. Program execution continues even if the file is not found.

When it is absolutely essential to include a file, require it. For the same reasons I gave for using include_once, I recommend that you generally stick with require_once whenever you need to require a file (see Example 5-8).

Example 5-8. Requiring a PHP file only once

```php
<?php
  require_once "library.php";

  // Your code goes here
?>
```

PHP Version Compatibility

PHP is in an ongoing process of development, and there are multiple versions. If you need to check whether a particular function is available to your code, you can use the `function_exists` function, which checks all predefined and user-created functions.

Example 5-9 checks for the function `array_combine`, which is specific to PHP version 5.

Example 5-9. Checking for a function's existence

```php
<?php
  if (function_exists("array_combine"))
  {
    echo "Function exists";
  }
  else
  {
    echo "Function does not exist - better write our own";
  }
?>
```

Using code such as this, you can take advantage of features in newer versions of PHP and yet still have your code run on earlier versions, as long as you replicate any features that are missing. Your functions may be slower than the built-in ones, but at least your code will be much more portable.

You can also use the `phpversion` function to determine which version of PHP your code is running on. The returned result will be similar to the following, depending on version:

    5.4.21

PHP Objects

In much the same way that functions represent a huge increase in programming power over the early days of computing, where sometimes the best program navigation available was a very basic `GOTO` or `GOSUB` statement, *object-oriented programming* (OOP) takes the use of functions to a whole new level.

Once you get the hang of condensing reusable bits of code into functions, it's not that great a leap to consider bundling the functions and their data into objects.

Let's take a social networking site that has many parts. One part handles all user functions; that is, code to enable new users to sign up and existing users to modify their details. In standard PHP, you might create a few functions to handle this and embed some calls to the MySQL database to keep track of all the users.

Imagine how much easier it would be to create an object to represent the current user. To do this, you could create a class, perhaps called `User`, that would contain all the code required for handling users and all the variables needed for manipulating the data within the class. Then, whenever you need to manipulate a user's data, you could simply create a new object with the User class.

You could treat this new object as if it were the actual user. For example, you could pass the object a name, password, and email address; ask it whether such a user already exists; and, if not, have it create a new user with those attributes. You could even have an instant messaging object, or one for managing whether two users are friends.

Terminology

When creating a program to use objects, you need to design a composite of data and code called a *class*. Each new object based on this class is called an *instance* (or *occurrence*) of that class.

The data associated with an object is called its *properties*; the functions it uses are called *methods*. In defining a class, you supply the names of its properties and the code for its methods. See Figure 5-3 for a jukebox metaphor for an object. Think of the CDs that it holds in the carousel as its properties; the method of playing them is to press buttons on the front panel. There is also the slot for inserting coins (the method used to activate the object), and the laser disc reader (the method used to retrieve the music, or properties, from the CDs).

When you're creating objects, it is best to use *encapsulation*, or writing a class in such a way that only its methods can be used to manipulate its properties. In other words, you deny outside code direct access to its data. The methods you supply are known as the object's *interface*.

This approach makes debugging easy: you have to fix faulty code only within a class. Additionally, when you want to upgrade a program, if you have used proper encapsulation and maintained the same interface, you can simply develop new replacement classes, debug them fully, and then swap them in for the old ones. If they don't work, you can swap the old ones back in to immediately fix the problem before further debugging the new classes.

Once you have created a class, you may find that you need another class that is similar to it but not quite the same. The quick and easy thing to do is to define a new class using *inheritance*. When you do this, your new class has all the properties of the one it has inherited from. The original class is now called the *superclass*, and the new one is the *subclass* (or *derived* class).

Figure 5-3. A jukebox: a great example of a self-contained object

In our jukebox example, if you invent a new jukebox that can play a video along with the music, you can inherit all the properties and methods from the original jukebox superclass and add some new properties (videos) and new methods (a movie player).

An excellent benefit of this system is that if you improve the speed or any other aspect of the superclass, its subclasses will receive the same benefit.

Declaring a Class

Before you can use an object, you must define a class with the `class` keyword. Class definitions contain the class name (which is case-sensitive), its properties, and its methods. Example 5-10 defines the class `User` with two properties: `$name` and `$password` (indicated by the `public` keyword—see "Property and Method Scope in PHP 5" on page 123). It also creates a new instance (called `$object`) of this class.

Example 5-10. Declaring a class and examining an object

```
<?php
  $object = new User;
  print_r($object);
```

```
  class User
  {
    public $name, $password;

    function save_user()
    {
      echo "Save User code goes here";
    }
  }
?>
```

Here I have also used an invaluable function called print_r. It asks PHP to display information about a variable in human-readable form. The _r stands for "in human-readable format." In the case of the new object $object, it prints the following:

```
User Object
(
  [name]    =>
  [password] =>
)
```

However, a browser compresses all the whitespace, so the output in a browser is slightly harder to read:

```
User Object ( [name] => [password] => )
```

In any case, the output says that $object is a user-defined object that has the properties name and password.

Creating an Object

To create an object with a specified class, use the new keyword, like this: object = new Class. Here are a couple of ways in which we could do this:

```
$object = new User;
$temp   = new User('name', 'password');
```

On the first line, we simply assign an object to the User class. In the second, we pass parameters to the call.

A class may require or prohibit arguments; it may also allow arguments, but not require them.

Accessing Objects

Let's add a few lines more to Example 5-10 and check the results. Example 5-11 extends the previous code by setting object properties and calling a method.

Example 5-11. Creating and interacting with an object

```php
<?php
  $object = new User;
  print_r($object); echo "<br>";

  $object->name     = "Joe";
  $object->password = "mypass";
  print_r($object); echo "<br>";

  $object->save_user();

  class User
  {
    public $name, $password;

    function save_user()
    {
      echo "Save User code goes here";
    }
  }
?>
```

As you can see, the syntax for accessing an object's property is *$object->property*. Likewise, you call a method like this: *$object->method()*.

You should note that the example property and method do not have $ signs in front of them. If you were to preface them with $ signs, the code would not work, as it would try to reference the value inside a variable. For example, the expression $object-> $property would attempt to look up the value assigned to a variable named $property (let's say that value is the string brown) and then attempt to reference the property $object->brown. If $property is undefined, an attempt to reference $object->NULL would occur and cause an error.

When looked at using a browser's View Source facility, the output from Example 5-11 is:

```
User Object
(
  [name]     =>
  [password] =>
)
User Object
(
  [name]     => Joe
  [password] => mypass
)
Save User code goes here
```

Again, print_r shows its utility by providing the contents of $object before and after property assignment. From now on, I'll omit print_r statements, but if you are working along with this book on your development server, you can put some in to see exactly what is happening.

You can also see that the code in the method save_user was executed via the call to that method. It printed the string reminding us to create some code.

 You can place functions and class definitions anywhere in your code, before or after statements that use them. Generally, though, it is considered good practice to place them toward the end of a file.

Cloning Objects

Once you have created an object, it is passed by reference when you pass it as a parameter. In the matchbox metaphor, this is like keeping several threads attached to an object stored in a matchbox, so that you can follow any attached thread to access it.

In other words, making object assignments does not copy objects in their entirety. You'll see how this works in Example 5-12, where we define a very simple User class with no methods and only the property name.

Example 5-12. Copying an object?

```php
<?php
  $object1        = new User();
  $object1->name = "Alice";
  $object2        = $object1;
  $object2->name = "Amy";

  echo "object1 name = " . $object1->name . "<br>";
  echo "object2 name = " . $object2->name;

  class User
  {
    public $name;
  }
?>
```

We've created the object $object1 and assigned the value Alice to the name property. Then we create $object2, assigning it the value of $object1, and assign the value Amy just to the name property of $object2—or so we might think. But this code outputs the following:

```
object1 name = Amy
object2 name = Amy
```

What has happened? Both $object1 and $object2 refer to the *same* object, so changing the name property of $object2 to Amy also sets that property for $object1.

To avoid this confusion, you can use the clone operator, which creates a new instance of the class and copies the property values from the original instance to the new instance. Example 5-13 illustrates this usage.

Example 5-13. Cloning an object

```php
<?php
  $object1         = new User();
  $object1->name = "Alice";
  $object2         = clone $object1;
  $object2->name = "Amy";

  echo "object1 name = " . $object1->name . "<br>";
  echo "object2 name = " . $object2->name;

  class User
  {
    public $name;
  }
?>
```

Voilà! The output from this code is what we initially wanted:

```
object1 name = Alice
object2 name = Amy
```

Constructors

When creating a new object, you can pass a list of arguments to the class being called. These are passed to a special method within the class, called the *constructor*, which initializes various properties.

In the past, you would normally give this method the same name as the class, as in Example 5-14.

Example 5-14. Creating a constructor method

```php
<?php
  class User
  {
    function User($param1, $param2)
    {
      // Constructor statements go here
      public $username = "Guest";
    }
  }
?>
```

However, PHP 5 provides a more logical approach to naming the constructor, which is to use the function name __construct (i.e., construct preceded by two underscore characters), as in Example 5-15.

Example 5-15. Creating a constructor method in PHP 5

```php
<?php
  class User
  {
    function __construct($param1, $param2)
    {
      // Constructor statements go here
      public $username = "Guest";
    }
  }
?>
```

PHP 5 Destructors

Also new in PHP 5 is the ability to create *destructor* methods. This ability is useful when code has made the last reference to an object or when a script reaches the end. Example 5-16 shows how to create a destructor method.

Example 5-16. Creating a destructor method in PHP 5

```php
<?php
  class User
  {
    function __destruct()
    {
      // Destructor code goes here
    }
  }
?>
```

Writing Methods

As you have seen, declaring a method is similar to declaring a function, but there are a few differences. For example, method names beginning with a double underscore (__) are reserved and you should not create any of this form.

You also have access to a special variable called $this, which can be used to access the current object's properties. To see how it works, take a look at Example 5-17, which contains a different method from the User class definition called get_password.

Example 5-17. Using the variable $this in a method

```php
<?php
  class User
  {
    public $name, $password;

    function get_password()
    {
      return $this->password;
```

```
    }
  }
?>
```

`get_password` uses the `$this` variable to access the current object and then return the value of that object's `password` property. Note how the preceding `$` of the property `$password` is omitted when we use the `->` operator. Leaving the `$` in place is a typical error you may run into, particularly when you first use this feature.

Here's how you would use the class defined in Example 5-17:

```
$object            = new User;
$object->password = "secret";

echo $object->get_password();
```

This code prints the password `secret`.

Static Methods in PHP 5

If you are using PHP 5, you can also define a method as *static*, which means that it is called on a class, not on an object. A static method has no access to any object properties and is created and accessed as in Example 5-18.

Example 5-18. Creating and accessing a static method

```
<?php
  User::pwd_string();

  class User
  {
    static function pwd_string()
    {
      echo "Please enter your password";
    }
  }
?>
```

Note how we call the class itself, along with the static method, using a double colon (also known as the *scope resolution* operator), not `->`. Static functions are useful for performing actions relating to the class itself, but not to specific instances of the class. You can see another example of a static method in Example 5-21.

 If you try to access `$this->property`, or other object properties from within a static function, you will receive an error message.

Declaring Properties

It is not necessary to explicitly declare properties within classes, as they can be implicitly defined when first used. To illustrate this, in Example 5-19 the class User has no properties and no methods but is legal code.

Example 5-19. Defining a property implicitly

```php
<?php
  $object1       = new User();
  $object1->name = "Alice";

  echo $object1->name;

  class User {}
?>
```

This code correctly outputs the string Alice without a problem, because PHP implicitly declares the variable $object1->name for you. But this kind of programming can lead to bugs that are infuriatingly difficult to discover, because name was declared from outside the class.

To help yourself and anyone else who will maintain your code, I advise that you get into the habit of always declaring your properties explicitly within classes. You'll be glad you did.

Also, when you declare a property within a class, you may assign a default value to it. The value you use must be a constant and not the result of a function or expression. Example 5-20 shows a few valid and invalid assignments.

Example 5-20. Valid and invalid property declarations

```php
<?php
  class Test
  {
    public $name  = "Paul Smith"; // Valid
    public $age   = 42;           // Valid
    public $time  = time();       // Invalid - calls a function
    public $score = $level * 2;   // Invalid - uses an expression
  }
?>
```

Declaring Constants

In the same way that you can create a global constant with the define function, you can define constants inside classes. The generally accepted practice is to use uppercase letters to make them stand out, as in Example 5-21.

Example 5-21. Defining constants within a class

```php
<?php
  Translate::lookup();

  class Translate
  {
    const ENGLISH = 0;
    const SPANISH = 1;
    const FRENCH  = 2;
    const GERMAN  = 3;
    // ...

    static function lookup()
    {
      echo self::SPANISH;
    }
  }
?>
```

You can reference constants directly, using the self keyword and double colon operator. Note that this code calls the class directly, using the double colon operator at line 1, without creating an instance of it first. As you would expect, the value printed when you run this code is 1.

Remember that once you define a constant, you can't change it.

Property and Method Scope in PHP 5

PHP 5 provides three keywords for controlling the scope of properties and methods:

public

> These properties are the default when you are declaring a variable using the var or public keywords, or when a variable is implicitly declared the first time it is used. The keywords var and public are interchangeable because, although deprecated, var is retained for compatibility with previous versions of PHP. Methods are assumed to be public by default.

protected

> These properties and methods (*members*) can be referenced only by the object's class methods and those of any subclasses.

private

> These members can be referenced only by methods within the same class—not by subclasses.

Here's how to decide which you need to use:

- Use `public` when outside code *should* access this member and extending classes *should* also inherit it.
- Use `protected` when outside code *should not* access this member but extending classes *should* inherit it.
- Use `private` when outside code *should not* access this member and extending classes also *should not* inherit it.

Example 5-22 illustrates the use of these keywords.

Example 5-22. Changing property and method scope

```php
<?php
  class Example
  {
    var $name    = "Michael"; // Same as public but deprecated
    public $age = 23;         // Public property
    protected $usercount;     // Protected property

    private function admin() // Private method
    {
      // Admin code goes here
    }
  }
?>
```

Static Properties and Methods

Most data and methods apply to instances of a class. For example, in a User class, you want to do such things as set a particular user's password or check when the user has been registered. These facts and operations apply separately to each user and therefore use instance-specific properties and methods.

But occasionally you'll want to maintain data about a whole class. For instance, to report how many users are registered, you will store a variable that applies to the whole User class. PHP provides static properties and methods for such data.

As shown briefly in Example 5-18, declaring members of a class `static` makes them accessible without an instantiation of the class. A property declared `static` cannot be directly accessed within an instance of a class, but a static method can.

Example 5-23 defines a class called `Test` with a static property and a public method.

Example 5-23. Defining a class with a static property

```php
<?php
  $temp = new Test();

  echo "Test A: " . Test::$static_property . "<br>";
  echo "Test B: " . $temp->get_sp()       . "<br>";
  echo "Test C: " . $temp->static_property . "<br>";

  class Test
  {
    static $static_property = "I'm static";

    function get_sp()
    {
      return self::$static_property;
    }
  }
?>
```

When you run this code, it returns the following output:

```
Test A: I'm static
Test B: I'm static

Notice: Undefined property: Test::$static_property
Test C:
```

This example shows that the property $static_property could be directly referenced from the class itself via the double colon operator in Test A. Also, Test B could obtain its value by calling the get_sp method of the object $temp, created from class Test. But Test C failed, because the static property $static_property was not accessible to the object $temp.

Note how the method get_sp accesses $static_property using the keyword self. This is the way in which a static property or constant can be directly accessed within a class.

Inheritance

Once you have written a class, you can derive subclasses from it. This can save lots of painstaking code rewriting: you can take a class similar to the one you need to write, extend it to a subclass, and just modify the parts that are different. You achieve this using the extends operator.

In Example 5-24, the class Subscriber is declared a subclass of User by means of the extends operator.

Example 5-24. Inheriting and extending a class

```php
<?php
  $object            = new Subscriber;
  $object->name      = "Fred";
  $object->password  = "pword";
  $object->phone     = "012 345 6789";
  $object->email     = "fred@bloggs.com";
  $object->display();

  class User
  {
    public $name, $password;

    function save_user()
    {
      echo "Save User code goes here";
    }
  }

  class Subscriber extends User
  {
    public $phone, $email;

    function display()
    {
      echo "Name:  " . $this->name     . "<br>";
      echo "Pass:  " . $this->password . "<br>";
      echo "Phone: " . $this->phone    . "<br>";
      echo "Email: " . $this->email;
    }
  }
?>
```

The original User class has two properties, $name and $password, and a method to save
the current user to the database. Subscriber extends this class by adding an additional
two properties, $phone and $email, and includes a method of displaying the properties
of the current object using the variable $this, which refers to the current values of the
object being accessed. The output from this code is:

```
Name:  Fred
Pass:  pword
Phone: 012 345 6789
Email: fred@bloggs.com
```

The parent operator

If you write a method in a subclass with the same name as one in its parent class, its
statements will override those of the parent class. Sometimes this is not the behavior
you want and you need to access the parent's method. To do this, you can use the parent
operator, as in Example 5-25.

Example 5-25. Overriding a method and using the parent operator

```php
<?php
  $object = new Son;
  $object->test();
  $object->test2();

  class Dad
  {
    function test()
    {
      echo "[Class Dad] I am your Father<br>";
    }
  }

  class Son extends Dad
  {
    function test()
    {
      echo "[Class Son] I am Luke<br>";
    }

    function test2()
    {
      parent::test();
    }
  }
?>
```

This code creates a class called Dad and then a subclass called Son that inherits its properties and methods, and then overrides the method test. Therefore, when line 2 calls the method test, the new method is executed. The only way to execute the overridden test method in the Dad class is to use the parent operator, as shown in function test2 of class Son. The code outputs the following:

```
[Class Son] I am Luke
[Class Dad] I am your Father
```

If you wish to ensure that your code calls a method from the current class, you can use the self keyword, like this:

```
self::method();
```

Subclass constructors

When you extend a class and declare your own constructor, you should be aware that PHP will not automatically call the constructor method of the parent class. If you want to be certain that all initialization code is executed, subclasses should always call the parent constructors, as in Example 5-26.

Example 5-26. Calling the parent class constructor

```php
<?php
  $object = new Tiger();

  echo "Tigers have...<br>";
  echo "Fur: " . $object->fur . "<br>";
  echo "Stripes: " . $object->stripes;

  class Wildcat
  {
    public $fur; // Wildcats have fur

    function __construct()
    {
      $this->fur = "TRUE";
    }
  }

  class Tiger extends Wildcat
  {
    public $stripes; // Tigers have stripes

    function __construct()
    {
      parent::__construct(); // Call parent constructor first
      $this->stripes = "TRUE";
    }
  }
?>
```

This example takes advantage of inheritance in the typical manner. The Wildcat class has created the property $fur, which we'd like to reuse, so we create the Tiger class to inherit $fur and additionally create another property, $stripes. To verify that both constructors have been called, the program outputs the following:

```
Tigers have...
Fur: TRUE
Stripes: TRUE
```

Final methods

When you wish to prevent a subclass from overriding a superclass method, you can use the final keyword. Example 5-27 shows how.

Example 5-27. Creating a final method

```php
<?php
  class User
  {
    final function copyright()
    {
      echo "This class was written by Joe Smith";
    }
  }
?>
```

Once you have digested the contents of this chapter, you should have a strong feel for what PHP can do for you. You should be able to use functions with ease and, if you wish, write object-oriented code. In Chapter 6, we'll finish off our initial exploration of PHP by looking at the workings of PHP arrays.

Questions

1. What is the main benefit of using a function?
2. How many values can a function return?
3. What is the difference between accessing a variable by name and by reference?
4. What is the meaning of *scope* in PHP?
5. How can you incorporate one PHP file within another?
6. How is an object different from a function?
7. How do you create a new object in PHP?
8. What syntax would you use to create a subclass from an existing one?
9. How can you call an initializing piece of code when an object is created?
10. Why is it a good idea to explicitly declare properties within a class?

See "Chapter 5 Answers" on page 642 in Appendix A for the answers to these questions.

CHAPTER 6

PHP Arrays

In Chapter 3, I gave a very brief introduction to PHP's arrays—just enough for a little taste of their power. In this chapter, I'll show you many more things that you can do with arrays, some of which—if you have ever used a strongly typed language such as C—may surprise you with their elegance and simplicity.

Arrays are an example of what has made PHP so popular. Not only do they remove the tedium of writing code to deal with complicated data structures, they also provide numerous ways to access data while remaining amazingly fast.

Basic Access

We've already looked at arrays as if they were clusters of matchboxes glued together. Another way to think of an array is like a string of beads, with the beads representing variables that can be numeric, string, or even other arrays. They are like bead strings, because each element has its own location and (with the exception of the first and last ones) each has other elements on either side.

Some arrays are referenced by numeric indices; others allow alphanumeric identifiers. Built-in functions let you sort them, add or remove sections, and walk through them to handle each item through a special kind of loop. And by placing one or more arrays inside another, you can create arrays of two, three, or any number of dimensions.

Numerically Indexed Arrays

Let's assume that you've been tasked with creating a simple website for a local office supply company and you're currently working on the section devoted to paper. One way to manage the various items of stock in this category would be to place them in a numeric array. You can see the simplest way of doing so in Example 6-1.

Example 6-1. Adding items to an array

```php
<?php
  $paper[] = "Copier";
  $paper[] = "Inkjet";
  $paper[] = "Laser";
  $paper[] = "Photo";

  print_r($paper);
?>
```

In this example, each time you assign a value to the array `$paper`, the first empty location within that array is used to store the value, and a pointer internal to PHP is incremented to point to the next free location, ready for future insertions. The familiar `print_r` function (which prints out the contents of a variable, array, or object) is used to verify that the array has been correctly populated. It prints out the following:

```
Array
(
   [0] => Copier
   [1] => Inkjet
   [2] => Laser
   [3] => Photo
)
```

The previous code could also have been written as shown in Example 6-2, where the exact location of each item within the array is specified. But, as you can see, that approach requires extra typing and makes your code harder to maintain if you want to insert or remove supplies from the array. So unless you wish to specify a different order, it's usually better to simply let PHP handle the actual location numbers.

Example 6-2. Adding items to an array using explicit locations

```php
<?php
  $paper[0] = "Copier";
  $paper[1] = "Inkjet";
  $paper[2] = "Laser";
  $paper[3] = "Photo";

  print_r($paper);
?>
```

The output from these examples is identical, but you are not likely to use `print_r` in a developed website, so Example 6-3 shows how you might print out the various types of paper the website offers using a `for` loop.

Example 6-3. Adding items to an array and retrieving them

```php
<?php
  $paper[] = "Copier";
  $paper[] = "Inkjet";
  $paper[] = "Laser";
  $paper[] = "Photo";

  for ($j = 0 ; $j < 4 ; ++$j)
    echo "$j: $paper[$j]<br>";
?>
```

This example prints out the following:

```
0: Copier
1: Inkjet
2: Laser
3: Photo
```

So far, you've seen a couple of ways in which you can add items to an array and one way of referencing them, but PHP offers many more—which I'll get to shortly. But first, we'll look at another type of array.

Associative Arrays

Keeping track of array elements by index works just fine, but can require extra work in terms of remembering which number refers to which product. It can also make code hard for other programmers to follow.

This is where associative arrays come into their own. Using them, you can reference the items in an array by name rather than by number. Example 6-4 expands on the previous code by giving each element in the array an identifying name and a longer, more explanatory string value.

Example 6-4. Adding items to an associative array and retrieving them

```php
<?php
  $paper['copier'] = "Copier & Multipurpose";
  $paper['inkjet'] = "Inkjet Printer";
  $paper['laser']  = "Laser Printer";
  $paper['photo']  = "Photographic Paper";

  echo $paper['laser'];
?>
```

In place of a number (which doesn't convey any useful information, aside from the position of the item in the array), each item now has a unique name that you can use to reference it elsewhere, as with the echo statement—which simply prints out Laser Printer. The names (copier, inkjet, etc.) are called *indexes* or *keys* and the items assigned to them (such as "Laser Printer") are called *values*.

This very powerful feature of PHP is often used when you are extracting information from XML and HTML. For example, an HTML parser such as those used by a search engine could place all the elements of a web page into an associative array whose names reflect the page's structure:

```
$html['title'] = "My web page";
$html['body']  = "... body of web page ...";
```

The program would also probably break down all the links found within a page into another array, and all the headings and subheadings into another. When you use associative rather than numeric arrays, the code to refer to all of these items is easy to write and debug.

Assignment Using the array Keyword

So far, you've seen how to assign values to arrays by just adding new items one at a time. Whether you specify keys, specify numeric identifiers, or let PHP assign numeric identifiers implicitly, this is a long-winded approach. A more compact and faster assignment method uses the array keyword. Example 6-5 shows both a numeric and an associative array assigned using this method.

Example 6-5. Adding items to an array using the array keyword

```
<?php
  $p1 = array("Copier", "Inkjet", "Laser", "Photo");

  echo "p1 element: " . $p1[2] . "<br>";

  $p2 = array('copier' => "Copier & Multipurpose",
              'inkjet' => "Inkjet Printer",
              'laser'  => "Laser Printer",
              'photo'  => "Photographic Paper");

  echo "p2 element: " . $p2['inkjet'] . "<br>";
?>
```

The first half of this snippet assigns the old, shortened product descriptions to the array $p1. There are four items, so they will occupy slots 0 through 3. Therefore, the echo statement prints out the following:

    p1 element: Laser

The second half assigns associative identifiers and accompanying longer product descriptions to the array $p2 using the format *index => value*. The use of => is similar to the regular = assignment operator, except that you are assigning a value to an *index* and not to a *variable*. The index is then inextricably linked with that value, unless it is assigned a new value. The echo command therefore prints out:

    p2 element: Inkjet Printer

You can verify that $p1 and $p2 are different types of array, because both of the following commands, when appended to the code, will cause an Undefined index or Undefined offset error, as the array identifier for each is incorrect:

```php
echo $p1['inkjet']; // Undefined index
echo $p2[3];        // Undefined offset
```

The foreach ... as Loop

The creators of PHP have gone to great lengths to make the language easy to use. So, not content with the loop structures already provided, they added another one especially for arrays: the foreach ... as loop. Using it, you can step through all the items in an array, one at a time, and do something with them.

The process starts with the first item and ends with the last one, so you don't even have to know how many items there are in an array.

Example 6-6 shows how foreach ... as can be used to rewrite Example 6-3.

Example 6-6. Walking through a numeric array using foreach ... as

```php
<?php
  $paper = array("Copier", "Inkjet", "Laser", "Photo");
  $j = 0;

  foreach($paper as $item)
  {
    echo "$j: $item<br>";
    ++$j;
  }
?>
```

When PHP encounters a foreach statement, it takes the first item of the array and places it in the variable following the as keyword; and each time control flow returns to the foreach, the next array element is placed in the as keyword. In this case, the variable $item is set to each of the four values in turn in the array $paper. Once all values have been used, execution of the loop ends. The output from this code is exactly the same as Example 6-3.

Now let's see how foreach works with an associative array by taking a look at Example 6-7, which is a rewrite of the second half of Example 6-5.

Example 6-7. Walking through an associative array using foreach ... as

```php
<?php
  $paper = array('copier' => "Copier & Multipurpose",
                 'inkjet' => "Inkjet Printer",
                 'laser'  => "Laser Printer",
                 'photo'  => "Photographic Paper");
```

```
  foreach($paper as $item => $description)
    echo "$item: $description<br>";
?>
```

Remember that associative arrays do not require numeric indexes, so the variable $j is not used in this example. Instead, each item of the array $paper is fed into the key/value pair of variables $item and $description, from which they are printed out. The displayed result of this code is as follows:

```
copier: Copier & Multipurpose
inkjet: Inkjet Printer
laser: Laser Printer
photo: Photographic Paper
```

As an alternative syntax to foreach ... as, you can use the list function in conjunction with the each function, as in Example 6-8.

Example 6-8. Walking through an associative array using each and list

```
<?php
  $paper = array('copier' => "Copier & Multipurpose",
                 'inkjet' => "Inkjet Printer",
                 'laser'  => "Laser Printer",
                 'photo'  => "Photographic Paper");

  while (list($item, $description) = each($paper))
    echo "$item: $description<br>";
?>
```

In this example, a while loop is set up and will continue looping until the each function returns a value of FALSE. The each function acts like foreach: it returns an array containing a key/value pair from the array $paper and then moves its built-in pointer to the next pair in that array. When there are no more pairs to return, each returns FALSE.

The list function takes an array as its argument (in this case, the key/value pair returned by the function each) and then assigns the values of the array to the variables listed within parentheses.

You can see how list works a little more clearly in Example 6-9, where an array is created out of the two strings Alice and Bob and then passed to the list function, which assigns those strings as values to the variables $a and $b.

Example 6-9. Using the list function

```
<?php
  list($a, $b) = array('Alice', 'Bob');
  echo "a=$a b=$b";
?>
```

The output from this code is:

```
a=Alice b=Bob
```

So you can take your pick when walking through arrays. Use `foreach ... as` to create a loop that extracts values to the variable following the `as`, or use the `each` function and create your own looping system.

Multidimensional Arrays

A simple design feature in PHP's array syntax makes it possible to create arrays of more than one dimension. In fact, they can be as many dimensions as you like (although it's a rare application that goes further than three).

That feature makes it possible to include an entire array as a part of another one, and to be able to keep doing so, just like the old rhyme: "Big fleas have little fleas upon their backs to bite 'em. Little fleas have lesser fleas, add flea, ad infinitum."

Let's look at how this works by taking the associative array in the previous example and extending it; see Example 6-10.

Example 6-10. Creating a multidimensional associative array

```php
<?php
  $products = array(

    'paper' =>  array(

      'copier' => "Copier & Multipurpose",
      'inkjet' => "Inkjet Printer",
      'laser'  => "Laser Printer",
      'photo'  => "Photographic Paper"),

    'pens' => array(

      'ball'   => "Ball Point",
      'hilite' => "Highlighters",
      'marker' => "Markers"),

    'misc' => array(

      'tape'   => "Sticky Tape",
      'glue'   => "Adhesives",
      'clips'  => "Paperclips"
    )
  );

  echo "<pre>";

  foreach($products as $section => $items)
    foreach($items as $key => $value)
      echo "$section:\t$key\t($value)<br>";
```

```
    echo "</pre>";
?>
```

To make things clearer now that the code is starting to grow, I've renamed some of the elements. For example, because the previous array $paper is now just a subsection of a larger array, the main array is now called $products. Within this array, there are three items—paper, pens, and misc—each of which contains another array with key/value pairs.

If necessary, these subarrays could have contained even further arrays. For example, under ball there might be many different types and colors of ballpoint pens available in the online store. But for now, I've restricted the code to a depth of just two.

Once the array data has been assigned, I use a pair of nested foreach ... as loops to print out the various values. The outer loop extracts the main sections from the top level of the array, and the inner loop extracts the key/value pairs for the categories within each section.

As long as you remember that each level of the array works the same way (it's a key/value pair), you can easily write code to access any element at any level.

The echo statement makes use of the PHP escape character \t, which outputs a tab. Although tabs are not normally significant to the web browser, I let them be used for layout by using the <pre> ... </pre> tags, which tell the web browser to format the text as preformatted and monospaced, and *not* to ignore whitespace characters such as tabs and line feeds. The output from this code looks like the following:

```
paper:  copier  (Copier & Multipurpose)
paper:  inkjet  (Inkjet Printer)
paper:  laser   (Laser Printer)
paper:  photo   (Photographic Paper)
pens:   ball    (Ball Point)
pens:   hilite  (Highlighters)
pens:   marker  (Markers)
misc:   tape    (Sticky Tape)
misc:   glue    (Adhesives)
misc:   clips   (Paperclips)
```

You can directly access a particular element of the array using square brackets, like this:

```
echo $products['misc']['glue'];
```

which outputs the value Adhesives.

You can also create numeric multidimensional arrays that are accessed directly by indexes rather than by alphanumeric identifiers. Example 6-11 creates the board for a chess game with the pieces in their starting positions.

Example 6-11. Creating a multidimensional numeric array

```php
<?php
  $chessboard = array(
    array('r', 'n', 'b', 'q', 'k', 'b', 'n', 'r'),
    array('p', 'p', 'p', 'p', 'p', 'p', 'p', 'p'),
    array(' ', ' ', ' ', ' ', ' ', ' ', ' ', ' '),
    array(' ', ' ', ' ', ' ', ' ', ' ', ' ', ' '),
    array(' ', ' ', ' ', ' ', ' ', ' ', ' ', ' '),
    array(' ', ' ', ' ', ' ', ' ', ' ', ' ', ' '),
    array('P', 'P', 'P', 'P', 'P', 'P', 'P', 'P'),
    array('R', 'N', 'B', 'Q', 'K', 'B', 'N', 'R')
  );

  echo "<pre>";

  foreach($chessboard as $row)
  {
    foreach ($row as $piece)
      echo "$piece ";

    echo "<br>";
  }

  echo "</pre>";
?>
```

In this example, the lowercase letters represent black pieces and the uppercase white. The key is r = rook, n = knight, b = bishop, k = king, q = queen, and p = pawn. Again, a pair of nested foreach ... as loops walks through the array and displays its contents. The outer loop processes each row into the variable $row, which itself is an array, because the $chessboard array uses a subarray for each row. This loop has two statements within it, so curly braces enclose them.

The inner loop then processes each square in a row, outputting the character ($piece) stored in it, followed by a space (to square up the printout). This loop has a single statement, so curly braces are not required to enclose it. The <pre> and </pre> tags ensure that the output displays correctly, like this:

```
r n b q k b n r
p p p p p p p p



P P P P P P P P
R N B Q K B N R
```

You can also directly access any element within this array using square brackets, like this:

```php
echo $chessboard[7][3];
```

This statement outputs the uppercase letter Q, the eighth element down and the fourth along (remembering that array indexes start at 0, not 1).

Using Array Functions

You've already seen the list and each functions, but PHP comes with numerous other functions for handling arrays. The full list is at *http://tinyurl.com/arraysinphp*. However, some of these functions are so fundamental that it's worth taking the time to look at them here.

is_array

Arrays and variables share the same namespace. This means that you cannot have a string variable called $fred and an array also called $fred. If you're in doubt and your code needs to check whether a variable is an array, you can use the is_array function like this:

```
echo (is_array($fred)) ? "Is an array" : "Is not an array";
```

Note that if $fred has not yet been assigned a value, an Undefined variable message will be generated.

count

Although the each function and foreach ... as loop structure are excellent ways to walk through an array's contents, sometimes you need to know exactly how many elements there are in your array, particularly if you will be referencing them directly. To count all the elements in the top level of an array, use a command such as the following:

```
echo count($fred);
```

Should you wish to know how many elements there are altogether in a multidimensional array, you can use a statement such as:

```
echo count($fred, 1);
```

The second parameter is optional and sets the mode to use. It should be either a 0 to limit counting to only the top level, or 1 to force recursive counting of all subarray elements too.

sort

Sorting is so common that PHP provides a built-in function. In its simplest form, you would use it like this:

```
sort($fred);
```

Unlike some other functions, sort will act directly on the supplied array rather than returning a new array of sorted elements. Instead, it returns TRUE on success and FALSE on error and also supports a few flags, but the main two that you might wish to use force sorting to be made either numerically or as strings, like this:

```
sort($fred, SORT_NUMERIC);
sort($fred, SORT_STRING);
```

You can also sort an array in reverse order using the rsort function, like this:

```
rsort($fred, SORT_NUMERIC);
rsort($fred, SORT_STRING);
```

shuffle

There may be times when you need the elements of an array to be put in random order, such as when you're creating a game of playing cards:

```
shuffle($cards);
```

Like sort, shuffle acts directly on the supplied array and returns TRUE on success or FALSE on error.

explode

This is a very useful function with which you can take a string containing several items separated by a single character (or string of characters) and then place each of these items into an array. One handy example is to split up a sentence into an array containing all its words, as in Example 6-12.

Example 6-12. Exploding a string into an array using spaces

```
<?php
  $temp = explode(' ', "This is a sentence with seven words");
  print_r($temp);
?>
```

This example prints out the following (on a single line when viewed in a browser):

```
Array
(
  [0] => This
  [1] => is
  [2] => a
  [3] => sentence
  [4] => with
  [5] => seven
  [6] => words
)
```

The first parameter, the delimiter, need not be a space or even a single character. Example 6-13 shows a slight variation.

Example 6-13. Exploding a string delimited with *** into an array

```php
<?php
  $temp = explode('***', "A***sentence***with***asterisks");
  print_r($temp);
?>
```

The code in Example 6-13 prints out the following:

```
Array
(
  [0] => A
  [1] => sentence
  [2] => with
  [3] => asterisks
)
```

extract

Sometimes it can be convenient to turn the key/value pairs from an array into PHP variables. One such time might be when you are processing the $_GET or $_POST variables as sent to a PHP script by a form.

When a form is submitted over the Web, the web server unpacks the variables into a global array for the PHP script. If the variables were sent using the GET method, they will be placed in an associative array called $_GET; if they were sent using POST, they will be placed in an associative array called $_POST.

You could, of course, walk through such associative arrays in the manner shown in the examples so far. However, sometimes you just want to store the values sent into variables for later use. In this case, you can have PHP do the job automatically for you:

```php
extract($_GET);
```

So, for example, if the query string parameter q is sent to a PHP script along with the associated value Hi there, a new variable called $q will be created and assigned that value.

Be careful with this approach, though, because if any extracted variables conflict with ones that you have already defined, your existing values will be overwritten. To avoid this possibility, you can use one of the many additional parameters available to this function, like this:

```php
extract($_GET, EXTR_PREFIX_ALL, 'fromget');
```

In this case, all the new variables will begin with the given prefix string followed by an underscore, so $q will become $fromget_q. I strongly recommend that you use this version of the function when handling the $_GET and $_POST arrays, or any other array whose keys could be controlled by the user, because malicious users could submit keys chosen deliberately to overwrite commonly used variable names and compromise your website.

compact

There are also times when you want to use compact, the inverse of extract, to create an array from variables and their values. Example 6-14 shows how you might use this function.

Example 6-14. Using the compact function

```php
<?php
  $fname        = "Doctor";
  $sname        = "Who";
  $planet       = "Gallifrey";
  $system       = "Gridlock";
  $constellation = "Kasterborous";

  $contact = compact('fname', 'sname', 'planet', 'system', 'constellation');

  print_r($contact);
?>
```

The result of running Example 6-14 is:

```
Array
(
    [fname] => Doctor
    [sname] => Who
    [planet] => Gallifrey
    [system] => Gridlock
    [constellation] => Kasterborous
)
```

Note how compact requires the variable names to be supplied in quotes, not preceded by a $ symbol. This is because compact is looking for a list of variable names.

Another use of this function is for debugging, when you wish to quickly view several variables and their values, as in Example 6-15.

Example 6-15. Using compact to help with debugging

```php
<?php
  $j       = 23;
  $temp    = "Hello";
  $address = "1 Old Street";
  $age     = 61;

  print_r(compact(explode(' ', 'j temp address age')));
?>
```

This works by using the `explode` function to extract all the words from the string into an array, which is then passed to the `compact` function, which in turn returns an array to `print_r`, which finally shows its contents.

If you copy and paste the `print_r` line of code, you only need to alter the variables named there for a quick printout of a group of variables' values. In this example, the output is:

```
Array
(
  [j] => 23
  [temp] => Hello
  [address] => 1 Old Street
  [age] => 61
)
```

reset

When the `foreach ... as` construct or the `each` function walks through an array, it keeps an internal PHP pointer that makes a note of which element of the array it should return next. If your code ever needs to return to the start of an array, you can issue `reset`, which also returns the value of that element. Examples of how to use this function are:

```
reset($fred);         // Throw away return value
$item = reset($fred); // Keep first element of the array in $item
```

end

As with `reset`, you can move PHP's internal array pointer to the final element in an array using the `end` function, which also returns the value of the element, and can be used as in these examples:

```
end($fred);
$item = end($fred);
```

This chapter concludes your basic introduction to PHP, and you should now be able to write quite complex programs using the skills you have learned. In the next chapter, we'll look at using PHP for common, practical tasks.

Questions

1. What is the difference between a numeric and an associative array?
2. What is the main benefit of the `array` keyword?
3. What is the difference between `foreach` and `each`?
4. How can you create a multidimensional array?

5. How can you determine the number of elements in an array?

6. What is the purpose of the `explode` function?

7. How can you set PHP's internal pointer into an array back to the first element of the array?

See "Chapter 6 Answers" on page 643 in Appendix A for the answers to these questions.

CHAPTER 7

Practical PHP

Previous chapters went over the elements of the PHP language. This chapter builds on your new programming skills to teach you some common but important practical tasks. You will learn the best ways to manage string handling to achieve clear and concise code that displays in web browsers exactly how you want it to, including advanced date and time management. You'll also find out how to create and otherwise modify files, including those uploaded by users.

Using printf

You've already seen the `print` and `echo` functions, which simply output text to the browser. But a much more powerful function, `printf`, controls the format of the output by letting you put special formatting characters in a string. For each formatting character, `printf` expects you to pass an argument that it will display using that format. For instance, the following example uses the `%d` conversion specifier to display the value 3 in decimal:

```
printf("There are %d items in your basket", 3);
```

If you replace the `%d` with `%b`, the value 3 would be displayed in binary (`11`). Table 7-1 shows the conversion specifiers supported.

Table 7-1. The printf conversion specifiers

Specifier	Conversion action on argument arg	Example (for an arg of 123)
%	Display a % character (no `arg` is required).	%
b	Display `arg` as a binary integer.	1111011
c	Display ASCII character for the `arg`.	{
d	Display `arg` as a signed decimal integer.	123
e	Display `arg` using scientific notation.	1.23000e+2

Specifier	Conversion action on argument arg	Example (for an arg of 123)
f	Display arg as floating point.	123.000000
o	Display arg as an octal integer.	173
s	Display arg as a string.	123
u	Display arg as an unsigned decimal.	123
x	Display arg in lowercase hexadecimal.	7b
X	Display arg in uppercase hexadecimal.	7B

You can have as many specifiers as you like in a printf function, as long as you pass a matching number of arguments, and as long as each specifier is prefaced by a % symbol. Therefore, the following code is valid, and will output "My name is Simon. I'm 33 years old, which is 21 in hexadecimal":

```
printf("My name is %s. I'm %d years old, which is %X in hexadecimal",
    'Simon', 33, 33);
```

If you leave out any arguments, you will receive a parse error informing you that a right bracket,), was unexpectedly encountered.

A more practical example of printf sets colors in HTML using decimal. For example, suppose you know you want a color that has a triplet value of 65 red, 127 green, and 245 blue, but don't want to convert this to hexadecimal yourself. An easy solution is:

```
printf("<span style='color:#%X%X%X'>Hello</span>", 65, 127, 245);
```

Check the format of the color specification between the apostrophes (' ') carefully. First comes the pound, or hash, sign (#) expected by the color specification. Then come three %X format specifiers, one for each of your numbers. The resulting output from this command is:

```
<span style='color:#417FF5'>Hello</span>
```

Usually, you'll find it convenient to use variables or expressions as arguments to printf. For instance, if you stored values for your colors in the three variables $r, $g, and $b, you could create a darker color with:

```
printf("<span style='color:#%X%X%X'>Hello</span>", $r-20, $g-20, $b-20);
```

Precision Setting

Not only can you specify a conversion type, you can also set the precision of the displayed result. For example, amounts of currency are usually displayed with only two digits of precision. However, after a calculation, a value may have a greater precision than this, such as 123.42 / 12, which results in 10.285. To ensure that such values are correctly stored internally, but displayed with only two digits of precision, you can insert the string ".2" between the % symbol and the conversion specifier:

```
printf("The result is: $%.2f", 123.42 / 12);
```

The output from this command is:

```
The result is $10.29
```

But you actually have even more control than that, because you can also specify whether to pad output with either zeros or spaces by prefacing the specifier with certain values. Example 7-1 shows four possible combinations.

Example 7-1. Precision setting

```php
<?php
  echo "<pre>"; // Enables viewing of the spaces

  // Pad to 15 spaces
  printf("The result is $%15f\n", 123.42 / 12);

  // Pad to 15 spaces, fill with zeros
  printf("The result is $%015f\n", 123.42 / 12);

  // Pad to 15 spaces, 2 decimal places precision
  printf("The result is $%15.2f\n", 123.42 / 12);

  // Pad to 15 spaces, 2 decimal places precision, fill with zeros
  printf("The result is $%015.2f\n", 123.42 / 12);

  // Pad to 15 spaces, 2 decimal places precision, fill with # symbol
  printf("The result is $%'#15.2f\n", 123.42 / 12);
?>
```

The output from this example looks like this:

```
The result is $       10.285000
The result is $00000010.285000
The result is $          10.29
The result is $000000000010.29
The result is $##########10.29
```

The way it works is simple if you go from right to left (see Table 7-2). Notice that:

- The rightmost character is the conversion specifier. In this case, it is f for floating point.

- Just before the conversion specifier, if there is a period and a number together, then the precision of the output is specified as the value of the number.

- Regardless of whether there's a precision specifier, if there is a number, then that represents the amount of characters to which the output should be padded. In the previous example, this is 15 characters. If the output is already equal to or greater than the padding length, then this argument is ignored.

- The leftmost parameter allowed after the % symbol is a 0, which is ignored unless a padding value has been set, in which case the output is padded with zeros instead of spaces. If a pad character other than zero or a space is required, you can use any one of your choice as long as you preface it with a single quotation mark, like this: '#.

- On the left is the % symbol, which starts the conversion.

Table 7-2. Conversion specifier components

Start conversion	Pad character	Number of pad characters	Display precision	Conversion specifier	Examples
%		15		f	10.285000
%	0	15	.2	f	000000000010.29
%	'#	15	.4	f	########10.2850

String Padding

You can also pad strings to required lengths (as you can with numbers), select different padding characters, and even choose between left and right justification. Example 7-2 shows various examples.

Example 7-2. String padding

```php
<?php
  echo "<pre>"; // Enables viewing of the spaces

  $h = 'Rasmus';

  printf("[%s]\n",        $h); // Standard string output
  printf("[%12s]\n",      $h); // Right justify with spaces to width 12
  printf("[%-12s]\n",     $h); // Left justify with spaces
  printf("[%012s]\n",     $h); // Zero padding
  printf("[%'#12s]\n\n",  $h); // Use the custom padding character '#'

  $d = 'Rasmus Lerdorf';         // The original creator of PHP

  printf("[%12.8s]\n",    $d); // Right justify, cutoff of 8 characters
  printf("[%-12.12s]\n",  $d); // Left justify, cutoff of 12 characters
  printf("[%-'@12.10s]\n", $d); // Left justify, pad '@', cutoff 10 chars
?>
```

Note how for purposes of layout in a web page, I've used the <pre> HTML tag to preserve all the spaces and the \n newline character after each of the lines to be displayed. The output from this example is as follows:

```
[Rasmus]
[      Rasmus]
[Rasmus      ]
[000000Rasmus]
[######Rasmus]
```

```
[    Rasmus L]
[Rasmus Lerdo]
[Rasmus Ler@@]
```

When you are specifying a padding value, if a string is already of equal or greater length than that value it will be ignored, *unless* a cutoff value is given that shortens the string back to less than the padding value.

Table 7-3 shows a breakdown of the components available to string conversion specifiers.

Table 7-3. String conversion specifier components

Start conversion	Left/right justify	Padding character	Number of pad characters	Cutoff	Conversion specifier	Examples (using "Rasmus")
%					s	[Rasmus]
%	-		10		s	[Rasmus]
%		'#	8	.4	s	[####Rasm]

Using sprintf

Often, you don't want to output the result of a conversion but need it to use elsewhere in your code. This is where the `sprintf` function comes in. With it, you can send the output to another variable rather than to the browser.

You might use it simply to make a conversion, as in the following example, which returns the hexadecimal string value for the RGB color group 65, 127, 245 in `$hexstring`:

```
$hexstring = sprintf("%X%X%X", 65, 127, 245);
```

Or you may wish to store output ready to display later on:

```
$out = sprintf("The result is: $%.2f", 123.42 / 12);
echo $out;
```

Date and Time Functions

To keep track of the date and time, PHP uses standard Unix timestamps, which are simply the number of seconds since the start of January 1, 1970. To determine the current timestamp, you can use the `time` function:

```
echo time();
```

Because the value is stored as seconds, to obtain the timestamp for this time next week, you would use the following, which adds 7 days times 24 hours times 60 minutes times 60 seconds to the returned value:

```
echo time() + 7 * 24 * 60 * 60;
```

If you wish to create a timestamp for a given date, you can use the mktime function. Its output is the timestamp 946684800 for the first second of the first minute of the first hour of the first day of the year 2000:

```
echo mktime(0, 0, 0, 1, 1, 2000);
```

The parameters to pass are, in order from left to right:

- The number of the hour (0–23)
- The number of the minute (0–59)
- The number of seconds (0–59)
- The number of the month (1–12)
- The number of the day (1–31)
- The year (1970–2038, or 1901–2038 with PHP 5.1.0+ on 32-bit signed systems)

 You may ask why you are limited to the years 1970 through 2038. Well, it's because the original developers of Unix chose the start of the year 1970 as the base date that no programmer should need to go before! Luckily, because (as of version 5.1.0) PHP supports systems using a signed 32-bit integer for the timestamp, dates from 1901 to 2038 are allowed on them. However, that introduces a problem even worse than the original because the Unix designers also decided that nobody would be using Unix after about 70 years or so, and therefore believed they could get away with storing the timestamp as a 32-bit value—which will run out on January 19, 2038! This will create what has come to be known as the Y2K38 bug (much like the millennium bug, which was caused by storing years as two-digit values, and which also had to be fixed). PHP introduced the DateTime class in version 5.2 to overcome this issue, but it will work only on 64-bit architecture.

To display the date, use the date function, which supports a plethora of formatting options, enabling you to display the date any way you could wish. The format is as follows:

```
date($format, $timestamp);
```

The parameter $format should be a string containing formatting specifiers as detailed in Table 7-4, and $timestamp should be a Unix timestamp. For the complete list of specifiers, see *http://php.net/manual/en/function.date.php*. The following command will output the current date and time in the format "Thursday July 6th, 2017 - 1:38pm":

```
echo date("l F jS, Y - g:ia", time());
```

Table 7-4. The major date function format specifiers

Format	Description	Returned value
Day specifiers		
d	Day of month, two digits, with leading zeros	01 to 31
D	Day of the week, three letters	Mon to Sun
j	Day of the month, no leading zeros	1 to 31
l	Day of week, full names	Sunday to Saturday
N	Day of week, numeric, Monday to Sunday	1 to 7
S	Suffix for day of month (useful with specifier j)	st, nd, rd, or th
w	Day of week, numeric, Sunday to Saturday	0 to 6
z	Day of year	0 to 365
Week specifier		
W	Week number of year	01 to 52
Month specifiers		
F	Month name	January to December
m	Month number with leading zeros	01 to 12
M	Month name, three letters	Jan to Dec
n	Month number, no leading zeros	1 to 12
t	Number of days in given month	28 to 31
Year specifiers		
L	Leap year	1 = Yes, 0 = No
y	Year, 2 digits	00 to 99
Y	Year, 4 digits	0000 to 9999
Time specifiers		
a	Before or after midday, lowercase	am or pm
A	Before or after midday, uppercase	AM or PM
g	Hour of day, 12-hour format, no leading zeros	1 to 12
G	Hour of day, 24-hour format, no leading zeros	00 to 23
h	Hour of day, 12-hour format, with leading zeros	01 to 12
H	Hour of day, 24-hour format, with leading zeros	00 to 23
i	Minutes, with leading zeros	00 to 59
s	Seconds, with leading zeros	00 to 59

Date Constants

There are a number of useful constants that you can use with the date command to return the date in specific formats. For example, date(DATE_RSS) returns the current date and time in the valid format for an RSS feed. Some of the more commonly used constants are:

DATE_ATOM
> This is the format for Atom feeds. The PHP format is "Y-m-d\TH:i:sP" and example output is "2018-08-16T12:00:00+00:00".

DATE_COOKIE
> This is the format for cookies set from a web server or JavaScript. The PHP format is "l, d-M-y H:i:s T" and example output is "Thursday, 16-Aug-18 12:00:00 UTC".

DATE_RSS
> This is the format for RSS feeds. The PHP format is "D, d M Y H:i:s O" and example output is "Thu, 16 Aug 2018 12:00:00 UTC".

DATE_W3C
> This is the format for the World Wide Web Consortium. The PHP format is "Y-m-d\TH:i:sP" and example output is "2018-08-16T12:00:00+00:00".

The complete list can be found at *http://php.net/manual/en/class.datetime.php*.

Using checkdate

You've seen how to display a valid date in a variety of formats. But how can you check whether a user has submitted a valid date to your program? The answer is to pass the month, day, and year to the checkdate function, which returns a value of TRUE if the date is valid, or FALSE if it is not.

For example, if February 30 of any year is input, it will always be an invalid date. Example 7-3 shows code that you could use for this. As it stands, it will find the given date invalid.

Example 7-3. Checking for the validity of a date

```php
<?php
  $month = 9;      // September (only has 30 days)
  $day   = 31;     // 31st
  $year  = 2018;   // 2018

  if (checkdate($month, $day, $year)) echo "Date is valid";
  else echo "Date is invalid";
?>
```

File Handling

Powerful as it is, MySQL is not the only (or necessarily the best) way to store all data on a web server. Sometimes it can be quicker and more convenient to directly access files on the hard disk. Cases in which you might need to do this are modifying images such as uploaded user avatars, or log files that you wish to process.

First, though, a note about file naming: if you are writing code that may be used on various PHP installations, there is no way of knowing whether these systems are case-sensitive. For example, Windows and Mac OS X filenames are not case-sensitive, but Linux and Unix ones are. Therefore, you should always assume that the system is case-sensitive and stick to a convention such as all lowercase filenames.

Checking Whether a File Exists

To determine whether a file already exists, you can use the `file_exists` function, which returns either TRUE or FALSE, and is used like this:

```
if (file_exists("testfile.txt")) echo "File exists";
```

Creating a File

At this point, *testfile.txt* doesn't exist, so let's create it and write a few lines to it. Type Example 7-4 and save it as *testfile.php*.

Example 7-4. Creating a simple text file

```php
<?php // testfile.php
  $fh = fopen("testfile.txt", 'w') or die("Failed to create file");

  $text = <<<_END
Line 1
Line 2
Line 3
_END;

  fwrite($fh, $text) or die("Could not write to file");
  fclose($fh);
  echo "File 'testfile.txt' written successfully";
?>
```

When you run this in a browser, all being well, you will receive the message File 'test file.txt' written successfully. If you receive an error message, your hard disk may be full or, more likely, you may not have permission to create or write to the file, in which case you should modify the attributes of the destination folder according to your operating system. Otherwise, the file *testfile.txt* should now be residing in the same folder in which you saved the *testfile.php* program. Try opening the file in a text or program editor—the contents will look like this:

```
Line 1
Line 2
Line 3
```

This simple example shows the sequence that all file handling takes:

1. Always start by opening the file. You do this through a call to fopen.

2. Then you can call other functions; here we write to the file (fwrite), but you can also read from an existing file (fread or fgets) and do other things.

3. Finish by closing the file (fclose). Although the program does this for you when it ends, you should clean up after yourself by closing the file when you're finished.

Every open file requires a file resource so that PHP can access and manage it. The preceding example sets the variable $fh (which I chose to stand for *file handle*) to the value returned by the fopen function. Thereafter, each file handling function that accesses the opened file, such as fwrite or fclose, must be passed $fh as a parameter to identify the file being accessed. Don't worry about the content of the $fh variable; it's a number PHP uses to refer to internal information about the file—you just pass the variable to other functions.

Upon failure, FALSE will be returned by fopen. The previous example shows a simple way to capture and respond to the failure: it calls the die function to end the program and give the user an error message. A web application would never abort in this crude way (you would create a web page with an error message instead), but this is fine for our testing purposes.

Notice the second parameter to the fopen call. It is simply the character w, which tells the function to open the file for writing. The function creates the file if it doesn't already exist. Be careful when playing around with these functions: if the file already exists, the w mode parameter causes the fopen call to delete the old contents (even if you don't write anything new!).

There are several different mode parameters that can be used here, as detailed in Table 7-5.

Table 7-5. The supported fopen modes

Mode	Action	Description
'r'	Read from file start.	Open for reading only; place the file pointer at the beginning of the file. Return FALSE if the file doesn't already exist.
'r+'	Read from file start and allow writing.	Open for reading and writing; place the file pointer at the beginning of the file. Return FALSE if the file doesn't already exist.

Mode	Action	Description
'w'	Write from file start and truncate file.	Open for writing only; place the file pointer at the beginning of the file and truncate the file to zero length. If the file doesn't exist, attempt to create it.
'w+'	Write from file start, truncate file, and allow reading.	Open for reading and writing; place the file pointer at the beginning of the file and truncate the file to zero length. If the file doesn't exist, attempt to create it.
'a'	Append to file end.	Open for writing only; place the file pointer at the end of the file. If the file doesn't exist, attempt to create it.
'a+'	Append to file end and allow reading.	Open for reading and writing; place the file pointer at the end of the file. If the file doesn't exist, attempt to create it.

Reading from Files

The easiest way to read from a text file is to grab a whole line through `fgets` (think of the final s as standing for *string*), as in Example 7-5.

Example 7-5. Reading a file with fgets

```php
<?php
  $fh = fopen("testfile.txt", 'r') or
    die("File does not exist or you lack permission to open it");

  $line = fgets($fh);
  fclose($fh);
  echo $line;
?>
```

If you created the file as shown in Example 7-4, you'll get the first line:

    Line 1

Or you can retrieve multiple lines or portions of lines through the `fread` function, as in Example 7-6.

Example 7-6. Reading a file with fread

```php
<?php
  $fh = fopen("testfile.txt", 'r') or
    die("File does not exist or you lack permission to open it");

  $text = fread($fh, 3);
  fclose($fh);
  echo $text;
?>
```

I've requested three characters in the `fread` call, so the program displays the following:

    Lin

The `fread` function is commonly used with binary data. But if you use it on text data that spans more than one line, remember to count newline characters.

Copying Files

Let's try out the PHP copy function to create a clone of *testfile.txt*. Type in Example 7-7 and save it as *copyfile.php*, and then call up the program in your browser.

Example 7-7. Copying a file

```php
<?php // copyfile.php
  copy('testfile.txt', 'testfile2.txt') or die("Could not copy file");
  echo "File successfully copied to 'testfile2.txt'";
?>
```

If you check your folder again, you'll see that you now have the new file *testfile2.txt* in it. By the way, if you don't want your programs to exit on a failed copy attempt, you could try the alternate syntax in Example 7-8.

Example 7-8. Alternate syntax for copying a file

```php
<?php // copyfile2.php
  if (!copy('testfile.txt', 'testfile2.txt')) echo "Could not copy file";
  else echo "File successfully copied to 'testfile2.txt'";
?>
```

Moving a File

To move a file, rename it with the rename function, as in Example 7-9.

Example 7-9. Moving a file

```php
<?php // movefile.php
  if (!rename('testfile2.txt', 'testfile2.new'))
    echo "Could not rename file";
  else echo "File successfully renamed to 'testfile2.new'";
?>
```

You can use the rename function on directories, too. To avoid any warning messages, if the original file doesn't exist, you can call the file_exists function first to check.

Deleting a File

Deleting a file is just a matter of using the unlink function to remove it from the filesystem, as in Example 7-10.

Example 7-10. Deleting a file

```php
<?php // deletefile.php
  if (!unlink('testfile2.new')) echo "Could not delete file";
  else echo "File 'testfile2.new' successfully deleted";
?>
```

Whenever you access files on your hard disk directly, you must also always ensure that it is impossible for your filesystem to be compromised. For example, if you are deleting a file based on user input, you must make absolutely certain it is a file that can be safely deleted and that the user is allowed to delete it.

As with moving a file, a warning message will be displayed if the file doesn't exist, which you can avoid by using `file_exists` to first check for its existence before calling `unlink`.

Updating Files

Often, you will want to add more data to a saved file, which you can do in many ways. You can use one of the append write modes (see Table 7-5), or you can simply open a file for reading and writing with one of the other modes that supports writing, and move the file pointer to the correct place within the file that you wish to write to or read from.

The *file pointer* is the position within a file at which the next file access will take place, whether it's a read or a write. It is not the same as the *file handle* (as stored in the variable `$fh` in Example 7-4), which contains details about the file being accessed.

You can see this in action by typing Example 7-11 and saving it as *update.php*. Then call it up in your browser.

Example 7-11. Updating a file

```php
<?php // update.php
  $fh   = fopen("testfile.txt", 'r+') or die("Failed to open file");
  $text = fgets($fh);

  fseek($fh, 0, SEEK_END);
  fwrite($fh, "$text") or die("Could not write to file");
  fclose($fh);

  echo "File 'testfile.txt' successfully updated";
?>
```

This program opens *testfile.txt* for both reading and writing by setting the mode with `'r+'`, which puts the file pointer right at the start. It then uses the `fgets` function to read in a single line from the file (up to the first line feed). After that, the `fseek` function is called to move the file pointer right to the file end, at which point the line of text that was extracted from the start of the file (stored in `$text`) is then appended to file's end and the file is closed. The resulting file now looks like this:

```
Line 1
Line 2
Line 3
Line 1
```

The first line has successfully been copied and then appended to the file's end.

As used here, in addition to the $fh file handle, the fseek function was passed two other parameters, 0 and SEEK_END. SEEK_END tells the function to move the file pointer to the end of the file and 0 tells it how many positions it should then be moved backward from that point. In the case of Example 7-11, a value of 0 is used, because the pointer is required to remain at the file's end.

There are two other seek options available to the fseek function: SEEK_SET and SEEK_CUR. The SEEK_SET option tells the function to set the file pointer to the exact position given by the preceding parameter. Thus, the following example moves the file pointer to position 18:

```
fseek($fh, 18, SEEK_SET);
```

SEEK_CUR sets the file pointer to the current position *plus* the value of the given offset. Therefore, if the file pointer is currently at position 18, the following call will move it to position 23:

```
fseek($fh, 5, SEEK_CUR);
```

Although this is not recommended unless you have very specific reasons for it, it is even possible to use text files such as this (but with fixed line lengths) as simple flat file databases. Your program can then use fseek to move back and forth within such a file to retrieve, update, and add new records. You can also delete records by overwriting them with zero characters, and so on.

Locking Files for Multiple Accesses

Web programs are often called by many users at the same time. If more than one person tries to write to a file simultaneously, it can become corrupted. And if one person writes to it while another is reading from it, the file is all right but the person reading it can get odd results. To handle simultaneous users, you must use the file locking flock function. This function queues up all other requests to access a file until your program releases the lock. So, whenever your programs use write access on files that may be accessed concurrently by multiple users, you should also add file locking to them, as in Example 7-12, which is an updated version of Example 7-11.

Example 7-12. Updating a file with file locking

```
<?php
  $fh   = fopen("testfile.txt", 'r+') or die("Failed to open file");
  $text = fgets($fh);

  if (flock($fh, LOCK_EX))
  {
    fseek($fh, 0, SEEK_END);
    fwrite($fh, "$text") or die("Could not write to file");
    flock($fh, LOCK_UN);
```

```
    }
    fclose($fh);
    echo "File 'testfile.txt' successfully updated";
?>
```

There is a trick to file locking to preserve the best possible response time for your website visitors: perform it directly before a change you make to a file, and then unlock it immediately afterward. Having a file locked for any longer than this will slow down your application unnecessarily. This is why the calls to flock in Example 7-12 are directly before and after the fwrite call.

The first call to flock sets an exclusive file lock on the file referred to by $fh using the LOCK_EX parameter:

```
flock($fh, LOCK_EX);
```

From this point onward, no other processes can write to (or even read from) the file until you release the lock by using the LOCK_UN parameter, like this:

```
flock($fh, LOCK_UN);
```

As soon as the lock is released, other processes are again allowed access to the file. This is one reason why you should reseek to the point you wish to access in a file each time you need to read or write data, because another process could have changed the file since the last access.

However, did you notice that the call to request an exclusive lock is nested as part of an if statement? This is because flock is not supported on all systems; thus, it is wise to check whether you successfully secured a lock, just in case one could not be obtained.

Something else you must consider is that flock is what is known as an *advisory* lock. This means that it locks out only other processes that call the function. If you have any code that goes right in and modifies files without implementing flock file locking, it will always override the locking and could wreak havoc on your files.

By the way, implementing file locking and then accidentally leaving it out in one section of code can lead to an extremely hard-to-locate bug.

 flock will not work on NFS and many other networked filesystems. Also, when using a multithreaded server like ISAPI, you may not be able to rely on flock to protect files against other PHP scripts running in parallel threads of the same server instance. Additionally, flock is not supported on any system using the old FAT filesystem (such as older versions of Windows).

Reading an Entire File

A handy function for reading in an entire file without having to use file handles is file_get_contents. It's very easy to use, as you can see in Example 7-13.

Example 7-13. Using file_get_contents

```php
<?php
  echo "<pre>";  // Enables display of line feeds
  echo file_get_contents("testfile.txt");
  echo "</pre>"; // Terminates pre tag
?>
```

But the function is actually a lot more useful than that, because you can also use it to fetch a file from a server across the Internet, as in Example 7-14, which requests the HTML from the O'Reilly home page, and then displays it as if the user had surfed to the page itself. The result will be similar to Figure 7-1.

Example 7-14. Grabbing the O'Reilly home page

```php
<?php
  echo file_get_contents("http://oreilly.com");
?>
```

Figure 7-1. The O'Reilly home page grabbed with file_get_contents

Uploading Files

Uploading files to a web server is a subject that seems daunting to many people, but it actually couldn't be much easier. All you need to do to upload a file from a form is choose a special type of encoding called *multipart/form-data*, and your browser will handle the rest. To see how this works, type the program in Example 7-15 and save it as *upload.php*. When you run it, you'll see a form in your browser that lets you upload a file of your choice.

Example 7-15. Image uploader upload.php

```
<?php // upload.php
  echo <<<_END
    <html><head><title>PHP Form Upload</title></head><body>
    <form method='post' action='upload.php' enctype='multipart/form-data'>
    Select File: <input type='file' name='filename' size='10'>
    <input type='submit' value='Upload'>
    </form>
_END;

  if ($_FILES)
  {
    $name = $_FILES['filename']['name'];
    move_uploaded_file($_FILES['filename']['tmp_name'], $name);
    echo "Uploaded image '$name'<br><img src='$name'>";
  }

  echo "</body></html>";
?>
```

Let's examine this program a section at a time. The first line of the multiline echo statement starts an HTML document, displays the title, and then starts the document's body.

Next we come to the form that selects the POST method of form submission, sets the target for posted data to the program *upload.php* (the program itself), and tells the web browser that the data posted should be encoded via the content type of multipart/form-data.

With the form set up, the next lines display the prompt "Select File:" and then request two inputs. The first request is for a file; it uses an input type of file, a name of filename, and an input field with a width of 10 characters.

The second requested input is just a Submit button that is given the label Upload (which replaces the default button text of Submit Query). And then the form is closed.

This short program shows a common technique in web programming in which a single program is called twice: once when the user first visits a page, and again when the user presses the Submit button.

The PHP code to receive the uploaded data is fairly simple, because all uploaded files are placed into the associative system array $_FILES. Therefore, a quick check to see whether $_FILES contains anything is sufficient to determine whether the user has up-loaded a file. This is done with the statement if ($_FILES).

The first time the user visits the page, before uploading a file, $_FILES is empty, so the program skips this block of code. When the user uploads a file, the program runs again and discovers an element in the $_FILES array.

Once the program realizes that a file was uploaded, the actual name, as read from the uploading computer, is retrieved and placed into the variable $name. Now all that's nec-essary is to move the file from the temporary location in which PHP stored the uploaded file to a more permanent one. We do this using the move_uploaded_file function, passing it the original name of the file, with which it is saved to the current directory.

Finally, the uploaded image is displayed within an IMG tag, and the result should look like Figure 7-2.

 If you run this program and then receive warning messages such as Permission denied for the move_uploaded_file function call, then you may not have the correct permissions set for the folder in which the program is running.

Figure 7-2. Uploading an image as form data

Using $_FILES

Five things are stored in the $_FILES array when a file is uploaded, as shown in Table 7-6 (where file is the file upload field name supplied by the submitting form).

Table 7-6. The contents of the $_FILES array

Array element	Contents
$_FILES['*file*']['*name*']	The name of the uploaded file (e.g., *smiley.jpg*)
$_FILES['*file*']['*type*']	The content type of the file (e.g., *image/jpeg*)
$_FILES['*file*']['*size*']	The file's size in bytes
$_FILES['*file*']['*tmp_name*']	The name of the temporary file stored on the server
$_FILES['*file*']['*error*']	The error code resulting from the file upload

Content types used to be known as *MIME (Multipurpose Internet Mail Extension)* types, but because their use later expanded to the whole Internet, now they are often called *Internet media types*. Table 7-7 shows some of the more frequently used types that turn up in $_FILES['*file*']['*type*'].

Table 7-7. Some common Internet media content types

application/pdf	image/gif	multipart/form-data	text/xml
application/zip	image/jpeg	text/css	video/mpeg
audio/mpeg	image/png	text/html	video/mp4
audio/x-wav	image/tiff	text/plain	video/quicktime

Validation

I hope it now goes without saying (although I'll do so anyway) that form data validation is of the utmost importance, due to the possibility of users attempting to hack into your server.

In addition to maliciously formed input data, some of the things you also have to check are whether a file was actually received and, if so, whether the right type of data was sent.

Taking all this into account, Example 7-16, *upload2.php*, is a rewrite of *upload.php*.

Example 7-16. A more secure version of upload.php

```php
<?php // upload2.php
  echo <<<_END
    <html><head><title>PHP Form Upload</title></head><body>
    <form method='post' action='upload2.php' enctype='multipart/form-data'>
    Select a JPG, GIF, PNG or TIF File:
    <input type='file' name='filename' size='10'>
    <input type='submit' value='Upload'></form>
_END;

  if ($_FILES)
  {
    $name = $_FILES['filename']['name'];
```

```
switch($_FILES['filename']['type'])
{
  case 'image/jpeg': $ext = 'jpg'; break;
  case 'image/gif':  $ext = 'gif'; break;
  case 'image/png':  $ext = 'png'; break;
  case 'image/tiff': $ext = 'tif'; break;
  default:           $ext = '';    break;
}
if ($ext)
{
  $n = "image.$ext";
  move_uploaded_file($_FILES['filename']['tmp_name'], $n);
  echo "Uploaded image '$name' as '$n':<br>";
  echo "<img src='$n'>";
}
else echo "'$name' is not an accepted image file";
}
else echo "No image has been uploaded";

echo "</body></html>";
?>
```

The non-HTML section of code has been expanded from the half-dozen lines of Example 7-15 to more than 20 lines, starting at if ($_FILES).

As with the previous version, this if line checks whether any data was actually posted, but there is now a matching else near the bottom of the program that echoes a message to screen when nothing has been uploaded.

Within the if statement, the variable $name is assigned the value of the filename as retrieved from the uploading computer (just as before), but this time we won't rely on the user having sent us valid data. Instead, a switch statement is used to check the uploaded content type against the four types of image this program supports. If a match is made, the variable $ext is set to the three-letter file extension for that type. Should no match be found, the file uploaded was not of an accepted type and the variable $ext is set to the empty string "".

The next section of code then checks the variable $ext to see whether it contains a string and, if so, creates a new filename called $n with the base name *image* and the extension stored in $ext. This means that the program is in full control over the name of the file to be created, as it can be only one of *image.jpg*, *image.gif*, *image.png*, or *image.tif*.

Safe in the knowledge that the program has not been compromised, the rest of the PHP code is much the same as in the previous version. It moves the uploaded temporary image to its new location and then displays it, while also displaying the old and new image names.

Don't worry about having to delete the temporary file that PHP creates during the upload process, because if the file has not been moved or renamed, it will be automatically removed when the program exits.

After the if statement there is a matching else, which is executed only if an unsupported image type was uploaded, in which case it displays an appropriate error message.

When you write your own file uploading routines, I strongly advise you to use a similar approach and have pre-chosen names and locations for uploaded files. That way, no attempts to add pathnames and other malicious data to the variables you use can get through. If this means that more than one user could end up having a file uploaded with the same name, you could prefix such files with their user's name, or save them to individually created folders for each user.

But if you must use a supplied filename, you should sanitize it by allowing only alphanumeric characters and the period, which you can do with the following command, using a regular expression (see Chapter 17) to perform a search and replace on $name:

```php
$name = preg_replace("/[^A-Za-z0-9.]/", "", $name);
```

This leaves only the characters A–Z, a–z, 0–9, and periods in the string $name, and strips out everything else.

Even better, to ensure that your program will work on all systems, regardless of whether they are case-sensitive or case-insensitive, you should probably use the following command instead, which changes all uppercase characters to lowercase at the same time:

```php
$name = strtolower(ereg_replace("[^A-Za-z0-9.]", "", $name));
```

Sometimes you may encounter the media type of image/pjpeg, which indicates a progressive JPEG, but you can safely add this to your code as an alias of image/jpeg, like this:

```php
case 'image/pjpeg':
case 'image/jpeg': $ext = 'jpg'; break;
```

System Calls

Sometimes PHP will not have the function you need to perform a certain action, but the operating system it is running on may. In such cases, you can use the exec system call to do the job.

For example, to quickly view the contents of the current directory, you can use a program such as Example 7-17. If you are on a Windows system, it will run as is using the Windows dir command. On Linux, Unix, or Mac OS X, comment out or remove the first line and uncomment the second to use the ls system command. You may wish to type this program, save it as *exec.php*, and call it up in your browser.

Example 7-17. Executing a system command

```php
<?php // exec.php
  $cmd = "dir";    // Windows
  // $cmd = "ls"; // Linux, Unix & Mac

  exec(escapeshellcmd($cmd), $output, $status);

  if ($status) echo "Exec command failed";
  else
  {
    echo "<pre>";
    foreach($output as $line) echo htmlspecialchars("$line\n");
    echo "</pre>";
  }
?>
```

The htmlspecialchars function is called to turn any special characters returned by the system into ones that HTML can understand and properly display, neatening the output. Depending on the system you are using, the result of running this program will look something like this (from a Windows dir command):

```
Volume in drive C is Hard Disk
Volume Serial Number is DC63-0E29

Directory of C:\Program Files (x86)\Zend\Apache2\htdocs

09/02/2014  12:03    <DIR>           .
09/02/2014  12:03    <DIR>           ..
28/04/2013  08:30             5,336 chars.php
12/02/2012  13:08             1,406 favicon.ico
20/01/2014  12:52             4,202 index.html
09/02/2014  11:49                76 info.php
21/03/2013  09:52               110 test.htm
01/04/2013  13:06           182,459 test.php
               6 File(s)        193,589 bytes
               9 Dir(s)  1,811,290,472,448 bytes free
```

exec takes three arguments:

- The command itself (in the previous case, $cmd)
- An array in which the system will put the output from the command (in the previous case, $output)
- A variable to contain the returned status of the call (in the previous case, $status)

If you wish, you can omit the $output and $status parameters, but you will not know the output created by the call or even whether it completed successfully.

You should also note the use of the `escapeshellcmd` function. It is a good habit to always use this when issuing an `exec` call, because it sanitizes the command string, preventing the execution of arbitrary commands, should you supply user input to the call.

 The system calling functions are typically disabled on shared web hosts, as they pose a security risk. You should always try to solve your problems within PHP if you can, and go to the system directly only if it is really necessary. Also, going to the system is relatively slow and you need to code two implementations if your application is expected to run on both Windows and Linux/Unix systems.

XHTML or HTML5?

Because XHTML documents need to be well formed, you can parse them using standard XML parsers—unlike HTML, which requires a lenient HTML-specific parser. For this reason, XHTML never really caught on, and when the time came to devise a new standard, the World Wide Web Consortium chose to support HTML5 rather than the newer XHTML2 standard.

HTML5 has some of the features of both HTML4 and XHTML, but is much simpler to use and less strict to validate and, happily, there is now just a single document type you need to place at the head of an HTML5 document (instead of the variety of strict, transitional, and frameset types previously required), namely:

```
<!DOCTYPE html>
```

Just the simple word `html` is sufficient to tell the browser that your web page is designed for HTML5 and, because all the latest versions of the most popular browsers have been supporting most of the HTML5 specification since 2011 or so, this document type is generally the only one you need, unless you choose to cater to older browsers.

For all intents and purposes, when writing HTML documents, web developers can safely ignore the old XHTML document types and syntax (such as using <br /> instead of the simpler <br> tag). But if you find yourself having to cater to a very old browser or an unusual application that relies on XHTML, then you can get more information on how to do that at *http://xhtml.com*.

Questions

1. Which `printf` conversion specifier would you use to display a floating-point number?

2. What `printf` statement could be used to take the input string "Happy Birthday" and output the string "**Happy"?

3. To send the output from `printf` to a variable instead of to a browser, what alternative function would you use?

4. How would you create a Unix timestamp for 7:11 a.m. on May 2, 2016?

5. Which file access mode would you use with `fopen` to open a file in write and read mode, with the file truncated and the file pointer at the start?

6. What is the PHP command for deleting the file *file.txt*?

7. Which PHP function is used to read in an entire file in one go, even from across the Web?

8. Which PHP superglobal variable holds the details on uploaded files?

9. Which PHP function enables the running of system commands?

10. Which of the following tag styles is preferred in HTML5: <hr> or <hr />?

See "Chapter 7 Answers" on page 643 in Appendix A for the answers to these questions.

CHAPTER 8

Introduction to MySQL

With well over 10 million installations, MySQL is probably the most popular database management system for web servers. Developed in the mid-1990s, it's now a mature technology that powers many of today's most-visited Internet destinations.

One reason for its success must be the fact that, like PHP, it's free to use. But it's also extremely powerful and exceptionally fast—it can run on even the most basic of hardware, and it hardly puts a dent in system resources.

MySQL is also highly scalable, which means that it can grow with your website (for the latest benchmarks, see *http://mysql.com/why-mysql/benchmarks*).

MySQL Basics

A *database* is a structured collection of records or data stored in a computer system and organized in such a way that it can be quickly searched and information can be rapidly retrieved.

The *SQL* in MySQL stands for *Structured Query Language*. This language is loosely based on English and also used in other databases such as Oracle and Microsoft SQL Server. It is designed to allow simple requests from a database via commands such as:

```
SELECT title FROM publications WHERE author = 'Charles Dickens';
```

A MySQL database contains one or more *tables*, each of which contains *records* or *rows*. Within these rows are various *columns* or *fields* that contain the data itself. Table 8-1 shows the contents of an example database of five publications detailing the author, title, type, and year of publication.

Table 8-1. Example of a simple database

Author	Title	Type	Year
Mark Twain	The Adventures of Tom Sawyer	Fiction	1876
Jane Austen	Pride and Prejudice	Fiction	1811
Charles Darwin	The Origin of Species	Non-Fiction	1856
Charles Dickens	The Old Curiosity Shop	Fiction	1841
William Shakespeare	Romeo and Juliet	Play	1594

Each row in the table is the same as a row in a MySQL table, and each element within a row is the same as a MySQL field.

To uniquely identify this database, I'll refer to it as the *publications* database in the examples that follow. And, as you will have observed, all these publications are considered to be classics of literature, so I'll call the table within the database that holds the details *classics*.

Summary of Database Terms

The main terms you need to acquaint yourself with for now are:

Database
> The overall container for a collection of MySQL data

Table
> A subcontainer within a database that stores the actual data

Row
> A single record within a table, which may contain several fields

Column
> The name of a field within a row

I should note that I'm not trying to reproduce the precise terminology used in academic literature about relational databases, but just to provide simple, everyday terms to help you quickly grasp basic concepts and get started with a database.

Accessing MySQL via the Command Line

There are three main ways in which you can interact with MySQL: using a command line, via a web interface such as phpMyAdmin, and through a programming language like PHP. We'll start doing the third of these in Chapter 10, but for now, let's look at the first two.

Starting the Command-Line Interface

The following sections describe relevant instructions for Windows, OS X, and Linux.

Windows users

If you installed the Zend Server Free Edition WAMP (as explained in Chapter 2), you will be able to access the MySQL executable from one of the following directories (the first on 32-bit computers, and the second on 64-bit machines):

```
C:\Program Files\Zend\MySQL55\bin
C:\Program Files (x86)\Zend\MySQL55\bin
```

 If you installed Zend Server in a place other than *Program Files* (or *Program Files (x86)*), you will need to use that directory instead.

By default, the initial MySQL user will be *root* and will not have had a password set. Seeing as this is a development server that only you should be able to access, we won't worry about creating one yet.

So, to enter MySQL's command-line interface, select Start→Run, enter CMD into the Run box, and press Return. This will call up a Windows Command Prompt. From there, enter one of the following (making any appropriate changes as just discussed):

```
"C:\Program Files\Zend\MySQL55\bin\mysql" -u root
"C:\Program Files (x86)\Zend\MySQL55\bin\mysql" -u root
```

 Note the quotation marks surrounding the path and filename. These are present because the name contains spaces, which the Command Prompt doesn't correctly interpret, and the quotation marks group the parts of the filename into a single string for the command program to understand.

This command tells MySQL to log you in as user *root*, without a password. You will now be logged into MySQL and can start entering commands. So, to be sure everything is working as it should be, enter the following (the results should look similar to the output shown in Figure 8-1):

```
SHOW databases;
```

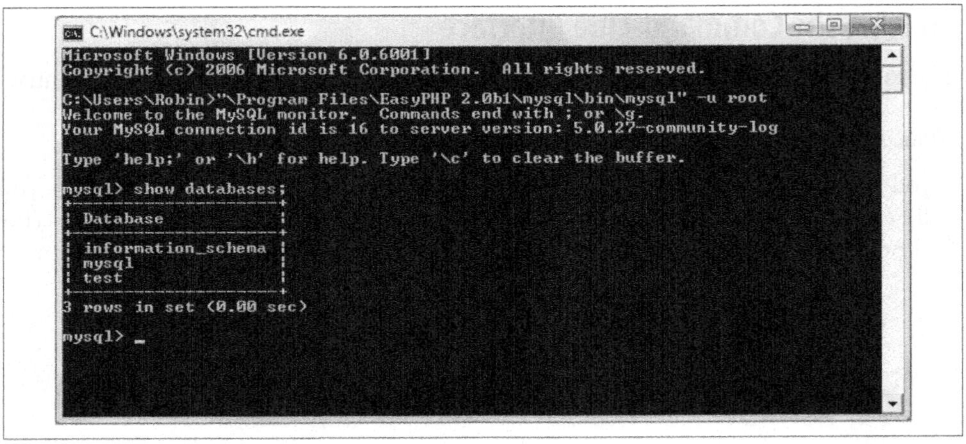

Figure 8-1. Accessing MySQL from a Windows Command Prompt

If this has not worked and you get an error, make sure that you have correctly installed MySQL along with Zend Server (as described in Chapter 2). Otherwise, you are ready to move on to the next section, "Using the Command-Line Interface" on page 177.

OS X users

To proceed with this chapter, you should have installed Zend Server as detailed in Chapter 2. You should also have the web server already running and the MySQL server started.

To enter the MySQL command-line interface, start the Terminal program (which should be available in Finder→Utilities). Then call up the MySQL program, which will have been installed in the directory */usr/local/zend/mysql/bin*.

By default, the initial MySQL user is *root*, and it will have a password of *root* too. So, to start the program, type the following:

```
/usr/local/zend/mysql/bin/mysql -u root
```

This command tells MySQL to log you in as user *root* and not to request your password. To verify that all is well, type the following (the result should look like the output shown in Figure 8-2):

```
SHOW databases;
```

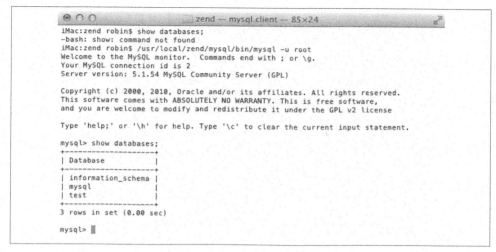

Figure 8-2. Accessing MySQL from the OS X Terminal program

If you receive an error such as `Can't connect to local MySQL server through socket`, you haven't started up the MySQL server, so make sure you followed the advice in Chapter 2 about configuring MySQL to start when OS X starts.

You should now be ready to move on to the next section, "Using the Command-Line Interface" on page 177.

Linux users

On a system running a Unix-like operating system such as Linux, you will almost certainly already have PHP and MySQL installed and running, and you will be able to enter the examples in the next section. But first you should type the following to log into your MySQL system:

```
mysql -u root -p
```

This tells MySQL to log you in as the user *root* and to request your password. If you have a password, enter it; otherwise, just press Return.

Once you are logged in, type the following to test the program (you should see something like Figure 8-3 in response):

```
SHOW databases;
```

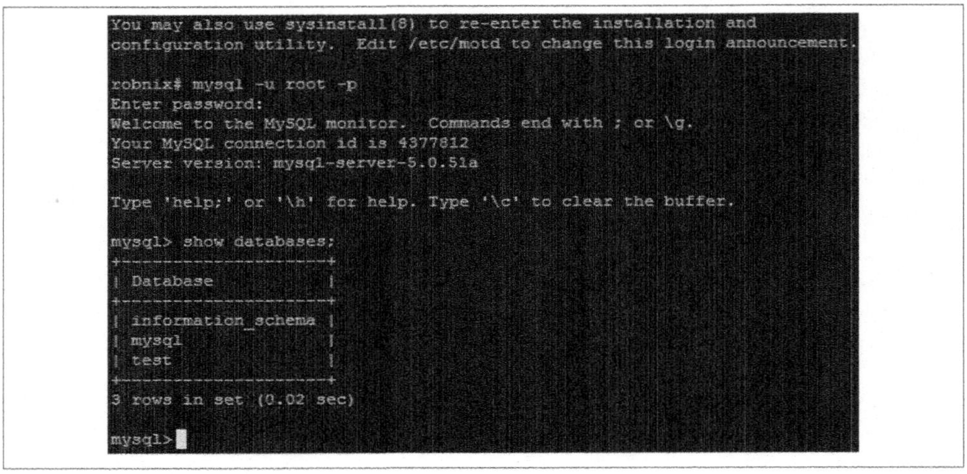

```
You may also use sysinstall(8) to re-enter the installation and
configuration utility.  Edit /etc/motd to change this login announcement.

robnix# mysql -u root -p
Enter password:
Welcome to the MySQL monitor.  Commands end with ; or \g.
Your MySQL connection id is 4377812
Server version: mysql-server-5.0.51a

Type 'help;' or '\h' for help. Type '\c' to clear the buffer.

mysql> show databases;
+--------------------+
| Database           |
+--------------------+
| information_schema |
| mysql              |
| test               |
+--------------------+
3 rows in set (0.02 sec)

mysql>
```

Figure 8-3. Accessing MySQL using Linux

If this procedure fails at any point, refer to the section "Installing a LAMP on Linux" on page 38 in Chapter 2 to ensure that you have MySQL properly installed. Otherwise, you should now be ready to move on to the next section, "Using the Command-Line Interface" on page 177.

MySQL on a remote server

If you are accessing MySQL on a remote server, you should Telnet (or preferably, for security, use SSH) into the remote machine, which will probably be a Linux/FreeBSD/ Unix type of box. Once in there, you might find that things are a little different, depending on how the system administrator has set the server up, especially if it's a shared hosting server. Therefore, you need to ensure that you have been given access to MySQL and that you have your username and password. Armed with these, you can then type the following, where *username* is the name supplied:

```
mysql -u username -p
```

Enter your password when prompted. You can then try the following command, which should result in something like Figure 8-3:

```
SHOW databases;
```

There may be other databases already created, and the *test* database may not be there.

Bear in mind also that system administrators have ultimate control over everything and that you can encounter some unexpected setups. For example, you may find that you are required to preface all database names that you create with a unique identifying string to ensure that you do not conflict with databases created by other users.

Therefore, if you have any problems, talk with your system administrator, who will get you sorted out. Just let the sysadmin know that you need a username and password. You should also ask for the ability to create new databases or, at a minimum, to have at least one database created for you ready to use. You can then create all the tables you require within that database.

Using the Command-Line Interface

From here on out, it makes no difference whether you are using Windows, Mac OS X, or Linux to access MySQL directly, as all the commands used (and errors you may receive) are identical.

The semicolon

Let's start with the basics. Did you notice the semicolon (;) at the end of the SHOW databases; command that you typed? The semicolon is used by MySQL to separate or end commands. If you forget to enter it, MySQL will issue a prompt and wait for you to do so. The required semicolon was made part of the syntax to let you enter multiple-line commands, which can be convenient because some commands get quite long. It also allows you to issue more than one command at a time by placing a semicolon after each one. The interpreter gets them all in a batch when you press the Enter (or Return) key and executes them in order.

 It's very common to receive a MySQL prompt instead of the results of your command; it means that you forgot the final semicolon. Just enter the semicolon and press the Enter key, to get what you want.

There are six different prompts that MySQL may present you with (see Table 8-2), so you will always know where you are during a multiline input.

Table 8-2. MySQL's six command prompts

MySQL prompt	Meaning
mysql>	Ready and waiting for a command
->	Waiting for the next line of a command
'>	Waiting for the next line of a string started with a single quote
">	Waiting for the next line of a string started with a double quote
`>	Waiting for the next line of a string started with a backtick
/*>	Waiting for the next line of a comment started with /*

Canceling a command

If you are partway through entering a command and decide you don't wish to execute it after all, whatever you do *don't press Control-C!* That will close the program. Instead, you can enter \c and press Return. Example 8-1 shows how to use it.

Example 8-1. Canceling a line of input

```
meaningless gibberish to mysql \c
```

When you enter that line, MySQL will ignore everything you typed and issue a new prompt. Without the \c, it would have displayed an error message. Be careful, though: if you have opened a string or comment, close it first before using the \c or MySQL will think the \c is just part of the string. Example 8-2 shows the right way to do this.

Example 8-2. Canceling input from inside a string

```
this is "meaningless gibberish to mysql" \c
```

Also note that using \c after a semicolon will not work, as it is then a new statement.

MySQL Commands

You've already seen the SHOW command, which lists tables, databases, and many other items. The commands you'll probably use most often are listed in Table 8-3.

Table 8-3. A selection of common MySQL commands

Command	Action
ALTER	Alter a database or table
BACKUP	Backup a table
\c	Cancel input
CREATE	Create a database
DELETE	Delete a row from a table
DESCRIBE	Describe a table's columns
DROP	Delete a database or table
EXIT (CTRL-C)	Exit
GRANT	Change user privileges
HELP (\h, \?)	Display help
INSERT	Insert data
LOCK	Lock table(s)
QUIT (\q)	Same as EXIT
RENAME	Rename a table
SHOW	List details about an object
SOURCE	Execute a file

Command	Action
STATUS (\s)	Display the current status
TRUNCATE	Empty a table
UNLOCK	Unlock table(s)
UPDATE	Update an existing record
USE	Use a database

I'll cover most of these as we proceed, but first, you need to remember a couple of points about MySQL commands:

- SQL commands and keywords are case-insensitive. CREATE, create, and CrEaTe all mean the same thing. However, for the sake of clarity, the recommended style is to use uppercase.

- Table names are case-sensitive on Linux and OS X, but case-insensitive on Windows. So for portability purposes, you should always choose a case and stick to it. The recommended style is to use lowercase for tables.

Creating a database

If you are working on a remote server and have only a single user account and access to a single database that was created for you, move on to the section "Creating a table" on page 181. Otherwise, get the ball rolling by issuing the following command to create a new database called *publications*:

```
CREATE DATABASE publications;
```

A successful command will return a message that doesn't mean much yet—Query OK, 1 row affected (0.00 sec)—but will make sense soon. Now that you've created the database, you want to work with it, so issue:

```
USE publications;
```

You should now see the message Database changed and will then be set to proceed with the following examples.

Creating users

Now that you've seen how easy it is to use MySQL, and created your first database, it's time to look at how you create users, as you probably won't want to grant your PHP scripts root access to MySQL; it could cause a real headache should you get hacked.

To create a user, issue the GRANT command, which takes the following form (don't type this in; it's not an actual working command):

```
GRANT PRIVILEGES ON database.object TO 'username'@'hostname'
    IDENTIFIED BY 'password';
```

All this should be pretty straightforward, with the possible exception of the `data base.object` part, which refers to the database itself and the objects it contains, such as tables (see Table 8-4).

Table 8-4. Example parameters for the GRANT command

Arguments	Meaning
`*.*`	All databases and all their objects
`database.*`	Only the database called *database* and all its objects
`database.object`	Only the database called *database* and its object called *object*

So let's create a user who can access just the new *publications* database and all its objects, by entering the following (replacing the username *jim* and the password *mypasswd* with ones of your choosing):

```
GRANT ALL ON publications.* TO 'jim'@'localhost' IDENTIFIED BY 'mypasswd';
```

What this does is allow the user *jim@localhost* full access to the *publications* database using the password *mypasswd*. You can test whether this step has worked by entering `quit` to exit and then rerunning MySQL the way you did before, but instead of entering **-u root -p**, type **-u jim -p**, or whatever username you created. See Table 8-5 for the correct command for your operating system. Modify it as necessary if the *mysql* client program is installed in a different directory on your system.

Table 8-5. Starting MySQL and logging in as jim@localhost

OS	Example command
Windows	`"C:\Program Files\Zend\MySQL55\bin\mysql" -u jim -p`
Mac OS X	`/Applications/MAMP/Library/bin/mysql -u jim -p`
Linux	`mysql -u jim -p`

All you have to do now is enter your password when prompted and you will be logged in. By the way, if you prefer, you can place your password immediately following the `-p` (without any spaces) to avoid having to enter it when prompted. But this is considered a poor practice, because if other people are logged into your system, there may be ways for them to look at the command you entered and find out your password.

You can grant only privileges that *you* already have, and you must also have the privilege to issue GRANT commands. There is a whole range of privileges you can choose to grant if you are not granting all privileges. For further details, visit *http://tinyurl.com/mysqlgrant*, which also covers the REVOKE command, which can remove privileges once granted.

Also be aware that if you create a new user but do not specify an IDENTIFIED BY clause, the user will have no password, a situation that is very insecure and should be avoided.

Creating a table

At this point, you should now be logged into MySQL with ALL privileges granted for the database *publications* (or a database that was created for you), so you're ready to create your first table. Make sure the correct database is in use by typing the following (replacing *publications* with the name of your database if it is different):

```
USE publications;
```

Now enter the commands in Example 8-3 one line at a time.

Example 8-3. Creating a table called classics

```
CREATE TABLE classics (
  author VARCHAR(128),
  title VARCHAR(128),
  type VARCHAR(16),
  year CHAR(4)) ENGINE MyISAM;
```

You could also issue this command on a single line like this:

```
CREATE TABLE classics (author VARCHAR(128), title VARCHAR(128),
type VARCHAR(16), year CHAR(4)) ENGINE MyISAM;
```

but MySQL commands can be long and complicated, so I recommend one line per instruction until you are comfortable with longer lines.

MySQL should then issue the response Query OK, 0 rows affected, along with how long it took to execute the command. If you see an error message instead, check your syntax carefully. Every parenthesis and comma counts, and typing errors are easy to make. In case you are wondering, the ENGINE MyISAM tells MySQL the type of database engine to use for this table.

To check whether your new table has been created, type:

```
DESCRIBE classics;
```

All being well, you will see the sequence of commands and responses shown in Example 8-4, where you should particularly note the table format displayed.

Example 8-4. A MySQL session: creating and checking a new table

```
mysql> USE publications;
Database changed
mysql> CREATE TABLE classics (
    -> author VARCHAR(128),
    -> title VARCHAR(128),
    -> type VARCHAR(16),
    -> year CHAR(4)) ENGINE MyISAM;
Query OK, 0 rows affected (0.03 sec)

mysql> DESCRIBE classics;
+--------+--------------+------+-----+---------+-------+
| Field  | Type         | Null | Key | Default | Extra |
+--------+--------------+------+-----+---------+-------+
| author | varchar(128) | YES  |     | NULL    |       |
| title  | varchar(128) | YES  |     | NULL    |       |
| type   | varchar(16)  | YES  |     | NULL    |       |
| year   | char(4)      | YES  |     | NULL    |       |
+--------+--------------+------+-----+---------+-------+
4 rows in set (0.00 sec)
```

The DESCRIBE command is an invaluable debugging aid when you need to ensure that you have correctly created a MySQL table. You can also use it to remind yourself about a table's field or column names and the types of data in each one. Let's look at each of the headings in detail:

Field
> The name of each field or column within a table.

Type
> The type of data being stored in the field.

Null
> Whether a field is allowed to contain a value of NULL.

Key
> MySQL supports *keys* or *indexes*, which are quick ways to look up and search for data. The Key heading shows what type of key (if any) has been applied.

Default
> The default value that will be assigned to the field if no value is specified when a new row is created.

Extra
> Additional information, such as whether a field is set to auto-increment.

Data Types

In Example 8-3, you may have noticed that three of the table's fields were given the data type of VARCHAR, and one was given the type CHAR. The term VARCHAR stands for *VARiable length CHARacter string*, and the command takes a numeric value that tells MySQL the maximum length allowed for a string stored in this field.

This data type is very useful, as MySQL can then plan the size of databases and perform lookups and searches more easily. The downside is that if you ever attempt to assign a string value longer than the length allowed, it will be truncated to the maximum length declared in the table definition.

The year field, however, has more predictable values, so instead of VARCHAR we use the more efficient CHAR(4) data type. The parameter of 4 allows for four bytes of data, supporting all years from –999 to 9999; a byte comprises 8 bits and can have the values 00000000 through 11111111, which are 0 to 255 in decimal.

You could, of course, just store two-digit values for the year, but if your data is going to still be needed in the following century, or may otherwise wrap around, it will have to be sanitized first—much like the "millennium bug" that would have caused dates beginning on January 1, 2000, to be treated as 1900 on many of the world's biggest computer installations.

> The reason I didn't use the YEAR data type in the *classics* table is because it supports only the year 0000, and years 1901 through 2155. This is because MySQL stores the year in a single byte for reasons of efficiency, but it also means that only 256 years are available, and the publication years of the titles in the *classics* table are well before this.

Both CHAR and VARCHAR accept text strings and impose a limit on the size of the field. The difference is that every string in a CHAR field has the specified size. If you put in a smaller string, it is padded with spaces. A VARCHAR field does not pad the text; it lets the size of the field vary to fit the text that is inserted. But VARCHAR requires a small amount of overhead to keep track of the size of each value. So CHAR is slightly more efficient if the sizes are similar in all records, whereas VARCHAR is more efficient if sizes can vary a lot and get large. In addition, the overhead causes access to VARCHAR data to be slightly slower than to CHAR data.

The CHAR data type

Table 8-6 lists the CHAR data types. All these types offer a parameter that sets the maximum (or exact) length of the string allowed in the field. As the table shows, each type has a built-in maximum number of bytes it can occupy.

Table 8-6. MySQL's CHAR data types

Data type	Bytes used	Examples
CHAR(*n*)	exactly *n* (< 256)	CHAR(5) *"Hello" uses 5 bytes* CHAR(57) *"Goodbye" uses 57 bytes*
VARCHAR(*n*)	up to *n* (< 65,536)	VARCHAR(7) *"Morning" uses 7 bytes* VARCHAR(100) *"Night" uses 5 bytes*

The BINARY data type

The BINARY data type is used for storing strings of full bytes that do not have an associated character set. For example, you might use the BINARY data type to store a GIF image (see Table 8-7).

Table 8-7. MySQL's BINARY data types

Data type	Bytes used	Examples
BINARY(*n*) or BYTE(*n*)	exactly *n* (< 256)	As CHAR but contains binary data
VARBINARY(*n*)	up to *n* (< 65,536)	As VARCHAR but for binary data

The TEXT and VARCHAR data types

The differences between TEXT and VARCHAR are small:

- Prior to version 5.0.3, MySQL would remove leading and trailing spaces from VARCHAR fields.
- TEXT fields cannot have default values.
- MySQL indexes only the first *n* characters of a TEXT column (you specify *n* when you create the index).

What this means is that VARCHAR is the better and faster data type to use if you need to search the entire contents of a field. If you will never search more than a certain number of leading characters in a field, you should probably use a TEXT data type (see Table 8-8).

Table 8-8. MySQL's TEXT data types

Data type	Bytes used	Attributes
TINYTEXT(*n*)	up to *n* (< 256)	Treated as a string with a character set
TEXT(*n*)	up to *n* (< 65,536)	Treated as a string with a character set
MEDIUMTEXT(*n*)	up to *n* (< 1.67e+7)	Treated as a string with a character set
LONGTEXT(*n*)	up to *n* (< 4.29e+9)	Treated as a string with a character set

The BLOB data type

The term BLOB stands for *Binary Large OBject* and therefore, as you would think, the BLOB data type is most useful for binary data in excess of 65,536 bytes in size. The main other difference between the BLOB and BINARY data types is that BLOBs cannot have default values (see Table 8-9).

Table 8-9. MySQL's BLOB data types

Data type	Bytes used	Attributes
TINYBLOB(*n*)	up to *n* (< 256)	Treated as binary data—no character set
BLOB(*n*)	up to *n* (<= 65,536)	Treated as binary data—no character set
MEDIUMBLOB(*n*)	up to *n* (< 1.67e+7)	Treated as binary data—no character set
LONGBLOB(*n*)	up to *n* (< 4.29e+9)	Treated as binary data—no character set

Numeric data types

MySQL supports various numeric data types from a single byte up to double-precision floating-point numbers. Although the most memory that a numeric field can use up is 8 bytes, you are well advised to choose the smallest data type that will adequately handle the largest value you expect. Your databases will be small and quickly accessible.

Table 8-10 lists the numeric data types supported by MySQL and the ranges of values they can contain. In case you are not acquainted with the terms, a signed number is one with a possible range from a minus value, through 0, to a positive one, and an unsigned one has a value ranging from 0 to a positive one. They can both hold the same number of values; just picture a signed number as being shifted halfway to the left so that half its values are negative and half are positive. Note that floating-point values (of any precision) may only be signed.

Table 8-10. MySQL's numeric data types

Data type	Bytes used	Minimum value		Maximum value	
		Signed	Unsigned	Signed	Unsigned
TINYINT	1	−128	0	127	255
SMALLINT	2	−32,768	0	32,767	65,535
MEDIUMINT	3	−8.38e+6	0	8.38e+6	1.67e+7
INT or INTEGER	4	−2.15e+9	0	2.15e+9	4.29e+9
BIGINT	8	−9.22e+18	0	9.22e+18	1.84e+19
FLOAT	4	−3.40e+38	*n/a*	3.40e+38	*n/a*
DOUBLE or REAL	8	−1.80e+308	*n/a*	1.80e+308	*n/a*

To specify whether a data type is signed or unsigned, use the UNSIGNED qualifier. The following example creates a table called *tablename* with a field in it called *fieldname* of the data type UNSIGNED INTEGER:

```
CREATE TABLE tablename (fieldname INT UNSIGNED);
```

When creating a numeric field, you can also pass an optional number as a parameter, like this:

```
CREATE TABLE tablename (fieldname INT(4));
```

But you must remember that, unlike BINARY and CHAR data types, this parameter does not indicate the number of bytes of storage to use. It may seem counterintuitive, but what the number actually represents is the display width of the data in the field when it is retrieved. It is commonly used with the ZEROFILL qualifier like this:

```
CREATE TABLE tablename (fieldname INT(4) ZEROFILL);
```

What this does is cause any numbers with a width of less than four characters to be padded with one or more zeros, sufficient to make the display width of the field four characters long. When a field is already of the specified width or greater, no padding takes place.

DATE and TIME

The main remaining data types supported by MySQL relate to the date and time and can be seen in Table 8-11.

Table 8-11. MySQL's DATE and TIME data types

Data type	Time/date format
DATETIME	'0000-00-00 00:00:00'
DATE	'0000-00-00'
TIMESTAMP	'0000-00-00 00:00:00'
TIME	'00:00:00'
YEAR	0000 (Only years 0000 and 1901–2155)

The DATETIME and TIMESTAMP data types display the same way. The main difference is that TIMESTAMP has a very narrow range (from the years 1970 through 2037), whereas DATETIME will hold just about any date you're likely to specify, unless you're interested in ancient history or science fiction.

TIMESTAMP is useful, however, because you can let MySQL set the value for you. If you don't specify the value when adding a row, the current time is automatically inserted. You can also have MySQL update a TIMESTAMP column each time you change a row.

The AUTO_INCREMENT data type

Sometimes you need to ensure that every row in your database is guaranteed to be unique. You could do this in your program by carefully checking the data you enter and making sure that there is at least one value that differs in any two rows, but this approach is error-prone and works only in certain circumstances. In the *classics* table, for instance, an author may appear multiple times. Likewise, the year of publication will also be frequently duplicated, and so on. It would be hard to guarantee that you have no duplicate rows.

The general solution is to use an extra column just for this purpose. In a while, we'll look at using a publication's ISBN (International Standard Book Number), but first I'd like to introduce the AUTO_INCREMENT data type.

As its name implies, a column given this data type will set the value of its contents to that of the column entry in the previously inserted row, plus 1. Example 8-5 shows how to add a new column called *id* to the table *classics* with auto-incrementing.

Example 8-5. Adding the auto-incrementing column id

```
ALTER TABLE classics ADD id INT UNSIGNED NOT NULL AUTO_INCREMENT KEY;
```

This is your introduction to the ALTER command, which is very similar to the CREATE command. ALTER operates on an existing table, and can add, change, or delete columns. Our example adds a column named *id* with the following characteristics:

INT UNSIGNED
Makes the column take an integer large enough for you to store more than 4 billion records in the table.

NOT NULL
Ensures that every column has a value. Many programmers use NULL in a field to indicate that the field doesn't have any value. But that would allow duplicates, which would violate the whole reason for this column's existence. So we disallow NULL values.

AUTO_INCREMENT
Causes MySQL to set a unique value for this column in every row, as described earlier. We don't really have control over the value that this column will take in each row, but we don't care: all we care about is that we are guaranteed a unique value.

KEY
An auto-increment column is useful as a key, because you will tend to search for rows based on this column, as explained in the section "Indexes" on page 192.

Each entry in the column *id* will now have a unique number, with the first starting at 1 and the others counting upward from there. And whenever a new row is inserted, its *id* column will automatically be given the next number in sequence.

Rather than applying the column retroactively, you could have included it by issuing the CREATE command in slightly different format. In that case, the command in Example 8-3 would be replaced with Example 8-6. Check the final line in particular.

Example 8-6. Adding the auto-incrementing id column at table creation

```
CREATE TABLE classics (
 author VARCHAR(128),
 title VARCHAR(128),
 type VARCHAR(16),
 year CHAR(4),
 id INT UNSIGNED NOT NULL AUTO_INCREMENT KEY) ENGINE MyISAM;
```

If you wish to check whether the column has been added, use the following command to view the table's columns and data types:

```
DESCRIBE classics;
```

Now that we've finished with it, the *id* column is no longer needed, so if you created it using Example 8-5, you should now remove the column using the command in Example 8-7.

Example 8-7. Removing the id column

```
ALTER TABLE classics DROP id;
```

Adding data to a table

To add data to a table, use the INSERT command. Let's see this in action by populating the table *classics* with the data from Table 8-1, using one form of the INSERT command repeatedly (Example 8-8).

Example 8-8. Populating the classics table

```
INSERT INTO classics(author, title, type, year)
 VALUES('Mark Twain','The Adventures of Tom Sawyer','Fiction','1876');
INSERT INTO classics(author, title, type, year)
 VALUES('Jane Austen','Pride and Prejudice','Fiction','1811');
INSERT INTO classics(author, title, type, year)
 VALUES('Charles Darwin','The Origin of Species','Non-Fiction','1856');
INSERT INTO classics(author, title, type, year)
 VALUES('Charles Dickens','The Old Curiosity Shop','Fiction','1841');
INSERT INTO classics(author, title, type, year)
 VALUES('William Shakespeare','Romeo and Juliet','Play','1594');
```

After every second line, you should see a Query OK message. Once all lines have been entered, type the following command, which will display the table's contents (the result should look like Figure 8-4):

```
SELECT * FROM classics;
```

Don't worry about the SELECT command for now—we'll come to it in the section "Querying a MySQL Database" on page 198. Suffice it to say that, as typed, it will display all the data you just entered.

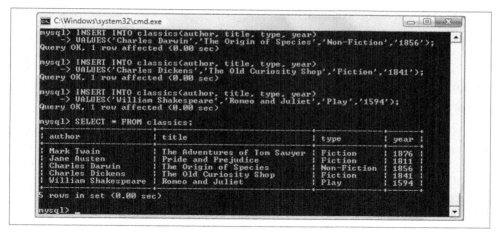

Figure 8-4. Populating the classics table and viewing its contents

Let's go back and look at how we used the INSERT command. The first part, INSERT INTO classics, tells MySQL where to insert the following data. Then, within parentheses, the four column names are listed—*author, title, type*, and *year*—all separated by commas. This tells MySQL that these are the fields into which the data is to be inserted.

The second line of each INSERT command contains the keyword VALUES followed by four strings within parentheses, and separated by commas. This supplies MySQL with the four values to be inserted into the four columns previously specified. (As always, my choice of where to break the lines was arbitrary.)

Each item of data will be inserted into the corresponding column, in a one-to-one correspondence. If you accidentally listed the columns in a different order from the data, the data would go into the wrong columns. And the number of columns must match the number of data items.

Renaming a table

Renaming a table, like any other change to the structure or meta information about a table, is achieved via the ALTER command. So, for example, to change the name of table *classics* to *pre1900*, use the following command:

```
ALTER TABLE classics RENAME pre1900;
```

If you tried that command, you should revert the table name by entering the following, so that later examples in this chapter will work as printed:

```
ALTER TABLE pre1900 RENAME classics;
```

Changing the data type of a column

Changing a column's data type also makes use of the ALTER command, this time in conjunction with the MODIFY keyword. So to change the data type of column *year* from CHAR(4) to SMALLINT (which requires only two bytes of storage and so will save disk space), enter the following:

```
ALTER TABLE classics MODIFY year SMALLINT;
```

When you do this, if the conversion of data type makes sense to MySQL, it will automatically change the data while keeping the meaning. In this case, it will change each string to a comparable integer, and so on, as the string is recognizable as referring to an integer.

Adding a new column

Let's suppose that you have created a table and populated it with plenty of data, only to discover you need an additional column. Not to worry. Here's how to add the new column *pages*, which will be used to store the number of pages in a publication:

```
ALTER TABLE classics ADD pages SMALLINT UNSIGNED;
```

This adds the new column with the name *pages* using the UNSIGNED SMALLINT data type, sufficient to hold a value of up to 65,535—hopefully that's more than enough for any book ever published!

And, if you ask MySQL to describe the updated table using the DESCRIBE command, as follows, you will see the change has been made (see Figure 8-5):

```
DESCRIBE classics;
```

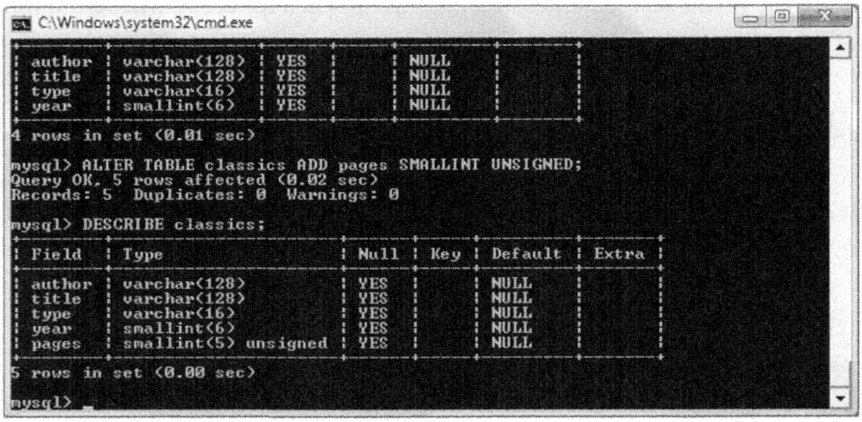

Figure 8-5. Adding the new pages column and viewing the table

---

Renaming a column

Looking again at Figure 8-5, you may decide that having a column named *type* can be confusing, because that is the name used by MySQL to identify data types. Again, no problem—let's change its name to *category*, like this:

```
ALTER TABLE classics CHANGE type category VARCHAR(16);
```

Note the addition of VARCHAR(16) on the end of this command. That's because the CHANGE keyword requires the data type to be specified, even if you don't intend to change it, and VARCHAR(16) was the data type specified when that column was initially created as *type*.

Removing a column

Actually, upon reflection, you might decide that the page count column *pages* isn't actually all that useful for this particular database, so here's how to remove that column using the DROP keyword:

```
ALTER TABLE classics DROP pages;
```

 Remember that DROP is irreversible and you should always use it with caution, because you could inadvertently delete entire tables (and even databases) with it if you are not careful!

Deleting a table

Deleting a table is very easy indeed. But, because I don't want you to have to reenter all the data for the *classics* table, let's quickly create a new table, verify its existence, and then delete it by typing the commands in Example 8-9. The result of these four commands should look like Figure 8-6.

Example 8-9. Creating, viewing, and deleting a table

```
CREATE TABLE disposable(trash INT);
DESCRIBE disposable;
DROP TABLE disposable;
SHOW tables;
```

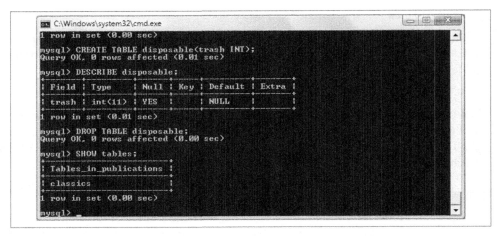

Figure 8-6. Creating, viewing, and deleting a table

Indexes

As things stand, the table *classics* works and can be searched without problem by MySQL—until it grows to more than a couple of hundred rows, that is. At that point, database accesses will get slower and slower with every new row added, because MySQL has to search through every row whenever a query is issued. This is like searching through every book in a library whenever you need to look something up.

Of course, you don't have to search libraries that way, because they have either a card index system or, most likely, a database of their own. And the same goes for MySQL, because at the expense of a slight overhead in memory and disk space, you can create a "card index" for a table that MySQL will use to conduct lightning-fast searches.

Creating an Index

The way to achieve fast searches is to add an *index*, either when creating a table or at any time afterward. But the decision is not so simple. For example, there are different index types such as a regular INDEX, PRIMARY KEY, and FULLTEXT. Also, you must decide which columns require an index, a judgment that requires you to predict whether you will be searching any of the data in that column. Indexes can also get complicated, because you can combine multiple columns in one index. And even when you've decided that, you still have the option of reducing index size by limiting the amount of each column to be indexed.

If we imagine the searches that may be made on the *classics* table, it becomes apparent that all of the columns may need to be searched. However, if the *pages* column created in the section "Adding a new column" on page 190 had not been deleted, it would probably not have needed an index, as most people would be unlikely to search for books by the number of pages they have. Anyway, go ahead and add an index to each of the columns, using the commands in Example 8-10.

Example 8-10. Adding indexes to the classics table

```
ALTER TABLE classics ADD INDEX(author(20));
ALTER TABLE classics ADD INDEX(title(20));
ALTER TABLE classics ADD INDEX(category(4));
ALTER TABLE classics ADD INDEX(year);
DESCRIBE classics;
```

The first two commands create indexes on both the *author* and *title* columns, limiting each index to only the first 20 characters. For instance, when MySQL indexes the following title:

```
The Adventures of Tom Sawyer
```

It will actually store in the index only the first 20 characters:

```
The Adventures of To
```

This is done to minimize the size of the index, and to optimize database access speed. I chose 20 because it's likely to be sufficient to ensure uniqueness for most strings in these columns. If MySQL finds two indexes with the same contents, it will have to waste time going to the table itself and checking the column that was indexed to find out which rows really matched.

With the *category* column, currently only the first character is required to identify a string as unique (F for Fiction, N for Non-Fiction, and P for Play), but I chose an index of four characters to allow for future category types that may be unique only after four characters. You can also re-index this column later, when you have a more complete set of categories. And finally, I set no limit to the *year* column's index, because it's an integer, not a string.

The results of issuing these commands (and a DESCRIBE command to confirm that they worked) can be seen in Figure 8-7, which shows the key MUL for each column. This key means that multiple occurrences of a value may occur within that column, which is exactly what we want, as authors may appear many times, the same book title could be used by multiple authors, and so on.

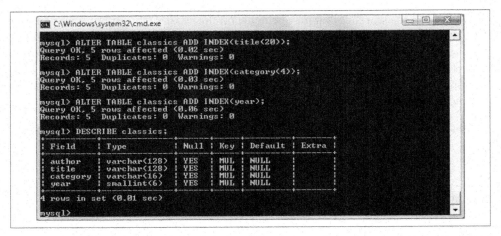

Figure 8-7. Adding indexes to the classics table

Using CREATE INDEX

An alternative to using ALTER TABLE to add an index is to use the CREATE INDEX command. They are equivalent, except that CREATE INDEX cannot be used to create a PRIMARY KEY (see the section "Primary keys" on page 195). The format of this command is shown in the second line of Example 8-11.

Example 8-11. These two commands are equivalent

```
ALTER TABLE classics ADD INDEX(author(20));
CREATE INDEX author ON classics (author(20));
```

Adding indexes when creating tables

You don't have to wait until after creating a table to add indexes. In fact, doing so can be time consuming, as adding an index to a large table can take a very long time. Therefore, let's look at a command that creates the table *classics* with indexes already in place.

Example 8-12 is a reworking of Example 8-3 in which the indexes are created at the same time as the table. Note that to incorporate the modifications made in this chapter, this version uses the new column name *category* instead of *type* and sets the data type of *year* to SMALLINT instead of CHAR(4). If you want to try it out without first deleting your current *classics* table, change the word *classics* in line 1 to something else like *classics1*, then drop *classics1* after you have finished with it.

Example 8-12. Creating the table classics with indexes

```
CREATE TABLE classics (
 author VARCHAR(128),
 title VARCHAR(128),
 category VARCHAR(16),
 year SMALLINT,
```

```
INDEX(author(20)),
INDEX(title(20)),
INDEX(category(4)),
INDEX(year)) ENGINE MyISAM;
```

Primary keys

So far, you've created the table *classics* and ensured that MySQL can search it quickly by adding indexes, but there's still something missing. All the publications in the table can be searched, but there is no single unique key for each publication to enable instant accessing of a row. The importance of having a key with a unique value for each row will come up when we start to combine data from different tables.

The section "The AUTO_INCREMENT data type" on page 186 briefly introduced the idea of a primary key when creating the auto-incrementing column *id*, which could have been used as a primary key for this table. However, I wanted to reserve that task for a more appropriate column: the internationally recognized ISBN number.

So let's go ahead and create a new column for this key. Now, bearing in mind that ISBNs are 13 characters long, you might think that the following command would do the job:

```
ALTER TABLE classics ADD isbn CHAR(13) PRIMARY KEY;
```

But it doesn't. If you try it, you'll get the error Duplicate entry for key 1. The reason is that the table is already populated with some data and this command is trying to add a column with the value NULL to each row, which is not allowed, as all values must be unique in any column having a primary key index. However, if there were no data already in the table, this command would work just fine, as would adding the primary key index upon table creation.

In our current situation, we have to be a bit sneaky and create the new column without an index, populate it with data, and then add the index retrospectively using the commands in Example 8-13. Luckily, each of the years is unique in the current set of data, so we can use the *year* column to identify each row for updating. Note that this example uses the UPDATE and WHERE keywords, which are explained in more detail in the section "Querying a MySQL Database" on page 198.

Example 8-13. Populating the isbn column with data and using a primary key

```
ALTER TABLE classics ADD isbn CHAR(13);
UPDATE classics SET isbn='9781598184891' WHERE year='1876';
UPDATE classics SET isbn='9780582506206' WHERE year='1811';
UPDATE classics SET isbn='9780517123201' WHERE year='1856';
UPDATE classics SET isbn='9780099533474' WHERE year='1841';
UPDATE classics SET isbn='9780192814968' WHERE year='1594';
ALTER TABLE classics ADD PRIMARY KEY(isbn);
DESCRIBE classics;
```

Once you have typed these commands, the results should look like Figure 8-8. Note that the keywords `PRIMARY KEY` replace the keyword `INDEX` in the `ALTER TABLE` syntax (compare Examples 8-10 and 8-13).

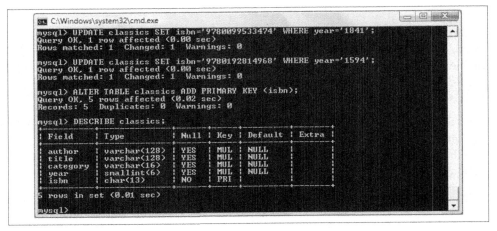

Figure 8-8. Retrospectively adding a primary key to the classics table

To have created a primary key when the table *classics* was created, you could have used the commands in Example 8-14. Again, rename *classics* in line 1 to something else if you wish to try this example for yourself, and then delete the test table afterward.

Example 8-14. Creating the table classics with a primary key

```
CREATE TABLE classics (
 author VARCHAR(128),
 title VARCHAR(128),
 category VARCHAR(16),
 year SMALLINT,
 isbn CHAR(13),
 INDEX(author(20)),
 INDEX(title(20)),
 INDEX(category(4)),
 INDEX(year),
 PRIMARY KEY (isbn)) ENGINE MyISAM;
```

Creating a FULLTEXT index

Unlike a regular index, MySQL's `FULLTEXT` allows super-fast searches of entire columns of text. It stores every word in every data string in a special index that you can search using "natural language," in a similar manner to a search engine.

Actually, it's not strictly true that MySQL stores *all* the words in a FULLTEXT index, because it has a built-in list of more than 500 words that it chooses to ignore because they are so common that they aren't very helpful for searching anyway. This list, called *stopwords*, includes *the, as, is, of,* and so on. The list helps MySQL run much more quickly when performing a FULLTEXT search and keeps database sizes down. Appendix C contains the full list of stopwords.

Here are some things that you should know about FULLTEXT indexes:

- FULLTEXT indexes can be used only with MyISAM tables, the type used by MySQL's default storage engine (MySQL supports at least 10 different storage engines). If you need to convert a table to MyISAM, you can usually use the MySQL command `ALTER TABLE tablename ENGINE = MyISAM;`.
- FULLTEXT indexes can be created for CHAR, VARCHAR, and TEXT columns only.
- A FULLTEXT index definition can be given in the CREATE TABLE statement when a table is created, or added later using ALTER TABLE (or CREATE INDEX).
- For large data sets, it is *much* faster to load your data into a table that has no FULLTEXT index and then create the index than to load data into a table that has an existing FULLTEXT index.

To create a FULLTEXT index, apply it to one or more records as in Example 8-15, which adds a FULLTEXT index to the pair of columns *author* and *title* in the table *classics* (this index is in addition to the ones already created and does not affect them).

Example 8-15. Adding a FULLTEXT index to the table classics

```
ALTER TABLE classics ADD FULLTEXT(author,title);
```

You can now perform FULLTEXT searches across this pair of columns. This feature could really come into its own if you could now add the entire text of these publications to the database (particularly as they're out of copyright protection) and they would be fully searchable. See the section "MATCH ... AGAINST" on page 202 for a description of searches using FULLTEXT.

 If you find that MySQL is running slower than you think it should be when accessing your database, the problem is usually related to your indexes. Either you don't have an index where you need one, or the indexes are not optimally designed. Tweaking a table's indexes will often solve such a problem. Performance is beyond the scope of this book, but in Chapter 9 I give you a few tips so you know what to look for.

Querying a MySQL Database

So far, we've created a MySQL database and tables, populated them with data, and added indexes to make them fast to search. Now it's time to look at how these searches are performed, and the various commands and qualifiers available.

SELECT

As you saw in Figure 8-4, the SELECT command is used to extract data from a table. In that section, I used its simplest form to select all data and display it—something you will never want to do on anything but the smallest tables, because all the data will scroll by at an unreadable pace. Let's now examine SELECT in more detail.

The basic syntax is:

```
SELECT something FROM tablename;
```

The *something* can be an * (asterisk) as you saw before, which means "every column," or you can choose to select only certain columns. For instance, Example 8-16 shows how to select just the *author* and *title* and just the *title* and *isbn*. The result of typing these commands can be seen in Figure 8-9.

Example 8-16. Two different SELECT statements

```
SELECT author,title FROM classics;
SELECT title,isbn FROM classics;
```

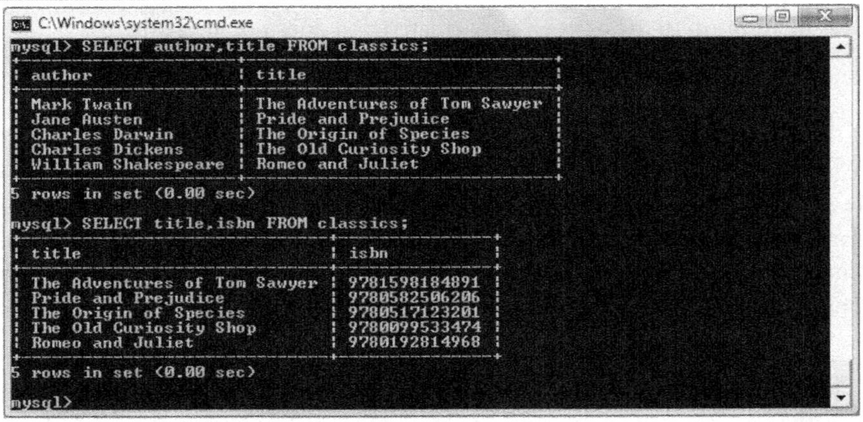

Figure 8-9. The output from two different SELECT statements

SELECT COUNT

Another replacement for the *something* parameter is COUNT, which can be used in many ways. In Example 8-17, it displays the number of rows in the table by passing * as a parameter, which means "all rows." As you'd expect, the result returned is 5, as there are five publications in the table.

Example 8-17. Counting rows

```
SELECT COUNT(*) FROM classics;
```

SELECT DISTINCT

This qualifier (and its synonym `DISTINCTROW`) allows you to weed out multiple entries when they contain the same data. For instance, suppose that you want a list of all authors in the table. If you select just the *author* column from a table containing multiple books by the same author, you'll normally see a long list with same author names over and over. But by adding the `DISTINCT` keyword, you can show each author just once. So let's test that out by adding another row that repeats one of our existing authors (Example 8-18).

Example 8-18. Duplicating data

```
INSERT INTO classics(author, title, category, year, isbn)
  VALUES('Charles Dickens','Little Dorrit','Fiction','1857', '9780141439969');
```

Now that Charles Dickens appears twice in the table, we can compare the results of using `SELECT` with and without the `DISTINCT` qualifier. Example 8-19 and Figure 8-10 show that the simple `SELECT` lists Dickens twice, and the command with the `DISTINCT` qualifier shows him only once.

Example 8-19. With and without the DISTINCT qualifier

```
SELECT author FROM classics;
SELECT DISTINCT author FROM classics;
```

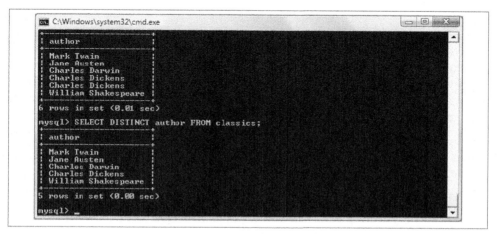

Figure 8-10. Selecting data with and without DISTINCT

DELETE

When you need to remove a row from a table, use the DELETE command. Its syntax is similar to the SELECT command and allows you to narrow down the exact row or rows to delete using qualifiers such as WHERE and LIMIT.

Now that you've seen the effects of the DISTINCT qualifier, if you entered Example 8-18, you should remove *Little Dorrit* by entering the commands in Example 8-20.

Example 8-20. Removing the new entry

```
DELETE FROM classics WHERE title='Little Dorrit';
```

This example issues a DELETE command for all rows whose *title* column contains the string Little Dorrit.

The WHERE keyword is very powerful, and important to enter correctly; an error could lead a command to the wrong rows (or have no effect in cases where nothing matches the WHERE clause). So now we'll spend some time on that clause, which is the heart and soul of SQL.

WHERE

The WHERE keyword enables you to narrow down queries by returning only those *where* a certain expression is true. Example 8-20 returns only the rows where the column exactly matches the string Little Dorrit, using the equality operator =. Example 8-21 shows a couple more examples of using WHERE with =.

Example 8-21. Using the WHERE keyword

```
SELECT author,title FROM classics WHERE author="Mark Twain";
SELECT author,title FROM classics WHERE isbn="9781598184891 ";
```

Given our current table, the two commands in Example 8-21 display the same results. But we could easily add more books by Mark Twain, in which case the first line would display all titles he wrote and the second line would continue (because we know the ISBN is unique) to display The Adventures of Tom Sawyer. In other words, searches using a unique key are more predictable, and you'll see further evidence later of the value of unique and primary keys.

You can also do pattern matching for your searches using the LIKE qualifier, which allows searches on parts of strings. This qualifier should be used with a % character before or after some text. When placed before a keyword, % means "anything before" and after a keyword it means "anything after." Example 8-22 performs three different queries, one for the start of a string, one for the end, and one for anywhere in a string. You can see the results of these commands in Figure 8-11.

Example 8-22. Using the LIKE qualifier

```
SELECT author,title FROM classics WHERE author LIKE "Charles%";
SELECT author,title FROM classics WHERE title LIKE "%Species";
SELECT author,title FROM classics WHERE title LIKE "%and%";
```

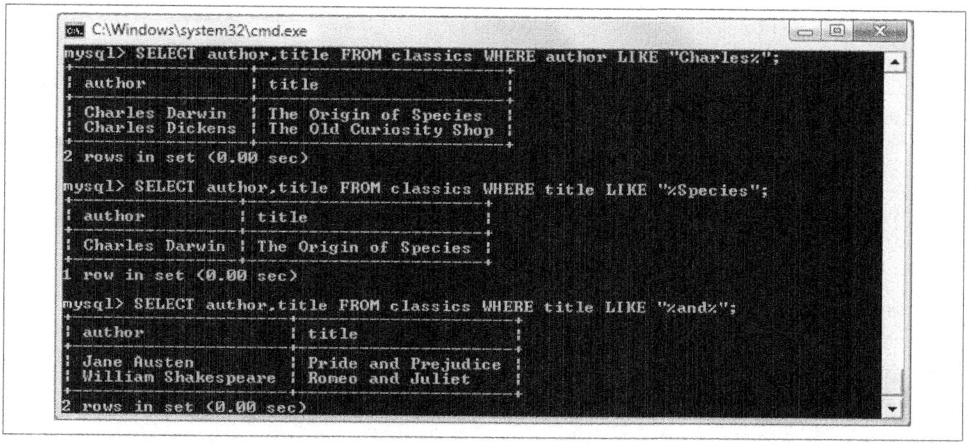

Figure 8-11. Using WHERE with the LIKE qualifier

The first command outputs the publications by both Charles Darwin and Charles Dickens because the LIKE qualifier was set to return anything matching the string Charles followed by any other text. Then just The Origin of Species is returned, because it's the only row whose column ends with the string Species. Last, both Pride and Prejudice and Romeo and Juliet are returned, because they both matched the string and anywhere in the column.

The % will also match if there is nothing in the position it occupies; in other words, it can match an empty string.

LIMIT

The LIMIT qualifier enables you to choose how many rows to return in a query, and where in the table to start returning them. When passed a single parameter, it tells MySQL to start at the beginning of the results and just return the number of rows given in that parameter. If you pass it two parameters, the first indicates the offset from the start of the results where MySQL should start the display, and the second indicates how many to return. You can think of the first parameter as saying, "Skip this number of results at the start."

Example 8-23 includes three commands. The first returns the first three rows from the table. The second returns two rows starting at position 1 (skipping the first row). The last command returns a single row starting at position 3 (skipping the first three rows). Figure 8-12 shows the results of issuing these three commands.

Example 8-23. Limiting the number of results returned

```
SELECT author,title FROM classics LIMIT 3;
SELECT author,title FROM classics LIMIT 1,2;
SELECT author,title FROM classics LIMIT 3,1;
```

Figure 8-12. Restricting the rows returned with LIMIT

> Be careful with the LIMIT keyword, because offsets start at 0, but the number of rows to return starts at 1. So LIMIT 1,3 means return *three* rows starting from the *second* row.

MATCH ... AGAINST

The MATCH ... AGAINST construct can be used on columns that have been given a FULLTEXT index (see the section "Creating a FULLTEXT index" on page 196). With it, you can make natural-language searches as you would in an Internet search engine. Unlike the use of WHERE ... = or WHERE ... LIKE, MATCH ... AGAINST lets you enter multiple words in a search query and checks them against all words in the FULLTEXT columns. FULLTEXT indexes are case-insensitive, so it makes no difference what case is used in your queries.

Assuming that you have added a FULLTEXT index to the *author* and *title* columns, enter the three queries shown in Example 8-24. The first asks for any of these columns that contain the word *and* to be returned. Because *and* is a stopword, MySQL will ignore it and the query will always produce an empty set—no matter what is stored in the

---

columns. The second query asks for any rows that contain both of the words *old* and *shop* anywhere in them, in any order, to be returned. And the last query applies the same kind of search for the words *tom* and *sawyer*. Figure 8-13 shows the results of these queries.

Example 8-24. Using MATCH ... AGAINST on FULLTEXT indexes

```
SELECT author,title FROM classics
 WHERE MATCH(author,title) AGAINST('and');
SELECT author,title FROM classics
 WHERE MATCH(author,title) AGAINST('old shop');
SELECT author,title FROM classics
 WHERE MATCH(author,title) AGAINST('tom sawyer');
```

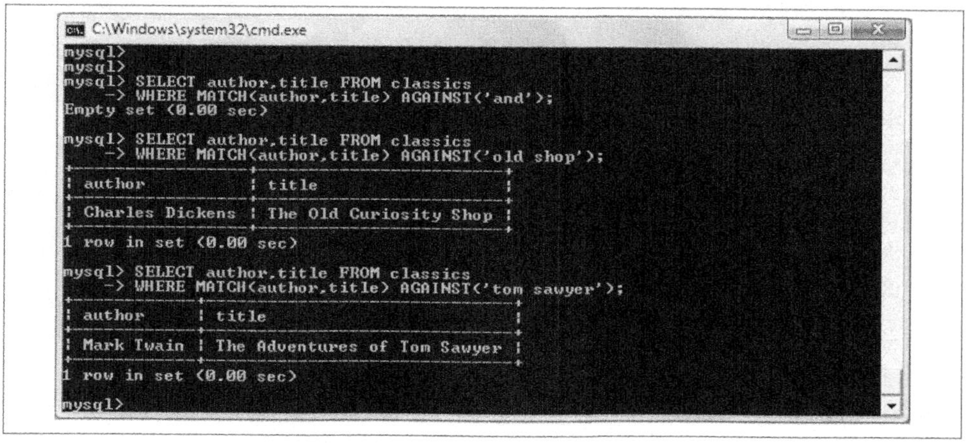

Figure 8-13. Using MATCH ... AGAINST on a FULLTEXT index

MATCH ... AGAINST ... IN BOOLEAN MODE

If you wish to give your MATCH ... AGAINST queries even more power, use Boolean mode. This changes the effect of the standard FULLTEXT query so that it searches for any combination of search words, instead of requiring all search words to be in the text. The presence of a single word in a column causes the search to return the row.

Boolean mode also allows you to preface search words with a + or – sign to indicate whether they must be included or excluded. If normal Boolean mode says, "Any of these words will do," a plus sign means "This word must be present; otherwise, don't return the row." A minus sign means "This word must not be present; its presence disqualifies the row from being returned."

Example 8-25 illustrates Boolean mode through two queries. The first asks for all rows containing the word *charles* and not the word *species* to be returned. The second uses double quotes to request that all rows containing the exact phrase *origin of* be returned. Figure 8-14 shows the results of these queries.

Example 8-25. Using MATCH ... AGAINST ... IN BOOLEAN MODE

```
SELECT author,title FROM classics
 WHERE MATCH(author,title)
 AGAINST('+charles -species' IN BOOLEAN MODE);
SELECT author,title FROM classics
 WHERE MATCH(author,title)
 AGAINST('"origin of"' IN BOOLEAN MODE);
```

Figure 8-14. Using MATCH ... AGAINST ... IN BOOLEAN MODE

As you would expect, the first request returns only The Old Curiosity Shop by Charles Dickens, because any rows containing the word *species* have been excluded, so Charles Darwin's publication is ignored.

> There is something of interest to note in the second query: the stop-word *of* is part of the search string, but is still used by the search because the double quotation marks override stopwords.

UPDATE ... SET

This construct allows you to update the contents of a field. If you wish to change the contents of one or more fields, you need to first narrow in on just the field or fields to be changed, in much the same way you use the SELECT command. Example 8-26 shows the use of UPDATE ... SET in two different ways. You can see the results in Figure 8-15.

Example 8-26. Using UPDATE ... SET

```
UPDATE classics SET author='Mark Twain (Samuel Langhorne Clemens)'
 WHERE author='Mark Twain';
UPDATE classics SET category='Classic Fiction'
 WHERE category='Fiction';
```

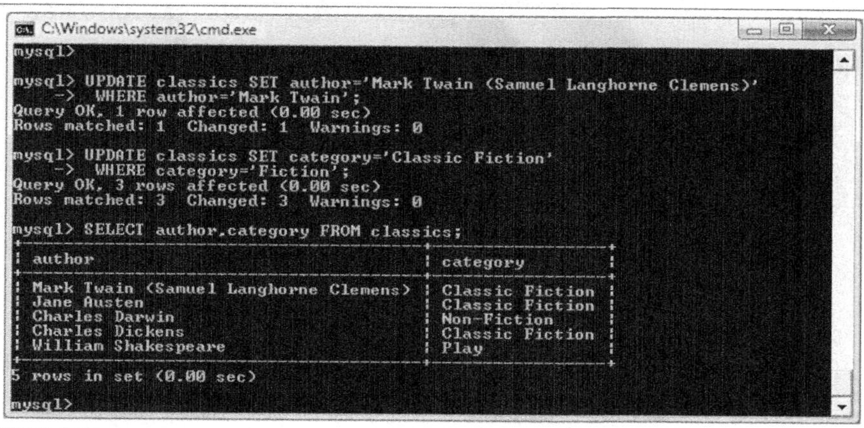

Figure 8-15. Updating columns in the classics table

In the first query, Mark Twain's real name of Samuel Langhorne Clemens was appended to his pen name in brackets, which affected only one row. The second query, however, affected three rows, because it changed all occurrences of the word *Fiction* in the *category* column to the term *Classic Fiction*.

When performing an update, you can also make use of the qualifiers you have already seen, such as LIMIT, and the following ORDER BY and GROUP BY keywords.

ORDER BY

ORDER BY sorts returned results by one or more columns in ascending or descending order. Example 8-27 shows two such queries, the results of which can be seen in Figure 8-16.

Example 8-27. Using ORDER BY

```
SELECT author,title FROM classics ORDER BY author;
SELECT author,title FROM classics ORDER BY title DESC;
```

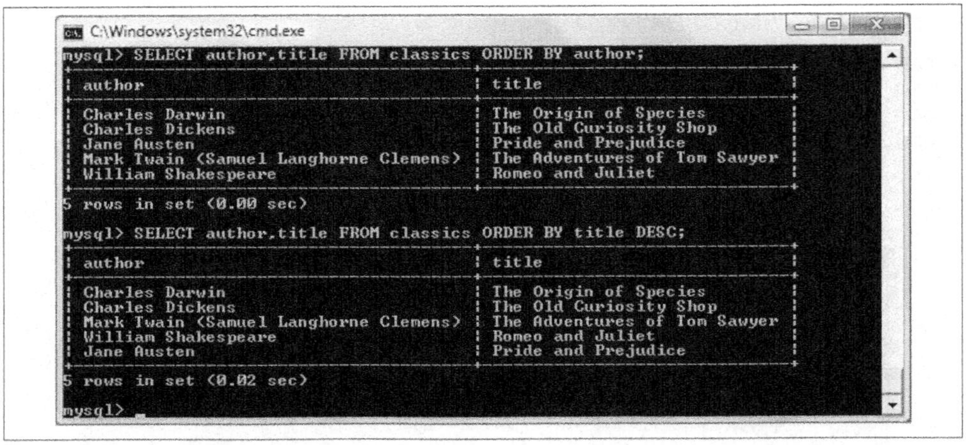

Figure 8-16. Sorting the results of requests

As you can see, the first query returns the publications by *author* in ascending alphabetical order (the default), and the second returns them by *title* in descending order.

If you wanted to sort all the rows by *author* and then by descending *year* of publication (to view the most recent first), you would issue the following query:

```
SELECT author,title,year FROM classics ORDER BY author,year DESC;
```

This shows that each ascending and descending qualifier applies to a single column. The DESC keyword applies only to the preceding column, *year*. Because you allow *author* to use the default sort order, it is sorted in ascending order. You could also have explicitly specified ascending order for that column, with the same results:

```
SELECT author,title,year FROM classics ORDER BY author ASC,year DESC;
```

GROUP BY

In a similar fashion to ORDER BY, you can group results returned from queries using GROUP BY, which is good for retrieving information about a group of data. For example, if you want to know how many publications there are of each category in the *classics* table, you can issue the following query:

```
SELECT category,COUNT(author) FROM classics GROUP BY category;
```

which returns the following output:

```
+-----------------+-----------------+
| category        | COUNT(author)   |
+-----------------+-----------------+
| Classic Fiction |               3 |
| Non-Fiction     |               1 |
| Play            |               1 |
+-----------------+-----------------+
3 rows in set (0.00 sec)
```

Joining Tables Together

It is quite normal to maintain multiple tables within a database, each holding a different type of information. For example, consider the case of a *customers* table that needs to be able to be cross-referenced with publications purchased from the *classics* table. Enter the commands in Example 8-28 to create this new table and populate it with three customers and their purchases. Figure 8-17 shows the result.

Example 8-28. Creating and populating the customers table

```
CREATE TABLE customers (
 name VARCHAR(128),
 isbn VARCHAR(13),
 PRIMARY KEY (isbn)) ENGINE MyISAM;
INSERT INTO customers(name,isbn)
 VALUES('Joe Bloggs','9780099533474');
INSERT INTO customers(name,isbn)
 VALUES('Mary Smith','9780582506206');
INSERT INTO customers(name,isbn)
 VALUES('Jack Wilson','9780517123201');
SELECT * FROM customers;
```

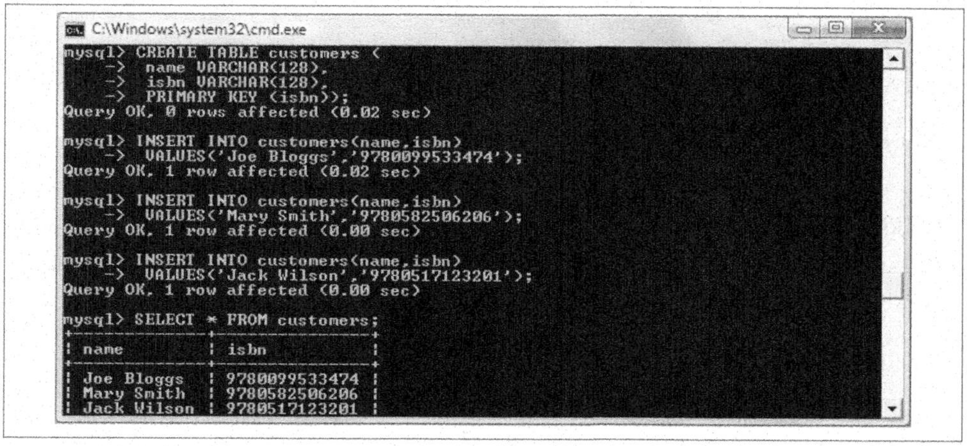

Figure 8-17. Creating the customers table

There's also a shortcut for inserting multiple rows of data, as in Example 8-28, in which you can replace the three separate INSERT INTO queries with a single one listing the data to be inserted, separated by commas, like this:

```
INSERT INTO customers(name,isbn) VALUES
('Joe Bloggs','9780099533474'),
('Mary Smith','9780582506206'),
('Jack Wilson','9780517123201');
```

Of course, in a proper table containing customers' details there would also be addresses, phone numbers, email addresses, and so on, but they aren't necessary for this explanation. While creating the new table, you should have noticed that it has something in common with the *classics* table: a column called *isbn*. Because it has the same meaning in both tables (an ISBN refers to a book, and always the same book), we can use this column to tie the two tables together into a single query, as in Example 8-29.

Example 8-29. Joining two tables into a single SELECT

```
SELECT name,author,title from customers,classics
 WHERE customers.isbn=classics.isbn;
```

The result of this operation is the following:

```
+-------------+-----------------+------------------------+
| name        | author          | title                  |
+-------------+-----------------+------------------------+
| Joe Bloggs  | Charles Dickens | The Old Curiosity Shop |
| Mary Smith  | Jane Austen     | Pride and Prejudice    |
| Jack Wilson | Charles Darwin  | The Origin of Species  |
+-------------+-----------------+------------------------+
3 rows in set (0.00 sec)
```

See how this query has neatly tied both tables together to show the publications purchased from the *classics* table by the people in the *customers* table?

NATURAL JOIN

Using NATURAL JOIN, you can save yourself some typing and make queries a little clearer. This kind of join takes two tables and automatically joins columns that have the same name. So, to achieve the same results as from Example 8-29, you would enter:

```
SELECT name,author,title FROM customers NATURAL JOIN classics;
```

JOIN...ON

If you wish to specify the column on which to join two tables, use the JOIN ... ON construct, as follows, to achieve results identical to those of Example 8-29:

```
SELECT name,author,title FROM customers
 JOIN classics ON customers.isbn=classics.isbn;
```

Using AS

You can also save yourself some typing and improve query readability by creating aliases using the AS keyword. Follow a table name with AS and the alias to use. The following code, therefore, is also identical in action to Example 8-29. Aliases can be particularly useful when you have long queries that reference the same table names many times.

```
SELECT name,author,title from
 customers AS cust, classics AS class
  WHERE cust.isbn=class.isbn;
```

The result of this operation is the following:

```
+------------+----------------+------------------------+
| name       | author         | title                  |
+------------+----------------+------------------------+
| Joe Bloggs | Charles Dickens | The Old Curiosity Shop |
| Mary Smith | Jane Austen    | Pride and Prejudice    |
| Jack Wilson | Charles Darwin | The Origin of Species  |
+------------+----------------+------------------------+
3 rows in set (0.00 sec)
```

Using Logical Operators

You can also use the logical operators AND, OR, and NOT in your MySQL WHERE queries to further narrow down your selections. Example 8-30 shows one instance of each, but you can mix and match them in any way you need.

Example 8-30. Using logical operators

```
SELECT author,title FROM classics WHERE
 author LIKE "Charles%" AND author LIKE "%Darwin";
SELECT author,title FROM classics WHERE
 author LIKE "%Mark Twain%" OR author LIKE "%Samuel Langhorne Clemens%";
SELECT author,title FROM classics WHERE
 author LIKE "Charles%" AND author NOT LIKE "%Darwin";
```

I've chosen the first query, because Charles Darwin might be listed in some rows by his full name, *Charles Robert Darwin*. Thus, the query returns publications as long as the *author* column starts with *Charles* and ends with *Darwin*. The second query searches for publications written using either *Mark Twain*'s pen name or his real name, *Samuel Langhorne Clemens*. The third query returns publications written by authors with the first name *Charles* but not the surname *Darwin*.

MySQL Functions

You might wonder why anyone would want to use MySQL functions when PHP comes with a whole bunch of powerful functions of its own. The answer is very simple: the MySQL functions work on the data right there in the database. If you were to use PHP, you would first have to extract raw data from MySQL, manipulate it, and then perform the database query you first wanted.

Having functions built into MySQL substantially reduces the time needed for performing complex queries, as well as their complexity. If you wish to learn more about the available string and date/time functions, you can visit the following URLs:

- *http://tinyurl.com/mysqlstrings*
- *http://tinyurl.com/mysqldates*

However, to get you started, Appendix D describes a subset containing the most useful of these functions.

Accessing MySQL via phpMyAdmin

Although to use MySQL you have to learn these main commands and how they work, once you understand them, it can be much quicker and simpler to use a program such as *phpMyAdmin* to manage your databases and tables.

However, you will need to install phpMyAdmin before you can use it. To do this, call up the Zend UI by entering the following into your browser, and log in (as shown in Figure 8-18):

```
http://localhost:10081/ZendServer/
```

Figure 8-18. The Zend Dashboard

Now click on the left and right arrows to the right of the DEPLOY SAMPLE APPS section until you see the phpMyAdmin logo and click it to initiate the download; then click Next when you're finished. Click Next again, after you have viewed the README information, to call up the Application Details screen (see Figure 8-19).

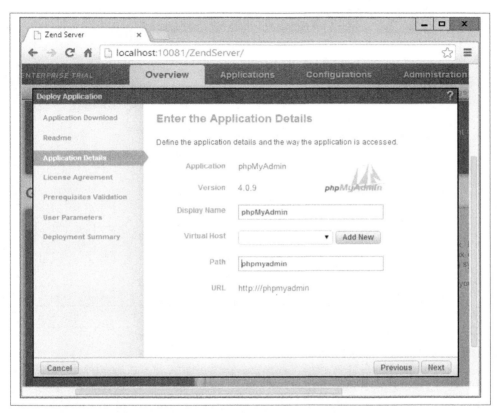

Figure 8-19. Configuring phpMyAdmin for Zend

Here you should probably accept the defaults for Display Name and Virtual Host, but will need to specify a directory name for phpMyAdmin in order to keep it away from your document root files. I have entered the name *phpmyadmin* (all in lowercase so that I won't have to enter any capital letters whenever I type the URL to call it up).

Continue clicking Next and accepting any license agreements until you get to the screen in Figure 8-20. Here you should select the "Use HTTP (Apache) Basic Authentication?" checkbox and supply a login and password. The default login is *DBadmin*, but I have chosen to use simply *admin*; your login and password are up to you. Unless you have configured them differently, you can probably leave the IP, Port, Database User, and Password as displayed.

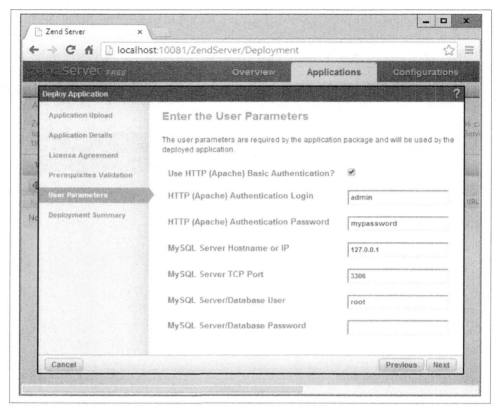

Figure 8-20. Entering phpMyAdmin user parameters

Now click Next, review the summary displayed, and when ready, click the Deploy button. After a few seconds, you should see that the application was successfully deployed, at which point you'll be ready to access phpMyAdmin by entering the following into your browser:

```
http://localhost/phpmyadmin
```

This will bring up the dialog shown in Figure 8-21, where you should enter your username and password before clicking the Log In button.

Figure 8-21. Logging into phpMyAdmin

Your browser should now look like Figure 8-22, and you're ready to use phpMyAdmin in place of the MySQL command line.

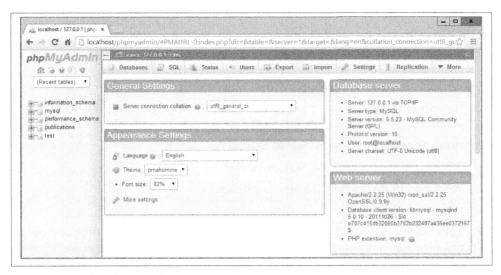

Figure 8-22. The phpMyAdmin main screen

Full details on this installation process are on the Zend website at the following (shortened) URL: *http://tinyurl.com/installpma*.

Using phpMyAdmin

In the lefthand pane of the main phpMyAdmin screen, you can click on the drop-down menu that says "(Databases)" to select any database you wish to work with. This will open the database and display its tables.

From here you can perform all the main operations, such as creating new databases, adding tables, creating indexes, and much more. To read the supporting documentation for phpMyAdmin, visit *https://docs.phpmyadmin.net*.

If you worked with me through the examples in this chapter, congratulations—it's been quite a long journey. You've come all the way from learning how to create a MySQL database through issuing complex queries that combine multiple tables, to using Boolean operators and leveraging MySQL's various qualifiers.

In the next chapter, we'll start looking at how to approach efficient database design, advanced SQL techniques, and MySQL functions and transactions.

Questions

1. What is the purpose of the semicolon in MySQL queries?
2. Which command would you use to view the available databases or tables?
3. How would you create a new MySQL user on the local host called *newuser* with a password of *newpass* and with access to everything in the database *newdatabase*?
4. How can you view the structure of a table?
5. What is the purpose of a MySQL index?
6. What benefit does a FULLTEXT index provide?
7. What is a stopword?
8. Both SELECT DISTINCT and GROUP BY cause the display to show only one output row for each value in a column, even if multiple rows contain that value. What are the main differences between SELECT DISTINCT and GROUP BY?

9. Using the SELECT ... WHERE construct, how would you return only rows containing the word *Langhorne* somewhere in the *author* column of the *classics* table used in this chapter?

10. What needs to be defined in two tables to make it possible for you to join them together?

See "Chapter 8 Answers" on page 644 in Appendix A for the answers to these questions.

CHAPTER 9

Mastering MySQL

Chapter 8 provided you with a good grounding in the practice of using relational databases with structured query language. You've learned about creating databases and the tables they comprise, as well as inserting, looking up, changing, and deleting data.

With that knowledge under your belt, we now need to look at how to design databases for maximum speed and efficiency. For example, how do you decide what data to place in which table? Well, over the years, a number of guidelines have been developed that—if you follow them—ensure your databases will be efficient and capable of growing as you feed them more and more data.

Database Design

It's very important that you design a database correctly before you start to create it; otherwise, you are almost certainly going to have to go back and change it by splitting up some tables, merging others, and moving various columns about in order to achieve sensible relationships that MySQL can easily use.

Sitting down with a sheet of paper and a pencil and writing down a selection of the queries that you think you and your users are likely to ask is an excellent starting point. In the case of an online bookstore's database, some of your questions could be:

- How many authors, books, and customers are in the database?
- Which author wrote a certain book?
- Which books were written by a certain author?
- What is the most expensive book?
- What is the best-selling book?
- Which books have not sold this year?

- Which books did a certain customer buy?
- Which books have been purchased together?

Of course, there are many more queries that you could make on such a database, but even this small sample will begin to give you insights into how to lay out your tables. For example, books and ISBNs can probably be combined into one table, because they are closely linked (we'll examine some of the subtleties later). In contrast, books and customers should be in separate tables, because their connection is very loose. A customer can buy any book, and even multiple copies of a book, yet a book can be bought by many customers and be ignored by still more potential customers.

When you plan to do a lot of searches on something, it can often benefit by having its own table. And when couplings between things are loose, it's best to put them in separate tables.

Taking into account those simple rules of thumb, we can guess we'll need at least three tables to accommodate all these queries:

Authors
> There will be lots of searches for authors, many of whom have collaborated on titles, and many of whom will be featured in collections. Listing all the information about each author together, linked to that author, will produce optimal results for searches—hence an *authors* table.

Books
> Many books appear in different editions. Sometimes they change publisher and sometimes they have the same titles as other, unrelated books. So the links between books and authors are complicated enough to call for a separate table.

Customers
> It's even more clear why customers should get their own table, as they are free to purchase any book by any author.

Primary Keys: The Keys to Relational Databases

Using the power of relational databases, we can define information for each author, book, and customer in just one place. Obviously, what interests us is the links between them—such as who wrote each book and who purchased it—but we can store that information just by making links between the three tables. I'll show you the basic principles, and then it just takes practice for it to feel natural.

The magic involves giving every author a unique identifier. Do the same for every book and for every customer. We saw the means of doing that in the previous chapter: the *primary key*. For a book, it makes sense to use the ISBN, although you then have to deal with multiple editions that have different ISBNs. For authors and customers, you can just assign arbitrary keys, which the AUTO_INCREMENT feature that you saw in the last chapter makes easy.

In short, every table will be designed around some object that you're likely to search for a lot—an author, book, or customer, in this case—and that object will have a primary key. Don't choose a key that could possibly have the same value for different objects. The ISBN is a rare case for which an industry has provided a primary key that you can rely on to be unique for each product. Most of the time, you'll create an arbitrary key for this purpose, using AUTO_INCREMENT.

Normalization

The process of separating your data into tables and creating primary keys is called *normalization*. Its main goal is to make sure each piece of information appears in the database only once. Duplicating data is very inefficient, because it makes databases larger than they need to be and therefore slows down access. But, more importantly, the presence of duplicates creates a strong risk that you'll update only one row of duplicated data, creating inconsistencies in a database and potentially causing serious errors.

Thus, if you list the titles of books in the *authors* table as well as the *books* table, and you have to correct a typographic error in a title, you'll have to search through both tables and make sure you make the same change every place the title is listed. It's better to keep the title in one place and use the ISBN in other places.

But in the process of splitting a database into multiple tables, it's important not to go too far and create more tables than is necessary, which would also lead to inefficient design and slower access.

Luckily, E. F. Codd, the inventor of the relational model, analyzed the concept of normalization and split it into three separate schemas called *First*, *Second*, and *Third Normal Form*. If you modify a database to satisfy each of these forms in order, you will ensure that your database is optimally balanced for fast access, and minimum memory and disk space usage.

To see how the normalization process works, let's start with the rather monstrous database in Table 9-1, which shows a single table containing all of the author names, book titles, and (fictional) customer details. You could consider it a first attempt at a table intended to keep track of which customers have ordered books. Obviously this is inefficient design, because data is duplicated all over the place (duplications are highlighted), but it represents a starting point.

Table 9-1. A highly inefficient design for a database table

Author 1	Author 2	Title	ISBN	Price $US	Customer Name	Customer Address	Purchase Date
David Sklar	Adam Trachtenberg	PHP Cookbook	0596101015	44.99	Emma Brown	1565 Rainbow Road, Los Angeles, CA 90014	Mar 03 2009
Danny Goodman		Dynamic HTML	0596527403	59.99	**Darren Ryder**	**4758 Emily Drive, Richmond, VA 23219**	**Dec 19 2008**
Hugh E Williams	David Lane	PHP and MySQL	0596005436	44.95	Earl B. Thurston	862 Gregory Lane, Frankfort, KY 40601	Jun 22 2009
David Sklar	Adam Trachtenberg	PHP Cookbook	0596101015	44.99	**Darren Ryder**	**4758 Emily Drive, Richmond, VA 23219**	**Dec 19 2008**
Rasmus Lerdorf	Kevin Tatroe & Peter MacIntyre	Programming PHP	0596006815	39.99	David Miller	3647 Cedar Lane, Waltham, MA 02154	Jan 16 2009

In the following three sections, we will examine this database design, and you'll see how we can improve it by removing the various duplicate entries and splitting the single table into multiple tables, each containing one type of data.

First Normal Form

For a database to satisfy the *First Normal Form*, it must fulfill three requirements:

- There should be no repeating columns containing the same kind of data.
- All columns should contain a single value.
- There should be a primary key to uniquely identify each row.

Looking at these requirements in order, you should notice straightaway that the *Author 1* and *Author 2* columns constitute repeating data types. So we already have a target column for pulling into a separate table, as the repeated *Author* columns violate Rule 1.

Second, there are three authors listed for the final book, *Programming PHP*. I've handled that by making Kevin Tatroe and Peter MacIntyre share the *Author 2* column, which violates Rule 2—yet another reason to transfer the *Author* details to a separate table.

However, Rule 3 is satisfied, because the primary key of ISBN has already been created.

Table 9-2 shows the result of removing the *Authors* columns from Table 9-1. Already it looks a lot less cluttered, although there remain duplications that are highlighted.

Table 9-2. The result of stripping the Authors columns from Table 9-1

Title	ISBN	Price $US	Customer Name	Customer Address	Purchase Date
PHP Cookbook	*0596101015*	*44.99*	Emma Brown	1565 Rainbow Road, Los Angeles, CA 90014	Mar 03 2009
Dynamic HTML	0596527403	59.99	**Darren Ryder**	**4758 Emily Drive, Richmond, VA 23219**	**Dec 19 2008**
PHP and MySQL	0596005436	44.95	Earl B. Thurston	862 Gregory Lane, Frankfort, KY 40601	Jun 22 2009
PHP Cookbook	*0596101015*	*44.99*	**Darren Ryder**	**4758 Emily Drive, Richmond, VA 23219**	**Dec 19 2008**
Programming PHP	0596006815	39.99	David Miller	3647 Cedar Lane, Waltham, MA 02154	Jan 16 2009

The new *Authors* table shown in Table 9-3 is small and simple. It just lists the ISBN of a title along with an author. If a title has more than one author, additional authors get their own rows. At first, you may feel ill at ease with this table, because you can't tell which author wrote which book. But don't worry: MySQL can quickly tell you. All you have to do is tell it which book you want information for, and MySQL will use its ISBN to search the *Authors* table in a matter of milliseconds.

Table 9-3. The new Authors table

ISBN	Author
0596101015	David Sklar
0596101015	Adam Trachtenberg
0596527403	Danny Goodman
0596005436	Hugh E Williams
0596005436	David Lane
0596006815	Rasmus Lerdorf
0596006815	Kevin Tatroe
0596006815	Peter MacIntyre

As I mentioned earlier, the ISBN will be the primary key for the *Books* table, when we get around to creating that table. I mention that here in order to emphasize that the ISBN is not, however, the primary key for the *Authors* table. In the real world, the *Authors* table would deserve a primary key, too, so that each author would have a key to uniquely identify him or her.

So, in the *Authors* table, the ISBN is just a column for which—for the purposes of speeding up searches—we'll probably make a key, but not the primary key. In fact, it *cannot* be the primary key in this table, because it's not unique: the same ISBN appears multiple times whenever two or more authors have collaborated on a book.

Because we'll use it to link authors to books in another table, this column is called a *foreign* key.

Keys (also called *indexes*) have several purposes in MySQL. The fundamental reason for defining a key is to make searches faster. You've seen examples in Chapter 8 in which keys are used in WHERE clauses for searching. But a key can also be useful to uniquely identify an item. Thus, a unique key is often used as a primary key in one table, and as a foreign key to link rows in that table to rows in another table.

Second Normal Form

The First Normal Form deals with duplicate data (or redundancy) across multiple columns. The *Second Normal Form* is all about redundancy across multiple rows. In order to achieve Second Normal Form, your tables must already be in First Normal Form. Once this has been done, we achieve Second Normal Form by identifying columns whose data repeats in different places and then removing them to their own tables.

So let's look again at Table 9-2. Notice how Darren Ryder bought two books and therefore his details are duplicated. This tells us that the *Customer* columns need to be pulled into their own tables. Table 9-4 shows the result of removing the *Customer* columns from Table 9-2.

Table 9-4. The new Titles table

ISBN	Title	Price
0596101015	PHP Cookbook	44.99
0596527403	Dynamic HTML	59.99
0596005436	PHP and MySQL	44.95
0596006815	Programming PHP	39.99

As you can see, all that's left in Table 9-4 are the *ISBN*, *Title*, and *Price* columns for four unique books, so this now constitutes an efficient and self-contained table that satisfies the requirements of both the First and Second Normal Forms. Along the way, we've managed to reduce the information to data closely related to book titles. This table could also include years of publication, page counts, numbers of reprints, and so on, as these details are also closely related. The only rule is that we can't put in any column that could have multiple values for a single book, because then we'd have to list the same book in multiple rows and would thus violate Second Normal Form. Restoring an *Author* column, for instance, would violate this normalization.

However, looking at the extracted *Customer* columns, now in Table 9-5, we can see that there's still more normalization work to do, because Darren Ryder's details are still duplicated. And it could also be argued that First Normal Form Rule 2 (all columns should contain a single value) has not been properly complied with, because the addresses really need to be broken into separate columns for *Address*, *City*, *State*, and *Zip code*.

Table 9-5. The Customer details from Table 9-2

ISBN	Customer Name	Customer Address	Purchase Date
0596101015	Emma Brown	1565 Rainbow Road, Los Angeles, CA 90014	Mar 03 2009
0596527403	Darren Ryder	4758 Emily Drive, Richmond, VA 23219	Dec 19 2008
0596005436	Earl B. Thurston	862 Gregory Lane, Frankfort, KY 40601	Jun 22 2009
0596101015	Darren Ryder	4758 Emily Drive, Richmond, VA 23219	Dec 19 2008
0596006815	David Miller	3647 Cedar Lane, Waltham, MA 02154	Jan 16 2009

What we have to do is split this table further to ensure that each customer's details are entered only once. Because the ISBN is not and cannot be used as a primary key to identify customers (or authors), a new key must be created.

Table 9-6 is the result of normalizing the *Customers* table into both First and Second Normal Forms. Each customer now has a unique customer number called *CustNo*, which is the table's primary key and will most likely have been created via AUTO_INCRE MENT. All the parts of customer addresses have also been separated into distinct columns to make them easily searchable and updateable.

Table 9-6. The new Customers table

CustNo	Name	Address	City	State	Zip
1	Emma Brown	1565 Rainbow Road	Los Angeles	CA	90014
2	Darren Ryder	4758 Emily Drive	Richmond	VA	23219
3	Earl B. Thurston	862 Gregory Lane	Frankfort	KY	40601
4	David Miller	3647 Cedar Lane	Waltham	MA	02154

At the same time, in order to normalize Table 9-6, we had to remove the information on customer purchases, because otherwise, there would be multiple instances of customer details for each book purchased. Instead, the purchase data is now placed in a new table called *Purchases* (see Table 9-7).

Table 9-7. The new Purchases table

CustNo	ISBN	Date
1	0596101015	Mar 03 2009
2	0596527403	Dec 19 2008
2	0596101015	Dec 19 2008
3	0596005436	Jun 22 2009
4	0596006815	Jan 16 2009

Here the *CustNo* column from Table 9-6 is reused as a key to tie both the *Customers* and the *Purchases* tables together. Because the ISBN column is also repeated here, this table can be linked with either of the *Authors* or the *Titles* tables, too.

The *CustNo* column can be a useful key in the *Purchases* table, but it's not a primary key. A single customer can buy multiple books (and even multiple copies of one book), so the *CustNo* column is not a primary key. In fact, the *Purchases* table has no primary key. That's all right, because we don't expect to need to keep track of unique purchases. If one customer buys two copies of the same book on the same day, we'll just allow two rows with the same information. For easy searching, we can define both *CustNo* and *ISBN* as keys—just not as primary keys.

 There are now four tables, one more than the three we had initially assumed would be needed. We arrived at this decision through the normalization processes, by methodically following the First and Second Normal Form rules, which made it plain that a fourth table called *Purchases* would also be required.

The tables we now have are *Authors* (Table 9-3), *Titles* (Table 9-4), *Customers* (Table 9-6), and *Purchases* (Table 9-7), and we can link each table to any other using either the *CustNo* or the *ISBN* keys.

For example, to see which books Darren Ryder has purchased, you can look him up in Table 9-6, the *Customers* table, where you will see his *CustNo* is 2. Armed with this number, you can now go to Table 9-7, the *Purchases* table; looking at the ISBN column here, you will see that he purchased titles 0596527403 and 0596101015 on December 19, 2008. This looks like a lot of trouble for a human, but it's not so hard for MySQL.

To determine what these titles were, you can then refer to Table 9-4, the *Titles* table, and see that the books he bought were *Dynamic HTML* and *PHP Cookbook*. Should you wish to know the authors of these books, you could also use the ISBNs you just looked up on Table 9-3, the *Authors* table, and you would see that ISBN 0596527403, *Dynamic HTML*, was written by Danny Goodman, and that ISBN 0596101015, *PHP Cookbook*, was written by David Sklar and Adam Trachtenberg.

Third Normal Form

Once you have a database that complies with both the First and Second Normal Forms, it is in pretty good shape and you might not have to modify it any further. However, if you wish to be very strict with your database, you can ensure that it adheres to the *Third Normal Form*, which requires that data that is *not* directly dependent on the primary key but *is* dependent on another value in the table should also be moved into separate tables, according to the dependence.

For example, in Table 9-6, the *Customers* table, it could be argued that the *State*, *City*, and *Zip code* keys are not directly related to each customer, because many other people will have the same details in their addresses, too. However, they are directly related to each other, in that the street *Address* relies on the *City*, and the *City* relies on the *State*.

Therefore, to satisfy Third Normal Form for Table 9-6, you would need to split it into Tables 9-8 through 9-11.

Table 9-8. *Third Normal Form Customers table*

CustNo	Name	Address	Zip
1	Emma Brown	1565 Rainbow Road	90014
2	Darren Ryder	4758 Emily Drive	23219
3	Earl B. Thurston	862 Gregory Lane	40601
4	David Miller	3647 Cedar Lane	02154

Table 9-9. *Third Normal Form Zip codes table*

Zip	CityID
90014	1234
23219	5678
40601	4321
02154	8765

Table 9-10. *Third Normal Form Cities table*

CityID	Name	StateID
1234	Los Angeles	5
5678	Richmond	46
4321	Frankfort	17
8765	Waltham	21

Table 9-11. *Third Normal Form States table*

StateID	Name	Abbreviation
5	California	CA
46	Virginia	VA
17	Kentucky	KY
21	Massachusetts	MA

So, how would you use this set of four tables instead of the single Table 9-6? Well, you would look up the *Zip code* in Table 9-8, then find the matching *CityID* in Table 9-9. Given this information, you could then look up the city *Name* in Table 9-10 and then also find the *StateID*, which you could use in Table 9-11 to look up the State's *Name*.

Although using the Third Normal Form in this way may seem like overkill, it can have advantages. For example, take a look at Table 9-11, where it has been possible to include both a state's name and its two-letter abbreviation. It could also contain population details and other demographics, if you desired.

Table 9-10 could also contain even more localized demographics that could be useful to you and/or your customers. By splitting up these pieces of data, you can make it easier to maintain your database in the future, should it be necessary to add columns.

Deciding whether to use the Third Normal Form can be tricky. Your evaluation should rest on what data you may need to add at a later date. If you are absolutely certain that the name and address of a customer is all that you will ever require, you probably will want to leave out this final normalization stage.

On the other hand, suppose you are writing a database for a large organization such as the U.S. Postal Service. What would you do if a city were to be renamed? With a table such as Table 9-6, you would need to perform a global search and replace on every instance of that city. But if you have your database set up according to the Third Normal Form, you would have to change only a single entry in Table 9-10 for the change to be reflected throughout the entire database.

Therefore, I suggest that you ask yourself two questions to help you decide whether to perform a Third Normal Form normalization on any table:

- Is it likely that many new columns will need to be added to this table?
- Could any of this table's fields require a global update at any point?

If either of the answers is yes, you should probably consider performing this final stage of normalization.

When Not to Use Normalization

Now that you know all about normalization, I'm going to tell you why you should throw these rules out of the window on high-traffic sites. That's right—you should never fully normalize your tables on sites that will cause MySQL to thrash.

Normalization requires spreading data across multiple tables, and this means making multiple calls to MySQL for each query. On a very popular site, if you have normalized tables, your database access will slow down considerably once you get above a few dozen concurrent users, because they will be creating hundreds of database accesses between them. In fact, I would go so far as to say you should denormalize any commonly looked-up data as much as you can.

You see, if you have data duplicated across your tables, you can substantially reduce the number of additional requests that need to be made, because most of the data you want is available in each table. This means that you can simply add an extra column to a query and that field will be available for all matching results.

Of course, you have to deal with the downsides previously mentioned, such as using up large amounts of disk space, and ensuring that you update every single duplicate copy of data when one of them needs modifying.

Multiple updates can be computerized, though. MySQL provides a feature called *triggers* that make automatic changes to the database in response to changes you make. (Triggers are, however, beyond the scope of this book.) Another way to propagate redundant data is to set up a PHP program to run regularly and keep all copies in sync. The program reads changes from a "master" table and updates all the others. (You'll see how to access MySQL from PHP in the next chapter.)

However, until you are very experienced with MySQL, I recommend that you fully normalize all your tables (at least to First and Second Normal Form), as this will instill the habit and put you in good stead. Only when you actually start to see MySQL logjams should you consider looking at denormalization.

Relationships

MySQL is called a *relational* database management system because its tables store not only data, but the *relationships* among the data. There are three categories of relationships.

One-to-One

A one-to-one relationship is like a (traditional) marriage: each item has a relationship to only one item of the other type. This is surprisingly rare. For instance, an author can write multiple books, a book can have multiple authors, and even an address can be associated with multiple customers. Perhaps the best example in this chapter so far of a one-to-one relationship is the relationship between the name of a state and its two-character abbreviation.

However, for the sake of argument, let's assume that there can only ever be one customer at any address. In such a case, the Customers–Addresses relationship in Figure 9-1 is a one-to-one relationship: only one customer lives at each address, and each address can have only one customer.

Table 9-8a (Customers)		Table 9-8b (Addresses)	
CustNo	Name	Address	Zip
1	Emma Brown ---------------------	1565 Rainbow Road	90014
2	Darren Ryder -----------------------	4758 Emily Drive	23219
3	Earl B. Thurston ---------------------	862 Gregory Lane	40601
4	David Miller----------------------------	3647 Cedar Lane	02154

Figure 9-1. The Customers table, Table 9-8, split into two tables

Usually, when two items have a one-to-one relationship, you just include them as columns in the same table. There are two reasons for splitting them into separate tables:

- You want to be prepared in case the relationship changes later.
- The table has a lot of columns and you think that performance or maintenance would be improved by splitting it.

Of course, when you come to build your own databases in the real world, you will have to create one-to-many Customer–Address relationships (*one* address, *many* customers).

One-to-Many

One-to-many (or many-to-one) relationships occur when one row in one table is linked to many rows in another table. You have already seen how Table 9-8 would take on a one-to-many relationship if multiple customers were allowed at the same address, which is why it would have to be split up if that were the case.

So, looking at Table 9-8a within Figure 9-1, you can see that it shares a one-to-many relationship with Table 9-7 because there is only one of each customer in Table 9-8a. However Table 9-7, the *Purchases* table, can (and does) contain more than one purchase from customers. Therefore *one* customer has a relationship with *many* purchases.

You can see these two tables alongside each other in Figure 9-2, where the dashed lines joining rows in each table start from a single row in the lefthand table but can connect to more than one row on the righthand table. This one-to-many relationship is also the preferred scheme to use when describing a many-to-one relationship, in which case you would normally swap the left and right tables to view them as a one-to-many relationship.

Table 9-8a (Customers)			Table 9-7. (Purchases)		
CustNo	Name		CustNo	ISBN	Date
1	Emma Brown ----------------------- 1			0596101015	Mar 03 2009
2	Darren Ryder ---------------------- 2			0596527403	Dec 19 2008
	----------------- 2			0596101015	Dec 19 2008
3	Earl B. Thurston ----------------------- 3			0596005436	Jun 22 2009
4	David Miller---------------------------- 4			0596006815	Jan 16 2009

Figure 9-2. Illustrating the relationship between two tables

Many-to-Many

In a many-to-many relationship, many rows in one table are linked to many rows in another table. To create this relationship, add a third table containing the same key column from each of the other tables. This third table contains nothing else, as its sole purpose is to link up the other tables.

Table 9-12 is just such a table. It was extracted from Table 9-7, the *Purchases* table, but omits the purchase date information. It contains a copy of the ISBN of every title sold, along with the customer number of each purchaser.

Table 9-12. An intermediary table

Customer	ISBN
1	0596101015
2	0596527403
2	0596101015
3	0596005436
4	0596006815

With this intermediary table in place, you can traverse all the information in the database through a series of relations. You can take an address as a starting point and find out the authors of any books purchased by the customer living at that address.

For example, let's suppose that you want to find out about purchases in the 23219 zip code. Look that zip code up in Table 9-8b, and you'll find that customer number 2 has bought at least one item from the database. At this point, you can use Table 9-8a to find out his or her name, or use the new intermediary Table 9-12 to see the book(s) purchased.

From here, you will find that two titles were purchased and can follow them back to Table 9-4 to find the titles and prices of these books, or to Table 9-3 to see who the authors were.

If it seems to you that this is really combining multiple one-to-many relationships, then you are absolutely correct. To illustrate, Figure 9-3 brings three tables together.

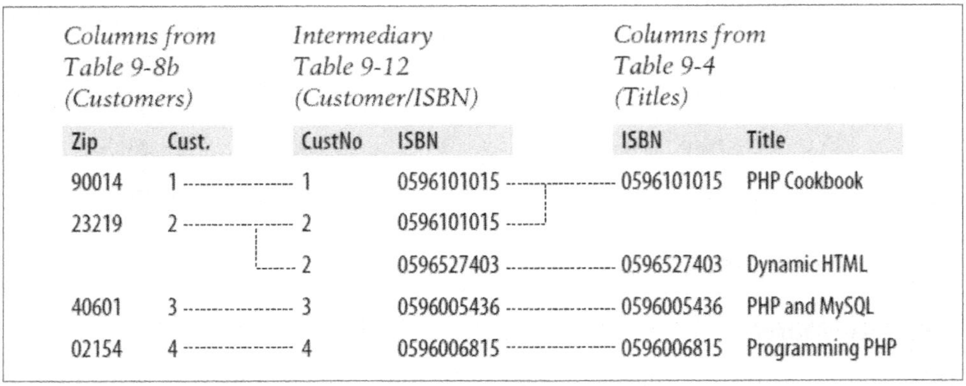

Columns from Table 9-8b (Customers)		Intermediary Table 9-12 (Customer/ISBN)		Columns from Table 9-4 (Titles)	
Zip	Cust.	CustNo	ISBN	ISBN	Title
90014	1 ---------------- 1		0596101015 ----------┐--------	0596101015	PHP Cookbook
23219	2 ---------┐---- 2		0596101015 ------┘		
	└---- 2		0596527403 ----------------	0596527403	Dynamic HTML
40601	3 ---------------- 3		0596005436 ----------------	0596005436	PHP and MySQL
02154	4 ---------------- 4		0596006815 ----------------	0596006815	Programming PHP

Figure 9-3. Creating a many-to-many relationship via a third table

Follow any zip code in the lefthand table to associated customer IDs. From there, you can link to the middle table, which joins the left and right tables by linking customer IDs and ISBNs. Now all you have to do is follow an ISBN over to the righthand table to see which book it relates to.

You can also use the intermediary table to work your way backward from book titles to zip codes. The *Titles* table can tell you the ISBN, which you can use in the middle table to find ID numbers of customers who bought the books, and finally, the *Customers* table matches the customer ID numbers to the customers' zip codes.

Databases and Anonymity

An interesting aspect of using relations is that you can accumulate a lot of information about some item—such as a customer—without actually knowing who that customer is. Note that in the previous example we went from customers' zip codes to customers' purchases, and back again, without finding out the name of a customer. Databases can be used to track people, but they can also be used to help preserve people's privacy while still finding useful information.

Transactions

In some applications, it is vitally important that a sequence of queries runs in the correct order and that every single query successfully completes. For example, suppose that you are creating a sequence of queries to transfer funds from one bank account to another. You would not want either of the following events to occur:

- You add the funds to the second account, but when you try to subtract them from the first account the update fails, and now both accounts have the funds.

- You subtract the funds from the first bank account, but the update request to add them to the second account fails, and the funds have now disappeared into thin air.

As you can see, not only is the order of queries important in this type of transaction, but it is also vital that all parts of the transaction complete successfully. But how can you ensure this happens, because surely after a query has occurred, it cannot be undone? Do you have to keep track of all parts of a transaction and then undo them all one at a time if any one fails? The answer is absolutely not, because MySQL comes with powerful transaction handling features to cover just these types of eventualities.

In addition, transactions allow concurrent access to a database by many users or programs at the same time. MySQL handles this seamlessly by ensuring that all transactions are queued and that users or programs take their turns and don't tread on each other's toes.

Transaction Storage Engines

To be able to use MySQL's transaction facility, you have to be using MySQL's *InnoDB* storage engine. This is easy to do, as it's simply another parameter that you use when creating a table. So go ahead and create a table of bank accounts by typing the commands in Example 9-1. (Remember that to do this you will need access to the MySQL command line, and must also have already selected a suitable database in which to create this table.)

Example 9-1. Creating a transaction-ready table

```
CREATE TABLE accounts (
number INT, balance FLOAT, PRIMARY KEY(number)
) ENGINE InnoDB;
DESCRIBE accounts;
```

The final line of this example displays the contents of the new table so you can ensure that it was correctly created. The output from it should look like this:

```
+---------+----------+------+-----+---------+-------+
| Field   | Type     | Null | Key | Default | Extra |
+---------+----------+------+-----+---------+-------+
| number  | int(11)  | NO   | PRI | 0       |       |
| balance | float    | YES  |     | NULL    |       |
+---------+----------+------+-----+---------+-------+
2 rows in set (0.00 sec)
```

Now let's create two rows within the table so that you can practice using transactions. Enter the commands in Example 9-2.

Example 9-2. Populating the accounts table

```
INSERT INTO accounts(number, balance) VALUES(12345, 1025.50);
INSERT INTO accounts(number, balance) VALUES(67890, 140.00);
SELECT * FROM accounts;
```

The third line displays the contents of the table to confirm that the rows were correctly inserted. The output should look like this:

```
+--------+---------+
| number | balance |
+--------+---------+
|  12345 |  1025.5 |
|  67890 |     140 |
+--------+---------+
2 rows in set (0.00 sec)
```

With this table created and prepopulated, you are now ready to start using transactions.

Using BEGIN

Transactions in MySQL start with either a BEGIN or a START TRANSACTION statement. Type the commands in Example 9-3 to send a transaction to MySQL.

Example 9-3. A MySQL transaction

```
BEGIN;
UPDATE accounts SET balance=balance+25.11 WHERE number=12345;
COMMIT;
SELECT * FROM accounts;
```

The result of this transaction is displayed by the final line, and should look like this:

```
+--------+---------+
| number | balance |
+--------+---------+
|  12345 | 1050.61 |
|  67890 |     140 |
+--------+---------+
2 rows in set (0.00 sec)
```

As you can see, the balance of account number 12345 was increased by 25.11 and is now 1050.61. You may also have noticed the COMMIT command in Example 9-3, which is explained next.

Using COMMIT

When you are satisfied that a series of queries in a transaction has successfully completed, issue a COMMIT command to commit all the changes to the database. Until it receives a COMMIT, MySQL considers all the changes you make to be merely temporary.

This feature gives you the opportunity to cancel a transaction by not sending a COMMIT but by issuing a ROLLBACK command instead.

Using ROLLBACK

Using the ROLLBACK command, you can tell MySQL to forget all the queries made since the start of a transaction and to end the transaction. See this in action by entering the funds transfer transaction in Example 9-4.

Example 9-4. A funds transfer transaction

```
BEGIN;
UPDATE accounts SET balance=balance-250 WHERE number=12345;
UPDATE accounts SET balance=balance+250 WHERE number=67890;
SELECT * FROM accounts;
```

Once you have entered these lines, you should see the following result:

```
+--------+----------+
| number | balance  |
+--------+----------+
|  12345 |   800.61 |
|  67890 |      390 |
+--------+----------+
2 rows in set (0.00 sec)
```

The first bank account now has a value that is 250 less than before, and the second has been incremented by 250; you have transferred a value of 250 between them. But let's assume that something went wrong and you wish to undo this transaction. All you have to do is issue the commands in Example 9-5.

Example 9-5. Canceling a transaction using ROLLBACK

```
ROLLBACK;
SELECT * FROM accounts;
```

You should now see the following output, showing that the two accounts have had their previous balances restored, due to the entire transaction being canceled via the ROLL BACK command:

```
+--------+----------+
| number | balance  |
+--------+----------+
|  12345 |  1050.61 |
|  67890 |      140 |
+--------+----------+
2 rows in set (0.00 sec)
```

Using EXPLAIN

MySQL comes with a powerful tool for investigating how the queries you issue to it are interpreted. Using EXPLAIN, you can get a snapshot of any query to find out whether you could issue it in a better or more efficient way. Example 9-6 shows how to use it with the accounts table you created earlier.

Example 9-6. Using the EXPLAIN command

```
EXPLAIN SELECT * FROM accounts WHERE number='12345';
```

The results of this EXPLAIN command should look like the following:

```
+--+-----------+--------+-----+-------------+-------+-------+----+----+-----+
|id|select_type|table   |type |possible_keys|key    |key_len|ref |rows|Extra|
+--+-----------+--------+-----+-------------+-------+-------+----+----+-----+
| 1|SIMPLE     |accounts|const|PRIMARY      |PRIMARY|4      |const|  1|     |
+--+-----------+--------+-----+-------------+-------+-------+----+----+-----+
1 row in set (0.00 sec)
```

The information that MySQL is giving you here is as follows:

select_type
> The selection type is SIMPLE. If you were joining tables together, this would show the join type.

table
> The current table being queried is accounts.

type
> The query type is const. From worst to best, the possible values can be ALL, index, range, ref, eq_ref, const, system, and NULL.

possible_keys
> There is a possible PRIMARY key, which means that accessing should be fast.

key
> The key actually used is PRIMARY. This is good.

key_len
> The key length is 4. This is the number of bytes of the index that MySQL will use.

ref
> The ref column displays which columns or constants are used with the key. In this case, a constant key is being used.

rows
> The number of rows that needs to be searched by this query is 1. This is good.

Whenever you have a query that seems to be taking longer than you think it should to execute, try using EXPLAIN to see where you can optimize it. You will discover which keys (if any) are being used, their lengths, and so on, and will be able to adjust your query or the design of your table(s) accordingly.

 When you have finished experimenting with the temporary *accounts* table, you may wish to remove it by entering the following command:

```
DROP TABLE accounts;
```

Backing Up and Restoring

Whatever kind of data you are storing in your database, it must have some value to you, even if it's only the cost of the time required for reentering it should the hard disk fail. Therefore, it's important that you keep backups to protect your investment. Also, there will be times when you have to migrate your database over to a new server; the best way to do this is usually to back it up first. It is also important that you test your backups from time to time to ensure that they are valid and will work if they need to be used.

Thankfully, backing up and restoring MySQL data is easy with the mysqldump command.

Using mysqldump

With mysqldump, you can dump a database or collection of databases into one or more files containing all the instructions necessary to re-create all your tables and repopulate them with your data. It can also generate files in *CSV (Comma-Separated Values)* and other delimited text formats, or even in XML format. Its main drawback is that you must make sure that no one writes to a table while you're backing it up. There are various ways to do this, but the easiest is to shut down the MySQL server before mysqldump and start up the server again after mysqldump finishes.

Or you can lock the tables you are backing up before running mysqldump. To lock tables for reading (as we want to read the data), issue the following command from the MySQL command line:

```
LOCK TABLES tablename1 READ, tablename2 READ ...
```

Then, to release the lock(s), enter:

```
UNLOCK TABLES;
```

By default, the output from mysqldump is simply printed out, but you can capture it in a file through the > redirect symbol.

The basic format of the `mysqldump` command is:

```
mysqldump -u user -ppassword database
```

However, before you can dump the contents of a database, you must make sure that `mysqldump` is in your path, or that you specify its location as part of your command. Table 9-13 shows the likely locations of the program for the different installations and operating systems covered in Chapter 2. If you have a different installation, it may be in a slightly different location.

 If you are using OS X with `mysqldump` and receive the error 2002: `Can't connect to local MySQL server through socket '/tmp/mysql.sock' (2)` when trying to connect, you may be able to remedy this by issuing the following instruction:

```
ln -s /usr/local/zend/mysql/tmp/mysql.sock /tmp/mysql.sock
```

Table 9-13. Likely locations of mysqldump for different installations

Operating System & Program	Likely folder location
Windows 32-bit Zend Server	*C:\Program Files\Zend\MySQL55\bin*
Windows 64-bit Zend Server	*C:\Program Files (x86)\Zend\MySQL55\bin*
OS X Zend Server	*/usr/local/zend/mysql/bin*
Linux Zend Server	*/usr/local/zend/mysql/bin*

So, to dump the contents of the *publications* database that you created in Chapter 8 to the screen, enter `mysqldump` (or the full path if necessary) and the command in Example 9-7.

Example 9-7. Dumping the publications database to screen

```
mysqldump -u user -ppassword publications
```

Make sure that you replace *user* and *password* with the correct details for your installation of MySQL. If there is no password set for the user, you can omit that part of the command, but the `-u user` part is mandatory—unless you have root access without a password and are executing as root (not recommended). The result of issuing this command will look something like Figure 9-4.

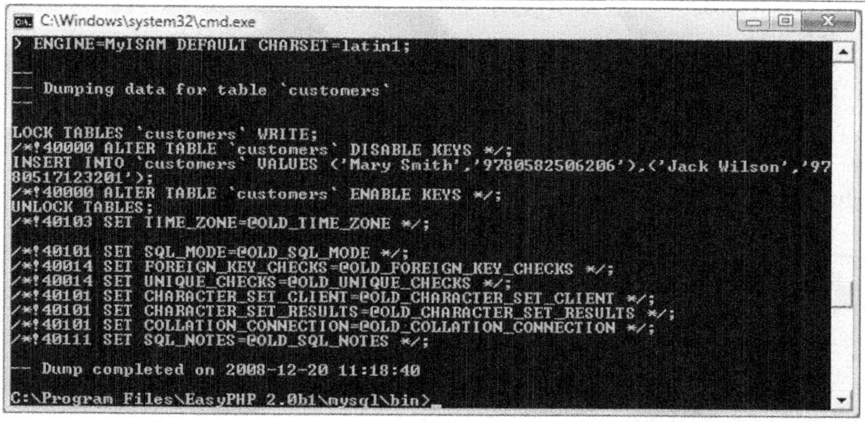

```
C:\Windows\system32\cmd.exe
> ENGINE=MyISAM DEFAULT CHARSET=latin1;


-- Dumping data for table `customers`

LOCK TABLES `customers` WRITE;
/*!40000 ALTER TABLE `customers` DISABLE KEYS */;
INSERT INTO `customers` VALUES ('Mary Smith','9780582506206'),('Jack Wilson','97
80517123201');
/*!40000 ALTER TABLE `customers` ENABLE KEYS */;
UNLOCK TABLES;
/*!40103 SET TIME_ZONE=@OLD_TIME_ZONE */;

/*!40101 SET SQL_MODE=@OLD_SQL_MODE */;
/*!40014 SET FOREIGN_KEY_CHECKS=@OLD_FOREIGN_KEY_CHECKS */;
/*!40014 SET UNIQUE_CHECKS=@OLD_UNIQUE_CHECKS */;
/*!40101 SET CHARACTER_SET_CLIENT=@OLD_CHARACTER_SET_CLIENT */;
/*!40101 SET CHARACTER_SET_RESULTS=@OLD_CHARACTER_SET_RESULTS */;
/*!40101 SET COLLATION_CONNECTION=@OLD_COLLATION_CONNECTION */;
/*!40111 SET SQL_NOTES=@OLD_SQL_NOTES */;

-- Dump completed on 2008-12-20 11:18:40

C:\Program Files\EasyPHP 2.0b1\mysql\bin>
```

Figure 9-4. Dumping the publications database to screen

Creating a Backup File

Now that you have mysqldump working, and have verified it outputs correctly to the screen, you can send the backup data directly to a file using the > redirect symbol. Assuming that you wish to call the backup file *publications.sql*, type the command in Example 9-8 (remembering to replace *user* and *password* with the correct details).

Example 9-8. Dumping the publications database to file

```
mysqldump -u user -ppassword publications > publications.sql
```

The command in Example 9-8 stores the backup file into the current directory. If you need it to be saved elsewhere, you should insert a file path before the filename. You must also ensure that the directory you are backing up to has the right permissions set to allow the file to be written.

If you echo the backup file to screen or load it into a text editor, you will see that it comprises sequences of SQL commands such as the following:

```
DROP TABLE IF EXISTS `classics`;
CREATE TABLE `classics` (
  `author` varchar(128) default NULL,
  `title` varchar(128) default NULL,
  `category` varchar(16) default NULL,
  `year` smallint(6) default NULL,
  `isbn` char(13) NOT NULL default '',
  PRIMARY KEY  (`isbn`),
  KEY `author` (`author`(20)),
  KEY `title` (`title`(20)),
```

```
KEY `category` (`category`(4)),
KEY `year` (`year`),
FULLTEXT KEY `author_2` (`author`,`title`)
) ENGINE=MyISAM DEFAULT CHARSET=latin1;
```

This is smart code that can be used to restore a database from a backup, even if it currently exists, because it will first drop any tables that need to be re-created, thus avoiding potential MySQL errors.

Backing up a single table

To back up only a single table from a database (such as the *classics* table from the *publications* database), you should first lock the table from within the MySQL command line, by issuing a command such as the following:

```
LOCK TABLES publications.classics READ;
```

This ensures that MySQL remains running for read purposes, but writes cannot be made. Then, while keeping the MySQL command line open, use another terminal window to issue the following command from the operating system command line:

```
mysqldump -u user -ppassword publications classics > classics.sql
```

You must now release the table lock by entering the following command from the MySQL command line in the first terminal window, which unlocks all tables that have been locked during the current session:

```
UNLOCK TABLES;
```

Backing up all tables

If you want to back up all your MySQL databases at once (including the system databases such as *mysql*), you can use a command such as the one in Example 9-9, which would enable you to restore an entire MySQL database installation. Remember to use locking where required.

Example 9-9. Dumping all the MySQL databases to file

```
mysqldump -u user -ppassword --all-databases > all_databases.sql
```

 Of course, there's a lot more than just a few lines of SQL code in backed-up database files. I recommend that you take a few minutes to examine a couple in order to familiarize yourself with the types of commands that appear in backup files and how they work.

Restoring from a Backup File

To perform a restore from a file, call the *mysql* executable, passing it the file to restore from using the < symbol. So, to recover an entire database that you dumped using the *--all-databases* option, use a command such as that in Example 9-10.

Example 9-10. Restoring an entire set of databases

```
mysql -u user -ppassword < all_databases.sql
```

To restore a single database, use the -D option followed by the name of the database, as in Example 9-11, where the *publications* database is being restored from the backup made in Example 9-8.

Example 9-11. Restoring the publications database

```
mysql -u user -ppassword -D publications < publications.sql
```

To restore a single table to a database, use a command such as that in Example 9-12, where just the *classics* table is being restored to the *publications* database.

Example 9-12. Restoring the classics table to the publications database

```
mysql -u user -ppassword -D publications < classics.sql
```

Dumping Data in CSV Format

As previously mentioned, the `mysqldump` program is very flexible and supports various types of output, such as the CSV format. Example 9-13 shows how you can dump the data from the *classics* and *customers* tables in the *publications* database to the files *classics.txt* and *customers.txt* in the folder *c:/temp*. By default, on Zend Server the user should be *root* and no password is used. On OS X or Linux systems, you should modify the destination path to an existing folder.

Example 9-13. Dumping data to CSV format files

```
mysqldump -u user -ppassword --no-create-info --tab=c:/temp
  --fields-terminated-by=',' publications
```

This command is quite long and is shown here wrapped over several lines, but you must type it all as a single line. The result is the following:

```
Mark Twain (Samuel Langhorne Clemens)','The Adventures
of Tom Sawyer','Classic Fiction','1876','9781598184891
Jane Austen','Pride and Prejudice','Classic Fiction','1811','9780582506206
Charles Darwin','The Origin of Species','Non-Fiction','1856','9780517123201
Charles Dickens','The Old Curiosity Shop','Classic Fiction','1841','9780099533474
William Shakespeare','Romeo and Juliet','Play','1594','9780192814968

Mary Smith','9780582506206
Jack Wilson','9780517123201
```

Planning Your Backups

The golden rule to backing up is to do so as often as you find practical. The more valuable the data, the more often you should back it up, and the more copies you should make. If your database gets updated at least once a day, you should really back it up on a daily basis. If, on the other hand, it is not updated very often, you could probably get by with less frequent backups.

 You should also consider making multiple backups and storing them in different locations. If you have several servers, it is a simple matter to copy your backups between them. You would also be well advised to make physical backups of removable hard disks, thumb drives, CDs or DVDs, and so on, and to keep these in separate locations—preferably somewhere like a fireproof safe.

Once you've digested the contents of this chapter, you will be proficient in using both PHP and MySQL; the next chapter will show you how to bring these two technologies together.

Questions

1. What does the word *relationship* mean in reference to a relational database?
2. What is the term for the process of removing duplicate data and optimizing tables?
3. What are the three rules of the First Normal Form?
4. How can you make a table satisfy the Second Normal Form?
5. What do you put in a column to tie together two tables that contain items having a one-to-many relationship?
6. How can you create a database with a many-to-many relationship?
7. What commands initiate and end a MySQL transaction?
8. What feature does MySQL provide to enable you to examine how a query will work in detail?
9. What command would you use to back up the database *publications* to a file called *publications.sql*?

See "Chapter 9 Answers" on page 645 in Appendix A for the answers to these questions.

CHAPTER 10

Accessing MySQL Using PHP

If you worked through the previous chapters, you're proficient in using both MySQL and PHP. In this chapter, you will learn how to integrate the two by using PHP's built-in functions to access MySQL.

Querying a MySQL Database with PHP

The reason for using PHP as an interface to MySQL is to format the results of SQL queries in a form visible in a web page. As long as you can log into your MySQL installation using your username and password, you can also do so from PHP. However, instead of using MySQL's command line to enter instructions and view output, you will create query strings that are passed to MySQL. When MySQL returns its response, it will come as a data structure that PHP can recognize instead of the formatted output you see when you work on the command line. Further PHP commands can retrieve the data and format it for the web page.

 To get you started, in this chapter I use the standard, procedural `mysql` function calls, so that you'll be up and running quickly, and able to maintain older PHP code. However, the new object-oriented `mysqli` functions (the `i` stands for improved) are becoming the recommended way to interface with MySQL from PHP, so in the following chapter I'll show you how to use these too (or instead, because the old functions have become deprecated and could be removed from PHP at some point).

The Process

The process of using MySQL with PHP is:

1. Connect to MySQL.
2. Select the database to use.
3. Build a query string.
4. Perform the query.
5. Retrieve the results and output them to a web page.
6. Repeat Steps 3 to 5 until all desired data has been retrieved.
7. Disconnect from MySQL.

We'll work through these sections in turn, but first it's important to set up your login details in a secure manner so people snooping around on your system have trouble getting access to your database.

Creating a Login File

Most websites developed with PHP contain multiple program files that will require access to MySQL and will thus need the login and password details. Therefore, it's sensible to create a single file to store these and then include that file wherever it's needed. Example 10-1 shows such a file, which I've called *login.php*. Type the example, replacing placeholder values (such as *username*) with the actual values you use for your MySQL database, and save it to the web development directory you set up in Chapter 2. We'll be making use of the file shortly. The hostname localhost should work as long as you're using a MySQL database on your local system, and the database *publications* should work if you're typing the examples I've used so far.

Example 10-1. The login.php file

```
<?php // login.php
  $db_hostname = 'localhost';
  $db_database = 'publications';
  $db_username = 'username';
  $db_password = 'password';
?>
```

The enclosing <?php and ?> tags are especially important for the *login.php* file in Example 10-1, because they mean that the lines between can be interpreted *only* as PHP code. If you were to leave them out and someone were to call up the file directly from your website, it would display as text and reveal your secrets. But, with the tags in place, all that person will see is a blank page. The file will correctly include in your other PHP files.

The $db_hostname variable will tell PHP which computer to use when connecting to a database. This is required, because you can access MySQL databases on any computer connected to your PHP installation, and that potentially includes any host anywhere on the Web. However, the examples in this chapter will be working on the local server. So, in place of specifying a domain such as *mysql.myserver.com*, you can just use the word localhost (or the IP address 127.0.0.1).

The database we'll be using, $db_database, is the one called *publications*, which you probably created in Chapter 8, or the one you were provided with by your server administrator (in which case you have to modify *login.php* accordingly).

The variables $db_username and $db_password should be set to the username and password that you have been using with MySQL.

 Another benefit of keeping these login details in a single place is that you can change your password as frequently as you like and there will be only one file to update when you do, no matter how many PHP files access MySQL.

Connecting to MySQL

Now that you have the *login.php* file saved, you can include it in any PHP files that will need to access the database by using the require_once statement. This is preferable to an include statement, as it will generate a fatal error if the file is not found. And believe me, not finding the file containing the login details to your database *is* a fatal error.

Also, using require_once instead of require means that the file will be read in only when it has not previously been included, which prevents wasteful duplicate disk accesses. Example 10-2 shows the code to use.

Example 10-2. Connecting to a MySQL server

```php
<?php
  require_once 'login.php';
  $db_server = mysql_connect($db_hostname, $db_username, $db_password);

  if (!$db_server) die("Unable to connect to MySQL: " . mysql_error());
?>
```

This example runs PHP's mysql_connect function, which requires three parameters: the *hostname*, *username*, and *password* of a MySQL server. Upon success it returns an *identifier* to the server; otherwise, FALSE is returned. Notice that the second line uses an if statement with the die function, which does what it sounds like and quits from PHP with an error message if $db_server is not TRUE.

The die message explains that it was not possible to connect to the MySQL database, and—to help identify why this happened—includes a call to the mysql_error function. This function outputs the error text from the last called MySQL function.

The database server pointer $db_server will be used in some of the following examples to identify the MySQL server to be queried. By using identifiers this way, we can connect to and access multiple MySQL servers from a single PHP program.

 The die function is great for when you are developing PHP code, but of course you will want more user-friendly error messages on a production server. In this case you won't abort your PHP program, but format a message that will be displayed when the program exits normally, such as:

```
function mysql_fatal_error($msg)
{
    $msg2 = mysql_error();
    echo <<< _END
We are sorry, but it was not possible to complete
the requested task. The error message we got was:

    <p>$msg: $msg2</p>

Please click the back button on your browser
and try again. If you are still having problems,
please <a href="mailto:admin@server.com">email
our administrator</a>. Thank you.
_END;
}
```

Selecting a database

Having successfully connected to MySQL, you are now ready to select the database that you will be using. Example 10-3 shows how to do this.

Example 10-3. Selecting a database

```
<?php
  mysql_select_db($db_database)
    or die("Unable to select database: " . mysql_error());
?>
```

The command to select the database is mysql_select_db. Pass it the name of the database you want and the server to which you connected. As with the previous example, a die statement has been included to provide an error message and explanation, should the selection fail—the only difference being that there is no need to retain the return value from the mysql_select_db function, as it simply returns either TRUE or FALSE. Therefore the PHP or statement was used, which means "if the previous command failed, do the following." Note that for the or to work, there must be no semicolon at the end of the first line of code.

Building and executing a query

Sending a query to MySQL from PHP is as simple as issuing it using the `mysql_query` function. Example 10-4 shows you how to use it.

Example 10-4. Querying a database

```php
<?php
  $query  = "SELECT * FROM classics";
  $result = mysql_query($query);

  if (!$result) die ("Database access failed: " . mysql_error());
?>
```

First, the variable `$query` is set to the query to be made. In this case, it is asking to see all rows in the table *classics*. Note that, unlike with MySQL's command line, no semicolon is required at the tail of the query, because the `mysql_query` function is used to issue a complete query; it cannot be used for queries sent in multiple parts, one at a time. Therefore, MySQL knows the query is complete and doesn't look for a semicolon.

This function returns a result that we place in the variable `$result`. Having used MySQL at the command line, you might think that the contents of `$result` will be the same as the result returned from a command-line query, with horizontal and vertical lines, and so on. However, this is not the case with the result returned to PHP. Instead, upon success, `$result` will contain a *resource* that can be used to extract the results of the query. You'll see how to extract the data in the next section. Upon failure, `$result` contains `FALSE`. So the example finishes by checking `$result`. If it's `FALSE`, it means that there was an error, and the `die` command is executed.

Fetching a result

Once you have a resource returned from a `mysql_query` function, you can use it to retrieve the data you want. The simplest way to do this is to fetch the cells you want, one at a time, using the `mysql_result` function. Example 10-5 combines and extends the previous examples into a program that you can type and run yourself to retrieve the returned results. I suggest that you save it in the same folder as *login.php* and give it the name *query.php*.

Example 10-5. Fetching results one cell at a time

```php
<?php // query.php
  require_once 'login.php';
  $db_server = mysql_connect($db_hostname, $db_username, $db_password);

  if (!$db_server) die("Unable to connect to MySQL: " . mysql_error());

  mysql_select_db($db_database)
    or die("Unable to select database: " . mysql_error());
```

```
$query  = "SELECT * FROM classics";
$result = mysql_query($query);

if (!$result) die ("Database access failed: " . mysql_error());

$rows = mysql_num_rows($result);

for ($j = 0 ; $j < $rows ; ++$j)
{
  echo 'Author: '   . mysql_result($result,$j,'author')   . '<br>';
  echo 'Title: '    . mysql_result($result,$j,'title')    . '<br>';
  echo 'Category: ' . mysql_result($result,$j,'category') . '<br>';
  echo 'Year: '     . mysql_result($result,$j,'year')     . '<br>';
  echo 'ISBN: '     . mysql_result($result,$j,'isbn')     . '<br><br>';
}
?>
```

The final 10 lines of code are the new ones, so let's look at them. They start by setting the variable $rows to the value returned by a call to mysql_num_rows. This function reports the number of rows returned by a query.

Armed with the row count, we enter a for loop that extracts each cell of data from each row using the mysql_result function. The parameters supplied to this function are the resource $result, which was returned by mysql_query, the row number $j, and the name of the column from which to extract the data.

The results from each call to mysql_result are then incorporated within echo statements to display one field per line, with an additional line feed between rows. Figure 10-1 shows the result of running this program.

As you may recall, we populated the *classics* table with five rows in Chapter 8, and indeed, five rows of data are returned by *query.php*. But, as it stands, this code is actually extremely inefficient and slow, because a total of 25 calls are made to the function mysql_result in order to retrieve all the data, a single cell at a time. Luckily, there is a much better way of retrieving the data, which is getting a single row at a time using the mysql_fetch_row function.

 In Chapter 9, I talked about First, Second, and Third Normal Form, so you may have now noticed that the *classics* table doesn't satisfy these, because both author and book details are included within the same table. That's because we created this table before encountering normalization. However, for the purposes of illustrating access to MySQL from PHP, reusing this table avoids the hassle of typing in a new set of test data, so we'll stick with it for the time being.

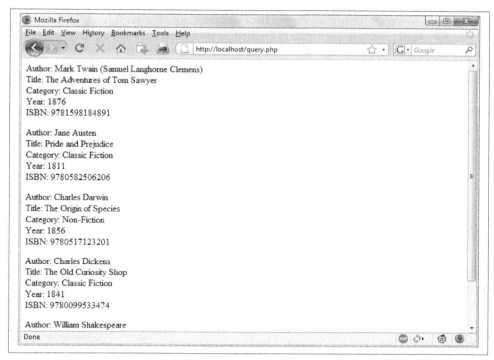

Figure 10-1. The output from the query.php program in Example 10-5

Fetching a row

It was important to show how you can fetch a single cell of data from MySQL, but now let's look at a much more efficient method. Replace the `for` loop of *query.php* (in Example 10-5) with the new loop in Example 10-6, and you will find that you get exactly the same result that was displayed in Figure 10-1.

Example 10-6. Replacement for loop for fetching results one row at a time

```php
<?php
  for ($j = 0 ; $j < $rows ; ++$j)
  {
    $row = mysql_fetch_row($result);

    echo 'Author: ' .    $row[0] . '<br>';
    echo 'Title: ' .     $row[1] . '<br>';
    echo 'Category: ' .  $row[2] . '<br>';
    echo 'Year: ' .      $row[3] . '<br>';
    echo 'ISBN: ' .      $row[4] . '<br><br>';
  }
?>
```

In this modified code, only one-fifth of the calls are made to a MySQL-calling function (a full 80% less), because each row is fetched in its entirety via the `mysql_fetch_row` function. This returns a single row of data in an array, which is then assigned to the variable `$row`.

All that's necessary, then, is to reference each element of the array `$row` in turn (starting at an offset of 0). Therefore `$row[0]` contains the *Author* data, `$row[1]` the *Title*, and so on, because each column is placed in the array in the order in which it appears in the MySQL table. Also, by using `mysql_fetch_row` instead of `mysql_result`, you use substantially less PHP code and achieve much faster execution time, due to simply referencing each item of data by offset rather than by name.

Closing a connection

When you have finished using a database, you should close the connection. You do so by issuing the command in Example 10-7.

Example 10-7. Closing a MySQL server connection

```
<?php
  mysql_close($db_server);
?>
```

We have to pass the identifier returned by `mysql_connect` back in Example 10-2, which we stored in the variable `$db_server`.

> All database connections are automatically closed when PHP exits, so it doesn't matter that the connection wasn't closed in Example 10-5. But in longer programs, where you may continually open and close database connections, you are strongly advised to close each one as soon as you're finished accessing it.

A Practical Example

It's time to write our first example of inserting data in and deleting it from a MySQL table using PHP. I recommend that you type Example 10-8 and save it to your web development directory using the filename *sqltest.php*. You can see an example of the program's output in Figure 10-2.

> Example 10-8 creates a standard HTML form. Chapter 12 explains forms in detail, but in this chapter I take form handling for granted and just deal with database interaction.

Example 10-8. Inserting and deleting using sqltest.php

```php
<?php // sqltest.php
  require_once 'login.php';
  $db_server = mysql_connect($db_hostname, $db_username, $db_password);

  if (!$db_server) die("Unable to connect to MySQL: " . mysql_error());

  mysql_select_db($db_database, $db_server)
    or die("Unable to select database: " . mysql_error());

  if (isset($_POST['delete']) && isset($_POST['isbn']))
  {
    $isbn  = get_post('isbn');
    $query = "DELETE FROM classics WHERE isbn='$isbn'";

    if (!mysql_query($query, $db_server))
      echo "DELETE failed: $query<br>" .
      mysql_error() . "<br><br>";
  }

  if (isset($_POST['author']) &&
      isset($_POST['title']) &&
      isset($_POST['category']) &&
      isset($_POST['year']) &&
      isset($_POST['isbn']))
  {
    $author   = get_post('author');
    $title    = get_post('title');
    $category = get_post('category');
    $year     = get_post('year');
    $isbn     = get_post('isbn');

    $query = "INSERT INTO classics VALUES" .
      "('$author', '$title', '$category', '$year', '$isbn')";

    if (!mysql_query($query, $db_server))
      echo "INSERT failed: $query<br>" .
      mysql_error() . "<br><br>";
  }

  echo <<<_END
  <form action="sqltest.php" method="post"><pre>
    Author <input type="text" name="author">
     Title <input type="text" name="title">
  Category <input type="text" name="category">
      Year <input type="text" name="year">
      ISBN <input type="text" name="isbn">
           <input type="submit" value="ADD RECORD">
  </pre></form>
_END;

  $query  = "SELECT * FROM classics";
```

```
$result = mysql_query($query);

if (!$result) die ("Database access failed: " . mysql_error());
$rows = mysql_num_rows($result);

for ($j = 0 ; $j < $rows ; ++$j)
{
  $row = mysql_fetch_row($result);
  echo <<<_END
<pre>
  Author $row[0]
   Title $row[1]
Category $row[2]
    Year $row[3]
    ISBN $row[4]
</pre>
<form action="sqltest.php" method="post">
<input type="hidden" name="delete" value="yes">
<input type="hidden" name="isbn" value="$row[4]">
<input type="submit" value="DELETE RECORD"></form>
_END;
  }

  mysql_close($db_server);

  function get_post($var)
  {
    return mysql_real_escape_string($_POST[$var]);
  }
?>
```

At over 80 lines of code, this program may appear daunting, but don't worry—you've already covered many of them in Example 10-5, and what the code does is actually quite simple.

It first checks for any inputs that may have been made and then either inserts new data into the table *classics* of the *publications* database or deletes a row from it, according to the input supplied. Regardless of whether there was input, the program then outputs all rows in the table to the browser. So let's see how it works.

The first section of new code starts by using the isset function to check whether values for all the fields have been posted to the program. Upon confirmation, each of the lines within the if statement calls the function get_post, which appears at the end of the program. This function has one small but critical job: fetching the input from the browser.

Figure 10-2. The output from Example 10-8, sqltest.php

The $_POST Array

I mentioned in an earlier chapter that a browser sends user input through either a GET request or a POST request. The POST request is usually preferred, and we use it here. The web server bundles up all of the user input (even if the form was filled out with a hundred fields) and puts in into an array named $_POST.

$_POST is an associative array, which you encountered in Chapter 6. Depending on whether a form has been set to use the POST or the GET method, either the $_POST or the $_GET associative array will be populated with the form data. They can both be read in exactly the same way.

Each field has an element in the array named after that field. So, if a form contained a field named isbn, the $_POST array contains an element keyed by the word isbn. The PHP program can read that field by referring to either $_POST['isbn'] or $_POST["isbn"] (single and double quotes have the same effect in this case).

If the $_POST syntax still seems complex to you, rest assured that you can just use the convention I've shown in Example 10-8, copy the user's input to other variables, and forget about $_POST after that. This is normal in PHP programs: they retrieve all the fields from $_POST at the beginning of the program and then ignore it.

 There is no reason to write to an element in the $_POST array. Its only purpose is to communicate information from the browser to the program, and you're better off copying data to your own variables before altering it.

So, back to the get_post function: it passes each item it retrieves through the mysql_real_escape_string function to strip out any characters that a hacker may have inserted in order to break into or alter your database.

Deleting a Record

Prior to checking whether new data has been posted, the program checks whether the variable $_POST['delete'] has a value. If so, the user has clicked on the DELETE RECORD button to erase a record. In this case, the value of $isbn will also have been posted.

As you'll recall, the ISBN uniquely identifies each record. The HTML form appends the ISBN to the DELETE FROM query string created in the variable $query, which is then passed to the mysql_query function to issue it to MySQL. mysql_query returns either TRUE or FALSE, and FALSE causes an error message to be displayed explaining what went wrong.

If $_POST['delete']) is not set (and there is therefore no record to be deleted), $_POST['author']) and other posted values are checked. If they have all been given values, then $query is set to an INSERT INTO command, followed by the five values to be inserted. The variable is then passed to mysql_query, which upon completion returns either TRUE or FALSE. If FALSE is returned, an error message is displayed.

Displaying the Form

Next we get to the part of code that displays the little form at the top of Figure 10-2. You should recall the echo <<<_END structure from previous chapters, which outputs everything between the _END tags.

Instead of the echo command, the program could also drop out of PHP using ?>, issue the HTML, and then reenter PHP processing with <?php. Whichever style used is a matter of programmer preference, but I always recommend staying within PHP code for these reasons:

- It makes it very clear when debugging (and also for other users) that everything within a *.php* file is PHP code. Therefore, there is no need to go hunting for dropouts to HTML.

- When you wish to include a PHP variable directly within HTML, you can just type it. If you had dropped back to HTML, you would have had to temporarily reenter PHP processing, output the variable, and then drop back out again.

The HTML form section simply sets the form's action to *sqltest.php*. This means that when the form is submitted, the contents of the form fields will be sent to the file *sqltest.php*, which is the program itself. The form is also set up to send the fields as a POST rather than a GET request. This is because GET requests are appended to the URL being submitted to and can look messy in your browser. They also allow users to easily modify submissions and try to hack your server. Therefore, whenever possible, you should use POST submissions, which also have the benefit of hiding the posted data from view.

Having output the form fields, the HTML displays a Submit button with the name ADD RECORD and closes the form. Note the use of the <pre> and </pre> tags here, which have been used to force a monospaced font and allow all the inputs to line up neatly. The carriage returns at the end of each line are also output when inside <pre> tags.

Querying the Database

Next, the code returns to the familiar territory of Example 10-5 where, in the following four lines of code, a query is sent to MySQL asking to see all the records in the *classics* table. After that, $rows is set to a value representing the number of rows in the table and a for loop is entered to display the contents of each row.

I have altered the next bit of code to simplify things. Instead of using the <br> tags for line feeds in Example 10-5, I have chosen to use a <pre> tag to line up the display of each record in a pleasing manner.

After the display of each record, there is a second form that also posts to *sqltest.php* (the program itself) but this time contains two hidden fields: delete and isbn. The delete field is set to "yes" and isbn to the value held in $row[4], which contains the ISBN for the record. Then a Submit button with the name DELETE RECORD is displayed and the form is closed. A curly brace then completes the for loop, which will continue until all records have been displayed.

Finally, you see the definition for the function `get_post`, which we've already looked at. And that's it—our first PHP program to manipulate a MySQL database. So, let's check out what it can do.

Once you have typed the program (and corrected any typing errors), try entering the following data into the various input fields to add a new record for the book *Moby Dick* to the database:

```
Herman Melville
Moby Dick
Fiction
1851
9780199535729
```

Running the Program

When you have submitted this data using the ADD RECORD button, scroll down to the bottom of the web page to see the new addition. It should look like Figure 10-3.

Figure 10-3. The result of adding Moby Dick to the database

Now let's look at how deleting a record works by creating a dummy record. So try entering just the number 1 in each of the five fields and click on the ADD RECORD button. If you now scroll down, you'll see a new record consisting just of 1s. Obviously this record isn't useful in this table, so now click on the DELETE RECORD button and scroll down again to confirm that the record has been deleted.

 Assuming that everything worked, you are now able to add and delete records at will. Try doing this a few times, but leave the main records in place (including the new one for *Moby Dick*), as we'll be using them later. You could also try adding the record with all 1s again a couple of times and note the error message that you receive the second time, indicating that there is already an ISBN with the number 1.

Practical MySQL

You are now ready to look at some practical techniques that you can use in PHP to access the MySQL database, including tasks such as creating and dropping tables; inserting, updating, and deleting data; and protecting your database and website from malicious users. Note that the following examples assume that you've created the *login.php* program discussed earlier in this chapter.

Creating a Table

Let's assume you are working for a wildlife park and need to create a database to hold details about all the types of cats it houses. You are told that there are nine *families* of cats—Lion, Tiger, Jaguar, Leopard, Cougar, Cheetah, Lynx, Caracal, and Domestic—so you'll need a column for that. Then each cat has been given a *name*, so that's another column, and you also want to keep track of their *ages*, which is another. Of course, you will probably need more columns later, perhaps to hold dietary requirements, inoculations, and other details, but for now that's enough to get going. A unique identifier is also needed for each animal, so you also decide to create a column for that called *id*.

Example 10-9 shows the code you might use to create a MySQL table to hold this data, with the main query assignment in bold text.

Example 10-9. Creating a table called cats

```php
<?php
  require_once 'login.php';
  $db_server = mysql_connect($db_hostname, $db_username, $db_password);

  if (!$db_server) die("Unable to connect to MySQL: " . mysql_error());

  mysql_select_db($db_database)
    or die("Unable to select database: " . mysql_error());
```

```
$query = "CREATE TABLE cats (
  id SMALLINT NOT NULL AUTO_INCREMENT,
  family VARCHAR(32) NOT NULL,
  name VARCHAR(32) NOT NULL,
  age TINYINT NOT NULL,
  PRIMARY KEY (id)
)";

$result = mysql_query($query);

if (!$result) die ("Database access failed: " . mysql_error());
?>
```

As you can see, the MySQL query looks pretty similar to how you would type it directly in the command line, except that there is no trailing semicolon, as none is needed when you are accessing MySQL from PHP.

Describing a Table

When you aren't logged into the MySQL command line, here's a handy piece of code that you can use to verify that a table has been correctly created from inside a browser. It simply issues the query DESCRIBE cats and then outputs an HTML table with four headings—*Column*, *Type*, *Null*, and *Key*—underneath which all columns within the table are shown. To use it with other tables, simply replace the name cats in the query with that of the new table (see Example 10-10).

Example 10-10. Describing the table cats

```
<?php
  require_once 'login.php';
  $db_server = mysql_connect($db_hostname, $db_username, $db_password);

  if (!$db_server) die("Unable to connect to MySQL: " . mysql_error());

  mysql_select_db($db_database)
    or die("Unable to select database: " . mysql_error());

  $query  = "DESCRIBE cats";
  $result = mysql_query($query);

  if (!$result) die ("Database access failed: " . mysql_error());

  $rows = mysql_num_rows($result);

  echo "<table><tr><th>Column</th><th>Type</th><th>Null</th><th>Key</th></tr>";

  for ($j = 0 ; $j < $rows ; ++$j)
  {
    $row = mysql_fetch_row($result);
    echo "<tr>";
```

```php
  for ($k = 0 ; $k < 4 ; ++$k)
    echo "<td>$row[$k]</td>";

  echo "</tr>";
  }

  echo "</table>";
?>
```

The output from the program should look like this:

```
Column Type        Null Key
id     smallint(6) NO   PRI
family varchar(32) NO
name   varchar(32) NO
age    tinyint(4)  NO
```

Dropping a Table

Dropping a table is very easy to do and is therefore very dangerous, so be careful. Example 10-11 shows the code that you need. However, I don't recommend that you try it until you have been through the other examples, as it will drop the table *cats* and you'll have to re-create it using Example 10-9.

Example 10-11. Dropping the table cats

```php
<?php
  require_once 'login.php';
  $db_server = mysql_connect($db_hostname, $db_username, $db_password);

  if (!$db_server) die("Unable to connect to MySQL: " . mysql_error());

  mysql_select_db($db_database)
    or die("Unable to select database: " . mysql_error());

  $query  = "DROP TABLE cats";
  $result = mysql_query($query);

  if (!$result) die ("Database access failed: " . mysql_error());
?>
```

Adding Data

Let's add some data to the table using the code in Example 10-12.

Example 10-12. Adding data to table cats

```php
<?php
  require_once 'login.php';
  $db_server = mysql_connect($db_hostname, $db_username, $db_password);
```

```php
    if (!$db_server) die("Unable to connect to MySQL: " . mysql_error());

    mysql_select_db($db_database)
      or die("Unable to select database: " . mysql_error());

    $query  = "INSERT INTO cats VALUES(NULL, 'Lion', 'Leo', 4)";
    $result = mysql_query($query);

    if (!$result) die ("Database access failed: " . mysql_error());
?>
```

You may wish to add a couple more items of data by modifying $query as follows and calling up the program in your browser again:

```php
$query = "INSERT INTO cats VALUES(NULL, 'Cougar', 'Growler', 2)";
$query = "INSERT INTO cats VALUES(NULL, 'Cheetah', 'Charly', 3)";
```

By the way, notice the NULL value passed as the first parameter? This is because the *id* column is of type AUTO_INCREMENT, and MySQL will decide what value to assign according to the next available number in sequence, so we simply pass a NULL value, which will be ignored.

Of course, the most efficient way to populate MySQL with data is to create an array and insert the data with a single query.

Retrieving Data

Now that some data has been entered into the *cats* table, Example 10-13 shows how you can check that it was correctly inserted.

Example 10-13. Retrieving rows from the cats table

```php
<?php
  require_once 'login.php';
  $db_server = mysql_connect($db_hostname, $db_username, $db_password);

  if (!$db_server) die("Unable to connect to MySQL: " . mysql_error());

  mysql_select_db($db_database)
    or die("Unable to select database: " . mysql_error());

  $query  = "SELECT * FROM cats";
  $result = mysql_query($query);

  if (!$result) die ("Database access failed: " . mysql_error());

  $rows = mysql_num_rows($result);

  echo "<table><tr> <th>Id</th> <th>Family</th><th>Name</th><th>Age</th></tr>";

  for ($j = 0 ; $j < $rows ; ++$j)
  {
```

```
    $row = mysql_fetch_row($result);
    echo "<tr>";

    for ($k = 0 ; $k < 4 ; ++$k)
      echo "<td>$row[$k]</td>";

    echo "</tr>";
  }

  echo "</table>";
?>
```

This code simply issues the MySQL query SELECT * FROM cats and then displays all
the rows returned. Its output is as follows:

```
Id Family   Name    Age
1  Lion     Leo     4
2  Cougar   Growler 2
3  Cheetah  Charly  3
```

Here you can see that the *id* column has correctly auto-incremented.

Updating Data

Changing data that you have already inserted is also quite simple. Did you notice the
spelling of Charly for the cheetah's name? Let's correct that to Charlie, as in
Example 10-14.

Example 10-14. Renaming Charly the cheetah to Charlie

```
<?php
  require_once 'login.php';
  $db_server = mysql_connect($db_hostname, $db_username, $db_password);

  if (!$db_server) die("Unable to connect to MySQL: " . mysql_error());

  mysql_select_db($db_database)
    or die("Unable to select database: " . mysql_error());

  $query  = "UPDATE cats SET name='Charlie' WHERE name='Charly'";
  $result = mysql_query($query);

  if (!$result) die ("Database access failed: " . mysql_error());
?>
```

If you run Example 10-13 again, you'll see that it now outputs the following:

```
Id Family   Name    Age
1  Lion     Leo     4
2  Cougar   Growler 2
3  Cheetah  Charlie 3
```

Deleting Data

Growler the cougar has been transferred to another zoo, so it's time to remove him from the database; see Example 10-15.

Example 10-15. Removing Growler the cougar from the cats table

```php
<?php
  require_once 'login.php';
  $db_server = mysql_connect($db_hostname, $db_username, $db_password);

  if (!$db_server) die("Unable to connect to MySQL: " . mysql_error());

  mysql_select_db($db_database)
    or die("Unable to select database: " . mysql_error());

  $query  = "DELETE FROM cats WHERE name='Growler'";
  $result = mysql_query($query);

  if (!$result) die ("Database access failed: " . mysql_error());
?>
```

This uses a standard DELETE FROM query, and when you run Example 10-13, you can see that the row has been removed in the following output:

```
Id Family  Name    Age
1  Lion    Leo     4
3  Cheetah Charlie 3
```

Using AUTO_INCREMENT

When using AUTO_INCREMENT, you cannot know what value has been given to a column before a row is inserted. Instead, if you need to know it, you must ask MySQL afterward using the mysql_insert_id function. This need is common: for instance, when you process a purchase, you might insert a new customer into a *Customers* table and then refer to the newly created *CustId* when inserting a purchase into the purchase table.

Example 10-12 can be rewritten as Example 10-16 to display this value after each insert.

Example 10-16. Adding data to table cats and reporting the insertion id

```php
<?php
  require_once 'login.php';
  $db_server = mysql_connect($db_hostname, $db_username, $db_password);

  if (!$db_server) die("Unable to connect to MySQL: " . mysql_error());

  mysql_select_db($db_database)
    or die("Unable to select database: " . mysql_error());

  $query  = "INSERT INTO cats VALUES(NULL, 'Lynx', 'Stumpy', 5)";
  $result = mysql_query($query);
```

```
echo "The Insert Id was: " . mysql_insert_id();

if (!$result) die ("Database access failed: " . mysql_error());
?>
```

The contents of the table should now look like the following (note how the previous *id* value of 2 is *not* reused, as this could cause complications in some instances):

```
Id Family  Name     Age
1  Lion    Leo      4
3  Cheetah Charlie  3
4  Lynx    Stumpy   5
```

Using insert IDs

It's very common to insert data in multiple tables: a book followed by its author, or a customer followed by his purchase, and so on. When doing this with an auto-increment column, you will need to retain the insert ID returned for storing in the related table.

For example, let's assume that these cats can be "adopted" by the public as a means of raising funds, and that when a new cat is stored in the *cats* table, we also want to create a key to tie it to the animal's adoptive owner. The code to do this is similar to that in Example 10-16, except that the returned insert ID is stored in the variable $insertID, and is then used as part of the subsequent query:

```
$query    = "INSERT INTO cats VALUES(NULL, 'Lynx', 'Stumpy', 5)";
$result   = mysql_query($query);
$insertID = mysql_insert_id();

$query    = "INSERT INTO owners VALUES($insertID, 'Ann', 'Smith')";
$result   = mysql_query($query);
```

Now the cat is connected to its "owner" through the cat's unique ID, which was created automatically by AUTO_INCREMENT.

Using locks

A completely safe procedure for linking tables through the insert ID is to use locks (or transactions, as described in Chapter 9). It can slow down response time a bit when there are many people submitting data to the same table, but it can also be worth it. The sequence is:

1. Lock the first table (e.g., *cats*).

2. Insert data into the first table.

3. Retrieve the unique ID from the first table through mysql_insert_id.

4. Unlock the first table.

5. Insert data into the second table.

You can safely release the lock before inserting data into the second table, because the insert ID has been retrieved and is stored in a program variable. You could also use a transaction instead of locking, but that slows down the MySQL server even more.

Performing Additional Queries

OK, that's enough feline fun. To explore some slightly more complex queries, we need to revert to using the *customers* and *classics* tables that you created in Chapter 8. There will be two customers in the *customers* table; the *classics* table holds the details of a few books. They also share a common column of ISBNs, called *isbn*, that we can use to perform additional queries.

For example, to display all of the customers along with the titles and authors of the books they have bought, you can use the code in Example 10-17.

Example 10-17. Performing a secondary query

```php
<?php
  require_once 'login.php';
  $db_server = mysql_connect($db_hostname, $db_username, $db_password);

  if (!$db_server) die("Unable to connect to MySQL: " . mysql_error());

  mysql_select_db($db_database)
    or die("Unable to select database: " . mysql_error());

  $query  = "SELECT * FROM customers";
  $result = mysql_query($query);

  if (!$result) die ("Database access failed: " . mysql_error());

  $rows = mysql_num_rows($result);

  for ($j = 0 ; $j < $rows ; ++$j)
  {
    $row = mysql_fetch_row($result);
    echo "$row[0] purchased ISBN $row[1]:<br>";

    $subquery  = "SELECT * FROM classics WHERE isbn='$row[1]'";
    $subresult = mysql_query($subquery);

    if (!$subresult) die ("Database access failed: " . mysql_error());

    $subrow = mysql_fetch_row($subresult);

    echo "  '$subrow[1]' by $subrow[0]<br>";
  }
?>
```

This program uses an initial query to the *customers* table to look up all the customers and then, given the ISBN of the book each customer purchased, makes a new query to the *classics* table to find out the title and author for each. The output from this code should be as follows:

```
Mary Smith purchased ISBN 9780582506206:
  'Pride and Prejudice' by Jane Austen
Jack Wilson purchased ISBN 9780517123201:
  'The Origin of Species' by Charles Darwin
```

 Of course, although it wouldn't illustrate performing additional queries, in this particular case you could also return the same information using a NATURAL JOIN query (see Chapter 8), like this:

```
SELECT name,isbn,title,author FROM customers
    NATURAL JOIN classics;
```

Preventing SQL Injection

It may be hard to understand just how dangerous it is to pass user input unchecked to MySQL. For example, suppose you have a simple piece of code to verify a user, and it looks like this:

```
$user  = $_POST['user'];
$pass  = $_POST['pass'];
$query = "SELECT * FROM users WHERE user='$user' AND pass='$pass'";
```

At first glance, you might think this code is perfectly fine. If the user enters values of fredsmith and mypass for $user and $pass, respectively, then the query string, as passed to MySQL, will be as follows:

```
SELECT * FROM users WHERE user='fredsmith' AND pass='mypass'
```

This is all well and good, but what if someone enters the following for $user (and doesn't even enter anything for $pass)?

```
admin' #
```

Let's look at the string that would be sent to MySQL:

```
SELECT * FROM users WHERE user='admin' #' AND pass=''
```

Do you see the problem there? In MySQL, the # symbol represents the start of a comment. Therefore, the user will be logged in as *admin* (assuming there is a user *admin*), without having to enter a password. In the following, the part of the query that will be executed is shown in bold; the rest will be ignored.

SELECT * FROM users WHERE user='admin' #' AND pass=''

But you should count yourself very lucky if that's all a malicious user does to you. At least you might still be able to go into your application and undo any changes the user makes as *admin*. But what about the case in which your application code removes a user from the database? The code might look something like this:

```
$user  = $_POST['user'];
$pass  = $_POST['pass'];
$query = "DELETE FROM users WHERE user='$user' AND pass='$pass'";
```

Again, this looks quite normal at first glance, but what if someone entered the following for $user?

```
anything' OR 1=1 #
```

This would be interpreted by MySQL as:

DELETE FROM users WHERE user='anything' OR 1=1 #' AND pass=''

Ouch—that SQL query will always be TRUE and therefore you've lost your whole *users* database! So what can you do about this kind of attack?

Well, the first thing is not to rely on PHP's built-in *magic quotes*, which automatically escape any characters such as single and double quotes by prefacing them with a backslash (\). Why? Because this feature can be turned off; many programmers do so in order to put their own security code in place. So there is no guarantee that this hasn't happened on the server you are working on. In fact, the feature was deprecated as of PHP 5.3.0 and has been removed in PHP 6.0.0.

Instead, you should always use the function mysql_real_escape_string for all calls to MySQL. Example 10-18 is a function you can use that will remove any magic quotes added to a user-inputted string and then properly sanitize it for you.

Example 10-18. How to properly sanitize user input for MySQL

```php
<?php
  function mysql_fix_string($string)
  {
    if (get_magic_quotes_gpc()) $string = stripslashes($string);
    return mysql_real_escape_string($string);
  }
?>
```

The get_magic_quotes_gpc function returns TRUE if magic quotes are active. In that case, any slashes that have been added to a string have to be removed, or the function mysql_real_escape_string could end up double-escaping some characters, creating corrupted strings. Example 10-19 illustrates how you would incorporate mysql_fix_string within your own code.

Example 10-19. How to safely access MySQL with user input

```php
<?php
  $user  = mysql_fix_string($_POST['user']);
  $pass  = mysql_fix_string($_POST['pass']);
  $query = "SELECT * FROM users WHERE user='$user' AND pass='$pass'";
```

```
  function mysql_fix_string($string)
  {
    if (get_magic_quotes_gpc()) $string = stripslashes($string);
    return mysql_real_escape_string($string);
  }
?>
```

 Remember that you can use `mysql_real_escape_string` only when a MySQL database is actively open; otherwise, an error will occur.

Using Placeholders

Another way—this one virtually bulletproof—to prevent SQL injections is to use a feature called *placeholders*. The idea is to predefine a query using ? characters where the data will appear. Then, instead of calling a MySQL query directly, you call the predefined one, passing the data to it. This has the effect of ensuring that every item of data entered is inserted directly into the database and cannot be interpreted as SQL queries. In other words, SQL injections become impossible.

The sequence of queries to execute when using MySQL's command line would be like that in Example 10-20.

Example 10-20. Using placeholders

```
PREPARE statement FROM "INSERT INTO classics VALUES(?,?,?,?,?)";

SET @author   = "Emily Brontë",
    @title    = "Wuthering Heights",
    @category = "Classic Fiction",
    @year     = "1847",
    @isbn     = "9780553212587";

EXECUTE statement USING @author,@title,@category,@year,@isbn;

DEALLOCATE PREPARE statement;
```

The first command prepares a statement called `statement` for inserting data into the *classics* table. As you can see, in place of values or variables for the data to insert, the statement contains a series of ? characters. These are the placeholders.

The next five lines assign values to MySQL variables according to the data to be inserted. Then the predefined statement is executed, passing these variables as parameters. Finally, the statement is removed, in order to return the resources it was using.

In PHP, the code for this procedure looks like Example 10-21 (assuming that you have created *login.php* with the correct details to access the database).

Example 10-21. Using placeholders with PHP

```php
<?php
  require 'login.php';
  $db_server = mysql_connect($db_hostname, $db_username, $db_password);

  if (!$db_server) die("Unable to connect to MySQL: " . mysql_error());

  mysql_select_db($db_database)
    or die("Unable to select database: " . mysql_error());

  $query = 'PREPARE statement FROM "INSERT INTO classics VALUES(?,?,?,?,?)"';
  mysql_query($query);

  $query = 'SET @author = "Emily Brontë",' .
           '@title = "Wuthering Heights",' .
           '@category = "Classic Fiction",' .
           '@year = "1847",' .
           '@isbn = "9780553212587"';
  mysql_query($query);

  $query = 'EXECUTE statement USING @author,@title,@category,@year,@isbn';
  mysql_query($query);

  $query = 'DEALLOCATE PREPARE statement';
  mysql_query($query);
?>
```

Once you have prepared a statement, until you deallocate it you can use it as often as you wish. Such statements are commonly used within a loop to quickly insert data into a database by assigning values to the MySQL variables and then executing the statement. This approach is more efficient than creating the entire statement from scratch on each pass through the loop.

Preventing HTML Injection

There's another type of injection you need to concern yourself about—not for the safety of your own websites, but for your users' privacy and protection. That's *cross-site scripting*, also referred to as *XSS*.

This occurs when you allow HTML, or more often JavaScript code, to be input by a user and then displayed back by your website. One place this is common is in a comment form. What happens most often is that a malicious user will try to write code that steals cookies from your site's users, allowing him or her to discover username and password pairs or other information. Even worse, the malicious user might launch an attack to download a Trojan onto a user's computer.

But preventing this is as simple as calling the `htmlentities` function, which strips out all HTML markup codes and replaces them with a form that displays the characters, but does not allow a browser to act on them. For example, consider the following HTML:

```
<script src='http://x.com/hack.js'>
</script><script>hack();</script>
```

This code loads in a JavaScript program and then executes malicious functions. But if it is first passed through `htmlentities`, it will be turned into the following, totally harmless string:

```
&lt;script src='http://x.com/hack.js'&gt;
&lt;/script&gt;&lt;script&gt;hack();&lt;/script&gt;
```

Therefore, if you are ever going to display anything that your users enter, either immediately or after storing it in a database, you need to first sanitize it with `htmlentities`. To do this, I recommend that you create a new function, like the first one in Example 10-22, which can sanitize for both SQL and XSS injections.

Example 10-22. Functions for preventing both SQL and XSS injection attacks

```php
<?php
  function mysql_entities_fix_string($string)
  {
    return htmlentities(mysql_fix_string($string));
  }

  function mysql_fix_string($string)
  {
    if (get_magic_quotes_gpc()) $string = stripslashes($string);
    return mysql_real_escape_string($string);
  }
?>
```

The `mysql_entities_fix_string` function first calls `mysql_fix_string` and then passes the result through `htmlentities` before returning the fully sanitized string. Example 10-23 shows your new "ultimate protection" version of Example 10-19.

Example 10-23. How to safely access MySQL and prevent XSS attacks

```php
<?php
  $user  = mysql_entities_fix_string($_POST['user']);
  $pass  = mysql_entities_fix_string($_POST['pass']);
  $query = "SELECT * FROM users WHERE user='$user' AND pass='$pass'";

  function mysql_entities_fix_string($string)
  {
    return htmlentities(mysql_fix_string($string));
  }

  function mysql_fix_string($string)
  {
```

```
    if (get_magic_quotes_gpc()) $string = stripslashes($string);
    return mysql_real_escape_string($string);
  }
?>
```

Now that you have learned how to integrate PHP with MySQL and avoid malicious user input, the next chapter will explain how to use the improved MySQLi extension for your MySQL queries.

Questions

1. What is the standard PHP function for connecting to a MySQL database?

2. When is the mysql_result function not optimal?

3. Give one reason why using the POST form method is usually better than GET.

4. How can you determine the most recently entered value of an AUTO_INCREMENT column?

5. Which PHP function escapes a string, making it suitable for use with MySQL?

6. Which function can be used to prevent XSS injection attacks?

See "Chapter 10 Answers" on page 646 in Appendix A for the answers to these questions.

CHAPTER 11

Using the mysqli Extension

Now that you understand how to access a MySQL database using PHP and the procedural mysql extensions, it's time to learn how to do this with the improved mysqli extension. This is an object-oriented system, but there is a procedural version available if you prefer, and I'll show you how to use both.

Querying a MySQL Database with mysqli

In this chapter, I replicate a number of the previous one's examples, but rewrite them to use mysqli. This should serve as an excellent example of how you can bring any legacy code you encounter up-to-date.

Creating a Login File

Creating a login file is no different with mysqli than before, so it will look something like Example 11-1.

Example 11-1. The login.php file

```php
<?php // login.php
  $db_hostname = 'localhost';
  $db_database = 'publications';
  $db_username = 'username';
  $db_password = 'password';
?>
```

As in the previous chapter, the database we'll be using is the one called *publications*, and the variables $db_username and $db_password should be set to the username and password that you have been using with MySQL.

Connecting to MySQL

With the *login.php* file saved, you access the database with the `require_once` statement, and connect to the server in the manner shown in Example 11-2.

Example 11-2. Connecting to a MySQL server with mysqli

```php
<?php
  require_once 'login.php';
  $connection = new mysqli($db_hostname, $db_username, $db_password, $db_database);

  if ($connection->connect_error) die($connection->connect_error)
?>
```

This example creates a new object called `$connection` by calling the `mysqli` method with all the values retrieved from *login.php*. Note the improved error checking, which we achieve by referencing the `$connection->connect_error` property. If it is TRUE, we call the `die` function and display details explaining the error. The `connect_error` property of `$connection` contains a string detailing the connection error.

The `$connection` object will be used in the following examples to access the MySQL database.

Building and executing a query

Sending a query to MySQL from PHP with `mysqli` is as simple as issuing it using the query method. Example 11-3 shows you how to use it.

Example 11-3. Querying a database with mysqli

```php
<?php
  $query  = "SELECT * FROM classics";
  $result = $connection->query($query);

  if (!$result) die($connection->error);
?>
```

As in Chapter 10, the variable `$query` is set to the query to be made, but here this value is passed to the query method of the `$connection` object, which returns a result that we place in the object `$result`. We've done everything we need with `$connection` and turn to `$result` to enjoy what has been returned from the connection. The `$result` will be FALSE if there was an error; otherwise, it will be an object that can be accessed. The error property of `$connection` contains a string detailing any error.

Fetching a result

Once you have an object returned in `$result`, you can use it to retrieve the data you want, one item at a time, using the `fetch_assoc` method of the object. Example 11-4 combines and extends the previous examples into a program that you can type and run yourself to retrieve these results (as depicted in Figure 11-1). I suggest that you save this script using the filename *query-mysqli.php*.

Example 11-4. Fetching results with mysqli, one cell at a time

```php
<?php // query-mysqli.php
  require_once 'login.php';
  $connection =
    new mysqli($db_hostname, $db_username, $db_password, $db_database);

  if ($connection->connect_error) die($connection->connect_error)

  $query  = "SELECT * FROM classics";
  $result = $connection->query($query);

  if (!$result) die($connection->error);

  $rows = $result->num_rows;

  for ($j = 0 ; $j < $rows ; ++$j)
  {
    $result->data_seek($j);
    echo 'Author: '   . $result->fetch_assoc()['author']   . '<br>';
    $result->data_seek($j);
    echo 'Title: '    . $result->fetch_assoc()['title']    . '<br>';
    $result->data_seek($j);
    echo 'Category: ' . $result->fetch_assoc()['category'] . '<br>';
    $result->data_seek($j);
    echo 'Year: '     . $result->fetch_assoc()['year']     . '<br>';
    $result->data_seek($j);
    echo 'ISBN: '     . $result->fetch_assoc()['isbn']     . '<br><br>';
  }

  $result->close();
  $connection->close();
?>
```

Here, to seek to the correct row each time around the loop, we call the `data_seek` method of `$result` before fetching each item of data. Then we call the `fetch_assoc` method to retrieve the value stored in each cell, and output the result using `echo` commands.

You will probably agree that all this data seeking is rather cumbersome and that there ought to be a more efficient method of achieving the same result. And, indeed, there is a better method, which is to extract a row at a time.

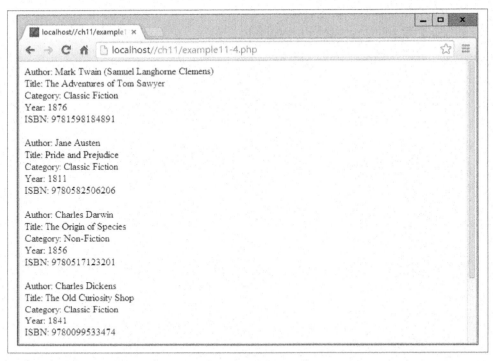

Figure 11-1. The result of running Example 11-4

Fetching a row

To fetch one row at a time, replace the `for` loop from Example 11-4 with the one high-lighted in bold in Example 11-5, and you will find that you get exactly the same result that was displayed in Figure 11-1. You may wish to save this revised file as *fetchrow-mysqli.php*.

Example 11-5. Fetching results with mysqli, one row at a time

```php
<?php //fetchrow-mysqli.php
  require_once 'login.php';
  $connection =
    new mysqli($db_hostname, $db_username, $db_password, $db_database);

  if ($connection->connect_error) die($connection->connect_error);

  $query  = "SELECT * FROM classics";
  $result = $connection->query($query);

  if (!$result) die($connection->error);

  $rows = $result->num_rows;
```

```
for ($j = 0 ; $j < $rows ; ++$j)
{
  $result->data_seek($j);
  $row = $result->fetch_array(MYSQLI_ASSOC);

  echo 'Author: '   . $row['author']   . '<br>';
  echo 'Title: '    . $row['title']    . '<br>';
  echo 'Category: ' . $row['category'] . '<br>';
  echo 'Year: '     . $row['year']     . '<br>';
  echo 'ISBN: '     . $row['isbn']     . '<br><br>';
}

$result->close();
$connection->close();
?>
```

In this modified code, only one-fifth of the interrogations of the $result object are made, and only one seek into the object is made in each iteration of the loop, because each row is fetched in its entirety via the fetch_array method. This returns a single row of data as an array, which is then assigned to the array $row.

The fetch_array method can return three types of array according to the value passed to it:

MYSQLI_NUM

Numeric array. Each column appears in the array in the order in which you defined it when you created (or altered) the table. In our case, the zeroth element of the array contains the Author column, element 1 contains the Title, and so on.

MYSQLI_ASSOC

Associative array. Each key is the name of a column. Because items of data are referenced by column name (rather than index number), use this option where possible in your code to make debugging easier and help other programmers better manage your code.

MYSQLI_BOTH

Associative and numeric array.

Associative arrays are usually more useful than numeric ones because you can refer to each column by name, such as $row['author'], instead of trying to remember where it is in the column order. So this script uses an associative array, leading us to pass MYSQLI_ASSOC.

Closing a connection

PHP will eventually return the memory it has allocated for objects after you have finished with the script, so in small scripts, you don't usually need to worry about releasing memory yourself. However, if you're allocating a lot of result objects or fetching large amounts of data, it can be a good idea to free the memory you have been using to prevent problems later in your script.

This becomes particularly important on higher traffic pages, because the amount of memory consumed in a session can rapidly grow. Therefore, note the calls to the close methods of the objects $result and $connection in the preceding scripts, as soon as each object is no longer needed.

Ideally, you should close each result object when you have finished using it, and then close the connection object when your script will not be accessing MySQL anymore. This best practice ensures that resources are returned to the system as quickly as possible to keep MySQL running optimally, and alleviates doubt over whether PHP will return unused memory in time for when you next need it.

A Practical Example

Now let's rewrite the procedural *sqltest.php* program from the previous chapter using mysqli. The conversion is pretty straightforward, as you can see in Example 11-6 (which you should save as *mysqlitest.php* if you intend to test it, because it continuously calls itself).

Example 11-6. Inserting and deleting using mysqlitest.php

```php
<?php // mysqlitest.php
  require_once 'login.php';
  $connection =
    new mysqli($db_hostname, $db_username, $db_password, $db_database);

  if ($connection->connect_error) die($connection->connect_error);

  if (isset($_POST['delete']) && isset($_POST['isbn']))
  {
    $isbn   = get_post($connection, 'isbn');
    $query  = "DELETE FROM classics WHERE isbn='$isbn'";
    $result = $connection->query($query);

    if (!$result) echo "DELETE failed: $query<br>" .
      $connection->error . "<br><br>";
  }

  if (isset($_POST['author'])   &&
      isset($_POST['title'])    &&
      isset($_POST['category']) &&
      isset($_POST['year'])     &&
      isset($_POST['isbn']))
  {
    $author   = get_post($connection, 'author');
    $title    = get_post($connection, 'title');
    $category = get_post($connection, 'category');
```

```php
    $year     = get_post($connection, 'year');
    $isbn     = get_post($connection, 'isbn');
    $query    = "INSERT INTO classics VALUES" .
      "('$author', '$title', '$category', '$year', '$isbn')";
    $result   = $connection->query($query);

    if (!$result) echo "INSERT failed: $query<br>" .
      $connection->error . "<br><br>";
  }

  echo <<<_END
  <form action="mysqlitest.php" method="post"><pre>
    Author <input type="text" name="author">
     Title <input type="text" name="title">
  Category <input type="text" name="category">
      Year <input type="text" name="year">
      ISBN <input type="text" name="isbn">
           <input type="submit" value="ADD RECORD">
  </pre></form>
_END;

  $query  = "SELECT * FROM classics";
  $result = $connection->query($query);

  if (!$result) die ("Database access failed: " . $connection->error);

  $rows = $result->num_rows;

  for ($j = 0 ; $j < $rows ; ++$j)
  {
    $result->data_seek($j);
    $row = $result->fetch_array(MYSQLI_NUM);

    echo <<<_END
  <pre>
    Author $row[0]
     Title $row[1]
  Category $row[2]
      Year $row[3]
      ISBN $row[4]
  </pre>
  <form action="mysqlitest.php" method="post">
  <input type="hidden" name="delete" value="yes">
  <input type="hidden" name="isbn" value="$row[4]">
  <input type="submit" value="DELETE RECORD"></form>
_END;
  }

  $result->close();
  $connection->close();

  function get_post($connection, $var)
```

```
    {
       return $connection->real_escape_string($_POST[$var]);
    }
?>
```

How this code works is explained in Chapter 10, so all we need to examine here are the differences between Examples 10-8 and 11-6. Let's work through them in order.

The first couple of lines pull in the code from *login.php* and create a $connection object to gain access to the database. Then there's the code for deleting an entry, which simply issues a DELETE command to the $connection object using the query method, and returns an error message if there's a problem.

Then, if new data has been posted to the program, it issues an INSERT command, again on the $connection object using the query method. In both instances, the $result object is given the result of this operation, which should be either TRUE or FALSE.

The final main part of the program deals with extracting data from the database and displaying it using the data_seek and fetch_array methods of the $result object. Unlike Example 11-5, however, in which an associative array was returned, here the fetch_array method is given the value MYSQLI_NUM so that a numeric array is returned; accordingly, the cells are referenced numerically (e.g., $row[0] for the author). The results are then displayed in each iteration of the loop, and finally the result object and connection are closed.

The function get_post has also been modified here to use the new real_escape_string method of a connection object, so now two values are passed to it (the connection and the string value).

Using mysqli Procedurally

If you prefer, there is an alternative set of functions you can use to access mysqli in a procedural (rather than object-oriented) manner.

So, instead of creating a $connection object like this:

```
$connection = new mysqli($db_hostname, $db_username, $db_password, $db_database);
```

You can use the following:

```
$link = mysqli_connect($db_hostname, $db_username, $db_password, $db_database);
```

To check that the connection has been made and handle it, you could use code such as this:

```
if (mysqli_connect_errno()) die(mysqli_connect_error());
```

And to make a MySQL query, you would use code such as the following:

```
$result = mysqli_query($link, "SELECT * FROM classics");
```

Upon return, `$result` will contain the data. You can find out the number of rows returned as follows:

```
$rows = mysqli_num_rows($result));
```

An integer is returned in `$rows`. You can fetch the actual data one row at a time in the following way, which returns a numeric array:

```
$row = mysqli_fetch_array($result, MYSQLI_NUM);
```

In this instance, `$row[0]` will contain the first column of data, `$row[1]` the second, and so on. As described in Example 11-5, rows can also be returned as associative arrays or as both types, depending on the value passed in the second argument.

Escaping strings procedurally with `mysqli` is as easy as using the following:

```
$escaped = mysqli_real_escape_string($link, $val);
```

For full details on using `mysqli` procedurally (and all other aspects of `mysqli`), visit *http://tinyurl.com/usingmysqli*.

Now that you have learned how to integrate PHP with MySQL in several different ways, the next chapter moves on to creating user-friendly forms and dealing with the data submitted from them.

Questions

1. How do you connect to a MySQL database using `mysqli`?
2. How do you submit a query to MySQL using `mysqli`?
3. How can you retrieve a string containing an error message when a `mysqli` error occurs?
4. How can you determine the number of rows returned by a `mysqli` query?
5. How can you retrieve a particular row of data from a set of `mysqli` results?
6. Which `mysqli` method can be used to properly escape user input to prevent code injection?
7. What negative effects can happen if you do not close the objects created by `mysqli` methods?

See "Chapter 11 Answers" on page 646 in Appendix A for the answers to these questions.

CHAPTER 12

Form Handling

The main way that website users interact with PHP and MySQL is through the use of HTML forms. These were introduced very early on in the development of the World Wide Web in 1993—even before the advent of ecommerce—and have remained a mainstay ever since, due to their simplicity and ease of use.

Of course, enhancements have been made over the years to add extra functionality to HTML form handling, so this chapter will bring you up to speed on state-of-the-art form handling and show you the best ways to implement forms for good usability and security. Plus, as you will see a little later on, the HTML5 specification has further improved the use of forms.

Building Forms

Handling forms is a multipart process. First a form is created, into which a user can enter the required details. This data is then sent to the web server, where it is interpreted, often with some error checking. If the PHP code identifies one or more fields that require reentering, the form may be redisplayed with an error message. When the code is satisfied with the accuracy of the input, it takes some action that usually involves the database, such as entering details about a purchase.

To build a form, you must have at least the following elements:

- An opening <form> and closing </form> tag
- A submission type specifying either a GET or POST method
- One or more input fields
- The destination URL to which the form data is to be submitted

Example 12-1 shows a very simple form created with PHP. Type it and save it as *formtest.php*.

Example 12-1. formtest.php—a simple PHP form handler

```php
<?php // formtest.php
  echo <<<_END
    <html>
      <head>
        <title>Form Test</title>
      </head>
      <body>
      <form method="post" action="formtest.php">
        What is your name?
        <input type="text" name="name">
        <input type="submit">
      </form>
      </body>
    </html>
_END;
?>
```

The first thing to notice about this example is that, as you have already seen in this book, rather than dropping in and out of PHP code, the echo <<<_END ... _END construct is used whenever multiline HTML must be output.

Inside of this multiline output is some standard code for commencing an HTML document, displaying its title, and starting the body of the document. This is followed by the form, which is set to send its data using the POST method to the PHP program *formtest.php*, which is the name of the program itself.

The rest of the program just closes all the items it opened: the form, the body of the HTML document, and the PHP echo <<<_END statement. The result of opening this program in a web browser is shown in Figure 12-1.

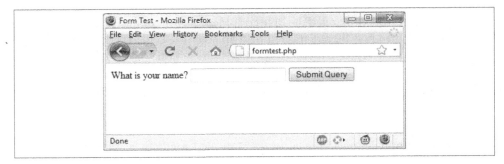

Figure 12-1. The result of opening formtest.php in a web browser

Retrieving Submitted Data

Example 12-1 is only one part of the multipart form handling process. If you enter a name and click the Submit Query button, absolutely nothing will happen other than the form being redisplayed. So now it's time to add some PHP code to process the data submitted by the form.

Example 12-2 expands on the previous program to include data processing. Type it or modify *formtest.php* by adding in the new lines, save it as *formtest2.php*, and try the program for yourself. The result of running this program and entering a name is shown in Figure 12-2.

Example 12-2. Updated version of formtest.php

```
<?php // formtest2.php
  if (isset($_POST['name'])) $name = $_POST['name'];
  else $name = "(Not entered)";

  echo <<<_END
    <html>
      <head>
        <title>Form Test</title>
      </head>
      <body>
        Your name is: $name<br>
        <form method="post" action="formtest2.php">
          What is your name?
          <input type="text" name="name">
          <input type="submit">
        </form>
      </body>
    </html>
_END;
?>
```

The only changes are a couple of lines at the start that check the $_POST associative array for the field *name* having been submitted. Chapter 10 introduced the $_POST associative array, which contains an element for each field in an HTML form. In Example 12-2, the input name used was *name* and the form method was POST, so element name of the $_POST array contains the value in $_POST['name'].

The PHP isset function is used to test whether $_POST['name'] has been assigned a value. If nothing was posted, the program assigns the value (Not entered); otherwise, it stores the value that was entered. Then a single line has been added after the <body> statement to display that value, which is stored in $name.

Figure 12-2. formtest.php with data handling

Notice how the <input> elements in this example do not use the /> form of self-closing, because in the new world of HTML5 this style is optional (and it was never actually required in HTML4 anyway; it was recommended purely because XHTML was planned to supersede HTML at some point—but this never happened). I'm always in favor of less work when programming, so I no longer use these characters except for actual XHTML (where this type of closing remains necessary), saving both a space and a slash for every self-closing tag.

register_globals: An Old Solution Hangs On

Before security became such a big issue, the default behavior of PHP was to assign the $_POST and $_GET arrays directly to PHP variables. For example, there would be no need to use the instruction $name=$_POST['name']; because $name would already be given that value automatically by PHP at the program start!

Initially (prior to version 4.2.0 of PHP), this seemed a very useful idea that saved a lot of extra code writing, but this practice has now been discontinued and the feature is disabled by default. Should you find register_globals enabled on a production web server for which you are developing, you should urgently ask your server administrator to disable it.

So why disable register_globals? It enables anyone to enter a GET input on the tail of a URL, like this: *http://myserver.com?override=1*. If your code were ever to use the variable $override and you forgot to initialize it (e.g., through $override=0;), the program could be compromised by such an exploit.

In fact, because many installations on the Web still have this gaping hole, I advise you to always initialize every variable you use, just in case your code will ever run on such a system. Initialization is also good programming practice, because you can comment each initialization to remind yourself and other programmers what each variable is for.

If you find yourself maintaining code that seems to assume values for certain variables for no apparent reason, you can make an educated guess that the programmer wrote the code using register_globals, and that these values are intended to be extracted from a POST or GET. If so, I recommend that you rewrite the code to load these variables explicitly from the correct $_POST or $_GET array.

Default Values

Sometimes it's convenient to offer your site visitors a default value in a web form. For example, suppose you put up a loan repayment calculator widget on a real estate website. It could make sense to enter default values of, say, 25 years and 6% interest, so that the user can simply type either the principle sum to borrow or the amount that she can afford to pay each month.

In this case, the HTML for those two values would be something like Example 12-3.

Example 12-3. Setting default values

```
<form method="post" action="calc.php"><pre>
     Loan Amount <input type="text" name="principle">
Monthly Repayment <input type="text" name="monthly">
  Number of Years <input type="text" name="years" value="25">
    Interest Rate <input type="text" name="rate"  value="6">
                  <input type="submit">
</pre></form>
```

If you wish to try this (and the other HTML code samples), save it with an *.html* (or *.htm*) file extension, such as *test.html* (or *test.htm*), and then load that file into your browser.

Take a look at the third and fourth inputs. By populating the value attribute, you display a default value in the field, which the users can then change if they wish. With sensible default values, you can often make your web forms more user-friendly by minimizing unnecessary typing. The result of the previous code looks like Figure 12-3. Of course, this was created just to illustrate default values and, because the program *calc.php* has not been written, the form will not do anything if submitted.

Default values are also used for hidden fields if you want to pass extra information from your web page to your program, in addition to what users enter. We'll look at hidden fields later in this chapter.

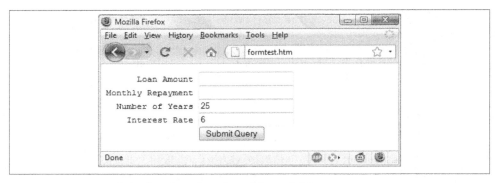

Figure 12-3. Using default values for selected form fields

Input Types

HTML forms are very versatile and allow you to submit a wide range of input types, from text boxes and text areas to checkboxes, radio buttons, and more.

Text boxes

The input type you will probably use most often is the text box. It accepts a wide range of alphanumeric text and other characters in a single-line box. The general format of a text box input is:

```
<input type="text" name="name" size="size" maxlength="length" value="value">
```

We've already covered the name and value attributes, but two more are introduced here: size and maxlength. The size attribute specifies the width of the box (in characters of the current font) as it should appear on the screen, and maxlength specifies the maximum number of characters that a user is allowed to enter into the field.

The only required attributes are type, which tells the web browser what type of input to expect, and name, for giving the input a name that will be used to process the field upon receipt of the submitted form.

Text areas

When you need to accept input of more than a short line of text, use a text area. This is similar to a text box, but, because it allows multiple lines, it has some different attributes. Its general format looks like this:

```
<textarea name="name" cols="width" rows="height" wrap="type">
</textarea>
```

The first thing to notice is that <textarea> has its own tag and is not a subtype of the <input> tag. It therefore requires a closing </textarea> to end input.

Instead of a default attribute, if you have default text to display, you must put it before the closing </textarea>, and it will then be displayed and be editable by the user, like this:

```
<textarea name="name" cols="width" rows="height" wrap="type">
  This is some default text.
</textarea>
```

To control the width and height, use the cols and rows attributes. Both use the character spacing of the current font to determine the size of the area. If you omit these values, a default input box will be created that will vary in dimensions depending on the browser used, so you should always define them to be certain about how your form will appear.

Lastly, you can control how the text entered into the box will wrap (and how any such wrapping will be sent to the server) using the wrap attribute. Table 12-1 shows the wrap types available. If you leave out the wrap attribute, soft wrapping is used.

Table 12-1. The wrap types available in a textarea input

Type	Action
off	Text does not wrap and lines appear exactly as the user types them.
soft	Text wraps but is sent to the server as one long string without carriage returns and line feeds.
hard	Text wraps and is sent to the server in wrapped format with soft returns and line feeds.

Checkboxes

When you want to offer a number of different options to a user, from which he can select one or more items, checkboxes are the way to go. The format to use is:

```
<input type="checkbox" name="name" value="value" checked="checked">
```

If you include the checked attribute, the box is already checked when the browser is displayed. The string you assign to the attribute should be either a double quote or the value "checked", or there should be no value assigned. If you don't include the attribute, the box is shown unchecked. Here is an example of creating an unchecked box:

```
I Agree <input type="checkbox" name="agree">
```

If the user doesn't check the box, no value will be submitted. But if he does, a value of "on" will be submitted for the field named agree. If you prefer to have your own value submitted instead of the word *on* (such as the number 1), you could use the following syntax:

```
I Agree <input type="checkbox" name="agree" value="1">
```

On the other hand, if you wish to offer a newsletter to your readers when submitting a form, you might want to have the checkbox already checked as the default value:

```
Subscribe? <input type="checkbox" name="news" checked="checked">
```

If you want to allow groups of items to be selected at one time, assign them all the same name. However, only the last item checked will be submitted, unless you pass an array as the name. For example, Example 12-4 allows the user to select his favorite ice creams (see Figure 12-4 for how it displays in a browser).

Example 12-4. Offering multiple checkbox choices

```
    Vanilla <input type="checkbox" name="ice" value="Vanilla">
  Chocolate <input type="checkbox" name="ice" value="Chocolate">
 Strawberry <input type="checkbox" name="ice" value="Strawberry">
```

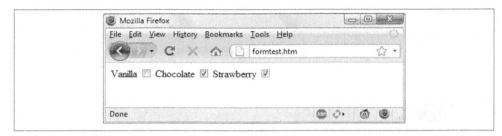

Figure 12-4. Using checkboxes to make quick selections

If only one of the checkboxes is selected, such as the second one, only that item will be submitted (the field named ice would be assigned the value "Chocolate"). But if two or more are selected, only the last value will be submitted, with prior values being ignored.

If you *want* exclusive behavior—so that only one item can be submitted—then you should use *radio buttons* (see the next section), but to allow multiple submissions, you have to slightly alter the HTML, as in Example 12-5 (note the addition of the square brackets, [], following the values of ice).

Example 12-5. Submitting multiple values with an array

```
    Vanilla <input type="checkbox" name="ice[]" value="Vanilla">
  Chocolate <input type="checkbox" name="ice[]" value="Chocolate">
 Strawberry <input type="checkbox" name="ice[]" value="Strawberry">
```

Now, when the form is submitted, if any of these items have been checked, an array called ice will be submitted that contains any and all values. In each case, you can extract either the single submitted value, or the array of values, to a variable like this:

```
    $ice = $_POST['ice'];
```

If the field ice has been posted as a single value, $ice will be a single string, such as "Strawberry". But if ice was defined in the form as an array (like Example 12-5), $ice will be an array, and its number of elements will be the number of values submitted. Table 12-2 shows the seven possible sets of values that could be submitted by this HTML for one, two, or all three selections. In each case, an array of one, two, or three items is created.

Table 12-2. The seven possible sets of values for the array $ice

One value submitted	Two values submitted	Three values submitted
$ice[0] => Vanilla	$ice[0] => Vanilla $ice[1] => Chocolate	$ice[0] => Vanilla $ice[1] => Chocolate
$ice[0] => Chocolate		$ice[2] => Strawberry
	$ice[0] => Vanilla	
$ice[0] => Strawberry	$ice[1] => Strawberry	
	$ice[0] => Chocolate	
	$ice[1] => Strawberry	

If $ice is an array, the PHP code to display its contents is quite simple and might look like this:

```
foreach($ice as $item) echo "$item<br>";
```

This uses the standard PHP foreach construct to iterate through the array $ice and pass each element's value into the variable $item, which is then displayed via the echo command. The <br> is just an HTML formatting device to force a new line after each flavor in the display. By default, checkboxes are square.

Radio buttons

Radio buttons are named after the push-in preset buttons found on many older radios, where any previously depressed button pops back up when another is pressed. They are used when you want only a single value to be returned from a selection of two or more options. All the buttons in a group must use the same name and, because only a single value is returned, you do not have to pass an array.

For example, if your website offers a choice of delivery times for items purchased from your store, you might use HTML like that in Example 12-6 (see Figure 12-5 to see how it displays).

Example 12-6. Using radio buttons

```
8am-Noon<input type="radio" name="time" value="1">
Noon-4pm<input type="radio" name="time" value="2" checked="checked">
 4pm-8pm<input type="radio" name="time" value="3">
```

Here, the second option of Noon–4pm has been selected by default. This default choice ensures that at least one delivery time will be chosen by the user, which can be changed to one of the other two options if preferred. Had one of the items not been already checked, the user might forget to select an option, and no value would be submitted at all for the delivery time. By default, radio buttons are round.

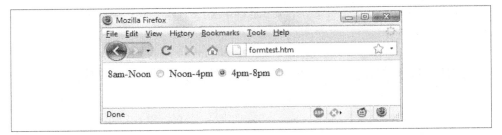

Figure 12-5. Selecting a single value with radio buttons

Hidden fields

Sometimes it is convenient to have hidden form fields so that you can keep track of the state of form entry. For example, you might wish to know whether a form has already been submitted. You can achieve this by adding some HTML in your PHP code, such as the following:

```
echo '<input type="hidden" name="submitted" value="yes">'
```

This is a simple PHP `echo` statement that adds an `input` field to the HTML form. Let's assume the form was created outside the program and displayed to the user. The first time the PHP program receives the input, this line of code has not run, so there will be no field named `submitted`. The PHP program re-creates the form, adding the `input` field. So when the visitor resubmits the form, the PHP program receives it with the `submitted` field set to `"yes"`. The code can simply check whether the field is present:

```
if (isset($_POST['submitted']))
{...
```

Hidden fields can also be useful for storing other details, such as a session ID string that you might create to identify a user, and so on.

 Never treat hidden fields as secure—because they are not. Someone could easily view the HTML containing them using a browser's View Source feature.

<select>

The `<select>` tag lets you create a drop-down list of options, offering either single or multiple selections. It conforms to the following syntax:

```
<select name="name" size="size" multiple="multiple">
```

The attribute `size` is the number of lines to display. Clicking on the display causes a list to drop down showing all the options. If you use the `multiple` attribute, a user can select multiple options from the list by pressing the Ctrl key when clicking. So to ask a user for his or her favorite vegetable from a choice of five, you might use HTML as in Example 12-7, which offers a single selection.

Example 12-7. Using select

```
Vegetables
<select name="veg" size="1">
  <option value="Peas">Peas</option>
  <option value="Beans">Beans</option>
  <option value="Carrots">Carrots</option>
  <option value="Cabbage">Cabbage</option>
  <option value="Broccoli">Broccoli</option>
</select>
```

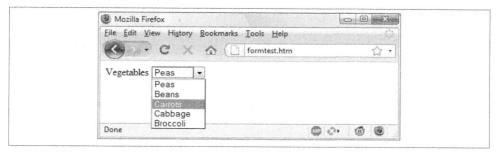

Figure 12-6. Creating a drop-down list with select

This HTML offers five choices, with the first one, *Peas*, preselected (due to it being the first item). Figure 12-6 shows the output where the list has been clicked on to drop it down, and the option *Carrots* has been highlighted. If you want to have a different default option offered first (such as *Beans*), use the `<selected>` tag, like this:

```
<option selected="selected" value="Beans">Beans</option>
```

You can also allow users to select more than one item, as in Example 12-8.

Example 12-8. Using select with the multiple attribute

```
Vegetables
<select name="veg" size="5" multiple="multiple">
  <option value="Peas">Peas</option>
  <option value="Beans">Beans</option>
  <option value="Carrots">Carrots</option>
  <option value="Cabbage">Cabbage</option>
  <option value="Broccoli">Broccoli</option>
</select>
```

This HTML is not very different; only the size has been changed to `"5"` and the attribute `multiple` has been added. But, as you can see from Figure 12-7, it is now possible to select more than one option by using the Ctrl key when clicking. You can leave out the size attribute if you wish, and the output will be the same; however, with a larger list, the drop-down box might take up too much screen space, so I recommend that you pick a suitable number of rows and stick with it. I also recommend against multiple select boxes smaller than two rows in height—some browsers may not correctly display the scroll bars needed to access it.

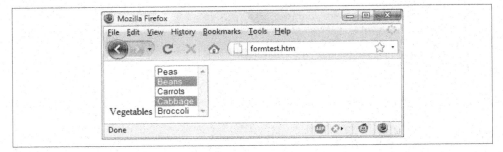

Figure 12-7. Using a select with the multiple attribute

You can also use the selected attribute within a multiple select and can, in fact, have more than one option preselected if you wish.

Labels

You can provide an even better user experience by utilizing the <label> tag. With it, you can surround a form element, making it selectable by clicking any visible part contained between the opening and closing <label> tags.

For example, going back to the example of choosing a delivery time, you could allow the user to click on the radio button itself *and* the associated text, like this:

```
<label>8am-Noon<input type="radio" name="time" value="1"></label>
```

The text will not be underlined like a hyperlink when you do this, but as the mouse passes over, it will change to an arrow instead of a text cursor, indicating that the whole item is clickable.

The submit button

To match the type of form being submitted, you can change the text of the submit button to anything you like by using the value attribute, like this:

```
<input type="submit" value="Search">
```

You can also replace the standard text button with a graphic image of your choice, using HTML such as this:

```
<input type="image" name="submit" src="image.gif">
```

Sanitizing Input

Now we return to PHP programming. It can never be emphasized enough that handling user data is a security minefield, and that it is essential to learn to treat all such data with utmost caution from the word go. It's actually not that difficult to sanitize user input from potential hacking attempts, but it must be done.

The first thing to remember is that regardless of what constraints you have placed in an HTML form to limit the types and sizes of inputs, it is a trivial matter for a hacker to use a browser's View Source feature to extract the form and modify it to provide malicious input to your website.

Therefore, you must never trust any variable that you fetch from either the $_GET or $_POST arrays until you have processed it. If you don't, users may try to inject JavaScript into the data to interfere with your site's operation, or even attempt to add MySQL commands to compromise your database.

Therefore, instead of just using code such as the following when reading in user input:

```php
$variable = $_POST['user_input'];
```

you should also use one or more of the following lines of code. For example, to prevent escape characters from being injected into a string that will be presented to MySQL, use the following. Remember that this function takes into account the current character set of a MySQL connection, so it must be used with a `mysqli` connection object (in this instance, `$connection`), as discussed in Chapter 11.

```php
$variable = $connection->real_escape_string($variable);
```

To get rid of unwanted slashes, use:

```php
$variable = stripslashes($variable);
```

And to remove any HTML from a string, use the following:

```php
$variable = htmlentities($variable);
```

For example, this would change a string of interpretable HTML code like `<b>hi</b>` into `&lt;b&gt;hi&lt;/b&gt;`, which displays as text, and won't be interpreted as HTML tags.

Finally, if you wish to strip HTML entirely from an input, use the following:

```php
$variable = strip_tags($variable);
```

In fact, until you know exactly what sanitization you require for a program, Example 12-9 shows a pair of functions that brings all these checks together to provide a very good level of security.

Example 12-9. The sanitizeString and sanitizeMySQL functions

```php
<?php
  function sanitizeString($var)
  {
    $var = stripslashes($var);
    $var = htmlentities($var);
    $var = strip_tags($var);
    return $var;
  }

  function sanitizeMySQL($connection, $var)
  { // Using the mysqli extension
    $var = $connection->real_escape_string($var);
    $var = sanitizeString($var);
    return $var;
  }
?>
```

Add this code to the end of your PHP programs, and you can then call it for each user input to sanitize, like this:

```php
$var = sanitizeString($_POST['user_input']);
```

Or, when you have an open MySQL connection, and a mysqli connection object (in this case, called $connection):

```php
$var = sanitizeMySQL($connection, $_POST['user_input']);
```

> If you use the procedural version of the mysqli extension, you will need to modify sanitizeMySQL to call the mysqli_real_es cape_string function, like this (in which case $connection will then be a handle, not an object):
>
> ```php
> $var = mysqli_real_escape_string($connection, $var);
> ```

An Example Program

So let's look at how a real life PHP program integrates with an HTML form by creating the program *convert.php* listed in Example 12-10. Enter it as shown and try it for yourself.

Example 12-10. A program to convert values between Fahrenheit and Celsius

```php
<?php // convert.php
  $f = $c = '';

  if (isset($_POST['f'])) $f = sanitizeString($_POST['f']);
  if (isset($_POST['c'])) $c = sanitizeString($_POST['c']);

  if ($f != '')
```

```php
  {
    $c = intval((5 / 9) * ($f - 32));
    $out = "$f °f equals $c °c";
  }
  elseif($c != '')
  {
    $f = intval((9 / 5) * $c + 32);
    $out = "$c °c equals $f °f";
  }
  else $out = "";

  echo <<<_END
<html>
  <head>
    <title>Temperature Converter</title>
  </head>
  <body>
    <pre>
      Enter either Fahrenheit or Celsius and click on Convert

      <b>$out</b>
      <form method="post" action="convert.php">
        Fahrenheit <input type="text" name="f" size="7">
           Celsius <input type="text" name="c" size="7">
                   <input type="submit" value="Convert">
      </form>
    </pre>
  </body>
</html>
_END;

  function sanitizeString($var)
  {
    $var = stripslashes($var);
    $var = htmlentities($var);
    $var = strip_tags($var);
    return $var;
  }
?>
```

When you call up *convert.php* in a browser, the result should look something like Figure 12-8.

To break the program down, the first line initializes the variables $c and $f in case they do not get posted to the program. The next two lines fetch the values of either the field named f or the one named c, for an input Fahrenheit or Celsius value. If the user inputs both, the Celsius is simply ignored and the Fahrenheit value is converted. As a security measure, the new function sanitizeString from Example 12-9 is also used.

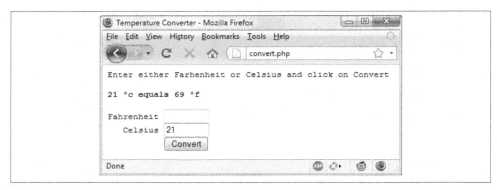

Figure 12-8. The temperature conversion program in action

So, having either submitted values or empty strings in both $f and $c, the next portion of code constitutes an if ... elseif ... else structure that first tests whether $f has a value. If not, it checks $c; otherwise, the variable $out is set to the empty string (more on that in a moment).

If $f is found to have a value, the variable $c is assigned a simple mathematical expression that converts the value of $f from Fahrenheit to Celsius. The formula used is Celsius = (5 ÷ 9) × (Fahrenheit − 32). The variable $out is then set to a message string explaining the conversion.

On the other hand, if $c is found to have a value, a complementary operation is performed to convert the value of $c from Celsius to Fahrenheit and assign the result to $f. The formula used is Fahrenheit = (9 ÷ 5) × Celsius + 32. As with the previous section, the string $out is then set to contain a message about the conversion.

In both conversions, the PHP intval function is called to convert the result of the conversion to an integer value. It's not necessary, but looks better.

With all the arithmetic done, the program now outputs the HTML, which starts with the basic head and title and then contains some introductory text before displaying the value of $out. If no temperature conversion was made, $out will have a value of NULL and nothing will be displayed, which is exactly what we want when the form hasn't yet been submitted. But if a conversion was made, $out contains the result, which is displayed.

After this, we come to the form, which is set to submit using the POST method to the file *convert.php* (the program itself). Within the form, there are two inputs for either a Fahrenheit or Celsius value to be entered. A submit button with the text Convert is then displayed, and the form is closed.

After outputting the HTML to close the document, we come finally to the function sanitizeString from Example 12-9. Try playing with the example by inputting different values into the fields; for a bit of fun, can you find a value for which Fahrenheit and Celsius are the same?

 All the examples in this chapter have used the POST method to send form data. I recommend this, as it's the neatest and most secure method. However, the forms can easily be changed to use the GET method, as long as values are fetched from the $_GET array instead of the $_POST array. Reasons to do this might include making the result of a search bookmarkable or directly linkable from another page.

What's New in HTML5?

With HTML5, developers can draw on a number of useful enhancements to form handling to make using forms easier than ever, including new attributes; color, date, and time pickers; and new input types—although some of these features are not yet implanted across all major browsers. The following new features, however, will work on all browsers.

The autocomplete Attribute

You can apply the autocomplete attribute to either the <form> element, or to any of the color, date, email, password, range, search, tel, text, or url types of the <input> element.

With autocomplete enabled, previous user inputs are recalled and automatically entered into fields as suggestions. You can also disable this feature by turning autocomplete off. Here's how to turn autocomplete on for an entire form but disable it for specific fields (highlighted in bold):

```
<form action='myform.php' method='post' autocomplete='on'>
  <input type='text'     name='username'>
  <input type='password' name='password' autocomplete='off'>
</form>
```

The autofocus Attribute

The autofocus attribute gives immediate focus to an element when a page loads. It can be applied to any <input>, <textarea>, or <button> element, like this:

```
<input type='text' name='query' autofocus='autofocus'>
```

 Browsers that use touch interfaces (such as Android, iOS, or Windows Phone) usually ignore the autofocus attribute, leaving it to the user to tap on a field to give it focus; otherwise, the zoom in, focusing, and pop-up keyboards this attribute would generate could quickly become very annoying.

Because this feature will cause the focus to move in to an input element, the backspace key will no longer take the user back a web page (although Alt-Left and Alt-Right will still move backward and forward within the browsing history).

The placeholder Attribute

The placeholder attribute lets you place into any blank input field a helpful hint to explain to users what they should enter. You use it like this:

```
<input type='text' name='name' size='50' placeholder='First & Last name'>
```

The input field will display the placeholder text as a prompt until the user starts typing, at which point the placeholder will disappear.

The required Attribute

The required attribute is used to ensure that a field has been completed before a form is submitted. You use it like this:

```
<input type='text' name='creditcard' required='required'>
```

If the browser detects attempted form submission with an uncompleted required input, a message is displayed prompting the user to complete the field.

Override Attributes

With override attributes, you can override form settings on an element-by-element basis. So, for example, using the formaction attribute you can specify that a submit button should submit a form to a different URL than is specified in the form itself, like the following (in which the default and overridden action URLs are shown in bold):

```
<form action='url1.php' method='post'>
  <input type='text' name='field'>
  <input type='submit' formaction='url2.php'>
</form>
```

HTML5 also brings support for the formenctype, formmethod, formnovalidate, and formtarget override attributes, which can be used in the same manner as formaction to override one of these settings.

The form overrides have been supported in most major browsers for a few years, but have only been featured in Internet Explorer since version 10.

The width and height Attributes

Using these new attributes, you can alter the dimensions of an input image, like this:

```
<input type='image' src='picture.png' width='120' height='80'>
```

Features Awaiting Full Implementation

Because HTML5 is still in its early days (even though it's been around for many years), browser developers have been implementing features according to their own schedules, so many parts of the specification are available only on some browsers. However, during the life of this edition more and more of them will become available across the board, so it's worth mentioning what's coming here so that you'll be ready to use them sooner rather than later.

The form Attribute

With HTML5, you no longer have to place <input> elements within <form> elements, because you can specify the form to which an input applies by supplying a form attribute. The following code shows a form being created, but with its input outside of the <form> and </form> tags:

```
<form action='myscript.php' method='post' id='form1'>
</form>

<input type='text' name='username' form='form1'>
```

To do this, you must give the form an ID using the id attribute, and this is the ID to which the form attribute of an input element must refer.

At the time of writing, this attribute is unsupported by Internet Explorer.

The list Attribute

HTML5 supports attaching lists to inputs to enable users to easily select from a predefined list. But, at the time of writing, only Firefox, Chrome, Opera, and IE support the list attribute. Nevertheless, once Safari picks it up, it will be a very handy feature, which you'll be able to use like this:

```
Select destination:
<input type='url' name='site' list='links'>

<datalist id='links'>
  <option label='Google' value='http://google.com'>
  <option label='Yahoo!' value='http://yahoo.com'>
  <option label='Bing'   value='http://bing.com'>
  <option label='Ask'    value='http://ask.com'>
</datalist>
```

The min and max Attributes

With the `min` and `max` attributes you can specify minimum and maximum values for inputs, but currently not in Firefox or IE. You use the attributes like this:

```
<input type='time' name='alarm' value='07:00' min='05:00' max='09:00'>
```

The browser will then either offer up and down selectors for the range of values allowed, or simply disallow values outside of that range. In tests, however, I have found this attribute to be flaky in some implementations, and suggest you fully test before implementing this feature, even when it is available on all browsers.

The step Attribute

Often used with `min` and `max`, the `step` attribute supports stepping through number or date values, like this:

```
<input type='time' name='meeting' value='12:00'
   min='09:00' max='16:00' step='3600'>
```

When you are stepping through date or time values, each unit represents one second. This attribute is not yet supported by Firefox or IE.

The color Input Type

The `color` input type calls up a color picker so that you can simply click on the color of your choice. You use it like this:

```
Choose a color <input type='color' name='color'>
```

Neither Firefox nor IE supports this input type at the time of writing.

The number and range Input Types

The `number` and `range` input types restrict input to either a number or a number within a specified range, like this:

```
<input type='number' name='age'>
<input type='range' name='num' min='0' max='100' value='50' step='1'>
```

Firefox does not appear to support the `number` input type at the time of writing.

Date and time Pickers

When you choose an input type of `date`, `month`, `week`, `time`, `datetime`, or `datetime-local`, a picker will pop up on supported browsers from which the user can make a selection, like this one, which inputs the time:

```
<input type='time' name='time' value='12:34'>
```

However, without support from IE or Firefox, these pickers are probably not worth using in your web pages yet.

There are a few other form-related enhancements to HTML5 that are still under development, and you can keep abreast of them at *http://tinyurl.com/h5forms*.

The next chapter will show you how to use cookies and authentication to store users' preferences and keep them logged in, and how to maintain a complete user session.

Questions

1. You can submit form data using either the POST or the GET method. Which associative arrays are used to pass this data to PHP?

2. What is register_globals, and why is it a bad idea?

3. What is the difference between a text box and a text area?

4. If a form has to offer three choices to a user, each of which is mutually exclusive so that only one of the three can be selected, which input type would you use, given a choice between checkboxes and radio buttons?

5. How can you submit a group of selections from a web form using a single field name?

6. How can you submit a form field without displaying it in the browser?

7. Which HTML tag is used to encapsulate a form element and supporting text or graphics, making the entire unit selectable with a mouse-click?

8. Which PHP function converts HTML into a format that can be displayed but will not be interpreted as HTML by a browser?

9. What form attribute can be used to help users complete input fields?

10. How can you ensure that an input is completed before a form gets submitted?

See "Chapter 12 Answers" on page 647 in Appendix A for the answers to these questions.

CHAPTER 13

Cookies, Sessions, and Authentication

As your web projects grow larger and more complicated, you will find an increasing need to keep track of your users. Even if you aren't offering logins and passwords, you will still often need to store details about a user's current session and possibly also recognize people when they return to your site.

Several technologies support this kind of interaction, ranging from simple browser cookies to session handling and HTTP authentication. Between them, they offer the opportunity for you to configure your site to your users' preferences and ensure a smooth and enjoyable transition through it.

Using Cookies in PHP

A *cookie* is an item of data that a web server saves to your computer's hard disk via a web browser. It can contain almost any alphanumeric information (as long as it's under 4 KB) and can be retrieved from your computer and returned to the server. Common uses include session tracking, maintaining data across multiple visits, holding shopping cart contents, storing login details, and more.

Because of their privacy implications, cookies can be read only from the issuing domain. In other words, if a cookie is issued by, for example, *oreilly.com*, it can be retrieved only by a web server using that domain. This prevents other websites from gaining access to details for which they are not authorized.

Due to the way the Internet works, multiple elements on a web page can be embedded from multiple domains, each of which can issue its own cookies. When this happens, they are referred to as *third-party cookies*. Most commonly, these are created by advertising companies in order to track users across multiple websites.

Because of this, most browsers allow users to turn cookies off either for the current server's domain, third-party servers, or both. Fortunately, most people who disable cookies do so only for third-party websites.

Cookies are exchanged during the transfer of headers, before the actual HTML of a web page is sent, and it is impossible to send a cookie once any HTML has been transferred. Therefore, careful planning of cookie usage is important. Figure 13-1 illustrates a typical request and response dialog between a web browser and web server passing cookies.

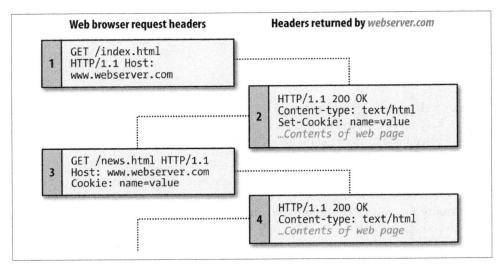

Figure 13-1. A browser/server request/response dialog with cookies

This exchange shows a browser receiving two pages:

1. The browser issues a request to retrieve the main page, *index.html*, at the website *http://www.webserver.com*. The first header specifies the file, and the second header specifies the server.

2. When the web server at *webserver.com* receives this pair of headers, it returns some of its own. The second header defines the type of content to be sent (*text/html*), and the third one sends a cookie of the name *name* and with the value *value*. Only then are the contents of the web page transferred.

3. Once the browser has received the cookie, it will then return it with every future request made to the issuing server until the cookie expires or is deleted. So, when the browser requests the new page */news.html*, it also returns the cookie *name* with the value *value*.

4. Because the cookie has already been set, when the server receives the request to send */news.html*, it does not have to resend the cookie, but just returns the requested page.

Setting a Cookie

Setting a cookie in PHP is a simple matter. As long as no HTML has yet been transferred, you can call the `setcookie` function, which has the following syntax (see Table 13-1):

```
setcookie(name, value, expire, path, domain, secure, httponly);
```

Table 13-1. The setcookie parameters

Parameter	Description	Example
name	The name of the cookie. This is the name that your server will use to access the cookie on subsequent browser requests.	username
value	The value of the cookie, or the cookie's contents. This can contain up to 4 KB of alphanumeric text.	Hannah
expire	(*Optional.*) Unix timestamp of the expiration date. Generally, you will probably use `time()` plus a number of seconds. If not set, the cookie expires when the browser closes.	time() + 2592000
path	(*Optional.*) The path of the cookie on the server. If this is a / (forward slash), the cookie is available over the entire domain, such as *www.webserver.com*. If it is a subdirectory, the cookie is available only within that subdirectory. The default is the current directory that the cookie is being set in, and this is the setting you will normally use.	/
domain	(*Optional.*) The Internet domain of the cookie. If this is *.webserver.com*, the cookie is available to all of *webserver.com* and its subdomains, such as *www.webserver.com* and *images.webserver.com*. If it is *images.webserver.com*, the cookie is available only to *images.webserver.com* and its subdomains such as *sub.images.webserver.com*, but not, say, to *www.webserver.com*.	.webserver.com
secure	(*Optional.*) Whether the cookie must use a secure connection (*https://*). If this value is TRUE, the cookie can be transferred only across a secure connection. The default is FALSE.	FALSE
httponly	(*Optional*; implemented since PHP version 5.2.0.) Whether the cookie must use the HTTP protocol. If this value is TRUE, scripting languages such as JavaScript cannot access the cookie. (Not supported in all browsers.) The default is FALSE.	FALSE

So, to create a cookie with the name `username` and the value `Hannah` that is accessible across the entire web server on the current domain, and will be removed from the browser's cache in seven days, use the following:

```
setcookie('username', 'Hannah', time() + 60 * 60 * 24 * 7, '/');
```

Accessing a Cookie

Reading the value of a cookie is as simple as accessing the $_COOKIE system array. For example, if you wish to see whether the current browser has the cookie called user name already stored and, if so, to read its value, use the following:

```
if (isset($_COOKIE['username'])) $username = $_COOKIE['username'];
```

Note that you can read a cookie back only after it has been sent to a web browser. This means that when you issue a cookie, you cannot read it in again until the browser reloads the page (or another with access to the cookie) from your website and passes the cookie back to the server in the process.

Destroying a Cookie

To delete a cookie, you must issue it again and set a date in the past. It is important for all parameters in your new setcookie call except the timestamp to be identical to the parameters when the cookie was first issued; otherwise, the deletion will fail. Therefore, to delete the cookie created earlier, you would use the following:

```
setcookie('username', 'Hannah', time() - 2592000, '/');
```

As long as the time given is in the past, the cookie should be deleted. However, I have used a time of 2592000 seconds (one month) in the past in case the client computer's date and time are not correctly set.

 You can try PHP cookies for yourself using the file *php-cookies.php* in this chapter's matching folder of the accompanying examples archive (available for free at *http://lpmj.net*). The folder also contains the file *javascript-cookies.htm*, which does the same thing using JavaScript.

HTTP Authentication

HTTP authentication uses the web server to manage users and passwords for the application. It's adequate for most applications that ask users to log in, although some applications have specialized needs or more stringent security requirements that call for other techniques.

To use HTTP authentication, PHP sends a header request asking to start an authentication dialog with the browser. The server must have this feature turned on in order for it to work, but because it's so common, your server is very likely to offer the feature.

Although it is usually installed with Apache, HTTP authentication may not necessarily be installed on the server you use. So attempting to run these examples may generate an error telling you that the feature is not enabled, in which case you must install the module, change the configuration file to load the module, or ask your system administrator to do these fixes.

After entering your URL into the browser or visiting via a link, the user will see an "Authentication Required" prompt pop up requesting two fields: User Name and Password (Figure 13-2 shows how this looks in Firefox).

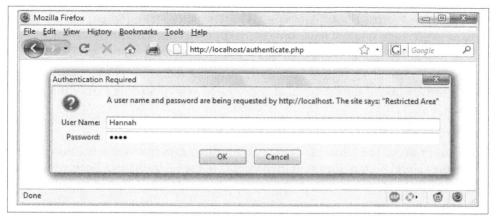

Figure 13-2. An HTTP authentication login prompt

Example 13-1 shows the code to make this happen.

Example 13-1. PHP authentication

```php
<?php
  if (isset($_SERVER['PHP_AUTH_USER']) &&
      isset($_SERVER['PHP_AUTH_PW']))
  {
    echo "Welcome User: " . $_SERVER['PHP_AUTH_USER'] .
        " Password: "    . $_SERVER['PHP_AUTH_PW'];
  }
  else
  {
    header('WWW-Authenticate: Basic realm="Restricted Section"');
    header('HTTP/1.0 401 Unauthorized');
    die("Please enter your username and password");
  }
?>
```

By default, the type of interface Zend Server uses is *cgi-fcgi*, which is incompatible with basic authentication. However, configuring Zend is beyond the scope of this book, so if you are using it for Examples 13-1 through 13-5, you may prefer to test them on a different server. To determine the interface of a server, you can call the php_sapi_name function, which will return a string such as 'cgi-fcgi', 'cli', and so on. Basic authentication is not recommended anyway on a production website, as it is very insecure, but you need to know how it works for maintaining legacy code. For further details, refer to *http://php.net/php_sapi_name*.

The first thing the program does is look for two particular values: $_SERVER['PHP_AUTH_USER'] and $_SERVER['PHP_AUTH_PW']. If they both exist, they represent the username and password entered by a user into an authentication prompt.

If either of the values does not exist, the user has not yet been authenticated and you display the prompt in Figure 13-2 by issuing the following header, where Basic realm is the name of the section that is protected and appears as part of the pop-up prompt:

```
WWW-Authenticate: Basic realm="Restricted Area"
```

If the user fills out the fields, the PHP program runs again from the top. But if the user clicks the Cancel button, the program proceeds to the following two lines, which send the following header and an error message:

```
HTTP/1.0 401 Unauthorized
```

The die statement causes the text "Please enter your username and password" to be displayed (see Figure 13-3).

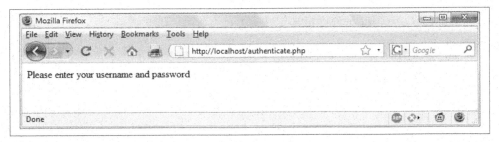

Figure 13-3. The result of clicking the Cancel button

Once a user has been authenticated, you will not be able to get the authentication dialog to pop up again unless the user closes and re-opens all browser windows, as the web browser will keep returning the same username and password to PHP. You may need to close and reopen your browser a few times as you work through this section and try different things out.

Now let's check for a valid username and password. The code in Example 13-1 doesn't require you to change much to add this check, other than modifying the previous welcome message code to test for a correct username and password, and then issuing a welcome message. A failed authentication causes an error message to be sent (see Example 13-2).

Example 13-2. PHP authentication with input checking

```php
<?php
  $username = 'admin';
  $password = 'letmein';

  if (isset($_SERVER['PHP_AUTH_USER']) &&
      isset($_SERVER['PHP_AUTH_PW']))
  {
    if ($_SERVER['PHP_AUTH_USER'] == $username &&
        $_SERVER['PHP_AUTH_PW']   == $password)
          echo "You are now logged in";
    else die("Invalid username / password combination");
  }
  else
  {
    header('WWW-Authenticate: Basic realm="Restricted Section"');
    header('HTTP/1.0 401 Unauthorized');
    die ("Please enter your username and password");
  }
?>
```

Incidentally, take a look at the wording of the error message: Invalid username / password combination. It doesn't say whether the username or the password or both were wrong—the less information you can give to a potential hacker, the better.

A mechanism is now in place to authenticate users, but only for a single username and password. Also, the password appears in clear text within the PHP file, and if someone managed to hack into your server, he would instantly know it. So let's look at a better way to handle usernames and passwords.

Storing Usernames and Passwords

Obviously MySQL is the natural way to store usernames and passwords. But again, we don't want to store the passwords as clear text, because our website could be compromised if the database were accessed by a hacker. Instead, we'll use a neat trick called a *one-way function*.

This type of function is easy to use and converts a string of text into a seemingly random string. Due to their one-way nature, such functions are virtually impossible to reverse, so their output can be safely stored in a database—and anyone who steals it will be none the wiser as to the passwords used.

In previous editions of this book I recommended using the *md5* hashing algorithm for your data security. Time marches on, however, and now md5 is considered easily hackable and therefore unsafe, while even its previously recommended replacement of *sha1* can apparently be hacked (plus sha1 and sha2 were designed by the NSA and therefore considerable caution is recommended for their use in highly secure implementations).

So now I have moved on to using the PHP hash function, passing it a version of the *ripemd* algorithm, which was designed by the open academic community and which (like md5) returns a 32-character hexadecimal number—so it can easily replace md5 in most databases. Use it like this:

```
$token = hash('ripemd128', 'mypassword');
```

That example happens to give $token the value:

```
7b694600c8a2a2b0897c719958713619
```

By using the hash function, you can keep up with future developments in security and simply pass the hashing algorithm to it that you wish to implement, resulting in less code maintenance (although you will probably have to accommodate larger hash lengths than 32 characters in your databases).

Salting

Unfortunately, hash on its own is not enough to protect a database of passwords, because it could still be susceptible to a brute force attack that uses another database of known 32-character hexadecimal tokens. Such databases do exist, as a quick Google search will verify, although probably only for md5 and sha1 or sha2 at the moment.

Thankfully, though, we can put a spanner in the works of any such attempts by *salting* all the passwords before they are sent to hash. Salting is simply a matter of adding some text that only we know about to each parameter to be encrypted, like this (with the salt highlighted in bold):

```
$token = hash('ripemd128', 'saltstringmypassword');
```

In this example, the text *saltstring* has been prepended to the password. Of course, the more obscure you can make the salt, the better. I like to use salts such as this:

```
$token = hash('ripemd128', 'hqb%$tmypasswordcg*l');
```

Here some random characters have been placed both before and after the password. Given just the database, and without access to your PHP code, it should now be next to impossible to work out the stored passwords.

All you have to do when verifying someone's login password is to add these same random strings back in before and after it, and then check the resulting token from a hash call against the one stored in the database for that user.

Let's create a MySQL table to hold some user details and add a couple of accounts. So type and save the program in Example 13-3 as *setupusers.php*, then open it in your browser.

Example 13-3. Creating a users table and adding two accounts

```php
<?php // setupusers.php
  require_once 'login.php';
  $connection =
    new mysqli($db_hostname, $db_username, $db_password, $db_database);

  if ($connection->connect_error) die($connection->connect_error);

  $query = "CREATE TABLE users (
    forename VARCHAR(32) NOT NULL,
    surname  VARCHAR(32) NOT NULL,
    username VARCHAR(32) NOT NULL UNIQUE,
    password VARCHAR(32) NOT NULL
  )";
  $result = $connection->query($query);
  if (!$result) die($connection->error);

  $salt1     = "qm&h*";
  $salt2     = "pg!@";

  $forename = 'Bill';
  $surname  = 'Smith';
  $username = 'bsmith';
  $password = 'mysecret';
  $token     = hash('ripemd128', "$salt1$password$salt2");

  add_user($connection, $forename, $surname, $username, $token);

  $forename = 'Pauline';
  $surname  = 'Jones';
  $username = 'pjones';
  $password = 'acrobat';
  $token     = hash('ripemd128', "$salt1$password$salt2");

  add_user($connection, $forename, $surname, $username, $token);

  function add_user($connection, $fn, $sn, $un, $pw)
  {
    $query = "INSERT INTO users VALUES('$fn', '$sn', '$un', '$pw')";
```

```
      $result = $connection->query($query);
      if (!$result) die($connection->error);
  }
?>
```

This program will create the table *users* within your *publications* database (or whichever database you set up for the *login.php* file in Chapter 10). In this table, it will create two users: Bill Smith and Pauline Jones. They have the usernames and passwords of *bsmith/ mysecret* and *pjones/acrobat*, respectively.

Using the data in this table, we can now modify Example 13-2 to properly authenticate users, and Example 13-4 shows the code needed to do this. Type it, save it as *authenti cate.php*, and call it up in your browser.

Example 13-4. PHP authentication using MySQL

```
<?php // authenticate.php
  require_once 'login.php';
  $connection =
    new mysqli($db_hostname, $db_username, $db_password, $db_database);

  if ($connection->connect_error) die($connection->connect_error);

  if (isset($_SERVER['PHP_AUTH_USER']) &&
      isset($_SERVER['PHP_AUTH_PW']))
  {
    $un_temp = mysql_entities_fix_string($connection, $_SERVER['PHP_AUTH_USER']);
    $pw_temp = mysql_entities_fix_string($connection, $_SERVER['PHP_AUTH_PW']);

    $query  = "SELECT * FROM users WHERE username='$un_temp'";
    $result = $connection->query($query);
    if (!$result) die($connection->error);
    elseif ($result->num_rows)
    {
      $row = $result->fetch_array(MYSQLI_NUM);

        $result->close();

      $salt1 = "qm&h*";
      $salt2 = "pg!@";
      $token = hash('ripemd128', "$salt1$pw_temp$salt2");

      if ($token == $row[3]) echo "$row[0] $row[1] :
        Hi $row[0], you are now logged in as '$row[2]'";
      else die("Invalid username/password combination");
    }
    else die("Invalid username/password combination");
  }
  else
  {
    header('WWW-Authenticate: Basic realm="Restricted Section"');
    header('HTTP/1.0 401 Unauthorized');
```

```
      die ("Please enter your username and password");
   }

   $connection->close();

   function mysql_entities_fix_string($connection, $string)
   {
      return htmlentities(mysql_fix_string($connection, $string));
   }

   function mysql_fix_string($connection, $string)
   {
      if (get_magic_quotes_gpc()) $string = stripslashes($string);
      return $connection->real_escape_string($string);
   }
?>
```

As you might expect at this point in the book, some of the examples such as this one are starting to get quite a bit longer. But don't be put off. The final 10 lines are simply Example 10-22 from Chapter 10. They are there to sanitize the user input—very important.

The only lines to really concern yourself with at this point start with the assigning of two variables, $un_temp and $pw_temp, using the submitted username and password, highlighted in bold text. Next, a query is issued to MySQL to look up the user $un_temp and, if a result is returned, to assign the first row to $row. (Because usernames are unique, there will be only one row.) Then the two salts are created in $salt1 and $salt2, which are then added before and after the submitted password $pw_temp. This string is then passed to the hash function, which returns a 32-character hexadecimal value in $token.

Now all that's necessary is to check $token against the value stored in the database, which happens to be in the fourth column—which is column 3 when starting from 0. So $row[3] contains the previous token calculated for the salted password. If the two match, a friendly welcome string is output, calling the user by his or her first name (see Figure 13-4). Otherwise, an error message is displayed. As mentioned before, the error message is the same regardless of whether such a username exists, as this provides minimal information to potential hackers or password guessers.

You can try this out for yourself by calling up the program in your browser and entering a username of bsmith and password of mysecret (or pjones and acrobat), the values that were saved in the database by Example 13-3.

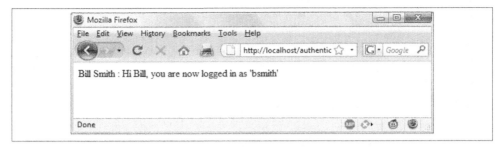

Figure 13-4. Bill Smith has now been authenticated

 By sanitizing input immediately after it is encountered, you will block any malicious HTML, JavaScript, or MySQL attacks before they can get any further, and will not have to sanitize this data again. Remember, however, that if a user has characters such as < or & in a password (for example), these will be expanded to < or & by the htmlemtities function. But as long as your code allows for strings that may end up larger than the provided input width, and as long as you always run passwords through this sanitization, you'll be just fine.

Using Sessions

Because your program can't tell what variables were set in other programs—or even what values the same program set the previous time it ran—you'll sometimes want to track what your users are doing from one web page to another. You can do this by setting hidden fields in a form, as seen in Chapter 10, and checking the value of the fields after the form is submitted, but PHP provides a much more powerful and simpler solution in the form of *sessions*. These are groups of variables that are stored on the server but relate only to the current user. To ensure that the right variables are applied to the right users, PHP saves a cookie in the users' web browsers to uniquely identify them.

This cookie has meaning only to the web server and cannot be used to ascertain any information about a user. You might ask about those users who have their cookies turned off. Well, that's not a problem as of PHP 4.2.0, because it will identify when this is the case and place a cookie token in the GET portion of each URL request instead. Either way, sessions provide a solid way of keeping track of your users.

Starting a Session

Starting a session requires calling the PHP function session_start before any HTML has been output, similarly to how cookies are sent during header exchanges. Then, to begin saving session variables, you just assign them as part of the $_SESSION array, like this:

```
$_SESSION['variable'] = $value;
```

They can then be read back just as easily in later program runs, like this:

```
$variable = $_SESSION['variable'];
```

Now assume that you have an application that always needs access to the username, password, first name, and last name of each user, as stored in the table *users*, which you should have created a little earlier. So let's further modify *authenticate.php* from Example 13-4 to set up a session once a user has been authenticated.

Example 13-5 shows the changes needed. The only difference is the content of the `if ($token == $row[3])` section, which we now start by opening a session and saving these four variables into it. Enter this program (or modify Example 13-4) and save it as *authenticate2.php*. But don't run it in your browser yet, as you will also need to create a second program in a moment.

Example 13-5. Setting a session after successful authentication

```php
<?php //authenticate2.php
  require_once 'login.php';
  $connection =
    new mysqli($db_hostname, $db_username, $db_password, $db_database);

  if ($connection->connect_error) die($connection->connect_error);

  if (isset($_SERVER['PHP_AUTH_USER']) &&
      isset($_SERVER['PHP_AUTH_PW']))
  {
    $un_temp = mysql_entities_fix_string($connection, $_SERVER['PHP_AUTH_USER']);
    $pw_temp = mysql_entities_fix_string($connection, $_SERVER['PHP_AUTH_PW']);

    $query = "SELECT * FROM users WHERE username='$un_temp'";
    $result = $connection->query($query);

    if (!$result) die($connection->error);
    elseif ($result->num_rows)
    {
        $row = $result->fetch_array(MYSQLI_NUM);

        $result->close();

        $salt1 = "qm&h*";
        $salt2 = "pg!@";
      $token = hash('ripemd128', "$salt1$pw_temp$salt2");

        if ($token == $row[3])
        {
            session_start();
            $_SESSION['username'] = $un_temp;
            $_SESSION['password'] = $pw_temp;
            $_SESSION['forename'] = $row[0];
```

```
            $_SESSION['surname']  = $row[1];
            echo "$row[0] $row[1] : Hi $row[0],
                you are now logged in as '$row[2]'";
            die ("<p><a href=continue.php>Click here to continue</a></p>");
      }
      else die("Invalid username/password combination");
  }
  else die("Invalid username/password combination");
}
else
{
  header('WWW-Authenticate: Basic realm="Restricted Section"');
  header('HTTP/1.0 401 Unauthorized');
  die ("Please enter your username and password");
}

$connection->close();

function mysql_entities_fix_string($connection, $string)
{
  return htmlentities(mysql_fix_string($connection, $string));
}

function mysql_fix_string($connection, $string)
{
  if (get_magic_quotes_gpc()) $string = stripslashes($string);
  return $connection->real_escape_string($string);
}
?>
```

One other addition to the program is the "Click here to continue" link with a destination URL of *continue.php*. This will be used to illustrate how the session will transfer to another program or PHP web page. So create *continue.php* by entering the program in Example 13-6 and saving it.

Example 13-6. Retrieving session variables

```
<?php // continue.php
  session_start();

  if (isset($_SESSION['username']))
  {
    $username = $_SESSION['username'];
    $password = $_SESSION['password'];
    $forename = $_SESSION['forename'];
    $surname  = $_SESSION['surname'];

    echo "Welcome back $forename.<br>
        Your full name is $forename $surname.<br>
        Your username is '$username'
        and your password is '$password'.";
  }
```

```
    else echo "Please <a href='authenticate2.php'>click here</a> to log in.";
?>
```

Now you are ready to call up *authenticate2.php* into your browser. Enter a username of
bsmith and password of mysecret (or pjones and acrobat) when prompted, and click
the link to load in *continue.php*. When your browser calls it up, the result should be
something like Figure 13-5.

Figure 13-5. Maintaining user data with sessions

Sessions neatly confine to a single program the extensive code required to authenticate
and log in a user. Once a user has been authenticated and you have created a session,
your program code becomes very simple indeed. You need only to call up
session_start and look up any variables to which you need access from $_SESSION.

In Example 13-6, a quick test of whether $_SESSION['username'] has a value is enough
to let you know that the current user is authenticated, because session variables are
stored on the server (unlike cookies, which are stored on the web browser) and can
therefore be trusted.

If $_SESSION['username'] has not been assigned a value, no session is active, so the
last line of code in Example 13-6 directs users to the login page at *authenticate2.php*.

 The *continue.php* program prints back the value of the user's password to show you how session variables work. In practice, you already know that the user is logged in, so you shouldn't need to keep
track of (or display) any passwords, and in fact doing so would be a
security risk.

Ending a Session

When the time comes to end a session, usually when a user requests to log out from
your site, you can use the session_destroy function in association, as in
Example 13-7. That example provides a useful function for totally destroying a session,
logging a user out, and unsetting all session variables.

Example 13-7. A handy function to destroy a session and its data

```php
<?php
  function destroy_session_and_data()
  {
    session_start();
    $_SESSION = array();
    setcookie(session_name(), '', time() - 2592000, '/');
    session_destroy();
  }
?>
```

To see this in action, you could modify *continue.php* as in Example 13-8.

Example 13-8. Retrieving session variables and then destroying the session

```php
<?php
  session_start();

  if (isset($_SESSION['username']))
  {
    $username = $_SESSION['username'];
    $password = $_SESSION['password'];
    $forename = $_SESSION['forename'];
    $surname  = $_SESSION['surname'];

    destroy_session_and_data();

    echo "Welcome back $forename.<br>
          Your full name is $forename $surname.<br>
          Your username is '$username'
          and your password is '$password'.";

  }
  else echo "Please <a href='authenticate2.php'>click here</a> to log in.";

  function destroy_session_and_data()
  {
    $_SESSION = array();
    setcookie(session_name(), '', time() - 2592000, '/');
    session_destroy();
  }
?>
```

The first time you navigate from *authenticate2.php* to *continue.php*, it will display all the session variables. But, because of the call to destroy_session_and_data, if you then click on your browser's Reload button, the session will have been destroyed and you'll be prompted to return to the login page.

Setting a Timeout

There are other times when you might wish to close a user's session yourself, such as when the user has forgotten or neglected to log out, and you want the program to do so for his for her own security. You do this by setting the timeout after which a logout will automatically occur if there has been no activity.

To do this, use the `ini_set` function as follows. This example sets the timeout to exactly one day:

```
ini_set('session.gc_maxlifetime', 60 * 60 * 24);
```

If you wish to know what the current timeout period is, you can display it using the following:

```
echo ini_get('session.gc_maxlifetime');
```

Session Security

Although I mentioned that once you had authenticated a user and set up a session you could safely assume that the session variables were trustworthy, this isn't exactly the case. The reason is that it's possible to use *packet sniffing* (sampling of data) to discover session IDs passing across a network. Additionally, if the session ID is passed in the GET part of a URL, it might appear in external site server logs. The only truly secure way of preventing these from being discovered is to implement a *Secure Socket Layer (SSL)* and run HTTPS instead of HTTP web pages. That's beyond the scope of this book, although you may like to take a look at *http://apache-ssl.org* for details on setting up a secure web server.

Preventing session hijacking

When SSL is not a possibility, you can further authenticate users by storing their IP address along with their other details by adding a line such as the following when you store their session:

```
$_SESSION['ip'] = $_SERVER['REMOTE_ADDR'];
```

Then, as an extra check, whenever any page loads and a session is available, perform the following check. It calls the function `different_user` if the stored IP address doesn't match the current one:

```
if ($_SESSION['ip'] != $_SERVER['REMOTE_ADDR']) different_user();
```

What code you place in your `different_user` function is up to you. I recommend that you simply delete the current session and ask the user to log in again due to a technical error. Don't say any more than that, or you're giving away potentially useful information.

Of course, you need to be aware that users on the same proxy server, or sharing the same IP address on a home or business network, will have the same IP address. Again, if this is a problem for you, use SSL. You can also store a copy of the browser *user agent string* (a string that developers put in their browsers to identify them by type and version), which might also distinguish users due to the wide variety of browser types, versions, and computer platforms. Use the following to store the user agent:

```
$_SESSION['ua'] = $_SERVER['HTTP_USER_AGENT'];
```

And use this to compare the current agent string with the saved one:

```
if ($_SESSION['ua'] != $_SERVER['HTTP_USER_AGENT']) different_user();
```

Or, better still, combine the two checks like this and save the combination as a hash hexadecimal string:

```
$_SESSION['check'] = hash('ripemd128', $_SERVER['REMOTE_ADDR'] .
    $_SERVER['HTTP_USER_AGENT']);
```

And use this to compare the current and stored strings:

```
if ($_SESSION['check'] != hash('ripemd128', $_SERVER['REMOTE_ADDR'] .
    $_SERVER['HTTP_USER_AGENT'])) different_user();
```

Preventing session fixation

Session fixation happens when a malicious user tries to present a session ID to the server rather than letting the server create one. It can happen when a user takes advantage of the ability to pass a session ID in the GET part of a URL, like this:

```
http://yourserver.com/authenticate.php?PHPSESSID=123456789
```

In this example, the made-up session ID of 123456789 is being passed to the server. Now, consider Example 13-9, which is susceptible to session fixation. To see how, save it as *sessiontest.php*.

Example 13-9. A session susceptible to session fixation

```
<?php // sessiontest.php
  session_start();

  if (!isset($_SESSION['count'])) $_SESSION['count'] = 0;
  else ++$_SESSION['count'];

  echo $_SESSION['count'];
?>
```

Once it's saved, call it up in your browser using the following URL (prefacing it with the correct pathname, such as *http://localhost/*):

```
sessiontest.php?PHPSESSID=1234
```

Press Reload a few times, and you'll see the counter increase. Now try browsing to:

```
sessiontest.php?PHPSESSID=5678
```

Press Reload a few times here, and you should see it count up again from 0. Leave the counter on a different number than the first URL and then go back to the first URL and see how the number changes back. You have created two different sessions of your own choosing here, and you could easily create as many as you needed.

The reason this approach is so dangerous is that a malicious attacker could try to distribute these types of URLs to unsuspecting users, and if any of them followed these links, the attacker would be able to come back and take over any sessions that had not been deleted or expired!

In order to prevent this, add a simple check to change the session ID using `session_re generate_id`. This function keeps all current session variable values, but replaces the session ID with a new one that an attacker cannot know.

To do this, check for a special session variable that you arbitrarily invent. If it doesn't exist, you know that this is a new session, so you simply change the session ID and set the special session variable to note the change.

Example 13-10 shows how the code to do this might look, using the session variable `initiated`.

Example 13-10. Session regeneration

```php
<?php
  session_start();

  if (!isset($_SESSION['initiated']))
  {
    session_regenerate_id();
    $_SESSION['initiated'] = 1;
  }

  if (!isset($_SESSION['count'])) $_SESSION['count'] = 0;
  else ++$_SESSION['count'];

  echo $_SESSION['count'];
?>
```

This way, an attacker can come back to your site using any of the session IDs that he or she generated, but none of them will call up another user's session, as they will all have been replaced with regenerated IDs. If you want to be ultra-paranoid, you can even regenerate the session ID on each request.

Forcing cookie-only sessions

If you are prepared to require your users to enable cookies on your website, you can use the `ini_set` function like this:

```php
ini_set('session.use_only_cookies', 1);
```

With that setting, the ?PHPSESSID= trick will be completely ignored. If you use this security measure, I also recommend you inform your users that your site requires cookies, so they know what's wrong if they don't get the results they want.

Using a shared server

On a server shared with other accounts, you will not want to have all your session data saved into the same directory as theirs. Instead, you should choose a directory to which only your account has access (and that is not web-visible) to store your sessions, by placing an ini_set call near the start of a program, like this:

```
ini_set('session.save_path', '/home/user/myaccount/sessions');
```

The configuration option will keep this new value only during the program's execution, and the original configuration will be restored at the program's ending.

This sessions folder can fill up quickly; you may wish to periodically clear out older sessions according to how busy your server gets. The more it's used, the less time you will want to keep a session stored.

 Remember that your websites can and will be subject to hacking attempts. There are automated bots running riot around the Internet trying to find sites vulnerable to exploits. So whatever you do, whenever you are handling data that is not 100% generated within your own program, you should always treat it with the utmost caution.

At this point, you should now have a very good grasp of both PHP and MySQL, so in the next chapter it's time to introduce the third major technology covered by this book, JavaScript.

Questions

1. Why must a cookie be transferred at the start of a program?

2. Which PHP function stores a cookie on a web browser?

3. How can you destroy a cookie?

4. Where are the username and password stored in a PHP program when you are using HTTP authentication?

5. Why is the hash function a powerful security measure?

6. What is meant by "salting" a string?

7. What is a PHP session?

8. How do you initiate a PHP session?

9. What is session hijacking?

10. What is session fixation?

See "Chapter 13 Answers" on page 648 in Appendix A for the answers to these questions.

CHAPTER 14

Exploring JavaScript

JavaScript brings a dynamic functionality to your websites. Every time you see something pop up when you mouse over an item in the browser, or see new text, colors, or images appear on the page in front of your eyes, or grab an object on the page and drag it to a new location—all those things are done through JavaScript. It offers effects that are not otherwise possible, because it runs inside the browser and has direct access to all the elements in a web document.

JavaScript first appeared in the Netscape Navigator browser in 1995, coinciding with the addition of support for Java technology in the browser. Because of the initial incorrect impression that JavaScript was a spin-off of Java, there has been some long-term confusion over their relationship. However, the naming was just a marketing ploy to help the new scripting language benefit from the popularity of the Java programming language.

JavaScript gained new power when the HTML elements of the web page got a more formal, structured definition in what is called the *Document Object Model*, or *DOM*. The DOM makes it relatively easy to add a new paragraph or focus on a piece of text and change it.

Because both JavaScript and PHP support much of the structured programming syntax used by the C programming language, they look very similar to each other. They are both fairly high-level languages, too; for instance, they are weakly typed, so it's easy to change a variable to a new type just by using it in a new context.

Now that you have learned PHP, you should find JavaScript even easier. And you'll be glad you did, because it's at the heart of the Web 2.0 Ajax technology that provides the fluid web frontends that (along with HTML5 features) savvy web users expect these days.

JavaScript and HTML Text

JavaScript is a client-side scripting language that runs entirely inside the web browser. To call it up, you place it between opening `<script>` and closing `</script>` HTML tags. A typical HTML 4.01 "Hello World" document using JavaScript might look like Example 14-1.

Example 14-1. "Hello World" displayed using JavaScript

```
<html>
  <head><title>Hello World</title></head>
  <body>
    <script type="text/javascript">
      document.write("Hello World")
    </script>
    <noscript>
      Your browser doesn't support or has disabled JavaScript
    </noscript>
  </body>
</html>
```

 You may have seen web pages that use the HTML tag `<script lan guage="javascript">`, but that usage has now been deprecated. This example uses the more recent and preferred `<script type="text/ javascript">`, or you can just use `<script>` on its own if you like.

Within the `<script>` tags is a single line of JavaScript code that uses its equivalent of the PHP `echo` or `print` commands, `document.write`. As you'd expect, it simply outputs the supplied string to the current document, where it is displayed.

You may also have noticed that, unlike with PHP, there is no trailing semicolon (`;`). This is because a newline serves the same purpose as a semicolon in JavaScript. However, if you wish to have more than one statement on a single line, you do need to place a semicolon after each command except the last one. Of course, if you wish, you can add a semicolon to the end of every statement and your JavaScript will work fine.

The other thing to note in this example is the `<noscript>` and `</noscript>` pair of tags. These are used when you wish to offer alternative HTML to users whose browser does not support JavaScript or who have it disabled. Using these tags is up to you, as they are not required, but you really ought to use them because it's usually not that difficult to provide static HTML alternatives to the operations you provide using JavaScript. However, the remaining examples in this book will omit `<noscript>` tags, because we're focusing on what you can do with JavaScript, not what you can do without it.

When Example 14-1 is loaded, a web browser with JavaScript enabled will output the following (see Figure 14-1):

```
Hello World
```

Figure 14-1. JavaScript, enabled and working

A browser with JavaScript disabled will display the message in Figure 14-2.

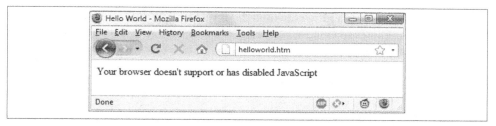

Figure 14-2. JavaScript has been disabled

Using Scripts Within a Document Head

In addition to placing a script within the body of a document, you can put it in the <head> section, which is the ideal place if you wish to execute a script when a page loads. If you place critical code and functions there, you can also ensure that they are ready to use immediately by any other script sections in the document that rely on them.

Another reason for placing a script in the document head is to enable JavaScript to write things such as meta tags into the <head> section, because the location of your script is the part of the document it writes to by default.

Older and Nonstandard Browsers

If you need to support browsers that do not offer scripting, you will need to use the HTML comment tags (<!-- and -->) to prevent them from encountering script code that they should not see. Example 14-2 shows how you add them to your script code.

Example 14-2. The "Hello World" example modified for non-JavaScript browsers

```
<html>
  <head><title>Hello World</title></head>
  <body>
    <script type="text/javascript"><!--
      document.write("Hello World")
    // --></script>
  </body>
</html>
```

Here an opening HTML comment tag (`<!--`) has been added directly after the opening `<script>` statement and a closing comment tag (`//  -->`) directly before the script is closed with `</script>`.

The double forward slash (`//`) is used by JavaScript to indicate that the rest of the line is a comment. It is there so that browsers that *do* support JavaScript will ignore the following `-->`, but non-JavaScript browsers will ignore the preceding `//`, and act on the `-->` by closing the HTML comment.

Although the solution is a little convoluted, all you really need to remember is to use the two following lines to enclose your JavaScript when you wish to support very old or non-standard browsers:

```
<script type="text/javascript"><!-
  (Your JavaScript goes here...)
// --></script>
```

However, the use of these comments is unnecessary for any browser released over the past several years.

There are a couple of other scripting languages you should know about. These include Microsoft's VBScript, which is based on the Visual Basic programming language, and Tcl, a rapid prototyping language. They are called up in a similar way to JavaScript, except they use types of `text/vbscript` and `text/tcl`, respectively. VBScript works only in Internet Explorer; use of it in other browsers requires a plugin. Tcl always needs a plug-in. So both should be considered nonstandard, and neither is covered in this book.

Including JavaScript Files

In addition to writing JavaScript code directly in HTML documents, you can include files of JavaScript code either from your website or from anywhere on the Internet. The syntax for this is:

```
<script type="text/javascript" src="script.js"></script>
```

Or, to pull a file in from the Internet, use:

```
<script type="text/javascript" src="http://someserver.com/script.js">
</script>
```

As for the script files themselves, they must *not* include any `<script>` or `</script>` tags, because they are unnecessary: the browser already knows that a JavaScript file is being loaded. Putting them in the JavaScript files will cause an error.

Including script files is the preferred way for you to use third-party JavaScript files on your website.

It is possible to leave out the `type="text/javascript"` parameters; all modern browsers default to assuming that the script contains JavaScript.

Debugging JavaScript Errors

When you're learning JavaScript, it's important to be able to track typing or other coding errors. Unlike PHP, which displays error messages in the browser, JavaScript handles error messages in a way that changes according to the browser used. Table 14-1 lists how to access JavaScript error messages in each of the five most commonly used browsers.

Table 14-1. Accessing JavaScript error messages in different browsers

Browser	How to access JavaScript error messages
Apple Safari	Safari does not have an Error Console enabled by default, but you can turn it on by selecting Safari→Preferences→Advanced→"Show Develop menu in menu bar." However, you may prefer to use the Firebug Lite JavaScript module (*http://getfirebug.com/firebuglite*), which many people find easier to use.
Google Chrome	Click the menu icon that looks like a page with a corner turned, then select Developer→JavaScript Console. You can also use the shortcut Ctrl-Shift-J on a PC, or Command-Shift-J on a Mac.
Microsoft Internet Explorer	Select Tools→Internet Options→Advanced, then uncheck the Disable Script Debugging box and check the "Display a Notification about Every Script Error" box.
Mozilla Firefox	Select Tools→Error Console or use the shortcut Ctrl-Shift-J on a PC, or Command-Shift-J on a Mac.
Opera	Select Tools→Advanced→Error Console.

OS X users: although I have shown you how to create an Error Console for JavaScript, you may prefer to use Google Chrome (for Intel OS X 10.5 or higher).

To try out whichever Error Console you are using, let's create a script with a minor error. Example 14-3 is much the same as Example 14-1, but the final double quotation mark has been left off the end of the string "Hello World"—a common syntax error.

Example 14-3. A JavaScript "Hello World" script with an error

```html
<html>
  <head><title>Hello World</title></head>
  <body>
    <script type="text/javascript">
      document.write("Hello World)
    </script>
  </body>
</html>
```

Enter the example and save it as *test.html*, then call it up in your browser. It should succeed only in displaying the title, not anything in the main browser window. Now call up the Error Console in your browser, and you should see a message such as the one in Example 14-4. To the right there will be a link to the source, which, when clicked, shows the error line highlighted (but does not indicate the position at which the error was encountered).

Example 14-4. A Mozilla Firefox Error Console message

```
SyntaxError: unterminated string literal
```

In Microsoft Internet Explorer, the error message will look like Example 14-5, and there's no helpful arrow, but you are given the line and position.

Example 14-5. A Microsoft Internet Explorer Error Console message

```
Unterminated string constant
```

Google Chrome and Opera will give the message in Example 14-6. Again, you'll be given the line error number but not the exact location.

Example 14-6. A Google Chrome/Opera Error Console message

```
Uncaught SyntaxError: Unexpected token ILLEGAL
```

And Apple Safari provides the message in Example 14-7, with a link to the source on the right stating the line number of the error. You can click the link to highlight the line, but it will not show where on the line the error occurred.

Example 14-7. An Opera Error Console message

```
SyntaxError: Unexpected EOF
```

If you find this support a little underwhelming, the Firebug plug-in (*http://getfire bug.com*) for Firefox (and now Chrome too) is very popular among JavaScript developers for debugging code, and is definitely worth a look.

If you will be entering the following code snippets to try them out, don't forget to surround them with `<script>` and `</script>` tags.

Using Comments

Due to their shared inheritance from the C programming language, PHP and JavaScript have many similarities, one of which is commenting. First, there's the single-line comment, like this:

```
// This is a comment
```

This style uses a pair of forward slash characters (//) to inform JavaScript that everything following is to be ignored. And then you also have multiline comments, like this:

```
/* This is a section
   of multiline comments
   that will not be
   interpreted */
```

Here you start a multiline comment with the sequence /* and end it with */. Just remember that you cannot nest multiline comments, so make sure that you don't comment out large sections of code that already contain multiline comments.

Semicolons

Unlike PHP, JavaScript generally does not require semicolons if you have only one statement on a line. Therefore, the following is valid:

```
x += 10
```

However, when you wish to place more than one statement on a line, you must separate them with semicolons, like this:

```
x += 10; y -= 5; z = 0
```

You can normally leave the final semicolon off, because the newline terminates the final statement.

There are exceptions to the semicolon rule. If the first character of a line is either a left parenthesis or a left bracket, then JavaScript will assume it follows on from the previous line. If this is not what you intend, then insert a semicolon between the two lines to separate them. Semicolons are also required by JavaScript bookmarklets because all the code must be on a single line. So, when in doubt, use a semicolon.

Variables

No particular character identifies a variable in JavaScript as the dollar sign does in PHP. Instead, variables use the following naming rules:

- A variable may include only the letters a–z, A–Z, 0–9, the $ symbol, and the underscore (_).
- No other characters, such as spaces or punctuation, are allowed in a variable name.
- The first character of a variable name can be only a–z, A–Z, $, or _ (no numbers).
- Names are case-sensitive. Count, count, and COUNT are all different variables.
- There is no set limit on variable name lengths.

And yes, you're right, that is a $ there in that list. It *is* allowed by JavaScript and *may* be the first character of a variable or function name. Although I don't recommend keeping the $ symbols, it means that you can port a lot of PHP code more quickly to JavaScript that way.

String Variables

JavaScript string variables should be enclosed in either single or double quotation marks, like this:

```
greeting = "Hello there"
warning  = 'Be careful'
```

You may include a single quote within a double-quoted string or a double quote within a single-quoted string. But you must escape a quote of the same type using the backslash character, like this:

```
greeting = "\"Hello there\" is a greeting"
warning  = '\'Be careful\' is a warning'
```

To read from a string variable, you can assign it to another one, like this:

```
newstring = oldstring
```

or you can use it in a function, like this:

```
status = "All systems are working"
document.write(status)
```

Numeric Variables

Creating a numeric variable is a simple as assigning a value, like these examples:

```
count       = 42
temperature = 98.4
```

Like strings, numeric variables can be read from and used in expressions and functions.

Arrays

JavaScript arrays are also very similar to those in PHP, in that an array can contain string or numeric data, as well as other arrays. To assign values to an array, use the following syntax (which in this case creates an array of strings):

```
toys = ['bat', 'ball', 'whistle', 'puzzle', 'doll']
```

To create a multidimensional array, nest smaller arrays within a larger one. So, to create a two-dimensional array containing the colors of a single face of a scrambled Rubik's Cube (where the colors red, green, orange, yellow, blue, and white are represented by their capitalized initial letters), you could use the following code:

```
face =
[
  ['R', 'G', 'Y'],
  ['W', 'R', 'O'],
  ['Y', 'W', 'G']
]
```

The previous example has been formatted to make it obvious what is going on, but it could also be written like this:

```
face = [['R', 'G', 'Y'], ['W', 'R', 'O'], ['Y', 'W', 'G']]
```

or even like this:

```
top = ['R', 'G', 'Y']
mid = ['W', 'R', 'O']
bot = ['Y', 'W', 'G']

face = [top, mid, bot]
```

To access the element two down and three along in this matrix, you would use the following (because array elements start at position 0):

```
document.write(face[1][2])
```

This statement will output the letter O for orange.

 JavaScript arrays are powerful storage structures, so Chapter 16 discusses them in much greater depth.

Operators

Operators in JavaScript, as in PHP, can involve mathematics, changes to strings, and comparison and logical operations (and, or, etc.). JavaScript mathematical operators look a lot like plain arithmetic; for instance, the following statement outputs 15:

```
document.write(13 + 2)
```

The following sections teach you about the various operators.

Arithmetic Operators

Arithmetic operators are used to perform mathematics. You can use them for the main four operations (addition, subtraction, multiplication, and division) as well as to find the modulus (the remainder after a division) and to increment or decrement a value (see Table 14-2).

Table 14-2. Arithmetic operators

Operator	Description	Example
+	Addition	j + 12
–	Subtraction	j – 22
*	Multiplication	j * 7
/	Division	j / 3.13
%	Modulus (division remainder)	j % 6
++	Increment	++j
--	Decrement	--j

Assignment Operators

The assignment operators are used to assign values to variables. They start with the very simple =, and move on to +=, -=, and so on. The operator += adds the value on the right side to the variable on the left, instead of totally replacing the value on the left. Thus, if count starts with the value 6, the statement:

```
count += 1
```

sets count to 7, just like the more familiar assignment statement:

```
count = count + 1
```

Table 14-3 lists the various assignment operators available.

Table 14-3. Assignment operators

Operator	Example	Equivalent to
=	j = 99	j = 99
+=	j += 2	j = j + 2
+=	j += 'string'	j = j + 'string'
-=	j -= 12	j = j - 12
*=	j *= 2	j = j * 2
/=	j /= 6	j = j / 6
%=	j %= 7	j = j % 7

Comparison Operators

Comparison operators are generally used inside a construct such as an `if` statement where you need to compare two items. For example, you may wish to know whether a variable you have been incrementing has reached a specific value, or whether another variable is less than a set value, and so on (see Table 14-4).

Table 14-4. Comparison operators

Operator	Description	Example
==	Is **equal** to	j == 42
!=	Is **not equal** to	j != 17
>	Is **greater than**	j > 0
<	Is **less than**	j < 100
>=	Is **greater than or equal** to	j >= 23
<=	Is **less than or equal** to	j <= 13
===	Is **equal** to (and of the same type)	j ===56
!==	Is **not equal** to (and of the same type)	j !== '1'

Logical Operators

Unlike PHP, JavaScript's logical operators do not include and and or equivalents to && and ||, and there is no xor operator (see Table 14-5).

Table 14-5. Logical operators

Operator	Description	Example
&&	And	j == 1 && k == 2
||	Or	j < 100 || j > 0
!	Not	! (j == k)

Variable Incrementing and Decrementing

The following forms of post- and pre-incrementing and decrementing you learned to use in PHP are also supported by JavaScript:

```
++x
--y
x += 22
y -= 3
```

String Concatenation

JavaScript handles string concatenation slightly differently from PHP. Instead of the . (period) operator, it uses the plus sign (+), like this:

```
document.write("You have " + messages + " messages.")
```

Assuming that the variable messages is set to the value 3, the output from this line of code will be:

You have 3 messages.

Just as you can add a value to a numeric variable with the += operator, you can also append one string to another the same way:

```
name =   "James"
name += " Dean"
```

Escaping Characters

Escape characters, which you've seen used to insert quotation marks in strings, can also insert various special characters such as tabs, newlines, and carriage returns. Here is an example using tabs to lay out a heading; it is included here merely to illustrate escapes, because in web pages, there are better ways to do layout:

```
heading = "Name\tAge\tLocation"
```

Table 14-6 details the escape characters available.

Table 14-6. JavaScript's escape characters

Character	Meaning
\b	Backspace
\f	Form feed
\n	New line
\r	Carriage return
\t	Tab
\'	Single quote (or apostrophe)
\"	Double quote

Character	Meaning
\\	Backslash
\XXX	An octal number between 000 and 377 that represents the Latin-1 character equivalent (such as \251 for the © symbol)
\xXX	A hexadecimal number between 00 and FF that represents the Latin-1 character equivalent (such as \xA9 for the © symbol)
\uXXXX	A hexadecimal number between 0000 and FFFF that represents the Unicode character equivalent (such as \u00A9 for the © symbol)

Variable Typing

Like PHP, JavaScript is a very loosely typed language; the *type* of a variable is determined only when a value is assigned and can change as the variable appears in different contexts. Usually, you don't have to worry about the type; JavaScript figures out what you want and just does it.

Take a look at Example 14-8, in which:

1. The variable n is assigned the string value 838102050, the next line prints out its value, and the typeof operator is used to look up the type.

2. n is given the value returned when the numbers 12345 and 67890 are multiplied together. This value is also 838102050, but it is a number, not a string. The type of variable is then looked up and displayed.

3. Some text is appended to the number n and the result is displayed.

Example 14-8. Setting a variable's type by assignment

```
<script>
  n = '838102050'       // Set 'n' to a string
  document.write('n = ' + n + ', and is a ' + typeof n + '<br>')

  n = 12345 * 67890;    // Set 'n' to a number
  document.write('n = ' + n + ', and is a ' + typeof n + '<br>')

  n += ' plus some text' // Change 'n' from a number to a string
  document.write('n = ' + n + ', and is a ' + typeof n + '<br>')
</script>
```

The output from this script looks like:

```
n = 838102050, and is a string
n = 838102050, and is a number
n = 838102050 plus some text, and is a string
```

If there is ever any doubt about the type of a variable, or you need to ensure that a variable has a particular type, you can force it to that type using statements such as the following (which respectively turn a string into a number and a number into a string):

```
n = "123"
n *= 1     // Convert 'n' into a number

n = 123
n += ""    // Convert 'n' into a string
```

Or, of course, you can always look up a variable's type using the typeof operator.

Functions

As with PHP, JavaScript functions are used to separate out sections of code that perform a particular task. To create a function, declare it in the manner shown in Example 14-9.

Example 14-9. A simple function declaration

```
<script>
  function product(a, b)
  {
    return a * b
  }
</script>
```

This function takes the two parameters passed, multiplies them together, and returns the product.

Global Variables

Global variables are ones defined outside of any functions (or within functions, but defined without the var keyword). They can be defined in the following ways:

```
        a = 123              // Global scope
    var b = 456              // Global scope
    if (a == 123) var c = 789 // Global scope
```

Regardless of whether you are using the var keyword, as long as a variable is defined outside of a function, it is global in scope. This means that every part of a script can have access to it.

Local Variables

Parameters passed to a function automatically have local scope; that is, they can be referenced only from within that function. However, there is one exception. Arrays are passed to a function by reference, so if you modify any elements in an array parameter, the elements of the original array will be modified.

To define a local variable that has scope only within the current function, and has not been passed as a parameter, use the `var` keyword. Example 14-10 shows a function that creates one variable with global scope and two with local scope.

Example 14-10. A function creating variables with global and local scope

```
<script>
  function test()
  {
        a = 123              // Global scope
     var b = 456             // Local scope
     if (a == 123) var c = 789 // Local scope
  }
</script>
```

To test whether scope setting has worked in PHP, we can use the `isset` function. But in JavaScript there isn't one, so Example 14-11 makes use of the `typeof` operator, which returns the string `undefined` when a variable is not defined.

Example 14-11. Checking the scope of the variables defined in function test

```
<script>
  test()

  if (typeof a != 'undefined') document.write('a = "' + a + '"<br>')
  if (typeof b != 'undefined') document.write('b = "' + b + '"<br>')
  if (typeof c != 'undefined') document.write('c = "' + c + '"<br>')

  function test()
  {
    a     = 123
    var b = 456

    if (a == 123) var c = 789
  }
</script>
```

The output from this script is the following single line:

```
a = "123"
```

This shows that only the variable a was given global scope, which is exactly what we would expect, because the variables b and c were given local scope by being prefaced with the var keyword.

If your browser issues a warning about b being undefined, the warning is correct but can be ignored.

The Document Object Model

The designers of JavaScript were very smart. Rather than just creating yet another scripting language (which would have still been a pretty good improvement at the time), they had the vision to build it around the *Document Object Model*, or *DOM*. This breaks down the parts of an HTML document into discrete *objects*, each with its own *properties* and *methods* and each subject to JavaScript's control.

JavaScript separates objects, properties, and methods using a period (one good reason why + is the string concatenation operator in JavaScript, rather than the period). For example, let's consider a business card as an object we'll call card. This object contains properties such as a name, address, phone number, and so on. In the syntax of JavaScript, these properties would look like this:

```
card.name
card.phone
card.address
```

Its methods are functions that retrieve, change, and otherwise act on the properties. For instance, to invoke a method that displays the properties of object card, you might use syntax such as:

```
card.display()
```

Have a look at some of the earlier examples in this chapter and look at where the statement document.write is used. Now that you understand how JavaScript is based around objects, you will see that write is actually a method of the document object.

Within JavaScript, there is a hierarchy of parent and child objects, which is what is known as the Document Object Model (see Figure 14-3).

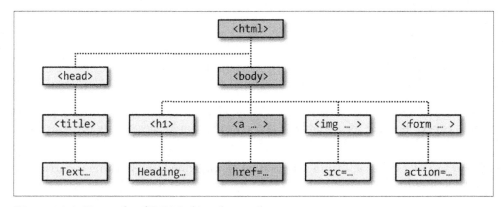

Figure 14-3. Example of DOM object hierarchy

The figure uses HTML tags that you are already familiar with to illustrate the parent/child relationship between the various objects in a document. For example, a URL within a link is part of the body of an HTML document. In JavaScript, it is referenced like this:

```
url = document.links.linkname.href
```

Notice how this follows the central column down. The first part, document, refers to the <html> and <body> tags; links.linkname to the <a> tag; and href to the href attribute.

Let's turn this into some HTML and a script to read a link's properties. Save Example 14-12 as *linktest.html*, then call it up in your browser.

 If you are using Microsoft Internet Explorer as your main development browser, skim through this section first (without trying the example), then read the section entitled "But It's Not That Simple" on page 340, and finally come back here and try the example with the getElementById modification discussed there. Without it, this example will not work for you.

Example 14-12. Reading a link URL with JavaScript

```
<html>
  <head>
    <title>Link Test</title>
  </head>
  <body>
    <a id="mylink" href="http://mysite.com">Click me</a><br>
    <script>
      url = document.links.mylink.href
      document.write('The URL is ' + url)
    </script>
  </body>
</html>
```

Note the short form of the <script> tags where I have omitted the parameter type="text/JavaScript" to save you some typing. If you wish, just for the purposes of testing this (and other examples), you could also omit everything outside of the <script> and </script> tags. The output from this example is:

<u>Click me</u>
The URL is http://mysite.com

The second line of output comes from the document.write method. Notice how the code follows the document tree down from document to links to mylink (the id given to the link) to href (the URL destination value).

There is also a short form that works equally well, which starts with the value in the id attribute: mylink.href. So you can replace this:

```
    url = document.links.mylink.href
```

with the following:

```
    url = mylink.href
```

But It's Not That Simple

If you tried Example 14-12 in Safari, Firefox, Opera, or Chrome, it will have worked just great. But in Internet Explorer it will fail, because Microsoft's implementation of JavaScript, called JScript, has many subtle differences from the recognized standards. Welcome to the world of advanced web development!

So what can we do about this? Well, in this case, instead of using the links child object of the parent document object, which Internet Explorer balks at, you have to replace it with a method to fetch the element by its id. Therefore, the following line:

```
    url = document.links.mylink.href
```

can be replaced with this one:

```
    url = document.getElementById('mylink').href
```

And now the script will work in all major browsers. Incidentally, when you don't have to look up the element by id, the short form that follows will still work in Internet Explorer, as well as the other browsers:

```
    url = mylink.href
```

Another Use for the $ Symbol

As mentioned earlier, the $ symbol is allowed in JavaScript variable and function names. Because of this, you may sometimes encounter strange-looking code like this:

```
    url = $('mylink').href
```

Some enterprising programmers have decided that the getElementById function is so prevalent in JavaScript that they have written a function to replace it called $, shown in Example 14-13.

Example 14-13. A replacement function for the getElementById method

```
<script>
  function $(id)
  {
    return document.getElementById(id)
  }
</script>
```

Therefore, as long as you have included the $ function in your code, syntax such as:

```
    $('mylink').href
```

can replace code such as:

```
document.getElementById('mylink').href
```

Using the DOM

The links object is actually an array of URLs, so the mylink URL in Example 14-12 can also be safely referred to on all browsers in the following way (because it's the first, and only, link):

```
url = document.links[0].href
```

If you want to know how many links there are in an entire document, you can query the length property of the links object like this:

```
numlinks = document.links.length
```

You can therefore extract and display all links in a document like this:

```
for (j=0 ; j < document.links.length ; ++j)
  document.write(document.links[j].href + '<br>')
```

The length of something is a property of every array, and many objects as well. For example, the number of items in your browser's web history can be queried like this:

```
document.write(history.length)
```

However, to stop websites from snooping on your browsing history, the history object stores only the number of sites in the array: you cannot read from or write to these values. But you can replace the current page with one from the history, if you know what position it has within the history. This can be very useful in cases in which you know that certain pages in the history came from your site, or you simply wish to send the browser back one or more pages, which you do with the go method of the history object. For example, to send the browser back three pages, issue the following command:

```
history.go(-3)
```

You can also use the following methods to move back or forward a page at a time:

```
history.back()
history.forward()
```

In a similar manner, you can replace the currently loaded URL with one of your choosing, like this:

```
document.location.href = 'http://google.com'
```

Of course, there's a whole lot more to the DOM than reading and modifying links. As you progress through the following chapters on JavaScript, you'll become quite familiar with the DOM and how to access it.

Questions

1. Which tags do you use to enclose JavaScript code?
2. By default, to which part of a document will JavaScript code output?
3. How can you include JavaScript code from another source in your documents?
4. Which JavaScript function is the equivalent of `echo` or `print` in PHP?
5. How can you create a comment in JavaScript?
6. What is the JavaScript string concatenation operator?
7. Which keyword can you use within a JavaScript function to define a variable that has local scope?
8. Give two cross-browser methods to display the URL assigned to the link with an id of `thislink`.
9. Which two JavaScript commands will make the browser load the previous page in its history array?
10. What JavaScript command would you use to replace the current document with the main page at the *oreilly.com* website?

See "Chapter 14 Answers" on page 648 in Appendix A for the answers to these questions.

CHAPTER 15

Expressions and Control Flow in JavaScript

In the previous chapter, I introduced the basics of JavaScript and the DOM. Now it's time to look at how to construct complex expressions in JavaScript and how to control the program flow of your scripts using conditional statements.

Expressions

JavaScript expressions are very similar to those in PHP. As you learned in Chapter 4, an expression is a combination of values, variables, operators, and functions that results in a value; the result can be a number, a string, or a Boolean value (which evaluates to either true or false).

Example 15-1 shows some simple expressions. For each line, it prints out a letter between a and d, followed by a colon and the result of the expressions. The <br> tag is there to create a line break and separate the output into four lines (remember that both <br> and <br /> are acceptable in HTML5, so I choose to use the former style for brevity).

Example 15-1. Four simple Boolean expressions

```
<script>
  document.write("a: " + (42 > 3) + "<br>")
  document.write("b: " + (91 < 4) + "<br>")
  document.write("c: " + (8 == 2) + "<br>")
  document.write("d: " + (4 < 17) + "<br>")
</script>
```

The output from this code is as follows:

```
a: true
b: false
c: false
d: true
```

Notice that both expressions a: and d: evaluate to true. But b: and c: evaluate to false. Unlike PHP (which would print the number 1 and nothing, respectively), actual strings of true and false are displayed.

In JavaScript, when you are checking whether a value is true or false, all values evaluate to true with the exception of the following, which evaluate to false: the string false itself, 0, -0, the empty string, null, undefined, and NaN (Not a Number, a computer engineering concept for an illegal floating-point operation such as division by zero).

Note how I am referring to true and false in lowercase. This is because, unlike in PHP, these values *must* be in lowercase in JavaScript. Therefore, only the first of the two following statements will display, printing the lowercase word true, because the second will cause a 'TRUE' is not defined error:

```
if (1 == true) document.write('true') // True
if (1 == TRUE) document.write('TRUE') // Will cause an error
```

 Remember that any code snippets you wish to type and try for yourself in an HTML file need to be enclosed within <script> and </script> tags.

Literals and Variables

The simplest form of an expression is a *literal*, which means something that evaluates to itself, such as the number 22 or the string Press Enter. An expression could also be a variable, which evaluates to the value that has been assigned to it. They are both types of expressions, because they return a value.

Example 15-2 shows three different literals and two variables, all of which return values, albeit of different types.

Example 15-2. Five types of literals

```
<script>
  myname = "Peter"
  myage  = 24
  document.write("a: " + 42     + "<br>") // Numeric literal
  document.write("b: " + "Hi"   + "<br>") // String literal
  document.write("c: " + true   + "<br>") // Constant literal
  document.write("d: " + myname + "<br>") // String variable
  document.write("e: " + myage  + "<br>") // Numeric variable
</script>
```

And, as you'd expect, you see a return value from all of these in the following output:

```
a: 42
b: Hi
c: true
d: Peter
e: 24
```

Operators let you create more complex expressions that evaluate to useful results. When you combine assignment or control-flow constructs with expressions, the result is a *statement*.

Example 15-3 shows one of each. The first assigns the result of the expression 366 - day_number to the variable days_to_new_year, and the second outputs a friendly message only if the expression days_to_new_year < 30 evaluates to true.

Example 15-3. Two simple JavaScript statements

```
<script>
  days_to_new_year = 366 - day_number;
  if (days_to_new_year < 30) document.write("It's nearly New Year")
</script>
```

Operators

JavaScript offers a lot of powerful operators that range from arithmetic, string, and logical operators to assignment, comparison, and more (see Table 15-1).

Table 15-1. JavaScript operator types

Operator	Description	Example
Arithmetic	Basic mathematics	a + b
Array	Array manipulation	a + b
Assignment	Assign values	a = b + 23
Bitwise	Manipulate bits within bytes	12 ^ 9
Comparison	Compare two values	a < b
Increment/decrement	Add or subtract one	a++
Logical	Boolean	a && b
String	Concatenation	a + 'string'

Each operator takes a different number of operands:

- *Unary* operators, such as incrementing (a++) or negation (-a), take a single operand.
- *Binary* operators, which represent the bulk of JavaScript operators—including addition, subtraction, multiplication, and division—take two operands.
- One *ternary* operator, which takes the form ? x : y. It's a terse single-line if statement that chooses between two expressions depending on a third one.

Operator Precedence

As with PHP, JavaScript utilizes operator precedence, in which some operators in an expression are considered more important than others and are therefore evaluated first. Table 15-2 lists JavaScript's operators and their precedences.

Table 15-2. The precedence of JavaScript operators (high to low)

Operator(s)	Type(s)
( ) [ ] .	Parentheses, call, and member
++ --	Increment/decrement
+ - ~ !	Unary, bitwise, and logical
* / %	Arithmetic
+ -	Arithmetic and string
<< >> >>>	Bitwise
< > <= >=	Comparison
== != === !==	Comparison
& ^ |	Bitwise
&&	Logical
||	Logical
? :	Ternary
= += -= *= /= %=	Assignment
<<= >>= >>>= &= ^= |=	Assignment
,	Separator

Associativity

Most JavaScript operators are processed in order from left to right in an equation. But some operators require processing from right to left instead. The direction of processing is called the operator's *associativity*.

This associativity becomes important in cases where you do not explicitly force precedence. For example, look at the following assignment operators, by which three variables are all set to the value 0:

```
level = score = time = 0
```

This multiple assignment is possible only because the rightmost part of the expression is evaluated first and then processing continues in a right-to-left direction. Table 15-3 lists operators and their associativity.

Table 15-3. Operators and associativity

Operator	Description	Associativity
++ --	Increment and decrement	None
new	Create a new object	Right
+ - ~ !	Unary and bitwise	Right
? :	Ternary	Right
= *= /= %= += -=	Assignment	Right
<<= >>= >>>= &= ^= |=	Assignment	Right
,	Separator	Left
+ - * / %	Arithmetic	Left
<< >> >>>	Bitwise	Left
< <= > >= == != === !==	Arithmetic	Left

Relational Operators

Relational operators test two operands and return a Boolean result of either `true` or `false`. There are three types of relational operators: *equality, comparison,* and *logical.*

Equality operators

The equality operator is == (which should not be confused with the = assignment operator). In Example 15-4, the first statement assigns a value and the second tests it for equality. As it stands, nothing will be printed out, because month is assigned the string value July, and therefore the check for it having a value of October will fail.

Example 15-4. Assigning a value and testing for equality

```
<script>
  month = "July"
  if (month == "October") document.write("It's the Fall")
</script>
```

If the two operands of an equality expression are of different types, JavaScript will convert them to whatever type makes best sense to it. For example, any strings composed entirely of numbers will be converted to numbers whenever compared with a number. In Example 15-5, a and b are two different values (one is a number and the other is a string), and we would therefore normally expect neither of the if statements to output a result.

Example 15-5. The equality and identity operators

```
<script>
  a = 3.1415927
  b = "3.1415927"
  if (a == b)  document.write("1")
  if (a === b) document.write("2")
</script>
```

However, if you run the example, you will see that it outputs the number 1, which means that the first `if` statement evaluated to `true`. This is because the string value of b was first temporarily converted to a number, and therefore both halves of the equation had a numerical value of 3.1415927.

In contrast, the second `if` statement uses the *identity* operator, three equals signs in a row, which prevents JavaScript from automatically converting types. This means that a and b are therefore found to be different, so nothing is output.

As with forcing operator precedence, whenever you're in doubt about how JavaScript will convert operand types, you can use the identity operator to turn this behavior off.

Comparison operators

Using comparison operators, you can test for more than just equality and inequality. JavaScript also gives you > (is greater than), < (is less than), >= (is greater than or equal to), and <= (is less than or equal to) to play with. Example 15-6 shows these operators in use.

Example 15-6. The four comparison operators

```
<script>
  a = 7; b = 11
  if (a > b)  document.write("a is greater than b<br>")
  if (a < b)  document.write("a is less than b<br>")
  if (a >= b) document.write("a is greater than or equal to b<br>")
  if (a <= b) document.write("a is less than or equal to b<br>")
</script>
```

In this example, where a is 7 and b is 11, the following is output (because 7 is less than 11, and also less than or equal to 11):

```
a is less than b
a is less than or equal to b
```

Logical operators

Logical operators produce true-or-false results, and are also known as *Boolean* operators. There are three of them in JavaScript (see Table 15-4).

Table 15-4. JavaScript's logical operators

Logical operator	Description
&& *(and)*	true if both operands are true
|| *(or)*	true if either operand is true
! *(not)*	true if the operand is false, or false if the operand is true

You can see how these can be used in Example 15-7, which outputs 0, 1, and true.

Example 15-7. The logical operators in use

```
<script>
  a = 1; b = 0
  document.write((a && b) + "<br>")
  document.write((a || b) + "<br>")
  document.write(( !b ) + "<br>")
</script>
```

The && statement requires both operands to be true if it is going to return a value of true, the || statement will be true if either value is true, and the third statement performs a NOT on the value of b, turning it from 0 into a value of true.

The || operator can cause unintentional problems, because the second operand will not be evaluated if the first is evaluated as true. In Example 15-8, the function getnext will never be called if finished has a value of 1.

Example 15-8. A statement using the || operator

```
<script>
  if (finished == 1 || getnext() == 1) done = 1
</script>
```

If you *need* getnext to be called at each if statement, you should rewrite the code as shown in Example 15-9.

Example 15-9. The if...or statement modified to ensure calling of getnext

```
<script>
  gn = getnext()
  if (finished == 1 OR gn == 1) done = 1;
</script>
```

In this case, the code in function getnext will be executed and its return value stored in gn before the if statement.

Table 15-6 shows all the possible variations of using the logical operators. You should also note that !true equals false and !false equals true.

Table 15-5. All possible logical expressions

Inputs		Operators and results	
a	b	&&	||
true	true	true	true
true	false	false	true
false	true	false	true
false	false	false	false

The with Statement

The `with` statement is not one that you've seen in earlier chapters on PHP, because it's exclusive to JavaScript. With it (if you see what I mean), you can simplify some types of JavaScript statements by reducing many references to an object to just one reference. References to properties and methods within the `with` block are assumed to apply to that object.

For example, take the code in Example 15-10, in which the `document.write` function never references the variable `string` by name.

Example 15-10. Using the with statement

```
<script>
  string = "The quick brown fox jumps over the lazy dog"

  with (string)
  {
    document.write("The string is " + length + " characters<br>")
    document.write("In uppercase it's: " + toUpperCase())
  }
</script>
```

Even though `string` is never directly referenced by `document.write`, this code still manages to output the following:

```
The string is 43 characters
In uppercase it's: THE QUICK BROWN FOX JUMPS OVER THE LAZY DOG
```

This is how the code works: the JavaScript interpreter recognizes that the `length` property and `toUpperCase()` method have to be applied to some object. Because they stand alone, the interpreter assumes they apply to the `string` object that you specified in the `with` statement.

Using onerror

There are more constructs not available in PHP. Using either the onerror event, or a combination of the try and catch keywords, you can catch JavaScript errors and deal with them yourself.

Events are actions that can be detected by JavaScript. Every element on a web page has certain events that can trigger JavaScript functions. For example, the onclick event of a button element can be set to call a function and make it run whenever a user clicks the button.

Example 15-11 illustrates how to use the onerror event.

Example 15-11. A script employing the onerror event

```
<script>
  onerror = errorHandler
  document.writ("Welcome to this website") // Deliberate error

  function errorHandler(message, url, line)
  {
    out  = "Sorry, an error was encountered.\n\n";
    out += "Error: " + message + "\n";
    out += "URL: "   + url     + "\n";
    out += "Line: "  + line    + "\n\n";
    out += "Click OK to continue.\n\n";
    alert(out);
    return true;
  }
</script>
```

The first line of this script tells the error event to use the new errorHandler function from now onward. This function takes three parameters—a message, a url, and a line number—so it's a simple matter to display all these in an alert pop up.

Then, to test the new function, we deliberately place a syntax error in the code with a call to document.writ instead of document.write (the final e is missing). Figure 15-1 shows the result of running this script in a browser. Using onerror this way can also be quite useful during the debugging process.

Figure 15-1. Using the onerror event with an alert method pop up

Using try ... catch

The `try` and `catch` keywords are more standard and more flexible than the `onerror` technique shown in the previous section. These keywords let you trap errors for a selected section of code, rather than all scripts in a document. However, they do not catch syntax errors, for which you need `onerror`.

The `try ... catch` construct is supported by all major browsers and is handy when you want to catch a certain condition that you are aware could occur in a specific part of your code.

For example, in Chapter 18 we'll be exploring Ajax techniques that make use of the `XMLHttpRequest` object. Unfortunately, this isn't available in the Internet Explorer browser (although it is in all other major browsers). Therefore, we can use `try` and `catch` to trap this case and do something else if the function is not available. Example 15-12 shows how.

Example 15-12. Trapping an error with try and catch

```
<script>
  try
  {
    request = new XMLHTTPRequest()
  }
  catch(err)
  {
    // Use a different method to create an XML HTTP Request object
  }
</script>
```

I won't go into how we implement the missing object in Internet Explorer here, but you can see how the system works. There's also another keyword associated with try and catch called finally that is always executed, regardless of whether an error occurs in the try clause. To use it, just add something like the following statements after a catch statement:

```
finally
{
  alert("The 'try' clause was encountered")
}
```

Conditionals

Conditionals alter program flow. They enable you to ask questions about certain things and respond to the answers you get in different ways. There are three types of non-looping conditionals: the if statement, the switch statement, and the ? operator.

The if Statement

Several examples in this chapter have already made use of if statements. The code within such a statement is executed only if the given expression evaluates to true. Multiline if statements require curly braces around them, but as in PHP, you can omit the braces for single statements. Therefore, the following statements are valid:

```
if (a > 100)
{
  b=2
  document.write("a is greater than 100")
}

if (b == 10) document.write("b is equal to 10")
```

The else Statement

When a condition has not been met, you can execute an alternative using an else statement, like this:

```
if (a > 100)
{
  document.write("a is greater than 100")
}
else
{
  document.write("a is less than or equal to 100")
}
```

Unlike PHP, JavaScript has no elseif statement, but that's not a problem, because you can use an else followed by another if to form the equivalent of an elseif statement, like this:

```
if (a > 100)
{
  document.write("a is greater than 100")
}
else if(a < 100)
{
  document.write("a is less than 100")
}
else
{
  document.write("a is equal to 100")
}
```

As you can see, you can use another else after the new if, which could equally be
followed by another if statement, and so on. Although I have shown braces on the
statements, because each is a single line, the whole previous example could be written
as follows:

```
if      (a > 100) document.write("a is greater than 100")
else if(a < 100) document.write("a is less than 100")
else              document.write("a is equal to 100")
```

The switch statement

The switch statement is useful when one variable or the result of an expression can
have multiple values, for each of which you want to perform a different function.

For example, the following code takes the PHP menu system we put together in Chapter 4 and converts it to JavaScript. It works by passing a single string to the main menu
code according to what the user requests. Let's say the options are Home, About, News,
Login, and Links, and we set the variable page to one of these according to the user's
input.

The code for this written using if ... else if ... might look like Example 15-13.

Example 15-13. A multiline if...else if... statement

```
<script>
  if      (page == "Home")  document.write("You selected Home")
  else if (page == "About") document.write("You selected About")
  else if (page == "News")  document.write("You selected News")
  else if (page == "Login") document.write("You selected Login")
  else if (page == "Links") document.write("You selected Links")
</script>
```

But using a switch construct, the code could look like Example 15-14.

Example 15-14. A switch construct

```
<script>
  switch (page)
  {
```

```
      case "Home":
        document.write("You selected Home")
        break
      case "About":
        document.write("You selected About")
        break
      case "News":
        document.write("You selected News")
        break
      case "Login":
        document.write("You selected Login")
        break
      case "Links":
        document.write("You selected Links")
        break
   }
</script>
```

The variable page is mentioned only once at the start of the switch statement. Thereafter, the case command checks for matches. When one occurs, the matching conditional statement is executed. Of course, a real program would have code here to display or jump to a page, rather than simply telling the user what was selected.

Breaking out

As you can see in Example 15-14, just as with PHP, the break command allows your code to break out of the switch statement once a condition has been satisfied. Remember to include the break unless you want to continue executing the statements under the next case.

Default action

When no condition is satisfied, you can specify a default action for a switch statement using the default keyword. Example 15-15 shows a code snippet that could be inserted into Example 15-14.

Example 15-15. A default statement to add to Example 15-14

```
default:
   document.write("Unrecognized selection")
   break
```

The ? Operator

The ternary operator (?), combined with the : character, provides a quick way of doing if ... else tests. With it you can write an expression to evaluate, then follow it with a ? symbol and the code to execute if the expression is true. After that, place a : and the code to execute if the expression evaluates to false.

Example 15-16 shows a ternary operator being used to print out whether the variable a is less than or equal to 5, and prints something either way.

Example 15-16. Using the ternary operator

```
<script>
  document.write(
    a <= 5 ?
    "a is less than or equal to 5" :
    "a is greater than 5"
  )
</script>
```

The statement has been broken up into several lines for clarity, but you would be more likely to use such a statement on a single line, in this manner:

```
size = a <= 5 ? "short" : "long"
```

Looping

Again, you will find many close similarities between JavaScript and PHP when it comes to looping. Both languages support while, do ... while, and for loops.

while Loops

A JavaScript while loop first checks the value of an expression and starts executing the statements within the loop only if that expression is true. If it is false, execution skips over to the next JavaScript statement (if any).

Upon completing an iteration of the loop, the expression is again tested to see if it is true and the process continues until such a time as the expression evaluates to false, or until execution is otherwise halted. Example 15-17 shows such a loop.

Example 15-17. A while loop

```
<script>
  counter=0

  while (counter < 5)
  {
    document.write("Counter: " + counter + "<br>")
    ++counter
  }
</script>
```

This script outputs the following:

```
Counter: 0
Counter: 1
Counter: 2
```

```
Counter: 3
Counter: 4
```

 If the variable counter were not incremented within the loop, it is quite possible that some browsers could become unresponsive due to a never-ending loop, and the page may not even be easy to terminate with Escape or the Stop button. So be careful with your JavaScript loops.

do ... while Loops

When you require a loop to iterate at least once before any tests are made, use a do ... while loop, which is similar to a while loop, except that the test expression is checked only after each iteration of the loop. So, to output the first seven results in the seven times table, you could use code such as that in Example 15-18.

Example 15-18. A do ... while loop

```
<script>
  count = 1

  do
  {
    document.write(count + " times 7 is " + count * 7 + "<br>")
  } while (++count <= 7)
</script>
```

As you might expect, this loop outputs the following:

```
1 times 7 is 7
2 times 7 is 14
3 times 7 is 21
4 times 7 is 28
5 times 7 is 35
6 times 7 is 42
7 times 7 is 49
```

for Loops

A for loop combines the best of all worlds into a single looping construct that allows you to pass three parameters for each statement:

- An initialization expression
- A condition expression
- A modification expression

These are separated by semicolons, like this: for (*expr1* ; *expr2* ; *expr3*). At the start of the first iteration of the loop, the initialization expression is executed. In the case of the code for the multiplication table for 7, count would be initialized to the value 1. Then, each time around the loop, the condition expression (in this case, count <= 7) is tested, and the loop is entered only if the condition is true. Finally, at the end of each iteration, the modification expression is executed. In the case of the multiplication table for 7, the variable count is incremented. Example 15-19 shows what the code would look like.

Example 15-19. Using a for loop

```
<script>
  for (count = 1 ; count <= 7 ; ++count)
  {
    document.write(count + "times 7 is " + count * 7 + "<br>");
  }
</script>
```

As in PHP, you can assign multiple variables in the first parameter of a for loop by separating them with a comma, like this:

```
for (i = 1, j = 1 ; i < 10 ; i++)
```

Likewise, you can perform multiple modifications in the last parameter, like this:

```
for (i = 1 ; i < 10 ; i++, --j)
```

Or you can do both at the same time:

```
for (i = 1, j = 1 ; i < 10 ; i++, --j)
```

Breaking Out of a Loop

The break command, which you'll recall is important inside a switch statement, is also available within for loops. You might need to use this, for example, when searching for a match of some kind. Once the match is found, you know that continuing to search will only waste time and make your visitor wait. Example 15-20 shows how to use the break command.

Example 15-20. Using the break command in a for loop

```
<script>
  haystack       = new Array()
  haystack[17] = "Needle"

  for (j = 0 ; j < 20 ; ++j)
  {
    if (haystack[j] == "Needle")
    {
      document.write("<br>- Found at location " + j)
      break
```

```
  }
  else document.write(j + ", ")
  }
</script>
```

This script outputs the following:

```
0, 1, 2, 3, 4, 5, 6, 7, 8, 9, 10, 11, 12, 13, 14, 15, 16,
- Found at location 17
```

The continue Statement

Sometimes you don't want to entirely exit from a loop, but instead wish to skip the remaining statements just for this iteration of the loop. In such cases, you can use the continue command. Example 15-21 shows this in use.

Example 15-21. Using the continue command in a for loop

```
<script>
  haystack      = new Array()
  haystack[4]  = "Needle"
  haystack[11] = "Needle"
  haystack[17] = "Needle"

  for (j = 0 ; j < 20 ; ++j)
  {
    if (haystack[j] == "Needle")
    {
      document.write("<br>- Found at location " + j + "<br>")
      continue
    }

    document.write(j + ", ")
  }
</script>
```

Notice how the second document.write call does not have to be enclosed in an else statement (as it did before), because the continue command will skip it if a match has been found. The output from this script is as follows:

```
0, 1, 2, 3,
- Found at location 4
5, 6, 7, 8, 9, 10,
- Found at location 11
12, 13, 14, 15, 16,
- Found at location 17
18, 19,
```

Explicit Casting

Unlike PHP, JavaScript has no explicit casting of types such as (int) or (float). Instead, when you need a value to be of a certain type, use one of JavaScript's built-in functions, shown in Table 15-6.

Table 15-6. JavaScript's type-changing functions

Change to type	Function to use
Int, Integer	parseInt()
Bool, Boolean	Boolean()
Float, Double, Real	parseFloat()
String	String()
Array	split()

So, for example, to change a floating-point number to an integer, you could use code such as the following (which displays the value 3):

```
n = 3.1415927
i = parseInt(n)
document.write(i)
```

Or you can use the compound form:

```
document.write(parseInt(3.1415927))
```

That's it for control flow and expressions. The next chapter focuses on the use of functions, objects, and arrays in JavaScript.

Questions

1. How are Boolean values handled differently by PHP and JavaScript?
2. What characters are used to define a JavaScript variable name?
3. What is the difference between unary, binary, and ternary operators?
4. What is the best way to force your own operator precedence?
5. When would you use the === (identity) operator?
6. What are the simplest two forms of expressions?
7. Name the three conditional statement types.
8. How do if and while statements interpret conditional expressions of different data types?

9. Why is a `for` loop more powerful than a `while` loop?

10. What is the purpose of the `with` statement?

See "Chapter 15 Answers" on page 649 in Appendix A for the answers to these questions.

CHAPTER 16

JavaScript Functions, Objects, and Arrays

Just like PHP, JavaScript offers access to functions and objects. In fact, JavaScript is actually based on objects, because—as you've seen—it has to access the DOM, which makes every element of an HTML document available to manipulate as an object.

The usage and syntax are also quite similar to those of PHP, so you should feel right at home as I take you through using functions and objects in JavaScript, as well as through an in-depth exploration of array handling.

JavaScript Functions

In addition to having access to dozens of built-in functions (or methods) such as write, which you have already seen being used in document.write, you can easily create your own functions. Whenever you have a more complex piece of code that is likely to be reused, you have a candidate for a function.

Defining a Function

The general syntax for a function is:

```
function function_name([parameter [, ...]])
{
    statements
}
```

The first line of the syntax indicates that:

- A definition starts with the word function.
- A name follows that must start with a letter or underscore, followed by any number of letters, digits, dollar symbols, or underscores.

- The parentheses are required.

- One or more parameters, separated by commas, are optional (indicated by the square brackets, which are not part of the function syntax).

Function names are case-sensitive, so all of the following strings refer to different functions: getInput, GETINPUT, and getinput.

In JavaScript there is a general naming convention for functions: the first letter of each word in a name is capitalized except for the very first letter, which is lowercase. Therefore, of the previous examples, getInput would be the preferred name used by most programmers. This convention is commonly referred to as *bumpyCaps*, *bumpyCase*, or *camelCase*.

The opening curly brace starts the statements that will execute when you call the function; a matching curly brace must close it. These statements may include one or more return statements, which force the function to cease execution and return to the calling code. If a value is attached to the return statement, the calling code can retrieve it.

The arguments Array

The arguments array is a member of every function. With it, you can determine the number of variables passed to a function and what they are. Take the example of a function called displayItems. Example 16-1 shows one way of writing it.

Example 16-1. Defining a function

```
<script>
  displayItems("Dog", "Cat", "Pony", "Hamster", "Tortoise")

  function displayItems(v1, v2, v3, v4, v5)
  {
    document.write(v1 + "<br>")
    document.write(v2 + "<br>")
    document.write(v3 + "<br>")
    document.write(v4 + "<br>")
    document.write(v5 + "<br>")
  }
</script>
```

When you call up this script in your browser, it will display the following:

```
Dog
Cat
Pony
Hamster
Tortoise
```

All of this is fine, but what if you wanted to pass more than five items to the function? Also, reusing the document.write call multiple times instead of employing a loop is wasteful programming. Luckily, the `arguments` array gives you the flexibility to handle a variable number of arguments. Example 16-2 shows how you can use it to rewrite the example in a much more efficient manner.

Example 16-2. Modifying the function to use the arguments array

```
<script>
  function displayItems()
  {
    for (j = 0 ; j < displayItems.arguments.length ; ++j)
      document.write(displayItems.arguments[j] + "<br>")
  }
</script>
```

Note the use of the `length` property, which you already encountered in the previous chapter, and also how the array `displayItems.arguments` is referenced using the variable `j` as an offset into it. I also chose to keep the function short and sweet by not surrounding the contents of the `for` loop in curly braces, as it contains only a single statement.

Using this technique, you now have a function that can take as many (or as few) arguments as you like and act on each argument as you desire.

Returning a Value

Functions are not used just to display things. In fact, they are mostly used to perform calculations or data manipulation and then return a result. The function `fixNames` in Example 16-3 uses the `arguments` array (discussed in the previous section) to take a series of strings passed to it and return them as a single string. The "fix" it performs is to convert every character in the arguments to lowercase except for the first character of each argument, which is set to a capital letter.

Example 16-3. Cleaning up a full name

```
<script>
  document.write(fixNames("the", "DALLAS", "CowBoys"))

  function fixNames()
  {
    var s = ""

    for (j = 0 ; j < fixNames.arguments.length ; ++j)
      s += fixNames.arguments[j].charAt(0).toUpperCase() +
           fixNames.arguments[j].substr(1).toLowerCase() + " "

    return s.substr(0, s.length-1)
  }
</script>
```

called with the parameters the, DALLAS, and CowBoys, for example, the function the string The Dallas Cowboys. Let's walk through the function.

nction first initializes the temporary (and local) variable s to the empty string. for loop iterates through each of the passed parameters, isolating the parameter's first character using the charAt method and converting it to uppercase with the toUpperCase method. The various methods shown in this example are all built into JavaScript and available by default.

Then the substr method is used to fetch the rest of each string, which is converted to lowercase using the toLowerCase method. A fuller version of the substr method here would specify how many characters are part of the substring as a second argument:

```
substr(1, (arguments[j].length) - 1 )
```

In other words, this substr method says, "Start with the character at position 1 (the second character) and return the rest of the string (the length minus one)." As a nice touch, though, the substr method assumes that you want the rest of the string if you omit the second argument.

After the whole argument is converted to our desired case, a space character is added to the end and the result is appended to the temporary variable s.

Finally, the substr method is used again to return the contents of the variable s, except for the final space—which is unwanted. We remove this by using substr to return the string up to, but not including, the final character.

This example is particularly interesting in that it illustrates the use of multiple properties and methods in a single expression. For example:

```
fixNames.arguments[j].substr(1).toLowerCase()
```

You have to interpret the statement by mentally dividing it into parts at the periods. JavaScript evaluates these elements of the statement from left to right as follows:

1. Start with the name of the function itself: fixNames.

2. Extract element j from the array arguments representing fixNames arguments.

3. Invoke substr with a parameter of 1 to the extracted element. This passes all but the first character to the next section of the expression.

4. Apply the method toLowerCase to the string that has been passed this far.

This practice is often referred to as *method chaining*. So, for example, if the string mixedCASE is passed to the example expression, it will go through the following transformations:

```
mixedCASE
ixedCASE
ixedcase
```

One final reminder: the s variable created inside the function is local, and therefore cannot be accessed outside the function. By returning s in the return statement, we made its value available to the caller, which could store or use it any way it wanted. But s itself disappears at the end of the function. Although we could make a function operate on global variables (and sometimes that's necessary), it's much better to just return the values you want to preserve and let JavaScript clean up all the other variables used by the function.

Returning an Array

In Example 16-3, the function returned only one parameter, but what if you need to return multiple parameters? You can do this by returning an array, as in Example 16-4.

Example 16-4. Returning an array of values

```
<script>
  words = fixNames("the", "DALLAS", "CowBoys")

  for (j = 0 ; j < words.length ; ++j)
    document.write(words[j] + "<br>")

  function fixNames()
  {
    var s = new Array()

    for (j = 0 ; j < fixNames.arguments.length ; ++j)
      s[j] = fixNames.arguments[j].charAt(0).toUpperCase() +
             fixNames.arguments[j].substr(1).toLowerCase()

  return s
}
</script>
```

Here the variable words is automatically defined as an array and populated with the returned result of a call to the function fixNames. Then a for loop iterates through the array and displays each member.

As for the fixNames function, it's almost identical to Example 16-3, except that the variable s is now an array, and after each word has been processed it is stored as an element of this array, which is returned by the return statement.

This function enables the extraction of individual parameters from its returned values, like the following (the output from which is simply The Cowboys):

```
    words = fixNames("the", "DALLAS", "CowBoys")
    document.write(words[0] + " " + words[2])
```

cript Objects

cript object is a step up from a variable, which can contain only one value at a
that objects can contain multiple values and even functions. An object groups
data together with the functions needed to manipulate it.

Declaring a Class

When creating a script to use objects, you need to design a composite of data and code
called a *class*. Each new object based on this class is called an *instance* (or *occurrence*)
of that class. As you've already seen, the data associated with an object is called its
properties, while the functions it uses are called *methods*.

Let's look at how to declare the class for an object called User that will contain details
about the current user. To create the class, just write a function named after the class.
This function can accept arguments (I'll show later how it's invoked) and can create
properties and methods for the objects in that class. The function is called a *constructor*.

Example 16-5 shows a constructor for the class User with three properties: forename,
username, and password. The class also defines the method showUser.

Example 16-5. Declaring the User class and its method

```
<script>
  function User(forename, username, password)
  {
    this.forename = forename
    this.username = username
    this.password = password

    this.showUser = function()
    {
      document.write("Forename: " + this.forename + "<br>")
      document.write("Username: " + this.username + "<br>")
      document.write("Password: " + this.password + "<br>")
    }
  }
</script>
```

The function is different from other functions we've seen so far in two ways:

- It refers to an object named this. When the program creates an instance of User
  by running this function, this refers to the instance being created. The same func‐
  tion can be called over and over with different arguments, and will create a new
  User each time with different values for the properties forename, and so on.

- A new function named `showUser` is created within the function. The syntax shown here is new and rather complicated, but its purpose is to tie `showUser` to the `User` class. Thus, `showUser` comes into being as a method of the `User` class.

The naming convention I have used is to keep all properties in lowercase and to use at least one uppercase character in method names, following the camelCase convention mentioned earlier in the chapter.

Example 16-5 follows the recommended way to write a class constructor, which is to include methods in the constructor function. However, you can also refer to functions defined outside the constructor, as in Example 16-6.

Example 16-6. Separately defining a class and method

```
<script>
  function User(forename, username, password)
  {
    this.forename = forename
    this.username = username
    this.password = password
    this.showUser = showUser
  }

  function showUser()
  {
    document.write("Forename: " + this.forename + "<br>")
    document.write("Username: " + this.username + "<br>")
    document.write("Password: " + this.password + "<br>")
  }
</script>
```

I show you this form because you are certain to encounter it when perusing other programmers' code.

Creating an Object

To create an instance of the class `User`, you can use a statement such as the following:

```
details = new User("Wolfgang", "w.a.mozart", "composer")
```

Or you can create an empty object, like this:

```
details = new User()
```

and then populate it later, like this:

```
details.forename = "Wolfgang"
details.username = "w.a.mozart"
details.password = "composer"
```

You can also add new properties to an object, like this:

```
                    details.greeting = "Hello"
```

You can verify that adding such new properties works with the following statement:

```
                    document.write(details.greeting)
```

Accessing Objects

To access an object, you can refer to its properties, as in the following two unrelated example statements:

```
                    name = details.forename
                    if (details.username == "Admin") loginAsAdmin()
```

So, to access the showUser method of an object of class User, you would use the following syntax, in which the object details has already been created and populated with data:

```
                    details.showUser()
```

Assuming the data supplied earlier, this code would display:

```
                    Forename: Wolfgang
                    Username: w.a.mozart
                    Password: composer
```

The prototype Keyword

The prototype keyword can save you a lot of memory. In the User class, every instance will contain the three properties and the method. Therefore, if you have 1,000 of these objects in memory, the method showUser will also be replicated 1,000 times. However, because the method is identical in every case, you can specify that new objects should refer to a single instance of the method instead of creating a copy of it. So, instead of using the following in a class constructor:

```
                    this.showUser = function()
```

you could replace it with this:

```
                    User.prototype.showUser = function()
```

Example 16-7 shows what the new constructor would look like.

Example 16-7. Declaring a class using the prototype keyword for a method

```
<script>
  function User(forename, username, password)
  {
    this.forename = forename
    this.username = username
    this.password = password

    User.prototype.showUser = function()
    {
      document.write("Forename: " + this.forename + "<br>")
```

```
      document.write("Username: " + this.username + "<br>")
      document.write("Password: " + this.password + "<br>")
   }
 }
</script>
```

This works because all functions have a `prototype` property, designed to hold properties and methods that are not replicated in any objects created from a class. Instead, they are passed to its objects by reference.

This means that you can add a `prototype` property or method at any time and all objects (even those already created) will inherit it, as the following statements illustrate.

```
User.prototype.greeting = "Hello"
document.write(details.greeting)
```

The first statement adds the `prototype` property of `greeting` with a value of `Hello` to the class `User`. In the second line, the object `details`, which has already been created, correctly displays this new property.

You can also add to or modify methods in a class, as the following statements illustrate:

```
User.prototype.showUser = function()
{
   document.write("Name "  + this.forename +
                  " User " + this.username +
                  " Pass " + this.password)
}

details.showUser()
```

You might add these lines to your script in a conditional statement (such as `if`), so they run if user activities cause you to decide you need a different `showUser` method. After these lines run, even if the object `details` has been created already, further calls to `details.showUser` will run the new function. The old definition of `showUser` has been erased.

Static methods and properties

When reading about PHP objects, you learned that classes can have static properties and methods as well as properties and methods associated with a particular instance of a class. JavaScript also supports static properties and methods, which you can conveniently store and retrieve from the class's `prototype`. Thus, the following statements set and read a static string from `User`:

```
User.prototype.greeting = "Hello"
document.write(User.prototype.greeting)
```

Extending JavaScript objects

The `prototype` keyword even lets you add functionality to a built-in object. For example, suppose that you would like to add the ability to replace all spaces in a string with nonbreaking spaces in order to prevent it from wrapping around. You can do this by adding a prototype method to JavaScript's default `String` object definition, like this:

```
String.prototype.nbsp = function()
{
  return this.replace(/ /g, ' ')
}
```

Here the `replace` method is used with a regular expression (see Chapter 17) to find and replace all single spaces with the string ` `. If you then enter the following command:

```
document.write("The quick brown fox".nbsp())
```

It will output the string `The quick brown fox`. Or here's a method you can add that will trim leading and trailing spaces from a string (once again using a regular expression):

```
String.prototype.trim = function()
{
  return this.replace(/^\s+|\s+$/g, '')
}
```

If you issue the following statement, the output will be the string `Please trim me` (with the leading and trailing spaces removed).

```
document.write("  Please trim me   ".trim())
```

If we break down the expression into its component parts, the two / characters mark the start and end of the expression, and the final g specifies a global search. Inside the expression, the `^\s+` part searches for one or more whitespace characters appearing at the start of the search string, while the `\s+$` part searches for one or more whitespace characters at the end of the search string. The | character in the middle acts to separate the alternatives.

The result is that when either of these expressions matches, the match is replaced with the empty string, thus returning a trimmed version of the string without any leading or trailing whitespace.

JavaScript Arrays

Array handling in JavaScript is very similar to PHP, although the syntax is a little different. Nevertheless, given all you have already learned about arrays, this section should be relatively straightforward for you.

Numeric Arrays

To create a new array, use the following syntax:

```
arrayname = new Array()
```

Or you can use the shorthand form, as follows:

```
arrayname = []
```

Assigning element values

In PHP, you could add a new element to an array by simply assigning it without speci-fying the element offset, like this:

```
$arrayname[] = "Element 1";
$arrayname[] = "Element 2";
```

But in JavaScript you use the push method to achieve the same thing, like this:

```
arrayname.push("Element 1")
arrayname.push("Element 2")
```

This allows you to keep adding items to an array without having to keep track of the number of items. When you need to know how many elements are in an array, you can use the length property, like this:

```
document.write(arrayname.length)
```

Alternatively, if you wish to keep track of the element locations yourself and place them in specific locations, you can use syntax such as this:

```
arrayname[0] = "Element 1"
arrayname[1] = "Element 2"
```

Example 16-8 shows a simple script that creates an array, loads it with some values, and then displays them.

Example 16-8. Creating, building, and printing an array

```
<script>
  numbers = []
  numbers.push("One")
  numbers.push("Two")
  numbers.push("Three")

  for (j = 0 ; j < numbers.length ; ++j)
    document.write("Element " + j + " = " + numbers[j] + "<br>")
</script>
```

The output from this script is:

```
Element 0 = One
Element 1 = Two
Element 2 = Three
```

Assignment using the array keyword

You can also create an array together with some initial elements using the `Array` keyword, like this:

```
numbers = Array("One", "Two", "Three")
```

There is nothing stopping you from adding more elements afterward as well.

So now you have a couple of ways you can add items to an array, and one way of referencing them, but JavaScript offers many more, which I'll get to shortly. But first we'll look at another type of array.

Associative Arrays

An associative array is one in which its elements are referenced by name rather than by numeric offset. To create an associative array, define a block of elements within curly braces. For each element, place the key on the left and the contents on the right of a colon (`:`). Example 16-9 shows how you might create an associative array to hold the contents of the "balls" section of an online sports equipment retailer.

Example 16-9. Creating and displaying an associative array

```
<script>
  balls = {"golf":    "Golf balls, 6",
           "tennis":  "Tennis balls, 3",
           "soccer":  "Soccer ball, 1",
           "ping":    "Ping Pong balls, 1 doz"}

  for (ball in balls)
    document.write(ball + " = " + balls[ball] + "<br>")
</script>
```

To verify that the array has been correctly created and populated, I have used another kind of `for` loop using the `in` keyword. This creates a new variable to use only within the array (`ball`, in this example) and iterates through all elements of the array to the right of the `in` keyword (`balls`, in this example). The loop acts on each element of `balls`, placing the key value into `ball`.

Using this key value stored in `ball`, you can also get the value of the current element of `balls`. The result of calling up the example script in a browser is as follows:

```
golf = Golf balls, 6
tennis = Tennis balls, 3
soccer = Soccer ball, 1
ping = Ping Pong balls, 1 doz
```

To get a specific element of an associative array, you can specify a key explicitly, in the following manner (in this case, outputting the value `Soccer ball, 1`):

```
document.write(balls['soccer'])
```

Multidimensional Arrays

To create a multidimensional array in JavaScript, just place arrays inside other arrays. For example, to create an array to hold the details of a two-dimensional checkerboard (8×8 squares), you could use the code in Example 16-10.

Example 16-10. Creating a multidimensional numeric array

```
<script>
  checkerboard = Array(
    Array(' ', 'o', ' ', 'o', ' ', 'o', ' ', 'o'),
    Array('o', ' ', 'o', ' ', 'o', ' ', 'o', ' '),
    Array(' ', 'o', ' ', 'o', ' ', 'o', ' ', 'o'),
    Array(' ', ' ', ' ', ' ', ' ', ' ', ' ', ' '),
    Array(' ', ' ', ' ', ' ', ' ', ' ', ' ', ' '),
    Array('O', ' ', 'O', ' ', 'O', ' ', 'O', ' '),
    Array(' ', 'O', ' ', 'O', ' ', 'O', ' ', 'O'),
    Array('O', ' ', 'O', ' ', 'O', ' ', 'O', ' '))

  document.write("<pre>")

  for (j = 0 ; j < 8 ; ++j)
  {
    for (k = 0 ; k < 8 ; ++k)
      document.write(checkerboard[j][k] + " ")

    document.write("<br>")
  }

  document.write("</pre>")
</script>
```

In this example, the lowercase letters represent black pieces, and the uppercase white. A pair of nested for loops walks through the array and displays its contents.

The outer loop contains two statements, so curly braces enclose them. The inner loop then processes each square in a row, outputting the character at location [j][k], followed by a space (to square up the printout). This loop contains a single statement, so curly braces are not required to enclose it. The <pre> and </pre> tags ensure that the output displays correctly, like this:

```
  o   o   o   o
o   o   o   o
  o   o   o   o


O   O   O   O
  O   O   O   O
O   O   O   O
```

You can also directly access any element within this array using square brackets, as follows:

```
document.write(checkerboard[7][2])
```

This statement outputs the uppercase letter O, the eighth element down and the third along—remember that array indexes start at 0, not 1.

Using Array Methods

Given the power of arrays, JavaScript comes ready-made with a number of methods for manipulating them and their data. Here is a selection of the most useful ones.

concat

The concat method concatenates two arrays, or a series of values within an array. For example, the following code outputs Banana,Grape,Carrot,Cabbage:

```
fruit = ["Banana", "Grape"]
veg   = ["Carrot", "Cabbage"]

document.write(fruit.concat(veg))
```

You can specify multiple arrays as arguments, in which case concat adds all their elements in the order that the arrays are specified.

Here's another way to use concat. This time, plain values are concatenated with the array pets, which outputs Cat,Dog,Fish,Rabbit,Hamster:

```
pets      = ["Cat", "Dog", "Fish"]
more_pets = pets.concat("Rabbit", "Hamster")

document.write(more_pets)
```

forEach (for non-IE browsers)

The forEach method in JavaScript is another way of achieving functionality similar to the PHP foreach keyword, but *only for browsers other than Internet Explorer*. To use it, you pass it the name of a function, which will be called for each element within the array. Example 16-11 shows how.

Example 16-11. Using the forEach method

```
<script>
  pets = ["Cat", "Dog", "Rabbit", "Hamster"]
  pets.forEach(output)

  function output(element, index, array)
  {
    document.write("Element at index " + index + " has the value " +
      element + "<br>")
```

```
  }
</script>
```

In this case, the function passed to forEach is called output. It takes three parameters: the element, its index, and the array. These can be used as required by your function. In this example, just the element and index values are displayed using the function document.write.

Once an array has been populated, the method is called like this:

```
pets.forEach(output)
```

The output from which is:

```
Element at index 0 has the value Cat
Element at index 1 has the value Dog
Element at index 2 has the value Rabbit
Element at index 3 has the value Hamster
```

forEach (a cross-browser solution)

Of course, as is its way, Microsoft chose not to support the forEach method, so the previous example will work only on non–Internet Explorer browsers. Therefore, until IE does support it, and to ensure cross-browser compatibility, you should use a statement such as the following instead of pets.forEach(output):

```
for (j = 0 ; j < pets.length ; ++j) output(pets[j], j)
```

join

With the join method, you can convert all the values in an array to strings and then join them together into one large string, placing an optional separator between them. Example 16-12 shows three ways of using this method.

Example 16-12. Using the join method

```
<script>
  pets = ["Cat", "Dog", "Rabbit", "Hamster"]

  document.write(pets.join()      + "<br>")
  document.write(pets.join(' ')   + "<br>")
  document.write(pets.join(' : ') + "<br>")
</script>
```

Without a parameter, join uses a comma to separate the elements; otherwise, the string passed to join is inserted between each element. The output of Example 16-12 looks like this:

```
Cat,Dog,Rabbit,Hamster
Cat Dog Rabbit Hamster
Cat : Dog : Rabbit : Hamster
```

push and pop

You already saw how the push method can be used to insert a value into an array. The inverse method is pop. It deletes the most recently inserted element from an array and returns it. Example 16-13 shows an example of its use.

Example 16-13. Using the push and pop methods

```
<script>
  sports = ["Football", "Tennis", "Baseball"]
  document.write("Start = "      + sports +  "<br>")

  sports.push("Hockey")
  document.write("After Push = " + sports +  "<br>")

  removed = sports.pop()
  document.write("After Pop = "  + sports +  "<br>")
  document.write("Removed = "    + removed + "<br>")
</script>
```

The three main statements of this script are shown in bold type. First, the script creates an array called sports with three elements and then pushes a fourth element into the array. After that, it pops that element back off. In the process, the various current values are displayed via document.write. The script outputs the following:

```
Start = Football,Tennis,Baseball
After Push = Football,Tennis,Baseball,Hockey
After Pop = Football,Tennis,Baseball
Removed = Hockey
```

The push and pop functions are useful in situations where you need to divert from some activity to do another, then return, as in Example 16-14.

Example 16-14. Using push and pop inside and outside of a loop

```
<script>
  numbers = []

  for (j = 0 ; j < 3 ; ++j)
  {
    numbers.push(j);
    document.write("Pushed " + j + "<br>")
  }

  // Perform some other activity here
  document.write("<br>")

  document.write("Popped " + numbers.pop() + "<br>")
  document.write("Popped " + numbers.pop() + "<br>")
  document.write("Popped " + numbers.pop() + "<br>")
</script>
```

The output from this example is:

Pushed 0
Pushed 1
Pushed 2

Popped 2
Popped 1
Popped 0

Using reverse

The reverse method simply reverses the order of all elements in an array. Example 16-15 shows this in action.

Example 16-15. Using the reverse method

```
<script>
  sports = ["Football", "Tennis", "Baseball", "Hockey"]
  sports.reverse()
  document.write(sports)
</script>
```

The original array is modified and the output from this script is:

Hockey,Baseball,Tennis,Football

sort

With the sort method, you can place all the elements of an array in alphabetical or other order, depending upon the parameters used. Example 16-16 shows four types of sort.

Example 16-16. Using the sort method

```
<script>
  // Alphabetical sort
  sports = ["Football", "Tennis", "Baseball", "Hockey"]
  sports.sort()
  document.write(sports + "<br>")

  // Reverse alphabetical sort
  sports = ["Football", "Tennis", "Baseball", "Hockey"]
  sports.sort().reverse()
  document.write(sports + "<br>")

  // Ascending numeric sort
  numbers = [7, 23, 6, 74]
  numbers.sort(function(a,b){return a - b})
  document.write(numbers + "<br>")

  // Descending numeric sort
  numbers = [7, 23, 6, 74]
  numbers.sort(function(a,b){return b - a})
```

```
  document.write(numbers + "<br>")
</script>
```

The first of the four example sections is the default sort method, *alphabetical sort*, while the second uses the default sort and then applies the reverse method to get a *reverse alphabetical sort*.

The third and fourth sections are a little more complicated; they use a function to compare the relationships between a and b. The function doesn't have a name, because it's used only in the sort. You have already seen the function named function to create an anonymous function; we used it to define a method in a class (the showUser method).

Here, function creates an anonymous function meeting the needs of the sort method. If the function returns a value greater than zero, the sort assumes that b comes before a. If the function returns a value less than zero, the sort assumes that a comes before b. The sort runs this function across all the values in the array to determine their order.

By manipulating the value returned (a - b in contrast to b - a), the third and fourth sections of Example 16-16 choose between an *ascending numerical sort* and a *descending numerical sort*.

And, believe it or not, this marks the end of your introduction to JavaScript. You should now have a core knowledge of the three main technologies covered in this book. The next chapter will look at some advanced techniques used across these technologies, such as pattern matching and input validation.

Questions

1. Are JavaScript functions and variable names case-sensitive or case-insensitive?

2. How can you write a function that accepts and processes an unlimited number of parameters?

3. Name a way to return multiple values from a function.

4. When you're defining a class, what keyword do you use to refer to the current object?

5. Do all the methods of a class have to be defined within the class definition?

6. What keyword is used to create an object?

7. How can you make a property or method available to all objects in a class without replicating the property or method within the object?

8. How can you create a multidimensional array?

9. What syntax is used to create an associative array?

10. Write a statement to sort an array of numbers in descending numerical order.

See "Chapter 16 Answers" on page 650 in Appendix A for the answers to these questions.

CHAPTER 17

JavaScript and PHP Validation and Error Handling

With your solid foundation in both PHP and JavaScript, it's time to bring these technologies together to create web forms that are as user-friendly as possible.

We'll be using PHP to create the forms and JavaScript to perform client-side validation to ensure that the data is as complete and correct as it can be before it is submitted. Final validation of the input will then be made by PHP, which will, if necessary, present the form again to the user for further modification.

In the process, this chapter will cover validation and regular expressions in both JavaScript and PHP.

Validating User Input with JavaScript

JavaScript validation should be considered an assistance more to your users than to your websites because, as I have already stressed many times, you cannot trust any data submitted to your server, even if it has supposedly been validated with JavaScript. This is because hackers can quite easily simulate your web forms and submit any data of their choosing.

Another reason you cannot rely on JavaScript to perform all your input validation is that some users disable JavaScript, or use browsers that don't support it.

So the best types of validation to do in JavaScript are checking that fields have content if they are not to be left empty, ensuring that email addresses conform to the proper format, and ensuring that values entered are within expected bounds.

The validate.html Document (Part One)

Let's begin with a general signup form, common on most sites that offer memberships or registered users. The inputs being requested will be *forename*, *surname*, *username*, *password*, *age*, and *email address*. Example 17-1 provides a good template for such a form.

Example 17-1. A form with JavaScript validation (part one)

```html
<!DOCTYPE html>
<html>
  <head>
    <title>An Example Form</title>
    <style>
      .signup {
        border:1px solid #999999;
        font:  normal 14px helvetica;
        color: #444444;
      }
    </style>
    <script>
      function validate(form)
      {
        fail  = validateForename(form.forename.value)
        fail += validateSurname(form.surname.value)
        fail += validateUsername(form.username.value)
        fail += validatePassword(form.password.value)
        fail += validateAge(form.age.value)
        fail += validateEmail(form.email.value)

        if   (fail == "")   return true
        else { alert(fail); return false }
      }
    </script>
  </head>
  <body>
    <table border="0" cellpadding="2" cellspacing="5" bgcolor="#eeeeee">
      <th colspan="2" align="center">Signup Form</th>
      <form method="post" action="adduser.php" onsubmit="return validate(this)">
        <tr><td>Forename</td>
          <td><input type="text" maxlength="32" name="forename"></td></tr>
        <tr><td>Surname</td>
          <td><input type="text" maxlength="32" name="surname"></td></tr>
        <tr><td>Username</td>
          <td><input type="text" maxlength="16" name="username"></td></tr>
        <tr><td>Password</td>
          <td><input type="text" maxlength="12" name="password"></td></tr>
        <tr><td>Age</td>
          <td><input type="text" maxlength="3"  name="age"></td></tr>
        <tr><td>Email</td>
          <td><input type="text" maxlength="64" name="email"></td></tr>
        <tr><td colspan="2" align="center"><input type="submit"
```

```
        value="Signup"></td></tr>
      </form>
    </table>
  </body>
</html>
```

As it stands, this form will display correctly but will not self-validate, because the main validation functions have not yet been added. Even so, save it as *validate.html*, and when you call it up in your browser, it will look like Figure 17-1.

Figure 17-1. The output from Example 17-1

Let's look at how this document is made up. The first few lines set up the document and use a little CSS to make the form look a little less plain. The parts of the document related to JavaScript come next and are shown in bold.

Between the <script> and </script> tags lies a single function called validate which itself calls up six other functions to validate each of the form's input fields. We'll get to these functions shortly. For now I'll just explain that they return either an empty string if a field validates, or an error message if it fails. If there are any errors, the final line of the script pops up an alert box to display them.

Upon passing validation, the validate function returns a value of true; otherwise, it returns false. The return values from validate are important, because if it returns false, the form is prevented from being submitted. This allows the user to close the alert pop up and make changes. If true is returned, no errors were encountered in the form's fields and so the form is allowed to be submitted.

The second part of this example features the HTML for the form with each field and its name placed within its own row of a table. This is pretty straightforward HTML, with the exception of the onSubmit="return validate(this)" statement within the opening <form> tag. Using onSubmit, you can cause a function of your choice to be called when a form is submitted. That function can perform some checking and return a value of either true or false to signify whether the form should be allowed to be submitted.

The this parameter is the current object (i.e., this form) and is passed to the just discussed validate function. The validate function receives this parameter as the object form.

As you can see, the only JavaScript used within the form's HTML is the call to return buried in the onSubmit attribute. Browsers with JavaScript disabled or not available will simply ignore the onSubmit attribute, and the HTML will display just fine.

The validate.html Document (Part Two)

Now we come to Example 17-2, a set of six functions that do the actual form field validation. I suggest that you type all of this second part and save it in the <script> ... </script> section of Example 17-1, which you should already have saved as *validate.html*.

Example 17-2. A form with JavaScript validation (part two)

```
function validateForename(field)
{
  return (field == "") ? "No Forename was entered.\n" : ""
}

function validateSurname(field)
{
  return (field == "") ? "No Surname was entered.\n" : ""
}

function validateUsername(field)
{
  if (field == "") return "No Username was entered.\n"
  else if (field.length < 5)
    return "Usernames must be at least 5 characters.\n"
  else if (/[^a-zA-Z0-9_-]/.test(field))
    return "Only a-z, A-Z, 0-9, - and _ allowed in Usernames.\n"
  return ""
}

function validatePassword(field)
{
  if (field == "") return "No Password was entered.\n"
  else if (field.length < 6)
    return "Passwords must be at least 6 characters.\n"
  else if (!/[a-z]/.test(field) || ! /[A-Z]/.test(field) ||
```

```
                        !/[0-9]/.test(field))
      return "Passwords require one each of a-z, A-Z and 0-9.\n"
    return ""
}

function validateAge(field)
{
  if (isNaN(field)) return "No Age was entered.\n"
  else if (field < 18 || field > 110)
    return "Age must be between 18 and 110.\n"
  return ""
}

function validateEmail(field)
{
  if (field == "") return "No Email was entered.\n"
    else if (!((field.indexOf(".") > 0) &&
               (field.indexOf("@") > 0)) ||
              /[^a-zA-Z0-9.@_-]/.test(field))
      return "The Email address is invalid.\n"
    return ""
}
```

We'll go through each of these functions in turn, starting with validateForename, so you can see how validation works.

Validating the forename

validateForename is quite a short function that accepts the parameter field, which is the value of the forename passed to it by the validate function.

If this value is the empty string, an error message is returned; otherwise, an empty string is returned to signify that no error was encountered.

If the user entered spaces in this field, it would be accepted by validateForename, even though it's empty for all intents and purposes. You can fix this by adding an extra statement to trim whitespace from the field before checking whether it's empty, use a regular expression to make sure there's something besides whitespace in the field, or—as I do here—just let the user make the mistake and allow the PHP program to catch it on the server.

Validating the surname

The validateSurname function is almost identical to validateForename in that an error is returned only if the surname supplied was the empty string. I chose not to limit the characters allowed in either of the name fields to allow for possibilities such as non-English and accented characters.

Validating the username

The `validateUsername` function is a little more interesting, because it has a more complicated job. It has to allow through only the characters `a-z`, `A-Z`, `0-9`, `_` and `-`, and ensure that usernames are at least five characters long.

The `if ... else` statements commence by returning an error if `field` has not been filled in. If it's not the empty string, but is fewer than five characters in length, another error message is returned.

Then the JavaScript `test` function is called, passing a regular expression (which matches any character that is *not* one of those allowed) to be matched against `field` (see the "Regular Expressions" on page 387 section). If even one character that isn't one of the acceptable characters is encountered, then the `test` function returns `true`, and subsequently `validateUser` returns an error string.

Validating the password

Similar techniques are used in the `validatePassword` function. First the function checks whether `field` is empty, and if it is, returns an error. Next, an error message is returned if a password is shorter than six characters.

One of the requirements we're imposing on passwords is that they must have at least one each of a lowercase, uppercase, and numerical character, so the `test` function is called three times, once for each of these cases. If any one of them returns `false`, one of the requirements was not met and so an error message is returned. Otherwise, the empty string is returned to signify that the password was OK.

Validating the age

`validateAge` returns an error message if `field` is not a number (determined by a call to the `isNaN` function), or if the age entered is lower than 18 or greater than 110. Your applications may well have different or no age requirements. Again, upon successful validation the empty string is returned.

Validating the email

In the last and most complicated example, the email address is validated with `validateEmail`. After checking whether anything was actually entered, and returning an error message if it wasn't, the function calls the JavaScript `indexOf` function twice. The first time a check is made to ensure there is a period (`.`) somewhere from at least the second character of the field, and the second checks that an `@` symbol appears somewhere at or after the second character.

If those two checks are satisfied, the `test` function is called to see whether any disallowed characters appear in the field. If any of these tests fail, an error message is returned. The allowed characters in an email address are uppercase and lowercase letters, numbers, and the _, -, period and @ characters, as detailed in the regular expression passed to the test method. If no errors are found, the empty string is returned to indicate successful validation. On the last line, the script and document are closed.

Figure 17-2 shows the result of the user clicking on the Signup button without having completed any fields.

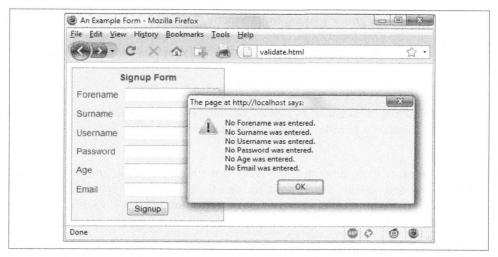

Figure 17-2. JavaScript form validation in action

Using a separate JavaScript file

Of course, because they are generic in construction and could apply to many types of validations you might require, these six functions make ideal candidates for moving out into a separate JavaScript file. For example, you could name the file something like *validate_functions.js* and include it right after the initial script section in Example 17-1, using the following statement:

```
<script src="validate_functions.js"></script>
```

Regular Expressions

Let's look a little more closely at the pattern matching we have been doing. We've achieved it using *regular expressions*, which are supported by both JavaScript and PHP. They make it possible to construct the most powerful of pattern-matching algorithms within a single expression.

Matching through metacharacters

Every regular expression must be enclosed in slashes. Within these slashes, certain characters have special meanings; they are called *metacharacters*. For instance, an asterisk (*) has a meaning similar to what you have seen if you use a shell or Windows Command Prompt (but not quite the same). An asterisk means, "the text you're trying to match may have any number of the preceding characters—or none at all."

For instance, let's say you're looking for the name "Le Guin" and know that someone might spell it with or without a space. Because the text is laid out strangely (for instance, someone may have inserted extra spaces to right-justify lines), you could have to search for a line such as:

```
The    difficulty  of   classifying Le    Guin's    works
```

So you need to match "LeGuin," as well as "Le" and "Guin" separated by any number of spaces. The solution is to follow a space with an asterisk:

```
/Le *Guin/
```

There's a lot more than the name "Le Guin" in the line, but that's OK. As long as the regular expression matches some part of the line, the test function returns a true value. What if it's important to make sure the line contains nothing but "Le Guin"? I'll show you how to ensure that later.

Suppose that you know there is always at least one space. In that case, you could use the plus sign (+), because it requires at least one of the preceding character to be present:

```
/Le +Guin/
```

Fuzzy character matching

The dot (.) is particularly useful, because it can match anything except a newline. Suppose that you are looking for HTML tags, which start with < and end with >. A simple way to do so is:

```
/<.*>/
```

The dot matches any character and the * expands it to match zero or more characters, so this is saying, "match anything that lies between < and >, even if there's nothing." You will match <>, <em>, <br>, and so on. But if you don't want to match the empty case, <>, you should use + instead of *, like this:

```
/<.+>/
```

The plus sign expands the dot to match one or more characters, saying, "match anything that lies between < and > as long as there's at least one character between them." You will match <em> and </em>, <h1> and </h1>, and tags with attributes such as:

```
<a href="www.mozilla.org">
```

Unfortunately, the plus sign keeps on matching up to the last > on the line, so you might end up with:

```
<h1><b>Introduction</b></h1>
```

A lot more than one tag! I'll show a better solution later in this section.

 If you use the dot on its own between the angle brackets, without following it with either a + or *, then it matches a single character; you will match <b> and <i> but *not* <em> or <textarea>.

If you want to match the dot character itself (.), you have to escape it by placing a backslash (\) before it, because otherwise it's a metacharacter and matches anything. As an example, suppose you want to match the floating-point number 5.0. The regular expression is:

```
/5\.0/
```

The backslash can escape any metacharacter, including another backslash (in case you're trying to match a backslash in text). However, to make things a bit confusing, you'll see later how backslashes sometimes give the following character a special meaning.

We just matched a floating-point number. But perhaps you want to match 5. as well as 5.0, because both mean the same thing as a floating-point number. You also want to match 5.00, 5.000, and so forth—any number of zeros is allowed. You can do this by adding an asterisk, as you've seen:

```
/5\.0*/
```

Grouping through parentheses

Suppose you want to match powers of increments of units, such as kilo, mega, giga, and tera. In other words, you want all the following to match:

```
1,000
1,000,000
1,000,000,000
1,000,000,000,000
...
```

The plus sign works here, too, but you need to group the string ,000 so the plus sign matches the whole thing. The regular expression is:

```
/1(,000)+ /
```

The parentheses mean "treat this as a group when you apply something such as a plus sign." 1,00,000 and 1,000,00 won't match because the text must have a 1 followed by one or more complete groups of a comma followed by three zeros.

The space after the + character indicates that the match must end when a space is encountered. Without it, 1,000,00 would incorrectly match because only the first 1,000 would be taken into account, and the remaining ,00 would be ignored. Requiring a space afterward ensures that matching will continue right through to the end of a number.

Character classes

Sometimes you want to match something fuzzy, but not so broad that you want to use a dot. Fuzziness is the great strength of regular expressions: they allow you to be as precise or vague as you want.

One of the key features supporting fuzzy matching is the pair of square brackets, [ ]. It matches a single character, like a dot, but inside the brackets you put a list of things that can match. If any of those characters appears, the text matches. For instance, if you wanted to match both the American spelling "gray" and the British spelling "grey," you could specify:

    /gr[ae]y/

After the gr in the text you're matching, there can be either an a or an e. But there must be only one of them: whatever you put inside the brackets matches exactly one character. The group of characters inside the brackets is called a *character class*.

Indicating a range

Inside the brackets, you can use a hyphen (-) to indicate a range. One very common task is matching a single digit, which you can do with a range as follows:

    /[0-9]/

Digits are such a common item in regular expressions that a single character is provided to represent them: \d. You can use it in place of the bracketed regular expression to match a digit:

    /\d/

Negation

One other important feature of the square brackets is *negation* of a character class. You can turn the whole character class on its head by placing a caret (^) after the opening bracket. Here it means, "Match any characters *except* the following." So let's say you want to find instances of "Yahoo" that lack the following exclamation point. (The name of the company officially contains an exclamation point!) You could do it as follows:

    /Yahoo[^!]/

The character class consists of a single character—an exclamation point—but it is inverted by the preceding ^. This is actually not a great solution to the problem—for instance, it fails if "Yahoo" is at the end of the line, because then it's not followed by *anything*, whereas the brackets must match a character. A better solution involves negative *lookahead* (matching something that is not followed by anything else), but that's beyond the scope of this book.

Some more complicated examples

With an understanding of character classes and negation, you're ready now to see a better solution to the problem of matching an HTML tag. This solution avoids going past the end of a single tag, but still matches tags such as <em> and </em> as well as tags with attributes such as:

```
<a href="www.mozilla.org">
```

One solution is:

```
/<[^>]+>/
```

That regular expression may look like I just dropped my teacup on the keyboard, but it is perfectly valid and very useful. Let's break it apart. Figure 17-3 shows the various elements, which I'll describe one by one.

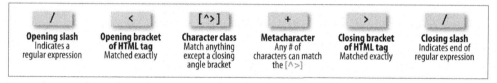

Figure 17-3. Breakdown of a typical regular expression

The elements are:

/

Opening slash that indicates this is a regular expression.

<

Opening bracket of an HTML tag. This is matched exactly; it is not a metacharacter.

[^>]

Character class. The embedded ^> means "match anything except a closing angle bracket."

+

Allows any number of characters to match the previous [^>], as long as there is at least one of them.

>

Closing bracket of an HTML tag. This is matched exactly.

/

Closing slash that indicates the end of the regular expression.

 Another solution to the problem of matching HTML tags is to use a nongreedy operation. By default, pattern matching is greedy, return-ing the longest match possible. Nongreedy matching finds the short-est possible match, and its use is beyond the scope of this book, but there are more details at *http://oreilly.com/catalog/regex/chapter/ ch04.html*.

We are going to look now at one of the expressions from Example 17-1, where the `validateUsername` function used:

    /[^a-zA-Z0-9_-]/

Figure 17-4 shows the various elements.

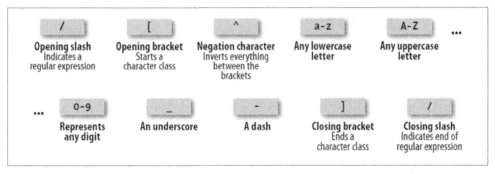

Figure 17-4. Breakdown of the validateUsername regular expression

Let's look at these elements in detail:

/

Opening slash that indicates this is a regular expression.

[

Opening bracket that starts a character class.

^

Negation character: inverts everything else between the brackets.

a-z

Represents any lowercase letter.

`A-Z`

Represents any uppercase letter.

`0-9`

Represents any digit.

`_`

An underscore.

`-`

A dash.

`]`

Closing bracket that ends a character class.

`/`

Closing slash that indicates the end of the regular expression.

There are two other important metacharacters. They "anchor" a regular expression by requiring that it appear in a particular place. If a caret (^) appears at the beginning of the regular expression, the expression has to appear at the beginning of a line of text; otherwise, it doesn't match. Similarly, if a dollar sign ($) appears at the end of the regular expression, the expression has to appear at the end of a line of text.

 It may be somewhat confusing that ^ can mean "negate the character class" inside square brackets and "match the beginning of the line" if it's at the beginning of the regular expression. Unfortunately, the same character is used for two different things, so take care when using it.

We'll finish our exploration of regular expression basics by answering a question raised earlier: suppose you want to make sure there is nothing extra on a line besides the regular expression? What if you want a line that has "Le Guin" and nothing else? We can do that by amending the earlier regular expression to anchor the two ends:

```
/^Le *Guin$/
```

Summary of metacharacters

Table 17-1 shows the metacharacters available in regular expressions.

Table 17-1. Regular expression metacharacters

Metacharacters	Description
`/`	Begins and ends the regular expression
`.`	Matches any single character except the newline
`element*`	Matches *element* zero or more times

Metacharacters	Description
element+	Matches element one or more times
element?	Matches element zero or one times
[characters]	Matches a character out of those contained within the brackets
[^characters]	Matches a single character that is not contained within the brackets
(regex)	Treats the regex as a group for counting or a following *, +, or ?
left|right	Matches either left or right
[l-r]	Matches a range of characters between l and r
^	Requires match to be at the string's start
$	Requires match to be at the string's end
\b	Matches a word boundary
\B	Matches where there is not a word boundary
\d	Matches a single digit
\D	Matches a single nondigit
\n	Matches a newline character
\s	Matches a whitespace character
\S	Matches a nonwhitespace character
\t	Matches a tab character
\w	Matches a word character (a-z, A-Z, 0-9, and _)
\W	Matches a nonword character (anything but a-z, A-Z, 0-9, and _)
\x	x (useful if x is a metacharacter, but you really want x)
{n}	Matches exactly n times
{n,}	Matches n times or more
{min,max}	Matches at least min and at most max times

Provided with this table, and looking again at the expression /[^a-zA-Z0-9_]/, you can see that it could easily be shortened to /[^\w]/ because the single metacharacter \w (with a lowercase w) specifies the characters a-z, A-Z, 0-9, and _.

In fact, we can be cleverer than that, because the metacharacter \W (with an uppercase W) specifies all characters *except* for a-z, A-Z, 0-9, and _. Therefore, we could also drop the ^ metacharacter and simply use /[\W]/ for the expression.

To give you more ideas of how this all works, Table 17-2 shows a range of expressions and the patterns they match.

Table 17-2. Some example regular expressions

Example	Matches
r	The first *r* in *The quick brown*
rec[ei][ei]ve	Either of *receive* or *recieve* (but also *receeve* or *reciive*)
rec[ei]{2}ve	Either of *receive* or *recieve* (but also *receeve* or *reciive*)
rec(ei|ie)ve	Either of *receive* or *recieve* (but not *receeve* or *reciive*)
cat	The word *cat* in *I like cats and dogs*
cat|dog	Either of the words *cat* or *dog* in *I like cats and dogs*
\.	. (the \ is necessary because . is a metacharacter)
5\.0*	*5.*, *5.0*, *5.00*, *5.000*, etc.
[a-f]	Any of the characters *a, b, c, d, e* or *f*
cats$	Only the final *cats* in *My cats are friendly cats*
^my	Only the first *my* in *my cats are my pets*
\d{2,3}	Any two- or three-digit number (*00* through *999*)
7(,000)+	*7,000*; *7,000,000*; *7,000,000,000*; *7,000,000,000,000*; etc.
[\w]+	Any word of one or more characters
[\w]{5}	Any five-letter word

General modifiers

Some additional modifiers are available for regular expressions:

- /g enables "global" matching. When using a replace function, specify this modifier to replace all matches, rather than only the first one.
- /i makes the regular expression match case-insensitive. Thus, instead of /[a-zA-Z]/, you could specify /[a-z]/i or /[A-Z]/i.
- /m enables multiline mode, in which the caret (^) and dollar ($) match before and after any newlines in the subject string. Normally, in a multiline string, ^ matches only at the start of the string and $ matches only at the end of the string.

For example, the expression /cats/g will match both occurrences of the word *cats* in the sentence *I like cats and cats like me*. Similarly, /dogs/gi will match both occurrences of the word *dogs* (*Dogs* and *dogs*) in the sentence *Dogs like other dogs*, because you can use these specifiers together.

Using Regular Expressions in JavaScript

In JavaScript, you will use regular expressions mostly in two methods: test (which you have already seen) and replace. Whereas test just tells you whether its argument matches the regular expression, replace takes a second parameter: the string to replace the text that matches. Like most functions, `replace` generates a new string as a return value; it does not change the input.

To compare the two methods, the following statement just returns `true` to let us know that the word *cats* appears at least once somewhere within the string:

```
document.write(/cats/i.test("Cats are funny. I like cats."))
```

But the following statement replaces both occurrences of the word *cats* with the word *dogs*, printing the result. The search has to be global (`/g`) to find all occurrences, and case-insensitive (`/i`) to find the capitalized *Cats*:

```
document.write("Cats are friendly. I like cats.".replace(/cats/gi,"dogs"))
```

If you try out the statement, you'll see a limitation of `replace`: because it replaces text with exactly the string you tell it to use, the first word *Cats* is replaced by *dogs* instead of *Dogs*.

Using Regular Expressions in PHP

The most common regular expression functions that you are likely to use in PHP are `preg_match`, `preg_match_all`, and `preg_replace`.

To test whether the word *cats* appears anywhere within a string, in any combination of upper- and lowercase, you could use `preg_match` like this:

```
$n = preg_match("/cats/i", "Cats are crazy. I like cats.");
```

Because PHP uses 1 for TRUE and 0 for FALSE, the preceding statement sets $n to 1. The first argument is the regular expression and the second is the text to match. But `preg_match` is actually a good deal more powerful and complicated, because it takes a third argument that shows what text matched:

```
$n = preg_match("/cats/i", "Cats are curious. I like cats.", $match);
echo "$n Matches: $match[0]";
```

The third argument is an array (here, given the name $match). The function puts the text that matches into the first element, so if the match is successful you can find the text that matched in $match[0]. In this example, the output lets us know that the matched text was capitalized:

1 Matches: Cats

If you wish to locate all matches, you use the `preg_match_all` function, like this:

```
$n = preg_match_all("/cats/i", "Cats are strange. I like cats.", $match);
echo "$n Matches: ";
for ($j=0 ; $j < $n ; ++$j) echo $match[0][$j]." ";
```

As before, $match is passed to the function and the element $match[0] is assigned the matches made, but this time as a subarray. To display the subarray, this example iterates through it with a `for` loop.

When you want to replace part of a string, you can use `preg_replace` as shown here. This example replaces all occurrences of the word *cats* with the word *dogs*, regardless of case:

```
echo preg_replace("/cats/i", "dogs", "Cats are furry. I like cats.");
```

 The subject of regular expressions is a large one and entire books have been written about it. If you would like further information, I suggest the Wikipedia entry (*http://wikipedia.org/wiki/Regular_expression*), or Jeffrey Friedl's excellent book *Mastering Regular Expressions*.

Redisplaying a Form After PHP Validation

OK, back to form validation. So far we've created the HTML document *validate.html*, which will post through to the PHP program *adduser.php*, but only if JavaScript validates the fields or if JavaScript is disabled or unavailable.

So now it's time to create *adduser.php* to receive the posted form, perform its own validation, and then present the form again to the visitor if the validation fails. Example 17-3 contains the code that you should type and save (or download from the companion website).

Example 17-3. The adduser.php program

```php
<?php // adduser.php

// The PHP code

$forename = $surname = $username = $password = $age = $email = "";

if (isset($_POST['forename']))
  $forename = fix_string($_POST['forename']);
if (isset($_POST['surname']))
  $surname  = fix_string($_POST['surname']);
if (isset($_POST['username']))
  $username = fix_string($_POST['username']);
if (isset($_POST['password']))
  $password = fix_string($_POST['password']);
if (isset($_POST['age']))
  $age      = fix_string($_POST['age']);
if (isset($_POST['email']))
  $email    = fix_string($_POST['email']);

$fail  = validate_forename($forename);
$fail .= validate_surname($surname);
$fail .= validate_username($username);
$fail .= validate_password($password);
$fail .= validate_age($age);
$fail .= validate_email($email);
```

```php
echo "<!DOCTYPE html>\n<html><head><title>An Example Form</title>";

if ($fail == "")
{
  echo "</head><body>Form data successfully validated:
    $forename, $surname, $username, $password, $age, $email.</body></html>";

  // This is where you would enter the posted fields into a database,
  // preferably using hash encryption for the password.

  exit;
}

echo <<<_END

  <!-- The HTML/JavaScript section -->

  <style>
    .signup {
      border: 1px solid #999999;
      font:   normal 14px helvetica; color:#444444;
    }
  </style>

  <script>
    function validate(form)
    {
      fail  = validateForename(form.forename.value)
      fail += validateSurname(form.surname.value)
      fail += validateUsername(form.username.value)
      fail += validatePassword(form.password.value)
      fail += validateAge(form.age.value)
      fail += validateEmail(form.email.value)

      if (fail == "")      return true
      else { alert(fail); return false }
    }

    function validateForename(field)
    {
      return (field == "") ? "No Forename was entered.\n" : ""
    }

    function validateSurname(field)
    {
      return (field == "") ? "No Surname was entered.\n" : ""
    }

    function validateUsername(field)
    {
      if (field == "") return "No Username was entered.\n"
```

```
      else if (field.length < 5)
        return "Usernames must be at least 5 characters.\n"
      else if (/[^a-zA-Z0-9_-]/.test(field))
        return "Only a-z, A-Z, 0-9, - and _ allowed in Usernames.\n"
      return ""
    }

    function validatePassword(field)
    {
      if (field == "") return "No Password was entered.\n"
      else if (field.length < 6)
        return "Passwords must be at least 6 characters.\n"
      else if (!/[a-z]/.test(field) || ! /[A-Z]/.test(field) ||
              !/[0-9]/.test(field))
        return "Passwords require one each of a-z, A-Z and 0-9.\n"
      return ""
    }

    function validateAge(field)
    {
      if (isNaN(field)) return "No Age was entered.\n"
      else if (field < 18 || field > 110)
        return "Age must be between 18 and 110.\n"
      return ""
    }

    function validateEmail(field)
    {
      if (field == "") return "No Email was entered.\n"
        else if (!((field.indexOf(".") > 0) &&
                   (field.indexOf("@") > 0)) ||
                  /[^a-zA-Z0-9.@_-]/.test(field))
          return "The Email address is invalid.\n"
      return ""
    }
  </script>
</head>
<body>

  <table border="0" cellpadding="2" cellspacing="5" bgcolor="#eeeeee">
    <th colspan="2" align="center">Signup Form</th>

      <tr><td colspan="2">Sorry, the following errors were found<br>
        in your form: <p><font color=red size=1><i>$fail</i></font></p>
      </td></tr>

    <form method="post" action="adduser.php" onSubmit="return validate(this)">
      <tr><td>Forename</td>
        <td><input type="text" maxlength="32" name="forename" value="forename">
      </td></tr><tr><td>Surname</td>
        <td><input type="text" maxlength="32" name="surname"  value="surname">
      </td></tr><tr><td>Username</td>
```

```
        <td><input type="text" maxlength="16" name="username" value="username">
    </td></tr><tr><td>Password</td>
        <td><input type="text" maxlength="12" name="password" value="password">
    </td></tr><tr><td>Age</td>
        <td><input type="text" maxlength="3"  name="age"        value="age">
    </td></tr><tr><td>Email</td>
        <td><input type="text" maxlength="64" name="email"    value="email">
    </td></tr><tr><td colspan="2" align="center"><input type="submit"
        value="Signup"></td></tr>
    </form>
  </table>
  </body>
</html>

_END;

  // The PHP functions

  function validate_forename($field)
  {
      return ($field == "") ? "No Forename was entered<br>": "";
  }

  function validate_surname($field)
  {
      return($field == "") ? "No Surname was entered<br>" : "";
  }

  function validate_username($field)
  {
    if ($field == "") return "No Username was entered<br>";
    else if (strlen($field) < 5)
      return "Usernames must be at least 5 characters<br>";
    else if (preg_match("/[^a-zA-Z0-9_-]/", $field))
      return "Only letters, numbers, - and _ in usernames<br>";
    return "";
  }

  function validate_password($field)
  {
    if ($field == "") return "No Password was entered<br>";
    else if (strlen($field) < 6)
      return "Passwords must be at least 6 characters<br>";
    else if (!preg_match("/[a-z]/", $field) ||
             !preg_match("/[A-Z]/", $field) ||
             !preg_match("/[0-9]/", $field))
      return "Passwords require 1 each of a-z, A-Z and 0-9<br>";
    return "";
  }

  function validate_age($field)
  {
```

```
    if ($field == "") return "No Age was entered<br>";
    else if ($field < 18 || $field > 110)
      return "Age must be between 18 and 110<br>";
    return "";
  }

  function validate_email($field)
  {
    if ($field == "") return "No Email was entered<br>";
      else if (!((strpos($field, ".") > 0) &&
                 (strpos($field, "@") > 0)) ||
                 preg_match("/[^a-zA-Z0-9.@_-]/", $field))
          return "The Email address is invalid<br>";
    return "";
  }

  function fix_string($string)
  {
    if (get_magic_quotes_gpc()) $string = stripslashes($string);
    return htmlentities ($string);
  }
?>
```

 In this example, all input is sanitized prior to use, even passwords, which, because they may contain characters used to format HTML, will be changed into HTML entities. For example, & will become & and < will become <, and so on. If you will be using a hash function to store encrypted passwords, this will not be an issue as long as when you later check the password entered, it is sanitized in the same way, so that the same inputs will be compared.

The result of submitting the form with JavaScript disabled (and two fields incorrectly completed) is shown in Figure 17-5.

I have put the PHP section of this code (and changes to the HTML section) in a bold typeface so that you can more clearly see the difference between this and Examples 17-1 and 17-2.

If you browsed through this example (or typed it or downloaded it from the companion website (*http://lpmj.net*)), you'll have seen that the PHP code is almost a clone of the JavaScript code; the same regular expressions are used to validate each field in very similar functions.

But there are a couple of things to note. First, the fix_string function (right at the end) is used to sanitize each field and prevent any attempts at code injection from succeeding.

Also, you will see that the HTML from Example 17-1 has been repeated in the PHP code within a <<<_END ... _END; structure, displaying the form with the values that the visitor entered the previous time. You do this by simply adding an extra value parameter to each <input> tag (such as value="$forename").

This courtesy is highly recommended so that the user has to edit only the previously entered values, and doesn't have to type the fields all over again.

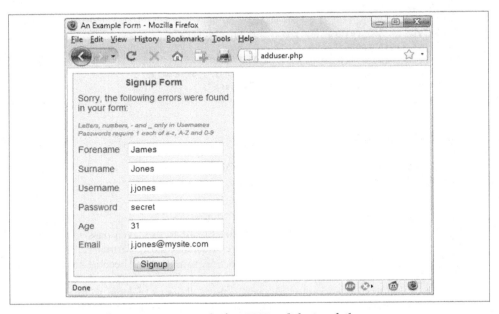

Figure 17-5. The form as represented after PHP validation fails

In the real world, you probably wouldn't start with an HTML form such as the one in Example 17-1. Instead, you'd be more likely to go straight ahead and write the PHP program in Example 17-3, which incorporates all the HTML. And, of course, you'd also need to make a minor tweak for the case when it's the first time the program is called up, to prevent it from displaying errors when all the fields are empty. You also might drop the six JavaScript functions into their own .js file for separate inclusion.

Now that you've seen how to bring all of PHP, HTML, and JavaScript together, the next chapter will introduce Ajax (Asynchronous JavaScript and XML), which uses JavaScript calls to the server in the background to seamlessly update portions of a web page, without having to resubmit the entire page to the web server.

Questions

1. What JavaScript method can you use to send a form for validation prior to submitting it?

2. What JavaScript method is used to match a string against a regular expression?

3. Write a regular expression to match any characters that are *not* in a word, as defined by regular expression syntax.

4. Write a regular expression to match either of the words *fox* or *fix*.

5. Write a regular expression to match any single word followed by any nonword character.

6. Using regular expressions, write a JavaScript function to test whether the word *fox* exists in the string The quick brown fox.

7. Using regular expressions, write a PHP function to replace all occurrences of the word *the* in The cow jumps over the moon with the word *my*.

8. What HTML attribute is used to precomplete form fields with a value?

See "Chapter 17 Answers" on page 651 in Appendix A for the answers to these questions.

CHAPTER 18

Using Ajax

The term *Ajax* was first coined in 2005. It stands for Asynchronous JavaScript and XML, which, in simple terms, means using a set of methods built into JavaScript to transfer data between the browser and a server in the background. An excellent example of this technology is Google Maps (see Figure 18-1), in which new sections of a map are downloaded from the server when needed, without requiring a page refresh.

Using Ajax not only substantially reduces the amount of data that must be sent back and forth, it also makes web pages seamlessly dynamic—allowing them to behave more like self-contained applications. The results are a much improved user interface and better responsiveness.

What Is Ajax?

The beginnings of Ajax as used today started with the release of Internet Explorer 5 in 1999, which introduced a new ActiveX object, XMLHttpRequest. ActiveX is Microsoft's technology for signing plug-ins that install additional software to your computer. Other browser developers later followed suit, but rather than using ActiveX, they all implemented the feature as a native part of the JavaScript interpreter.

However, even before then, an early form of Ajax had already surfaced that used hidden frames on a page that interacted with the server in the background. Chat rooms were early adopters of this technology, using it to poll for and display new message posts without requiring page reloads.

So let's see how to implement Ajax using JavaScript.

Figure 18-1. Google Maps is an excellent example of Ajax in action

Using XMLHttpRequest

Due to the differences between browser implementations of `XMLHttpRequest`, you must create a special function in order to ensure that your code will work on all major browsers.

To do this, you must understand the three ways of creating an `XMLHttpRequest` object:

- IE 5: `request = new ActiveXObject("Microsoft.XMLHTTP")`
- IE 6+: `request = new ActiveXObject("Msxml2.XMLHTTP")`
- All others: `request = new XMLHttpRequest()`

This is the case because Microsoft chose to implement a change with the release of Internet Explorer 6, while all other browsers use a slightly different method. Therefore, the code in Example 18-1 will work for all major browsers released over the last few years.

Example 18-1. A cross-browser Ajax function

```
<script>
  function ajaxRequest()
  {
    try // Non IE Browser?
    {   // Yes
      var request = new XMLHttpRequest()
    }
    catch(e1)
    {
      try // IE 6+?
      {   // Yes
        request = new ActiveXObject("Msxml2.XMLHTTP")
      }
      catch(e2)
      {
        try // IE 5?
        {   // Yes
          request = new ActiveXObject("Microsoft.XMLHTTP")
        }
        catch(e3) // There is no AJAX Support
        {
          request = false
        }
      }
    }
    return request
  }
</script>
```

You may remember the introduction to error handling in the previous chapter, using the try ... catch construct. Example 18-1 is a perfect illustration of its utility, because it uses the try keyword to execute the non-IE Ajax command, and upon success, jumps on to the final return statement, where the new object is returned.

Otherwise, a catch traps the error and the subsequent command is executed. Again, upon success, the new object is returned; otherwise, the final of the three commands is tried. If that attempt fails, then the browser doesn't support Ajax and the request object is set to false; otherwise, the object is returned. So there you have it: a cross-browser Ajax request function that you may wish to add to your library of useful JavaScript functions.

OK, so now you have a means of creating an XMLHttpRequest object, but what can you do with these objects? Well, each one comes with a set of properties (variables) and methods (functions), which are detailed in Tables 18-1 and 18-2.

Table 18-1. An XMLHttpRequest object's properties

Properties	Description
onreadystatechange	Specifies an event handling function to be called whenever the readyState property of an object changes.
readyState	An integer property that reports on the status of a request. It can have any of these values: 0 = Uninitialized, 1 = Loading, 2 = Loaded, 3 = Interactive, and 4 = Completed.
responseText	The data returned by the server in text format.
responseXML	The data returned by the server in XML format.
status	The HTTP status code returned by the server.
statusText	The HTTP status text returned by the server.

Table 18-2. An XMLHttpRequest object's methods

Methods	Description
abort()	Aborts the current request.
getAllResponseHeaders()	Returns all headers as a string.
getResponseHeader(*param*)	Returns the value of *param* as a string.
open('*method*', '*url*', '*asynch*')	Specifies the HTTP method to use (GET or POST), the target URL, and whether the request should be handled asynchronously (true or false).
send(*data*)	Sends data to the target server using the specified HTTP method.
setRequestHeader('*param*', '*value*')	Sets a header with a parameter/value pair.

These properties and methods give you control over what data you send to the server and receive back, as well as a choice of send and receive methods. For example, you can choose whether to request data in plain text (which could include HTML and other tags) or in XML format. You can also decide whether you wish to use the POST or GET method to send to the server.

Let's look at the POST method first by creating a very simple pair of documents: a combination of HTML and JavaScript, and a PHP program to interact via Ajax with the first. Hopefully you'll enjoy these examples, because they illustrate just what Web 2.0 and Ajax are all about. With a few lines of JavaScript, they request a web document from a third-party web server, which is then returned to the browser by your server and placed within a section of the current document.

Your First Ajax Program

Type and save the code in Example 18-2 as *urlpost.html*, but don't load it into your browser yet.

Example 18-2. urlpost.html

```
<!DOCTYPE html>
<html>
  <head>
    <title>AJAX Example</title>
  </head>
  <body style='text-align:center'>
    <h1>Loading a web page into a DIV</h1>
    <div id='info'>This sentence will be replaced</div>

    <script>
      params  = "url=amazon.com/gp/aw"
      request = new ajaxRequest()

      request.open("POST", "urlpost.php", true)
      request.setRequestHeader("Content-type",
        "application/x-www-form-urlencoded")
      request.setRequestHeader("Content-length", params.length)
      request.setRequestHeader("Connection", "close")

      request.onreadystatechange = function()
      {
        if (this.readyState == 4)
        {
          if (this.status == 200)
          {
            if (this.responseText != null)
            {
              document.getElementById('info').innerHTML =
                this.responseText
            }
            else alert("Ajax error: No data received")
          }
          else alert( "Ajax error: " + this.statusText)
        }
      }

      request.send(params)

      function ajaxRequest()
      {
        try
        {
          var request = new XMLHttpRequest()
        }
        catch(e1)
        {
          try
          {
            request = new ActiveXObject("Msxml2.XMLHTTP")
          }
          catch(e2)
```

```
        {
          try
          {
            request = new ActiveXObject("Microsoft.XMLHTTP")
          }
          catch(e3)
          {
            request = false
          }
        }
      }
      return request
    }
  </script>
 </body>
</html>
```

Let's go through this document and look at what it does, starting with the first six lines, which simply set up an HTML document and display a heading. The next line creates a DIV with the ID info, containing the text This sentence will be replaced by default. Later on, the text returned from the Ajax call will be inserted here.

The next six lines are required for making an HTTP POST Ajax request. The first sets the variable params to a *parameter=value* pair, which is what we'll send to the server. Then the Ajax object request is created. After this, the open method is called to set the object to make a POST request to *urlpost.php* in asynchronous mode. The last three lines in this group set up headers that are required for the receiving server to know that a POST request is coming.

The readyState property

Now we get to the nitty-gritty of an Ajax call, which all hangs on the readyState property. The "asynchronous" aspect of Ajax allows the browser to keep accepting user input and changing the screen, while our program sets the onreadystatechange property to call a function of our choice each time readyState changes. In this case, a nameless (or anonymous) inline function has been used, as opposed to a separate, named function. This type of function is known as a *callback* function, as it is called back each time readyState changes.

The syntax to set up the callback function using an inline, anonymous function is as follows:

```
request.onreadystatechange = function()
{
  if (this.readyState == 4)
  {
    // do something
  }
}
```

If you wish to use a separate, named function, the syntax is slightly different:

```
request.onreadystatechange = ajaxCallback

function ajaxCallback()
{
  if (this.readyState == 4)
  {
    // do something
  }
}
```

Looking at Table 18-1, you'll see that readyState can have five different values. But only one of them concerns us: value 4, which represents a completed Ajax call. Therefore, each time the new function gets called, it returns without doing anything until ready State has a value of 4. When our function detects that value, it next inspects the status of the call to ensure it has a value of 200, which means that the call succeeded. If it's not 200, an alert pop up displays the error message contained in statusText.

 You will notice that all of these object properties are referenced using this.readyState, this.status, and so on, rather than the object's current name, request, as in request.readyState or request.status. This is so that you can easily copy and paste the code and it will work with any object name, because the this keyword always refers to the current object.

So, having ascertained that the readyState is 4 and the status is 200, we test the responseText value to see whether it contains a value. If not, an error message is displayed in an alert box. Otherwise, the inner HTML of the DIV is assigned the value of responseText, like this:

```
document.getElementById('info').innerHTML = this.responseText
```

In this line, the element info is referenced via the getElementByID method, and then its innerHTML property is assigned the value that was returned by the Ajax call.

After all this setting up and preparation, the Ajax request is finally sent to the server via the following command, which passes the parameters already defined in the variable params:

```
request.send(params)
```

After that, all the preceding code is activated each time readyState changes.

The remainder of the document is the ajaxRequest function from Example 18-1, and the closing script and HTML tags.

The server half of the Ajax process

Now we get to the PHP half of the equation, which you can see in Example 18-3. Type it and save it as *urlpost.php*.

Example 18-3. urlpost.php

```php
<?php // urlpost.php
  if (isset($_POST['url']))
  {
    echo file_get_contents('http://' . SanitizeString($_POST['url']));
  }

  function SanitizeString($var)
  {
    $var = strip_tags($var);
    $var = htmlentities($var);
    return stripslashes($var);
  }
?>
```

As you can see, this is short and sweet, and as should be done with all posted data, it also makes use of the ever-important SanitizeString function. In this instance, unsanitized data could result in the user gaining an advantage over your code.

This program uses the file_get_contents PHP function to load in the web page at the URL supplied to it in the POST variable $_POST['url']. The file_get_contents function is versatile in that it loads in the entire contents of a file or web page from either a local or a remote server; it even takes into account moved pages and other redirects.

Once you have typed the program, you are ready to call up *urlpost.html* into your web browser and, after a few seconds, you should see the contents of the Amazon mobile front page loaded into the DIV that we created for that purpose. It won't be as fast as directly loading the web page, because it is transferred twice: once to the server and again from the server to your browser. The result should look like Figure 18-2.

Not only have we succeeded in making an Ajax call and having a response returned to JavaScript, we've also harnessed the power of PHP to enable the merging in of a totally unrelated web object. Incidentally, if we had tried to find a way to fetch the Amazon mobile web page directly via Ajax (without recourse to the PHP server-side module), we wouldn't have succeeded, because there are security blocks preventing cross-domain Ajax. So this little example also illustrates a handy solution to a very practical problem.

Figure 18-2. The Amazon mobile website has been loaded into a DIV

Using GET Instead of POST

As with submitting any form data, you have the option of submitting your data in the form of GET requests, and you will save a few lines of code if you do so. However, there is a downside: some browsers may cache GET requests, whereas POST requests will never be cached. You don't want to cache a request, because the browser will just redisplay what it got the last time instead of going to the server for fresh input. The solution to this is to use a workaround that adds a random parameter to each request, ensuring that each URL requested is unique.

Example 18-4 shows how you would achieve the same result as with Example 18-2, but using an Ajax GET request instead of POST.

Example 18-4. urlget.html

```
<!DOCTYPE html>
<html>
  <head>
    <title>AJAX Example</title>
  </head>
  <body style='text-align:center'>
```

```
<h1>Loading a web page into a DIV</h1>
<div id='info'>This sentence will be replaced</div>

<script>
  nocache = "&nocache=" + Math.random() * 1000000
  request = new ajaxRequest()
  request.open("GET", "urlget.php?url=amazon.com/gp/aw" + nocache, true)

  request.onreadystatechange = function()
  {
    if (this.readyState == 4)
    {
      if (this.status == 200)
      {
        if (this.responseText != null)
        {
          document.getElementById('info').innerHTML =
            this.responseText
        }
        else alert("Ajax error: No data received")
      }
      else alert( "Ajax error: " + this.statusText)
    }
  }

  request.send(null)

  function ajaxRequest()
  {
    try
    {
      var request = new XMLHttpRequest()
    }
    catch(e1)
    {
      try
      {
        request = new ActiveXObject("Msxml2.XMLHTTP")
      }
      catch(e2)
      {
        try
        {
          request = new ActiveXObject("Microsoft.XMLHTTP")
        }
        catch(e3)
        {
          request = false
        }
      }
    }
    return request
```

```
      }
    </script>
  </body>
</html>
```

The differences to note between the two documents are highlighted in bold, and described as follows:

- It is not necessary to send headers for a GET request.
- We call the open method using a GET request, supplying a URL with a string comprising a ? symbol followed by the parameter/value pair url=amazon.com/gp/aw.
- We start a second parameter/value pair using an & symbol, then set the value of the parameter nocache to a random value between 0 and a million. This is used to ensure that each URL requested is different, and therefore that no requests will be cached.
- The call to send now contains only a parameter of null, as no parameters are being passed via a POST request. Note that leaving the parameter out is not an option, as it would result in an error.

To accompany this new document, the PHP program must be modified to respond to a GET request, as in Example 18-5, *urlget.php*.

Example 18-5. urlget.php

```php
<?php
  if (isset($_GET['url']))
  {
    echo file_get_contents("http://".sanitizeString($_GET['url']));
  }

  function sanitizeString($var)
  {
    $var = strip_tags($var);
    $var = htmlentities($var);
    return stripslashes($var);
  }
?>
```

All that's different between this and Example 18-3 is that the references to $_POST have been replaced with $_GET. The end result of calling up *urlget.html* in your browser is identical to loading in *urlpost.html*.

Sending XML Requests

Although the objects we've been creating are called XMLHttpRequest objects, so far we have made absolutely no use of XML. This is where the Ajax term is a bit of a misnomer, because the technology actually allows you to request any type of textual data, only one of which is XML. As you have seen, we have requested an entire HTML document via Ajax, but we could equally have asked for a text page, a string or number, or even spreadsheet data.

So let's modify the previous example document and PHP program to fetch some XML data. To do this, first take a look at the PHP program, *xmlget.php*, shown in Example 18-6.

Example 18-6. xmlget.php

```php
<?php
  if (isset($_GET['url']))
  {
    header('Content-Type: text/xml');
    echo file_get_contents("http://".sanitizeString($_GET['url']));
  }

  function sanitizeString($var)
  {
    $var = strip_tags($var);
    $var = htmlentities($var);
    return stripslashes($var);
  }
?>
```

This program has been very slightly modified (shown in bold highlighting) to output the correct XML header before returning a fetched document. No checking is made here, as it is assumed that the calling Ajax will request an actual XML document.

Now on to the HTML document, *xmlget.html*, shown in Example 18-7.

Example 18-7. xmlget.html

```html
<!DOCTYPE html>
<html>
  <head>
    <title>AJAX Example</title>
  </head>
  <body>
    <h1>Loading a web page into a DIV</h1>
    <div id='info'>This sentence will be replaced</div>

    <script>
      nocache = "&nocache=" + Math.random() * 1000000
      url     = "rss.news.yahoo.com/rss/topstories"
      out     = "";

      request = new ajaxRequest()
      request.open("GET", "xmlget.php?url=" + url + nocache, true)

      request.onreadystatechange = function()
      {
```

```
        if (this.readyState == 4)
        {
          if (this.status == 200)
          {
            if (this.responseText != null)
            {
              titles = this.responseXML.getElementsByTagName('title')

              for (j = 0 ; j < titles.length ; ++j)
              {
                out += titles[j].childNodes[0].nodeValue + '<br>'
              }
              document.getElementById('info').innerHTML = out
            }
            else alert("Ajax error: No data received")
          }
          else alert( "Ajax error: " + this.statusText)
        }
      }

      request.send(null)

      function ajaxRequest()
      {
        try
        {
          var request = new XMLHttpRequest()
        }
        catch(e1)
        {
          try
          {
            request = new ActiveXObject("Msxml2.XMLHTTP")
          }
          catch(e2)
          {
            try
            {
              request = new ActiveXObject("Microsoft.XMLHTTP")
            }
            catch(e3)
            {
              request = false
            }
          }
        }
        return request
      }
    </script>
  </body>
</html>
```

Again, the changes have been highlighted in bold, so you can see that this code is substantially similar to previous versions, except that the URL now being requested, *rss.news.yahoo.com/rss/topstories*, contains an XML document, the Yahoo! News Top Stories feed.

The other big difference is the use of the `responseXML` property, which replaces the `responseText` property. Whenever a server returns XML data, `responseXML` will contain the XML returned.

However, `responseXML` doesn't simply contain a string of XML text: it is actually a complete XML document object that we can examine and parse using DOM tree methods and properties. This means it is accessible, for example, by the JavaScript `getElements ByTagName` method.

About XML

An XML document will generally take the form of the RSS feed shown in Example 18-8. However, the beauty of XML is that we can store this type of structure internally in a DOM tree (see Figure 18-3) to make it quickly searchable.

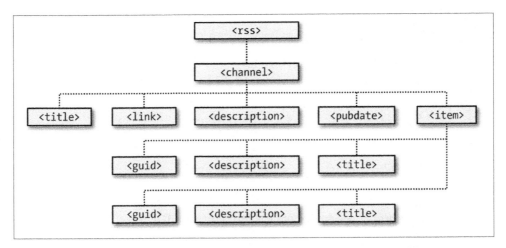

Figure 18-3. The DOM tree of Example 18-8

Example 18-8. An XML document

```
<?xml version="1.0" encoding="UTF-8"?>
<rss version="2.0">
  <channel>
    <title>RSS Feed</title>
    <link>http://website.com</link>
    <description>website.com's RSS Feed</description>
    <pubDate>Mon, 11 May 2020 00:00:00 GMT</pubDate>
```

```
<item>
  <title>Headline</title>
  <guid>http://website.com/headline</guid>
  <description>This is a headline</description>
</item>
<item>
  <title>Headline 2</title>
  <guid>http://website.com/headline2</guid>
  <description>The 2nd headline</description>
</item>
</channel>
</rss>
```

Therefore, using the `getElementsByTagName` method, you can quickly extract the values associated with various tags without a lot of string searching. This is exactly what we do in Example 18-7, where the following command is issued:

```
titles = this.responseXML.getElementsByTagName('title')
```

This single command has the effect of placing all the values of the `title` elements into the array `titles`. From there, it is a simple matter to extract them with the following expression (where `j` is the title to access):

```
titles[j].childNodes[0].nodeValue
```

All the titles are then appended to the string variable out and, once all have been processed, the result is inserted into the empty DIV at the document start. When you call up *xmlget.html* in your browser, the result will be something like Figure 18-4.

> As with all form data, you can use either the POST or the GET method when requesting XML data; your choice will make little difference to the result.

Why use XML?

You may ask why you would use XML other than for fetching XML documents such as RSS feeds. Well, the simple answer is that you don't have to, but if you wish to pass structured data back to your Ajax applications, it could be a real pain to send a simple, unorganized jumble of text that would need complicated processing in JavaScript.

Instead, you can create an XML document and pass that back to the Ajax function, which will automatically place it into a DOM tree, as easily accessible as the HTML DOM object with which you are now familiar.

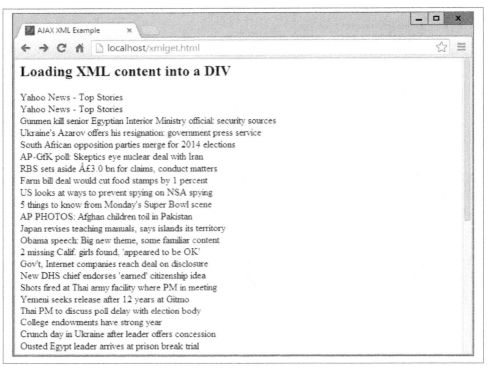

Figure 18-4. Fetching a Yahoo! XML news feed via Ajax

Using Frameworks for Ajax

Now that you know how to code your own Ajax routines, you might like to investigate some of the free frameworks that are available to make it even easier, as they offer many more advanced features. In particular, I would suggest you check out jQuery, which is probably the most commonly used framework.

You can download it (and get full documentation) from *http://jquery.com*, but be aware that there's an initially steep learning curve, as you have to familiarize yourself with the $ function it provides, which is used extensively for accessing jQuery's features. That said, once you understand how jQuery works, you'll find it can make your web development much easier and quicker due to the large number of ready-made features it offers.

Questions

1. Why is it necessary to write a function for creating new XMLHttpRequest objects?

2. What is the purpose of the try ... catch construct?

3. How many properties and how many methods does an XMLHttpRequest object have?

4. How can you tell when an Ajax call has completed?

5. How do you know whether an Ajax call completed successfully?

6. What XMLHttpRequest object's property returns an Ajax text response?

7. What XMLHttpRequest object's property returns an Ajax XML response?

8. How can you specify a callback function to handle Ajax responses?

9. What XMLHttpRequest method is used to initiate an Ajax request?

10. What are the main differences between an Ajax GET and POST request?

See "Chapter 18 Answers" on page 651 in Appendix A for the answers to these questions.

CHAPTER 19

Introduction to CSS

Using *CSS (Cascading Style Sheets)*, you can apply styles to your web pages to make them look exactly how you want. This works because CSS is connected to the DOM (Document Object Model), which I explained in Chapter 14.

With CSS and its integration with the DOM, you can quickly and easily restyle any element. For example, if you don't like the default look of the <h1>, <h2>, and other heading tags, you can assign new styles to override the default settings for the font family and size used, or whether bold or italics should be set, and many more properties too.

One way you can add styling to a web page is by inserting the required statements into the head of a web page between the <head> and </head> tags. So, to change the style of the <h1> tag, you might use the following code (I'll explain the syntax later):

```
<style>
   h1 { color:red; font-size:3em; font-family:Arial; }
</style>
```

Within an HTML page this might look like Example 19-1 (see Figure 19-1), which, like all the examples in this chapter, uses the standard HTML5 DOCTYPE declaration.

Example 19-1. A simple HTML page

```
<!DOCTYPE html>
<html>
  <head>
    <title>Hello World</title>
    <style>
      h1 { color:red; font-size:3em; font-family:Arial; }
    </style>
  </head>
  <body>
    <h1>Hello there</h1>
  </body>
</html>
```

Figure 19-1. Styling a tag, with the original style shown in the inset

Importing a Style Sheet

When you wish to style a whole site, rather than a single page, a better way to manage style sheets is to move them completely out of your web pages to separate files, and then import the ones you need. This lets you apply different style sheets for different layouts (such as web and print), without changing the HTML.

There are a couple of different ways you can achieve this, the first of which is by using the CSS `@import` directive like this:

```
<style>
  @import url('styles.css');
</style>
```

This statement tells the browser to fetch a style sheet with the name *styles.css*. The `@import` command is quite flexible in that you can create style sheets that themselves pull in other style sheets, and so on. You need to just make sure that there are no `<style>` or `</style>` tags in any of your external style sheets, or they will not work.

Importing CSS from Within HTML

You can also include a style sheet with the HTML `<link>` tag like this:

```
<link rel='stylesheet' type='text/css' href='styles.css'>
```

This has the exact same effect as the `@import` directive, except that `<link>` is an HTML-only tag and is not a valid style directive, so it cannot be used from within one style sheet to pull in another, and also cannot be placed within a pair of `<style>` ... `</style>` tags.

Just as you can use multiple @import directives within your CSS to include multiple external style sheets, you can also use as many <link> elements as you like in your HTML.

Embedded Style Settings

There's also nothing stopping you from individually setting or overriding certain styles for the current page on a case-by-case basis by inserting style declarations directly within HTML, like this (which results in italic, blue text within the tags):

```
<div style='font-style:italic; color:blue;'>Hello there</div>
```

But this should be reserved only for the most exceptional circumstances, as it breaks the separation of content and presentation.

Using IDs

A better solution for setting the style of an element is to assign an ID to it in the HTML, like this:

```
<div id='welcome'>Hello there</div>
```

This states that the contents of the <div> with the ID welcome should have applied to them the style defined in the welcome style setting. The matching CSS statement for this might look like the following

```
#welcome { font-style:italic; color:blue; }
```

 Note the use of the # symbol, which specifies that only the ID with the name welcome should be styled with this statement.

Using Classes

If you would like to apply the same style to many elements, you do not have to give each one a different ID because you can specify a class to manage them all, like this:

```
<div class='welcome'>Hello</div>
```

This states that the contents of this element (and any others that use the class) should have applied to them the style defined in the welcome class. Once a class is applied you can use the following rule, either in the page header or within an external style sheet for setting the styles for the class:

```
.welcome { font-style:italic; color:blue; }
```

Instead of the # symbol, which is reserved for IDs, class statements are prefaced with a . (period).

Using Semicolons

In CSS, semicolons are used to separate multiple CSS statements on the same line. But if there is only one statement in a rule (or in an inline style setting within an HTML tag), you can omit the semicolon, as you can for the final statement in a group.

However, to avoid hard-to-find CSS errors, you may prefer to always use a semicolon after every CSS setting. You can then copy and paste them, and otherwise modify properties, without worrying about removing semicolons where they aren't strictly necessary or having to add them where they are required.

CSS Rules

Each statement in a CSS rule starts with a *selector*, which is the item to which the rule will be applied. For example, in this assignment, h1 is the selector being given a font size 240% larger than the default:

```
h1 { font-size:240%; }
```

font-size is a *property*. Providing a value of 240% to the font-size property of the selector ensures that the contents of all <h1> ... </h1> pairs of tags will be displayed at a font size that is 240% of the default size. All changes in rules must be within the { and } symbols that follow the selector. In font-size:240%; the part before the : (colon) is the property, while the remainder is the value applied to it.

Last comes a ; (semicolon) to end the statement. In this instance, because font-size is the last property in the rule, the semicolon is not required (but it would be if another assignment were to follow).

Multiple Assignments

You can create multiple style declarations in a couple of different ways. First, you can concatenate them on the same line, like this:

```
h1 { font-size:240%; color:blue; }
```

This adds a second assignment that changes the color of all <h1> headings to blue. You can also place the assignments one per line, like the following:

```
h1 { font-size:240%;
color:blue; }
```

Or you can space out the assignments a little more, so that they line up below each other in a column at the colons, like this:

```
h1 {
  font-size:240%;
  color     :blue;
}
```

This way, you can easily see where each new set of rules begins, because the selector is always in the first column, and the assignments that follow are neatly lined up with all property values starting at the same horizontal offset. In the preceding examples, the final semicolon is unnecessary, but should you ever want to concatenate any such groups of statements into a single line, it is very quick to do with all semicolons already in place.

You can specify the same selector as many times as you want, and CSS combines all the properties. So the previous example could also be specified as:

```
h1 { font-size: 240%; }
h1 { color    : blue; }
```

 There is no right or wrong way to lay out your CSS, but I recommend that you at least try to keep each block of CSS consistent with itself, so that other people can take it in at a glance.

What if you specified the same property to the same selector twice?

```
h1 { color : red; }
h1 { color : blue; }
```

The last value specified—in this case, blue—would apply. In a single file, repeating the same property for the same selector would be pointless, but such repetition happens frequently in real-life web pages when multiple style sheets are applied. It's one of the valuable features of CSS, and where the term *cascading* comes from.

Using Comments

It is a good idea to comment your CSS rules, even if you describe only the main groups of statements rather than all or most of them. You can do this in two different ways. First, you can place a comment within a pair of /* ... */ tags, like this:

```
/* This is a CSS comment */
```

Or you can extend a comment over many lines, like this:

```
/*
    A Multi
    line
    comment
*/
```

When using multiline comments, note that you cannot nest single-line (or any other) comments within them. Doing so can lead to unpredictable errors.

Style Types

There are a number of different style types, ranging from the default styles set up by your browser (and any user styles you may have applied in your browser to override its defaults), through inline or embedded styles, to external style sheets. The styles defined in each type have a hierarchy of precedence, from low to high.

Default Styles

The lowest level of style precedence is the default styling applied by a web browser. These styles are created as a fallback for when a web page doesn't have any styles, and they are intended to be a generic set of styles that will display reasonably well in most instances.

Pre-CSS, these were the only styles applied to a document, and only a handful of them could be changed by a web page (such as font face, color, and size, and a few element sizing arguments).

User Styles

These are the next highest precedence of styles, and they are supported by most modern browsers but are implemented differently by each. If you would like to learn how to create your own default styles for browsing, use a search engine to enter your browser name followed by "user styles" (e.g., "Firefox user styles" or "Opera user styles") to find out how. Figure 19-2 shows a user style sheet being applied to Microsoft Internet Explorer.

If a user style is assigned that has already been defined as a browser default, it will then override the browser's default setting. Any styles not defined in a user style sheet will retain their default values as set up in the browser.

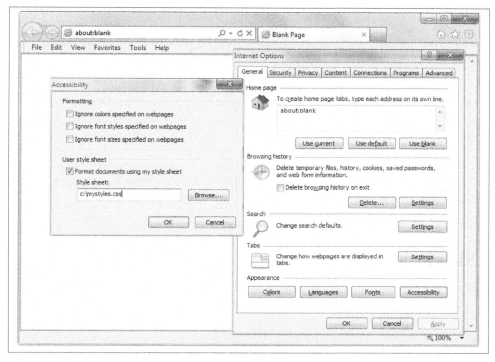

Figure 19-2. Applying a user style to Internet Explorer

External Style Sheets

The next types of styles are those assigned in an external style sheet. These settings will override any assigned either by the user or by the browser. External style sheets are the recommended way to create your styles because you can produce different style sheets for different purposes such as styling for general web use, for viewing on a mobile browser with a smaller screen, for printing purposes, and so on. Just apply the one needed for each type of media when you create the web page.

Internal Styles

Then there are internal styles, which you create within `<style>` ... `</style>` tags, and which take precedence over all the preceding style types. At this point, though, you are beginning to break the separation between styling and content, as any external style sheets loaded in at the same time will have a lower precedence.

Inline Styles

Finally, inline styles are where you assign a property directly to an element. They have the highest precedence of any style type, and are used like this:

```
<a href="http://google.com" style="color:green;">Visit Google</a>
```

In this example, the link specified will be displayed in green, regardless of any default or other color settings applied by any other type of style sheet, whether directly to this link or generically for all links.

 When you use this type of styling, you are breaking the separation between layout and content; therefore, it is recommended that you do so only when you have a very good reason.

CSS Selectors

The means by which you access one or more elements is called *selection*, and the part of a CSS rule that does this is known as a *selector*. As you might expect, there are many varieties of selector.

The Type Selector

The type selector works on types of HTML elements such as `<p>` or `<i>`. For example, the following rule will ensure that all text within `<p>` ... `</p>` tags is fully justified:

```
p { text-align:justify; }
```

The Descendant Selector

Descendant selectors let you apply styles to elements that are contained within other elements. For example, the following rule sets all text within `<b>` ... `</b>` tags to red, but only if they occur within `<p>` ... `</p>` tags (like this: `<p><b>Hello</b> there</p>`):

```
p b { color:red; }
```

Descendant selectors can continue nesting indefinitely, so the following is a perfectly valid rule to make the text blue within bold text, inside a list element of an unordered list:

```
ul li b { color:blue; }
```

As a practical example, suppose you want to use a different numbering system for an ordered list that is nested within another ordered list. You can achieve this in the following way, which will replace the default numeric numbering (starting from 1) with lowercase letters (starting from a):

```
<!DOCTYPE html>
<html>
  <head>
    <style>
      ol ol { list-style-type:lower-alpha; }
    </style>
  </head>
  <body>
    <ol>
      <li>One</li>
      <li>Two</li>
      <li>Three
        <ol>
          <li>One</li>
          <li>Two</li>
          <li>Three</li>
        </ol>
      </li>
    </ol>
  </body>
</html>
```

The result of loading this HTML into a web browser is as follows, in which you can see that the second list elements display differently:

1. One
2. Two
3. Three
   a. One
   b. Two
   c. Three

The Child Selector

The child selector is similar to the descendant selector but is more restrictive about when the style will be applied, by selecting only those elements that are direct children of another element. For example, the following code uses a descendant selector that will change any bold text within a paragraph to red, even if the bold text is itself within italics (like this `<p><i><b>Hello</b> there</i></p>`):

```
p b { color:red; }
```

In this instance, the word `Hello` displays in red. However, when this more general type of behavior is not required, a child selector can be used to narrow the scope of the selector. For example, the following child selector will set bold text to red only if the element is a direct child of a paragraph, and is not itself contained within another element:

```
p > b { color:red; }
```

Now the word `Hello` will not change color because it is not a direct child of the paragraph.

For a practical example, suppose you wish to embolden only those `<li>` elements that are direct children of `<ol>` elements. You can achieve this as follows, where the `<li>` elements that are direct children of `<ul>` elements do not get emboldened:

```
<!DOCTYPE html>
<html>
  <head>
    <style>
      ol > li { font-weight:bold; }
    </style>
  </head>
  <body>
    <ol>
      <li>One</li>
      <li>Two</li>
      <li>Three</li>
    </ol>
    <ul>
      <li>One</li>
      <li>Two</li>
      <li>Three</li>
    </ul>
  </body>
</html>
```

The result of loading this HTML into a browser will be as follows:

1. **One**
2. **Two**
3. **Three**

- One
- Two
- Three

The ID Selector

If you give an element an ID name (like this: `<div id='mydiv'>`) then you can directly access it from CSS in the following way, which changes all the text in the element to italic:

```
#mydiv { font-style:italic; }
```

IDs can be used only once within a document, so only the first occurrence found will receive the new property value assigned by a CSS rule. But in CSS you can directly reference any IDs that have the same name, as long as they occur within different element types, like this:

```
<div id='myid'>Hello</div> <span id='myid'>Hello</span>
```

Because IDs normally apply only to unique elements, the following rule will apply an underline to only the first occurrence of myid:

```
#myid { text-decoration:underline; }
```

However, you can ensure that CSS applies the rule to both occurrences like this:

```
span#myid { text-decoration:underline; }
div#myid  { text-decoration:underline; }
```

Or more succinctly like this (see "Selecting by Group" on page 435):

```
span#myid, div#myid { text-decoration:underline; }
```

 I don't recommend using this form of selection because any Java-Script that also must access these elements cannot easily do so because the commonly used getElementByID() function will return only the first occurrence. To reference any other instances, a program would have to search through the whole list of elements in the document—a trickier task to undertake. So it's generally better to always use unique ID names.

The Class Selector

When there are a number of elements in a page that you want to share the same styling, you can assign them all the same class name (like this: <span class='myclass'>); then, create a single rule to modify all those elements at once, as in the following rule, which creates a 10-pixel left margin offset for all elements using the class:

```
.myclass { margin-left:10px; }
```

In modern browsers, you can have HTML elements use more than one class by separating the class names with spaces, like this: <span class='class1 class2 class3'>. Remember, though, that some very old browsers only allow a single class name in a class argument.

You can narrow the scope of action of a class by specifying the types of elements to which it should apply. For example, the following rule applies the setting only to paragraphs that use the class main:

```
p.main { text-indent:30px; }
```

In this example, only paragraphs using the class main (like this: <p class="main">) will receive the new property value. Any other element types that may try to use the class (such as <div class="main">) will not be affected by this rule.

The Attribute Selector

Many HTML tags support attributes, and using this type of selector can save you from having to use IDs and classes to refer to them. For example, you can directly reference attributes in the following manner, which sets all elements with the attribute `type="submit"` to a width of 100 pixels:

```
[type="submit"] { width:100px; }
```

If you wish to narrow down the scope of the selector to, for example, only `form` input elements with that attribute type, you could use the following rule instead:

```
form input[type="submit"] { width:100px; }
```

 Attribute selectors also work on IDs and classes so that, for example, `[class~="classname"]` works exactly like the class selector `.classname` (except that the latter has a higher precedence). Likewise, `[id="idname"]` is equivalent to using the ID selector `#idname`. The class and ID selectors prefaced by # and . can therefore be viewed as shorthand for attribute selectors, but with a higher precedence. The `~=` operator matches an attribute even if it is one of a space-separated group of attributes.

The Universal Selector

The * wildcard or universal selector matches any element, so the following rule will make a complete mess of a document by giving a green border to all of its elements:

```
* { border:1px solid green; }
```

It's therefore unlikely that you will use the * on its own, but as part of a compound rule it can be very powerful. For example, the following rule will apply the same styling as the preceding one, but only to all paragraphs that are sub-elements of the element with the ID boxout, and only as long as they are not direct children:

```
#boxout * p {border:1px solid green; }
```

Let's look at what's going on here. The first selector following #boxout is a * symbol, so it refers to any element within the boxout object. The following p selector then narrows down the selection focus by changing the selector to apply only to paragraphs (as defined by the p) that are sub-elements of elements returned by the * selector. Therefore, this CSS rule performs the following actions (in which I use the terms *object* and *element* interchangeably):

1. Find the object with the ID of boxout.
2. Find all sub-elements of the object returned in step 1.

3. Find all p sub-elements of the objects returned in step 2 and, because this is the final selector in the group, also find all p sub- and sub-sub-elements (and so on) of the objects returned in step 2.

4. Apply the styles within the {and } characters to the objects returned in step 3.

The net result of this is that the green border is applied only to paragraphs that are grandchildren (or great-grandchildren, etc.) of the main element.

Selecting by Group

Using CSS you can apply a rule to more than one element, class, or any other type of selector at the same time by separating the selectors with commas. So, for example, the following rule will place a dotted orange line underneath all paragraphs, the element with the ID of idname, and all elements that use the class classname:

```
p, #idname, .classname { border-bottom:1px dotted orange; }
```

Figure 19-3 shows various selectors in use, with the rules applied to them alongside.

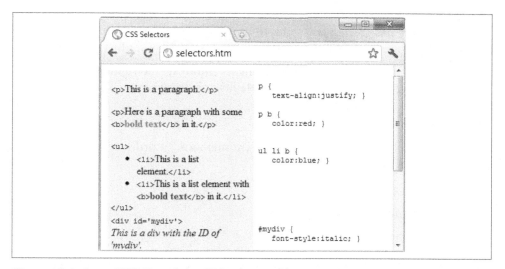

Figure 19-3. Some HTML and the CSS rules used by it

The CSS Cascade

One of the most fundamental things about CSS properties is that they cascade, which is why they are called Cascading Style Sheets. But what does this mean?

Cascading is a method used to resolve potential conflicts between the various types of style sheet a browser supports, and apply them in order of precedence by who created them, the method used to create the style, and the types of properties selected.

Style Sheet Creators

There are three main types of style sheet supported by all modern browsers. In order of precedence from high to low, they are:

1. Those created by a document's author
2. Those created by the user
3. Those created by the browser

These three sets of style sheets are processed in reverse order. First, the defaults in the web browser are applied to the document. Without these defaults, web pages that don't use style sheets would look terrible. They include the font face, size, and color; element spacing; table borders and spacing; and all the other reasonable standards a user would expect.

Next, if the user has created any styles to use instead of the standard ones, these are applied, replacing any of the browser's default styles that may conflict.

Last, any styles created by the current document's author are then applied, replacing any that have been created either as browser defaults or by the user.

Style Sheet Methods

Style sheets can be created via three different methods. In order of precedence from high to low, they are:

1. As inline styles
2. In an embedded style sheet
3. As an external style sheet

Again, these methods of style sheet creation are applied in reverse order of precedence. Therefore, all external style sheets are processed first, and their styles are applied to the document.

Next, any embedded styles (within `<style>` ... `</style>` tags) are processed, and any that conflict with external rules are given precedence and will override them.

Last, any styles applied directly to an element as an inline style (such as `<div style="...">` ... `</div>`) are given the highest precedence, and override all previously assigned properties.

Style Sheet Selectors

There are three different ways of selecting elements to be styled. Going from highest to lowest order of precedence, they are:

- Referencing by individual ID or attribute selector
- Referencing in groups by class
- Referencing by element tags (such as <p> or <b>)

Selectors are processed according to the number and types of elements affected by a rule, which is a little different from the previous two methods for resolving conflicts. This is because rules do not have to apply only to one type of selector at a time, and may reference many different selectors.

Therefore, we need a method to determine the precedence of rules that can contain any combinations of selectors. It does this by calculating the specificity of each rule by ordering them from the widest to narrowest scope of action.

Calculating Specificity

We calculate the specificity of a rule by creating three-part numbers based on the selector types in the numbered list in the previous section. These compound numbers start off looking like [0,0,0]. When processing a rule, each selector that references an ID increments the first number by 1, so that the compound number would become [1,0,0].

Let's look at the following rule, which has seven references, with three of them to the IDs #heading, #main, and #menu. So the compound number becomes [3,0,0].

```
#heading #main #menu .text .quote p span {
  // Rules go here;
}
```

Then the number of classes in the selector is placed in the second part of the compound number. In this example, there are two of them (.text and .quote), so the compound number becomes [3,2,0].

Finally, all selectors that reference element tags are counted, and this number is placed in the last part of the compound number. In the example, there are two (p and span), so the final compound number becomes [3,2,2], which is all that is needed to compare this rule's specificity with another, such as the following:

```
#heading #main .text .quote .news p span {
  // Rules go here;
}
```

Here, although seven elements are also referenced, there are now only two ID references, but there are three class references, which results in the compound number [2,3,2]. Because 322 is greater than 232, the former example has precedence over the latter.

In cases where there are nine or fewer of each type in a compound number, you can convert it directly to a decimal number, which in this case is 352. Rules with a lower number than this will have lower precedence, and those with a higher number will have greater precedence. Where two rules share the same value, the most recently applied one wins.

Using a different number base

Where there are more than nine of a type in a number, you have to work in a higher number base. For example, you can't convert the compound number [11,7,19] to decimal by simply concatenating the three parts. Instead, you can convert the number to a higher base such as base 20 (or higher if there are more than 19 of any type).

To do this, multiply the three parts out and add the results like this, starting with the rightmost number and working left:

```
          20 ×  19 =   380
       20×20 ×   7 =  2800
    20×20×20 ×  11 = 88000
 Total in decimal = 91180
```

On the left, replace the values of 20 with the base you are using. Once all of the compound numbers of a set of rules are converted from this base to decimal, it is easy to determine the specificity, and therefore the precedence, of each.

Thankfully, the CSS processor handles all of this for you, but knowing how it works helps you to properly construct rules and understand what precedence they will have.

Some rules are more equal than others

Where two or more style rules are exactly equivalent, only the most recently processed rule will take precedence. However, you can force a rule to a higher precedence than other equivalent rules using the !important declaration, like this:

```
p { color:#ff0000 !important; }
```

When you do this, all previous equivalent settings are overridden (including ones using !important) and any equivalent rules that are processed later will be ignored. So, for example, the second of the two following rules would normally take precedence, but because of the use of !important in the prior assignment, the second one is ignored:

```
p { color:#ff0000 !important; }
p { color:#ffff00 }
```

User style sheets can be created for specifying default browser styles, and they may use the !important declaration, in which case the user's style setting will take precedence over the same properties specified in the current web page. However, on very old browsers using CSS 1, this feature isn't supported.

The Difference Between Div and Span Elements

Both <div> and <span> elements are types of containers, but with some different qualities. By default, a <div> element has infinite width (at least to the browser edge), which you can see by applying a border to one, like this:

```
<div style="border:1px solid green;">Hello</div>
```

A <span> element, however, is only as wide as the text it contains. Therefore, the following line of HTML creates a border only around the word Hello, which does not extend to the righthand edge of the browser.

```
<span style="border:1px solid green;">Hello</span>
```

Also, <span> elements follow text or other objects as they wrap around, and can therefore have a complicated border. For example, in Example 19-2, I used CSS to make the background of all <div> elements yellow, to make all <span> elements cyan, and to add a border to both, before then creating a few example <span> and <div> sections.

Example 19-2. Div and span example

```
<!DOCTYPE html>
<html>
  <head>
    <title>Div and span example</title>
    <style>
      div, span { border          :1px solid black; }
      div       { background-color:yellow;          }
      span      { background-color:cyan;            }
    </style>
  </head>
  <body>
    <div>This text is within a div tag</div>
    This isn't. <div>And this is again.</div><br>

    <span>This text is inside a span tag.</span>
    This isn't. <span>And this is again.</span><br><br>

    <div>This is a larger amount of text in a div that wraps around
    to the next line of the browser</div><br>

    <span>This is a larger amount of text in a span that wraps around
    to the next line of the browser</span>
  </body>
</html>
```

Figure 19-4 shows what this example looks like in a web browser. Although it is printed only in shades of gray in this book, the figure clearly shows how <div> elements extend to the righthand edge of a browser, and force the following content to appear at the start of the first available position below them.

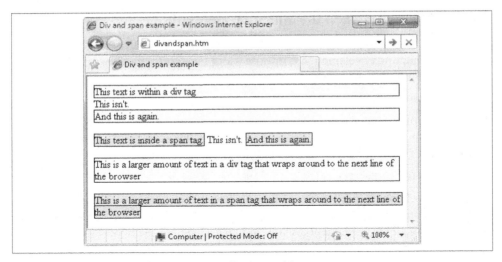

Figure 19-4. A variety of elements of differing width

The figure also shows how `<span>` elements keep to themselves and take up only the space required to hold their content, without forcing subsequent content to appear below them.

For example, in the bottom two examples of the figure, you can also see that when `<div>` elements wrap around the screen edge they retain a rectangular shape, whereas `<span>` elements simply follow the flow of the text (or other contents) they contain.

Because `<div>` tags can only be rectangular, they are better suited for containing objects such as images, boxouts, quotations, and so on, while `<span>` tags are best used for holding text or other attributes that are placed one after another inline, and which should flow from left to right (or right to left in some languages).

Measurements

CSS supports an impressive range of units of measurement, enabling you to tailor your web pages precisely to specific values, or by relative dimensions. The ones I generally use (and believe you will also find the most useful) are pixels, points, ems, and percent, but here's the complete list:

Pixels

The size of a pixel varies according to the dimensions and pixel depth of the user's monitor. One pixel equals the width/height of a single dot on the screen, and so this measurement is best suited to monitors. For example:

```
.classname { margin:5px; }
```

Points

A point is equivalent in size to 1/72 of an inch. The measurement comes from a print design background and is best suited for that medium, but is also commonly used on monitors. For example:

```
.classname { font-size:14pt; }
```

Inches

An inch is the equivalent of 72 points and is also a measurement type best suited for print. For example:

```
.classname { width:3in; }
```

Centimeters

Centimeters are another unit of measurement best suited for print. One centimeter is a little over 28 points. For example:

```
.classname { height:2cm; }
```

Millimeters

A millimeter is 1/10 of a centimeter (or almost 3 points). Millimeters are another measure best suited to print. For example:

```
.classname { font-size:5mm; }
```

Picas

A pica is another print typographic measurement, which is equivalent to 12 points. For example:

```
.classname { font-size:1pc; }
```

Ems

An em is equal to the current font size and is therefore one of the more useful measurements for CSS because it is used to describe relative dimensions. For example:

```
.classname { font-size:2em; }
```

Exs

An ex is also related to the current font size; it is equivalent to the height of a lowercase letter *x*. This is a less popular unit of measurement that is most often used as a good approximation for helping to set the width of a box that will contain some text. For example:

```
.classname { width:20ex; }
```

Percent

This unit is related to the em in that it is exactly 100 times greater (when used on a font). Whereas 1 em equals the current font size, the same size is 100 in percent. When not relating to a font, this unit is relative to the size of the container of the property being accessed. For example:

```
.classname { height:120%; }
```

Figure 19-5 shows each of these measurement types in turn being used to display text in almost identical sizes.

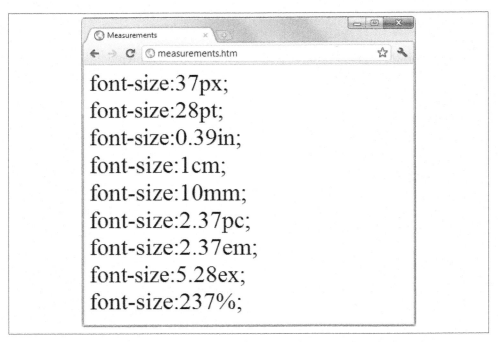

Figure 19-5. Different measurements that display almost the same

Fonts and Typography

There are four main font properties that you can style using CSS: `family`, `style`, `size`, and `weight`. Between them, you can fine-tune the way text displays in your web pages and/or when printed.

font-family

The `font-family` property assigns the font to use. It also supports listing a variety of fonts in order of preference from left to right, so that styling can fall back gracefully when the user doesn't have the preferred font installed. For example, to set the default font for paragraphs, you might use a CSS rule such as this:

```
p { font-family:Verdana, Arial, Helvetica, sans-serif; }
```

Where a font name is made up of two or more words, you must enclose the name in quotation marks, like this:

```
p { font-family:"Times New Roman", Georgia, serif; }
```

 Because they should be available on virtually all web browsers and operating systems, the safest font families to use on a web page are *Arial, Helvetica, Times New Roman, Times, Courier New,* and *Courier.* The *Verdana, Georgia, Comic Sans MS, Trebuchet MS, Arial Black,* and *Impact* fonts are safe for Mac and PC use, but may not be installed on other operating systems such as Linux. Other common but less safe fonts are *Palatino, Garamond, Bookman,* and *Avant Garde.* If you use one of the less safe fonts, make sure you offer fallbacks of one or more safer fonts in your CSS so that your web pages will degrade gracefully on browsers without your preferred fonts.

Figure 19-6 shows these two sets of CSS rules being applied.

Figure 19-6. Selecting font families

font-style

With the font-style property you can choose to display a font normally, in italics, or obliquely. The following rules create three classes (normal, italic, and oblique) that can be applied to elements to create these effects:

```
.normal  { font-style:normal;  }
.italic  { font-style:italic;  }
.oblique { font-style:oblique; }
```

font-size

As described in the earlier section on measurements, there are a large number of ways you can change a font's size. But these all boil down to two main types: fixed and relative. A fixed setting looks like the following rule, which sets the default paragraph font size to 14 point:

```
p { font-size:14pt; }
```

Alternatively, you may wish to work with the current default font size, using it to style various types of text such as headings. In the following rules, relative sizes of some headers are defined, with the <h4> tag starting off 20% bigger than the default, and with each greater size another 40% larger than the previous one:

```
h1 { font-size:240%; }
h2 { font-size:200%; }
h3 { font-size:160%; }
h4 { font-size:120%; }
```

Figure 19-7 shows a selection of font sizes in use.

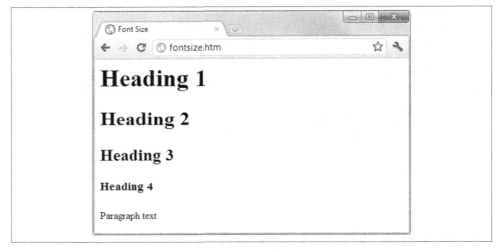

Figure 19-7. Setting four heading sizes and the default paragraph size

font-weight

Using the font-weight property you can choose how boldly to display a font. It supports a number of values, but the main ones you will use are likely to be normal and bold, like this:

```
.bold { font-weight:bold; }
```

Managing Text Styles

Regardless of the font in use, you can further modify the way text displays by altering its decoration, spacing, and alignment. There is a crossover between the text and font properties, though, in that effects such as italics or bold text are achieved via the font-style and font-weight properties, while others such as underlining require the text-decoration property.

Decoration

With the text-decoration property, you can apply effects to text such as underline, line-through, overline, and blink. The following rule creates a new class called over that applies overlines to text (the weight of over, under, and through lines will match that of the font):

```
.over { text-decoration:overline; }
```

In Figure 19-8 you can see a selection of font styles, weight, and decorations.

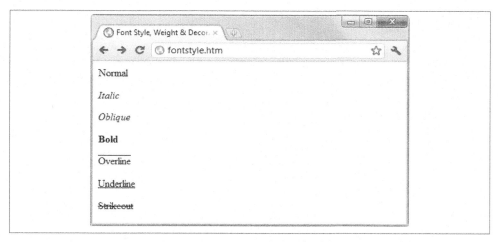

Figure 19-8. Examples of the styles and decoration rules available

Spacing

A number of different properties allow you to modify line, word, and letter spacing. For example, the following rules change the line spacing for paragraphs by modifying the line-height property to be 25% greater, while the word-spacing property is set to 30 pixels, and letter-spacing is set to 3 pixels:

```
p {
    line-height   :125%;
    word-spacing  :30px;
    letter-spacing:3px;
}
```

Alignment

Four types of text alignment are available in CSS: `left`, `right`, `center`, and `justify`. In the following rule, default paragraph text is set to full justification:

```
p { text-align:justify; }
```

Transformation

There are four properties available for transforming text: `none`, `capitalize`, `upper case`, and `lowercase`. The following rule creates a class called `upper` that will ensure that all text is displayed in uppercase when it is used:

```
.upper { text-transform:uppercase; }
```

Indenting

Using the `text-indent` property, you can indent the first line of a block of text by a specified amount. The following rule indents the first line of every paragraph by 20 pixels, although a different unit of measurement or a percent increase could also be applied:

```
p { text-indent:20px; }
```

In Figure 19-9, the following rules have been applied to a section of text:

```
p {          line-height   :150%;
             word-spacing  :10px;
             letter-spacing:1px;
}
.justify   { text-align      :justify;    }
.uppercase { text-transform:uppercase; }
.indent    { text-indent     :20px;       }
```

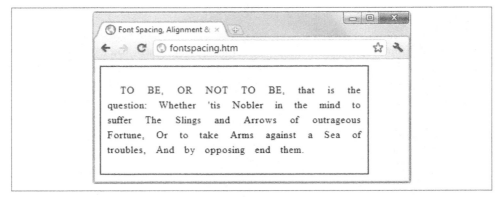

Figure 19-9. Indenting, uppercase, and spacing rules being applied

CSS Colors

You can apply colors to the foreground and background of text and objects using the color and background-color properties (or by supplying a single argument to the background property). The colors specified can be one of the named colors (such as red or blue), colors created from hexadecimal RGB triplets (such as #ff0000 or #0000ff), or colors created using the rgb CSS function.

The standard 16 color names as defined by the W3C (*http://w3.org*) standards organization are: aqua, black, blue, fuchsia, gray, green, lime, maroon, navy, olive, purple, red, silver, teal, white, and yellow. The following rule uses one of these names to set the background color for an object with the ID of object:

```
#object { background-color:silver; }
```

In this rule, the foreground color of text in all <div> elements is set to yellow (because on a computer display, hexadecimal levels of ff red, plus ff green, plus 00 blue creates the color yellow):

```
div { color:#ffff00; }
```

Or, if you don't wish to work in hexadecimal, you can specify your color triplets using the rgb function, as in the following rule, which changes the background color of the current document to aqua:

```
body { background-color:rgb(0, 255, 255); }
```

 If you prefer not to work in ranges of 256 levels per color, you can use percentages in the rgb function instead, with values from 0 to 100 ranging from the lowest (0) through to the highest (100) amount of a primary color, like this: rgb(58%, 95%, 74%). You can also use floating-point values for even finer color control, like this: rgb(23.4%, 67.6%, 15.5%).

Short Color Strings

There is also a short form of the hex digit string in which only the first of each 2-byte pair is used for each color. For example, instead of assigning the color #fe4692, you instead use #f49, omitting the second hex digit from each pair, which equates to a color value of #ff4499.

This results in almost the same color and is useful where exact colors are not required. The difference between a six-digit and three-digit string is that the former supports 16 million different colors, while the latter supports four thousand.

Wherever you intend to use a color such as #883366, this is the direct equivalent of #836 (because the repeated digits are implied by the shorter version), and you can use either string to create the exact same color.

Gradients

In place of using a solid background color, you can choose to apply a gradient, which will then automatically flow from a given initial color to a final color of your choice. It is best used in conjunction with a simple color rule so that browsers that don't support gradients will at least display a solid color.

Example 19-3 uses a rule to display an orange gradient (or simply plain orange on non-supporting browsers) as shown in the middle section of Figure 19-10.

Example 19-3. Creating a linear gradient

```
<!DOCTYPE html>
<html>
  <head>
    <title>Creating a linear gradient</title>
    <style>
      .orangegrad {
        background:orange;
        background:linear-gradient(top, #fb0, #f50);
        background:-moz-linear-gradient(top, #fb0, #f50);
        background:-webkit-linear-gradient(top, #fb0, #f50);
        background:-o-linear-gradient(top, #fb0, #f50);
        background:-ms-linear-gradient(top, #fb0, #f50); }
    </style>
  </head>
  <body>
    <div class='orangegrad'>Black text<br>
    on an orange<br>linear gradient</div>
  </body>
</html>
```

 As shown in the preceding example, many CSS rules require browser-specific prefixes such as -moz-, -webkit-, -o-, and -ms- (for Mozilla-based browsers such as Firefox; WebKit-based browsers such as Apple Safari, Google Chrome, and the iOS and Android browsers; and the Opera and Microsoft browsers). *http://caniuse.com* lists the major CSS rules and attributes, and whether browser-specific versions are required.

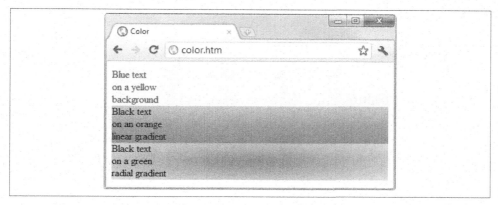

Figure 19-10. A solid background color, a linear gradient, and a radial gradient

To create a gradient, choose where it will begin out of top, bottom, left, right, and center (or any combination, such as top left or center right), enter the start and end colors you require, and then apply either the linear-gradient or radial-gradient rule, making sure you also supply rules for all browsers that you are targeting.

You can also use more than just a start and end color by also supplying what are termed *stop* colors in between as additional arguments. In this case, for example, if five arguments are supplied, each argument will control the color change over a fifth of the area represented by its location in the argument list.

Positioning Elements

Elements within a web page fall where they are placed in the document, but you can move them about by changing an element's position property from the default of static to one of absolute, relative, or fixed.

Absolute Positioning

An element with absolute positioning is removed from the document, and any other elements that are capable will flow into its released space. You can then position the object anywhere you like within the document using the top, right, bottom, and left properties. It will then rest on top of (or behind) other elements.

So, for example, to move an object with the ID of object to the absolute location of 100 pixels down from the document start and 200 pixels in from the left, you would apply the following rules to it (you can also use any of the other units of measurement supported by CSS):

```
#object {
  position:absolute;
  top      :100px;
  left     :200px;
}
```

Relative Positioning

Likewise, you can move the object relative to the location it would occupy in the normal document flow. So, for example, to move object 10 pixels down and 10 pixels to the right of its normal location, you would use the following rules:

```
#object {
  position:relative;
  top      :10px;
  left     :10px;
}
```

Fixed Positioning

The final positioning property setting lets you move an object to an absolute location, but only within the current browser viewport. Then, when the document is scrolled, the object remains exactly where it has been placed, with the main document scrolling beneath it—a great way to create dock bars and other similar devices. To fix the object to the top-left corner of the browser window, you would use the following rules:

```
#object {
  position:fixed;
  top      :0px;
  left     :0px;
}
```

In Figure 19-11, Example 19-4 has been loaded into a browser, and the browser has been reduced in width and height so that you must scroll down to see all of the web page.

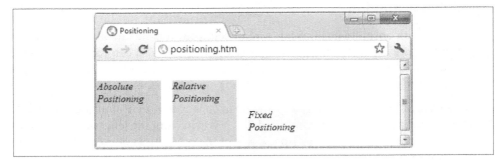

Figure 19-11. Using different positioning values

When this is done, it is immediately obvious that the element with fixed positioning remains in place even through scrolling. You can also see that the element with absolute positioning is located exactly at 100 pixels down, with 0 horizontal offset, while the element with relative positioning is actually moved up by 8 pixels and then offset from the left margin by 110 pixels in order to line up alongside the first element.

Example 19-4. Applying different positioning values

```
<!DOCTYPE html>
<html>
  <head>
    <title>Positioning</title>
    <style>
      #object1 {
        position  :absolute;
        background:pink;
        width     :100px;
        height    :100px;
        top       :100px;
        left      :0px;
      }
      #object2 {
        position  :relative;
        background:lightgreen;
        width     :100px;
        height    :100px;
        top       :-8px;
        left      :110px;
      }
      #object3 {
        position  :fixed;
        background:yellow;
        width     :100px;
        height    :100px;
        top       :100px;
        left      :236px;
      }
    </style>
  </head>
  <body>
      <br><br><br><br><br>
    <div id='object1'>Absolute Positioning</div>
    <div id='object2'>Relative Positioning</div>
    <div id='object3'>Fixed Positioning</div>
  </body>
</html>
```

In the figure, the element with fixed positioning initially lines up with the other two elements, but has stayed put while the others have been scrolled up the page, and now appears offset below them.

Pseudo-Classes

There are a number of selectors and classes that are used only within a style sheet and do not have any matching tags or attributes within any HTML. Their task is to classify elements using characteristics other than their name, attributes, or content—that is, characteristics that cannot be deduced from the document tree. These include *pseudo-classes* such as link and visited. There are also pseudo-elements that make a selection, which may consist of partial elements such as first-line or first-letter.

Pseudo-classes and pseudo-elements are separated by a : (colon) character. For example, to create a class called bigfirst for emphasizing the first letter of an element, you would use a rule such as the following:

```
.bigfirst:first-letter {
  font-size:400%;
  float     :left;
}
```

When the bigfirst class is applied to an element, the first letter will be displayed much enlarged, with the remaining text shown at normal size, neatly flowing around it (due to the float property) as if the first letter were an image or other object. Pseudo-classes include hover, link, active, and visited, all of which are mostly useful for applying to anchor elements, as in the following rules, which set the default color of all links to blue, and that of links that have already been visited to light blue:

```
a:link    { color:blue;      }
a:visited { color:lightblue; }
```

The following rules are interesting in that they use the hover pseudo-class so that they are applied only when the mouse is placed over the element. In this example, they change the link to white text on a red background, providing a dynamic effect you would normally only expect from using JavaScript code:

```
a:hover {
  color     :white;
  background:red;
}
```

Here I have used the background property with a single argument, instead of the longer background-color property.

The active pseudo-class is also dynamic in that it effects a change to a link during the time between the mouse button being clicked and released, as with this rule, which changes the link color to dark blue:

```
a:active { color:darkblue; }
```

Another interesting dynamic pseudo-class is focus, which is applied only when an element is given focus by the user selecting it with the keyboard or mouse. The following rule uses the universal selector to always place a mid-gray, dotted, 2-pixel border around the currently focused object:

```
*:focus { border:2px dotted #888888; }
```

Example 19-5 displays two links and an input field, as shown in Figure 19-12. The first link shows up as gray because it has already been visited in this browser, but the second link has not and displays in blue. The Tab key has been pressed and the focus of input is now the input field, so its background has changed to yellow. When either of the links is clicked it will display in purple, and when hovered over it will appear red.

Example 19-5. Link and focus pseudo-classes

```
<!DOCTYPE html>
<html>
  <head>
    <title>Pseudo-classes</title>
    <style>
      a:link    { color:blue; }
      a:visited { color:gray; }
      a:hover   { color:red; }
      a:active  { color:purple; }
      *:focus   { background:yellow; }
    </style>
  </head>
  <body>
    <a href='http://google.com'>Link to Google'</a><br>
    <a href='nowhere'>Link to nowhere'</a><br>
    <input type='text'>
  </body>
</html>
```

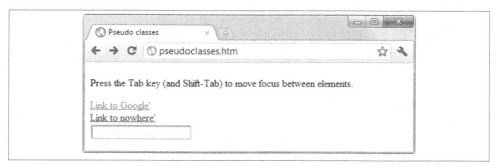

Figure 19-12. Pseudo-classes applied to a selection of elements

Other pseudo-classes are also available, and you can get more information on them at *http://tinyurl.com/pseudoclasses*.

Beware of applying the `focus` pseudo-class to the universal selector, `*`, as shown in this example; Internet Explorer regards an unfocused document as actually having focus applied to the entire web page, and (in this instance) the whole page will turn yellow until Tab is pressed or focus is otherwise applied to one of the page's elements.

Shorthand Rules

To save space, groups of related CSS properties can be concatenated into a single shorthand assignment. For example, I have already used the shorthand for creating a border a few times, as in the `focus` rule in the previous section:

```
*:focus { border:2px dotted #ff8800; }
```

This is actually a shorthand concatenation of the following rule set:

```
*:focus {
  border-width:2px;
  border-style:dotted;
  border-color:#ff8800;
}
```

When using a shorthand rule, you need only apply the properties up to the point where you wish to change values. So you could use the following to set only a border's width and style, choosing not to set its color:

```
*:focus { border:2px dotted; }
```

The order in which the properties are placed in a shorthand rule can be important, and misplacing them is a common way to get unexpected results. There are far too many to detail in this chapter, so if you wish to use shorthand CSS you will need to look up the default properties and their order of application using a CSS manual or search engine. To get you started, I recommend visiting *http://dustin diaz.com/css-shorthand*.

The Box Model and Layout

The CSS properties affecting the layout of a page are based around the *box model* (see Chapter 14 for more details), a nested set of properties surrounding an element. Virtually all elements have (or can have) these properties, including the document body, whose margin you can, for example, remove with the following rule:

```
body { margin:0px; }
```

The box model of an object starts at the outside, with the object's margin. Inside this is the border, then there is padding between the border and the inner contents, and finally there's the object's contents.

Once you have the hang of the box model, you will be well on your way to creating professionally laid-out pages, as these properties alone will make up much of your page styling.

Setting Margins

The margin is the outermost level of the box model. It separates elements from each other and its use is quite smart. For example, assume you have chosen to give a number of elements a default margin of 10 pixels around each. When they are placed on top of each other, this would create a gap of 20 pixels (the total of the adjacent border widths).

CSS overcomes this potential issue, however: when two elements with borders are positioned directly one above the other, only the larger of the two margins is used to separate them. If both margins are the same width, just one of the widths is used. This way, you are much more likely to get the result you want. But you should note that the margins of absolutely positioned or inline elements do not collapse.

The margins of an element can be changed en masse with the `margin` property, or individually with `margin-left`, `margin-top`, `margin-right`, and `margin-bottom`. When setting the `margin` property, you can supply one, two, three, or four arguments, which have the effects commented in the following rules:

```
/* Set all margins to 1 pixel */
margin:1px;

/* Set top and bottom to 1 pixel, and left and right to 2 */
margin:1px 2px;

/* Set top to 1 pixel, left and right to 2, and bottom to 3 */
margin:1px 2px 3px;

/* Set top to 1 pixel, right to 2, bottom to 3, and left to 4 */
margin:1px 2px 3px 4px;
```

Figure 19-13 shows Example 19-6 loaded into a browser, with the `margin` property rule (highlighted in bold) applied to a square element that has been placed inside a table element. The table has been given no dimensions, so it will simply wrap as closely around the inner `<div>` element as it can. As a consequence, there is a margin of 10 pixels above it, 20 pixels to its right, 30 pixels below it, and 40 pixels to its left.

Example 19-6. How margins are applied

```
<!DOCTYPE html>
<html>
  <head>
    <title>Margins</title>
    <style>
      #object1 {
        background   :lightgreen;
        border-style:solid;
        border-width:1px;
        font-family :"Courier New";
        font-size   :9px;
        width        :100px;
        height       :100px;
        padding      :5px;
        margin        :10px 20px 30px 40px;
      }
      table {
        padding      :0;
        border       :1px solid black;
        background   :cyan;
      }
    </style>
  </head>
  <body>
    <table>
      <tr>
        <td>
          <div id='object1'>margin:<br>10px 20px 30px 40px;</div>
        </td>
      </tr>
    </table>
  </body>
</html>
```

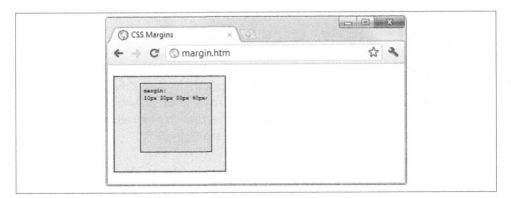

Figure 19-13. The outer table expands according to the margin widths

---

Applying Borders

The border level of the box model is similar to the margin except that there is no collapsing. It is the next level as we move into the box model. The main properties used to modify borders are `border`, `border-left`, `border-top`, `border-right`, and `border-bottom`, and each of these can have other subproperties added as suffixes, such as `-color`, `-style`, and `-width`.

The four ways to access individual property settings used for the `margin` property also apply with the `border-width` property, so all the following are valid rules:

```
/* All borders */
border-width:1px;

/* Top/bottom left/right */
border-width:1px 5px;

/* Top left/right bottom */
border-width:1px 5px 10px;

/* Top right bottom left */
border-width:1px 5px 10px 15px;
```

Figure 19-14 shows each of these rules applied in turn to a group of square elements. In the first one, you can clearly see that all borders have a width of 1 pixel. The second element, however, has a top and bottom border width of 1 pixel, while its side widths are 5 pixels each.

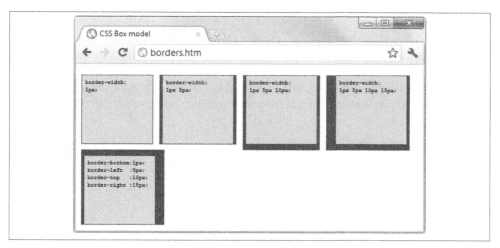

Figure 19-14. Applying long- and shorthand border rule values

The third element has a 1 pixel wide top, its sides are 5 pixels wide, and its bottom is 10 pixels wide. The fourth element has a 1-pixel top border width, a 5-pixel right border width, a 10-pixel bottom border width, and a 15-pixel left border width.

The final element, under the previous ones, doesn't use the shorthand rules; instead, it has each of the border widths set separately. As you can see, it takes a lot more typing to achieve the same result.

Adjusting Padding

The deepest of the box model levels (other than the contents of an element) is the padding, which is applied inside any borders and/or margins. The main properties used to modify padding are `padding`, `padding-left`, `padding-top`, `padding-right`, and `padding-bottom`.

The four ways of accessing individual property settings used for the `margin` and `border` properties also apply with the `padding` property, so all the following are valid rules:

```
/* All padding */
padding:1px;

/* Top/bottom and left/right */
padding:1px 2px;

/* Top, left/right and bottom */
padding:1px 2px 3px;

/* Top, right, bottom and left */
padding:1px 2px 3px 4px;
```

Figure 19-15 shows the padding rule (shown in bold) in Example 19-7 applied to some text within a table cell (as defined by the rule `display:table-cell;`, which makes the encapsulating `<div>` element display like a table cell), which has been given no dimensions so it will simply wrap as closely around the text as it can. As a consequence there is padding of 10 pixels above the inner element, 20 pixels to its right, 30 pixels below it, and 40 pixels to its left.

Example 19-7. Applying padding

```
<!DOCTYPE html>
<html>
  <head>
    <title>Padding</title>
    <style>
      #object1 {
        border-style:solid;
        border-width:1px;
        background   :orange;
        color        :darkred;
        font-family :Arial;
```

```
        font-size    :12px;
        text-align   :justify;
        display      :table-cell;
        width        :148px;
        padding      :10px 20px 30px 40px; }
    </style>
  </head>
  <body>
    <div id='object1'>To be, or not to be that is the question:
    Whether 'tis Nobler in the mind to suffer
    The Slings and Arrows of outrageous Fortune,
    Or to take Arms against a Sea of troubles,
    And by opposing end them.</div>
  </body>
</html>
```

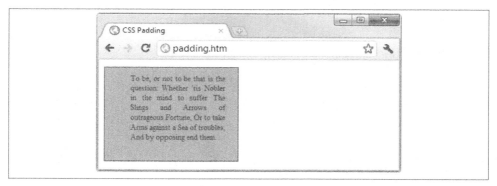

Figure 19-15. Applying different padding values to an object

Object Contents

Deep within the box model levels, at its center, lies an element that can be styled in all the ways discussed in this chapter, and which can (and usually will) contain further sub-elements, which in turn may contain sub-sub-elements, and so on, each with its own styling and box model settings.

Questions

1. Which directive do you use to import one style sheet into another (or the `<style>` section of some HTML)?

2. What HTML tag can you use to import a style sheet into a document?

3. Which HTML tag attribute is used to directly embed a style into an element?

4. What is the difference between a CSS ID and a CSS class?

5. Which characters are used to prefix (a) IDs, and (b) class names in a CSS rule?

6. In CSS rules, what is the purpose of the semicolon?

7. How can you add a comment to a style sheet?

8. Which character is used by CSS to represent any element?

9. How can you select a group of different elements and/or element types in CSS?

10. Given a pair of CSS rules with equal precedence, how can you make one have greater precedence over the other?

See "Chapter 19 Answers" on page 652 in Appendix A for the answers to these questions.

CHAPTER 20

Advanced CSS with CSS3

The first implementation of CSS was drawn up in 1996, was released in 1999, and has been supported by all browser releases since 2001. The standard for this version, CSS1, was revised in 2008. Beginning in 1998, developers began drawing up the second specification, CSS2; its standard was completed in 2007 and revised in 2009.

Development for the CSS3 specification commenced in 2001, with some features being proposed as recently as 2009. Therefore, the development process will likely continue for some time before a final recommendation for CSS3 is approved. And even though CSS3 isn't yet complete, people are already beginning to put forward suggestions for CSS4.

In this chapter, I'll take you through the CSS3 features that have already been generally adopted by the major browsers. Some of these features provide functionality that hitherto could be provided only with JavaScript.

I recommend using CSS3 to implement dynamic features where you can, instead of JavaScript. The features provided by CSS make document attributes part of the document itself, instead of being tacked on through JavaScript. Making them part of the document is a cleaner design.

Attribute Selectors

In the previous chapter, I detailed the various CSS attribute selectors, which I will now quickly recap. Selectors are used in CSS to match HTML elements, and there are 10 different types, as detailed in Table 20-1.

Table 20-1. CSS selectors, pseudo-classes, and pseudo-elements

Selector type	Example
Universal selector	`* { color:#555; }`
Type selectors	`b { color:red; }`
Class selectors	`.classname { color:blue; }`
ID selectors	`#idname { background:cyan; }`
Descendant selectors	`span em { color:green; }`
Child selectors	`div > em { background:lime; }`
Adjacent sibling selectors	`i + b { color:gray; }`
Attribute selectors	`a[href='info.htm'] { color:red; }`
Pseudo-classes	`a:hover { font-weight:bold; }`
Pseudo-elements	`P::first-letter { font-size:300%; }`

The CSS3 designers decided that most of these selectors work just fine the way they are, but they made three enhancements so that you can more easily match elements based on the contents of their attributes.

For example, in CSS2, you can use a selector such as `a[href='info.htm']` to match the string `info.htm` when found in an `href` attribute, but there's no way to match only a portion of a string. That's where CSS3's three new operators—^, $, and *—come to the rescue. If one directly precedes the = symbol, you can match the start, end, or any part of a string, respectively.

The ^ Operator

This operator matches at the start of a string so, for example, the following will match any `href` attribute whose value begins with the string `http://website`:

```
a[href^='http://website']
```

Therefore, the following element will match:

```
<a href='http://website.com'>
```

But this will not:

```
<a href='http://mywebsite.com'>
```

The $ Operator

To match only at the end of a string, you can use a selector such as the following, which will match any `img` tag whose `src` attribute ends with `.png`:

```
img[src$='.png']
```

For example, the following will match:

```
<img src='photo.png'>
```

But this will not:

```
<img src='snapshot.jpg'>
```

The * Operator

To match any substring anywhere in the attribute, you can use a selector such as the following to find any links on a page that have the string `google` anywhere within them:

```
a[href*='google']
```

For example, the HTML segment `<a href='http://google.com'>` will match, while the segment `<a href='http://gmail.com'>` will not.

The box-sizing Property

The W3C box model specifies that the width and height of an object should refer only to the dimensions of an element's content, ignoring any padding or border. But some web designers have expressed a desire to specify dimensions that refer to an entire element, including any padding and border.

To provide this feature, CSS3 lets you choose the box model you wish to use with the `box-sizing` property. For example, to use the total width and height of an object including padding and borders, you would use this declaration:

```
box-sizing:border-box;
```

Or, to have an object's width and height refer only to its content, you would use this declaration (the default):

```
box-sizing:content-box;
```

 Safari and Mozilla-based browsers (such as Firefox) require their own prefixes to this declaration (`-webkit-` and `-moz-`). For further details, refer to *http://caniuse.com*.

CSS3 Backgrounds

CSS3 provides two new properties: `background-clip` and `background-origin`. Between them, you can specify where a background should start within an element, and how to clip the background so that it doesn't appear in parts of the box model where you don't want it to.

To accomplish these, both properties support the following values:

border-box
> Refers to the outer edge of the border

padding-box
> Refers to the outer edge of the padding area

content-box
> Refers to the outer edge of the content area

The background-clip Property

The background-clip property specifies whether the background should be ignored (clipped) if it appears within either the border or padding area of an element. For example, the following declaration states that the background may display in all parts of an element, all the way to the outer edge of the border:

```
background-clip:border-box;
```

To keep the background from appearing within the border area of an element, you can restrict it to only the section of an element inside the outer edge of its padding area, like this:

```
background-clip:padding-box;
```

Or to restrict the background to display only within the content area of an element, you would use this declaration:

```
background-clip:content-box;
```

Figure 20-1 shows three rows of elements displayed in the Safari web browser, in which the first row uses border-box for the background-clip property, the second uses padding-box, and the third uses content-box.

In the first row, the inner box (an image file that has been loaded into the top left of the element, with repeating disabled) is allowed to display anywhere in the element. You can also clearly see it displayed in the border area of the first box because the border has been set to dotted.

In the second row, neither the background image nor the background shading displays in the border area, because they have been clipped to the padding area with a background-clip property value of padding-box.

Then, in the third row, both the background shading and the image have been clipped to display only within the inner content area of each element (shown inside a light-colored, dotted box), using a background-clip property of content-box.

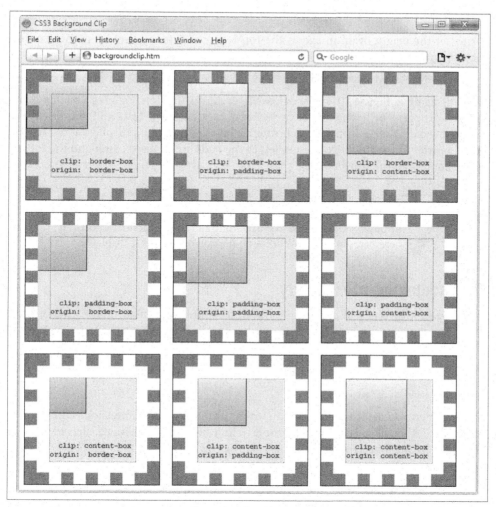

Figure 20-1. Different ways of combining CSS3 background properties

The background-origin Property

With the background-origin property, you can control where a background image will be located by specifying where the top left of the image should start. For example, the following declaration states that the background image's origin should be the top-left corner of the outer edge of the border:

```
background-origin:border-box;
```

To set the origin of an image to the top-left outer corner of the padding area, you would use this declaration:

```
background-origin:padding-box;
```

Or to set the origin of an image to the top-left corner of an element's inner content section, you would use this declaration:

```
background-origin:content-box;
```

Looking again at Figure 20-1, you can see in each row the first box uses a `background-origin` property of `border-box`, the second uses `padding-box`, and the third uses `content-box`. Consequently, in each row the smaller inner box displays at the top left of the border in the first box, the top left of the padding in the second, and the top left of the content in the third box.

 The only differences to note between the rows, with regard to the origins of the inner box in Figure 20-1, are that in rows two and three the inner box is clipped to the padding and content areas, respectively; therefore, outside these areas no portion of the box is displayed.

The background-size Property

In the same way that you can specify the width and height of an image when used in the `<img>` tag, you can now also do so for background images on the latest versions of all browsers.

You apply the property as follows (where *ww* is the width and *hh* is the height):

```
background-size:wwpx hhpx;
```

If you prefer, you can use only one argument, and then both dimensions will be set to that value. Also, if you apply this property to a block-level element such as a `<div>` (rather than one that is inline such as a `<span>`), you can specify the width and/or height as a percentage, instead of a fixed value.

If you wish to scale only one dimension of a background image, and then have the other one scale automatically to retain the same proportions, you can use the value `auto` for the other dimension, like this:

```
background-size:100px auto;
```

This sets the width to 100 pixels, and the height to a value proportionate to the increase or decrease in width.

 Different browsers may require different versions of the various background property names, so refer to *http://caniuse.com* when using them to ensure you are applying all the versions required for the browsers you are targeting.

Multiple Backgrounds

With CSS3 you can now attach multiple backgrounds to an element, each of which can use the previously discussed CSS3 background properties. Figure 20-2 shows an example of this; eight different images have been assigned to the background, to create the four corners and four edges of the certificate border.

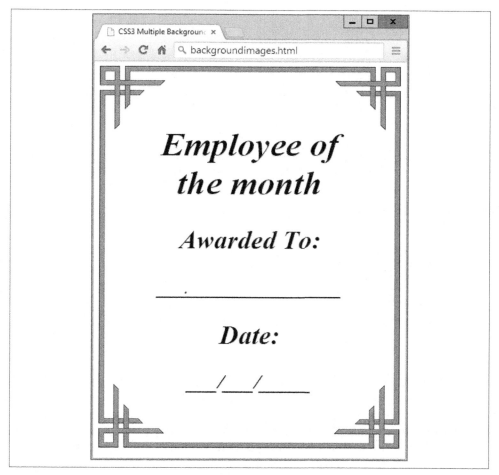

Figure 20-2. A background created with multiple images

To display multiple background images in a single CSS declaration, separate them with commas. Example 20-1 shows the HTML and CSS that was used to create the background in Figure 20-2.

Example 20-1. Using multiple images in a background

```
<!DOCTYPE html>
<html> <!-- backgroundimages.html -->
  <head>
    <title>CSS3 Multiple Backgrounds Example</title>
    <style>
      .border {
        font-family:'Times New Roman';
        font-style :italic;
        font-size  :170%;
        text-align :center;
        padding    :60px;
        width      :350px;
        height     :500px;
        background :url('b1.gif') top    left  no-repeat,
                    url('b2.gif') top    right no-repeat,
                    url('b3.gif') bottom left  no-repeat,
                    url('b4.gif') bottom right no-repeat,
                    url('ba.gif') top          repeat-x,
                    url('bb.gif') left         repeat-y,
                    url('bc.gif') right        repeat-y,
                    url('bd.gif') bottom       repeat-x
      }
    </style>
  </head>
  <body>
    <div class='border'>
      <h1>Employee of the month</h1>
      <h2>Awarded To:</h2>
      <h3>_____</h3>
      <h2>Date:</h2>
      <h3>___/___/_____</h3>
    </div>
  </body>
</html>
```

Looking at the CSS section, you see that the first four lines of the background declaration place the corner images into the four corners of the element, and the final four place the edge images, which are handled last because the order of priority for background images goes from high to low. In other words, where they overlap, additional background images will appear behind already placed images. If the GIFs were in the reverse order, the repeating edge images would display on top of the corners, which would be incorrect.

 Using this CSS, you can resize the containing element to any dimensions and the border will always correctly resize to fit, which is much easier than using tables or multiple elements for the same effect.

CSS3 Borders

CSS3 also brings a lot more flexibility to the way borders can be presented, by allowing you to independently change the colors of all four border edges, to display images for the edges and corners, to provide a radius value for applying rounded corners to borders, and to place box shadows underneath elements.

The border-color Property

There are two ways you can apply colors to a border. First, you can pass a single color to the property, as follows:

```
border-color:#888;
```

This property sets all the borders of an element to mid-gray. You can also set border colors individually, like this (which sets the border colors to various shades of gray):

```
border-top-color    :#000;
border-left-color   :#444;
border-right-color  :#888;
border-bottom-color :#ccc;
```

You can also set all the colors individually with a single declaration, as follows:

```
border-color:#f00 #0f0 #880 #00f;
```

This declaration sets the top border color to #f00, the right one to #0f0, the bottom one to #880, and the left one to #00f (red, green, orange, and blue, respectively). You can also use color names for the arguments.

The border-radius Property

Prior to CSS3, talented web developers came up with numerous different tweaks and fixes in order to achieve rounded borders, generally using <table> or <div> tags.

But now adding rounded borders to an element is really simple, and it works on the latest versions of all major browsers, as shown in Figure 20-3, in which a 10-pixel border is displayed in different ways. Example 20-2 shows the HTML for this.

Example 20-2. The border-radius property

```
<!DOCTYPE html>
<html> <!-- borderradius.html -->
  <head>
    <title>CSS3 Border Radius Examples</title>
    <style>
      .box {
        margin-bottom:10px;
        font-family :'Courier New', monospace;
        font-size   :12pt;
        text-align  :center;
```

```
      padding        :10px;
      width          :380px;
      height         :75px;
      border         :10px solid #006;
    }
    .b1 {
      -moz-border-radius     :40px;
      -webkit-border-radius:40px;
      border-radius          :40px;
    }
    .b2 {
      -moz-border-radius     :40px 40px 20px 20px;
      -webkit-border-radius:40px 40px 20px 20px;
      border-radius          :40px 40px 20px 20px;
    }
    .b3 {
      -moz-border-radius-topleft          :20px;
      -moz-border-radius-topright         :40px;
      -moz-border-radius-bottomleft       :60px;
      -moz-border-radius-bottomright      :80px;
      -webkit-border-top-left-radius      :20px;
      -webkit-border-top-right-radius     :40px;
      -webkit-border-bottom-left-radius   :60px;
      -webkit-border-bottom-right-radius:80px;
      border-top-left-radius              :20px;
      border-top-right-radius             :40px;
      border-bottom-left-radius           :60px;
      border-bottom-right-radius          :80px;
    }
    .b4 {
      -moz-border-radius-topleft          :40px 20px;
      -moz-border-radius-topright         :40px 20px;
      -moz-border-radius-bottomleft       :20px 40px;
      -moz-border-radius-bottomright      :20px 40px;
      -webkit-border-top-left-radius      :40px 20px;
      -webkit-border-top-right-radius     :40px 20px;
      -webkit-border-bottom-left-radius   :20px 40px;
      -webkit-border-bottom-right-radius:20px 40px;
      border-top-left-radius              :40px 20px;
      border-top-right-radius             :40px 20px;
      border-bottom-left-radius           :20px 40px;
      border-bottom-right-radius          :20px 40px;
    }
  </style>
</head>
<body>
  <div class='box b1'>
    border-radius:40px;
  </div>

  <div class='box b2'>
    border-radius:40px 40px 20px 20px;
```

```
    </div>

    <div class='box b3'>
      border-top-left-radius    :20px;<br>
      border-top-right-radius   :40px;<br>
      border-bottom-left-radius :60px;<br>
      border-bottom-right-radius:80px;
    </div>

    <div class='box b4'>
      border-top-left-radius    :40px 20px;<br>
      border-top-right-radius   :40px 20px;<br>
      border-bottom-left-radius :20px 40px;<br>
      border-bottom-right-radius:20px 40px;
    </div>
  </body>
</html>
```

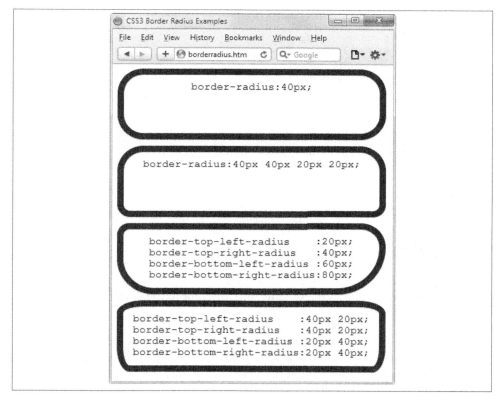

Figure 20-3. Mixing and matching various border radius properties

So, for example, to create a rounded border with a radius of 20 pixels, you could simply use the following declaration:

```
border-radius:20px;
```

 Although most browsers will work fine with border radius properties (including IE), some current (and many older) versions of the major browsers use different property names. So, if you wish to support them all, you will need to also use the relevant browser-specific prefixes, such as -moz- and -webkit-. To ensure that Example 20-2 works in all browsers, I have included all the required prefixes.

You can specify a separate radius for each of the four corners, like this (applied in a clockwise direction starting from the top-left corner):

```
border-radius:10px 20px 30px 40px;
```

If you prefer, you can also address each corner of an element individually, like this:

```
border-top-left-radius     :20px;
border-top-right-radius    :40px;
border-bottom-left-radius  :60px;
border-bottom-right-radius:80px;
```

And, when referencing individual corners, you can supply two arguments to choose a different vertical and horizontal radius (giving more interesting and subtle borders) like this:

```
border-top-left-radius     :40px 20px;
border-top-right-radius    :40px 20px;
border-bottom-left-radius  :20px 40px;
border-bottom-right-radius:20px 40px;
```

The first argument is the horizontal, and the second is the vertical radius.

Box Shadows

To apply a box shadow, specify a horizontal and vertical offset from the object, the amount of blurring to add to the shadow, and the color to use, like this:

```
box-shadow:15px 15px 10px #888;
```

The two instances of 15px specify the vertical and horizontal offset from the element, and these values can be negative, zero, or positive. The 10px specifies the amount of blurring, with smaller values resulting in less blurring. And the #888 is the color for the shadow, which can be any valid color value. The result of this declaration can be seen in Figure 20-4.

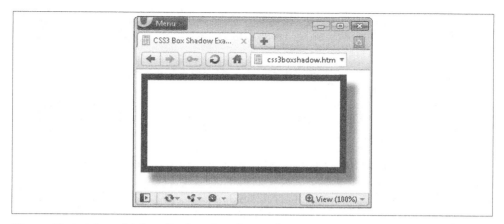

Figure 20-4. A box shadow displayed under an element

 You must use the WebKit and Mozilla prefixes to this property for those browsers.

Element Overflow

In CSS2, you can indicate what to do when one element is too large to be fully contained by its parent by setting the overflow property to hidden, visible, scroll, or auto. But with CSS3, you can now separately apply these values in the horizontal or vertical directions, too, as with these example declarations:

```
overflow-x:hidden;
overflow-x:visible;
overflow-y:auto;
overflow-y:scroll;
```

Multicolumn Layout

One of the most requested features by web developers is multiple columns, and this has finally been realized in CSS3, with Internet Explorer 10 being the last major browser to adopt it.

Now, flowing text over multiple columns is as easy as specifying the number of columns, and then (optionally) choosing the spacing between them and the type of dividing line (if any), as shown in Figure 20-5 (created using Example 20-3).

Figure 20-5. Flowing text in multiple columns

Example 20-3. Using CSS to create multiple columns

```html
<!DOCTYPE html>
<html> <!-- multiplecolumns.html -->
  <head>
    <title>Multiple Columns</title>
    <style>
      .columns {
        text-align          :justify;
        font-size           :16pt;
        -moz-column-count   :3;
        -moz-column-gap     :1em;
        -moz-column-rule    :1px solid black;
        -webkit-column-count:3;
        -webkit-column-gap  :1em;
        -webkit-column-rule :1px solid black;
        column-count        :3;
        column-gap          :1em;
        column-rule         :1px solid black;
      }
    </style>
  </head>
<body>
  <div class='columns'>
    Now is the winter of our discontent
    Made glorious summer by this sun of York;
    And all the clouds that lour'd upon our house
    In the deep bosom of the ocean buried.
    Now are our brows bound with victorious wreaths;
    Our bruised arms hung up for monuments;
    Our stern alarums changed to merry meetings,
    Our dreadful marches to delightful measures.
    Grim-visaged war hath smooth'd his wrinkled front;
    And now, instead of mounting barded steeds
    To fright the souls of fearful adversaries,
```

```
        He capers nimbly in a lady's chamber
        To the lascivious pleasing of a lute.
      </div>
    </body>
</html>
```

Within the `.columns` class, the first two lines simply tell the browser to right-justify the text and to set it to a font size of `16pt`. These declarations aren't needed for multiple columns, but they improve the text display. The remaining lines set up the element so that, within it, text will flow over three columns, with a gap of `1em` between the columns, and with a single-pixel border down the middle of each gap.

 In Example 20-3, Mozilla- and WebKit-based browsers require browser-specific prefixes to the declarations.

Colors and Opacity

The ways in which you can define colors have been greatly expanded with CSS3, and you can now also use CSS functions to apply colors in the common formats RGB (Red, Green, and Blue), RGBA (Red, Green, Blue, and Alpha), HSL (Hue, Saturation, and Luminance), and HSLA (Hue, Saturation, Luminance, and Alpha). The Alpha value specifies a color's transparency, which allows underlying elements to show through.

HSL Colors

To define a color with the `hsl` function, you must first choose a value for the hue between `0` and `359` from a color wheel. Any higher color numbers simply wrap around to the beginning again, so the value of `0` is red, and so are the values `360` and `720`.

In a color wheel, the primary colors of red, green, and blue are separated by 120 degrees, so that pure red is `0`, green is `120`, and blue is `240`. The numbers between these values represent shades comprising different proportions of the primary colors on either side.

Next you need the saturation level, which is a value between 0% and 100%. This specifies how washed-out or vibrant a color will appear. The saturation values commence in the center of the wheel with a mid-gray color (a saturation of 0%) and then become more and more vivid as they progress to the outer edge (a saturation of 100%).

All that's left then is for you to decide how bright you want the color to be, by choosing a luminance value of between 0% and 100%. A value of 50% for the luminance gives the fullest, brightest color; decreasing the value (down to a minimum of 0%) darkens the color until it displays as black; and increasing the value (up to a maximum of 100%)

lightens the color until it shows as white. You can visualize this as if you are mixing levels of either black or white into the color.

Therefore, for example, to choose a fully saturated yellow color with standard percent brightness, you would use a declaration such as this:

```
color:hsl(60, 100%, 50%);
```

Or, for a darker blue color, you might use a declaration such as:

```
color:hsl(240, 100%, 40%);
```

You can also use this (and all other CSS color functions) with any property that expects a color, such as `background-color`, and so on.

HSLA Colors

To provide even further control over how colors will appear, you can use the `hsla` function, supplying it with a fourth (or alpha) level for a color, which is a floating-point value between 0 and 1. A value of 0 specifies that the color is totally transparent, while 1 means it is fully opaque.

Here's how you would choose a fully saturated yellow color with standard brightness and 30% opacity:

```
color:hsla(60, 100%, 50%, 0.3);
```

Or, for a fully saturated but lighter blue color with 82% opacity, you might use this declaration:

```
color:hsla(240, 100%, 60%, 0.82);
```

RGB Colors

You will probably be more familiar with using the RGB system of selecting a color, as it's similar to using the #nnnnnn and #nnn color formats. For example, to apply a yellow color to a property, you can use either of the following declarations (the first supporting 16 million colors, and the second four thousand):

```
color:#ffff00;
color:#ff0;
```

You can also use the CSS `rgb` function to achieve the same result, but you use decimal numbers instead of hexadecimal (where 255 decimal is `ff` hexadecimal):

```
color:rgb(255, 255, 0);
```

But even better than that, you don't even have to think in amounts of up to 256 anymore, because you can specify percentage values, like this:

```
color:rgb(100%, 100%, 0);
```

In fact, you can now get very close to a desired color by simply thinking about its primary colors. For example, green and blue make cyan, so to create a color close to cyan, but with more blue in it than green, you could make a good first guess at 0% red, 40% green, and 60% blue, and try a declaration such as this:

```
color:rgb(0%, 40%, 60%);
```

RGBA Colors

As with the hsla function, the rgba function supports a fourth alpha argument, so you can, for example, apply the previous cyan-like color with an opacity of 40% by using a declaration such as this:

```
color:rgba(0%, 40%, 60%, 0.4);
```

The opacity Property

The opacity property provides the same alpha control as the hsla and rgba functions, but lets you modify an object's opacity (or transparency if you prefer) separately from its color.

To use it, apply a declaration such as the following to an element (which in this example sets the opacity to 25%, or 75% transparent):

```
opacity:0.25;
```

 WebKit- and Mozilla-based browsers require browser-specific prefixes to this property. And for backward compatibility with releases of Internet Explorer prior to version 9, you should add the following declaration (in which the opacity value is multiplied by 100):

```
filter:alpha(opacity='25');
```

Text Effects

A number of new effects can now be applied to text with the help of CSS3, including text shadows, text overlapping, and word wrapping.

The text-shadow Property

The text-shadow property is similar to the box-shadow property and takes the same set of arguments: a horizontal and vertical offset, an amount for the blurring, and the color to use. For example, the following declaration offsets the shadow by 3 pixels both horizontally and vertically, and displays the shadow in dark gray, with a blurring of 4 pixels:

```
text-shadow:3px 3px 4px #444;
```

The result of this declaration looks like Figure 20-6, and works in all recent versions of all major browsers (but not IE9 or lower).

Figure 20-6. Applying a shadow to text

The text-overflow Property

When using any of the CSS overflow properties with a value of `hidden`, you can also use the `text-overflow` property to place an ellipsis (three dots) just before the cutoff to indicate that some text has been truncated, like this:

```
text-overflow:ellipsis;
```

Without this property, when the text "To be, or not to be. That is the question." is truncated, the result will look like Figure 20-7; with the declaration applied, however, the result is like Figure 20-8.

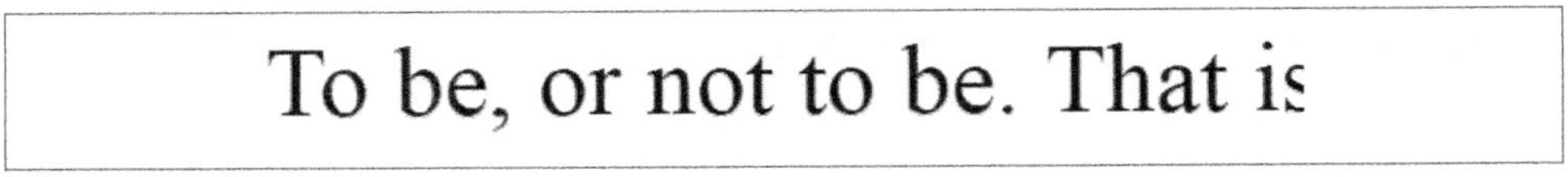

Figure 20-7. The text is automatically truncated

Figure 20-8. Instead of being cut off, the text trails off using an ellipsis

For this to work, three things are required:

- The element should have an `overflow` property that is not visible, such as `overflow:hidden`.
- The element must have the `white-space:nowrap` property set to constrain the text.
- The width of the element must be less than that of the text to truncate.

The word-wrap Property

When you have a really long word that is wider than the element containing it, it will either overflow or be truncated. But as an alternative to using the `text-overflow` property and truncating text, you can use the `word-wrap` property with a value of `break-word` to wrap long lines, like this:

```
word-wrap:break-word;
```

For example, in Figure 20-9 the word *Honorificabilitudinitatibus* is too wide for the containing box (whose righthand edge is shown as a solid vertical line between the letters *t* and *a*) and, because no overflow properties have been applied, it has overflowed its bounds.

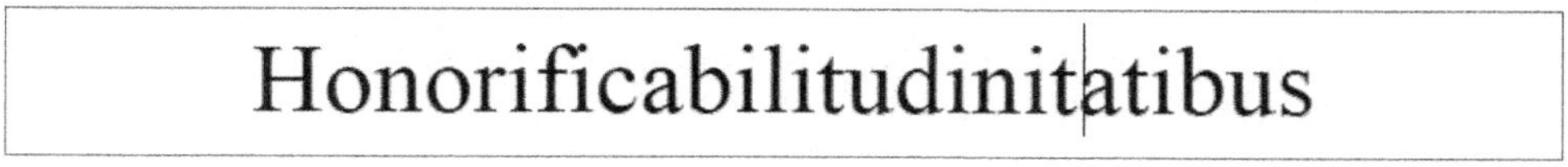

Honorificabilitudinit|atibus

Figure 20-9. The word is too wide for its container and has overflowed

But in Figure 20-10 the `word-wrap` property of the element has been assigned a value of `break-word`, so the word has neatly wrapped around to the next line.

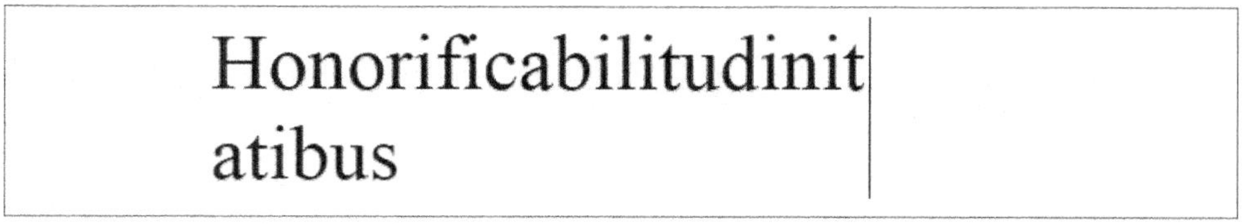

Honorificabilitudinit|
atibus

Figure 20-10. The word now wraps at the righthand edge

Web Fonts

The use of CSS3 web fonts vastly increases the typography available to web designers by allowing fonts to be loaded in and displayed from across the Web, not just from the user's computer. To achieve this, declare a web font using `@font-face`, like this:

```
@font-face
{
  font-family:FontName;
  src:url('FontName.otf');
}
```

The `url` function requires a value containing the path or URL of a font. On most browsers, you can use either TrueType (*.ttf*) or OpenType (*.otf*) fonts, but Internet Explorer restricts you to TrueType fonts that have been converted to EOT (*.eot*).

To tell the browser the type of font, you can use the `format` function, like this (for OpenType fonts):

```
@font-face
{
  font-family:FontName;
  src:url('FontName.otf') format('opentype');
}
```

Or this for TrueType fonts:

```
@font-face
{
  font-family:FontName;
  src:url('FontName.ttf') format('truetype');
}
```

However, because Microsoft Internet Explorer accepts only EOT fonts, it ignores `@font-face` declarations that contain the `format` function.

Google Web Fonts

One of the best ways to use web fonts is to load them in for free from Google's servers. To find out more about this, check out the Google Fonts website (*http://google.com/fonts*) (see Figure 20-11), where you can get access to over 630 font families, and counting!

To show you how easy it is to use one of these fonts, here's how you load a Google font (in this case, Lobster) into your HTML for use in <h1> headings:

```
<!DOCTYPE html>
<html>
  <head>
    <style>
      h1 { font-family:'Lobster', arial, serif; }
    </style>
    <link href='http://fonts.googleapis.com/css?family=Lobster'
      rel='stylesheet' type='text/css'>
  </head>
  <body>
    <h1>Hello</h1>
  </body>
</html>
```

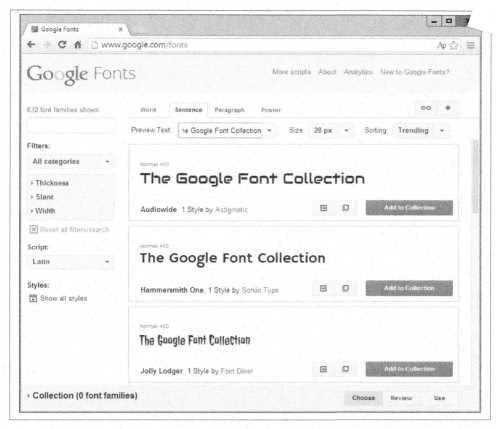

Figure 20-11. It's easy to include Google's web fonts

Transformations

Using transformations, you can skew, rotate, stretch, and squash elements in any of up to three dimensions (yes, 3D is supported, but only in WebKit-based browsers for now). This makes it easy to create great effects by stepping out of the uniform rectangular layout of <div> and other elements, because now they can be shown at a variety of angles and in many different forms.

To perform a transformation, use the transform property (which unfortunately has browser-specific prefixes for Mozilla, WebKit, Opera, and Microsoft browsers, so once again you'll need to refer to *http://caniuse.com*).

You can apply various properties to the transform property, starting with the value none, which resets an object to a nontransformed state:

```
transform:none;
```

You can supply one or more of the following functions to the `transform` property:

`matrix`
> Transforms an object by applying a matrix of values to it

`translate`
> Moves an element's origin

`scale`
> Scales an object

`rotate`
> Rotates an object

`skew`
> Skews an object

There are also single versions of many of these functions, such as `translateX`, `scaleY`, and so on.

So, for example, to rotate an element clockwise by 45 degrees, you could apply this declaration to it:

```
transform:rotate(45deg);
```

At the same time, you could enlarge this object, as in the following declaration, which enlarges its width by 1.5 times and its height by 2 times, and then performs the rotation (Figure 20-12 shows an object before the transformations are applied, and then afterward):

```
transform:scale(1.5, 2) rotate(45deg);
```

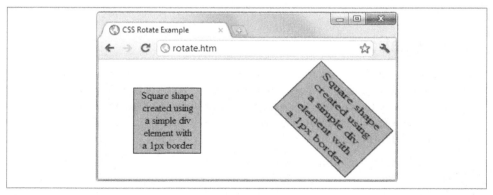

Figure 20-12. An object before and after transformation

3D Transformations

You can also transform objects in three dimensions using the following CSS3 3D transformation features:

`perspective`
: Releases an element from 2D space and creates a third dimension within which it can move

`transform-origin`
: Sets the location at which all lines converge to a single point

`translate3d`
: Moves an element to another location in its 3D space

`scale3d`
: Rescales one or more dimensions

`rotate3d`
: Rotates an element around any of the X, Y, and Z axes.

Figure 20-13 shows a 2D object that has been rotated in 3D space with a CSS rule such as the following:

```
transform:perspective(200px) rotateX(10deg) rotateY(20deg) rotateZ(30deg);
```

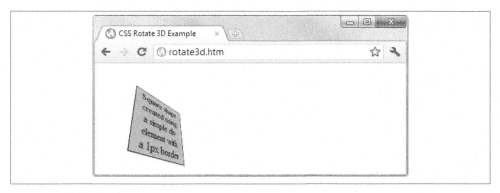

Figure 20-13. A figure rotated in 3D space

For more information, refer to the tutorial at *http://tinyurl.com/3dcsstransforms*.

Transitions

Also appearing on all the latest versions of the major browsers (including Internet Explorer 10, but not lower versions) is a dynamic new feature called *transitions*. These specify an animation effect you want to occur when an element is transformed, and the browser will automatically take care of all the in-between frames for you.

There are four properties you should supply in order to set up a transition, as follows:

```
transition-property        :property;
transition-duration        :time;
transition-delay           :time;
transition-timing-function:type;
```

You must preface these properties with the relevant browser prefixes for Mozilla, WebKit, Opera, and Microsoft browsers.

Properties to Transition

Transitions have properties such as height and border-color. Specify the properties you want to change in the CSS property named transition-property (here the word *property* is used by different tools to mean different things). You can include multiple properties by separating them with commas, like this:

```
transition-property:width, height, opacity;
```

Or, if you want absolutely everything about an element to transition (including colors), use the value all, like this:

```
transition-property:all;
```

Transition Duration

The transition-duration property requires a value of 0 seconds or greater, like the following, which specifies that the transition should take 1.25 seconds to complete:

```
transition-duration:1.25s;
```

Transition Delay

If the transition-delay property is given a value greater than 0 seconds (the default), it introduces a delay between the initial display of the element and the beginning of the transition. The following starts the transition after a 0.1-second delay:

```
transition-delay:0.1s;
```

If the transition-delay property is given a value of less than 0 seconds (in other words, a negative value), the transition will execute the moment the property is changed, but will appear to have begun execution at the specified offset, partway through its cycle.

Transition Timing

The `transition-timing` function property requires one of the following values:

ease
> Start slowly, get faster, and then end slowly.

linear
> Transition at constant speed.

ease-in
> Start slowly, and then go quickly until finished.

ease-out
> Start quickly, stay fast until near the end, and then end slowly.

ease-in-out
> Start slowly, go fast, and then end slowly.

Using any of the values containing the word *ease* ensures that the transition looks extra fluid and natural, unlike a linear transition that somehow seems more mechanical. And if these aren't sufficiently varied for you, you can also create your own transitions using the `cubic-bezier` function.

For example, following are the declarations used to create the preceding five transition types, illustrating how you can easily create your own:

```
transition-timing-function:cubic-bezier(0.25, 0.1, 0.25, 1);
transition-timing-function:cubic-bezier(0,    0,   1,    1);
transition-timing-function:cubic-bezier(0.42, 0,   1,    1);
transition-timing-function:cubic-bezier(0,    0,   0.58, 1);
transition-timing-function:cubic-bezier(0.42, 0,   0.58, 1);
```

Shorthand Syntax

You may find it easier to use the shorthand version of this property and include all the values in a single declaration like the following, which will transition all properties in a linear fashion, over a period of .3 seconds, after an initial (optional) delay of .2 seconds:

```
transition:all .3s linear .2s;
```

Doing so will save you the trouble of entering many very similar declarations, particularly if you are supporting all the major browser prefixes.

Example 20-4 illustrates how you might use transitions and transformations together. The CSS creates a square, orange element with some text in it, and a hover pseudo-class specifying that when the mouse passes over the object it should rotate by 180 degrees and change from orange to yellow (see Figure 20-14).

Example 20-4. A transition on hover effect

```
<!DOCTYPE html>
<html>
  <head>
    <title>Transitioning on hover</title>
    <style>
      #square {
        position           :absolute;
        top                :50px;
        left               :50px;
        width              :100px;
        height             :100px;
        padding            :2px;
        text-align         :center;
        border-width       :1px;
        border-style       :solid;
        background         :orange;
        transition         :all .8s ease-in-out;
        -moz-transition    :all .8s ease-in-out;
        -webkit-transition :all .8s ease-in-out;
        -o-transition      :all .8s ease-in-out;
        -ms-transition     :all .8s ease-in-out;
      }
      #square:hover {
        background         :yellow;
        -moz-transform     :rotate(180deg);
        -webkit-transform  :rotate(180deg);
        -o-transform       :rotate(180deg);
        -ms-transform      :rotate(180deg);
        transform          :rotate(180deg);
      }
    </style>
  </head>
  <body>
    <div id='square'>
      Square shape<br>
      created using<br>
      a simple div<br>
      element with<br>
      a 1px border
    </div>
  </body>
</html>
```

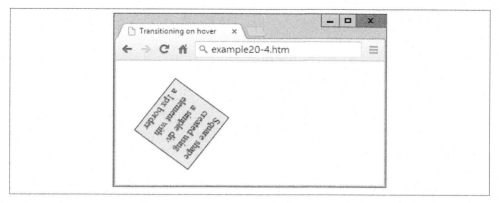

Figure 20-14. The object rotates and changes color when hovered over

The sample code caters to all the different browsers by providing browser-specific versions of the declarations. On all the latest browsers (including IE10 or higher), the object will rotate clockwise when hovered over, while slowly changing from orange to yellow.

CSS transitions are smart in that when they are canceled, they smoothly return to their original value. So if you move the mouse away before the transition has completed, it will instantly reverse and start transition back to its initial state.

Questions

1. What do the CSS3 attribute selector operators ^=, $=, and *= do?
2. What property do you use to specify the size of a background image?
3. With which property can you specify the radius of a border?
4. How can you flow text over multiple columns?
5. Name the four functions with which you can specify CSS colors.
6. How would you create a gray text shadow under some text, offset diagonally to the bottom right by 5 pixels, with a blurring of 3 pixels?
7. How can you indicate with an ellipsis that text is truncated?
8. How can you include a Google Web Font in a web page?
9. What CSS declaration would you use to rotate an object by 90 degrees?
10. How do you set up a transition on an object so that when any of its properties are changed, the change will transition immediately in a linear fashion over the course of half a second?

See "Chapter 20 Answers" on page 653 in Appendix A for the answers to these questions.

Accessing CSS from JavaScript

With a good understanding of the DOM and CSS now under your belt, you'll learn in this chapter how to access both the DOM and CSS directly from JavaScript, enabling you to create highly dynamic and responsive websites.

I'll also show you how to use interrupts so that you can create animations or provide any code that must continue running (such as a clock). Finally, I'll explain how you can add new elements to or remove existing ones from the DOM so that you don't have to pre-create elements in HTML just in case JavaScript may need to access them later.

Revisiting the getElementById Function

In Chapter 14, I mentioned the common usage of the $ character as a function name to provide easier access to the getElementById function. In fact, major frameworks such as jQuery use this new $ function, and substantially extend its functionality too.

I would also like to provide you with an enhanced version of this function, so that you can handle DOM elements and CSS styles quickly and efficiently. However, to avoid conflicting with frameworks that use the $ character, I'll simply use the uppercase O, because it's the first letter of the word *Object*, which is what will be returned when the function is called (the object represented by the ID passed to the function).

The O function

Here's what the bare-bones O function looks like:

```
function O(obj)
{
  return document.getElementById(obj)
}
```

This alone saves 22 characters of typing each time it's called. But I choose to extend the function a little by allowing either an ID name or an object to be passed to this function, as shown in the complete version of the function in Example 21-1.

Example 21-1. The O() function

```
function O(obj)
{
  if (typeof obj == 'object') return obj
  else return document.getElementById(obj)
}
```

If an object is passed to the function, it just returns that object back again. Otherwise, it assumes that an ID is passed and returns the object to which the ID refers.

But why on earth would I want to add this first statement, which simply returns the object passed to it?

The S Function

The answer to this question becomes clear when you look at a partner function called S, which gives you easy access to the style (or CSS) properties of an object, as shown in Example 21-1.

Example 21-2. The S() function

```
function S(obj)
{
  return O(obj).style
}
```

The S in this function name is the first letter of *Style*, and the function performs the task of returning the style property (or subobject) of the element referred to. Because the embedded O function accepts either an ID or an object, you can pass either an ID or an object to S as well.

Let's look at what's going on here by taking a <div> element with the ID of myobj and setting its text color to green, like this:

```
<div id='myobj'>Some text</div>

<script>
  O('myobj').style.color = 'green'
</script>
```

The preceding code will do the job, but it's much simpler to call the new S function, like this:

```
S('myobj').color = 'green'
```

Now consider the case in which the object returned by calling O is stored in, for example, an object called fred, like this:

```
fred = O('myobj')
```

Because of the way function S works, we can still call it to change the text color to green, like this:

```
S(fred).color = 'green'
```

This means that whether you wish to access an object directly or via its ID, you can do so by passing it to either the O or S function as required. Just remember that when you pass an object (rather than an ID), you must not place it in quotation marks.

The C Function

So far I've provided you with two simple functions that make it easy for you to access any element on a web page, and any style property of an element. Sometimes, though, you will want to access more than one element at a time, and you can do this by assigning a CSS class name to each such element, like these examples, which both employ the class myclass:

```
<div class='myclass'>Div contents</fiv>
<p class='myclass'>Paragraph contents</p>
```

If you want to access all elements on a page that use a particular class, you can use the C function (for the first letter of *Class*), shown in Example 21-3, to return an array containing all the objects that match a class name provided.

Example 21-3. The C() function

```
function C(name)
{
  var elements = document.getElementsByTagName('*')
  var objects  = []

  for (var i = 0 ; i < elements.length ; ++i)
    if (elements[i].className == name)
      objects.push(elements[i])

  return objects
}
```

Let's break this example down. First, the argument name contains the class name for which you are trying to retrieve objects. Then, inside the function, a new object called elements is created that contains all the elements in the document, as returned by a call to getElementsByTagName with an argument of '*', which means "find all elements":

```
var elements = document.getElementsByTagName('*')
```

Then a new array called `objects` is created, into which all the matching objects found will be placed:

```
var objects = []
```

Next, a `for` loop iterates through all the elements in the `elements` object using the variable `i` as the index:

```
for (var i = 0 ; i < elements.length ; ++i)
```

Each time around the loop, if an element's `className` property is the same as the string value passed in the argument `name`, the object is pushed onto the `objects` array:

```
if (elements[i].className == name)
   objects.push(elements[i])
```

Finally, once the loop has completed, the `objects` array will contain all the elements in the document that use the class name in `name`, so it is returned by the function:

```
return objects
```

To use this function simply call it as follows, saving the returned array so that you can access each of the elements individually as required or (more likely to be the case) en masse via a loop:

```
myarray = C('myclass')
```

Now you can do whatever you like with the objects returned, such as, for example, setting their `textDecoration` style property to `'underline'`, as follows:

```
for (i = 0 ; i < myarray.length ; ++i)
   S(myarray[i]).textDecoration = 'underline'
```

This code iterates through the objects in `myarray[]` and then uses the `S` function to reference each one's style property, setting its `textDecoration` property to `'underline'`.

Including the Functions

I use the `O` and `S` functions in the examples for the remainder of this chapter, as they make the code shorter and easier to follow. Therefore, I have saved them in the file *OSC.js* (along with the `C` function, as I think you'll find it extremely useful) in the *Chapter 21* folder of the accompanying archive of examples, freely downloadable from the companion website (*http://lpmj.net*).

You can include these functions in any web page using the following statement—preferably in its `<head>` section, anywhere before any script that relies on calling them:

```
<script src='OSC.js'></script>
```

The contents of *OSC.js* are shown in Example 21-4.

Example 21-4. The OSC.js file

```
function O(obj)
{
  if (typeof obj == 'object') return obj
  else return document.getElementById(obj)
}

function S(obj)
{
  return O(obj).style
}

function C(name)
{
  var elements = document.getElementsByTagName('*')
  var objects  = []

  for (var i = 0 ; i < elements.length ; ++i)
    if (elements[i].className == name)
      objects.push(elements[i])

  return objects
}
```

Accessing CSS Properties from JavaScript

The `textDecoration` property I used in an earlier example represents a CSS property that is normally hyphenated like this: `text-decoration`. But because JavaScript reserves the hyphen character for use as a mathematical operator, whenever you access a hyphenated CSS property, you must omit the hyphen and set the character immediately following it to uppercase.

Another example of this is the `font-size` property, which is referenced in JavaScript as `fontSize` when placed after a period operator, like this:

```
myobject.fontSize = '16pt'
```

An alternative to this is to be more long-winded and use the `setAttribute` function, which does support (and in fact requires) standard CSS property names, like this:

```
myobject.setAttribute('style', 'font-size:16pt')
```

Some older versions of Microsoft Internet Explorer are picky in certain instances about using the JavaScript-style CSS property names when applying the browser-specific `-ms-` prefixed versions of the rules. If you encounter this, use the `setAttribute` function and you should be all right.

Some Common Properties

Using JavaScript, you can modify any property of any element in a web document, in a similar manner to using CSS. I've already shown you how to access CSS properties using either the JavaScript short form or the `setAttribute` function to use exact CSS property names, so I won't bore you by detailing all of these hundreds of properties. Rather, I'd like to show you how to access just a few of the CSS properties as an overview of some of the things you can do.

First, then, let's look at modifying a few CSS properties from JavaScript using Example 21-5, which loads in the three earlier functions, creates a `<div>` element, and then issues JavaScript statements within a `<script>` section of HTML, to modify various of its attributes (see Figure 21-1).

Example 21-5. Accessing CSS properties from JavaScript

```
<!DOCTYPE html>
<html>
  <head>
    <title>Accessing CSS Properties</title>
    <script src='OSC.js'></script>
  </head>
  <body>
    <div id='object'>Div Object</div>

    <script>
      S('object').border     = 'solid 1px red'
      S('object').width      = '100px'
      S('object').height     = '100px'
      S('object').background = '#eee'
      S('object').color      = 'blue'
      S('object').fontSize   = '15pt'
      S('object').fontFamily = 'Helvetica'
      S('object').fontStyle  = 'italic'
    </script>
  </body>
</html>
```

You gain nothing by modifying properties like this, because you could just as easily have included some CSS directly, but shortly we'll be modifying properties in response to user interaction—and then you'll see the real power of combining JavaScript and CSS.

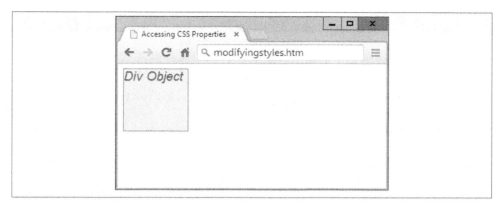

Figure 21-1. Modifying styles from JavaScript

Other Properties

JavaScript also opens up access to a very wide range of other properties, such as the width and height of the browser and of any pop-up or in-browser windows or frames, handy information such as the parent window (if there is one), and the history of URLs visited this session.

All these properties are accessed from the `window` object via the period operator (e.g., `window.name`), and Table 21-1 lists them all, along with descriptions of each.

Table 21-1. Common window properties

Properties	Sets and/or returns
closed	Returns a Boolean value indicating whether a window has been closed or not
defaultStatus	Sets or returns the default text in the status bar of a window
document	Returns the document object for the window
frames	Returns an array of all the frames and iframes in the window
history	Returns the history object for the window
innerHeight	Sets or returns the inner height of a window's content area
innerWidth	Sets or returns the inner width of a window's content area
length	Returns the number of frames and iframes in a window
location	Returns the location object for the window
name	Sets or returns the name of a window
navigator	Returns the navigator object for the window
opener	Returns a reference to the window that created the window
outerHeight	Sets or returns the outer height of a window, including tool and scroll bars
outerWidth	Sets or returns the outer width of a window, including tool and scroll bars
pageXOffset	Returns the pixels the document has been scrolled horizontally from the left of the window

Properties	Sets and/or returns
pageYOffset	Returns the pixels the document has been scrolled vertically from the top of the window
parent	Returns the parent window of a window
screen	Returns the screen object for the window
screenLeft	Returns the x coordinate of the window relative to the screen in all recent browsers except Mozilla Firefox (for which you should use screenX)
screenTop	Returns the y coordinate of the window relative to the screen in all recent browsers except Mozilla Firefox (for which you should use screenY)
screenX	Returns the x coordinate of the window relative to the screen in all recent browsers except Opera, which returns incorrect values; not supported in versions of IE prior to 9
screenY	Returns the y coordinate of the window relative to the screen in all recent browsers except Opera, which returns incorrect values; not supported in versions of IE prior to 9
self	Returns the current window
status	Sets or returns the text in the status bar of a window
top	Returns the top browser window

There are a few points to note about some of these properties:

- The defaultStatus and status properties can be set only if users have modified their browsers to allow it (very unlikely).

- The history object cannot be read from (so you cannot see where your visitors have been surfing). But it supports the length property to determine how long the history is, and the back, forward, and go methods to navigate to specific pages in the history.

- When you need to know how much space there is available in a current window of the web browser, just read the values in window.innerHeight and window.inner Width. I often use these values for centering in-browser pop-up alert or "confirm dialog" windows.

- The screen object supports the read properties availHeight, availWidth, color Depth, height, pixelDepth, and width, and is therefore great for determining information about the user's display.

 Many of these properties can be invaluable when you're targeting mobile phones and tablet devices, as they will tell you exactly how much screen space you have to work with, the type of browser being used, and more.

These few items of information will get you started and already provide you with many new and interesting things you can do with JavaScript. But, in fact, there are far more properties and methods available than can be covered in this chapter. However, now that you know how to access and use properties, all you need is a resource listing them all, so I recommend that you check out *http://tinyurl.com/domproperties* as a good starting point.

Inline JavaScript

Using `<script>` tags isn't the only way you can execute JavaScript statements; you can also access JavaScript from within HTML tags, which makes for great dynamic interactivity.

For example, to add a quick effect when the mouse passes over an object, you can use code such as that in the `<img>` tag in Example 21-6, which displays an apple by default, but replaces it with an orange when the mouse passes over, and restores the apple again when the mouse leaves.

Example 21-6. Using inline JavaScript

```
<!DOCTYPE html>
<html>
  <head>
    <title>Inline JavaScript</title>
  </head>
  <body>
    <img src='apple.png'
      onmouseover="this.src='orange.png'"
      onmouseout="this.src='apple.png'">
  </body>
</html>
```

The this Keyword

In the preceding example, you see the `this` keyword in use. It tells the JavaScript to operate on the calling object, namely the `<img>` tag. You can see the result in Figure 21-2, where the mouse has yet to pass over the apple.

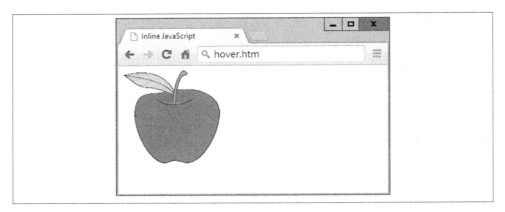

Figure 21-2. Inline mouse hover JavaScript example

 When supplied from an inline JavaScript call, the this keyword represents the calling object. When used in class methods, it represents an object to which the method applies.

Attaching Events to Objects in a Script

The preceding code is the equivalent of providing an ID to the `<img>` tag, and then attaching the actions to the tag's mouse events, like Example 21-7.

Example 21-7. Non-inline JavaScript

```
<!DOCTYPE html>
<html>
  <head>
    <title>Non-inline JavaScript</title>
    <script src='OSC.js'></script>
  </head>
  <body>
    <img id='object' src='apple.png'>

    <script>
      O('object').onmouseover = function() { this.src = 'orange.png' }
      O('object').onmouseout  = function() { this.src = 'apple.png'  }
    </script>
  </body>
</html>
```

In the HTML section, this example gives the `<img>` element an ID of `object`, then proceeds to manipulate it separately in the JavaScript section, by attaching anonymous functions to each event.

Attaching to Other Events

Whether you're using inline or separate JavaScript, there are several events to which you can attach actions, providing a wealth of additional features you can offer your users. Table 21-2 lists these events and details when they will be triggered.

Table 21-2. Events and when they are triggered

Event	Occurs
onabort	When an image's loading is stopped before completion
onblur	When an element loses focus
onchange	When any part of a form has changed
onclick	When an object is clicked
ondblclick	When an object is double-clicked
onerror	When a JavaScript error is encountered
onfocus	When an element gets focus
onkeydown	When a key is being pressed (including Shift, Alt, Ctrl, and Esc)
onkeypress	When a key is being pressed (not including Shift, Alt, Ctrl, and Esc)
onkeyup	When a key is released
onload	When an object has loaded
onmousedown	When the mouse button is pressed over an element
onmousemove	When the mouse is moved over an element
onmouseout	When the mouse leaves an element
onmouseover	When the mouse passes over an element from outside it
onmouseup	When the mouse button is released
onsubmit	When a form is submitted
onreset	When a form is reset
onresize	When the browser is resized
onscroll	When the document is scrolled
onselect	When some text is selected
onunload	When a document is removed

> Make sure you attach events to objects that make sense. For example, an object that is not a form will not respond to the onsubmit event.

Adding New Elements

With JavaScript you are not limited to manipulating the elements and objects supplied to a document in its HTML. In fact, you can create objects at will by inserting them into the DOM.

For example, suppose you need a new <div> element. Example 21-8 shows one way you can add it to the web page.

Example 21-8. Inserting an element into the DOM

```
<!DOCTYPE html>
<html>
  <head>
    <title>Adding Elements</title>
    <script src='OSC.js'></script>
  </head>
  <body>
    This is a document with only this text in it.<br><br>

    <script>
      alert('Click OK to add an element')

      newdiv    = document.createElement('div')
      newdiv.id = 'NewDiv'
      document.body.appendChild(newdiv)

      S(newdiv).border = 'solid 1px red'
      S(newdiv).width  = '100px'
      S(newdiv).height = '100px'
      newdiv.innerHTML = "I'm a new object inserted in the DOM"
      tmp              = newdiv.offsetTop

      alert('Click OK to remove the element')
      pnode = newdiv.parentNode
      pnode.removeChild(newdiv)
      tmp = pnode.offsetTop
    </script>
  </body>
</html>
```

Figure 21-3 shows this code being used to add a new <div> element to a web document. First, the new element is created with `createElement`, then the `appendChild` function is called and the element gets inserted into the DOM.

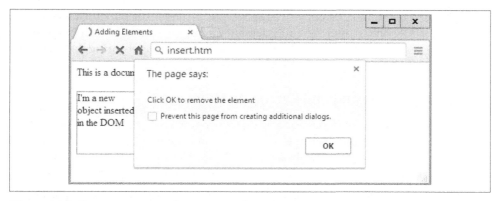

Figure 21-3. Inserting a new element into the DOM

After this, various properties are assigned to the element, including some text for its inner HTML. And then, to make sure the new element is instantly revealed, its offset Top property is read into the throwaway variable tmp. This forces a DOM refresh and makes the element display in any browser that might otherwise delay before doing so—particularly Internet Explorer.

This new element is exactly the same as if it had been included in the original HTML, and has all the same properties and methods available.

 I sometimes use the technique of creating new elements when I want to create in-browser pop-up windows, because it doesn't rely on there having to be a spare <div> element available in the DOM.

Removing Elements

You can also remove elements from the DOM, including ones that you didn't insert using JavaScript; it's even easier than adding an element. It works like this, assuming the element to remove is in the object element:

```
element.parentNode.removeChild(element)
```

This code accesses the element's parentNode object so that it can remove the element from that node. Then it calls the removeChild method on that object, passing the object to be removed. However, to ensure the DOM instantly refreshes on all browsers, you may prefer to replace the preceding single statement with something like the following:

```
pnode = element.parentNode
pnode.removeChild(element)
tmp   = pnode.offsetTop
```

This first statement makes a copy of `element.parentNode` (the parent element of the object) in `pnode`, which (after the child element is removed) has its `offsetTop` property looked up (and discarded in the throwaway variable `tmp`), thus ensuring that the DOM is fully refreshed.

Alternatives to Adding and Removing Elements

Inserting an element is intended for adding totally new objects into a web page. But if all you intend to do is hide and reveal objects according to an `onmouseover` or other event, don't forget that there are always a couple of CSS properties you can use for this purpose, without taking such drastic measures as creating and deleting DOM elements.

For example, when you want to make an element invisible but leave it in place (and with all the elements surrounding it remaining in their positions), you can simply set the object's `visibility` property to `'hidden'`, like this:

```
myobject.visibility = 'hidden'
```

And to redisplay the object, you can use the following:

```
myobject.visibility = 'visible'
```

You can also collapse elements down to occupy zero width and height (with all objects around it filling in the freed-up space), like this:

```
myobject.display = 'none'
```

To then restore an element to its original dimensions, you would use the following:

```
myobject.display = 'block'
```

And, of course, there's always the `innerHTML` property, with which you can change the HTML applied to an element, like this for example:

```
mylement.innerHTML = '<b>Replacement HTML</b>'
```

Or you can use the O function I outlined earlier, like this:

```
O('someid').innerHTML = 'New contents'
```

Or you can make an element seem to disappear, like this:

```
O('someid').innerHTML = ''
```

Don't forget other useful CSS properties you can access from JavaScript, such as `opacity` for setting the visibility of an object to somewhere between visible and invisible, or `width` and `height` for resizing an object. And, of course, using the `position` property with values of `'absolute'`, `'static'`, or `'relative'`, you can even locate an object anywhere in (or outside) the browser window that you like.

Using Interrupts

JavaScript provides access to *interrupts*, a method by which you can ask the browser to call your code after a set period of time, or even to keep calling it at specified intervals. This gives you a means of handling background tasks such as Ajax communications, or even things like animating web elements.

To accomplish this, you have two types of interrupt: `setTimeout` and `setInterval`, which have accompanying `clearTimeout` and `clearInterval` functions for turning them off again.

Using setTimeout

When you call `setTimeout`, you pass it some JavaScript code or the name of a function, and the value in milliseconds representing how long to wait before the code should be executed, like this:

```
setTimeout(dothis, 5000)
```

And your `dothis` function might look like this:

```
function dothis()
{
  alert('This is your wakeup alert!');
}
```

 In case you're wondering, you cannot simply specify `alert()` (with brackets) as a function to be called by `setTimeout`, because the function would be executed immediately. Only when you provide a function name without argument brackets (e.g., `alert`) can you safely pass the function name so that its code will be executed only when the timeout occurs.

Passing a string

When you need to provide an argument to a function, you can also pass a string value to the `setTimeout` function, which will not be executed until the correct time, like this:

```
setTimeout("alert('Hello!')", 5000)
```

In fact, you can provide as many lines of JavaScript code as you like, if you place a semicolon after each statement, like this:

```
setTimeout("document.write('Starting'); alert('Hello!')", 5000)
```

Repeating timeouts

One technique some programmers use to provide repeating interrupts with setTime
out is to call the setTimeout function from the code called by it, as with the following,
which will initiate a never-ending loop of alert windows:

```
setTimeout(dothis, 5000)

function dothis()
{
  setTimeout(dothis, 5000)
  alert('I am annoying!')
}
```

Now the alert will pop up every five seconds.

Canceling a Timeout

Once a timeout has been set up, you can cancel it if you previously saved the value
returned from the initial call to setTimeout, like this:

```
handle = setTimeout(dothis, 5000)
```

Armed with the value in handle, you can now cancel the interrupt at any point up until
its due time, like this:

```
clearTimeout(handle)
```

When you do this, the interrupt is completely forgotten, and the code assigned to it will
not get executed.

Using setInterval

An easier way to set up regular interrupts is to use the setInterval function. It works
in just the same way, except that having popped up after the interval you specify in
milliseconds, it will do so again after that interval again passes, and so on forever, unless
you cancel it.

Example 21-9 uses this function to display a simple clock in the browser, as shown in
Figure 21-4.

Example 21-9. A clock created using interrupts

```
<!DOCTYPE html>
<html>
  <head>
    <title>Using setInterval</title>
    <script src='OSC.js'></script>
  </head>
  <body>
    The time is: <span id='time'>00:00:00</span><br>
```

```
      <script>
        setInterval("showtime(O('time'))", 1000)

        function showtime(object)
        {
          var date = new Date()
          object.innerHTML = date.toTimeString().substr(0,8)
        }
      </script>
    </body>
</html>
```

Figure 21-4. Maintaining the correct time with interrupts

Every time `ShowTime` is called, it sets the object `date` to the current date and time with a call to `Date`:

```
var date = new Date()
```

Then the `innerHTML` property of the object passed to `showtime` (namely, `object`) is set to the current time in hours, minutes, and seconds, as determined by a call to `toTime String`. This returns a string such as `09:57:17 UTC+0530`, which is then truncated to just the first eight characters with a call to the `substr` function:

```
object.innerHTML = date.toTimeString().substr(0,8)
```

Using the function

To use this function, you first have to create an object whose `innerHTML` property will be used for displaying the time, like this HTML:

```
The time is: <span id='time'>00:00:00</span>
```

Then, from a `<script>` section of code, a call is placed to the `setInterval` function, like this:

```
setInterval("showtime(O('time'))", 1000)
```

It then passes a string to `setInterval`, containing the following statement, which is set to execute once a second (every 1,000 milliseconds):

```
showtime(O('time'))
```

In the rare situation where somebody has disabled JavaScript (which people sometimes do for security reasons), your JavaScript will not run and the user will see the original `00:00:00`.

Canceling an interval

In order to stop a repeating interval, when you first set up the interval with a call to `setInterval`, you must make a note of the interval's handle, like this:

```
handle = setInterval("showtime(O('time'))", 1000)
```

Now you can stop the clock at any time by issuing the following call:

```
clearInterval(handle)
```

You can even set up a timer to stop the clock after a certain amount of time, like this:

```
setTimeout("clearInterval(handle)", 10000)
```

This statement will issue an interrupt in 10 seconds that will clear the repeating intervals.

Using Interrupts for Animation

By combining a few CSS properties with a repeating interrupt, you can produce all manner of animations and effects.

For example, the code in Example 21-10 moves a square shape across the top of a browser, all the time ballooning in size, as shown in Figure 21-5, before starting all over again when LEFT is reset to 0.

Example 21-10. A simple animation

```
<!DOCTYPE html>
<html>
  <head>
    <title>Simple Animation</title>
    <script src='OSC.js'></script>
    <style>
      #box {
        position  :absolute;
        background:orange;
        border    :1px solid red;
      }
    </style>
  </head>
  <body>
    <div id='box'></div>
```

```
<script>
  SIZE = LEFT = 0

  setInterval(animate, 30)

  function animate()
  {
    SIZE += 10
    LEFT += 3

    if (SIZE == 200) SIZE = 0
    if (LEFT == 600) LEFT = 0

    S('box').width  = SIZE + 'px'
    S('box').height = SIZE + 'px'
    S('box').left   = LEFT + 'px'
  }
</script>
</body>
</html>
```

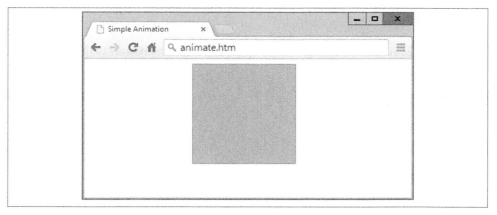

Figure 21-5. This object slides in from the left while changing size

In the document's <head>, the box object is set to a background color of 'orange' with a border value of '1px solid red', and its position property is set to absolute so that it is allowed to be moved around in the browser.

Then, in the animate function, the global variables SIZE and LEFT are continuously updated and then applied to the width, height, and left style attributes of the box object (with 'px' added after each to specify that the values are in pixels), thus animating it at a frequency of once every 30 milliseconds—giving a rate of 33.33 frames per second (1,000/30 milliseconds).

Questions

1. What are the O, S, and C functions provided to do?

2. Name two ways to modify a CSS attribute of an object.

3. Which properties provide the width and height available in a browser window?

4. How can you make something happen when the mouse passes both over and out of an object?

5. Which JavaScript function creates new elements, and which appends them to the DOM?

6. How can you make an element (a) invisible, and (b) collapse to zero dimensions?

7. Which function creates a single event at a future time?

8. Which function sets up repeating events at set intervals?

9. How can you release an element from its location in a web page to enable it to be moved around?

10. What delay between events should you set (in milliseconds) to achieve an animation rate of 50 frames per second?

See "Chapter 21 Answers" on page 654 in Appendix A for the answers to these questions.

Introduction to HTML5

HTML5 represents a substantial leap forward in web design, layout, and usability. It provides a simple way to manipulate graphics in a web browser without resorting to plug-ins such as Flash, offers methods to insert audio and video into web pages (again without plug-ins), and irons out several annoying inconsistencies that crept into HTML during its evolution.

In addition, HTML5 includes numerous other enhancements such as geolocation handling, web workers to manage background tasks, improved form handling, access to bundles of local storage (far in excess of the limited capabilities of cookies), and even the facility to turn web pages into web applications for mobile browsers.

What's curious about HTML5, though, is that it has been an ongoing evolution, in which different browsers have adopted different features at different times. Fortunately, all the biggest and most popular HTML5 additions are finally now supported by all major browsers (those with more than 1% or so of the market, such as Chrome, Internet Explorer, Firefox, Safari, and Opera, and the Android and iOS browsers).

But with HTML5 having only been officially submitted to the W3C in early 2013, there remain a number of features outstanding in several browsers, which I outline later in the book so you will be prepared when they are adopted.

Nevertheless, we are now fully into the second big surge toward dynamic web interactivity (the first being the adoption of what became known as Web 2.0). I would hesitate to call it Web 3.0, though, because the term *HTML5* says it all to most people, and in my view it could be considered a later version of Web 2.0 (maybe something like Web 2.7).

Actually, I think it will be very interesting to see what Web 3.0 will turn out to be. If I were to hazard a prediction, though, I would say it will result from the application of artificial intelligence (AI) in the form of much more capable versions of software such as Apple's Siri, Microsoft's Cortana, and IBM's Watson, combined with wearable technology that uses visual and voice input—like Google Glass and the Galaxy Gear watch—rather than keyboards. I look forward to covering these things in future editions of this book.

But for now, having written about what's to come in HTML5 for some years, and now that so many parts of the specification are usable on virtually all devices and browsers, I'm pleased to finally be able to bring it into this edition of the book. So let me take you on an overview of what's available to you in HTML5 right now.

The Canvas

Originally introduced by Apple for the WebKit rendering engine (which had itself originated in the KDE HTML layout engine) for its Safari browser (and now also implemented in iOS, Android, Kindle, Chrome, BlackBerry, Opera, and Tizen), the *canvas* element enables us to draw graphics in a web page without having to rely on a plug-in such as Java or Flash. After being standardized, the canvas was adopted by all other browsers and is now a mainstay of modern web development.

Like other HTML elements, a canvas is simply an element within a web page with defined dimensions, and within which you can use JavaScript to draw graphics. You create a canvas using the <canvas> tag, to which you must also assign an ID so that JavaScript will know which canvas it is accessing (as you can have more than one canvas on a page).

In Example 22-1, I've created a <canvas> element, with the ID mycanvas, that contains some text that is displayed only in browsers that don't support the canvas. Beneath this there is a section of JavaScript, which draws the Japanese flag on the canvas (as shown in Figure 22-1).

Example 22-1. Using the HTML5 canvas element

```
<!DOCTYPE html>
<html>
  <head>
    <title>The HTML5 Canvas</title>
    <script src='OSC.js'></script>
  </head>
  <body>
    <canvas id='mycanvas' width='320' height='240'>
      This is a canvas element given the ID <i>mycanvas</i>
      This text is only visible in non-HTML5 browsers
    </canvas>

    <script>
      canvas            = O('mycanvas')
      context           = canvas.getContext('2d')
      context.fillStyle = 'red'
      S(canvas).border  = '1px solid black'
```

```
        context.beginPath()
        context.moveTo(160, 120)
        context.arc(160, 120, 70, 0, Math.PI * 2, false)
        context.closePath()
        context.fill()
      </script>
    </body>
  </html>
```

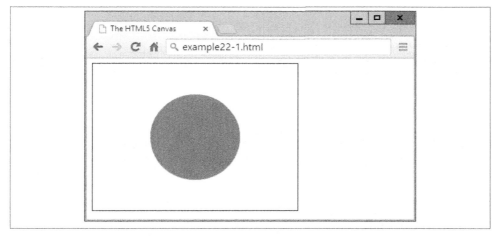

Figure 22-1. Drawing the Japanese flag using an HTML5 canvas

At this point it's not necessary to detail exactly what is going on, as I explain that in the following chapter, but you should already see how using the canvas is not hard, but does require learning a few new JavaScript functions. Note that this example draws on the *OSC.js* set of functions from the previous chapter to help keep the code neat and compact.

Geolocation

Using *geolocation*, your browser can return information to a web server about your location. This information can come from a GPS chip in the computer or mobile device you're using, from your IP address, or from analysis of nearby WiFi hotspots. For security purposes, the user is always in control and can refuse to provide this information on a one-off basis, or can enable settings to either permanently block or allow access to this data from one or all websites.

There are numerous uses for this technology, including giving you turn-by-turn navigation; providing local maps; notifying you of nearby restaurants, WiFi hotspots, or other places; letting you know which friends are near you; directing you to the nearest gas station; and more.

Example 22-2 will display a Google map of the user's location, as long as the browser supports geolocation and the user grants access to his location (as shown in Figure 22-2). Otherwise, it will display an error.

Example 22-2. Displaying the map at a user's location

```
<!DOCTYPE html>
<html>
  <head>
    <title>Geolocation Example</title>
    <script src='OSC.js'></script>
    <script src="https://maps.googleapis.com/maps/api/js?sensor=false"></script>
  </head>
  <body>
    <div id='status'></div>
    <div id='map'></div>

    <script>
      if (typeof navigator.geolocation == 'undefined')
        alert("Geolocation not supported.")
      else
        navigator.geolocation.getCurrentPosition(granted, denied)

      function granted(position)
      {
        O('status').innerHTML = 'Permission Granted'
        S('map').border       = '1px solid black'
        S('map').width        = '640px'
        S('map').height       = '320px'

        var lat   = position.coords.latitude
        var long  = position.coords.longitude
        var gmap  = O('map')
        var gopts =
        {
          center: new google.maps.LatLng(lat, long),
          zoom: 9, mapTypeId: google.maps.MapTypeId.ROADMAP
        }
        var map = new google.maps.Map(gmap, gopts)
      }

      function denied(error)
      {
        var message

        switch(error.code)
        {
          case 1: message = 'Permission Denied'; break;
          case 2: message = 'Position Unavailable'; break;
```

```
        case 3: message = 'Operation Timed Out'; break;
        case 4: message = 'Unknown Error'; break;
      }

      O('status').innerHTML = message
    }
  </script>
  </body>
</html>
```

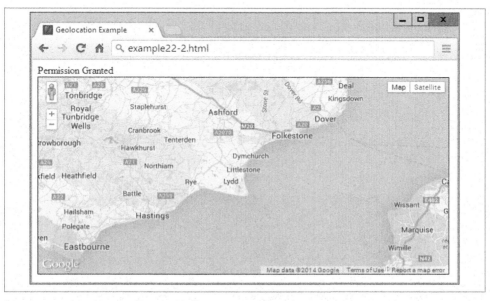

Figure 22-2. The user's location has been used to display a map

Again, here is not the place to describe how this all works, as I will detail that in Chapter 25. For now, though, this example serves to show you how easy managing geolocation can be, especially given that much of the code is dedicated to handling errors and calling up the Google map, so the core geolocation code you need is actually minimal.

Audio and Video

Another great addition to HTML5 is support for in-browser audio and video. While playing these types of media can be a little complicated due to the variety of encoding types and licenses, the <audio> and <video> elements provide the flexibility you need to display the types of media you have available.

In Example 22-3, the same video file has been encoded in different formats to ensure that all major browsers are accounted for. Browsers will simply select the first type they recognize and play it, as shown in Figure 22-3.

Example 22-3. Playing a video with HTML5

```
<!DOCTYPE html>
<html>
  <head>
    <title>HTML5 Video</title>
  </head>
  <body>
    <video width='560' height='320' controls>
      <source src='movie.mp4'  type='video/mp4'>
      <source src='movie.webm' type='video/webm'>
      <source src='movie.ogv'  type='video/ogg'>
    </video>
  </body>
</html>
```

Figure 22-3. Displaying video using HTML5

Inserting audio into a web page is just as easy, as you will discover in Chapter 24.

Forms

As you already saw in Chapter 12, HTML5 forms are in the process of being enhanced, but support across all browsers remains patchy. What you *can* safely use today has been detailed in Chapter 12, and future editions of this book will include other aspects of forms as they become adopted across the board. In the meantime, you can keep up-to-date with the latest developments on HTML5 forms at *http://tinyurl.com/h5forms*.

Local Storage

With local storage, your ability to save data on a local device is substantially increased from the meager space provided by cookies. This opens up the possibility of your using web apps to work on documents offline and then only syncing them with the web server when an Internet connection is available. It also raises the prospect of storing small databases locally for access with WebSQL, perhaps for keeping a copy of your music collection's details, or all your personal statistics as part of a diet or weight loss plan, for example. In Chapter 25, I show you how to make the most of this new facility in your web projects.

Web Workers

It has been possible to run interrupt-driven applications in the background using Java-Script for many years, but it is a clumsy and inefficient process. It makes much more sense to let the underlying browser technology run background tasks on your behalf, which it can do far more quickly than you can by continuously interrupting the browser to check how things are going.

Instead, with web workers you set everything up and pass your code to the web browser, which then runs it. When anything significant occurs, your code simply has to notify the browser, which then reports back to your main code. In the meantime, your web page can be doing nothing or a number of other tasks, and can forget about the background task until it makes itself known.

In Chapter 25, I demonstrate how you can use web workers to create a simple clock and to calculate prime numbers.

Web Applications

More and more these days, web pages are beginning to resemble apps, and with HTML5 they can become web apps very easily. All you have to do is tell the web browser about the resources used in your application, and it will download them to where they can be run and accessed locally, offline, and without any Internet connection if necessary.

Chapter 25 shows how you can do this to turn the clock example in the web workers section into a web app.

Microdata

Also in Chapter 25, I show how you can mark up your code with *microdata* to make it totally understandable to any browser or other technology that needs to access it. Microdata is sure to become more and more important to search engine optimization too, so it's important that you begin to incorporate it or at least understand what information it can provide about your websites.

Summary

As you can see, there's quite a lot to HTML5, and it's all goodies that many people waited a long time for—but they're finally here. Starting with the canvas, the following few chapters will explain these features to you in glorious detail, so you can be up and running with them, and enhancing your websites, in no time.

Questions

1. What new HTML5 element enables drawing of graphics in web pages?
2. What programming language is required to access many of the advanced HTML5 features?
3. Which tags would you use to incorporate audio and video in a web page?
4. What feature is new in HTML5 and offers greater capability than cookies?
5. Which HTML5 technology supports running background JavaScript tasks?

See "Chapter 22 Answers" on page 655 in Appendix A for the answers to these questions.

The HTML5 Canvas

Although the collective term given to the new web technologies is *HTML5*, they are not all simply HTML tags and properties. Such is the case with the canvas element. Yes, you create a canvas using the <canvas> tag, and maybe supply a width and height, and can modify it a little with CSS, but to actually write to (or read from) a canvas, you must use JavaScript.

Thankfully, the JavaScript you need to learn is minimal and very easy to implement, plus I've already provided you with a set of three ready-made functions in Chapter 21 (in the file *OSC.js*) that make accessing objects such as the canvas even more straight-forward. So let's dive right in and start using the new <canvas> tag.

Creating and Accessing a Canvas

In the previous chapter, I showed you how to draw a simple circle to display the Japanese flag, as in Example 23-1. Let's now look at what exactly is going on.

Example 23-1. Displaying the Japanese flag using a canvas

```
<!DOCTYPE html>
<html>
  <head>
    <title>The HTML5 Canvas</title>
    <script src='OSC.js'></script>
  </head>
  <body>
    <canvas id='mycanvas' width='320' height='240'>
      This is a canvas element given the ID <i>mycanvas</i>
      This text is only visible in non-HTML5 browsers
    </canvas>

    <script>
      canvas            = O('mycanvas')
```

```
      context            = canvas.getContext('2d')
      context.fillStyle = 'red'
      S(canvas).border  = '1px solid black'

      context.beginPath()
      context.moveTo(160, 120)
      context.arc(160, 120, 70, 0, Math.PI * 2, false)
      context.closePath()
      context.fill()
    </script>
  </body>
</html>
```

First, the `<!DOCTYPE html>` declaration is issued to tell the browser that the document will use HTML5. After this, a title is displayed and the three functions in the *OSC.js* file are loaded in.

In the body of the document, a `canvas` element is defined, given an ID of `mycanvas`, and given a width and height of 320 by 240 pixels.

This is followed by a section of JavaScript that styles and draws on the canvas. We begin by creating a `canvas` object by calling the O function on the `canvas` element. As you will recall, this calls the `document.getElementById` function, and is therefore a much shorter way of referencing the element.

This is all stuff you've seen before, but next comes something new:

```
context = canvas.getContext('2d')
```

This command calls the `getContext` method of the new `canvas` object just created, requesting two-dimensional access to the canvas by passing the value `'2d'`.

 As you might guess, there are plans for a three-dimensional context available for the canvas (probably based on the OpenGL ES API), which will support the argument `'3d'`. But for now, if you want to display 3D on a canvas you'll need to do the math yourself and "fake" it in 2D. Or you could investigate WebGL (which is based on OpenGL ES). There's no room to cover it here, but you can find a great tutorial at *http://learningwebgl.com*.

Armed with this context in the object `context`, we prime the subsequent drawing commands by setting the `fillStyle` property of context to the value `'red'`:

```
context.fillStyle = 'red'
```

Then the S function is called to set the border property of the canvas to a 1-pixel, solid black line to outline the flag image:

```
S(canvas).border = '1px solid black'
```

With everything prepared, a path is opened on the context and the drawing position is moved to the location 160,120:

```
context.beginPath()
context.moveTo(160, 120)
```

After that, an arc is drawn centered on that coordinate, with a radius of 70 pixels, beginning at an angle of 0 degrees (which is the righthand edge of the circle as you look at it), and continuing all the way around the circle in radians as determined by a value of $2 \times \pi$:

```
context.arc(160, 120, 70, 0, Math.PI * 2, false)
```

The final value of false indicates a clockwise direction for drawing the arc; a value of true would indicate that the drawing should occur in a counterclockwise direction.

Finally, we close and fill the path, using the preselected value in the fillStyle property that we set to 'red' a few lines earlier:

```
context.closePath()
context.fill()
```

The result of loading this document into a web browser looks like Figure 22-1 in the previous chapter.

The toDataURL Function

When you have created an image in a canvas, you will sometimes want to make a copy of it, perhaps to repeat elsewhere on a web page, to save to local storage, or to upload to a web server. This is particularly handy because users cannot use drag and drop to save a canvas image.

To illustrate how you do this, for Example 23-2 I have added a few lines of code to the previous example (highlighted in bold). These create a new <img> element with the ID 'myimage', give it a solid black border, and then copy the canvas image into the <img> element (see Figure 23-1).

Example 23-2. Copying a canvas image

```
<!DOCTYPE html>
<html>
  <head>
    <title>The HTML5 Canvas</title>
    <script src='OSC.js'></script>
  </head>
  <body>
    <canvas id='mycanvas' width='320' height='240'>
      This is a canvas element given the ID <i>mycanvas</i>
      This text is only visible in non-HTML5 browsers
    </canvas>
```

```
    <img id='myimage'>

    <script>
      canvas            = O('mycanvas')
      context           = canvas.getContext('2d')
      context.fillStyle = 'red'
      S(canvas).border  = '1px solid black'

      context.beginPath()
      context.moveTo(160, 120)
      context.arc(160, 120, 70, 0, Math.PI * 2, false)
      context.closePath()
      context.fill()

      S('myimage').border = '1px solid black'
      O('myimage').src    = canvas.toDataURL()
    </script>
  </body>
</html>
```

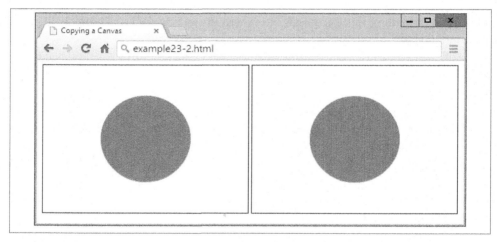

Figure 23-1. The image on the right is copied from the lefthand canvas

If you try this code for yourself, you will notice that while you cannot drag and drop the lefthand canvas image, you can do so with the righthand picture, which you could also save to local storage or upload to a web server using the right JavaScript (and PHP on the server end).

Specifying an Image Type

When creating an image from a canvas, you can specify the type of image you want out of *.jpg* and *.png*. The default is *.png* (`'image/png'`), but should you prefer *.jpg* you can alter the call to `toDataURL`. At the same time, you can also specify the amount of compression to use between 0 (for lowest quality) and 1 (for highest quality). The following uses a compression value of 0.4, and should generate a reasonably good-looking image at a fairly low file size:

```
O('myimage').src = canvas.toDataURL('image/jpeg', 0.4)
```

 Keep in mind that the `toDataURL` method applies to a canvas object, not to any context created from that object.

Now that you know how to create canvas images and then copy or otherwise use them, it's time to look at the individual drawing commands available, starting with rectangles.

The fillRect Method

There are two different methods you can call for drawing rectangles, the first of which is `fillRect`. To use it, you simply supply the top-left coordinates of your rectangle, followed by the width and height in pixels, like this:

```
context.fillRect(20, 20, 600, 200)
```

By default, the rectangle will be filled with black, but you can use any other color you like by first issuing a command such as the following, where the argument can be any acceptable CSS color name or value:

```
context.fillStyle = 'blue'
```

The clearRect Method

You can also draw a rectangle in which all its color values (red, green, blue, and alpha transparency) have been set to 0, like the following, which uses the same order of coordinates, and width and height arguments:

```
context.clearRect(40, 40, 560, 160)
```

Once the `clearRect` method is applied, the new clear rectangle will strip all color from the area it covers, leaving only any underlying CSS color that has been applied to the `canvas` element.

The strokeRect Method

When you want only an outlined rectangle, you can use a command such as the following, which will use the default of black or the currently selected stroke color:

```
context.strokeRect(60, 60, 520, 120)
```

To change the color used, you can first issue a command such as the following, supplying any valid CSS color argument:

```
context.strokeStyle = 'green'
```

Combining These Commands

In Example 23-3, the preceding rectangle-drawing commands have been combined to display the image shown in Figure 23-2.

Example 23-3. Drawing several rectangles

```
<!DOCTYPE html>
<html>
  <head>
    <title>Drawing Rectangles</title>
    <script src='OSC.js'></script>
  </head>
  <body>
    <canvas id='mycanvas' width='640' height='240'></canvas>

    <script>
      canvas               = O('mycanvas')
      context              = canvas.getContext('2d')
      S(canvas).background = 'lightblue'
      context.fillStyle    = 'blue'
      context.strokeStyle  = 'green'

      context.fillRect(  20, 20, 600, 200)
      context.clearRect( 40, 40, 560, 160)
      context.strokeRect(60, 60, 520, 120)
    </script>
  </body>
</html>
```

Later in this chapter, you'll see how you can further modify output by changing stroke types and widths, but first let's turn to modifying fills by applying gradients.

Figure 23-2. Drawing concentric rectangles

The createLinearGradient Method

There are a couple of different ways you can apply a gradient to a fill, but the simplest is with the createLinearGradient method. You specify start and end *x* and *y* coordinates relative to the canvas (not the object being filled). This allows for greater subtlety. For example, you can specify that a gradient begin at the far left and end at the far right of a canvas, but apply it only within the area defined in a fill command, as done in Example 23-4.

Example 23-4. Applying a gradient fill

```
gradient = context.createLinearGradient(0, 80, 640,80)
gradient.addColorStop(0, 'white')
gradient.addColorStop(1, 'black')
context.fillStyle = gradient
context.fillRect(80, 80, 480,80)
```

 For brevity and clarity in this and many of the following examples, only the salient lines of code are shown. The complete examples with the surrounding HTML, setup, and other sections of code are available to freely download from the companion website (*http://lpmj.net*).

In Example 23-4, we create a gradient fill object named gradient using the createLi nearGradient method of the context object. The start position of 0,80 is halfway down the lefthand canvas edge, while the end of 640,80 is halfway down the righthand edge.

Then a couple of color stops are provided such that the very first color of the gradient is white, and the final color is black. The gradient will then transition smoothly between these colors across the canvas from left to right.

With the `gradient` object now ready, it is applied to the `fillStyle` property of `context`, so that the final `fillRect` call can use it. In this call, the fill is applied only in a central rectangular area of the canvas, so, although the gradient goes from the far left to the far right of the canvas, the portion of it shown is only from 80 pixels in and down from the top-left corner, to a width of 480 and depth of 80 pixels. The result (when added to the previous example code) looks like Figure 23-3.

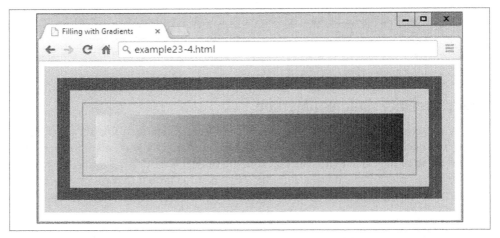

Figure 23-3. The central rectangle has a horizontal gradient fill

By specifying different start and end coordinates for a gradient, you can make it slant in any direction, as demonstrated with Example 23-5 and shown in Figure 23-4.

Example 23-5. A variety of gradients at different angles and colors

```
gradient = context.createLinearGradient(0, 0, 160, 0)
gradient.addColorStop(0, 'white')
gradient.addColorStop(1, 'black')
context.fillStyle = gradient
context.fillRect(20, 20, 135, 200)

gradient = context.createLinearGradient(0, 0, 0, 240)
gradient.addColorStop(0, 'yellow')
gradient.addColorStop(1, 'red')
context.fillStyle = gradient
context.fillRect(175, 20, 135, 200)

gradient = context.createLinearGradient(320, 0, 480, 240)
gradient.addColorStop(0, 'green')
```

```
gradient.addColorStop(1, 'purple')
context.fillStyle = gradient
context.fillRect(330, 20, 135, 200)

gradient = context.createLinearGradient(480, 240, 640, 0)
gradient.addColorStop(0, 'orange')
gradient.addColorStop(1, 'magenta')
context.fillStyle = gradient
context.fillRect(485, 20, 135, 200)
```

Figure 23-4. A range of different linear gradients

In this example, I chose to place the gradients directly on top of the areas to be filled in order to more clearly show the maximum variation in color from start to end.

To create your gradient, determine the direction in which you want it to flow and then locate two points to represent the start and end. No matter what values you supply for these points, the gradient will smoothly transition in the direction given, even if the points are outside the fill area.

The addColorStop Method in Detail

You can use as many color stops in a gradient as you like, not just the two start and end colors used so far in these examples. This makes it possible to clearly describe almost any type of gradient effect you can imagine. To do this, you must specify the percent of the gradient that each color should take up, by allocating a floating-point start position along the gradient range between 0 and 1. You do not enter a color's end position, as it is deduced from the start position of the next color stop, or the gradient end if there isn't another color.

In the preceding examples, only the two start and end values were chosen, but to create a rainbow effect you could set up your color stops as shown in Example 23-6 (and displayed in Figure 23-5).

Example 23-6. Adding multiple color stops

```
gradient.addColorStop(0.00, 'red')
gradient.addColorStop(0.14, 'orange')
gradient.addColorStop(0.28, 'yellow')
gradient.addColorStop(0.42, 'green')
gradient.addColorStop(0.56, 'blue')
gradient.addColorStop(0.70, 'indigo')
gradient.addColorStop(0.84, 'violet')
```

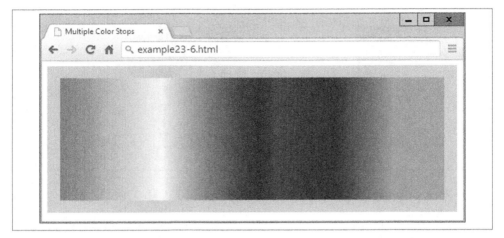

Figure 23-5. A rainbow effect with seven stop colors

In Example 23-6, all the colors are spaced roughly equidistantly (with each color given 14% of the gradient, and the final one 16%), but you don't have to stick to that; you can squish several colors near each other, while spacing others out. It's entirely up to you as to how many colors you use and where in the gradient they start and end.

The createRadialGradient Method

You aren't restricted to only linear gradients in HTML; you can create radial gradients on a canvas too. It's a little more complex than with a linear gradient, but not much more so.

What you need to do is pass the center location as a pair of *x* and *y* coordinates, along with a radius in pixels. These are used as the start of the gradient and outer circumference, respectively. Then you also pass another set of coordinates and a radius to specify the end of the gradient.

So, for example, to create a gradient that simply starts at the center of a circle and then expands out, you could issue a command such as the one in Example 23-7 (and displayed in Figure 23-6).

Example 23-7. Creating a radial gradient

```
gradient = context.createRadialGradient (320, 120, 0, 320, 120, 320)
```

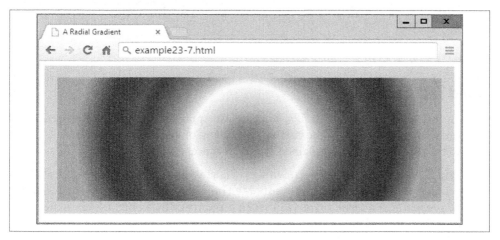

Figure 23-6. A centered radial gradient

Or you can be fancy and move the location of the start and end of a radial gradient, as in Example 23-8 (displayed in Figure 23-7), which starts centered on location 0,120 with a radius of 0 pixels, and ends centered at 480,120 with a radius of 480 pixels.

Example 23-8. Stretching a radial gradient

```
gradient = context.createRadialGradient(0, 120, 0, 480, 120, 480)
```

By manipulating the figures supplied to this method, you can create a wide range of weird and wonderful effects—try it for yourself with the supplied examples.

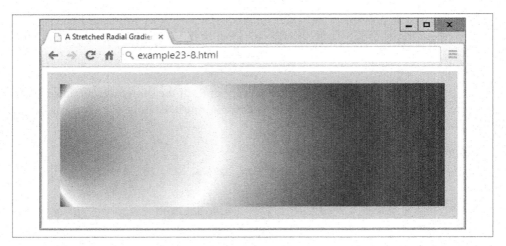

Figure 23-7. A stretched radial gradient

Using Patterns for Fills

In a similar manner to gradient fills, you can also apply an image as a fill pattern. This can be an image anywhere in the current document, or even one created from a canvas via the `toDataURL` method (explained earlier in this chapter).

Example 23-9 loads a 100×100-pixel image (the yin-yang symbol) into the new image object `image`, and then the `onload` event of the object has a function attached to it that creates a repeating pattern for the `fillStyle` property of the context. This is then used to fill a 600×200-pixel area within the canvas, as shown in Figure 23-8.

Example 23-9. Using an image for a pattern fill

```
image     = new Image()
image.src = 'image.png'

image.onload = function()
{
  pattern            = context.createPattern(image, 'repeat')
  context.fillStyle = pattern
  context.fillRect(20, 20, 600, 200)
}
```

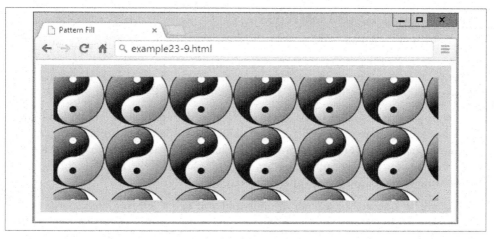

Figure 23-8. Tiling an image by using it as a pattern fill

We create the pattern using the `createPattern` method, which also supports nonrepeating patterns, or ones that just repeat in the x- or y-axes. We achieve this by passing one of the following values to it as the second argument after the image to use:

`repeat`
Repeat the image both vertically and horizontally.

`repeat-x`
Repeat the image horizontally.

`repeat-y`
Repeat the image vertically.

`no-repeat`
Do not repeat the image.

The fill pattern is based on the entire canvas area, so where the fill command is set to apply only to a smaller area within the canvas, the images appear cut off at the top and left.

 If the `onload` event had not been used in this example and, instead, the code was simply executed as soon as encountered, the image might not have already loaded in time, and may not be displayed. Attaching to this event ensures that the image is available for use in the canvas, because the event triggers only upon successful loading of an image.

Writing Text to the Canvas

As you would expect from a set of graphics features, writing to the canvas with text is fully supported with a variety of font, alignment, and fill methods. But why would you want to write text to the canvas when there's already such good support for web fonts in CSS these days?

Well, suppose you wish to display a graph or table with graphical elements. You'll surely also want to label parts of it. What's more, using the available commands you can produce much more than simply a colored font. So let's start by assuming you've been tasked to create a header for a website on basket weaving, called WickerpediA (actually there's already one of these, but let's go ahead anyway).

To start with, you need to select a suitable font and size it appropriately, perhaps as in Example 23-10, in which a font style of bold, a size of 140 pixels, and a typeface of Times have been selected. Also, the textBaseline property has been set to top so that the strokeText method can pass coordinates of 0,0 for the top-left origin of the text, placing it at the top left of the canvas. Figure 23-9 shows what this looks like.

Example 23-10. Writing text to the canvas

```
context.font        = 'bold 140px Times'
context.textBaseline = 'top'
context.strokeText('WickerpediA', 0, 0)
```

Figure 23-9. The text has been written to the canvas

The strokeText Method

To write text to the canvas, send the text string and a pair of coordinates to the stroke Text method, like this:

```
context.strokeText('WickerpediA', 0, 0)
```

The *x* and *y* coordinates supplied will be used as a relative reference by the textBase Line and textAlign properties.

This method—using line drawing—is only one way of drawing text to the canvas. So, in addition to all the following properties that affect text, line drawing properties such as lineWidth (detailed later in this chapter) will also affect how text displays.

The textBaseLine Property

The textBaseLine property can be given any of the following values:

top
> Aligns to the top of the text

middle
> Aligns to the middle of the text

alphabetic
> Aligns to the alphabetic baseline of the text

bottom
> Aligns to the bottom of the font

The font Property

The font style can be any of bold, italic, or normal (the default), or a combination of italic bold, and the size values can be specified in em, ex, px, %, in, cm, mm, pt, or pc measures, just as with CSS. The font should be one available to the current browser, which generally means one of Helvetica, Impact, Courier, Times, or Arial, or you can choose the default Serif or Sans-serif font of the user's system. However, if you know that a particular font is available to the browser, you can use it.

If you want to use a font such as Times New Roman, which incorporates spaces in its name, you should change the relevant line to something like this, in which the outer quotes are different than the ones surrounding the font name:

```
context.font = 'bold 140px "Times New Roman"'
```

The textAlign Property

As well as choosing how to align your text vertically, you can specify horizontal alignment by giving the textAlign property one of the following values:

start
> Aligns the text to the left if the document direction is left to right; otherwise, right. This is the default setting.

end
> Aligns the text to the right if the document direction is left to right; otherwise, left.

left
    Aligns the text to the left.

right
    Aligns the text to the right.

center
    Centers the text.

You use the property like this:

```
context.textAlign = 'center'
```

In the case of the current example, you need the text left-aligned so that it butts up neatly to the edge of the canvas, so the `textAlign` property is not used, and therefore the default left alignment occurs.

The fillText Method

You can also choose to use a fill property to fill in canvas text, which can be any of a solid color, a linear or radial gradient, or a pattern fill. So let's use a pattern fill for your heading, based on the texture of a wicker basket, as in Example 23-11, the result of which is shown in Figure 23-10.

Example 23-11. Filling in the text with a pattern

```
image       = new Image()
image.src = 'wicker.jpg'

image.onload = function()
{
  pattern            = context.createPattern(image, 'repeat')
  context.fillStyle = pattern
  context.fillText(  'WickerpediA', 0, 0)
  context.strokeText('WickerpediA', 0, 0)
}
```

Figure 23-10. The text now has a pattern fill

For good measure I also kept the strokeText call in this example to ensure a black outline to the text; without it, there wasn't enough definition at the edges.

A wide variety of other fill types or patterns can also be used here, and the simplicity of the canvas makes it easy to experiment. What's more: if you wish, once you have the heading just right, you can also choose to save a copy by issuing a call toDataURL, as detailed earlier in the chapter. Then you can use the image as a logo for uploading to other sites, for example.

The measureText Method

When working with canvas text, you may sometimes need to know how much space it will occupy so that you can best position it. You can achieve this with the measure Text method, as follows (assuming all the various text properties have already been defined at this point):

```
metrics = context.measureText('WickerpediA')
width   = metrics.width
```

Because the height of the text in pixels is equal to the font size in points when the font is defined, the metrics object doesn't provide a height metric.

Drawing Lines

The canvas provides a plethora of line drawing functions to cater to almost every need, including choices of lines, line caps and joins, and paths and curves of all types. But let's start with a property I touched on in the previous section on writing text to the canvas.

The lineWidth Property

All the canvas methods that draw using lines make use of lineWidth and a number of other line properties. Using it is as simple as specifying a line width in pixels, like this, which sets the width to 3 pixels:

```
context.lineWidth = 3
```

The lineCap and lineJoin Properties

When lines you draw come to an end and they are more than a pixel wide, you can choose how this *line cap* (as it is called) should appear by using the lineCap property, which can have the values butt, round, or square. For example:

```
context.lineCap = 'round'
```

Also, when you are joining lines together that are wider than a single pixel, it is important to specify exactly how they should meet. You achieve this with the lineJoin property, which can have values of round, bevel, or miter, like this:

```
                context.lineJoin = 'bevel'
```

Example 23-12 (shown here in full because it's a little more complicated) applies all three values of each property used in combination, creating the informative result shown in Figure 23-11. The beginPath, closePath, moveTo, and lineTo methods used by this example are explained next.

Example 23-12. Displaying combinations of line caps and joins

```
<!DOCTYPE html>
<html>
  <head>
    <title>Drawing Lines</title>
    <script src='OSC.js'></script>
  </head>
  <body>
    <canvas id='mycanvas' width='535' height='360'></canvas>

    <script>
      canvas              = O('mycanvas')
      context             = canvas.getContext('2d')
      S(canvas).background = 'lightblue'
      context.fillStyle   = 'red'
      context.font        = 'bold 13pt Courier'
      context.strokeStyle = 'blue'
      context.textBaseline = 'top'
      context.textAlign   = 'center'
      context.lineWidth   = 20
      caps                = [' butt', ' round', 'square']
      joins               = [' round', ' bevel', ' miter']

      for (j = 0 ; j < 3 ; ++j)
      {
        for (k = 0 ; k < 3 ; ++k)
        {
          context.lineCap  = caps[j]
          context.lineJoin = joins[k]

          context.fillText(' cap:' + caps[j],  88 + j * 180, 45 + k * 120)
          context.fillText('join:' + joins[k], 88 + j * 180, 65 + k * 120)

          context.beginPath()
          context.moveTo( 20 + j * 180, 100 + k * 120)
          context.lineTo( 20 + j * 180,  20 + k * 120)
          context.lineTo(155 + j * 180,  20 + k * 120)
          context.lineTo(155 + j * 180, 100 + k * 120)
          context.stroke()
          context.closePath()
        }
      }
    </script>
```

```
    </body>
</html>
```

This code sets up a few properties and then nests a pair of loops: one for the line caps and one for the joins. Inside the central loop, the current values for the lineCap and lineJoin properties are first set, and then displayed in the canvas with the fillText method.

Using these settings, the code then draws nine shapes with a 20-pixel-wide line, each of which has a different combination of line cap and join settings, as shown in Figure 23-11.

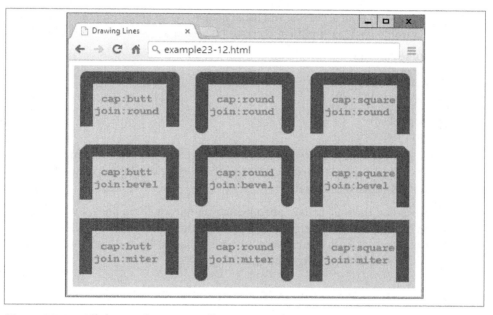

Figure 23-11. All the combinations of line caps and joins

As you can see, butted line caps are short, square ones are longer, and the round ones are somewhere between the two. At the same time, rounded line joins are curved, beveled ones are cut across the corner, and mitered ones have sharp corners. Line joins also apply to joins at angles other than 90 degrees.

The miterLimit Property

If you find that your mitered joins get cut off too short, you can extend them using the miterLimit property, like this:

```
context.miterLimit = 15
```

The default value is 10, so you can reduce the miter limit too. If `miterLimit` is not set to a sufficiently large enough value for a miter, then sharply mitered joins will simply bevel instead. So, if you are having trouble with your pointed miters, simply increase the value you supply for `miterLimit` until the miter displays.

Using Paths

The previous example made use of two methods to set up paths for the line drawing methods to follow. The `beginPath` method sets the start of a path, and `closePath` sets the end. Inside each path you can then use various methods for moving the location of drawing, and creating lines, curves, and other shapes. So let's examine the relevant section from Example 23-12, simplified to create just a single instance of the pattern:

```
context.beginPath()
context.moveTo(20, 100)
context.lineTo(20,  20)
context.lineTo(155, 20)
context.lineTo(155,100)
context.stroke()
context.closePath()
```

In this code snippet, a path is started in the first line, and then the drawing location is moved to a position 20 pixels across and 100 down from the top-left corner of the canvas, using a call to the `moveTo` method.

This is followed by three calls to `lineTo`, which then draw three lines, first upward to the location 20,20, then to the right to 155,20, and then down again to 155,100. Once this path has been set out, the `stroke` method is called to lay it down, and finally the path is closed because it's no longer needed.

It is essential to close paths as soon as you finish with them; otherwise, you can get some very unexpected results when using multiple paths.

The moveTo and LineTo Methods

The `moveTo` and `LineTo` methods both take simple *x* and *y* coordinates as their arguments, with the difference being that `MoveTo` picks up an imaginary pen from the current location and then moves it to a new one, while `LineTo` draws a line from the current location of the imaginary pen to the new one specified. Or, at least, a line will be drawn if the `stroke` method is called, but not otherwise. So let's just say that `LineTo` creates a *potential* drawn line, but it could equally be part of the outline for a fill area, for example.

The stroke Method

The stroke method has the job of actually drawing all the lines created so far in a path onto the canvas. If it is issued from inside an unclosed path, this has the effect of immediately drawing everything up to the most recent imaginary pen location.

However, if you close a path and then issue a call to stroke, it has the effect of also joining a path from the current location back to the start location, which in this example would turn the shapes into rectangles (which we don't want because we need to see the line caps as well as joins).

 This joining effect on closing a path is required (as you will see a little later) so that paths are properly closed before any fill methods are used on them; otherwise, they might overflow the bounds of the path.

The rect Method

Should it have been necessary to create four-sided rectangles instead of the three-sided shapes in the preceding example (and you didn't wish to close the path yet), another lineTo call could have been issued to join everything up, like this (highlighted in bold):

```
context.beginPath()
context.moveTo(20, 100)
context.lineTo(20, 20)
context.lineTo(155, 20)
context.lineTo(155, 100)
context.lineTo(20, 100)
context.closePath()
```

But there's a much simpler way to draw outlined rectangles, which is with the rect method, like this:

```
rect(20, 20, 155, 100)
```

In just a single call, this command takes two pairs of x and y coordinates and draws a rectangle with its top-left corner at location 20,20, and bottom-right corner at 155,100.

Filling Areas

Using paths, you can create complicated areas that can also be filled in with solid, gradient, or pattern fills. In Example 23-13, some basic trigonometry is used to create a complex star pattern. I won't detail how the math works because that's not important to the example (although if you want to play with the code, try changing the values assigned to points, and the scale1 and scale2 variables, for different effects).

All you really need to look at, however, are the lines highlighted in bold, in which a path is started, a pair of `lineTo` calls defines the shape, the path is closed, and then the `stroke` and `fill` methods are used to draw the shape outline in orange and fill it in with yellow (as shown in Figure 23-12).

Example 23-13. Filling in a complex path

```
<!DOCTYPE html>
<html>
  <head>
    <title>Drawing Lines</title>
    <script src='OSC.js'></script>
  </head>
  <body>
    <canvas id='mycanvas' width='320' height='320'></canvas>

    <script>
      canvas              = O('mycanvas')
      context             = canvas.getContext('2d')
      S(canvas).background = 'lightblue'
      context.strokeStyle = 'orange'
      context.fillStyle   = 'yellow'

      orig   = 160
      points = 21
      dist   = Math.PI / points * 2
      scale1 = 150
      scale2 = 80

      context.beginPath()

      for (j = 0 ; j < points ; ++j)
      {
        x = Math.sin(j * dist)
        y = Math.cos(j * dist)
        context.lineTo(orig + x * scale1, orig + y * scale1)
        context.lineTo(orig + x * scale2, orig + y * scale2)
      }

      context.closePath()
      context.stroke()
      context.fill()
    </script>
  </body>
</html>
```

Figure 23-12. Drawing and filling in a complex path

With paths it's possible to create as complex an object as you like, either using formulae or loops (as in this example), or simply with a long string of moveTo and/or LineTo or other calls.

The clip Method

Sometimes when you are building a path, you may want to ignore sections of the canvas (perhaps if you are drawing partly "behind" another object, and wish only the visible part to display. You can achieve this using the clip method, which creates a boundary outside of which stroke, fill, or other methods will not have any effect.

To illustrate this, Example 23-14 creates an effect similar to window blinds by moving the imaginary pen pointer to the lefthand edge, then drawing a lineTo over to the righthand edge, another down by 30 pixels, and then another back to the lefthand edge, and so on. This creates a sort of snaking pattern in which a series of 30-pixel-deep, horizontal bars are drawn on the canvas, as shown in Figure 23-13.

Example 23-14. Creating a clip area

```
context.beginPath()

for (j = 0 ; j < 10 ; ++j)
{
  context.moveTo(20,  j * 48)
  context.lineTo(620, j * 48)
  context.lineTo(620, j * 48 + 30)
  context.lineTo(20,  j * 48 + 30)
}

context.stroke()
context.closePath()
```

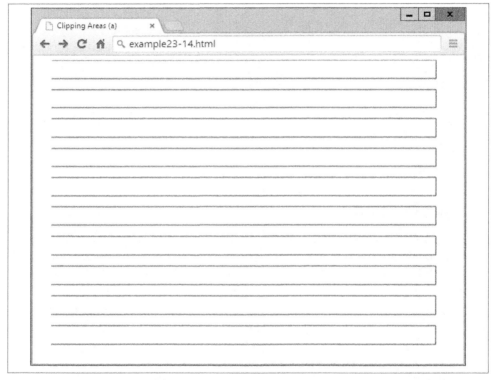

Figure 23-13. A path of horizontal bars

To turn this example into a clipped area of the canvas, you simply need to replace the call to stroke (highlighted in bold in the example) with one to clip, like this:

```
context.clip()
```

Now the outline of the bars won't be seen, but the clipping area will be in place. To illustrate this, Example 23-15 makes this method substitution and then adds to the previous example by drawing a simple picture on the canvas, of green grass below a blue sky containing a shining sun (modified from Example 23-12), with the changes highlighted in bold, and as shown in Figure 23-14.

Example 23-15. Drawing within the clipped area's bounds

```
context.fillStyle = 'white'
context.strokeRect(20, 20, 600, 440) // Black border
context.fillRect(  20, 20, 600, 440) // White background

context.beginPath()

for (j = 0 ; j < 10 ; ++j)
{
  context.moveTo(20,  j * 48)
  context.lineTo(620, j * 48)
  context.lineTo(620, j * 48 + 30)
  context.lineTo(20,  j * 48 + 30)
}

context.clip()
context.closePath()

context.fillStyle   = 'blue'          // Blue sky
context.fillRect(20, 20,  600, 320)
context.fillStyle   = 'green'         // Green grass
context.fillRect(20, 320, 600, 140)
context.strokeStyle = 'orange'
context.fillStyle   = 'yellow'

orig   = 170
points = 21
dist   = Math.PI / points * 2
scale1 = 130
scale2 = 80

context.beginPath()

for (j = 0 ; j < points ; ++j)
{
  x = Math.sin(j * dist)
  y = Math.cos(j * dist)
  context.lineTo(orig + x * scale1, orig + y * scale1)
  context.lineTo(orig + x * scale2, orig + y * scale2)
}

context.closePath()
context.stroke()                       // Sun outline
context.fill()                         // Sun fill
```

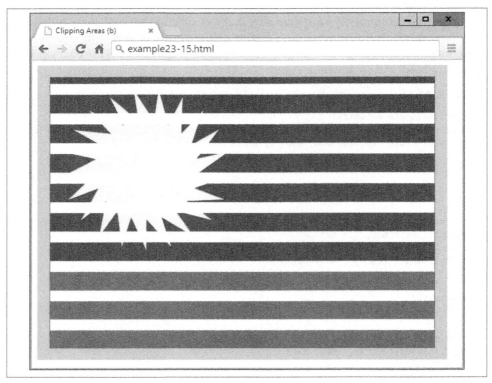

Figure 23-14. Drawing occurs only within the allowed clipped area

OK, we're not going to win any competitions here, but you can see how powerful clipping can be when used effectively.

The isPointInPath Method

Sometimes you need to know whether a particular point lies in a path you've constructed. However, you will probably only want to use this function if you're quite proficient with JavaScript and writing a fairly complex program—and will generally call it as part of a conditional `if` statement, like this:

```
if (context.isPointInPath(23, 87))
{
    // Do something here
}
```

If the location specified lies along any of the points in the path, the method returns the value `true`, so the contents of the `if` statement are executed. Otherwise, the value `false` is returned, and the contents of the `if` don't get executed.

A perfect use for the isPointInPath method is for creating games using the canvas in which you wish to check for a missile hitting a target, a ball hitting a wall or bat, or similar boundary conditions.

Working with Curves

In addition to straight paths, you can create an almost infinite variety of curved paths, with a selection of different methods, ranging from simple arcs and circles to complex quadratic and Bézier curves.

Actually, you don't need to use paths to create many lines, rectangles, and curves, because you can draw them directly by simply calling their methods. But using paths gives you more precise control, so I tend to almost always draw on the canvas within defined paths, as with the following examples.

The arc Method

The arc method requires you to pass it the *x* and *y* location of the center of the arc, and the radius in pixels. As well as these values, you need to pass a pair of radian offsets and an optional direction, like this:

```
context.arc(55, 85, 45, 0, Math.PI / 2, false)
```

Because the default direction is clockwise (a value of false), this can be omitted, or changed to true to draw the arc in a counterclockwise direction.

Example 23-16 creates three sets of four arcs, the first two of which draw in a clockwise direction, and the third of which draws counterclockwise. Additionally, the first set of four arcs has its paths closed before the stroke method is called, so the start and end points are joined up, whereas the other two sets of arcs are drawn before the path is closed, so they are not joined up.

Example 23-16. Drawing a variety of arcs

```
context.strokeStyle = 'blue'
arcs =
[
  Math.PI,
  Math.PI * 2,
  Math.PI / 2,
  Math.PI / 180 * 59
]

for (j = 0 ; j < 4 ; ++j)
{
  context.beginPath()
  context.arc(80 + j * 160, 80, 70, 0, arcs[j])
```

```
    context.closePath()
    context.stroke()
}

context.strokeStyle = 'red'

for (j = 0 ; j < 4 ; ++j)
{
  context.beginPath()
  context.arc(80 + j * 160, 240, 70, 0, arcs[j])
  context.stroke()
  context.closePath()
}

context.strokeStyle = 'green'

for (j = 0 ; j < 4 ; ++j)
{
  context.beginPath()
  context.arc(80 + j * 160, 400, 70, 0, arcs[j], true)
  context.stroke()
  context.closePath()
}
```

To create shorter code, I drew all the arcs using loops, so that the length of each arc is stored in the array arcs. These values are in radians, and because a radian is equivalent to $180 \div \pi$ (π being the ratio of a circle's circumference to its diameter, or approximately 3.1415927), they evaluate as follows:

Math.PI
> Equivalent to 180 degrees

Math.PI * 2
> Equivalent to 360 degrees

Math.PI / 2
> Equivalent to 90 degrees

Math.PI / 180 * 59
> Equivalent to 59 degrees

Figure 23-15 shows the three rows of arcs and illustrates both the use of the direction argument true in the final set, and the importance of carefully choosing where you close paths depending on whether you want to draw a line connecting the start and end points.

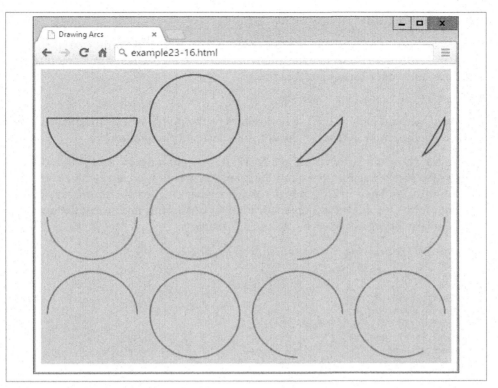

Figure 23-15. A variety of arc types

If you prefer to work with degrees instead of radians, you could create a new `Math` library function, like this:

```
Math.degreesToRadians = function(degrees)
{
  return degrees * Math.PI / 180
}
```

And then replace the array-creating code, starting at the second line of Example 23-16, with the following:

```
arcs =
[
  Math.degreesToRadians(180),
  Math.degreesToRadians(360),
  Math.degreesToRadians(90),
  Math.degreesToRadians(59)
]
```

The arcTo Method

Rather than creating a whole arc at once, you can choose to arc from the current location in the path to another one, like the following call to arcTo (which simply requires two pairs of x and y coordinates and a radius):

```
context.arcTo(100, 100, 200, 200, 100)
```

The locations you pass to the method represent the points where imaginary tangent lines touch the circumference of the arc at its start and end points.

To illustrate how this works, Example 23-17 draws eight different arcs with radii from 0 up to 280 pixels. Each time around the loop, a new path is created with a start point at location 20,20. Then an arc is drawn using imaginary tangent lines from that location to position 240,20, and from there to location 460,20. In this instance, it defines a pair of tangents at 90 degrees to each other, in a V shape.

Example 23-17. Drawing eight arcs of different radii

```
for (j = 0 ; j <= 280 ; j += 40)
{
  context.beginPath()
  context.moveTo(20, 20)
  context.arcTo(240, 240, 460, 20, j)
  context.lineTo(460, 20)
  context.stroke()
  context.closePath()
}
```

The arcTo method draws only up to the point at which the arc touches the second imaginary tangent. So, after each call to arcTo, the lineTo method creates the remainder of the line from wherever arcTo left off to location 460,20. Then the result is drawn to the canvas with a call to stroke, and the path is closed.

As you can see in Figure 23-16, when arcTo is called with a radius value of 0 it creates a sharp join. In this case, it's a right angle (but if the two imaginary tangents are at other angles to each other, then the join will be at that angle). Then, as the radius increases in size, you can see the arcs getting larger and larger.

Essentially, what you can best use arcTo for is to curve from one section of drawing to another, following an arc based on the previous and subsequent positions, as if they were tangential to the arc to be created. If this sounds complicated, don't worry: you'll soon get the hang of it and find it's actually a handy and logical way to draw arcs.

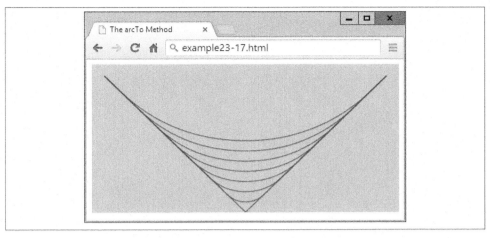

Figure 23-16. Drawing arcs of different radii

The quadraticCurveTo Method

Useful as arcs are, they are only one type of curve and can be limiting for more complex designs. But have no fear: there are still more ways to draw curves—for example, by using the quadraticCurveTo method. With this method, you can place an imaginary attractor near (or far from) a curve to pull it in that direction, in a similar way to the path of an object in space being pulled by the gravity of the planets and stars it passes. Unlike with gravity, though, the farther away the attractor is, the *more* it pulls!

In Example 23-18, there are six calls to this method, creating the path for a fluffy cloud, which is then filled in white. Figure 23-17 illustrates how the angles of the dashed line outside the cloud represent the attractor points applied to each curve.

Example 23-18. Drawing a cloud with quadratic curves

```
context.beginPath()
context.moveTo(180, 60)
context.quadraticCurveTo(240,   0, 300,  60)
context.quadraticCurveTo(460,  30, 420, 100)
context.quadraticCurveTo(480, 210, 340, 170)
context.quadraticCurveTo(240, 240, 200, 170)
context.quadraticCurveTo(100, 200, 140, 130)
context.quadraticCurveTo( 40,  40, 180,  60)
context.fillStyle = 'white'
context.fill()
context.closePath()
```

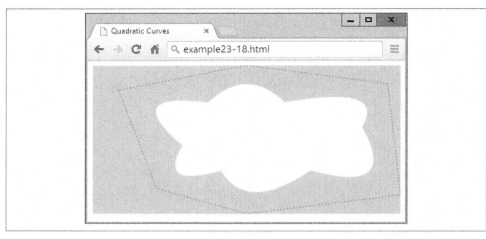

Figure 23-17. Drawing with quadratic curves

Incidentally, to achieve the dotted line around the cloud in this image I used the `stroke` method in conjunction with the `setLineDash` method, which takes a list representing the dash and space lengths. In this instance, I used `setLineDash([2, 3])`, but you can create dash lines as complicated as you like, such as `setLineDash([1, 2, 1, 3, 5, 1, 2, 4])`. However, I haven't documented this feature because it's been implemented only in IE, Opera, and Chrome so far. Fingers crossed that it'll be added to the other browsers soon, though, as it will be a great enhancement for creating contours and boundaries for mapping purposes, for example.

The bezierCurveTo Method

If you still don't find quadratic curves flexible enough for your needs, how about having access to two attractors for each curve? Using this method, you can do just that, as in Example 23-19, where a curve is created between location 24,20 and 240,220, but with invisible attractors off the canvas (in this case) at locations 720,480 and −240,−240. Figure 23-18 shows how this curve gets warped.

Example 23-19. Creating a Bézier curve with two attractors

```
context.beginPath()
context.moveTo(240, 20)
context.bezierCurveTo(720, 480, -240, -240, 240, 220)
context.stroke()
context.closePath()
```

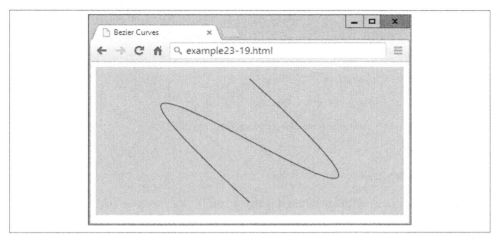

Figure 23-18. A Bézier curve with two attractors

Attractors do not need to be at opposite sides of a canvas, because you can place them anywhere, and when they are near each other, they will exert a combined pull (rather than opposing pulls, as in the preceding example). Using these various types of curve methods, it's possible for you to draw every type of curve you could ever need.

Manipulating Images

Not only can you draw and write on the canvas with graphical methods, you can also place images on or extract them from a canvas. And you're not limited to simple copy and paste commands, because you can stretch and distort images when reading or writing them, and also have full control over compositing and shadow effects.

The drawImage Method

Using the drawImage method, you can take an image object that was loaded from a website, uploaded to a server, or even extracted from a canvas, and draw it onto a canvas. The method supports a wide variety of arguments, many of which are optional, but at its simplest you call drawImage as follows, in which just the image and a pair of x and y coordinates are passed:

```
context.drawImage(myimage, 20, 20)
```

This command draws the image contained in the myimage object onto the canvas with the context of context, with its top-left corner at location 20,20.

To ensure that an image has been loaded before you use it, best practice is to enclose your image-handling code within a function that is triggered only upon image load, like this:

```
myimage     = new Image()
myimage.src = 'image.gif'

myimage.onload = function()
{
  context.drawImage(myimage, 20, 20)
}
```

Resizing an Image

If you need to resize an image when it is placed on the canvas, you add a second pair of arguments to the call representing the width and height you require, like this (highlighted in bold):

```
context.drawImage(myimage, 140,  20, 220, 220)
context.drawImage(myimage, 380,  20,  80, 220)
```

Here the image is placed at two locations: the first is at 140,20, where the image is enlarged (from a 100-pixel square to a 220-pixel square), while the second goes to location 380,20 with the image being squashed horizontally and expanded vertically, to a width and height of 80×220 pixels.

Selecting an Image Area

You're not stuck having to use an entire image; it's also possible to choose an area within an image when using drawImage. This can be handy, for example, if you wish to place all the graphical images you intend to use in a single image file, and then just grab the sections of the image that you need. This is a trick developers often use to speed up page loading and decrease server hits.

It's a little trickier to do this, though, because rather than add more arguments at the end of the list for this method, when extracting a portion of an image you must place those arguments first.

So, for example, to place an image at location 20,140, you might issue this command:

```
context.drawImage(myimage, 20, 140)
```

And to give it a width and height of 100×100 pixels, you would modify the call like this (highlighted in bold):

```
context.drawImage(myimage, 20, 140, 100, 100)
```

But, for example, to grab (or crop) just a 40×40-pixel subsection with its top-left corner at location 30,30 of the image, you would call the method like this (with the new arguments in bold):

```
context.drawImage(myimage, 30, 30, 40, 40, 20, 140)
```

And to resize the grabbed portion to 100 pixels square, you would use the following:

```
context.drawImage(myimage, 30, 30, 40, 40, 20, 140, 100, 100)
```

 I find this very confusing and cannot think of a logical reason for why this method works this way. But, because it does, I'm afraid there's nothing you can do other than force yourself to remember which arguments go where under which conditions.

Example 23-20 uses a variety of calls to the drawImage method to obtain the result shown in Figure 23-19. To make things clearer, I have spaced out the arguments so that values in each column provide the same information.

Example 23-20. Various ways of drawing an image on the canvas

```
myimage     = new Image()
myimage.src = 'image.png'

myimage.onload = function()
{
  context.drawImage(myimage,                   20,  20           )
  context.drawImage(myimage,                  140,  20, 220, 220)
  context.drawImage(myimage,                  380,  20,  80, 220)
  context.drawImage(myimage, 30, 30, 40, 40,  20, 140, 100, 100)
}
```

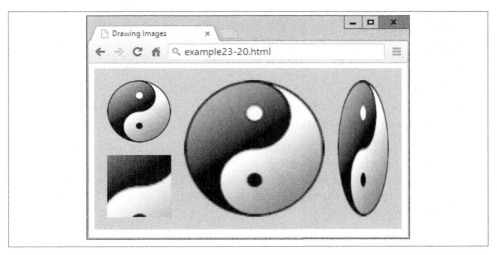

Figure 23-19. Drawing images to a canvas with resizing and cropping

Copying from a Canvas

You can also use a canvas as a source image for drawing to the same (or another) canvas. Just supply the canvas object name in place of an image object, and use all the remaining arguments in the same way as you would with an image.

 At this point, I would have loved to show you how to use a `<video>` element (explained in the following chapter) as an image source for drawing on the canvas. But sadly, Internet Explorer doesn't yet support this functionality, so it's still too early to recommend the exciting features you can create this way—such as live video manipulation, colorization, embossing, and much more. However, if you're curious, you can learn more about how you can combine video with the canvas at *http://html5doctor.com/video-canvas-magic*.

Adding Shadows

When you draw an image (or image section) or, indeed, anything else on the canvas, you can also specify a shadow that should be placed under it by setting one or more of the following properties:

shadowOffsetX
> The horizontal offset, in pixels, by which the shadow should be shifted to the right (or to the left if the value is negative).

shadowOffsetY
> The vertical offset, in pixels, by which the shadow should be shifted down (or up if the value is negative).

shadowBlur
> The number of pixels over which to blur the shadow's outline.

shadowColor
> The base color to use for the shadow. If a blur is in use, this color will blend with the background in the blurred area.

These properties can apply to text and lines as well as solid images, as in Example 23-21, in which some text, an image, and an object created using a path all have shadows added to them. In Figure 23-20, you can see the shadows intelligently flow around the visible portions of images, not just their rectangular boundaries.

Example 23-21. Applying shadows when drawing on the canvas

```
myimage      = new Image()
myimage.src = 'apple.png'

orig   = 95
points = 21
dist   = Math.PI / points * 2
scale1 = 75
scale2 = 50

myimage.onload = function()
{
  context.beginPath()

  for (j = 0 ; j < points ; ++j)
  {
    x = Math.sin(j * dist)
    y = Math.cos(j * dist)
    context.lineTo(orig + x * scale1, orig + y * scale1)
    context.lineTo(orig + x * scale2, orig + y * scale2)
  }

  context.closePath()

  context.shadowOffsetX = 5
  context.shadowOffsetY = 5
  context.shadowBlur    = 6
  context.shadowColor   = '#444'
  context.fillStyle     = 'red'
  context.stroke()
  context.fill()

  context.shadowOffsetX = 2
  context.shadowOffsetY = 2
  context.shadowBlur    = 3
  context.shadowColor   = 'yellow'
  context.font          = 'bold 36pt Times'
  context.textBaseline  = 'top'
  context.fillStyle     = 'green'
  context.fillText('Sale now on!', 200, 5)

  context.shadowOffsetX = 3
  context.shadowOffsetY = 3
  context.shadowBlur    = 5
  context.shadowColor   = 'black'
  context.drawImage(myimage, 245, 45)
}
```

Figure 23-20. Shadows under different types of drawing objects

Editing at the Pixel Level

Not only does the HTML5 canvas provide you with a powerful range of drawing methods, it also lets you get your hands dirty and work under the hood directly at the pixel level with a trio of powerful methods.

The getImageData Method

With the `getImageData` method, you can grab a portion (or all) of a canvas so that you can alter the retrieved data in any way you like, and then save it back or elsewhere in the canvas (or to another canvas).

To illustrate how this works, Example 23-22 first loads in a ready-made image and draws it onto a canvas. Then the canvas data is read back into an object called `idata`, where all the colors are averaged together to change each pixel to greyscale, and then tweaked a little to shift each color toward sepia, as shown in Figure 23-21.

Example 23-22. Manipulating image data

```
myimage       = new Image()
myimage.src = 'photo.jpg'

myimage.onload = function()
{
  context.drawImage(myimage, 0, 0)
  idata = context.getImageData(0, 0, myimage.width, myimage.height)

  for (y = 0 ; y < myimage.height ; ++y)
  {
    pos = y * myimage.width * 4

    for (x = 0 ; x < myimage.width ; ++x)
```

```
    {
      average =
      (
        idata.data[pos]     +
        idata.data[pos + 1] +
        idata.data[pos + 2]
      ) / 3

      idata.data[pos]     = average + 50
      idata.data[pos + 1] = average
      idata.data[pos + 2] = average - 50
      pos += 4;
    }
  }
  context.putImageData(idata, 320, 0)
}
```

Figure 23-21. Converting an image to sepia

The data Array

This image manipulation works thanks to the `data` array, which is a property of the `idata` object returned by the call to `getImageData`. This method returns an array containing all the picture pixel data in its component parts of red, green, blue, and alpha transparency. Therefore, four items of data are used to store each colored pixel.

All the data is stored sequentially in the data array, such that the value for red is followed by that for blue, then green, and then alpha; then, the next item in the array is the red value for the following pixel, and so on, like the following (for the pixel at location 0,0):

```
idata.data[0] // Red level
idata.data[1] // Green level
idata.data[2] // Blue level
idata.data[3] // Alpha level
```

Location 1,0 then follows, like this:

```
idata.data[4] // Red level
idata.data[5] // Green level
idata.data[6] // Blue level
idata.data[7] // Alpha level
```

In this image, everything continues in the same fashion until the rightmost pixel of the image in row 0 (which is the 320th pixel, at location 319,0) is reached. At that point, the value 319 is multiplied by 4 (the number of items of data in each pixel) to arrive at the following array elements, which contain this pixel's data:

```
idata.data[1276] // Red level
idata.data[1277] // Green level
idata.data[1278] // Blue level
idata.data[1279] // Alpha level
```

Then the data pointer moves all the way back to the first column of the image, but this time of row 1, at location 0,1 which (because each row in this image is 320 pixels wide), is at an offset of $(0 \times 4) + (1 \times 320 \times 4)$, or 1,280:

```
idata.data[1280] // Red level
idata.data[1281] // Green level
idata.data[1282] // Blue level
idata.data[1283] // Alpha level
```

So, if the image data is stored in `idata`, the image width in `w`, and the pixel location to access in `x` and `y`, the key formulae to use when directly accessing image data is:

```
red   = idata.data[x * 4 + y * w * 4    ]
green = idata.data[x * 4 + y * w * 4 + 1]
blue  = idata.data[x * 4 + y * w * 4 + 2]
alpha = idata.data[x * 4 + y * w * 4 + 3]
```

Using this knowledge, we create the sepia effect in Figure 32-12 by taking just the red, blue, and green components of each pixel and averaging them, like this (where `pos` is a variable pointer to the location in the array of the current pixel):

```
average =
(
  idata.data[pos]     +
  idata.data[pos + 1] +
  idata.data[pos + 2]
) / 3
```

With `average` now containing the average color value (which we attain by adding all the pixel values and dividing by three), this value is written back to all colors of the pixel, but with the red boosted by a value of 50, and the blue reduced by the same amount:

```
idata.data[pos]     = average + 50
idata.data[pos + 1] = average
idata.data[pos + 2] = average - 50
```

The result is to increase the red and reduce the blue level of each pixel (of what would otherwise now become a monochrome image, if only the average value were written back to these colors), giving it a sepia cast.

If you'd like to perform more advanced image manipulations, you may wish to refer to the following (third-party) web pages, which cover using convolution on an HTML5 canvas in detail:

- *http://tinyurl.com/convolut1*
- *http://tinyurl.com/convolut2*

The putImageData Method

When you've modified the image data array to your requirements, all you need to do to write it to the canvas is call the `putImageData` method, passing it the `idata` object and the coordinates of the top-left corner at which it should appear—as in the previous example, and as follows, which (in this case) places the modified copy of the image to the right of the original:

```
context.putImageData(idata, 320, 0)
```

If you wish to modify only part of a canvas, you don't have to grab the entire canvas; just fetch a section containing the area in which you are interested. And neither do you have to write back image data to the location from where you got it; image data can be written to any part of a canvas.

The createImageData Method

You don't have to create an object directly from a canvas; you can also create a new one with blank data by calling the `createImageData` method. The following example creates an object with a width of 320 and height of 240 pixels:

```
idata = createImageData(320, 240)
```

Alternatively, you can create a new object from an existing object, like this:

```
newimagedataobject = createImageData(imagedata)
```

It's then up to you what you do with these objects to add pixel data to them or otherwise modify them, how you paste them onto the canvas or create other objects from them, and so on.

Advanced Graphical Effects

Among the more advanced features available on the HTML5 canvas are the ability to assign various compositing and transparency effects, as well as to apply powerful transformations such as scaling, stretching, and rotating.

The globalCompositeOperation Property

There are 12 different methods available to fine-tune the way you place an object on the canvas, taking into account existing and future objects. These are called *compositing* options, and they are applied like this:

```
context.globalCompositeOperationProperty = 'source-over'
```

The compositing types are as follows:

source-over
: The default. The source image is copied over the destination image.

source-in
: Only parts of the source image that will appear within the destination are shown, and the destination image is removed. Any alpha transparency in the source image causes the destination under it to be removed.

source-out
: Only parts of the source image that do not appear within the destination are shown, and the destination image is removed. Any alpha transparency in the source image causes the destination under it to be removed.

source-atop
: The source image is displayed where it overlays the destination. The destination image is displayed where the destination image is opaque and the source image is transparent. Other regions are transparent.

destination-over
: The source image is drawn under the destination image.

destination-in
: The destination image displays where the source and destination image overlap, but not in any areas of source image transparency. The source image does not display.

destination-out
: Only those parts of the destination outside of the source image's nontransparent sections are shown. The source image does not display.

destination-atop

> The source image displays where the destination is not displayed. Where the destination and source overlap, the destination image is displayed. Any transparency in the source image prevents that area of the destination image being shown.

lighter

> The sum of the source and destination is applied such that where they do not overlap, they display as normal; where they do overlap, the sum of both images is shown, but lightened.

darker

> The sum of the source and destination is applied such that where they do not overlap, they display as normal; where they do overlap, the sum of both images is shown, but darkened.

copy

> The source image is copied over the destination. Any transparent area of the source causes any destination that it overlaps to not display.

xor

> Where the source and destination images do not overlap, they display as normal. Where they do overlap, their color values are exclusive-ored.

Example 23-23 illustrates the effect of all of these compositing types by creating 12 different canvases, each with two objects (a filled circle and the yin-yang image) offset from each other but overlapping.

Example 23-23. Using all 12 types of compositing effects

```
image     = new Image()
image.src = 'image.png'

image.onload = function()
{
  types =
  [
    'source-over',     'source-in',         'source-out',
    'source-atop',     'destination-over',  'destination-in',
    'destination-out', 'destination-atop',  'lighter',
    'darker',          'copy',              'xor'
  ]

  for (j = 0 ; j < 12 ; ++j)
  {
    canvas                 = O('c' + (j + 1))
    context                = canvas.getContext('2d')
    S(canvas).background    = 'lightblue'
    context.fillStyle       = 'red'

    context.arc(50, 50, 50, 0, Math.PI * 2, false)
```

```
        context.fill()
        context.globalCompositeOperation = types[j]
        context.drawImage(image, 20, 20, 100, 100)
    }
}
```

As with some others in this chapter, this example (downloadable from the companion website) includes some HTML and/or CSS to enhance the display, which isn't shown here because it's not essential to the program's operation.

This program uses a for loop to iterate through each compositing type, as stored in the array types. Each time around the loop, a new context is created on the next of the 12 canvas elements already created in some earlier HTML (not shown), with the IDs of c1 through c12.

In each canvas a 100-pixel-diameter red circle is first placed at the top left, and then the compositing type is selected and the yin-yang image is placed over the circle but offset to the right and down by 20 pixels. Figure 23-22 shows the results of each compositing type in action. As you can see, it's possible to achieve a very wide variety of effects.

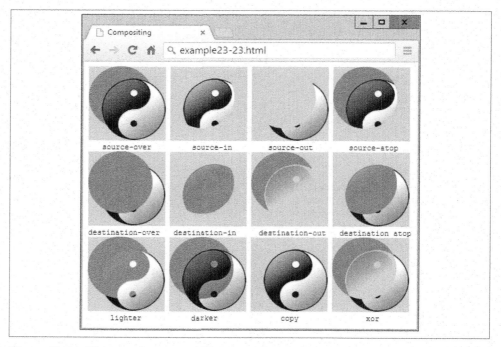

Figure 23-22. The 12 compositing effects in action

The globalAlpha Property

When drawing on the canvas, you can specify the amount of transparency to apply using the globalAlpha property, which supports values from 0 (fully transparent) to 1 (fully opaque). The following command sets the alpha to a value of 0.9, such that future draw operations will be 90% opaque (or 10% transparent):

```
context.globalAlpha = 0.9
```

This property can be used with all other properties, including the compositing options.

Transformations

The canvas supports four functions for applying transformations to elements when drawing them to the HTML5 canvas: scale, rotate, translate, and transform. They can be used alone, or together to produce even more interesting effects.

The scale Method

You can scale future drawing operations by first calling the scale method, supplying horizontal and vertical scaling factors, which can be negative, zero, or positive values.

In Example 23-24, the yin-yang image is drawn to the canvas at its original size of 100×100 pixels. Then scaling of 3 times horizontally and 2 times vertically is applied, and the drawImage function is called again to place the stretched image next to the original. Finally, scaling is reapplied with values of 0.33 and 0.5 to restore everything back to normal, and the image is once more drawn, this time below the original. Figure 23-23 shows the result.

Example 23-24. Scaling up and down in size

```
context.drawImage(myimage, 0, 0)
context.scale(3, 2)
context.drawImage(myimage, 40, 0)
context.scale(.33, .5)
context.drawImage(myimage, 0, 100)
```

If you look carefully, you may notice that the copy image under the original is a little bit fuzzy due to the scaling up and then down.

 If you use negative values for one or more scaling parameters, you can reverse an element in either the horizontal or vertical direction (or both), at the same time as (or instead of) scaling. For example, the following flips the context to create a mirror image:

```
context.scale(-1, 1)
```

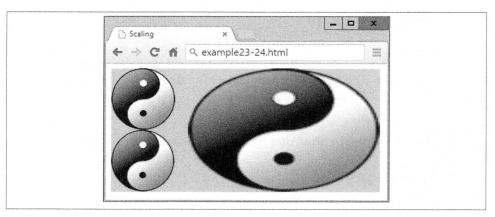

Figure 23-23. Scaling an image up and then down again

The save and restore Methods

If you need to use several scaling operations on different drawing elements, not only can you introduce fuzziness into the results, but it can be very time-consuming to calculate that a three times upward scaling requires a 0.33 value to scale back down again (and a two times upscale requires a value of 0.5 to reverse).

For this reason, you can call save to save the current context before issuing a scale call, and later return scaling back to normal by issuing a restore call. Check out the following, which can replace the code in Example 23-24:

```
context.drawImage(myimage, 0, 0)
context.save()
context.scale(3, 2)
context.drawImage(myimage, 40, 0)
context.restore()
context.drawImage(myimage, 0, 100)
```

The save and restore methods are very powerful because they don't just apply to image scaling. In fact, they apply across all the following properties, and can therefore be used at any time to save the current properties, and then restore them later: fillStyle, font, globalAlpha, globalCompositeOperation, lineCap, lineJoin, lineWidth, miterLi mit, shadowBlur, shadowColor, shadowOffsetX, shadowOffsetY, strokeStyle, textA lign, and textBaseline. The properties of the following methods are also managed by save and restore: scale, rotate, translate, and transform.

The rotate Method

Using the rotate method, you can choose the angle at which to apply an object (or any of the drawing methods) to the canvas, specified in radians, which are the same as 180 / π, or about 57 degrees, each.

Rotation takes place around the canvas origin, which, by default, is its top-left corner (but as you'll see shortly, this can be changed). Example 23-25 displays the yin-yang image four times, rotating each consecutive image by `Math.PI / 25` radians.

Example 23-25. Rotating an image

```
for (j = 0 ; j < 4 ; ++j)
{
  context.drawImage(myimage, 20 + j * 120 , 20)
  context.rotate(Math.PI / 25)
}
```

As you can see in Figure 23-24, the result may not be quite what you expect, because the image hasn't been rotated about itself. Rather, the rotations have taken place around the canvas origin at location 0,0. What's more, each new rotation has compounded the previous one. However, to correct for these things you can use the `translate` method in conjunction with the `save` and `restore` methods.

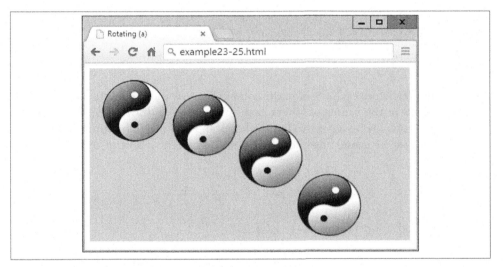

Figure 23-24. An image at four different rotations

 Radians are a sensible unit of measurement because there are $\pi \times 2$ radians in a complete circle. So π radians is a half circle, $\pi \div 2$ radians is a quarter circle, and $\pi \div 2 \times 3$ (or $\pi \times 1.5$) radians is three-quarters of a circle, and so on. To save having to remember the value of π, you can always refer to the value in `Math.PI`.

The translate Method

To change the origin of a rotation, you can call the `translate` method to shift it to somewhere else, which can be anywhere inside (or outside) the canvas or, more usually, somewhere within the destination location of the object (usually its center).

Example 23-26 performs this translation prior to each call to `rotate`, now resulting in the effect that was probably intended. Additionally, the `save` and `restore` methods are called before and after each operation to ensure that each rotation is applied independently, not compounded on the previous one.

Example 23-26. Rotating objects in place

```
w = myimage.width
h = myimage.height

for (j = 0 ; j < 4 ; ++j)
{
  context.save()
  context.translate(20 + w / 2 + j * (w + 20), 20 + h / 2)
  context.rotate(Math.PI / 5 * j)
  context.drawImage(myimage, -(w / 2), -(h / 2))
  context.restore()
}
```

In this example, before each rotation the context is saved and the origin is translated to a point exactly in the center of where each image will be drawn. We then issue the rotation and draw the image up and to the left of the new origin by supplying negative values, such that its center matches the origin point. The result of this is shown in Figure 23-25.

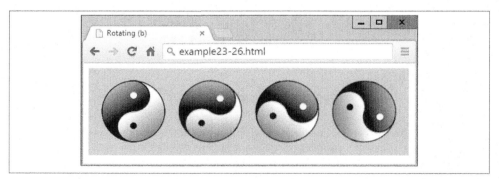

Figure 23-25. Rotating images in place

To recap: when you wish to rotate or transform (described next) an object in place, you should perform the following actions:

1. Save the context.
2. Translate the canvas origin to the center of where the object is to be placed.
3. Issue the rotation or transformation instruction.
4. Draw the object with any of the drawing methods supported, using a negative destination location point half the object's width to the left, and half its height upward.
5. Restore the context to revert the origin.

The transform Method

When you've exhausted all the other canvas features and still can't manipulate objects in just the way you need, it's time to turn to the transform method. With it you can apply a transformation matrix to the objects you draw to the canvas, giving you a multitude of possibilities, and powerful features that can combine scaling and rotating in a single instruction.

The transformation matrix used by this method is a 3×3 matrix of nine values, but only six of these are supplied externally to the transform method. So, rather than explain how this matrix multiplication works, I only need to explain the effects of its six arguments, which, in order, are:

1. Horizontal scale
2. Horizontal skew
3. Vertical skew
4. Vertical scale
5. Horizontal translate
6. Vertical translate

You can apply these values in many ways—for example, by emulating the scale method from Example 23-24 by replacing this call:

```
context.scale(3, 2)
```

with the following:

```
context.transform(3, 0, 0, 2, 0, 0)
```

Or, in the same way, you can replace this call from Example 23-26:

```
context.translate(20 + w / 2 + j * (w + 20), 20 + h / 2)
```

with the following:

```
context.transform(1, 0, 0, 1, 20 + w / 2 + j * (w + 20), 20 + h / 2)
```

Note how the horizontal and vertical scaling arguments are given values of 1 to ensure a 1:1 result, while the skew values are 0 to prevent the result from being skewed.

You could even combine the previous two lines of code to get a translation and scale at the same time, like this:

```
context.transform(3, 0, 0, 2, 20 + w / 2 + j * (w + 20), 20 + h / 2)
```

As you look at the skew arguments, as you might expect they result in an element being skewed in the direction specified (e.g., creating a rhombus from a square).

For example, Example 23-27 draws the yin-yang image on the canvas, followed by a skewed copy created with the transform method. The skew value can be any negative, zero, or positive amount, but I chose a horizontal value of 1, which has skewed the bottom of the image by one image width to the right, and pulled everything else along with it proportionally (see Figure 23-26).

Example 23-27. Creating an original and skewed image

```
context.drawImage(myimage, 20, 20)
context.transform(1, 0, 1, 1, 0, 0)
context.drawImage(myimage, 140, 20)
```

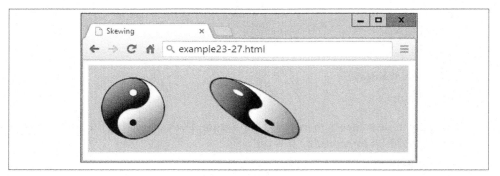

Figure 23-26. Horizontally skewing an object to the right

 You can even rotate an object with transform by supplying one negative and one opposite positive skew value. But beware: when you do this you'll modify the size of an element, and will therefore also need to adjust the scale arguments at the same time. Plus, you'll need to remember to translate the origin. Thus, I recommend sticking with the rotate method for this until you are fully experienced with using transform.

The setTransform Method

As an alternative to using the `save` and `restore` methods, you can set an absolute transform, which has the effect of resetting the transformation matrix and then applying the supplied values. Use the `setTransform` method just like `transform`, as in this example (which applies a horizontal positive skew with the value 1):

```
context.setTransform(1, 0, 1, 1, 0, 0)
```

 To learn more about transformation matrixes, see the comprehensive Wikipedia article on the subject (*http://wikipedia.org/wiki/Trans formation_matrix*).

Summary

As of writing, the HTML5 standard is still not 100% applied across all major browsers but, thankfully, most of the canvas functionality is. And even though there's more to come, such as 3D contexts, the HTML5 canvas already represents a tremendous new asset for web developers to continue making bigger, better, and more professional and compelling websites. In the following chapter, we'll take a look at two other major new enhancements to HTML: in-browser, plug-in-free audio and video.

Questions

1. How do you create a canvas element in HTML?
2. How do you give JavaScript access to a canvas element?
3. How do you start and finish the creation of a canvas path?
4. What method can you use to extract data from a canvas into an image?
5. How can you create gradient fills of more than two colors?
6. How can you adjust the width of lines when drawing?
7. Which method would you use to specify a section of a camera such that future drawing takes place only within that area?
8. How can you draw a complex curve with two imaginary attractors?
9. How many items of data per pixel are returned by the `getImageData` method?
10. Which two parameters to the `transform` method apply to scaling operations?

See "Chapter 23 Answers" on page 655 in Appendix A for the answers to these questions.

HTML5 Audio and Video

One of the biggest driving forces behind the growth of the Internet has been the insatiable demand from users for ever more multimedia in the form of audio and video. Initially, bandwidth was so precious that there was no such thing as live streaming, and it could take minutes or even hours to download an audio track, let alone a video.

The high cost of bandwidth and limited availability of fast modems drove the development of faster and more efficient compression algorithms, such MP3 audio and MPEG video, but even then the only way to download files in any reasonable length of time was to drastically reduce their quality.

One of my earlier Internet projects, back in 1997, was the UK's first online radio station licensed by the music authorities. Actually, it was more of a podcast (before the term was coined) because we made a daily half-hour show and then compressed it down to 8-bit, 11KHz mono using an algorithm originally developed for telephony, and it sounded like phone quality, or worse. Still, we quickly gained thousands of listeners who would download the show and then listen to it as they surfed to the sites discussed in it by means of a pop-up browser window containing a plug-in.

Thankfully for us, and everyone publishing multimedia, it soon became possible to offer greater audio and video quality, but still only by asking the user to download and install a plug-in player. Flash became the most popular of these players, after beating rivals such as RealAudio, but it gained a bad reputation as the cause of many a browser crash, and constantly required upgrading when new versions were released.

So it was generally agreed that the way ahead was to come up with some web standards for supporting multimedia directly within the browser. Of course, browser developers such as Microsoft and Google had differing visions of what these standards should look like, but after the dust had settled they had agreed on a subset of file types that all browsers should play natively, and these were introduced into the HTML5 specification.

Finally, it is now possible (as long as you encode your audio and video in a few different formats) to upload multimedia to a web server, place a couple of HTML tags in a web page, and have the media play on any major desktop browser, smartphone, or tablet device, without the user ever having to download a plug-in or make any other changes.

 There are still a lot of older browsers out there, so Flash remains important for supporting them. In this chapter, I show you how to add code to use Flash as a backup to HTML5 audio and video, to cover as many hardware and software combinations as possible.

About Codecs

The term *codec* stands for en*co*der/*dec*oder. It describes the functionality provided by software that encodes and decodes media such as audio and video. In HTML5 there are a number of different sets of codecs available, depending on the browser used.

Following are the codecs supported by the HTML5 `<audio>` tag (and also when audio is attached to HTML5 video):

AAC
> This audio codec, which stands for Advanced Audio Encoding, is the one used by Apple's iTunes store, and is a proprietary patented technology supported by Apple, Google, and Microsoft. It generally uses the *.aac* file extension. Its MIME type is `audio/aac`.

MP3
> This audio codec, which stands for MPEG Audio Layer 3, has been available for many years. While the term is often (incorrectly) used to refer to any type of digital audio, it is a proprietary patented technology that is supported by Apple, Google, Mozilla Firefox, and Microsoft. The file extension it uses is *.mp3*. Its MIME type is `audio/mpeg`.

PCM
> This audio codec, which stands for Pulse Coded Modulation, stores the full data as encoded by an analog-to-digital convertor, and is the format used for storing data on audio CDs. Because it does not use compression, it is called a *lossless* codec and its files are generally many times larger than AAC or MP3 files. It is supported by Apple, Mozilla Firefox, and Opera. Usually this type of file has the extension *.wav*. Its MIME type is `audio/wav`, but you may also see `audio/wave`.

Vorbis
> Sometimes referred to as Ogg Vorbis—because it generally uses the *.ogg* file extension—this audio codec is unencumbered by patents and free of royalty payments.

It is supported by Google Chrome, Mozilla Firefox, and Opera. Its MIME type is `audio/ogg`, or sometimes `audio/oga`.

The following list summarizes the major operating systems and browsers, along with the audio types their latest versions support:

- **Apple iOS:** AAC, MP3, PCM
- **Apple Safari:** AAC, MP3, PCM
- **Google Android:** 2.3+ AAC, MP3, Vorbis
- **Google Chrome:** AAC, MP3, Vorbis
- **Microsoft Internet Explorer:** AAC, MP3
- **Mozilla Firefox:** MP3, PCM, Vorbis
- **Opera:** PCM, Vorbis

The outcome of these different levels of codec support is that you always need at least two versions of each audio file to ensure it will play on all platforms. One of these should be Vorbis to support Opera, but for the second you have a choice of either AAC or MP3.

The <audio> Element

To cater to all platforms, you need to record or convert your content using multiple codecs and then list them all within <audio> and </audio> tags, as in Example 24-1. The nested <source> tags then contain the various media you wish to offer to a browser. Because the `controls` attribute is supplied, the result looks like Figure 24-1.

Example 24-1. Embedding three different types of audio files

```
<audio controls>
  <source src='audio.m4a' type='audio/aac'>
  <source src='audio.mp3' type='audio/mp3'>
  <source src='audio.ogg' type='audio/ogg'>
</audio>
```

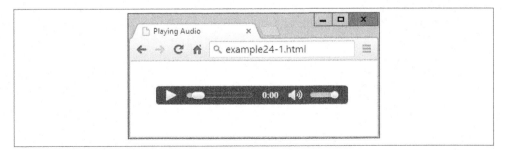

Figure 24-1. Playing an audio file

In this example, I included three different audio types, because that's perfectly acceptable, and can be a good idea if you wish to ensure that each browser can locate its preferred format rather than just one it knows how to handle. However, the example will still play on all platforms if one or the other (but not both) of the MP3 or the AAC files is dropped.

The <audio> element and its partner <source> tag support several attributes, as follows:

autoplay
    Causes the audio to start playing as soon as it is ready

controls
    Causes the control panel to be displayed

loop
    Sets the audio to play over and over

preload
    Causes the audio to begin loading even before the user selects Play

src
    Specifies the source location of an audio file

type
    Specifies the codec used in creating the audio

If you don't supply the controls attribute to the <audio> tag, and don't use the auto play attribute either, the sound will not play and there won't be a Play button for the user to click to start playback. This would leave you no option other than to offer this functionality in JavaScript, as in Example 24-2 (with the additional code required highlighted in bold), which provides the ability to play and pause the audio, as shown in Figure 24-2.

Example 24-2. Playing audio using JavaScript

```
<!DOCTYPE html>
<html>
  <head>
    <title>Playing Audio with JavaScript</title>
    <script src='OSC.js'></script>
  </head>
  <body>
    <audio id='myaudio'>
      <source src='audio.m4a' type='audio/aac'>
      <source src='audio.mp3' type='audio/mp3'>
      <source src='audio.ogg' type='audio/ogg'>
    </audio>

    <button onclick='playaudio()'>Play Audio</button>
    <button onclick='pauseaudio()'>Pause Audio</button>
```

```
  <script>
    function playaudio()
    {
      O('myaudio').play()
    }
    function pauseaudio()
    {
      O('myaudio').pause()
    }
  </script>
 </body>
</html>
```

Figure 24-2. HTML5 audio can be controlled with JavaScript

This works by calling the `play` or `pause` methods of the `myaudio` element when the buttons are clicked.

Supporting Non-HTML5 Browsers

It will probably be necessary to support older browsers for the foreseeable future by providing a fallback to Flash. Example 24-3 shows how you can do this using a Flash plug-in saved as *audioplayer.swf* (available, along with all the examples, in the free download at the companion website (*http://lpmj.net*)). The code to add is highlighted in bold.

Example 24-3. Providing a Flash fallback for non-HTML5 browsers

```
<audio controls>
  <object type="application/x-shockwave-flash"
    data="audioplayer.swf" width="300" height="30">
    <param name="FlashVars"
      value="mp3=audio.mp3&showstop=1&showvolume=1">
  </object>

  <source src='audio.m4a' type='audio/aac'>
  <source src='audio.mp3' type='audio/mp3'>
  <source src='audio.ogg' type='audio/ogg'>
</audio>
```

Here we take advantage of the fact that on non-HTML5 browsers, anything inside the `<audio>` tag (other than the `<source>` elements, which are ignored) will be acted on by the browser. Therefore, by placing an `<object>` element there that calls up a Flash player, we ensure that any non-HTML5 browsers will at least have a chance of playing the audio, as long as they have Flash installed, as shown in Figure 24-3.

Figure 24-3. The Flash audio player has been loaded

The particular audio player used in this example, *audioplayer.swf*, takes the following arguments and values to the `FlashVars` attribute of the `<param>` element:

`mp3`
> The URL of an MP3 audio file

`showstop`
> If 1, shows the stop button; otherwise, it is not displayed

`showvolume`
> If 1, shows the volume bar; otherwise, it is not displayed

As with many elements, you can easily resize the object to, for example, 300×30 pixels by providing these values to its `width` and `height` attributes.

The `<video>` Element

Playing video in HTML5 is quite similar to audio; you just use the `<video>` tag and provide `<source>` elements for the media you are offering. Example 24-4 shows how you do this with three different video codec types, as displayed in Figure 24-4.

Example 24-4. Playing HTML5 video

```
<video width='560' height='320' controls>
  <source src='movie.mp4'  type='video/mp4'>
  <source src='movie.webm' type='video/webm'>
  <source src='movie.ogv'  type='video/ogg'>
</video>
```

Figure 24-4. Playing HTML5 video

The Video Codecs

As with audio, there are a number of video codecs available, with differing support across multiple browsers. These codecs come in different containers, as follows:

MP4
A license-encumbered, multimedia container format standard specified as a part of MPEG-4, supported by Apple, Microsoft, and, to a lesser extent Google, which has its own WebM container format. Its MIME type is `video/mp4`.

OGG
A free, open container format maintained by the Xiph.Org Foundation. The creators of the Ogg format state that it is unrestricted by software patents and is designed to provide for efficient streaming and manipulation of high-quality digital multimedia. Its MIME type is `video/ogg`, or sometimes `video/ogv`.

WebM
An audio-video format designed to provide a royalty-free, open video compression format for use with HTML5 video. The project's development is sponsored by Google. There are two versions: VP8 and the newer VP9. Its MIME type is `video/webm`.

These may then contain one of the following video codecs:

H.264

> A patented, proprietary video codec for which playback is free for the end user, but which may incur royalty fees for all parts of the encoding and transmission process. At the time of writing, all of Apple, Google, Mozilla Firefox, and Microsoft Internet Explorer support this codec, while Opera (the remaining major browser) doesn't.

Theora

> This is a video codec unencumbered by patents, and free of royalty payments at all levels of encoding, transmission, and playback. This codec is supported by Google Chrome, Mozilla Firefox, and Opera.

VP8

> This video codec is similar to Theora but is owned by Google, which has published it as open source, making it royalty free. It is supported by Google Chrome, Mozilla Firefox, and Opera.

VP9

> Provides the same benefits as VP8, but is more powerful and uses half the bitrate.

The following list details the major operating systems and browsers, along with the video types their latest versions support:

- **Apple iOS:** MP4/H.264
- **Apple Safari:** MP4/H.264
- **Google Android:** MP4, OGG, WebM/H.264, Theora, VP8
- **Google Chrome:** MP4, OGG, WebM/H.264, Theora, VP8, VP9
- **Internet Explorer:** MP4/H.264
- **Mozilla Firefox:** MP4, OGG, WebM/H.264, Theora, VP8, VP9
- **Opera:** OGG, WebM/Theora, VP8

From this list, it's clear that MP4/H.264 is almost unanimously supported, except for the Opera browser. So if you're prepared to ignore the 1% or so of users this comprises (and hope that Opera will soon have to adopt the format anyway), you only need to supply your video using one file type: MP4/H.264. But for maximum viewing, you really ought to encode in OGG/Theora or OGG/VP8 as well (but not VP9, as it's not yet been adopted by Opera).

Therefore, the *movie.webm* file in Example 24-4 isn't strictly needed, but shows how you can add all the different file types you like, to give browsers the opportunity to play back the formats they prefer.

The `<video>` element and accompanying `<source>` tag support the following attributes:

---

autoplay

Causes the video to start playing as soon as it is ready

controls

Causes the control panel to be displayed

height

Specifies the height at which to display the video

loop

Sets the video to play over and over

muted

Mutes the audio output

poster

Lets you choose an image to display where the video will play

preload

Causes the video to begin loading before the user selects Play

src

Specifies the source location of a video file

type

Specifies the codec used in creating the video

width

Specifies the width at which to display the video

If you wish to control video playback from JavaScript, you can do so using code such as that in Example 24-5 (with the additional code required highlighted in bold), and shown in Figure 24-5.

Example 24-5. Controlling video playback from JavaScript

```
<!DOCTYPE html>
<html>
  <head>
    <title>Playing Video with JavaScript</title>
    <script src='OSC.js'></script>
  </head>
  <body>
    <video id='myvideo' width='560' height='320'>
      <source src='movie.mp4'  type='video/mp4'>
      <source src='movie.webm' type='video/webm'>
      <source src='movie.ogv'  type='video/ogg'>
    </video><br>

    <button onclick='playvideo()'>Play Video</button>
    <button onclick='pausevideo()'>Pause Video</button>
```

```
<script>
  function playvideo()
  {
    O('myvideo').play()
  }
  function pausevideo()
  {
    O('myvideo').pause()
  }
</script>
</body>
</html>
```

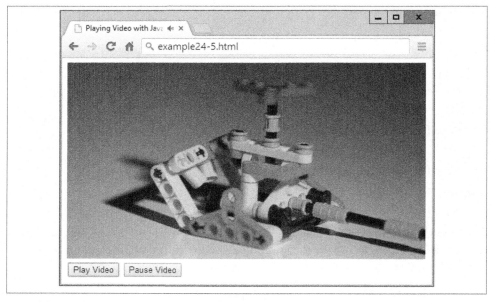

Figure 24-5. JavaScript is being used to control the video

This code is just like controlling audio from JavaScript. Simply call the play and/or pause methods of the myvideo object to play and pause the video.

Supporting Older Browsers

Also as with audio, older versions of browsers will still be in general use for a while to come, so it makes sense to offer a Flash video fallback to people with non-HTML5 browsers. Example 24-6, which uses the *flowplayer.swf* file (available in the free download at *http://lpmj.net*), shows how to do this (highlighted in bold), and Figure 24-6 shows how it displays in a browser that doesn't support HTML5 video.

Example 24-6. Providing Flash as a fallback video player

```
<video width='560' height='320' controls>
  <object width='560' height='320'
    type='application/x-shockwave-flash'
    data='flowplayer.swf'>
    <param name='movie' value='flowplayer.swf'>
    <param name='flashvars'
      value='config={"clip": {
        "url": "http://tinyurl.com/html5video-mp4",
        "autoPlay":false, "autoBuffering":true}}'>
    </object>

  <source src='movie.mp4'  type='video/mp4'>
  <source src='movie.webm' type='video/webm'>
  <source src='movie.ogv'  type='video/ogg'>
</video>
```

Figure 24-6. Flash provides a handy fallback for non-HTML5 browsers

This Flash video player is particular about security, so it won't play videos from a local filesystem, only from a web server, so I have supplied a file on the Web (*http://tinyurl.com/html5video-mp4*) for this example to play.

The arguments to supply to the `flashvars` attribute of the `<param>` element are:

url

A URL on a web server of a *.mp4* file to play

`autoPlay`

If `true`, plays automatically; otherwise, waits for the play button to be clicked

`autoBuffering`

If `true`, in order to minimize buffering later on with slow connections, before it starts playing the video will be preloaded sufficiently for the available bandwidth

For more information on the Flash *flowplayer* program (and an HTML5 version), check out *http://flowplayer.org*.

Summary

Using the information in this chapter, you will be able to embed any audio and video on almost all browsers and platforms without worrying about whether users may or may not be able to play it.

In the following chapter, I'll demonstrate the use of a number of other HTML5 features, including geolocation and local storage.

Questions

1. Which two HTML element tags are used to insert audio and video into an HTML5 document?

2. Which two audio codecs should you use to guarantee maximum playability on all platforms?

3. Which methods can you call to play and pause HTML5 media playback?

4. How can you support media playback in a non-HTML5 browser?

5. Which two video codecs should you use to guarantee maximum playability on all platforms?

See "Chapter 24 Answers" on page 656 in Appendix A for the answers to these questions.

Other HTML5 Features

In this final chapter on HTML5 I explain how to use geolocation, local storage, and web workers; show you how to allow web apps to run offline; and demonstrate the use of in-browser dragging and dropping.

Strictly speaking, most of these features (like much of HTML5) aren't really extensions to HTML, because you access them with JavaScript rather than with HTML markup. They are simply technologies that are being embraced by browser developers, and have been given the handy umbrella name of HTML5.

This means, though, that you need to have fully understood the JavaScript tutorial in this book in order to use them properly. That said, once you get the hang of them, you'll wonder how you ever did without these powerful new features.

Geolocation and the GPS Service

The *GPS (Global Positioning System)* service consists of multiple satellites orbiting the earth whose positions are very precisely known. When a GPS-enabled device tunes into them, the different times at which signals from these various satellites arrive enable the device to quite accurately know where it is; because the speed of light (and therefore radio waves) is a known constant, the time it takes a signal to get from a satellite to a GPS device indicates the satellite's distance.

By noting the different times at which signals arrive from different satellites, which are in precisely known orbital locations at any one time, a simple triangulation calculation gives the device its position relative to the satellites within a few meters or less.

Many mobile devices, such as phones and tablets, have GPS chips and can provide this information. But some don't, others have them tuned off, and others may be used indoors where they are shielded from the GPS satellites and therefore cannot receive any signals. In these cases, additional techniques may be used to attempt to determine your location.

Other Location Methods

If your device has mobile phone hardware but not GPS, it may attempt to triangulate its location by checking the timing of signals received from the various communication towers with which it can communicate (and whose positions are very precisely known). If there are a few towers, this can get almost as close to your location as GPS. But where there's only a single tower, the signal strength can be used to determine a rough radius around the tower, and the circle it creates represents the area in which you are likely to be located. This could place you anywhere within a mile or two of your actual location, down to within a few tens of meters.

Failing that, there may be known WiFi access points whose positions are known within range of your device, and because all access points have a unique identifying address called a *MAC (Media Access Control)* address, a reasonably good approximation of location can be obtained, perhaps to within a street or two. This is the type of information that Google Street View vehicles have been collecting.

And if that fails, the *IP (Internet Protocol)* address used by your device can be queried and used as a rough indicator of your location. Often, though, this provides only the location of a major switch belonging to your Internet provider, which could be dozens or even hundreds of miles away. But at the very least, your IP address can (usually) narrow down the country and sometimes the region you are in.

IP addresses are commonly used by media companies for restricting playback of their content by territory. However, it's a simple matter to set up proxy servers that use a forwarding IP address (in the territory that is blocking outside access) to fetch and pass content through the blockade directly to a "foreign" browser. Proxy servers are also often employed to disguise a user's real IP address or bypass censorship restrictions, and can be shared across many users on a WiFi hotspot. Therefore, if you locate someone by IP address, you can't be completely sure that you have identified the right location, or even country, and should treat this information as only a best guess.

Geolocation and HTML5

In Chapter 22, I briefly introduced HTML5 geolocation. Now it's time to look at it in depth, starting with the example I gave you before, shown again in Example 25-1.

Example 25-1. Displaying a map of your current location

```
<!DOCTYPE html>
<html>
  <head>
    <title>Geolocation Example</title>
    <script src='OSC.js'></script>
    <script src="https://maps.googleapis.com/maps/api/js?sensor=false"></script>
  </head>
  <body>
    <div id='status'></div>
    <div id='map'></div>

    <script>
      if (typeof navigator.geolocation == 'undefined')
        alert("Geolocation not supported.")
      else
        navigator.geolocation.getCurrentPosition(granted, denied)

      function granted(position)
      {
        O('status').innerHTML = 'Permission Granted'
        S('map').border       = '1px solid black'
        S('map').width        = '640px'
        S('map').height       = '320px'

        var lat   = position.coords.latitude
        var long  = position.coords.longitude
        var gmap  = O('map')
        var gopts =
        {
          center: new google.maps.LatLng(lat, long),
          zoom: 9, mapTypeId: google.maps.MapTypeId.ROADMAP
        }
        var map = new google.maps.Map(gmap, gopts)
      }

      function denied(error)
      {
        var message

        switch(error.code)
        {
          case 1: message = 'Permission Denied'; break;
          case 2: message = 'Position Unavailable'; break;
          case 3: message = 'Operation Timed Out'; break;
```

```
        case 4: message = 'Unknown Error'; break;
      }

      O('status').innerHTML = message
    }
  </script>
 </body>
</html>
```

Let's walk through this code and see how it works, starting with the <head> section, which displays a title; loads in the *OSC.js* file containing the O, S, and C functions I provided to make accessing HTML elements from JavaScript easier; and then also pulls in the JavaScript code for the Google Maps service, which is drawn on later in the program.

After this, two div elements are created—one for displaying the connection status, and the other for the map:

```
<div id='status'></div>
<div id='map'></div>
```

The remainder of the document is JavaScript, which immediately starts by interrogating the navigator.geolocation property. If the value returned is undefined, then geolocation is not supported by the browser and an error alert window is popped up.

Otherwise, the getCurrentPosition method of the property is called, passing it the names of two functions: granted and denied (remember that by passing function names we pass the actual function code, not the result of calling the function, which would be the case if the function names had brackets attached):

```
navigator.geolocation.getCurrentPosition(granted, denied)
```

These functions appear later in the script and are for handling the two possibilities of permission to provide the user's location data: granted or denied. The granted function comes first and is entered only if the data can be accessed.

In this function, the innerHTML property of the div element with the ID of status is set to the string Permission Granted to indicate success during the delay while the map is being fetched. Then the map div has some CSS styles applied to give it a border and set its dimensions:

```
O('status').innerHTML = 'Permission Granted'
S('map').border      = '1px solid black'
S('map').width       = '640px'
S('map').height      = '320px'
```

Next, the variables lat and long are given the values returned by the geolocation routines in the browser, and the object gmap is created to access the map div element:

```
var lat  = position.coords.latitude
var long = position.coords.longitude
var gmap = O('map')
```

After this, the object gopts is populated with the values in lat and long, the zoom level is set (in this case to 9), and the ROADMAP map type is selected:

```
var gopts =
{
  center: new google.maps.LatLng(lat, long),
  zoom: 9, mapTypeId: google.maps.MapTypeId.ROADMAP
}
```

Lastly, in this function, we create a new map object by passing gmap and gopts to the Map method of the google.maps object (the code for which you will recall was loaded in just after the *OSC.js* file).

```
var map = new google.maps.Map(gmap, gopts)
```

If permission is granted to access the user's location, the result looks like Figure 25-1.

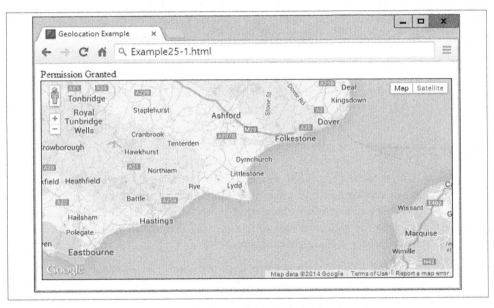

Figure 25-1. An interactive map of the user's location is displayed

If permission is denied or there is another issue, an error message is the only thing displayed, as output to the innerHTML property of the status div by the denied function, according to the problem encountered:

```
switch(error.code)
{
  case 1: message = 'Permission Denied'; break;
  case 2: message = 'Position Unavailable'; break;
  case 3: message = 'Operation Timed Out'; break;
  case 4: message = 'Unknown Error'; break;
}

O('status').innerHTML = message
```

The Google map will be fully interactive and zoomable by the user, who can also change the map type to satellite imagery.

You can set a different zoom level or imagery type by providing different values to the gopts object. For example, a value of 1 for zoom will zoom out the furthest, and 20 will zoom in the most. A value of SATELLITE for the google.maps.MapTypeId property will switch to satellite imagery, or HYBRID will combine map and satellite data together.

The sensor=false setting from the tail of the URL where the script is loaded in (near the start of the document) should be set to true if you know that the user's device has a GPS sensor; otherwise, leave it as it is. If you simply want to display a Google map for a specific location, and not access the user's location data, you can use the core code in the granted function, replacing the lat and long (and other) values with ones of your choosing. Also, if you would prefer to use Bing maps instead of Google, refer to *http://tinyurl.com/bingmap sapi*.

Local Storage

Cookies are an essential part of the modern Internet because they enable websites to save on each user's machine small snippets of information that can be used for tracking purposes. Now this isn't as ominous as it sounds, because most of the tracking going on helps web surfers by saving usernames and passwords, keeping them logged into a social network such as Twitter or Facebook, and more.

Cookies can also locally save your preferences for the way you access a website (rather than having those settings stored on the website's server) or can be used to keep track of a shopping cart as you build up an order on an ecommerce website.

But yes, they can also be used more aggressively to track the websites you frequent and gain a picture of your interests to try to target advertising more effectively. That's why the European Union now requires all websites within its borders to alert you to this, and let you disable cookies if you so choose.

But, as a web developer, think how useful it can be keeping data on user's devices, especially if you have a small budget for computer servers and disk space. For example, you could create in-browser web apps and services for editing word processing documents, spreadsheets, and graphic images, saving all this data offsite on users' computers and keeping your server purchasing budget as low as possible.

From the user's point of view, think about how much faster a document can be loaded up locally than from across the Web, especially on a slow connection. Plus, there's more security if you know that a website is not storing copies of your documents. Of course, you can never guarantee that a website or web app is totally secure, and should never work on highly sensitive documents using software (or hardware) that can go online. But for minimally private documents such as family photographs, you might feel more comfortable using a web app that saves locally than one that saves files to an external server.

Using Local Storage

The biggest problem with using cookies for local storage is that you can save a maximum of 4KB of data in each. Cookies also have to be passed back and forth on every page reload. And, unless your server uses *SSL (Secure Sockets Layer)* encryption, each time a cookie is transmitted it travels in the clear.

But with HTML5 you have access to a much larger local storage space (typically between 5MB and 10MB per domain depending on the browser) that remains over page loads, and between website visits (and even after powering a computer down and back up again). Also, the local storage data is not sent to the server on each page load.

You handle local storage data in key/value pairs. The key is the name assigned for referencing the data, and the value can hold any type of data, but it is saved as a string. All data is unique to the current domain, and for security reasons any local storage created by websites with different domains is separate from the current local storage, and is not accessible by any domain other than the one that stored the data.

The localStorage Object

You gain access to local storage by means of the localStorage object. To test whether this object is available, you query its type to check whether or not it has been defined, like this:

```
if (typeof localStorage == 'undefined')
{
  // Local storage is not available, tell the user and quit.
  // Or maybe offer to save data on the web server instead?
}
```

How you handle the lack of local storage being available will depend on what you intend to use it for, so the code you place inside the if statement will be up to you.

Once you've ascertained that local storage is available, you can start making use of it with the `setItem` and `getItem` methods of the `localStorage` object, like this:

```
localStorage.setItem('username', 'ceastwood')
localStorage.setItem('password', 'makemyday')
```

To later retrieve this data, pass the keys to the `getItem` method, like this:

```
username = localStorage.getItem('username')
password = localStorage.getItem('password')
```

Unlike saving and reading cookies, you can call these methods at any time you like, not simply before any headers have been sent by the web server. The saved values will remain in local storage until erased in the following manner:

```
localStorage.removeItem('username')
localStorage.removeItem('password')
```

Or, you can totally wipe the local storage for the current domain by calling the `clear` method, like this:

```
localStorage.clear()
```

Example 25-2 combines the preceding examples into a single document that displays the current values of the two keys in a pop-up alert message, which initially will be `null`. Then the keys and values are saved to local storage, retrieved, and redisplayed, this time having assigned values. Finally, the keys are removed and then an attempt at retrieving these values is again made, but the returned values are once again `null`. Figure 25-2 shows the second of these three alert messages.

Example 25-2. Getting, setting, and removing local storage data

```
if (typeof localStorage == 'undefined')
{
  alert("Local storage is not available")
}
else
{
  username = localStorage.getItem('username')
  password = localStorage.getItem('password')
  alert("The current values of 'username' and 'password' are\n\n" +
    username + " / " + password + "\n\nClick OK to assign values")

  localStorage.setItem('username', 'ceastwood')
  localStorage.setItem('password', 'makemyday')
  username = localStorage.getItem('username')
  password = localStorage.getItem('password')
  alert("The current values of 'username' and 'password' are\n\n" +
    username + " / " + password + "\n\nClick OK to clear values")

  localStorage.removeItem('username')
  localStorage.removeItem('password')
  username = localStorage.getItem('username')
```

```
password = localStorage.getItem('password')
alert("The current values of 'username' and 'password' are\n\n" +
  username + " / " + password)
}
```

Figure 25-2. Two keys and their values are read from local storage

 You are not restricted to just storing usernames and passwords; you can include virtually any and all data, and as many key/value pairs as you like, up to the available storage limit for your domain.

Web Workers

With *web workers*, you can create sections of JavaScript code that will run in the background, without having to set up and monitor interrupts. Instead, whenever it has something to report, your background process communicates with the main JavaScript through the use of an event.

This means the JavaScript interpreter gets to decide how to allocate time slices most efficiently, and your code only needs to worry about communicating with the background task whenever there's information to convey.

Example 25-3 shows how you can set up web workers to compute a repetitive task in the background—in this instance, calculating prime numbers.

Example 25-3. Setting up and communicating with a web worker

```html
<!DOCTYPE html>
<html>
  <head>
    <title>Web Workers</title>
    <script src='OSC.js'></script>
  </head>
  <body>
    Current highest prime number:
    <span id='result'>0</span>

    <script>
      if (!!window.Worker)
      {
        var worker = new Worker('worker.js')

        worker.onmessage = function (event)
        {
          O('result').innerHTML = event.data;
        }
      }
      else
      {
        alert("Web workers not supported")
      }
    </script>
  </body>
</html>
```

This example first creates a <span> element with the ID of result in which output from the web worker will be placed. Then, in the <script> section, window.Worker is tested via a !! pair of not operators. This has the effect of returning a Boolean value of true if the Worker method exists, and false otherwise. If it is not true, a message is displayed in the else section alerting us that web workers are not available.

Otherwise, a new worker object is created by calling Worker, passing it the filename *worker.js* (shown shortly). Then the onmessage event of the new worker object is attached to an anonymous function that places any message passed to it by *worker.js* into the innerHTML property of the previously created <span> element.

The web worker itself is saved in the file *worker.js*, in Example 25-4.

Example 25-4. The worker.js web worker

```javascript
var n = 1

search: while (true)
{
  n += 1
```

```
for (var i = 2; i <= Math.sqrt(n); i += 1)
{
  if (n % i == 0) continue search
}

postMessage(n)
}
```

This file assigns the value 1 to the variable n. It then loops continuously, incrementing n and checking it for primality by a brute-force method of testing all values from 1 to the square root of n to see if they divide exactly into n, with no remainder. Should a factor be found, the `continue` command stops the brute-force attack immediately because the number is not prime, and starts processing again at the next higher value of n.

However, if all possible factors are tested and none result in a zero remainder, then n must be prime, so its value is passed to `postMessage`, which sends a message back to the `onmessage` event of the object that set up this web worker.

The result looks like the following:

```
Current highest prime number: 30477191
```

To stop a web worker from running, issue a call to the `terminate` method of the `worker` object, like this:

```
worker.terminate()
```

If you wish to stop this particular example from running, you can enter the following into your browser's address bar:

```
javascript:worker.terminate()
```

Also note that due to the way Chrome handles security, you cannot use web workers on a filesystem, only from a web server (or running the files from `localhost` on a development server such as Zend Server, detailed in Chapter 2).

Offline Web Applications

By providing the right information to a browser, you can tell it how to download all the components of a web page to enable it to be loaded and run offline. The main file you need is a manifest file with the file extension *.appcache*. To illustrate a simple web app, I chose to create a clock, so the manifest file is given the filename *clock.appcache*, and looks like Example 25-5.

Example 25-5. The clock.appcache file

```
CACHE MANIFEST
clock.html
OSC.js
clock.css
clock.js
```

The first line in this file declares it to be a manifest file. The lines following list the files the browser needs to download and store, starting with Example 25-6, the *clock.html* file, and followed by the *OSC.js* file, which is the same one used by many examples in this book.

Example 25-6. The clock.html file

```
<!DOCTYPE html>
<html manifest='clock.appcache'>
  <head>
    <title>Offline Web Apps</title>
    <script src='OSC.js'></script>
    <script src='clock.js'></script>
    <link rel='stylesheet' href='clock.css'>
  </head>
  <body>
    <p>The time is: <output id='clock'></output></p>
  </body>
</html>
```

This file declares that it has a manifest file available from within the <html> tag, like this:

```
<html manifest='clock.appcache'>
```

 To support offline web apps, you will need to add the MIME type text/cache-manifest for the file extension *.appcache* to your server, in order for it to send the manifest file using the correct type. There's a neat shortcut you can use for this, which is to create a file called *.htaccess* in the same folder as the files to be made available offline, with the following contents:

```
AddType text/cache-manifest .appcache
```

The files *OSC.js*, *clock.js*, and *clock.css* are then imported and used by the document. The JavaScript in *clock.js* is listed in Example 25-7.

Example 25-7. The clock.js file

```
setInterval(function()
{
  O('clock').innerHTML = new Date()
}, 1000)
```

This is a very simple anonymous function attached to an interval that repeats once a second to save the current date and time into the `innerHTML` property of the `<output>` element that has the ID of `clock`.

The final file is the *clock.css* file (see Example 25-8), which simply applies bold styling to the `<output>` element.

Example 25-8. The clock.css file

```
output { font-weight:bold; }
```

As long as the *clock.appcache* file lists them all, these four files (*clock.html*, *OSC.js*, *clock.css*, and *clock.js*) together make up a working offline web application, which will be downloaded and made available locally by any web browser that understands offline web apps. When run, the output looks like this:

```
The time is: Thu Jul 19 2018 15:24:26 GMT+0000 (GMT Standard Time)
```

 For full details on the offline web applications specifications, you can check out the official website (*http://tinyurl.com/offlinewebapps*).

Drag and Drop

You can easily support dragging and dropping of objects on a web page by setting up event handlers for the `ondragstart`, `ondragover`, and `ondrop` events, as in Example 25-9.

Example 25-9. Dragging and dropping objects

```
<!DOCTYPE HTML>
<html>
  <head>
    <title>Drag and Drop</title>
    <script src='OSC.js'></script>
    <style>
      #dest {
        background:lightblue;
        border     :1px solid #444;
        width      :320px;
        height     :100px;
        padding    :10px;
      }
    </style>
  </head>
  <body>
    <div id='dest' ondrop='drop(event)' ondragover='allow(event)'></div><br>
    Drag the image below into the above element<br><br>
```

```
      <img id='source1' src='image1.png' draggable='true' ondragstart='drag(event)'>
      <img id='source2' src='image2.png' draggable='true' ondragstart='drag(event)'>
      <img id='source3' src='image3.png' draggable='true' ondragstart='drag(event)'>

      <script>
        function allow(event)
        {
          event.preventDefault()
        }

        function drag(event)
        {
          event.dataTransfer.setData('image/png', event.target.id)
        }

        function drop(event)
        {
          event.preventDefault()
          var data=event.dataTransfer.getData('image/png')
          event.target.appendChild(O(data))
        }
      </script>
    </body>
</html>
```

After setting up the HTML, title, and loading in the *OSC.js* file, this document styles the div element with the ID of dest, giving it a background color, border, set dimensions, and padding.

Then, in the <body> section, the div element is created, and its ondrop and ondrag over events have the event handler functions drop and allow attached to them. After this there's some text, and then three images are displayed with their draggable properties set to true, and the function drag is attached to the ondragstart event of each.

In the <script> section, the allow event handler function simply prevents the default action for dragging (which is to disallow it), while the drag event handler function calls the setData method of the dataTransfer object of the event, passing it the MIME type image/png and the target.id of the event (which is the object being dragged). The dataTransfer object holds the data that is being dragged during a drag-and-drop operation.

Finally, the drop event handler function also intercepts its default action so that dropping is allowed, and then it fetches the contents of the object being dragged from the data Transfer object, passing it the MIME type of the object. Then the dropped data is appended to the target (which is the dest div) using its appendChild method.

If you try this example for yourself, you'll be able to drag and drop the images into the div element, where they will stay, as shown in Figure 25-3.

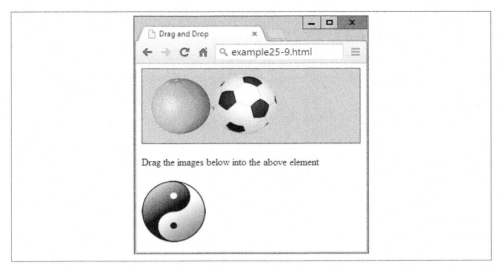

Figure 25-3. Two images have been dragged and dropped

Other events you can attach to include ondragenter for when a drag operation enters an element, ondragleave for when one leaves an element, and ondragend for when a dragging operation ends, which you can use, for example, to modify the cursor during these operations.

Cross Document Messaging

You've already seen messaging in use a little earlier, in the web worker section. I didn't go into any details, however, as it wasn't the core topic being discussed, and the message was being posted only to the same document anyway. But for obvious security reasons, cross-document messaging does need to be applied with caution, so you need to fully understand its workings if you plan to use it.

Before HTML5, browser developers disallowed cross-site scripting, but as well as blocking potential attack sites, this prevented communication between legitimate pages—meaning document interaction of any kind generally had to occur through Ajax and a third-party web server, which was cumbersome and fiddly to build and maintain.

But web messaging now allows scripts to interact across these boundaries by using some sensible security restraints to prevent malicious hacking attempts. It is achieved through use of the postMessage method, allowing plain-text messages to be sent from one domain to another.

This requires that JavaScript first obtain the Window object of the receiving document, letting messages post to a variety of other windows, frames, or iframes directly related to the sender's document. The received message event has the following attributes:

data

The incoming message

origin

The origin of the sender document, including the scheme, hostname, and port

source

The source window of the sender document

The code to send messages is just a single instruction, in which you pass the message to be sent and the domain to which it applies, as in Example 25-10.

Example 25-10. Sending web messages to an iframe

```html
<!DOCTYPE HTML>
<html>
  <head>
    <title>Web Messaging (a)</title>
    <script src='OSC.js'></script>
  </head>
  <body>
    <iframe id='frame' src='example25-11.html' width='360' height='75'></iframe>

    <script>
      count = 1

      setInterval(function()
      {
        O('frame').contentWindow.postMessage('Message ' + count++, '*')
      }, 1000)
    </script>
  </body>
</html>
```

Here the usual use is made of the *OSC.js* file to pull in the O function, and then an iframe element with the ID of `frame` is created, which loads in Example 25-11. Then, within the `<script>` section, the variable `count` is initialized to 1 and a repeating interval is set up to occur every second to post the string `'Message '` (using the `postMessage` method) along with the current value of `count`, which is then incremented. The `postMessage` call is attached to the `contentWindow` property of the iframe object, not the iframe object itself. This is important because web messaging requires posts to be made to a window, not to an object within a window.

Example 25-11. Receiving messages from another document

```html
<!DOCTYPE HTML>
<html>
  <head>
    <title>Web Messaging (b)</title>
    <style>
      #output {
```

```
        font-family:"Courier New";
        white-space:pre;
      }
    </style>
    <script src='OSC.js'></script>
  </head>
  <body>
    <div id='output'>Received messages will display here</div>

    <script>
      window.onmessage = function(event)
      {
        O('output').innerHTML =
          '<b>Origin:</b> ' + event.origin + '<br>' +
          '<b>Source:</b> ' + event.source + '<br>' +
          '<b>Data:</b>    ' + event.data
      }
    </script>
  </body>
</html>
```

This example sets up a little styling to make output clearer, then creates a div element with the ID output, in which the contents of received messages will be placed. In the <script> section there's a single anonymous function attached to the onmessage event of the window. In this function, the event.origin, event.source, and event.data property values are then displayed, as shown in Figure 25-4.

Figure 25-4. The iframe has so far received 17 messages

Web messaging works only across domains, so you cannot test it by loading files in from a filesystem; you must use a web server. As you can see from Figure 25-4, the origin is *http://localhost* because these examples are running on a local development server. The source is the Window object, and the current message value is Message 17.

At the moment, Example 25-10 is not at all secure because the domain value passed to postMessage is the wildcard *:

```
O('frame').contentWindow.postMessage('Message ' + count++, '*')
```

To direct messages only to documents originating from a particular domain, you can change this parameter. In the current case, a value of http://localhost would ensure that only documents loaded from the local server will be sent any messages, like this:

```
O('frame').contentWindow.postMessage('Message ' + count++, 'http://localhost')
```

Likewise, as it stands, the listener program displays any and all messages it receives. This is also not a very secure state of affairs, because malicious documents also present in the browser can attempt to send messages that unwary listener code in other documents might otherwise access. Therefore, you can restrict the messages your listeners react to using an if statement, like this:

```
window.onmessage = function(event)
{
  if (event.origin) == 'http://localhost')
  {
    O('output').innerHTML =
      '<b>Origin:</b> ' + event.origin + '<br>' +
      '<b>Source:</b> ' + event.source + '<br>' +
      '<b>Data:</b>    ' + event.data
  }
}
```

 If you always use the proper domain for the site you are working with, your web messaging communications will be more secure. However, be aware that because messages are sent in the clear, there may be insecurities in some browsers or browser plug-ins that might make this kind of communication insecure. One way to boost your security, then, is to create your own obfuscation or encryption scheme for all your web messages, and also consider introducing your own two-way communication protocols to verify each message as being authentic.

Normally, you won't alert the user to the origin or source values, and will simply make use of them for security checking. These examples, however, display those values to help you experiment with web messaging and see what is going on. As well as iframes, documents in pop-up windows and other tabs may also talk to each other using this method.

Microdata

Microdata is a subset of HTML designed to provide metadata to a document in order to make it have meaning to software, just as it has meaning to a reader of the document.

Microdata makes available the following new tag attributes: itemscope, itemtype, itemid, itemref, and itemprop. Using these, you can clearly define the properties of an item such as a book, providing a range of information that a computer can use to understand, for example, its authors, publishers, contents, and so on.

Or, more frequently these days, microdata is important for search engines and social networking sites. Example 25-12 creates a short bio for George Washington as if it were a profile on a social networking site, with microdata added to the various elements (shown highlighted in bold). The result looks like Figure 25-5, which will look the same with or without microdata, because it is never visible to the user.

Example 25-12. Adding microdata to HTML

```
<!DOCTYPE html>
<html>
  <head>
    <title>Microdata</title>
  </head>
  <body>
    <section itemscope itemtype='http://schema.org/Person'>
      <img itemprop='image' src='gw.jpg' alt='George Washington'
        align='left' style='margin-right:10px'>
      <h2 itemprop='name'>George Washington</h2>
      <p>I am the first <span itemprop='jobTitle'>US President</span>.
      My website is: <a itemprop='url'
        href='http://georgewashington.si.edu'>georgewashington.si.edu</a>.
      My address is:</p>
      <address itemscope itemtype='http://schema.org/PostalAddress'
        itemprop='address'>
        <span itemprop='streetAddress'>1600 Pennsylvania Avenue</span>,<br>
        <span itemprop='addressLocality'>Washington</span>,<br>
        <span itemprop='addressRegion'>DC</span>,<br>
        <span itemprop='postalCode'>20500</span>,<br>
        <span itemprop='addressCountry'>United States</span>.
      </address>
    </section>
  </body>
</html>
```

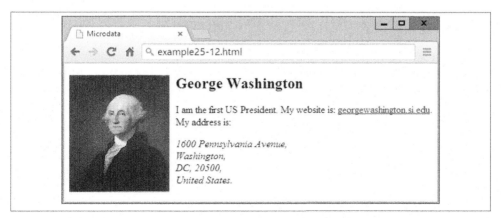

Figure 25-5. This document contains microdata, which is not visible

Browsers don't yet really do anything with microdata, but it's still very worth getting to know it. Using the right microdata gives lots of information to search engines like Google or Bing, and may help to promote clearly annotated pages in the rankings as compared to sites that don't implement microdata.

However, at some point browsers may also find a use for this information, and you'll be able to determine whether or not they support it by checking whether the getItems method exists, like this:

```
if (!!document.getItems)
{
  // Microdata is supported
}
else
{
  // Microdata is not supported
}
```

The !! pair of not operators is a shorthand way of returning a Boolean value representing the existence (or lack thereof) of the getItems method. If it exists, then true is returned and microdata is supported; otherwise, false is returned.

Currently, only the Mozilla Firefox and Opera browsers support accessing microdata, but the other browsers are sure to follow soon. When they do, you'll be able to extract this data in the following manner, in which (after the page has loaded) the data object is retrieved from a call to getItems, and the value for the key 'jobTitle' (just as an example) is retrieved by accessing the data object's properties object, and then fetching the latter object's textContent property:

```
window.onload = function()
{
  if (!!document.getItems)
  {
    data = document.getItems('http://schema.org/Person')[0]
    alert(data.properties['jobTitle'][0].textContent)
  }
}
```

Browsers that support this feature will display as Figure 25-6, but other browsers will not trigger the pop-up window.

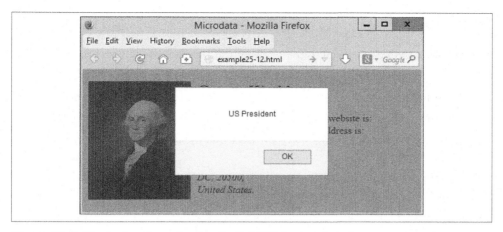

Figure 25-6. Displaying the value for the 'jobTitle' microdata key

Google has stated that it definitely uses microdata when it finds it, and that microdata is also the preferred snippet format for Google+, so it's well worth starting to add it to your HTML where applicable. For a complete breakdown of the myriad of microdata properties available, check out *http://schema.org*, which is also the reference for the microdata schemes as declared in the itemType properties.

Other HTML5 Tags

There are a number of other new HTML5 tags that have not yet been implemented in many browsers, and therefore I won't cover them (particularly because their specs could change). But, for the sake of completeness, these tags are <article>, <aside>, <details>, <figcaption>, <figure>, <footer>, <header>, <hgroup>, <keygen>, <mark>, <menuitem>, <meter>, <nav>, <output>, <progress>, <rp>, <rt>, <ruby>, <section>, <summary>, <time>, and <wbr>. You can get more information on these and all other HTML5 tags at *http://tinyurl.com/h5markup* (check out the elements sporting a NEW icon).

Summary

This concludes your introduction to HTML5. You now have a number of powerful new features with which to make even more dynamic and compelling websites. In the final chapter, I'll show you how you can bring all the different technologies in this book together to create a mini social networking site.

Questions

1. What method do you call to request geolocation data from a web browser?

2. How can you determine whether or not a browser supports local storage?

3. What method can you call to erase all local storage data for the current domain?

4. What is the best way for web workers to communicate with a main program?

5. How can your code inform a web browser that the document can be run offline as a local web app?

6. To support drag-and-drop operations, how can you prevent the default action of disallowing drag and drop for these events?

7. How can you make cross-document messaging more secure?

8. What is the purpose of microdata?

See "Chapter 25 Answers" on page 657 in Appendix A for the answers to these questions.

Bringing It All Together

Now that you've reached the end of your journey into learning the hows, whys, and wherefores of dynamic web programming, I want to leave you with a real example that you can sink your teeth into. In fact, it's a collection of examples, because I've put together a simple social networking project comprising all the main features you'd expect from such a site.

Across the various files, there are examples of MySQL table creation and database access, CSS style sheets, file inclusion, session control, DOM access, Ajax calls, event and error handling, file uploading, image manipulation, the HTML5 canvas, and a whole lot more.

Each example file is complete and self-contained, yet works with all the others to build a fully working social networking site, even including a style sheet you can modify to completely change the look and feel of the project. Being small and light, the end product is particularly usable on mobile platforms such as a smartphone or tablet, but will run equally well on a full-size desktop computer.

I leave it up to you to take any pieces of code you think you can use and expand on them for your own purposes. Perhaps you may even wish to build on these files to create a social networking site of your own.

Designing a Social Networking Site

Before writing any code, I sat down and came up with several things that I decided were essential to such a site. These included:

- A signup process
- A login form
- A logout facility
- Session control

- User profiles with uploaded thumbnails

- A member directory

- Adding members as friends

- Public and private messaging between members

- How to style the project

I decided to name the project *Robin's Nest*, but you have to modify only one line of code (in *functions.php*) to change this to a name of your choice.

On the Website

All the examples in this chapter can be found on the companion website (*http://lpmj.net*). You can also download the examples from there to your computer by clicking on the Download Examples link. This will download an archive file called *examples.zip*, which you should extract to a suitable location on your computer.

Of particular interest to this chapter, within the ZIP file is a folder called *robinsnest*, in which all the following examples have been saved with the correct filenames required by this sample application. So you can easily copy them all to your web development folder to try them out.

functions.php

Let's jump right into the project, starting with Example 26-1, *functions.php*, the include file of the main functions. This file contains a little more than just the functions, though, because I have added the database login details here instead of using yet another separate file. So the first half-dozen lines of code define the host, database name, username, and password of the database to use.

It doesn't matter what you call the database, as long as it already exists (see Chapter 8 for instructions on how to create a new database). Also make sure to correctly assign a MySQL username and password to $dbuser and $dbpass. With correct values, the subsequent two lines will open a connection to MySQL and select the database. The last of the initial instructions sets the name of the social networking site by assigning the value Robin's Nest to the variable $appname. If you want to change the name, this is the place to do so.

The Functions

The project uses five main functions:

createTable
> Checks whether a table already exists and, if not, creates it

queryMysql
> Issues a query to MySQL, outputting an error message if it fails

destroySession
> Destroys a PHP session and clears its data to log users out

sanitizeString
> Removes potentially malicious code or tags from user input

showProfile
> Displays a user's image and "about me" message if he has one

All of these should be obvious in their action to you by now, with the possible exception of showProfile, which looks for an image of the name *user.jpg* (where *user* is the username of the current user), and if it finds it, displays it. It also displays any "about me" text the user may have saved.

I have ensured that error handling is in place for all the functions that need it, so that they can catch any typographical or other errors you may introduce, and generate error messages. However, if you use any of this code on a production server, you will probably want to provide your own error-handling routines to make the code more user-friendly.

So enter Example 26-1 and save it as *functions.php* (or download it from the companion website), and you'll be ready to move on to the next section.

Example 26-1. functions.php

```php
<?php
  $dbhost  = 'localhost';    // Unlikely to require changing
  $dbname  = 'robinsnest';   // Modify these...
  $dbuser  = 'robinsnest';   // ...variables according
  $dbpass  = 'rnpassword';   // ...to your installation
  $appname = "Robin's Nest"; // ...and preference

  $connection = new mysqli($dbhost, $dbuser, $dbpass, $dbname);
  if ($connection->connect_error) die($connection->connect_error);

  function createTable($name, $query)
  {
    queryMysql("CREATE TABLE IF NOT EXISTS $name($query)");
    echo "Table '$name' created or already exists.<br>";
  }
```

```php
function queryMysql($query)
{
  global $connection;
  $result = $connection->query($query);
  if (!$result) die($connection->error);
  return $result;
}

function destroySession()
{
  $_SESSION=array();

  if (session_id() != "" || isset($_COOKIE[session_name()]))
    setcookie(session_name(), '', time()-2592000, '/');

  session_destroy();
}

function sanitizeString($var)
{
  global $connection;
  $var = strip_tags($var);
  $var = htmlentities($var);
  $var = stripslashes($var);
  return $connection->real_escape_string($var);
}

function showProfile($user)
{
  if (file_exists("$user.jpg"))
    echo "<img src='$user.jpg' style='float:left;'>";

  $result = queryMysql("SELECT * FROM profiles WHERE user='$user'");

  if ($result->num_rows)
  {
    $row = $result->fetch_array(MYSQLI_ASSOC);
    echo stripslashes($row['text']) . "<br style='clear:left;'><br>";
  }
}
?>
```

If you read a previous edition of this book, in which these examples used the old mysql extension, you should note that in order to reference the MySQL database using mysqli, you must apply the global keyword in the queryMysql and sanitizeString functions, to allow them to use the value in $connection.

header.php

For uniformity, each page of the project needs to have access to the same set of features. Therefore I placed these things in Example 26-2, *header.php*. This is the file that is actually included by the other files and it, in turn, includes *functions.php*. This means that only a single `require_once` is needed in each file.

header.php starts by calling the function `session_start`. As you'll recall from Chapter 12, this sets up a session that will remember certain values we want stored across different PHP files.

With the session started, the program then checks whether the session variable `user` is currently assigned a value. If so, a user has logged in and the variable `$loggedin` is set to TRUE.

After the main setup code in which a style sheet is loaded, a canvas element is created for the logo, and a div is also created. The file *javascript.js* (see Example 26-14, later on) is loaded to pull in the O, S, and C functions; these would normally be in the *OSC.js* file, but to keep the number of files down I've added them to the JavaScript used to create the logo.

Using the value of `$loggedin`, an `if` block displays one of two sets of menus. The non-logged-in set simply offers options of Home, Sign up, and Log in, whereas the logged-in version offers full access to the project's features. Additionally, if a user is logged in, his or her username is appended in brackets to the page title and placed after the main heading. We can freely refer to `$user` wherever we want to put in the name, because if the user is not logged in, that variable is empty and will have no effect on the output.

The styling applied to this file is in the file *styles.css* (Example 26-13, detailed at the end of this chapter) and includes creating a wide heading with a colored background, and turning the links in the lists to rounded buttons.

Example 26-2. header.php

```php
<?php
  session_start();

  echo "<!DOCTYPE html>\n<html><head>";

  require_once 'functions.php';

  $userstr = ' (Guest)';

  if (isset($_SESSION['user']))
  {
    $user     = $_SESSION['user'];
    $loggedin = TRUE;
    $userstr  = " ($user)";
  }
```

```
    else $loggedin = FALSE;

echo "<title>$appname$userstr</title><link rel='stylesheet' " .
    "href='styles.css' type='text/css'>"                        .
    "</head><body><center><canvas id='logo' width='624' "       .
    "height='96'>$appname</canvas></center>"                     .
    "<div class='appname'>$appname$userstr</div>"               .
    "<script src='javascript.js'></script>";

if ($loggedin)
  echo "<br ><ul class='menu'>" .
    "<li><a href='members.php?view=$user'>Home</a></li>" .
    "<li><a href='members.php'>Members</a></li>"       .
    "<li><a href='friends.php'>Friends</a></li>"       .
    "<li><a href='messages.php'>Messages</a></li>"     .
    "<li><a href='profile.php'>Edit Profile</a></li>"  .
    "<li><a href='logout.php'>Log out</a></li></ul><br>";
else
  echo ("<br><ul class='menu'>" .
    "<li><a href='index.php'>Home</a></li>"            .
    "<li><a href='signup.php'>Sign up</a></li>"        .
    "<li><a href='login.php'>Log in</a></li></ul><br>" .
    "<span class='info'>&#8658; You must be logged in to " .
    "view this page.</span><br><br>");
?>
```

 Using the <br> tag, as in the preceding example, is a quick-and-dirty way of creating spacing in page layout. In this instance it works well, but generally you will probably want to use CSS margins to fine-tune the spacing around elements.

setup.php

With the pair of included files written, it's now time to set up the MySQL tables they will use. We do this with Example 26-3, *setup.php*, which you should type and load into your browser before calling up any other files; otherwise, you'll get numerous MySQL errors.

The tables created are kept short and sweet, and have the following names and columns:

- members: username user (indexed), password pass
- messages: ID id (indexed), author auth (indexed), recipient recip, message type pm, message message
- friends: username user (indexed), friend's username friend
- profiles: username user (indexed), "about me" text

Because the function `createTable` first checks whether a table already exists, this program can be safely called multiple times without generating any errors.

It is very likely that you will need to add many more columns to these tables if you choose to expand on this project. If so, you may need to issue a MySQL DROP TABLE command before re-creating a table.

Example 26-3. setup.php

```
<!DOCTYPE html>
<html>
  <head>
    <title>Setting up database</title>
  </head>
  <body>

    <h3>Setting up...</h3>

<?php
  require_once 'functions.php';

  createTable('members',
              'user VARCHAR(16),
              pass VARCHAR(16),
              INDEX(user(6))');

  createTable('messages',
              'id INT UNSIGNED AUTO_INCREMENT PRIMARY KEY,
              auth VARCHAR(16),
              recip VARCHAR(16),
              pm CHAR(1),
              time INT UNSIGNED,
              message VARCHAR(4096),
              INDEX(auth(6)),
              INDEX(recip(6))');

  createTable('friends',
              'user VARCHAR(16),
              friend VARCHAR(16),
              INDEX(user(6)),
              INDEX(friend(6))');

  createTable('profiles',
              'user VARCHAR(16),
              text VARCHAR(4096),
              INDEX(user(6))');
?>

    <br>...done.
  </body>
</html>
```

For Example 26-3 to work, you must first ensure that you have already created the database specified in the variable $dbname in Example 26-1, and also have granted access to it by the user given the name in $dbuser, with the password in $dbpass.

index.php

This file is a trivial file but necessary nonetheless to give the project a home page. All it does is display a simple welcome message. In a finished application, this would be where you sell the virtues of your site to encourage signups.

Incidentally, seeing as all the MySQL tables have been created and the include files saved, you can now load Example 26-4, *index.php*, into your browser to get your first peek at the new application. It should look like Figure 26-1.

Example 26-4. index.php

```php
<?php
  require_once 'header.php';

  echo "<br><span class='main'>Welcome to $appname,";

  if ($loggedin) echo " $user, you are logged in.";
  else           echo ' please sign up and/or log in to join in.';
?>

    </span><br><br>
  </body>
</html>
```

signup.php

Now we need a module to enable users to join the new network, and that's Example 26-5, *signup.php*. This is a slightly longer program, but you've seen all its parts before.

Let's start by looking at the end block of HTML. This is a simple form that allows a username and password to be entered. But note the use of the empty span given the id of 'info'. This will be the destination of the Ajax call in this program that checks whether a desired username is available. See Chapter 18 for a complete description of how this works.

Figure 26-1. The main page of the site

Checking for Username Availability

Now go back to the program start and you'll see a block of JavaScript that starts with the function checkUser. This is called by the JavaScript onBlur event when focus is removed from the username field of the form. First it sets the contents of the span I mentioned (with the id of info) to an empty string, which clears it in case it previously had a value.

Next a request is made to the program *checkuser.php*, which reports whether the username user is available. The returned result of the Ajax call, a friendly message, is then placed in the info span.

After the JavaScript section comes some PHP code that you should recognize from the Chapter 16 discussion of form validation. This section also uses the sanitizeString function to remove potentially malicious characters before looking up the username in the database and, if it's not already taken, inserting the new username $user and password $pass.

Logging In

Upon successfully signing up, the user is then prompted to log in. A more fluid response at this point might be to automatically log in a newly created user, but because I don't want to overly complicate the code, I have kept the signup and login modules separate from each other. I'm sure you can easily implement this if you want to, however.

Example 26-5 uses the CSS class fieldname to arrange the form fields, aligning them neatly under each other in columns. When loaded into a browser (and in conjunction with *checkuser.php*, shown later), this program will look like Figure 26-2, where you can see that the Ajax call has identified that the username *Robin* is available. If you would like the password field to show only asterisks, change its type from text to password.

Example 26-5. signup.php

```php
<?php
  require_once 'header.php';

  echo <<< _END
    <script>
      function checkUser(user)
      {
        if (user.value == '')
        {
          O('info').innerHTML = ''
          return
        }

        params  = "user=" + user.value
        request = new ajaxRequest()
        request.open("POST", "checkuser.php", true)
        request.setRequestHeader("Content-type",
          "application/x-www-form-urlencoded")
        request.setRequestHeader("Content-length", params.length)
        request.setRequestHeader("Connection", "close")

        request.onreadystatechange = function()
        {
          if (this.readyState == 4)
            if (this.status == 200)
              if (this.responseText != null)
                O('info').innerHTML = this.responseText
        }
        request.send(params)
      }

      function ajaxRequest()
      {
        try { var request = new XMLHttpRequest() }
        catch(e1) {
          try { request = new ActiveXObject("Msxml2.XMLHTTP") }
          catch(e2) {
            try { request = new ActiveXObject("Microsoft.XMLHTTP") }
            catch(e3) {
              request = false
        } } }
```

```
        return request
      }
    </script>
    <div class='main'><h3>Please enter your details to sign up</h3>
_END;

  $error = $user = $pass = "";
  if (isset($_SESSION['user'])) destroySession();

  if (isset($_POST['user']))
  {
    $user = sanitizeString($_POST['user']);
    $pass = sanitizeString($_POST['pass']);

    if ($user == "" || $pass == "")
      $error = "Not all fields were entered<br><br>";
    else
    {
      $result = queryMysql("SELECT * FROM members WHERE user='$user'");

      if ($result->num_rows)
        $error = "That username already exists<br><br>";
      else
      {
        queryMysql("INSERT INTO members VALUES('$user', '$pass')");
        die("<h4>Account created</h4>Please Log in.<br><br>");
      }
    }
  }

  echo <<<_END
    <form method='post' action='signup.php'>$error
    <span class='fieldname'>Username</span>
    <input type='text' maxlength='16' name='user' value='$user'
      onBlur='checkUser(this)'><span id='info'></span><br>
    <span class='fieldname'>Password</span>
    <input type='text' maxlength='16' name='pass'
      value='$pass'><br>
_END;
?>

    <span class='fieldname'> </span>
    <input type='submit' value='Sign up'>
    </form></div><br>
  </body>
</html>
```

Figure 26-2. The signup page

 On a production server, I wouldn't recommend storing user passwords in the clear as I've done here (for reasons of space and simplicity). Instead, you should salt them and store them as one-way hash strings. See Chapter 13 for more details on how to do this.

checkuser.php

To go with *signup.php*, here's Example 26-6, *checkuser.php*, which looks up a username in the database and returns a string indicating whether it has already been taken. Because it relies on the functions `sanitizeString` and `queryMysql`, the program first includes the file *functions.php*.

Then, if the `$_POST` variable `user` has a value, the function looks it up in the database and, depending on whether it exists as a username, outputs either "Sorry, this username is taken" or "This username is available." Just checking the function `mysql_num_rows` against the result is sufficient for this, as it will return 0 for not found, or 1 if it is found.

The HTML entities ✘ and ✔ are also used to preface the string with either a cross or a checkmark.

Example 26-6. checkuser.php

```php
<?php
  require_once 'functions.php';

  if (isset($_POST['user']))
  {
    $user   = sanitizeString($_POST['user']);
    $result = queryMysql("SELECT * FROM members WHERE user='$user'");

    if ($result->num_rows)
      echo  "<span class='taken'> &#x2718; " .
            "This username is taken</span>";
    else
      echo "<span class='available'> &#x2714; " .
           "This username is available</span>";
  }
?>
```

login.php

With users now able to sign up to the site, Example 26-7, *login.php*, provides the code needed to let them log in. Like the signup page, it features a simple HTML form and some basic error checking, as well as using `sanitizeString` before querying the MySQL database.

The main thing to note here is that, upon successful verification of the username and password, the session variables `user` and `pass` are given the username and password values. As long as the current session remains active, these variables will be accessible by all the programs in the project, allowing them to automatically provide access to logged-in users.

You may be interested in the use of the `die` function upon successfully logging in. This is there because it combines an `echo` and an `exit` command in one, thus saving a line of code. For styling, this (and most of the files) applies the class `main` to indent the content from the lefthand edge.

When you call this program up in your browser, it should look like Figure 26-3. Note how the input type of `password` has been used here to mask the password with asterisks to prevent it from being viewed by anyone looking over the user's shoulder.

Example 26-7. login.php

```php
<?php
 require_once 'header.php';
 echo "<div class='main'><h3>Please enter your details to log in</h3>";
 $error = $user = $pass = "";

 if (isset($_POST['user']))
 {
   $user = sanitizeString($_POST['user']);
   $pass = sanitizeString($_POST['pass']);

   if ($user == "" || $pass == "")
       $error = "Not all fields were entered<br>";
   else
   {
     $result = queryMySQL("SELECT user,pass FROM members
       WHERE user='$user' AND pass='$pass'");

     if ($result->num_rows == 0)
     {
       $error = "<span class='error'>Username/Password
                 invalid</span><br><br>";
     }
     else
     {
       $_SESSION['user'] = $user;
       $_SESSION['pass'] = $pass;
       die("You are now logged in. Please <a href='members.php?view=$user'>" .
           "click here</a> to continue.<br><br>");
     }
   }
 }

 echo <<<_END
   <form method='post' action='login.php'>$error
   <span class='fieldname'>Username</span><input type='text'
     maxlength='16' name='user' value='$user'><br>
   <span class='fieldname'>Password</span><input type='password'
     maxlength='16' name='pass' value='$pass'>
_END;
?>

   <br>
   <span class='fieldname'> </span>
   <input type='submit' value='Login'>
   </form><br></div>
  </body>
</html>
```

Figure 26-3. The login page

profile.php

One of the first things that new users may want to do after signing up and logging in is to create a profile, which can be done via Example 26-8, *profile.php*. I think you'll find some interesting code here, such as routines to upload, resize, and sharpen images.

Let's start by looking at the main HTML at the end of the code. This is like the forms you've just seen, but this time it has the parameter `enctype='multipart/form-data'`. This allows us to send more than one type of data at a time, enabling the posting of an image as well as some text. There's also an input type of `file`, which creates a Browse button that a user can press to select a file to be uploaded.

When the form is submitted, the code at the start of the program is executed. The first thing it does is ensure that a user is logged in before allowing program execution to proceed. Only then is the page heading displayed.

Adding the "About Me" Text

Then the POST variable text is checked to see whether some text was posted to the program. If so, it is sanitized and all long whitespace sequences (including returns and line feeds) are replaced with a single space. This function incorporates a double security check, ensuring that the user actually exists in the database and that no attempted hacking can succeed before inserting this text into the database, where it will become the user's "about me" details.

If no text was posted, the database is queried to see whether any text already exists in order to prepopulate the textarea for the user to edit it.

Adding a Profile Image

Next we move on to the section where the $_FILES system variable is checked to see whether an image has been uploaded. If so, a string variable called $saveto is created, based on the user's username followed by the extension *.jpg*. For example, user Jill will cause $saveto to have the value *Jill.jpg*. This is the file where the uploaded image will be saved for use in the user's profile.

Following this, the uploaded image type is examined and is accepted only if it is a *jpeg*, *png*, or *gif* image. Upon success, the variable $src is populated with the uploaded image using one of the imagecreatefrom functions according to the image type uploaded. The image is now in a raw format that PHP can process. If the image is not of an allowed type, the flag $typeok is set to FALSE, preventing the final section of image upload code from being processed.

Processing the Image

First, we store the image's dimensions in $w and $h using the following statement, which is a quick way of assigning values from an array to separate variables:

```
list($w, $h) = getimagesize($saveto);
```

Then, using the value of $max (which is set to 100), we calculate new dimensions that will result in a new image of the same ratio, but with no dimension greater than 100 pixels. This results in giving the variables $tw and $th the new values needed. If you want smaller or larger thumbnails, simply change the value of $max accordingly.

Next, the function imagecreatetruecolor is called to create a new, blank canvas $tw wide and $th high in $tmp. Then imagecopyresampled is called to resample the image from $src, to the new $tmp. Sometimes resampling images can result in a slightly blurred copy, so the next piece of code uses the imageconvolution function to sharpen the image up a bit.

Finally, the image is saved as a *jpeg* file in the location defined by the variable $saveto, after which we remove both the original and the resized image canvases from memory using the imagedestroy function, returning the memory that was used.

Displaying the Current Profile

Last but not least, so that the user can see what the current profile looks like before editing it, the showProfile function from *functions.php* is called prior to outputting the form HTML. If no profile exists yet, nothing will be displayed.

When a profile image is displayed, CSS is applied to it to provide a border, shadow, and a margin to its right—to separate the profile text from the image. The result of loading Example 26-8 into a browser is shown in Figure 26-4, where you can see that the textarea has been prepopulated with the "about me" text.

Example 26-8. profile.php

```php
<?php
  require_once 'header.php';

  if (!$loggedin) die();

  echo "<div class='main'><h3>Your Profile</h3>";

  $result = queryMysql("SELECT * FROM profiles WHERE user='$user'");

  if (isset($_POST['text']))
  {
    $text = sanitizeString($_POST['text']);
    $text = preg_replace('/\s\s+/', ' ', $text);

    if ($result->num_rows)
        queryMysql("UPDATE profiles SET text='$text' where user='$user'");
    else queryMysql("INSERT INTO profiles VALUES('$user', '$text')");
  }
  else
  {
    if ($result->num_rows)
    {
      $row  = $result->fetch_array(MYSQLI_ASSOC);
      $text = stripslashes($row['text']);
    }
    else $text = "";
  }

  $text = stripslashes(preg_replace('/\s\s+/', ' ', $text));

  if (isset($_FILES['image']['name']))
  {
    $saveto = "$user.jpg";
    move_uploaded_file($_FILES['image']['tmp_name'], $saveto);
```

```php
    $typeok = TRUE;

    switch($_FILES['image']['type'])
    {
      case "image/gif":   $src = imagecreatefromgif($saveto); break;
      case "image/jpeg":  // Both regular and progressive jpegs
      case "image/pjpeg": $src = imagecreatefromjpeg($saveto); break;
      case "image/png":   $src = imagecreatefrompng($saveto); break;
      default:            $typeok = FALSE; break;
    }

    if ($typeok)
    {
      list($w, $h) = getimagesize($saveto);

      $max = 100;
      $tw  = $w;
      $th  = $h;

      if ($w > $h && $max < $w)
      {
        $th = $max / $w * $h;
        $tw = $max;
      }
      elseif ($h > $w && $max < $h)
      {
        $tw = $max / $h * $w;
        $th = $max;
      }
      elseif ($max < $w)
      {
        $tw = $th = $max;
      }

      $tmp = imagecreatetruecolor($tw, $th);
      imagecopyresampled($tmp, $src, 0, 0, 0, 0, $tw, $th, $w, $h);
      imageconvolution($tmp, array(array(-1, -1, -1),
        array(-1, 16, -1), array(-1, -1, -1)), 8, 0);
      imagejpeg($tmp, $saveto);
      imagedestroy($tmp);
      imagedestroy($src);
    }
  }

  showProfile($user);

  echo <<<_END
    <form method='post' action='profile.php' enctype='multipart/form-data'>
    <h3>Enter or edit your details and/or upload an image</h3>
    <textarea name='text' cols='50' rows='3'>$text</textarea><br>
_END;
?>
```

```
   Image: <input type='file' name='image' size='14'>
   <input type='submit' value='Save Profile'>
   </form></div><br>
  </body>
</html>
```

Figure 26-4. Editing a user profile

members.php

Using Example 26-9, *members.php*, your users will be able to find other members and choose to add them as friends (or drop them if they are already friends). This program has two modes. The first lists all members and their relationships to you, and the second shows a user's profile.

Viewing a User's Profile

The code for the latter mode comes first, where a test is made for the GET variable view. If it exists, a user wants to view someone's profile, so the program does that using the showProfile function, along with providing a couple of links to the user's friends and messages.

Adding and Dropping Friends

After that, the two GET variables, add and remove, are tested. If one or the other has a value, it will be the username of a user to either add or drop as a friend. We achieve this by looking up the user in the MySQL friends table and either inserting a friend username or removing it from the table.

And, of course, every posted variable is first passed through sanitizeString to ensure that it is safe to use with MySQL.

Listing All Members

The final section of code issues a SQL query to list all usernames. The code places the number returned in the variable $num before outputting the page heading.

A for loop then iterates through each and every member, fetching their details and then looking them up in the friends table to see if they are either being followed by or a follower of the user. If someone is both a follower and a followee, she is classed as a mutual friend.

The variable $t1 is nonzero when the user is following another member, and $t2 is nonzero when another member is following the user. Depending on these values, text is displayed after each username showing the relationship (if any) to the current user.

Icons are also displayed to show the relationships. A double pointing arrow means that the users are mutual friends. A left-pointing arrow indicates the user is following another member. And a right-pointing arrow indicates that another member is following the user.

Finally, depending on whether the user is following another member, a link is provided to either add or drop that member as a friend.

When you call Example 26-9 up in a browser, it will look like Figure 26-5. See how the user is invited to "follow" a non-following member, but if the member is already following the user, a "recip" link to reciprocate the friendship is offered. In the case of a user already following another member, the user can select "drop" to end the following.

Example 26-9. members.php

```php
<?php
  require_once 'header.php';

  if (!$loggedin) die();

  echo "<div class='main'>";

  if (isset($_GET['view']))
  {
    $view = sanitizeString($_GET['view']);

    if ($view == $user) $name = "Your";
    else                $name = "$view's";

    echo "<h3>$name Profile</h3>";
    showProfile($view);
    echo "<a class='button' href='messages.php?view=$view'>" .
        "View $name messages</a><br><br>";
    die("</div></body></html>");
  }

  if (isset($_GET['add']))
  {
    $add = sanitizeString($_GET['add']);

    $result = queryMysql("SELECT * FROM friends WHERE user='$add'
      AND friend='$user'");
    if (!$result->num_rows)
      queryMysql("INSERT INTO friends VALUES ('$add', '$user')");
  }
  elseif (isset($_GET['remove']))
  {
    $remove = sanitizeString($_GET['remove']);
    queryMysql("DELETE FROM friends WHERE user='$remove' AND friend='$user'");
  }

  $result = queryMysql("SELECT user FROM members ORDER BY user");
  $num     = $result->num_rows;

  echo "<h3>Other Members</h3><ul>";

  for ($j = 0 ; $j < $num ; ++$j)
  {
    $row = $result->fetch_array(MYSQLI_ASSOC);
    if ($row['user'] == $user) continue;
```

```
echo "<li><a href='members.php?view=" .
  $row['user'] . "'>" . $row['user'] . "</a>";
$follow = "follow";

$result1 = queryMysql("SELECT * FROM friends WHERE
  user='" . $row['user'] . "' AND friend='$user'");
$t1      = $result1->num_rows;
$result1 = queryMysql("SELECT * FROM friends WHERE
  user='$user' AND friend='" . $row['user'] . "'");
$t2      = $result1->num_rows;

if (($t1 + $t2) > 1) echo " &harr; is a mutual friend";
elseif ($t1)         echo " &larr; you are following";
elseif ($t2)      { echo " &rarr; is following you";
  $follow = "recip"; }

if (!$t1) echo " [<a href='members.php?add="    .
  $row['user'] . "'>$follow</a>]";
else      echo " [<a href='members.php?remove=" .
  $row['user'] . "'>drop</a>]";
  }
?>

    </ul></div>
  </body>
</html>
```

On a production server, there could be thousands or even hundreds of thousands of users, so you would probably substantially modify this program to include searching the "about me" text, support paging of the output a screen at a time, and so on.

Figure 26-5. Using the members module

friends.php

The module that shows a user's friends and followers is Example 26-10, *friends.php*. This interrogates the friends table just like the *members.php* program, but only for a single user. It then shows all of that user's mutual friends and followers along with the people he is following.

All the followers are saved into an array called $followers, and all the people being followed are placed in an array called $following. Then a neat piece of code is used to extract all those who are both following and followed by the user, like this:

```
$mutual = array_intersect($followers, $following);
```

The array_intersect function extracts all members common to both arrays and returns a new array containing only those people. This array is then stored in $mutual. Now it's possible to use the array_diff function for each of the $followers and $following arrays to keep only those people who are *not* mutual friends, like this:

```
$followers = array_diff($followers, $mutual);
$following = array_diff($following, $mutual);
```

This results in the array $mutual containing only mutual friends, $followers containing only followers (and no mutual friends), and $following containing only people being followed (and no mutual friends).

Now that we're armed with these arrays, it's a simple matter to separately display each category of members, as can be seen in Figure 26-6. The PHP sizeof function returns the number of elements in an array; here I use it just to trigger code when the size is nonzero (i.e., friends of that type exist).

Note how, by using the variables $name1, $name2, and $name3 in the relevant places, the code can tell when you're looking at your own friends list, using the words *Your* and *You are*, instead of simply displaying the username. The commented line can be uncommented if you wish to display the user's profile information on this screen.

Example 26-10. friends.php

```php
<?php
  require_once 'header.php';

  if (!$loggedin) die();

  if (isset($_GET['view'])) $view = sanitizeString($_GET['view']);
  else                      $view = $user;

  if ($view == $user)
  {
    $name1 = $name2 = "Your";
    $name3 =          "You are";
  }
  else
  {
    $name1 = "<a href='members.php?view=$view'>$view</a>'s";
    $name2 = "$view's";
    $name3 = "$view is";
  }

  echo "<div class='main'>";

  // Uncomment this line if you wish the user's profile to show here
  // showProfile($view);

  $followers = array();
  $following = array();

  $result = queryMysql("SELECT * FROM friends WHERE user='$view'");
  $num     = $result->num_rows;

  for ($j = 0 ; $j < $num ; ++$j)
  {
```

```php
    $row          = $result->fetch_array(MYSQLI_ASSOC);
    $followers[$j] = $row['friend'];
}

$result = queryMysql("SELECT * FROM friends WHERE friend='$view'");
$num    = $result->num_rows;

for ($j = 0 ; $j < $num ; ++$j)
{
    $row          = $result->fetch_array(MYSQLI_ASSOC);
    $following[$j] = $row['user'];
}

$mutual    = array_intersect($followers, $following);
$followers = array_diff($followers, $mutual);
$following = array_diff($following, $mutual);
$friends   = FALSE;

if (sizeof($mutual))
{
  echo "<span class='subhead'>$name2 mutual friends</span><ul>";
  foreach($mutual as $friend)
    echo "<li><a href='members.php?view=$friend'>$friend</a>";
  echo "</ul>";
  $friends = TRUE;
}

if (sizeof($followers))
{
  echo "<span class='subhead'>$name2 followers</span><ul>";
  foreach($followers as $friend)
    echo "<li><a href='members.php?view=$friend'>$friend</a>";
  echo "</ul>";
  $friends = TRUE;
}

if (sizeof($following))
{
  echo "<span class='subhead'>$name3 following</span><ul>";
  foreach($following as $friend)
    echo "<li><a href='members.php?view=$friend'>$friend</a>";
  echo "</ul>";
  $friends = TRUE;
}

if (!$friends) echo "<br>You don't have any friends yet.<br><br>";

echo "<a class='button' href='messages.php?view=$view'>" .
     "View $name2 messages</a>";
?>

    </div><br>
```

```
    </body>
</html>
```

Figure 26-6. Displaying a user's friends and followers

messages.php

The last of the main modules is Example 26-11, *messages.php*. The program starts by checking whether a message has been posted in the POST variable text. If so, it is inserted into the messages table. At the same time, the value of pm is also stored. This indicates whether a message is private or public. A 0 represents a public message and 1 is private.

Next, the user's profile and a form for entering a message are displayed, along with radio buttons to choose between a private or public message. After this, all the messages are shown, depending on whether they are private or public. If they are public, all users can see them, but private messages are visible only to the sender and recipient. This is all handled by a couple of queries to the MySQL database. Additionally, when a message is private, it is introduced by the word *whispered* and shown in italic.

Finally, the program displays a couple of links to refresh the messages (in case another user has posted one in the meantime) and to view the user's friends. The trick using the variables $name1 and $name2 is again used so that when you view your own profile the word *Your* is displayed instead of the username.

You can see the result of viewing this program with a browser in Figure 26-7. Note how users viewing their own messages are provided with links to erase any they don't want.

Example 26-11. messages.php

```php
<?php
  require_once 'header.php';

  if (!$loggedin) die();

  if (isset($_GET['view'])) $view = sanitizeString($_GET['view']);
  else                      $view = $user;

  if (isset($_POST['text']))
  {
    $text = sanitizeString($_POST['text']);

    if ($text != "")
    {
      $pm   = substr(sanitizeString($_POST['pm']),0,1);
      $time = time();
      queryMysql("INSERT INTO messages VALUES(NULL, '$user',
        '$view', '$pm', $time, '$text')");
    }
  }

  if ($view != "")
  {
    if ($view == $user) $name1 = $name2 = "Your";
    else
    {
      $name1 = "<a href='members.php?view=$view'>$view</a>'s";
      $name2 = "$view's";
    }

    echo "<div class='main'><h3>$name1 Messages</h3>";
    showProfile($view);

    echo <<<_END
      <form method='post' action='messages.php?view=$view'>
      Type here to leave a message:<br>
      <textarea name='text' cols='40' rows='3'></textarea><br>
      Public<input type='radio' name='pm' value='0' checked='checked'>
      Private<input type='radio' name='pm' value='1'>
```

```php
      <input type='submit' value='Post Message'></form><br>
_END;

    if (isset($_GET['erase']))
    {
      $erase = sanitizeString($_GET['erase']);
      queryMysql("DELETE FROM messages WHERE id=$erase AND recip='$user'");
    }

    $query  = "SELECT * FROM messages WHERE recip='$view' ORDER BY time DESC";
    $result = queryMysql($query);
    $num    = $result->num_rows;

    for ($j = 0 ; $j < $num ; ++$j)
    {
      $row = $result->fetch_array(MYSQLI_ASSOC);

      if ($row['pm'] == 0 || $row['auth'] == $user || $row['recip'] == $user)
      {
        echo date('M jS \'y g:ia:', $row['time']);
        echo " <a href='messages.php?view=" . $row['auth'] . "'>" .
          $row['auth']. "</a> ";

        if ($row['pm'] == 0)
          echo "wrote: &quot;" . $row['message'] . "&quot; ";
        else
          echo "whispered: <span class='whisper'>&quot;" .
            $row['message'] . "&quot;</span> ";

        if ($row['recip'] == $user)
          echo "[<a href='messages.php?view=$view" .
            "&erase=" . $row['id'] . "'>erase</a>]";

        echo "<br>";
      }
    }
  }

  if (!$num) echo "<br><span class='info'>No messages yet</span><br><br>";

  echo "<br><a class='button' href='messages.php?view=$view'>Refresh messages</a>";
?>

    </div><br>
  </body>
</html>
```

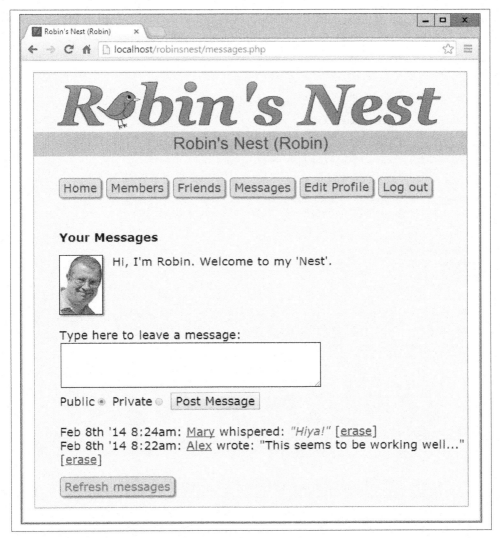

Figure 26-7. The messaging module

logout.php

The final ingredient in our social networking recipe is Example 26-12, *logout.php*, the logout page that closes a session and deletes any associated data and cookies. The result of calling up this program is shown in Figure 26-8, where the user is now asked to click on a link that will take her to the un-logged-in home page and remove the logged-in links from the top of the screen. Of course, you could write a JavaScript or PHP redirect to do this (probably a good idea if you wish to keep logout looking clean).

Example 26-12. logout.php

```php
<?php
  require_once 'header.php';

  if (isset($_SESSION['user']))
  {
    destroySession();
    echo "<div class='main'>You have been logged out. Please " .
         "<a href='index.php'>click here</a> to refresh the screen.";
  }
  else echo "<div class='main'><br>" .
            "You cannot log out because you are not logged in";
?>

    <br><br></div>
  </body>
</html>
```

Figure 26-8. The logout page

styles.css

The style sheet used for this project is shown in Example 26-13. There are a number of sets of declarations, as follows:

`*`

Sets the default font family and size for the project using the universal selector.

`body`

Sets the width of the project window, centers it horizontally, specifies a background color, and gives it a border.

`html`

Sets the background color of the HTML section.

`img`

Gives all images a border, shadow, and a righthand margin.

`li a` *and* `.button`

Remove underlines from hyperlinks in all `<a>` tags that are within a `<li>` element, and all elements employing the `button` class.

`li a:hover` *and* `.button:hover`

Set the color in which `<li>` elements and the `button` class should display text when hovered over.

`.appname`

Sets the properties for the heading (which uses the `appname` class), including centering, background and text colors, the font family and size, and the padding.

`.fieldname`

Sets the width of elements using the `fieldname` class by first floating them.

`.main`

This class applies an indent to elements that use it.

`.info`

This class is used for displaying important information. It sets a background and foreground text color, applies a border and padding, and indents elements that employ it.

`.menu li` *and* `.button`

These declarations ensure that all `<li>` elements and the `button` class display inline, have padding applied, and include a border, a background and foreground text color, a right margin, rounded borders, and a shadow—resulting in a button effect.

`.subhead`

Emphasizes sections of text.

`.taken, .available, .error,` *and* `.whisper`

These declarations set the colors and font styles to be used for displaying different types of information.

#logo

These rules style the logo text as a fallback in case a non-HTML5 browser is in use and the canvas logo doesn't get created.

Example 26-13. styles.css

```css
* {
  font-family:verdana,sans-serif;
  font-size   :14pt;
}

body {
  width      :700px;
  margin     :20px auto;
  background:#f8f8f8;
  border     :1px solid #888;
}

html {
  background:#fff
}

img {
  border             :1px solid black;
  margin-right       :15px;
  -moz-box-shadow    :2px 2px 2px #888;
  -webkit-box-shadow:2px 2px 2px #888;
  box-shadow         :2px 2px 2px #888;
}

li a, .button {
  text-decoration:none;
}

li a:hover, .button:hover {
  color:green;
}

.appname {
  text-align :center;
  background :#eb8;
  color      :#40d;
  font-family:helvetica;
  font-size  :20pt;
  padding    :4px;
}

.fieldname {
  float:left;
  width:120px;
}
```

```css
.main {
  margin-left:40px;
}

.info {
  background :lightgreen;
  color      :blue;
  border     :1px solid green;
  padding    :5px 10px;
  margin-left:40px;
}

.menu li, .button {
  display             :inline;
  padding             :4px 6px;
  border              :1px solid #777;
  background          :#ddd;
  color               :#d04;
  margin-right        :8px;
  border-radius       :5px;
  -moz-box-shadow     :2px 2px 2px #888;
  -webkit-box-shadow:2px 2px 2px #888;
  box-shadow          :2px 2px 2px #888;
}

.subhead {
  font-weight:bold;
}

.taken, .error {
  color:red;
}

.available {
  color:green;
}

.whisper {
  font-style:italic;
  color      :#006600;
}

#logo {
  font-family:Georgia;
  font-weight:bold;
  font-style :italic;
  font-size  :97px;
}
```

javascript.js

Finally, there's the JavaScript file (see Example 26-14), which contains the O, S, and C functions used throughout this book, along with some code to draw the logo for the site using an HTML5 canvas, as explained in Chapter 23.

Example 26-14. javascript.js

```
canvas              = O('logo')
context             = canvas.getContext('2d')
context.font        = 'bold italic 97px Georgia'
context.textBaseline = 'top'
image               = new Image()
image.src           = 'robin.gif'

image.onload = function()
{
  gradient = context.createLinearGradient(0, 0, 0, 89)
  gradient.addColorStop(0.00, '#faa')
  gradient.addColorStop(0.66, '#f00')
  context.fillStyle = gradient
  context.fillText(  "R  bin's Nest", 0, 0)
  context.strokeText("R  bin's Nest", 0, 0)
  context.drawImage(image, 64, 32)
}

function O(obj)
{
  if (typeof obj == 'object') return obj
  else return document.getElementById(obj)
}

function S(obj)
{
  return O(obj).style
}

function C(name)
{
  var elements = document.getElementsByTagName('*')
  var objects  = []

  for (var i = 0 ; i < elements.length ; ++i)
    if (elements[i].className == name)
      objects.push(elements[i])

  return objects
}
```

And that, as they say, is that. If you write anything based on this code or any other examples in this book, or have gained in any other way from it, then I am glad to have been of help and thank you for reading this book.

But before you go and try out your newly learned skills on the Web at large, browse through the appendixes that follow, as there's a lot of additional information there you should find useful.

Solutions to the Chapter Questions

Chapter 1 Answers

1. A web server (such as Apache), a server-side scripting language (PHP), a database (MySQL), and a client-side scripting language (JavaScript).

2. HyperText Markup Language: the web page itself, including text and markup tags.

3. Like nearly all database engines, MySQL accepts commands in Structured Query Language (SQL). SQL is the way that every user (including a PHP program) communicates with MySQL.

4. PHP runs on the server, whereas JavaScript runs on the client. PHP can communicate with the database to store and retrieve data, but it can't alter the user's web page quickly and dynamically. JavaScript has the opposite benefits and drawbacks.

5. Cascading Style Sheets: styling and layout rules applied to the elements in an HTML document.

6. Probably the most interesting new elements in HTML5 are `<audio>`, `<video>`, and `<canvas>`, although there are many others such as `<article>`, `<summary>`, `<footer>`, and more.

7. Some of these technologies are controlled by companies that accept bug reports and fix the errors like any software company. But open source software also depends on a community, so your bug report may be handled by any user who understands the code well enough. You may someday fix bugs in an open source tool yourself.

Chapter 2 Answers

1. WAMP stands for "Windows, Apache, MySQL, and PHP"; *M* in MAMP stands for Mac instead of Windows; and the *L* in LAMP stands for Linux. They all refer to a complete solution for hosting dynamic web pages.

2. Both 127.0.0.1 and http://localhost are ways of referring to the local computer. When a WAMP or MAMP is properly configured, you can type either into a browser's address bar to call up the default page on the local server.

3. FTP stands for File Transfer Protocol. An FTP program is used to transfer files back and forth between a client and a server.

4. It is necessary to FTP files to a remote server in order to update it, which can substantially increase development time if this action is carried out many times in a session.

5. Dedicated program editors are smart and can highlight problems in your code before you even run it.

Chapter 3 Answers

1. The tag used to start PHP interpreting code is <?php ... ?>, which can be shortened to <? ... ?> but is not recommended practice.

2. You can use // for a single-line comment or /* ... */ to span multiple lines.

3. All PHP statements must end with a semicolon (;).

4. With the exception of constants, all PHP variables must begin with $.

5. Variables hold a value that can be a string, a number, or other data.

6. $variable = 1 is an assignment statement, whereas $variable == 1 is a comparison operator. Use $variable = 1 to set the value of $variable. Use $variable == 1 to find out later in the program whether $variable equals 1. If you mistakenly use $variable = 1 where you meant to do a comparison, it will do two things you probably don't want: set $variable to 1 and return a true value all the time, no matter what its previous value was.

7. A hyphen is reserved for the subtraction operators. A construct like $current-user would be harder to interpret if hyphens were also allowed in variable names and, in any case, would lead programs to be ambiguous.

8. Variable names are case-sensitive. So, for example, $This_Variable is not the same as $this_variable.

9. You cannot use spaces in variable names, as this would confuse the PHP parser. Instead, try using the _ (underscore).

10. To convert one variable type to another, reference it and PHP will automatically convert it for you.

11. There is no difference between `++$j` and `$j++` unless the value of `$j` is being tested, assigned to another variable, or passed as a parameter to a function. In such cases, `++$j` increments `$j` before the test or other operation is performed, whereas `$j++` performs the operation and then increments `$j`.

12. Generally, the operators `&&` and `and` are interchangeable except where precedence is important, in which case `&&` has a high precedence, while `and` has a low one.

13. You can use multiple lines within quotations marks or the `<<<_END ... _END;` construct to create a multiline echo or assignment. The closing tag must begin at the start of a line, and end with a semicolon followed by a new line.

14. You cannot redefine constants because, by definition, once defined they retain their value until the program terminates.

15. You can use `\'` or `\"` to escape either a single or double quote.

16. The `echo` and `print` commands are similar in that they are both constructs, except that `print` behaves like a PHP function and takes a single argument, while `echo` can take multiple arguments.

17. The purpose of functions is to separate discrete sections of code into their own, self-contained sections that can be referenced by a single function name.

18. You can make a variable accessible to all parts of a PHP program by declaring it as `global`.

19. If you generate data within a function, you can convey the data to the rest of the program by returning a value or modifying a global variable.

20. When you combine a string with a number, the result is another string.

Chapter 4 Answers

1. In PHP, `TRUE` represents the value 1 and `FALSE` represents `NULL`, which can be thought of as "nothing" and is output as the empty string.

2. The simplest forms of expressions are literals (such as numbers and strings) and variables, which simply evaluate to themselves.

3. The difference between unary, binary, and ternary operators is the number of operands each requires (one, two, and three, respectively).

4. The best way to force your own operator precedence is to place parentheses around subexpressions to which you wish to give high precedence.

5. Operator associativity refers to the direction of processing (left to right or right to left).

6. You use the identity operator when you wish to bypass PHP's automatic operand type changing (also called *type casting*).

7. The three conditional statement types are `if`, `switch`, and the `?:` operator.

8. To skip the current iteration of a loop and move on to the next one, use a `continue` statement.

9. Loops using `for` statements are more powerful than `while` loops, because they support two additional parameters to control the loop handling.

10. Most conditional expressions in `if` and `while` statements are literal (or Boolean) and therefore trigger execution when they evaluate to `TRUE`. Numeric expressions trigger execution when they evaluate to a nonzero value. String expressions trigger execution when they evaluate to a nonempty string. A `NULL` value is evaluated as false and therefore does not trigger execution.

Chapter 5 Answers

1. Using functions avoids the need to copy or rewrite similar code sections many times over by combining sets of statements together so that they can be called by a simple name.

2. By default, a function can return a single value. But by utilizing arrays, references, and global variables, any number of values can be returned.

3. When you reference a variable by name, such as by assigning its value to another variable or by passing its value to a function, its value is copied. The original does not change when the copy is changed. But if you reference a variable, only a pointer (or reference) to its value is used, so that a single value is referenced by more than one name. Changing the value of the reference will change the original as well.

4. Scope refers to which parts of a program can access a variable. For example, a variable of global scope can be accessed by all parts of a PHP program.

5. To incorporate one file within another, you can use the `include` or `require` directives, or their safer variants, `include_once` and `require_once`.

6. A function is a set of statements referenced by a name that can receive and return values. An object may contain zero or many functions (which are then called methods) as well as variables (which are called properties), all combined in a single unit.

7. To create a new object in PHP, use the `new` keyword like this:

```
$object = new Class;
```

8. To create a subclass, use the `extends` keyword with syntax such as this:

```
class Subclass extends Parentclass ...
```

9. To call a piece of initializing code when an object is created, create a constructor method called __construct within the class and place your code there.

10. Explicitly declaring properties within a class is unnecessary, as they will be implicitly declared upon first use. But it is considered good practice as it helps with code readability and debugging, and is especially useful to other people who may have to maintain your code.

Chapter 6 Answers

1. A numeric array can be indexed numerically using numbers or numeric variables. An associative array uses alphanumeric identifiers to index elements.

2. The main benefit of the array keyword is that it enables you to assign several values at a time to an array without repeating the array name.

3. Both the each function and the foreach ... as loop construct return elements from an array; both start at the beginning and increment a pointer to make sure the next element is returned each time; and both return FALSE when the end of the array is reached. The difference is that the each function returns just a single element, so it is usually wrapped in a loop. The foreach ... as construct is already a loop, executing repeatedly until the array is exhausted or you explicitly break out of the loop.

4. To create a multidimensional array, you need to assign additional arrays to elements of the main array.

5. You can use the count function to count the number of elements in an array.

6. The purpose of the explode function is to extract sections from a string that are separated by an identifier, such as extracting words separated by spaces within a sentence.

7. To reset PHP's internal pointer into an array back to the first element, call the reset function.

Chapter 7 Answers

1. The conversion specifier you would use to display a floating-point number is %f.

2. To take the input string "Happy Birthday" and output the string "**Happy", you could use a printf statement such as:

```
printf("%'*7.5s", "Happy Birthday");
```

3. To send the output from printf to a variable instead of to a browser, you would use sprintf instead.

4. To create a Unix timestamp for 7:11am on May 2nd 2016, you could use the command:

```
$timestamp = mktime(7, 11, 0, 5, 2, 2016);
```

5. You would use the "w+" file access mode with `fopen` to open a file in write and read mode, with the file truncated and the file pointer at the start.

6. The PHP command for deleting the file *file.txt* is:

```
unlink('file.txt');
```

7. The PHP function `file_get_contents` is used to read in an entire file in one go. It will also read them from across the Internet if provided with a URL.

8. The PHP superglobal associative array `$_FILES` contains the details about uploaded files.

9. The PHP `exec` function enables the running of system commands.

10. In HTML5 you can use either the XHTML style of tag (such as <hr />) or the standard HTML4 style (such as <hr>). It's entirely up to you or your company's coding style.

Chapter 8 Answers

1. The semicolon is used by MySQL to separate or end commands. If you forget to enter it, MySQL will issue a prompt and wait for you to enter it. (In the answers in this section, I've left off the semicolon, because it looks strange in the text. But it must terminate every statement.)

2. To see the available databases, type SHOW databases. To see tables within a database that you are using, type SHOW tables. (These commands are case-insensitive.)

3. To create this new user, use the GRANT command like this:

```
GRANT PRIVILEGES ON newdatabase.* TO 'newuser'@'localhost'
    IDENTIFIED BY 'newpassword';
```

4. To view the structure of a table, type DESCRIBE tablename.

5. The purpose of a MySQL index is to substantially decrease database access times by maintaining indexes of one or more key columns, which can then be quickly searched to locate rows within a table.

6. A FULLTEXT index enables natural-language queries to find keywords, wherever they are in the FULLTEXT column(s), in much the same way as using a search engine.

7. A stopword is a word that is so common that it is considered not worth including in a FULLTEXT index or using in searches. However, it does participate in a search when it is part of a larger string bounded by double quotes.

8. `SELECT DISTINCT` essentially affects only the display, choosing a single row and eliminating all the duplicates. `GROUP BY` does not eliminate rows, but combines all the rows that have the same value in the column. Therefore, `GROUP BY` is useful for performing an operation such as `COUNT` on groups of rows. `SELECT DISTINCT` is not useful for that purpose.

9. To return only those rows containing the word *Langhorne* somewhere in the column *author* of the table *classics*, use a command such as:

```
SELECT * FROM classics WHERE author LIKE "%Langhorne%";
```

10. When you're joining two tables together, they must share at least one common column such as an ID number or, as in the case of the *classics* and *customers* tables, the *isbn* column.

Chapter 9 Answers

1. The term *relationship* refers to the connection between two pieces of data that have some association, such as a book and its author, or a book and the customer who bought the book. A relational database such as MySQL specializes in storing and retrieving such relations.

2. The process of removing duplicate data and optimizing tables is called *normalization*.

3. The three rules of First Normal Form are:

   - There should be no repeating columns containing the same kind of data.

   - All columns should contain a single value.

   - There should be a primary key to uniquely identify each row.

4. To satisfy Second Normal Form, columns whose data repeats across multiple rows should be removed to their own tables.

5. In a one-to-many relationship, the primary key from the table on the "one" side must be added as a separate column (a foreign key) to the table on the "many" side.

6. To create a database with many-to-many relationship, you create an intermediary table containing keys from two other tables. The other tables can then reference each other via the third.

7. To initiate a MySQL transaction, use either the `BEGIN` or the `START TRANSACTION` command. To terminate a transaction and cancel all actions, issue a `ROLLBACK` command. To terminate a transaction and commit all actions, issue a `COMMIT` command.

8. To examine how a query will work in detail, you can use the `EXPLAIN` command.

9. To back up the database *publications* to a file called *publications.sql*, you would use a command such as:

```
mysqldump -u user -ppassword publications > publications.sql
```

Chapter 10 Answers

1. The standard MySQL function used for connecting to a MySQL database is `mysql_connect`.

2. The `mysql_result` function is not optimal when more than one cell is being requested, because it fetches only a single cell from a database and therefore has to be called multiple times, whereas `mysql_fetch_row` will fetch an entire row.

3. The `POST` form method is generally better than `GET`, because the fields are posted directly, rather than being appended to the URL. This has several advantages, particularly in removing the possibility to enter spoof data at the browser's address bar. (It is not a complete defense against spoofing, however.)

4. To determine the last entered value of an `AUTO_INCREMENT` column, use the `mysql_insert_id` function.

5. The PHP function that escapes characters in a string, making it suitable for use with MySQL, is `mysql_real_escape_string`.

6. The function `htmlentities` can be used to prevent cross-site scripting injection attacks.

Chapter 11 Answers

1. To connect to a MySQL database with `mysqli` call the `mysqli` method, passing the hostname, username, password, and database. A connection object will be returned on success.

2. To submit a query to MySQL using `mysqli`, ensure you have first created a connection object to a database, and call its `query` method, passing the query string.

3. When a `mysqli` error occurs, the `error` property of the connection object contains the error message. If the error was in connecting to the database, then the `connect_error` property will contain the error message.

4. To determine the number of rows returned by a `mysqli` query, use the `num_rows` property of the result object.

5. To retrieve a specific row from a set of `mysqli` results, call the `data_seek` method of the result object, passing it the row number (starting from 0), then call the `fetch_array` or other retrieval method to obtain the required data.

6. To escape special characters in strings, you can call the `real_escape_string` method of a `mysqli` connection object, passing it the string to be escaped.

7. If you neglect to properly close objects created with `mysqli` methods, your programs carry the risk of running out of memory, especially on high-traffic websites. If there's a program flow logic error in your code, it also ensures you won't accidentally access old results.

Chapter 12 Answers

1. The associative arrays used to pass submitted form data to PHP are `$_GET` for the `GET` method and `$_POST` for the `POST` method.

2. The `register_globals` setting was the default in versions of PHP prior to 4.2.0. It was not a good idea, because it automatically assigned submitted form field data to PHP variables, thus opening up a security hole for potential hackers who could attempt to break into PHP code by initializing variables to values of their choice.

3. The difference between a text box and a text area is that although they both accept text for form input, a text box is a single line, whereas a text area can be multiple lines and include word wrapping.

4. To offer three mutually exclusive choices in a web form, you should use radio buttons, because checkboxes allow multiple selections.

5. Submit a group of selections from a web form using a single field name by using an array name with square brackets such as `choices[]`, instead of a regular field name. Each value is then placed into the array, whose length will be the number of elements submitted.

6. To submit a form field without the user seeing it, place it in a hidden field using the attribute `type="hidden"`.

7. You can encapsulate a form element and supporting text or graphics, making the entire unit selectable with a mouse-click, by using the `<label>` and `</label>` tags.

8. To convert HTML into a format that can be displayed but will not be interpreted as HTML by a browser, use the PHP `htmlentities` function.

9. You can help users complete fields with data they may have submitted elsewhere using the `autocomplete` attribute, which prompts the user with possible values.

10. To ensure that a form is not submitted with missing data, you can apply the `required` attribute to essential inputs.

Chapter 13 Answers

1. Cookies should be transferred before a web page's HTML, because they are sent as part of the headers.

2. To store a cookie on a web browser, use the `set_cookie` function.

3. To destroy a cookie, reissue it with `set_cookie`, but set its expiration date in the past.

4. Using HTTP authentication, the username and password are stored in `$_SERVER['PHP_AUTH_USER']` and `$_SERVER['PHP_AUTH_PW']`.

5. The `hash` function is a powerful security measure, because it is a one-way function that converts a string to a 32-character hexadecimal number that cannot be converted back, and is therefore almost uncrackable.

6. When a string is salted, extra characters (known only by the programmer) are added to it before `hash` conversion. This makes it nearly impossible for a brute-force dictionary attack to succeed.

7. A PHP session is a group of variables unique to the current user.

8. To initiate a PHP session, use the `session_start` function.

9. Session hijacking is where a hacker somehow discovers an existing session ID and attempts to take it over.

10. Session fixation is the attempt to force your own session ID onto a server rather than letting it create its own.

Chapter 14 Answers

1. To enclose JavaScript code, you use `<script>` and `</script>` tags.

2. By default, JavaScript code will output to the part of the document in which it resides. If it's in the head, it will output to the head; if in the body, it outputs to the body.

3. You can include JavaScript code from other sources in your documents by either copying and pasting them or, more commonly, including them as part of a `<script src='filename.js'>` tag.

4. The equivalent of the `echo` and `print` commands used in PHP is the JavaScript `document.write` function (or method).

5. To create a comment in JavaScript, preface it with `//` for a single-line comment or surround it with `/*` and `*/` for a multiline comment.

6. The JavaScript string concatenation operator is the + symbol.

7. Within a JavaScript function, you can define a variable that has local scope by preceding it with the `var` keyword upon first assignment.

8. To display the URL assigned to the link ID `thislink` in all main browsers, you can use the two following commands:

```
document.write(document.getElementById('thislink').href)
document.write(thislink.href)
```

9. The commands to change to the previous page in the browser's history array are:

```
history.back()
history.go(-1)
```

10. To replace the current document with the main page at the *oreilly.com* website, you could use the following command:

```
document.location.href = 'http://oreilly.com'
```

Chapter 15 Answers

1. The most noticeable difference between Boolean values in PHP and JavaScript is that PHP recognizes the keywords `TRUE`, `true`, `FALSE`, and `false`, whereas only `true` and `false` are supported in JavaScript. Additionally, in PHP `TRUE` has a value of 1 and `FALSE` is `NULL`; in JavaScript they are represented by `true` and `false`, which can be returned as string values.

2. Unlike PHP, no character is used (such as $) to define a JavaScript variable name. JavaScript variable names can start with and contain any uppercase and lowercase letters as well as underscores; names can also include digits, but not as the first character.

3. The difference between unary, binary, and ternary operators is the number of operands each requires (one, two, and three, respectively).

4. The best way to force your own operator precedence is to surround the parts of an expression to be evaluated first with parentheses.

5. You use the identity operator when you wish to bypass JavaScript's automatic operand type changing.

6. The simplest forms of expressions are literals (such as numbers and strings) and variables, which simply evaluate to themselves.

7. The three conditional statement types are `if`, `switch`, and the `?:` operator.

8. Most conditional expressions in `if` and `while` statements are literal or Boolean and therefore trigger execution when they evaluate to `TRUE`. Numeric expressions trigger execution when they evaluate to a nonzero value. String expressions trigger exe-

cution when they evaluate to a nonempty string. A NULL value is evaluated as false and therefore does not trigger execution.

9. Loops using for statements are more powerful than while loops, because they support two additional parameters to control loop handling.

10. The with statement takes an object as its parameter. Using it, you specify an object once; then for each statement within the with block, that object is assumed.

Chapter 16 Answers

1. JavaScript functions and variable name are case-sensitive. The variables Count, count, and COUNT are all different.

2. To write a function that accepts and processes an unlimited number of parameters, access parameters through the arguments array, which is a member of all functions.

3. One way to return multiple values from a function is to place them all inside an array and return the array.

4. When defining a class, use the this keyword to refer to the current object.

5. The methods of a class do not have to be defined within a class definition. If a method is defined outside the constructor, the method name must be assigned to the this object within the class definition.

6. New objects are created via the new keyword.

7. You can make a property or method available to all objects in a class without replicating the property or method within the object by using the prototype keyword to create a single instance, which is then passed by reference to all the objects in a class.

8. To create a multidimensional array, place subarrays inside the main array.

9. The syntax you would use to create an associative array is key : value, within curly braces, as in the following:

```
assocarray =
{
  "forename" : "Paul",
  "surname"  : "McCartney",
  "group"    : "The Beatles"
}
```

10. A statement to sort an array of numbers into descending numerical order would look like this:

```
numbers.sort(function(a, b){ return b - a })
```

Chapter 17 Answers

1. You can send a form for validation prior to submitting it by adding the JavaScript onsubmit attribute to the <form> tag. Make sure that your function returns true if the form is to be submitted and false otherwise.

2. To match a string against a regular expression in JavaScript, use the test method.

3. Regular expressions to match characters not in a word could be any of /[^\w]/, /[\W]/, /[^a-zA-Z0-9_]/, and so on.

4. A regular expression to match either of the words *fox* or *fix* could be /f[oi]x/.

5. A regular expression to match any single word followed by any nonword character could be /\w+\W/g.

6. A JavaScript function using regular expressions to test whether the word *fox* exists in the string "The quick brown fox" could be:

   ```
   document.write(/fox/.test("The quick brown fox"))
   ```

7. A PHP function using a regular expression to replace all occurrences of the word *the* in "The cow jumps over the moon" with the word *my* could be:

   ```
   $s=preg_replace("/the/i", "my", "The cow jumps over the moon");
   ```

8. The HTML attribute used to precomplete form fields with a value is value, which is placed within an <input> tag and takes the form value="*value*".

Chapter 18 Answers

1. It's necessary to write a function for creating new XMLHttpRequest objects, because Microsoft browsers use two different methods of creating them, while all other major browsers use a third. By writing a function to test the browser in use, you can ensure that code will work on all major browsers.

2. The purpose of the try ... catch construct is to set an error trap for the code inside the try statement. If the code causes an error, the catch section will be executed instead of a general error being issued.

3. An XMLHttpRequest object has six properties and six methods (see Tables 18-1 and 18-2).

4. You can tell that an Ajax call has completed when the readyState property of an object has a value of 4.

5. When an Ajax call successfully completes, the object's status will have a value of 200.

6. The `responseText` property of an `XMLHttpRequest` object contains the value returned by a successful Ajax call.

7. The `responseXML` property of an `XMLHttpRequest` object contains a DOM tree created from the XML returned by a successful Ajax call.

8. To specify a callback function to handle Ajax responses, assign the function name to the `XMLHttpRequest` object's `onreadystatechange` property. You can also use an unnamed, inline function.

9. To initiate an Ajax request, an `XMLHTTPRequest` object's send method is called.

10. The main differences between an Ajax `GET` and `POST` request are that `GET` requests append the data to the URL and not as a parameter of the send method, and `POST` requests pass the data as a parameter of the send method and require the correct form headers to be sent first.

Chapter 19 Answers

1. To import one style sheet into another, you use the `@import` directive like this:
   ```
   @import url('styles.css');
   ```

2. To import a style sheet into a document, you can use the HTML `<link>` tag, like this:
   ```
   <link rel='stylesheet' type='text/css' href='styles.css'>
   ```

3. To directly embed a style into an element, use the `style` attribute, like this:
   ```
   <div style='color:blue;'>
   ```

4. The difference between a CSS ID and a CSS class is that an ID is applied to only a single element, whereas a class can be applied to many elements.

5. In a CSS declaration, ID names are prefixed with a # character (e.g., `#myid`), and class names with a . character (e.g., `.myclass`).

6. In CSS, the semicolon is used as a separator between declarations.

7. To add a comment to a style sheet, you enclose it between /* and */ opening and closing comment markers.

8. In CSS, you can match any element using the * universal selector.

9. To select a group of different elements and/or element types in CSS, you place a comma between each element, ID, or class.

10. Given a pair of CSS declarations with equal precedence, to make one have greater precedence over the other, you append the `!important` declaration to it, like this:
    ```
    p { color:#ff0000 !important; }
    ```

Chapter 20 Answers

1. The CSS3 operators ^=, $=, and *= match the start, end, or any portion of a string, respectively.

2. The property you use to specify the size of a background image is background-size, like this:

```
background-size:800px 600px;
```

3. You can specify the radius of a border using the border-radius property, like this:

```
border-radius:20px;
```

4. To flow text over multiple columns, you use the column-count, column-gap, and column-rule properties or their browser-specific variants, like this:

```
column-count:3;
column-gap  :1em;
column-rule :1px solid black;
```

5. The four functions with which you can specify CSS colors are hsl, hsla, rgb, and rgba; for example:

```
color:rgba(0%,60%,40%,0.4);
```

6. To create a gray text shadow under some text, offset diagonally to the bottom right by 5 pixels, with a blurring of 3 pixels, you would use this declaration:

```
text-shadow:5px 5px 3px #888;
```

7. You can indicate that text is truncated with an ellipsis using this declaration:

```
text-overflow:ellipsis;
```

8. You include a Google Web Font in a web page by first selecting it from *http://google.com/fonts*. Then assuming, for example, you chose Lobster, include it in a <link> tag, like this:

```
<link href='http://fonts.googleapis.com/css?family=Lobster'
   rel='stylesheet' type='text/css'>
```

and also refer to the font in a CSS declaration such as this:

```
h1 { font-family:'Lobster', arial, serif; }
```

9. The CSS declaration you would you use to rotate an object by 90 degrees is:

```
transform:rotate(90deg);
```

10. To set up a transition on an object so that when any of its properties are changed the change will transition immediately in a linear fashion over the course of half a second, you would use this declaration:

```
transition:all .5s linear;
```

Chapter 21 Answers

1. The O function returns an object by its ID, the S function returns the `style` property of an object, and the C function returns an array of all objects that access a given class.

2. You can modify a CSS attribute of an object using the `setAttribute` function, like this:

    ```
    myobject.setAttribute('font-size', '16pt')
    ```

    You can also (usually) modify an attribute directly (using slightly modified property names where required), like this:

    ```
    myobject.fontSize = '16pt'
    ```

3. The properties that provide the width and height available in a browser window are `window.innerHeight` and `window.innerWidth`.

4. To make something happen when the mouse passes over and out of an object, attach to the `onmouseover` and `onmouseout` events.

5. To create a new element, use code such as:

    ```
    elem = document.createElement('span')
    ```

    To add the new element to the DOM, use code such as:

    ```
    document.body.appendChild(elem)
    ```

6. To make an element invisible, set its `visibility` property to `hidden` (or `visible` to restore it again). To collapse an element's dimensions to zero, set its `display` property to `none` (the value `block` is one way to restore it).

7. To set a single event at a future time, call the `setTimeout` function, passing it the code or function name to execute and the time delay in milliseconds.

8. To set up repeating events at regular intervals, use the `setInterval` function, passing it the code or function name to execute and the time delay between repeats in milliseconds.

9. To release an element from its location in a web page to enable it to be moved around, set its `position` property to `relative`, `absolute`, or `fixed`. To restore it to its original place, set the property to `static`.

10. To achieve an animation rate of 50 frames per second, you should set a delay between interrupts of 20 milliseconds. To calculate this value, divide 1,000 milliseconds by the desired frame rate.

Chapter 22 Answers

1. The new HTML5 element for drawing graphics in a web browser is the canvas element, created using the `<canvas>` tag.

2. You need to use JavaScript to access many of the new HTML5 technologies such as the canvas and geolocation.

3. To incorporate audio or video in a web page, you use the `<audio>` or `<video>` tags.

4. In HTML5, local storage offers far greater access to local user space than cookies, which are limited in the amount of data they can hold.

5. In HTML5 you can set up web workers to carry on background tasks for you. These workers are simply sections of JavaScript code.

Chapter 23 Answers

1. To create a canvas element in HTML, use a `<canvas>` tag and specify an ID that JavaScript can use to access it, like this:

   ```
   <canvas id='mycanvas'>
   ```

2. To give JavaScript access to a canvas element, ensure the element has been given an ID such as `mycanvas`, and then use the `document.getElementdById` function (or the `O` function from the *OSC.js* file supplied on the companion website) to return an object to the element. Finally, call `getContext` on the object to retrieve a 2D context to the canvas, like this:

   ```
   canvas  = document.getElementById('mycanvas')
   context = canvas.getContext('2d')
   ```

3. To start a canvas path, issue the `beginPath` method on the context. After creating a path, you close it by issuing `closePath` on the context, like this:

   ```
   context.beginPath()
      // Path creation commands go here
   context.closePath()
   ```

4. You can extract the data from a canvas using the `toDataURL` method, which can then be assigned to the `src` property of an image object, like this:

   ```
   image.src = canvas.toDataURL()
   ```

5. To create a gradient fill (either radial or linear) with more than two colors, specify all the colors required as stop colors assigned to a gradient object you have already created, and assign them each a starting point as a percent value of the complete gradient (between 0 and 1), like this:

```
gradient.addColorStop(0,    'green')
gradient.addColorStop(0.3,  'red')
gradient.addColorStop(0,79, 'orange')
gradient.addColorStop(1,    'brown')
```

6. To adjust the width of drawn lines, assign a value to the lineWidth property of the context, like this:

   ```
   context.lineWidth = 5
   ```

7. To ensure that future drawing takes place only within a certain area, you can create a path and then call the clip method.

8. A complex curve with two imaginary attractors is called a Bézier curve. To create one, call the bezierCurveTo method, supplying two pairs of *x* and *y* coordinates for the attractors, followed by another pair for the end point of the curve. A curve is then created from the current drawing location to the destination.

9. The getImageData method returns an array containing the specified pixel data, with the elements consecutively containing the red, green, blue, and alpha pixel values, so four items of data are returned per pixel.

10. The transform method takes six arguments (or parameters), which are in order: horizontal scale, horizontal skew, vertical skew, vertical scale, horizontal translate, and vertical translate. Therefore, the arguments that apply to scaling are numbers 1 and 4 in the list.

Chapter 24 Answers

1. To insert audio and video into an HTML5 document, use the <audio> and <video> tags.

2. To guarantee maximum audio playability on all platforms, you should use the OGG codec plus either the ACC or MP3 codec.

3. To play and pause HTML5 media playback, you can call the play and pause methods of an audio or video element.

4. To support media playback in a non-HTML5 browser, you can embed a Flash audio or video player inside any audio or video element, which will be activated if HTML5 media playing is not supported.

5. To guarantee maximum video playability on all platforms, you should use the MP4/H.264 codec, and the OGG/Theora or VP8 codec to support the Opera browser.

Chapter 25 Answers

1. To request geolocation data from a web browser, you call the following method, passing the names of two functions you have written for handling access or denial to the data:

   ```
   navigator.geolocation.getCurrentPosition(granted, denied)
   ```

2. To determine whether or not a browser supports local storage, test the `typeof` property of the `localStorage` object, like this:

   ```
   if (typeof localStorage == 'undefined')
      // Local storage is not available}
   ```

3. To erase all local storage data for the current domain, you can call the `localStorage.clear` method.

4. Web workers communicate with a main program most easily using the `postMessage` method to send information, and by attaching to the web worker object's `onmessage` event to retrieve it.

5. To inform a web browser that the document can be run offline as a local web app, create a file to use as a manifest; in that file, list the files required by the application, then link to the file in the `<html>` tag, like this:

   ```
   <html manifest='filename.appcache'>
   ```

6. You can prevent the default action of disallowing drag and drop for the events that handle these operations, by issuing a call to the event object's `preventDefault` method in your `ondragover` and `ondrop` event handlers.

7. To make cross-document messaging more secure, you should always supply a domain identifier when posting messages, and check for that identifier when receiving them, like this for posting:

   ```
   postMessage(message, 'http://mydomain.com')
   ```

   And this for receiving:

   ```
   if (event.origin) != 'http://mydomain.com') // Disallow
   ```

   You can also encrypt or obscure communications to discourage injection or eavesdropping.

8. The purpose of microdata is to make information more easily understandable by computer programs, such as search engines.

Online Resources

This appendix lists useful websites where you can get the material used in this book, or other resources that will enhance your web programs.

PHP Resource Sites

- *http://codewalkers.com*
- *http://developer.yahoo.com/php/*
- *http://easyphp.org*
- *http://forums.devshed.com*
- *http://free-php.net*
- *http://hotscripts.com/category/php/*
- *http://htmlgoodies.com/beyond/php/*
- *http://php.net*
- *http://php.resourceindex.com*
- *http://php-editors.com*
- *http://phpbuilder.com*
- *http://phpfreaks.com*
- *http://phpunit.de*
- *http://w3schools.com/php/*
- *http://zend.com*

MySQL Resource Sites

- *http://launchpad.net/mysql*
- *http://mysql.com*
- *http://php.net/mysql*
- *http://planetmysql.org*
- *http://oracle.com/us/sun*
- *http://w3schools.com/PHP/php_mysql_intro.asp*

JavaScript Resource Sites

- *http://developer.mozilla.org/en/JavaScript*
- *http://dynamicdrive.com*
- *http://javascript.about.com*
- *http://javascript.internet.com*
- *http://javascript.com*
- *http://javascriptkit.com*
- *http://w3schools.com/JS*
- *http://webreference.com/js*

CSS Resource Sites

- *http://freehtmlvalidator.com*
- *http://cssbasics.com*
- *http://dustindiaz.com/css-shorthand*
- *http://quirksmode.org/css/quirksmode.html*
- *http://css-discuss.incutio.com/wiki/Print_Stylesheets*

HTML5 Resource Sites

- *http://htmlvalidator.com*
- *http://caniuse.com*

- *http://html5test.com*
- *http://html5readiness.com*
- *http://html5demos.com*
- *http://html5-demos.appspot.com*
- *http://modernizr.com*
- *http://html5doctor.com*

AJAX Resource Sites

- *http://ajax.asp.net*
- *http://ajaxian.com*
- *http://ajaxmatters.com*
- *http://developer.mozilla.org/en/AJAX*
- *http://dojotoolkit.org*
- *http://jquery.com*
- *http://mochikit.com*
- *http://mootools.net*
- *http://openjs.com*
- *http://prototypejs.org*
- *http://sourceforge.net/projects/clean-ajax*
- *http://w3schools.com/Ajax*

Miscellaneous Resource Sites

- *http://onlinewebcheck.com*
- *http://apachefriends.org*
- *http://easyphp.org*
- *http://eclipse.org*
- *http://editra.org*
- *http://fireftp.mozdev.org*
- *http://sourceforge.net/projects/glossword*
- *http://mamp.info/en*

- *http://programmingforums.org*
- *http://putty.org*

O'Reilly Resource Sites

- *http://onlamp.com*
- *http://onlamp.com/php*
- *http://onlamp.com/onlamp/general/mysql.csp*
- *http://oreilly.com/ajax*
- *http://oreilly.com/javascript*
- *http://oreilly.com/mysql*
- *http://oreilly.com/php*
- *http://oreillynet.com/javascript*

MySQL's FULLTEXT Stopwords

This appendix contains the more than 500 *stopwords* referred to in the section "Creating a FULLTEXT index" on page 196 in Chapter 8. Stopwords are words that are considered so common as to not be worth searching for, or storing, in a FULLTEXT index. Theoretically, ignoring these words makes little difference to the results of most FULLTEXT searches, but makes MySQL databases considerably smaller and more efficient. The words are shown here in lowercase but apply to uppercase and mixed case versions, too:

A

a's, able, about, above, according, accordingly, across, actually, after, afterwards, again, against, ain't, all, allow, allows, almost, alone, along, already, also, although, always, am, among, amongst, an, and, another, any, anybody, anyhow, anyone, anything, anyway, anyways, anywhere, apart, appear, appreciate, appropriate, are, aren't, around, as, aside, ask, asking, associated, at, available, away, awfully

B

be, became, because, become, becomes, becoming, been, before, beforehand, behind, being, believe, below, beside, besides, best, better, between, beyond, both, brief, but, by

C

c'mon, c's, came, can, can't, cannot, cant, cause, causes, certain, certainly, changes, clearly, co, com, come, comes, concerning, consequently, consider, considering, contain, containing, contains, corresponding, could, couldn't, course, currently

D

definitely, described, despite, did, didn't, different, do, does, doesn't, doing, don't, done, down, downwards, during

E

each, edu, eg, eight, either, else, elsewhere, enough, entirely, especially, et, etc, even, ever, every, everybody, everyone, everything, everywhere, ex, exactly, example, except

F

far, few, fifth, first, five, followed, following, follows, for, former, formerly, forth, four, from, further, furthermore

G

get, gets, getting, given, gives, go, goes, going, gone, got, gotten, greetings

H

had, hadn't, happens, hardly, has, hasn't, have, haven't, having, he, he's, hello, help, hence, her, here, here's, hereafter, hereby, herein, hereupon, hers, herself, hi, him, himself, his, hither, hopefully, how, howbeit, however

I

i'd, i'll, i'm, i've, ie, if, ignored, immediate, in, inasmuch, inc, indeed, indicate, indicated, indicates, inner, insofar, instead, into, inward, is, isn't, it, it'd, it'll, it's, its, itself

J

just

K

keep, keeps, kept, know, knows, known

L

last, lately, later, latter, latterly, least, less, lest, let, let's, like, liked, likely, little, look, looking, looks, ltd

M

mainly, many, may, maybe, me, mean, meanwhile, merely, might, more, moreover, most, mostly, much, must, my, myself

N

name, namely, nd, near, nearly, necessary, need, needs, neither, never, nevertheless, new, next, nine, no, nobody, non, none, noone, nor, normally, not, nothing, novel, now, nowhere

O

obviously, of, off, often, oh, ok, okay, old, on, once, one, ones, only, onto, or, other, others, otherwise, ought, our, ours, ourselves, out, outside, over, overall, own

P

particular, particularly, per, perhaps, placed, please, plus, possible, presumably, probably, provides

Q

que, quite, qv

R

rather, rd, re, really, reasonably, regarding, regardless, regards, relatively, respectively, right

S

said, same, saw, say, saying, says, second, secondly, see, seeing, seem, seemed, seeming, seems, seen, self, selves, sensible, sent, serious, seriously, seven, several, shall, she, should, shouldn't, since, six, so, some, somebody, somehow, someone, something, sometime, sometimes, somewhat, somewhere, soon, sorry, specified, specify, specifying, still, sub, such, sup, sure

T

t's, take, taken, tell, tends, th, than, thank, thanks, thanx, that, that's, thats, the, their, theirs, them, themselves, then, thence, there, there's, thereafter, thereby, therefore, therein, theres, thereupon, these, they, they'd, they'll, they're, they've, think, third, this, thorough, thoroughly, those, though, three, through, throughout, thru, thus, to, together, too, took, toward, towards, tried, tries, truly, try, trying, twice, two

U

un, under, unfortunately, unless, unlikely, until, unto, up, upon, us, use, used, useful, uses, using, usually

V

value, various, very, via, viz, vs

W

want, wants, was, wasn't, way, we, we'd, we'll, we're, we've, welcome, well, went, were, weren't, what, what's, whatever, when, whence, whenever, where, where's, whereafter, whereas, whereby, wherein, whereupon, wherever, whether, which, while, whither, who, who's, whoever, whole, whom, whose, why, will, willing, wish, with, within, without, won't, wonder, would, would, wouldn't

Y

yes, yet, you, you'd, you'll, you're, you've, your, yours, yourself, yourselves

Z

zero

MySQL Functions

Having functions built into MySQL substantially reduces the speed of performing complex queries, as well as their complexity. If you wish to learn more about the available functions, you can visit the following URLs:

- String functions (*tinyurl.com/phpstringfuncs*)
- Date and time (*tinyurl.com/phpdateandtime*)

But, for easy reference, here are some of the most commonly used MySQL functions.

String Functions

CONCAT(*str1*, *str2*, ...)
> Returns the result of concatenating *str1*, *str2*, and any other parameters (or NULL if any argument is NULL). If any of the arguments are binary, then the result is a binary string; otherwise, the result is a non-binary string. The code returns the string "MySQL":

```
SELECT CONCAT('My', 'S', 'QL');
```

CONCAT_WS(*separator*, *str1*, *str2*, ...)
> This works in the same way as CONCAT except it inserts a separator between the items being concatenated. If the separator is NULL the result will be NULL, but NULL values can be used as other arguments, which will then be skipped. This code returns the string "Truman,Harry,S":

```
SELECT CONCAT_WS(',', 'Truman', 'Harry', 'S');
```

LEFT(*str*, *len*)
> Returns the leftmost *len* characters from the string *str* (or NULL if any argument is NULL). The following code returns the string "Chris":

```
SELECT LEFT('Christopher Columbus', '5');
```

RIGHT(*str, len*)

Returns the rightmost *len* characters from the string *str* (or NULL if any argument is NULL). This code returns the string "Columbus":

```
SELECT RIGHT('Christopher Columbus', '8');
```

MID(*str, pos, len*)

Returns up to *len* characters from the string *str* starting at position *pos*. If *len* is omitted, then all characters up to the end of the string are returned. You may use a negative value for *pos*, in which case it represents the character *pos* places from the end of the string. The first position in the string is 1. This code returns the string "stop":

```
SELECT MID('Christopher Columbus', '5', '4');
```

LENGTH(*str*)

Returns the length in bytes of the string *str*. Note that multibyte characters count as multiple bytes. If you need to know the actual number of characters in a string, use the CHAR_LENGTH function. This code returns the value 15:

```
SELECT LENGTH('Mark Zuckerberg');
```

LPAD(*str, len, padstr*)

Returns the string *str* padded to a length of *len* characters by prepending the string with *padstr* characters. If *str* is longer than *len*, then the string returned will be truncated to *len* characters. The example code returns the following strings:

```
 January
February
   March
   April
     May
```

Notice how all the strings have been padded to be eight characters long:

```
SELECT LPAD('January', '8', ' ');
SELECT LPAD('February', '8', ' ');
SELECT LPAD('March', '8', ' ');
SELECT LPAD('April', '8', ' ');
SELECT LPAD('May', '8', ' ');
```

RPAD

This is the same as the LPAD function except that the padding takes place on the right of the returned string. This code returns the string "Hi!!!":

```
SELECT RPAD('Hi', '5', '!');
```

LOCATE(*substr, str, pos*)

Returns the position of the first occurrence of *substr* in the string *str*. If the parameter *pos* is passed, the search begins at position *pos*. If *substr* is not found in *str*, a value of 0 is returned. This code returns the values 5 and 11, because the first function call returns the first encounter of the word *unit*, while the second one only starts to search at the seventh character, and so returns the second instance:

```
SELECT LOCATE('unit', 'Community unit');
SELECT LOCATE('unit', 'Community unit' 7);
```

LOWER(*str*)

This is the inverse of UPPER. Returns the string *str* with all the characters changed to lowercase. This code returns the string "queen elizabeth ii":

```
SELECT LOWER('Queen Elizabeth II');
```

UPPER(*str*)

This is the inverse of LOWER. It returns the string *str* with all the characters changed to uppercase. This code returns the string "I CAN'T HELP SHOUTING":

```
SELECT UPPER("I can't help shouting");
```

QUOTE(*str*)

Returns a quoted string that can be used as a properly escaped value in a SQL statement. The returned string is enclosed in single quotes with all instances of single quotes, backslashes, the ASCII NUL character, and Control-Z preceded by a backslash. If the argument *str* is NULL, the return value is the word NULL without enclosing quotes. The example code returns the following string:

```
'I\'m hungry'
```

Note how the " symbol has been replaced with \'.

```
SELECT QUOTE("I'm hungry");
```

REPEAT(*str, count*)

Returns a string comprising *count* copies of the string *str*. If *count* is less than 1, an empty string is returned. If either parameter is NULL then NULL is returned. This code returns the strings "Ho Ho Ho" and "Merry Christmas":

```
SELECT REPEAT('Ho ', 3), 'Merry Christmas';
```

REPLACE(*str, from, to*)

Returns the string *str* with all occurrences of the string *from* replaced with the string *to*. The search and replace is case-sensitive when searching for *from*. This code returns the string "Cheeseburger and Soda":

```
SELECT REPLACE('Cheeseburger and Fries', 'Fries', 'Soda');
```

TRIM([*specifier remove* FROM] *str*)

Returns the string *str* with all prefixes or suffixes removed. The *specifier* can be one of BOTH, LEADING, or TRAILING. If no *specifier* is supplied, then BOTH is assumed. The *remove* string is optional and, if omitted, spaces are removed. This code returns the strings "No Padding" and "Hello__":

```
SELECT TRIM('   No Padding   ');
SELECT TRIM(LEADING '_' FROM '__Hello__');
```

LTRIM(*str*) and RTRIM(*str*)

The function RTRIM returns the string *str* with any leading spaces removed, while the function RTRIM performs the same action on the string's tail. This code returns the strings "No Padding " and " No Padding":

```
SELECT LTRIM('   No Padding   ');
SELECT RTRIM('   No Padding   ');
```

Date Functions

Dates are an important part of most databases. Whenever financial transactions take place, the date has to be recorded, expiry dates of credit cards need to be noted for repeat billing purposes, and so on. So, as you might expect, MySQL comes with a wide variety of functions to make handling dates a breeze.

CURDATE()

Returns the current date in YYYY-MM-DD or YYYMMDD format, depending on whether the function is used in a numeric or string context. On the date May 2, 2018, the following code returns the values 2018-05-02 and 20180502:

```
SELECT CURDATE();
SELECT CURDATE() + 0;
```

DATE(*expr*)

Extracts the date part of the date or a DATETIME expression *expr*. This code returns the value 1961-05-02:

```
SELECT DATE('1961-05-02 14:56:23');
```

DATE_ADD(*date,* INTERVAL *expr unit*)

Returns the result of adding the expression *expr* using units *unit* to the *date*. The *date* argument is the starting date or DATETIME value, and *expr* may start with a - symbol for negative intervals. Table D-1 shows the interval types supported and the expected *expr* values. Note the examples in this table that show where it is necessary to surround the *expr* value with quotes for MySQL to correctly interpret them. If you are ever in doubt, adding the quotes will always work.

Table D-1. Expected expr values

Type	Expected expr value	Example
MICROSECOND	MICROSECONDS	111111
SECOND	SECONDS	11
MINUTE	MINUTES	11
HOUR	HOURS	11
DAY	DAYS	11
WEEK	WEEKS	11
MONTH	MONTHS	11
QUARTER	QUARTERS	1
YEAR	YEARS	11
SECOND_MICROSECOND	'SECONDS.MICROSECONDS'	11.22
MINUTE_MICROSECOND	'MINUTES.MICROSECONDS'	11.22
MINUTE_SECOND	'MINUTES:SECONDS'	'11:22'
HOUR_MICROSECOND	'HOURS.MICROSECONDS'	11.22
HOUR_SECOND	'HOURS:MINUTES:SECONDS'	'11:22:33'
HOUR_MINUTE	'HOURS:MINUTES'	'11:22'
DAY_MICROSECOND	'DAYS.MICROSECONDS'	11.22
DAY_SECOND	'DAYS HOURS:MINUTES:SECONDS'	'11 22:33:44'
DAY_MINUTE	'DAYS HOURS:MINUTES'	'11 22:33'
DAY_HOUR	'DAYS HOURS'	'11 22'
YEAR_MONTH	'YEARS-MONTHS'	'11-2'

You can also use the DATE_SUB function to subtract date intervals. However, it's not actually necessary for you to use the DATE_ADD or DATE_SUB functions, as you can use date arithmetic directly in MySQL. This code:

```
SELECT DATE_ADD('1975-01-01', INTERVAL 77 DAY);
SELECT DATE_SUB('1982-07-04', INTERVAL '3-11' YEAR_MONTH);
SELECT '2018-12-31 23:59:59' + INTERVAL 1 SECOND;
SELECT '2000-01-01' - INTERVAL 1 SECOND;
```

returns the following values:

```
1975-03-19
1978-08-04
2019-01-01 00:00:00
1999-12-31 23:59:59
```

Notice how the last two commands use date arithmetic directly without recourse to functions.

DATE_FORMAT(*date*, *format*)

This returns the *date* value formatted according to the *format* string. Table D-2 shows the specifiers that can be used in the *format* string. Note that the % character is required before each specifier, as shown. This code returns the given date and time as Friday May 4th 2018 03:02 AM:

```
SELECT DATE_FORMAT('2018-05-04 03:02:01', '%W %M %D %Y %h:%i %p');
```

Table D-2. DATE_FORMAT specifiers

Specifier	Description
%a	Abbreviated weekday name (Sun–Sat)
%b	Abbreviated month name (Jan–Dec)
%c	Month, numeric (0–12)
%D	Day of the month with English suffix (0th, 1st, 2nd, 3rd, …)
%d	Day of the month, numeric (00–31)
%e	Day of the month, numeric (0–31)
%f	Microseconds (000000–999999)
%H	Hour (00–23)
%h	Hour (01–12)
%I	Hour (01–12)
%i	Minutes, numeric (00–59)
%j	Day of year (001–366)
%k	Hour (0–23)
%l	Hour (1–12)
%M	Month name (January–December)
%m	Month, numeric (00–12)
%p	AM or PM
%r	Time, 12–hour (hh:mm:ss followed by AM or PM)
%S	Seconds (00–59)
%s	Seconds (00–59)
%T	Time, 24-hour (hh:mm:ss)
%U	Week (00–53), where Sunday is the first day of the week
%u	Week (00–53), where Monday is the first day of the week
%V	Week (01–53), where Sunday is the first day of the week; used with %X
%v	Week (01–53), where Monday is the first day of the week; used with %x
%W	Weekday name (Sunday–Saturday)
%w	Day of the week (0=Sunday–6=Saturday)
%X	Year for the week where Sunday is the first day of the week, numeric, four digits; used with %V

Specifier	Description
%x	Year for the week, where Monday is the first day of the week, numeric, four digits; used with %v
%Y	Year, numeric, four digits
%y	Year, numeric, two digits
%%	A literal % character

DAY(*date*)

Returns the day of the month for *date*, in the range 1 to 31 or 0 for dates that have a zero day part such as 0000-00-00 or 2018-00-00. You can also use the function DAYOFMONTH to return the same value. This code returns the value 3:

```
SELECT DAY('2018-02-03');
```

DAYNAME(*date*)

Returns the name of the weekday for the *date*. For example, this code returns the string "Saturday":

```
SELECT DAYNAME('2018-02-03');
```

DAYOFWEEK(*date*)

Returns the weekday index for *date* between 1 for Sunday through 7 for Saturday. This code returns the value 7:

```
SELECT DAYOFWEEK('2018-02-03');
```

DAYOFYEAR(*date*)

Returns the day of the year for *date* in the range 1 to 366. This code returns the value 34:

```
SELECT DAYOFYEAR('2018-02-03');
```

LAST_DAY(*date*)

Returns the last day of the month for the given DATETIME value *date*. If the argument is invalid, it returns NULL. This code:

```
SELECT LAST_DAY('2018-02-03');
SELECT LAST_DAY('2018-03-11');
SELECT LAST_DAY('2018-04-26');
```

returns the following values:

```
2018-02-28
2018-03-31
2018-04-30
```

As you'd expect, it correctly returns the 28th day of February, the 31st of March, and the 30th of April 2011.

MAKEDATE(*year*, *dayofyear*)

Returns a date given *year* and *dayofyear* values. If *dayofyear* is 0, the result is NULL. This code returns the date 2016-10-01:

```
SELECT MAKEDATE(2018,274);
```

MONTH(*date*)

Returns the month for *date* in the range 1 through 12 for January through December. Dates that have a zero month part, such as 0000-00-00 or 2016-00-00, return 0. This code returns the value 7:

```
SELECT MONTH('2018-07-11');
```

MONTHNAME(*date*)

Returns the full name of the month for *date*. This code returns the string "July":

```
SELECT MONTHNAME('2018-07-11');
```

SYSDATE()

Returns the current date and time as a value in either YYY-MM-DD HH:MM:SS or YYYMMDDHHMMSS format, depending on whether the function is used in a string or numeric context. The function NOW works in a similar manner, except that it returns the time and date only at the start of the current statement, whereas SYSDATE returns the time and date at the exact moment the function itself is called. On December 19, 2018, at 19:11:13, this code returns the values 2018-12-19 19:11:13 and 20181219191113.

```
SELECT SYSDATE();
SELECT SYSDATE() + 0;
```

YEAR(*date*)

Returns the year for *date* in the range 1000 to 9999, or 0 for the zero date. This code returns the year 1999.

```
SELECT YEAR('1999-08-07');
```

WEEK(*date* [, *mode*])

Returns the week number for *date*. If passed the optional *mode* parameter, the week number returned will be modified according to Table D-3. You can also use the function WEEKOFYEAR, which is equivalent to using the WEEK function with a *mode* of 3. This code returns the week number 14.

```
SELECT WEEK('2018-04-04', 1);
```

Table D-3. The modes supported by the WEEK function

Mode	First day of week	Range	Where week 1 is the first week...
0	Sunday	0–53	with a Sunday in this year
1	Monday	0–53	with more than three days this year
2	Sunday	1–53	with a Sunday in this year
3	Monday	1–53	with more than three days this year
4	Sunday	0–53	with more than three days this year
5	Monday	0–53	with a Monday in this year
6	Sunday	1–53	with more than three days this year
7	Monday	1–53	with a Monday in this year

WEEKDAY(*date*)

Returns the weekday index for *date* where 0=Monday through 6=Sunday. This code returns the value 2.

```
SELECT WEEKDAY('2018-04-04');
```

Time Functions

Sometimes you need to work with the time, rather than the date, and MySQL provides plenty of functions for you to do so.

CURTIME()

Returns the current time as a value in the format HH:MM:SS or HHMMSS.uuuuuu, depending on whether the function is used in a string or numeric context. The value is expressed using the current time zone. When the current time is 11:56:23, this code returns the values 11:56:23 and 115623.000000.

```
SELECT CURTIME();
SELECT CURTIME() + 0;
```

HOUR(*time*)

Returns the hour for *time*. This code returns the value 11.

```
SELECT HOUR('11:56:23');
```

MINUTE(*time*)

Returns the minute for *time*. This code returns the value 56.

```
SELECT MINUTE('11:56:23');
```

SECOND(*time*)

Returns the second for *time*. This code returns the value 23.

```
SELECT SECOND('11:56:23');
```

MAKETIME(*hour, minute, second*)

Returns a time value calculated from the *hour*, *minute*, and *second* arguments. This code returns the time 11:56:23.

```
SELECT MAKETIME(11, 56, 23);
```

TIMEDIFF(*expr1, expr2*)

Returns the difference between *expr1* and *expr2* (*expr1 – expr2*) as a time value. Both *expr1* and *expr2* must be TIME or DATETIME expressions of the same type. This code returns the value 01:37:38.

```
SELECT TIMEDIFF('2000-01-01 01:02:03', '1999-12-31 23:24:25');
```

UNIX_TIMESTAMP([*date*])

If called without the optional *date* argument, this function returns the number of seconds since 1970-01-01 00:00:00 UTC as an unsigned integer. If the *date* parameter is passed, then the value returned is the number of seconds since the 1970 start date until the given date. This command will not return the same value for everyone because the date given to it is interpreted as a local time (given in the user's time zone). This code will return the value 946684800 (the number of seconds up to the start of the new millennium) followed by a TIMESTAMP representing the current Unix time at the moment you run it.

```
SELECT UNIX_TIMESTAMP('2000-01-01');
SELECT UNIX_TIMESTAMP();
```

FROM_UNIXTIME(*unix_timestamp* [, *format*])

Returns the *unix_timestamp* parameter as either a string in YYY-MM-DD HH:MM:SS or YYYMMDDHHMMSS.uuuuuu format, depending on whether the function is used in a string or numeric context. If the optional *format* parameter is provided, the result is formatted according to the specifiers in Table 8-17. The precise value returned will depend on the user's local time. This code returns the strings "2000-01-01 00:00:00" and "Saturday January 1st 2000 12:00 AM".

```
SELECT FROM_UNIXTIME(946684800);
SELECT FROM_UNIXTIME(946684800, '%W %M %D %Y %h:%i %p');
```

Index

We'd like to hear your suggestions for improving our indexes. Send email to index@oreilly.com.

mysql_select_db function (PHP), 244

N

\n (newline) escape character, 60, 334
name attribute (forms), 281
__NAMESPACE__ constant (PHP), 64
naming conventions
    JavaScript function names, 364
    JavaScript variables, 330
    PHP constants, 122
    PHP constructor methods, 119
    PHP variables, 54, 69–70
NATURAL_JOIN clause (MySQL commands), 208, 263
nesting
    arrays, 331
    comments, 49, 329, 428
    constructs, 54
NetBeans IDE, 42
new keyword (PHP), 116
newline (\n) escape character, 60, 334
normalization
    about, 219
    First Normal Form, 220–221
    Second Normal Form, 222–224
    Third Normal Form, 224–226
    when not to use, 226
<noscript> tag, 324
Not (!) logical operator
    in JavaScript, 333, 348
    in PHP, 57, 82
not identical (!==) comparison operator (Java-Script), 333
NULL value, 74, 82
number input type (HTML5), 298
numbers
    converting number bases, 438
    numeric data types in MySQL, 185
    numeric variables in JavaScript, 330, 334
    numeric variables in PHP, 51, 63
numeric arrays
    in JavaScript, 373
    in PHP, 131–133, 138

O

(object) cast type, 99
object-oriented programming (OOP), 113

objects
    dragging and dropping, 593–595
    in JavaScript
        accessing objects, 370
        attaching events to objects, 498
        creating objects, 369
        declaring classes, 368
        DOM and, 338
        prototype keyword and, 370–372
        static methods and properties, 371
    in PHP
        about, 103, 113
        accessing objects, 116–118
        cloning objects, 118
        constructor methods, 119, 127
        creating objects, 116
        declaring classes, 115
        declaring constants, 122
        declaring properties, 122
        destructor methods, 120
        inheritance and, 114, 125–129, 125–129
        method scope, 123
        property scope, 123
        static methods, 121, 124
        static properties, 124
        terminology associated with, 114
        writing methods, 120
offsetTop property (JavaScript), 501
OGG format, 575
onabort event, 499
onblur event, 499
onchange event, 499
onclick event, 351, 499
ondblclick event, 499
ondragover event, 593
ondragstart event, 593
ondrop event, 593
one-to-many relationships in data, 228
one-to-one relationships in data, 227
one-way functions, 308
onerror event, 499
onerror event (JavaScript), 351
onfocus event, 499
onkeydown event, 499
onkeypress event, 499
onkeyup event, 499
onload event, 499
onmousedown event, 499
onmousemove event, 499

MySQL string functions, 667–670
in PHP
    concatenating strings, 58, 76
    converting string case, 105
    converting strings to numbers, 63
    escape characters, 59
    multiple-line commands and, 60
    padding strings, 150
    string types supported, 59
    string variables, 50
    strings as operators, 76, 78
stroke method (canvas), 537
strokeRect method (canvas), 522
strokeText method (canvas), 530
strrev function (PHP), 105
strtolower function (PHP), 106
strtoupper function (PHP), 105
Structured Query Language (SQL), 7, 171
str_repeat function (PHP), 105
style sheets, 424
    (see also CSS)
    browser support, 436
    !important declaration, 438
    importing, 424
    methods of creation, 436
    selecting elements for styling, 437
style types (CSS)
    about, 428
    default styles, 428
    external style sheets, 429
    inline styles, 430
    internal styles, 429
    user styles, 428
styles.css (social networking site), 632–636
subclasses (derived classes)
    about, 114
    calling parent constructors, 127
    extends operator and, 125
    parent operator and, 126
submit button in forms, 290
subtraction (−) operator
    in JavaScript, 332
    in PHP, 55
superclasses
    about, 114
    final methods and, 128
superglobal variables (PHP)
    about, 70
    security and, 71

SVG (Scalable Vector Graphics), 10
switch statement
    in JavaScript, 354
    in PHP, 88–90
SYSDATE function (MySQL), 674
system calls in PHP, 167–169

T

\t (tab) escape character, 60, 334
tab (\t) escape character, 60, 334
tables (MySQL)
    about, 171–172
    adding columns to, 190
    adding data to, 188, 257
    adding indexes to, 193–194
    backing up, 238
    changing data types of columns, 190
    creating, 181–182, 255
    creating transaction-ready, 231
    deleting, 191
    deleting data from, 260
    deleting records, 252
    describing, 256
    dropping, 257
    fetching rows, 247, 272–274
    joining together, 207–209
    locking for reading, 235, 261
    normalization and, 219–227
    practical example using PHP, 248–255
    removing columns in, 191
    renaming, 189
    renaming columns in, 191
    retrieving data from, 258
    updating data in, 259
tags (PHP), 139
ternary operators
    in JavaScript, 345, 355
    in PHP, 76, 78, 91
test method (JavaScript), 386, 388, 395
testing
    MAMP installation, 36–37
    WAMP installation, 28–30
text areas in forms, 284
text boxes in forms, 284
TEXT data type (MySQL), 184
text effect properties (CSS3), 477–479
text styles, managing, 444–446
text-align property (CSS), 446
text-decoration property (CSS), 445

user agent string, 318
user styles (CSS), 428
users and usernames
    creating users in MySQL, 179
    Gmail example, 12–14
    HTTP authentication and, 304–307
    social networking site example, 611
    storing, 307
    validating on forms, 385

V

validation
    form data using PHP, 165–167
    form data with JavaScript, 381–387
    redisplaying forms after, 397–402
value attribute (forms), 283, 290
var keyword (JavaScript), 336
VARBINARY data type (MySQL), 184
VARCHAR data type (MySQL), 183
variable substitution, 59
variables
    in JavaScript
        $ symbol in variables, 330, 340
        arrays, 331
        decrementing variables, 334
        global variables, 336
        incrementing variables, 334
        local variables, 336
        naming conventions, 330
        numeric variables, 330, 334
        string variables, 330
        variable typing, 335
        variables in expressions, 344
    in PHP
        $ symbol in variables, 49, 63, 117
        arrays, 52–54
        constants and, 63
        decrementing variables, 58
        incrementing variables, 58
        numeric variables, 51, 63
        returning values in, 110
        string variables, 50
        variable assignment, 57–60
        variable naming rules, 54, 69–70
        variable scope, 66–71, 111
        variable typing, 62
        variables in expressions, 75
VBScript (Microsoft), 326
version compatibility (PHP), 113

<video> element (HTML5)
    about, 513, 574
    attributes supported, 576
    browser considerations, 578
    codecs supported, 575
visibility property (CSS), 502
visited pseudo-class (CSS), 452
Vorbis (audio) codec, 570
VP8 (video) codec, 576
VP9 (video) codec, 576

W

W3C (World Wide Web Consortium)
    DATE_W3C constant, 154
    HTML5 standard, 10
    standard colors, 447
WAMPs
    about, 16
    alternative, 31
    installing on Windows, 16–28
    testing installation, 28–30
web applications (HTML5), 515, 591–593
web browsers (see browsers)
web fonts (CSS3), 479–481
web workers, 515, 589–591
WebM format, 575
WEEK function (MySQL), 674
week input type (HTML5), 298
WEEKDAY function (MySQL), 675
WHERE clause (MySQL commands), 195, 200
while statement
    in JavaScript, 356
    in PHP, 93–94
width attribute (HTML5), 297
window object
    closed property, 495
    defaultStatus property, 495
    document property, 495
    frames property, 495
    history property, 495
    innerHeight property, 495
    innerWidth property, 495
    length property, 495
    location property, 495
    name property, 495
    navigator property, 495
    opener property, 495
    outerHeight property, 495
    outerWidth property, 495

About the Author

Robin Nixon has worked with and written about computers since the early 1980s (his first computer was a Tandy TRS 80 Model 1 with a massive 4KB of RAM!). One of the websites he developed presented the world's first radio station licensed by the music copyright holders. In order to enable people to continue to surf while listening, Robin also developed the first known pop-up windows. He has also worked for one of Britain's main IT magazine publishers, where he held several roles including editorial, promotions, and cover disc editing, and has now written over 25 books on computing and web development.

Colophon

The animals on the cover of *Learning PHP, MySQL, JavaScript, CSS & HTML5* are sugar gliders (*Petaurus breviceps*). Sugar gliders are small, gray-furred creatures that grow to an adult length of six to seven-and-a-half inches. Their tails, which are distinguished by a black tip, are usually as long as their bodies. Membranes extend between their wrists and ankles and provide an aerodynamic surface that helps them glide between trees.

Sugar gliders are native to Australia and Tasmania. They prefer to live in the hollow parts of eucalyptus and other types of large trees with several other adult sugar gliders and their own children.

Though sugar gliders reside in groups and defend their territory together, they don't always live in harmony. One male will assert his dominance by marking the group's territory with his saliva and then by marking all group members with a distinctive scent produced from his forehead and chest glands. This ensures that members of the group will know when an outsider approaches; group members will fight off any sugar glider not bearing their scent. However, a sugar glider group will welcome and mark an outsider if one of their adult males dies (the group will typically replace a deceased adult female with one of their own female offspring).

Sugar gliders make popular pets because of their inquisitive, playful natures, and because many think they are cute. But there are disadvantages to keeping sugar gliders as pets: as they are exotic animals, sugar gliders need specialized, complicated diets consisting of items such as crickets, a variety of fruits and vegetables, and mealworms; healthy housing requires a cage or space no less than the size of an aviary; their distinctive scents can be bothersome to humans; as they are nocturnal creatures, they will bark, hiss, run, and glide all night long; it's not uncommon for them to lose control of their bowels while playing or eating; and in some states and countries, it is illegal to own sugar gliders as household pets.

The cover image is from *Dover's Animals*. The cover fonts are URW Typewriter and Guardian Sans. The text font is Adobe Minion Pro; the heading font is Adobe Myriad Condensed; and the code font is Dalton Maag's Ubuntu Mono.

Have it your way.

Get even more for your money.

Join the O'Reilly Community, and register the O'Reilly books you own. It's free, and you'll get:

- $4.99 ebook upgrade offer
- 40% upgrade offer on O'Reilly print books
- Membership discounts on books and events
- Free lifetime updates to ebooks and videos
- Multiple ebook formats, DRM FREE
- Participation in the O'Reilly community
- Newsletters
- Account management
- 100% Satisfaction Guarantee

Signing up is easy:

1. Go to: oreilly.com/go/register
2. Create an O'Reilly login.
3. Provide your address.
4. Register your books.

Note: English-language books only

To order books online:
oreilly.com/store

For questions about products or an order:
orders@oreilly.com

To sign up to get topic-specific email announcements and/or news about upcoming books, conferences, special offers, and new technologies:
elists@oreilly.com

For technical questions about book content:
booktech@oreilly.com

To submit new book proposals to our editors:
proposals@oreilly.com

O'Reilly books are available in multiple DRM-free ebook formats. For more information:
oreilly.com/ebooks

CPSIA information can be obtained at www.ICGtesting.com
Printed in the USA
BVOW08s1141141114

375132BV00001B/1/P